To Rule THE Waves

• • •

*How the British Navy
Shaped the Modern World*

ARTHUR HERMAN

HODDER &
STOUGHTON

Copyright © 2004 by Arthur Herman

First published in Great Britain in 2005 by Hodder and Stoughton
A division of Hodder Headline

The right of Arthur Herman to be identified as the Author of the Work
has been asserted by him in accordance with the
Copyright, Designs and Patents Act 1988.

1   3   5   7   9   10   8   6   4   2

A CIP catalogue record for this title is available from the British Library

ISBN 0 340 73418 3

Designed by Robert Bull

Map sources—page xv: James L. Stokesbury, *Navy and Empire* (New York: William Morrow,
1983); page 6: Rayner Unwin, *The Defeat of John Hawkins* (New York: Macmillan, 1960);
page 26: David Howarth, *Sovereign of the Seas* (New York: Atheneum, 1974); page 134: Tracy
W. McGregor Library of American History, Special Collections, University of Virginia;
page 285: Geoffrey Marcus, *Bay of Biscay* (Barre, Mass.: Barre Publishing Company, 1963);
page 355: David Howarth, *Sovereign of the Seas* (New York: Atheneum, 1974); page 387:
David Howarth, *Trafalgar: The Nelson Touch* (New York: Atheneum, 1969); page 445: C. J.
Bartlett, *Great Britain and Sea Power: 1815–1853* (Oxford: Clarendon Press, 1963); page 507:
Richard Hough, *The Great War at Sea: 1914–1918* (New York: Oxford University Press, 1983);
page 541: Martin Middlebrook and Patrick Mahoney, *Battleship: The Sinking of the* Prince of
Wales *and the* Repulse (New York: Charles Scribner's Sons, 1979); page 562: Robert Bull.

Printed and bound in Great Britain by
Mackays of Chatham Ltd, Chatham, Kent

Hodder Headline's policy is to use papers that are natural, renewable
and recyclable products and made from wood grown in sustainable forests.
The logging and manufacturing processes are expected to conform to the
environmental regulations of the country of origin

Hodder and Stoughton Ltd
A division of Hodder Headline
338 Euston Road
London NW1 3BH

To Barbara and Arthur Herman,
sine quibus non sum

The first article of an Englishman's political creed must be,
That he believeth in the sea.
—LORD HALIFAX, 1694

CONTENTS

MAPS

ACKNOWLEDGMENTS

My thanks go first to the researchers and staff at the National Maritime Museum, Greenwich, especially Janet Norton and Liz Verity, for their patient help in answering questions and finding documents. Thanks also to the staffs of the Docklands Museum in London; the British Library; the Australian National Maritime Museum in Sydney; the National Library of Scotland in Edinburgh; the Lauinger Library at Georgetown University, the Alderman Library at the University of Virginia; and special thanks to David Shafer, director of the Rappahannock County Library, for his help and enthusiasm for this project almost from the day it started.

My friend Charles Matheson read the entire manuscript, and his advice and suggestions proved invaluable, especially in the book's early stages. Commander Charles O'Brien, USN (Ret.) gave patient assistance with technical nautical matters, as did Admiral Ralph Ghormley, USN (Ret.) and John Tomlin, formerly of the Naval Surface Warfare Center in Carderock, Maryland, and Dean King. Allen Flint painstakingly went through the final manuscript with a discerning and erudite eye.

I owe another great debt to a quintet of eminent naval historians—Richard Harding, John B. Hattendorf, Andrew Lambert, N. A. M. Rodger, and Nicholas Tracy—who read selected chapters of the book, caught numerous mistakes, and answered even my most impertinent questions with unfailing courtesy. Patrick Robinson and Richard Aulie graciously offered their expertise on the chapters on the Falklands and on Captain Cook, respectively. Any remaining errors or omissions of fact in those chapters, or any others, are entirely my responsibility.

Will Hay helped out with the intricacies of nineteenth-century British politics and their impact on the Admiralty; John Meecham with the relations between Churchill and FDR. Paul Koda, as always, was my wise and useful sounding board as the project took shape, as was John Miller. Michael Barone, Jason Colosky, Ivor Tiefenbrun, and George Kerevan all contributed their ideas and encouragement.

My agents, Glen Hartley and Lynn Chu, took to the idea of a book on the British navy from the beginning, and have seen it through with their usual support and skill. My editor at Harper Collins, Tim Duggan, was the ideal taskmaster for this kind of project, and his assistant, John Williams, patiently coaxed me over the last fences and across the finish line.

My parents, Barbara and Arthur Herman, read the entire manuscript and have been my intellectual inspiration in more ways than I can count. That is why the book is dedicated to them.

My wife, Beth, believed in this project from the first, and she remained enthusiastic, cheerful, and supportive right to its end. No one could ask for a more wonderful companion on a journey such as this has been.

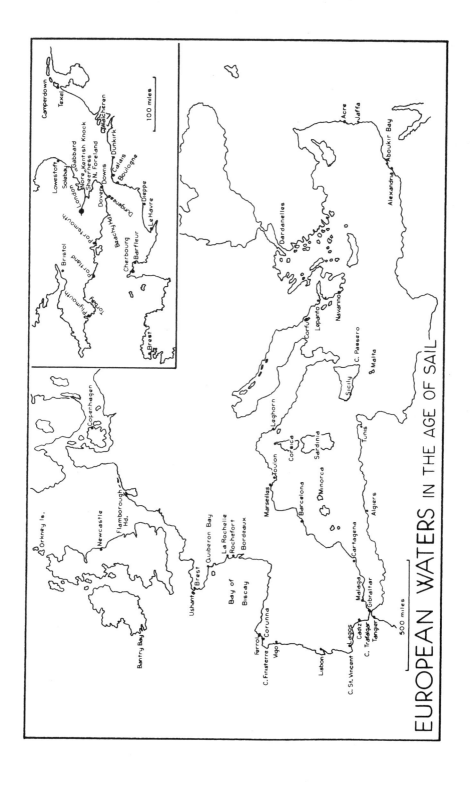

EUROPEAN WATERS IN THE AGE OF SAIL

INTRODUCTION

THE JOB OF the historian is not just to recount or explain the past but to show how things have come to be what they are.

This book will show how a single institution, the British navy, built the modern global system, which is *our* system, for better or worse. It did this first by challenging and toppling the global system forged by Spain and Portugal in the age of Columbus. Then it reshaped the world in the eighteenth and nineteenth centuries to fit the needs and desires of the British Empire. Those needs—access to markets, freedom of trade across international boundaries, an orderly state system that prefers peace to war, speedy communication and travel across open seas and skies—remain the principal features of globalization today.

Of course, a complicated historical development on this scale demands far more players and factors than just the British navy. But take it out of the picture, and the history of globalization becomes murkier, more haphazard, less inevitable and certain. Without it, a British Empire would have been unthinkable, and without a British Empire and its successor, the Commonwealth, half the world's independent nations would not exist today. Other nations *might* have built a modern unified world, but they probably would not have done it as quickly, efficiently, elegantly—or as humanely. In fact, not since the Roman legions has an ostensibly military force had so decisive an impact on the history of its own nation and the world.

An American, Captain Alfred Mahan, was the first to assert that the history of Western civilization has been the history of sea power, the ability of states and empires to exert control over the "wide common" of the oceans, and deny it to others. Through sea power even a small nation could dominate its neighbors, by controlling their access to resources while securing its own, and even a small nation could bend events, trends, geography, the globe itself to its will. This is the essence of what it means "to rule the waves."

In the sixteenth century, a handful of Elizabethan adventurers from Devon and Cornwall—John Hawkins, Francis Drake, Richard Grenville, Walter Raleigh—grasped these principles and used them to challenge the dominant world system of the day, which Spain and Portugal had built to exploit their empires in Asia and the New World. They inspired their fellow Englishmen to believe they would one day replace Spain and Portugal as rulers of the world, and rule an empire that would be aggressively English, militantly Protestant, and rely on control of the seas instead of phalanxes of standing armies. It was to achieve that end that John Hawkins remade the Royal Navy into the prototype of a modern seaforce.

The men of the sixteenth century still saw an English empire as a reflection of their own personal glory. Hawkins in the Caribbean, Drake in Panama, Martin Frobisher in the icebound reaches of Newfoundland, were all seekers after their own fortunes as well as servants of their nation and queen. But at the moment of crisis in 1588, they were able to come together to thwart the master of the global status quo, Philip II of Spain, and his Invincible Armada.

The failure of the Armada signaled the doom of the old system. After six decades of crisis and uncertainty, the elements for a new one finally arose, from the ranks of the Royal Navy that Hawkins had created and his successors nearly ruined. In the seventeenth century, the navy and sea power became irrevocable parts of the English national identity. The navy became the key to victory in the English Civil War (1642–48) and a key player on the world stage in the years of the Commonwealth and Oliver Cromwell's Protectorate. The restoration of monarchy in 1660 proved that no political power or faction, not even the king himself, could dare to challenge the navy's dominance over England's life and institutions.

The wars the Royal Navy fought against France in the eighteenth century only deepened the lessons of sea power. The navy made England's trade boom and prosper; it sustained its colonies and reshaped its politics; it drew England, Scotland, and Ireland together into a single United Kingdom. It enabled Great Britain to avoid prolonged land wars on the Continent, yet break the power of France, Europe's most powerful state. Thanks to its control of the seas, Britain was poised by the beginning of the nineteenth century to create its own global imperial system.

It would be unlike any other in history. While Britain itself maintained a polity based on limited government and the rule of law, its empire increasingly relied on trade rather than dominion, and cooperation with rather than conquest of, other sovereign states. All this was made possible by its navy. Sea power made sure that the nation's wealth depended on an active and expanding middle class. It removed the need for large standing armies and hence large intrusive government; it established safe and secure trade routes stretching from America and the Caribbean around the coast of Africa to India and China. It was this seagoing world system that Napoleon had to break in order to make himself absolute master of Europe. It was the Royal Navy, led by men like Horatio Nelson, that stopped him in his tracks, and preserved the liberty of Europe and the rest of the world.

The world system that emerged after 1815 would be one increasingly reliant on the Royal Navy as international policeman. The sea routes on which the British Empire depended were made accessible to other nations, as an expression of the British principle of free trade. The peace and security the navy brought to Britain's shores increasingly extended to other parts of the world. The personal liberty Englishmen enjoyed became a basic human right, as the navy wiped out the slave trade. British navy vessels regularly intervened to protect Briton and non-Briton alike from tyranny and violence. An empire, originally born out of ruthless ambition and brutality, had become the basis for a new progressive world order.

That order would survive the convulsions of the twentieth century, and the downfall of the British Empire itself. Britain passed its essential elements on to its successor, the United States and its navy. A *Pax Americana* would succeed the *Pax Britannica,* the reflection of American sea power and its ability to keep the world's sea lanes open. Even with the advent of new forms of warfare such as airpower and ballistic missiles, the sea remains the cornerstone of today's global system. Almost 95 percent of trade that crosses international boundaries is waterborne, as is 99.5 percent of the weight of all transcontinental trade.

Today the British navy may be only a shadow of its former self. But its legacy remains as powerful and relevant today as it was in the age of Nelson. The modern students of British sea power, from Alfred Mahan to Paul Kennedy and Nicholas Rodger, have all recognized the crucial link between the Royal Navy and Britain's national destiny. Likewise, historians of the British Empire have pointed out how that empire formed the essential features of our contemporary world order.

Just how those two histories relate to each other, and why, is what the reader discovers here. This is the story of how a navy forged a nation, then an empire—and then our world.

TO
Rule
THE
Waves

. . .

CHAPTER ONE

Incident at San Juan de Ulloa

A Sea-man hath a valiant heart,
And bears a noble minde,
He scorneth once to shrink or start
For any stormy wind.
　—ANONYMOUS BALLAD

FOR THREE DAYS the ships had struggled to hold their own against the hurricane. The wind out of the southeast had howled through the masts and rigging, tearing at their battered sails and smashing waves across their decks. There were five of them, sailing blind into the storm, in hour after hour of blackness. All they knew was that they were somewhere west of Cuba, and that they had to keep their ships pointed into the wind or else they could end up being thrown onto the coast of Spanish Florida. Their only guide through the perpetual darkness was the wildly tossing stern lantern of the *Jesus,* the flagship of their leader and commander, John Hawkins.

Storm-tossed ships: five tiny flyspecks in the midst of an empty hostile sea, and in the heart of a hostile empire. Yet without knowing it, they were about to alter history. A crucial moment had arrived in the struggle for global power. A new antagonist was about to enter the fray: England. John Hawkins's experiences over the next twelve days in September 1568 would mark the start of a century-long struggle with Spain for dominion over the New World, and also the start of the modern British navy.

No one would have been more surprised by this than John Hawkins. Thirty-five years old, small and spare, he was not a visionary but a man of action, a tough experienced mariner and the kind of man others naturally followed—even into a three-day hurricane. He had spent every moment of those three days on deck. Rain streamed from his hair and beard as he ordered men aloft to take in sail so that the hurricane wind did not snap off a weakened mast or spar like a matchstick. At one desperate point, he

I

had even been forced to cut away the top section of his mainmast to reduce the strain.

The *Jesus* was an old ship, a leaky tub with sprung timbers and a rotten hull. Now, after days of battering, she* was ready to give way completely. The carpenter came up from below and bellowed in his ear that the timbers around the stern post were about to burst. The gaps between them were so wide that fish were able to swim through into the hold, the carpenter said; if those timbers opened any wider, they would founder and sink.

This was John Hawkins's third trip into the Caribbean. His father, William Hawkins of Plymouth, was the first English merchant to gate-crash the trade monopoly Portugal and Spain enjoyed with their colonies in the New World. William Hawkins had made a fortune running goods from the Guinea coast—the two thousand miles of African coastline from the Senegal River to the mouth of the Niger—to Portuguese Brazil. His sons William and John had joined him on those dangerous transatlantic voyages when they were barely teenagers. But unlike his father, John Hawkins wanted more than just the occasional smuggling raid. He envisioned a regular trading network from Africa to America, with English ships offering the one commodity of which Spanish settlers could not get enough: slaves.

Slavery was a fact of life in the sixteenth century. The African slave trade was already the largest form of commerce in the world. No one had the least qualms about it, least of all Africa's own tribal rulers. It was also vital for running Spain's empire in America. Hawkins figured he could offer Spanish settlers slaves in greater quantities and at a lower price than they could get from their own merchants. Then they would pay him with the product from the New World everyone craved but which Spanish law forbade to all outsiders: gold and silver from the mines of Peru and Mexico. Once the trade got going, the Spanish colonies would flourish, England would prosper, and Hawkins would be a rich man—the uncrowned king of the New World.

In 1562 Hawkins sought permission for his first slaving voyage from Queen Elizabeth. "The voyage I pretend," he wrote, "is to load negroes in

---

*Why were ships invariably referred to as women? Because words for watercraft in Greek, Latin, Italian, and Spanish are almost all grammatically feminine (e.g., *nave*), which made English translators of books on navigation render the pronoun form as "she."

Guinea and sell them in the West Indies in truck of gold, pearls, and emeralds." He got her tacit approval, as well as backing of a large syndicate of London merchants. In October he set out from Plymouth for Tenerife, the central island of the Canaries and gateway to Africa and America. After stopping several Portuguese slave ships off Guinea and buying or hijacking their cargo (it is unclear which), Hawkins made his way across the Atlantic to Hispaniola, the island where Christopher Columbus had landed seventy years earlier and which was now a thriving Spanish colony.

Hawkins did a brisk business with the local planters. They liked being able to buy their black labor at a fraction of the official price of one hundred ducats per head. Hawkins returned triumphantly home in August of 1563, in ships laden with gold, silver, pearls, sugar, and hides—so much sugar and hides, in fact, that he had to hire two extra ships to carry it all. Everyone was happy, except of course the slaves (although Hawkins took better care of his expensive cargo, even outfitting them with shirts and shoes, than did slavers in later centuries), and the Spanish authorities, who had just seen their monopoly broken and their laws flouted.

Hawkins had done everything to try to accommodate and placate them even though the Spanish were Catholics and Hawkins a God-fearing Protestant. He appealed to the traditional alliance between England and Spain; he pointed out how the trade would benefit Spaniards, not just the English and himself. He had even shipped some of his goods on to Seville, so that he could pay customs just like any regular Spanish merchant (instead, the authorities seized the lot and threw Hawkins's men in prison). But in the end, Hawkins's position was clear. Law or no law, he was going to do business in the Spanish Caribbean. He had something to sell, and his customers were more than willing to buy. If King Philip II's officials in Spain and America did not like that, then they would have to find a way to stop him.

Hawkins's first voyage had been so successful that his second voyage in 1564 attracted some of the most important names in the kingdom as investors: the queen's favorite, Robert Dudley, Earl of Leicester; her first minister, William Cecil; William Herbert, Earl of Pembroke. The queen staked her own claim by contributing one of Her Majesty's own navy ships, the *Jesus of Lübeck,* an impressive high-prowed and high-sterned vessel of 700 tons with sixty-four guns of varying sizes and a crew of eighty. Her father, Henry VIII, had bought it from German merchants, and assessors estimated it was worth 2,000 pounds (only later did Hawkins discover how clumsy, leaking, and unseaworthy the old *Jesus* really was, and how Elizabeth had gotten into his deal on the cheap).

Even in the teeth of opposition from King Philip's government in Madrid, which sternly ordered that no one do business with that brigand and outlaw "Capitan Aquínez," Hawkins's second voyage was even more successful than his first. He returned to England on September 20, 1565, with all his slaves sold and all five of his ships intact, having lost only twenty men out of two hundred to drowning or disease, and returning for his delighted investors more than 60 percent profit.

But now, as he tossed helplessly in the hurricane force winds off the Florida coast almost three years later, Hawkins must have wondered if his luck had run out. It was as if this third voyage to the New World had been cursed from the beginning.

First, the two Portuguese pilots who were supposed to guide him further down the African coast disappeared while he was taking on supplies in London. Then, on July 30, just as they were preparing to leave for Plymouth and the final outfitting, a piece of heavy gear broke loose from the *Jesus* and killed a woman bystander.

When the *Jesus* and his four other vessels did reach Plymouth, Hawkins had an unpleasant run-in with a squadron of ships from Spanish Flanders. Their Flemish commander refused to dip his colors, as all foreign ships were required to do when they passed English navy ships in the Channel, and Hawkins had been forced to fire a shot across their bows to get him to comply. The same commander then had the audacity to ask to berth his ships alongside Hawkins in Plymouth harbor. The Flemish ships were passing England on their way to meet King Philip to take him on a tour of his Netherlands possessions, their commander said; but Hawkins doubted it. He suspected the Flemish were there to spy on him, and wanted to get close enough to learn what kind of cargo Hawkins was taking on and where he was going. Hawkins refused them any berths in Plymouth and so the Flemish sailed on.

Hawkins's bad luck continued as he came out of the Channel. He ran into four straight days of bad weather north of Finisterre, the westernmost tip of Brittany. Storms opened a seam in the *Jesus*'s hull so wide that they had to shove fifteen sheets of thick baize cloth into the gap to keep her from sinking. On reaching the Canary Islands, he had an argument with one of his men who drew his sword and cut a gash in Hawkins's forehead, narrowly missing his eye (the days when an English sailor did not dare to challenge his captain on pain of death were still far in the future).

Worst of all, when they finally reached Africa and the Guinea coast, they could not find any slaves. Every time the English landed to try to round up captives, the alert natives either fought them off or disappeared by running into the jungle. Hawkins lost seven men to poison dart wounds. Another two drowned when their small boat was rammed by a hippopotamus. Finally, in desperation, Hawkins had to strike a deal with two of the local chieftains to help them besiege the town of one of their enemies and split the prisoners between them.

The result was a grotesque horror, even by Elizabethan standards. For two days they besieged the great compound of grass huts with its wooden stockade, while Hawkins lost nine more men dead and twenty wounded. Then, fed up with the desultory pace, Hawkins led his men in a full frontal assault, smashing holes in the stockade with cannon brought on shore and rushing through the gaps with torches tied to their pikes and halberds to set the town alight. His African allies followed behind, but instead of helping to round up captives, they began a systematic massacre of men, women, and children. The terrified inhabitants fled the flames and the attackers. Thousands leaped into the river and adjoining swamps, and were drowned or trampled to death. All night the fires continued to burn, until the screams of the dying and drowning finally died away. In a horrible finale, their African allies cut up and roasted the bodies of their enemies, to consume them in cannibal ritual while the wounded and exhausted English were forced to watch.

The next morning came the final insult. Amid the smoldering ruins, Hawkins was left with only four hundred prisoners, instead of twice that number as he had been promised. But since that was the same number of slaves he had brought away on the previous voyage, and after the horrors of the previous night, he and his men were happy to get off the coast and away from Africa at last.

Once he arrived at the "Spanish Main," the Caribbean coast of South America, he found local officials were more uncooperative than ever. Sales in Barbaruta went well; but at Riohacha, Hawkins had to use cannon to intimidate the local governor into allowing him to set up an impromptu slave market on the beach, with English sailors roughly shoving their captives into line while Spanish settlers looked over their prospective purchases before stepping up to haggle and bargain under the blazing sun. Then came Santa Marta and finally Cartagena where, as Hawkins wrote later, "the governor was so strait" that the English were not even allowed to land to take on food and water. He was only two days

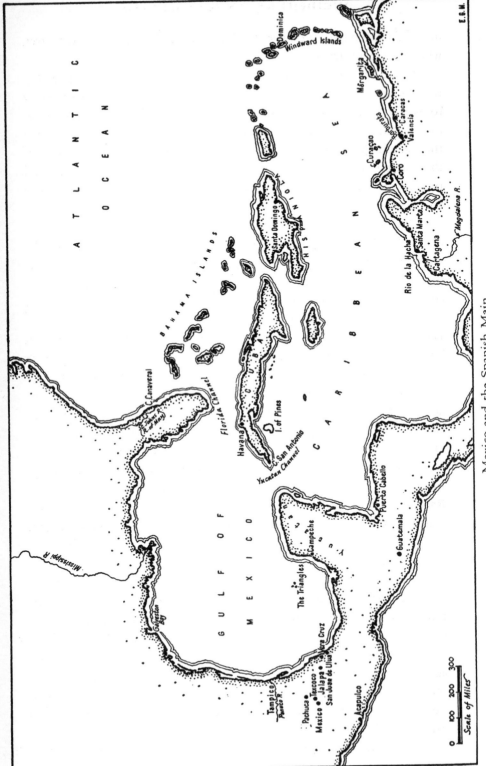

Mexico and the Spanish Main

out of Cartagena, short on supplies but with a hold full of gold and silver, when the storm struck.

Now, after three days of constant battling to keep his leaking flagship from sinking, Hawkins reached a hard decision. He would give up trying to fight the storm and would run with it, all the way back past Florida and into the Gulf of Mexico if necessary, in order to save his ships—as well as the bullion they were carrying. Hawkins ordered his men to hang out three lanterns, the signal for the others to bear away from the wind and run with it. Then the *Jesus*'s prow swung awkwardly as Hawkins tacked around to the south.

One by one the others followed. The *Minion*, 300 tons and commanded by John Hampton, was an even older ship than the *Jesus*, with the same high fore- and aft-castles. But the *Minion* was a seaworthy and seasoned veteran of Guinea coast voyages; like the *Jesus*, she carried a full complement of guns. Then, moving with more ease, came the *Swallow* of 100 tons and the *Angel* of 30, followed by the *Grace of God*. She was Hawkins's latest acquisition and named by him. She was not English at all but Portuguese-built, a fast-running barque with eight guns and a French captain whom Hawkins met when he was plying the African coast and who had decided to cast his lot with the enterprising Englishman. The last was the *Judith* of 50 tons, commanded by a squat and exuberant twenty-two-year-old skilled beyond his years, who also happened to be Hawkins's distant cousin. His name was Francis Drake.

In the surrounding storm and gloom, one ship missed the signal. Instead of bearing away, Captain Thomas Bolton and Master James Raunce kept their ship pointed into the wind—keeping station, as a mariner would say. The rest of the fleet bucketed along behind the *Jesus* and disappeared without noticing they had left one of their own behind.

For the next two days and nights the wind hurled them along the coast. The lashing wind in the rigging and braces had changed from a moan to a shriek, telling them that the hurricane was finally losing its force. The next day the rain stopped, and the wind suddenly shifted from the southeast to the north. Instead of the warm humid gales they had been fighting for almost a week, this wind felt cold, almost icy, as the sky once again began to grow black. Hawkins realized what was coming: the first of the winter season's northerly storms was about to hit his little fleet broadside. All he could do was once again "reef" or shorten the amount of sail exposed to the wind and brace himself for the next onslaught.

It came with less violence than the first storm but lasted almost as long. Timbers creaked and groaned, masts swayed and strained, and below decks barrels and guns pulled at their secure lashings with each pitch of the ship. The smaller ships, the *Judith* and the *Angel,* threatened to tip over or broach in the howling blast, which was pushing them deeper into the Gulf of Mexico. Day after day the *Jesus's* carpenters watched the bursting seams in her stern with alarm as water poured in, while exhausted men cranked away at the pump to spew it out and overboard.

Finally, on September 11, the storm blew itself out. The last clouds scudded past to the southwest. Hawkins and his men were in a part of the Gulf of Mexico none of them had seen before, off the southwest corner of Yucatan, and they were running low on food and water. They rode the freshening breeze all night and the next morning spotted two small sails on the horizon. Hawkins ordered two fast oared boats—pinnaces—out after them, catching one, whose Spanish captain told Hawkins that the only port ahead on their course was San Juan de Ulloa, fifteen miles south of the capital at Vera Cruz. It was four days' sailing.

He also told Hawkins something else. San Juan was where the annual Spanish treasure fleet from Seville picked up the bullion from the mines of Mexico, and the fleet was expected that month. If they arrived before the *Jesus* did, that would mean that the harbor would be swarming with well-armed Spanish galleons.

However, after checking once more below decks, Hawkins realized he had no choice. It was San Juan or sink. He ordered his helmsman to set course for the Mexican coast.

As night fell, the new watch came on deck and the hourglass marking the time was turned. Everyone on board the *Jesus* assembled around the mainmast. There they knelt and bared their heads, as the quartermaster began evening prayers. It was part of daily routine on Hawkins's ships, as one of his crewmen later remembered, "and everyone would recite the Psalms of David, Our Father, and the Creed, in the English tongue." Afterward Hawkins would offer his standard admonition: "Serve God daily, love one another, preserve your victuals, beware of fire, and keep good company"—meaning keep close together for safety's sake.

On September 15, Hawkins's lookouts spotted land, and before nightfall the little fleet dropped anchor in sight of San Juan de Ulloa. The place hardly deserved being called a harbor. It was a shingle of sand, separated from the barren mainland by a deep inlet four hundred yards wide. Barely a quarter-mile long and no wider than two hundred yards, "a bowshot across" as Hawkins put it, the island rose only three feet above high tide. A few small huts housed its Spanish garrison and some black laborers. Otherwise, there was nothing, either on the island or the mainland.

But it was the only safe deep harbor along the entire coast. Massive iron rings sunk in the sand kept ships safely moored, and even the strongest storms and gales left ships in San Juan inlet undisturbed. This was why the Spanish treasure fleet chose to load its gold and silver there, instead of north at Vera Cruz. And above the island, far beyond the beach and surrounding jungle and visible from many miles at sea, rose the great volcanic peak of Orizaba, its snow-covered peak silhouetted against the fading September sun.

Hawkins could make out ships in the inlet, but he could not tell how many or what kind. That night he no doubt consulted with his other captains, including Drake, and resolved on a plan. They would enter San Juan the next morning. However, they would show no English flags or other identification; only the battered royal standard, with the queen's coat of arms, would fly high from the top of the mainmast of the *Jesus,* and from the foretop of the *Minion.* The three Spanish vessels they had seized on their way to San Juan would accompany them as added protection and camouflage. By the time the San Juan garrison realized who he was, Hawkins hoped, it would be too late and his ships would already be in harbor.

The morning of the sixteenth of September found Hawkins and his ships cautiously making their way toward their uncertain rendezvous. Hawkins had no idea what to expect. However, he had ordered men armed with crossbows onto the sturdy platforms or "fighting tops" of the masts, and had his guns cleared for action.

For all the problems below decks, the *Jesus* cut an impressive figure above the waterline. The ship carried a towering forecastle in the bow and a massive aft-castle over the stern, which were both built to withstand waves of boarding parties or bombardment by the heaviest guns afloat. The aft-castle alone had four separate gun decks, each equipped with the various iron and bronze artillery pieces of the age. In addition, the ship was fitted with two fourteen-foot bronze culverins and nine even heavier cannons, each of which could hurl a twenty-five-pound ball into the hull of an enemy vessel with devastating effect. Unfortunately, all this armament and defensive timber also made a Tudor-era warship like the *Jesus* top-heavy and unstable—as the captain of another ship, the *Mary Rose,* found out one day in 1545, when too sharp a turn drove water into his open gunports, and carried him to the bottom of Portsmouth harbor.

Now, Hawkins watched intently as the *Jesus* slowly glided into San Juan. His men were poised on deck with their crossbows and pikes lying beside them, or were at their guns below, matches smoldering and ready to fire. The only sound was Hawkins's commands to his helmsman, who was one deck below him gripping the long rod or whipstaff that turned the rudder at the stern (the ship's wheel would not be invented for another century and a half). Hawkins could make out twelve ships moored in the habor, including a once-proud oceangoing carrack of 700 tons, but now stripped of its masts and left as a hulk at the inner side of the inlet. Then, as the *Jesus* came around the southwest corner of the island, he noticed another feature of the harbor: gun batteries pointing out to sea, including one, its Spanish crew standing at the ready, trained directly at him.

The entire harbor filled with an explosive crash as all five Spanish guns opened fire on the *Jesus,* and great plumes of smoke billowed out across the water. Hawkins was about to give the command to return fire when he realized it was a volley fired not in anger, but in salute. The Spanish assumed that he and his ships were part of the treasure *flota,* arriving to drop off cargo and supplies and await the bullion. Hawkins's deception had worked better than he thought. He had to take advantage of it before they realized their mistake.

It was not until the *Jesus* had dropped her anchors and crewmen had secured the bowline on shore, that the Spanish looked up and noticed that the faded blue and red banner flying from its mast was not that of Spain, but England. At once the cry went out: "The Lutherans are here!" The place flew into a panic. Men abandoned their posts, laborers their tools, and soldiers their weapons. They leapt into any boat or craft they could find, and began madly rowing for the shore. Some even ran into the water and began swimming for it. In a few minutes, the beach was empty while Hawkins's men quickly deployed and secured the island.

A single forlorn figure remained. It was the garrison commander, Captain Antonio Delgadillo. He had managed to keep his nerve while his men deserted him, although his position could hardly be called encouraging. Hawkins sent his second-in-command, Robert Barrett, to talk to him. Barrett was Drake's cousin and fluent in Spanish and Portuguese. He explained to Delgadillo, "They were the Queen of England's ships, come in there for victuals," and that Hawkins intended no harm. He needed time to refit and repair; he would pay for anything he used. All he asked was the permission and cooperation of the officials of San Juan.

Delgadillo was in no position to argue. All morning he had watched the ships come in, believing that they were the treasure fleet from Seville. He had even prepared the little five-gun salute to welcome the distinguished guest the fleet would be conveying to Mexico: Don Martín Enríquez de Almanza, the new viceroy of New Spain. Instead, it turned out to be that dreaded English outlaw Juan Aquínes, who now had the whole harbor under his guns and at his mercy. Delgadillo agreed to Hawkins's demands: he had no choice. Besides, as the Spanish official on Riohacha had said, when his subordinates reproached him for giving in to Hawkins too easily: "None of you knows John Hawkins. He is the sort of man who, when he talks to you, makes it impossible to deny him what he wants."

Inwardly, however, Hawkins was drawing a sigh of relief. He had made it in. As his other ships took their moorings one by one, he ordered the Spanish vessels and crews he had taken along with him to be released. He even had a letter drafted to send to the royal council or *audiencia* in Mexico City, stating his peaceful intentions and his desire to remain as a guest of Spain, "with no quarrel between us." (The letter never arrived; the Spanish officer dispatched to carry it made instead for Vera Cruz to alert the garrison there.) Hawkins kept only two Spaniards on board—a friendly easygoing nobleman named Villaneuva and a local official named Bustamente—in order to guarantee a safe stay in San Juan de Ulloa.

The afternoon passed and night fell on a harbor slowly returning to normal. Normal that is, except for its uninvited English visitors: *Jesus, Minion, Judith, Angel, Swallow,* and *Grace of God.* Hawkins could retire to his cabin and look forward to a day of strenuous hammering and repairs in the morning.

So it was with a sense of rude awakening that his lookouts called him out on deck at dawn. Sails had appeared on the horizon; several ships and large ones, almost certainly armed. Hawkins brought Bustamente up on deck to ask what they could be, but Hawkins had already guessed the answer: the treasure fleet.

Hawkins's position was an impossible one. With his guns and ships, he could deny them the harbor; but it would mean a full-scale fight, with a Spanish garrison at his back. He could not leave without running the same risk. On the other hand, if he allowed them in, he would be at their mercy. The *flota* would consist of at least some heavily armed galleons. And if they found out who he was, the close confines of his moorings would become a death trap.

Robert Barrett turned to ask for orders. "I am between two dangers," Hawkins muttered, "and forced to receive the one of them." By now Delgadillo had been summoned on board and he confirmed that it was indeed the treasure fleet. So Hawkins resolved to take the lesser of two evils. He would let the Spanish in, but on his terms. He dispatched Delgadillo in a small boat to tell the Spanish fleet's commander what those terms were.

By the time Delgadillo reached the fleet's great flagship, its commander Admiral Luxan and Viceroy Don Martín Enriquez already knew who was waiting for them in the harbor. Delgadillo had dispatched an earlier boat to them with news of the Englishmen's arrival as soon as he saw sails on the horizon. Now he told them Hawkins's proposal. Hawkins would allow the Spanish fleet into San Juan, but only after they had agreed to allow the English to remain as well. He wanted a signed agreement to that effect, in addition to an official exchange of hostages.

The viceroy exploded with rage. He was not in the habit of negotiating with pirates and renegades who violated Spanish territory. Tell him I have a thousand men with me, Enriquez told Delgadillo; I am the viceroy of the King of Spain and I will come into the harbor anytime I like.

Delgadillo made his way back and could see that the entire island of San Juan, including its shore batteries, had been taken over by the English in preparation for battle. As he swung on board the *Jesus,* gunpowder and shot were being shifted below and sawdust strewn on deck, with Hawkins himself helping out (the Spaniard remarked on this: no Spanish officer would allow himself to be seen doing manual labor). Dalgadillo saluted and conveyed the viceroy's message.

Hawkins paused and straightened. "I represent my queen's person," he said with a gruff laugh, "and am a vice-roy [literally, *in place of* the king] as well as he! And if he have a thousand men, my powder and shot will take the better place!"

Wearily, Delgadillo sailed the nine miles back to the convoy, which had been joined by all its ships—thirteen in all. Enriquez wanted to attack at once, but Admiral Luxan, an experienced sailor, explained the situation. The Spanish were in as tight a situation as the English. Hawkins now controlled the entrance to the harbor; an attack would mean being exposed to fire from the shore as well as from Hawkins's guns. The *flota* was running low on food and water; there was no other safe place to land anywhere on the coast, not even Vera Cruz. Enriquez would have to swallow his pride and negotiate with that devil Aquines.

The wrangling over terms and hostages took all night and most of the following morning, with Delgadillo ferrying messages back and forth. Then finally, on Saturday the eighteenth of September, Hawkins sent ten of his officers and men with Delgadillo to act as witnesses for the signing of the agreement, and to remain as hostages. The document they signed spelled out the division of the harbor between the two fleets, with sworn pledges before God, promising that "on pain of death, no occasion should be given, whereby any quarrel should grow to the breach" of the agreement. The Spanish officer returned to San Juan, with the ten Spanish hostages for Hawkins and a copy of the document. The deal was done. The Spanish could raise anchor and come into the harbor.

But Don Martín Enríquez was not yet ready to leave. He was planning a little surprise for John Hawkins. While Delgadillo's small vessel made its way south back to San Juan, the viceroy's attention shifted northward, toward Vera Cruz. The day before he had dispatched a boat there, ordering every man capable of bearing arms to join the fleet. That night they began to arrive: soldiers with breastplates, helmets, pikes, and muskets, squeezing into the lower decks alongside Enriquez's other troops. Enríquez had taken on almost two hundred additional men, out of sight of any English lookouts, before the weather began making it impossible for anyone to come safely alongside.

In fact, the weather turned bad for two full days, delaying the Spanish entry into San Juan de Ulloa until the twenty-first. Then the *flota* rode the morning tide into the harbor, sliding past the English-manned batteries and past the *Jesus* and *Minion,* which discreetly left their gunports open even as the ships formally saluted each other, "as the manner of the sea doth require," as one eyewitness remembered.

The work of getting everyone into their moorings and anchorages was complicated and took all day Tuesday and most of Wednesday. By the time they were done, there were almost thirty vessels moored along a few hundred yards of harbor. Hawkins had made it a condition that all the English ships be moored together. The *Minion* marked the line of separation between the two fleets, although it was so close to the nearest Spanish vessel that their bowsprits overlapped. The *Jesus* berthed next to her. *Grace of God,* Drake's *Judith,* the *Angel,* and the *Swallow* all lay on the seaward side. At the other end the Spanish ships were jammed so tightly together that sailors could walk from one deck on to the next, right up to the old empty hulk that lay alongside the *Minion.*

It was a tight situation in more ways than one, but Hawkins and his men were determined to make the best of it. English and Spanish sailors met warily on the beach and began to exchange greetings and goods. Sailors are sailors, after all, whatever country they come from, and since none wore uniforms (any more than officers did in the Elizabethan navy), with their beards and ragged patched clothing there was little to distinguish one from the other—except that the English sailors, by Hawkins's orders, all went ashore with a dagger or sword.

On board ship, too, everything gave the appearance of normality. All weapons were again stowed below. Hawkins exchanged formal salutations with his Spanish counterparts, Luxan and his vice admiral Ubilla, sent parties ashore to collect rope, timber, and nails (again, armed parties), and set to work to repair his ships. Only a very close Spanish observer might have noticed the ax that stood at the warpheads in the bows of every English vessel—ready to cut the mooring cable at a moment's notice.

All was quiet when Hawkins went to bed that night, although he must have felt uneasy. The Spanish had been almost too friendly, too ready and willing to give him the supplies he needed, too acquiescent in these novel arrangements. Too obliging, indeed, for proud men outmaneuvered by foreign intruders.

Then, as he lay in his cabin, he heard a noise.

Any captain on his ship senses when something is wrong or out of place, and Hawkins sensed that now. He sat up just as one of his men knocked on the cabin door. There were strange sounds, the man said, coming from the old Spanish hulk. Hawkins went up onto the moonlight-drenched deck and listened. There was no mistaking it. Someone was secretly moving men on board the hulk. Judging from the sound, they were armored men. The Spanish plan was suddenly clear: they were going to use the abandoned hulk as a Trojan horse, filling it secretly with soldiers so that they could storm across to the *Minion* and the *Jesus* without warning.

It was a trap—but the trap Hawkins had been waiting for. Now he knew the viceroy had had no intention of keeping his bargain. Now he had time to prepare for them. Hampton on board the *Minion* was aware of what was happening as well. Hawkins whispered to his men to double the watch but otherwise do nothing. Then, he went back to bed, his mind at ease. He would deal with the Spanish, and whatever it was they were planning, in the morning.

As dawn came up on September 22, there was still no sign of trouble. No Spanish soldiers or sailors were anywhere on the beach. Their ships lay still and motionless at their moorings. Hawkins checked the hulk. No sign of life. Still, he dispatched a man to warn Hampton and his crew to expect trouble, and told the steward to prepare an early dinner for 8:30 (instead of when an Elizabethan sailor usually dined, at 10:00). When battle came, at least he would have a full meal under his belt.

As the morning wore on with no move from the Spanish, Hawkins decided to break the tension. He dispatched Barrett to see the viceroy and ask him whether there were armed soldiers on board the abandoned hulk, in violation of the spirit of their agreement. Meanwhile, he got more disquieting news from his soldiers manning the guns on the island. They had seen carpenters cutting out extra gunports on the decks of some of the Spanish vessels. Barrett returned to report that Viceroy Enríquez denied that anything was happening on the hulk. Hawkins knew he was being lied to, as well as being lulled into a trap. In his mind, any agreement was now a dead letter.

His steward announced that dinner was ready. Before he went below, Hawkins sent Barrett back one last time, to ask point-blank: were there soldiers on board the hulk, or not? As he sat down at table with his remaining officers, his Spanish guest, Signor Villanueva, was all smiles and laughter. But as the steward, John Chamberlain, was about to put down a plate he saw out of the corner of his eye Villanueva move toward Hawkins with something metal in his hand. Quick as thought Chamberlain pinned Villanueva's arms behind his chair. The something clattered to the floor from Villanueva's hand. It was a dagger.

Villanueva blustered and denied everything as Hawkins sprang to his feet. He told his officers to bind the Spaniard hand and foot and keep him in his cabin. Then Hawkins grabbed a loaded crossbow from the wall and dashed up on deck.

There he had a clear view of the hulk, which was less than twenty yards away. A figure materialized on its deck. It was Vice Admiral Ubilla, with whom Hawkins had exchanged formal courtesies just yesterday— except now Ubilla was in full armor, with a small white flag in his hand and other armed soldiers behind him. Hawkins called out: Was this Spanish treachery? Ubilla replied that he was only doing his duty as an officer and gentleman, just as he knew Hawkins would do his.

"You are quite right," Hawkins roared, and aimed his crossbow and fired. His shot missed but one of his crewman also let loose a dart and the soldier next to Ubilla fell. Before he retreated for cover, Ubilla raised his arm and wildly waved his white flag. At that moment a trumpet sounded on board the *Almirante,* a loud clear note that shattered the silence of San Juan harbor.

All at once Spanish soldiers began to pour out of their ships and swarmed across the shingle bank. The English shore parties guarding the gun batteries were overwhelmed at once. The sailors on the *Minion* found themselves fighting off a tidal wave of boarders from the adjoining hulk. A short jump across and the Spaniards were on the English deck, flailing and slashing with their swords.

The scene was pandemonium. Hawkins watched the battle from the *Jesus's* towering forecastle as missiles and arrows shot past his head. He shouted to his men: "God and St George! Upon those traitorous villains and rescue the *Minion!*" They immediately swung down onto the *Minion's* beleaguered deck and pushed the Spanish back onto the hulk or into the water. But now Spaniards were scrambling onto the *Jesus* as well, as the hand-to-hand battle raged on both ships.

Even as the fight was growing hotter, English sailors were at the bow-lines, cutting the cables to cast off. The *Judith,* the closest to the sea, was the first out. Drake ordered his men aloft to raise sail and get under way. But the other ships were too close to shore to get any breeze to carry them out. Instead, they would have to warp out of harbor.

The term "warp out" conjures up the image of a lightning-quick get-away. In fact, there is probably no slower or more laborious way for a ship to go. It means sending out a kedge anchor in a boat ahead or astern of the ship and lowering it into the water to catch the bottom. Then crew-men man the capstan or anchor spool and haul in the cable until the ship is over the anchor. Then the anchor has to be pulled loose and raised, rowed out again to the end of its cable, lowered in the water, and the whole tedious process begins again. It is a technique of last resort, when a captain finds himself stuck fast on a sandbar, or with no wind—or, as in the case of San Juan de Ulloa, in a sheltered mooring that prevents any breeze from lifting his sails until he is almost out of harbor.

Warping is slow and backbreaking work in normal conditions. Under battle conditions, it seems unimaginable. But that was what the English now had to do if they were to get out of danger—and bring their guns to bear.

For the truth was, even as the Spanish boarders were still fighting desperately, and the crews of the *Jesus, Minion,* and the rest were straining at their capstans to get themselves out of their moorings, the mistake the viceroy had made was becoming clear. He had envisioned the surprise attack on Hawkins as a land battle. He had equipped his soldiers with the same weapons they would use in a normal infantry clash, and employed his sailors as boarders.

But Hawkins was prepared to fight a battle at sea. His ship's guns might fire slowly: each gun's crew took five minutes to get off a single shot (gun crews on Nelson's ships at Trafalgar could manage two shots every three minutes). But at this close range, they would not miss.

At first, things were too densely packed for anyone to fire. But as the *Minion* began to move with a backward lurch, the hulk drifted into her empty berth, exposing the deck and gunwales of the flagship *Almirante*. When the *Minion's* gun crews looked through their gunports, they could suddenly see a target. Almost at once all the guns on her port side roared out, sending hot metal into the *Almirante's* side.

Then as the English ships pulled apart, the *Jesus* joined in—with spectacular results. A shot from one of its great culverins ignited a gunpowder barrel on the *Almirante*. With a tremendous blast the entire starboard side of the ship blew apart, engulfing the ship in flames and black smoke.

As the stricken *Almirante* began to capsize, it was *Capitana's* turn. Shots ripped into her hull as timbers cracked and gave way. Since her sailors were with the boarding parties, there was no one to answer the English fire. The viceroy himself had to hide behind the mainmast as deadly splinters flew in all directions, killing and maiming the men around him.

Exultant, Hawkins surveyed the scene. Three of his men, including a youngster named Job Hartop, had swum out from the shingle to be picked up by the *Jesus*—they were all that was left of his shore parties. There was no sign of Barrett. But in spite of the confusion, it looked like the English ships were almost free. *Judith* was already out of the harbor, and the *Grace of God* and *Angel* were following. Only the *Swallow* seemed still stuck in her mooring. Meanwhile the *Jesus* and *Minion* had driven off their last attackers. Off his port beam, the *Capitana* was slowly sinking, while the *Almirante* was ablaze from end to end.

The English ships really did seem free—they had managed to pull themselves two cable lengths or almost four hundred yards from the nearest Spanish ships—when suddenly the bombardment from the shore started. The *Jesus* was still not far enough out to use her sails. With his men still laboriously warping the vessel along, Hawkins had to bear the brunt of it. The *Jesus's* high castles presented perfect targets for the Spanish gun crews, while her slow ungainly form struggled to maneuver.

Although the old ship could reply shot for shot, and could act as shield for the smaller *Minion,* it was a battle the *Jesus* could not sustain for long.

By now it was late afternoon. As the gun duel with the shore commenced, Hawkins called his mulatto page, Samuel, to bring him something to drink. The boy brought back beer in a silver cup which Hawkins drank to the bottom. He had just set it down to give an order when a Spanish shot swept it away. Hawkins called out to his men: "Fear nothing! God, who hath preserved us from this shot, will also deliver us from these traitors and villains!" The English redoubled their fire at the island.

Then a shot aimed high to cut the rigging severed the foremast just below its upper supports and it came crashing down on deck. Hawkins ordered the St. George banner to be tied to the stump that remained. He looked back into the harbor, where smoke from the *Almirante* continued to drift across the scene. The shore batteries were now firing on his other ships as well. The *Angel* was stricken and sinking, as was *Swallow.* The *Grace of God* had tried to escape heading out the opposite way in the north channel, but took a terrible pounding as it ran past the Spanish ships still in their moorings. Finally, its French captain had to set it alight and abandon ship, swimming out to be picked up by Hawkins and the *Jesus.* He explained that he had hoped to draw off the Spanish fire and torched his ship in the hope that it might ignite the rigging of the nearby Spanish galleons, but failed. "If you had done so," Hawkins roared over the din, clapping him on the back, "you had done well!"

A horrendous noise interrupted him. A shot had ploughed into the mainmast which, weakened by the earlier weeks of storms, now came crashing down on deck, killing twelve men, and slid overboard, dragging sails, braces, and bodies with it. The *Jesus* was now almost dead in the water as her firing slackened.

Hawkins signaled the *Minion* to come alongside. Sheltered in the shadow of the *Jesus*'s great bulk, the *Minion* was safe for the moment. Hawkins gave orders to Hampton: everything and everyone from the *Jesus* was transferring to the *Minion,* and everything that she could not carry would go into the *Judith.* Even now, Hawkins was signaling Drake to come alongside as well. Since they were still in range of the shore guns, there was no time to lose.

Once the *Judith* was laid up beside the *Minion,* work went quickly. Teams of men moved provisions, tools, and ammunition out of the battered *Jesus* and into the *Minion.* Hawkins supervised the transfer of goods on board as well, including his gold and silver—most of which passed on to Drake and the *Judith*. However, one great trunk stuffed with silver ingots was too heavy to move out of its deep hold and, to Hawkins's rage, had to be abandoned.

Last of all came the wounded. Men shot by arrows, pierced by sword or pike, maimed by musket or cannonball, or horribly gashed by flying splinters, were carried up on deck to be loaded onto the *Minion*. Then, suddenly, a cry came up: "Fireships!"

Hawkins turned. Out of the late afternoon gloom came a monstrous sight: an empty Spanish galleon, flames engulfing her masts and deck, was bearing directly down on the three English vessels. It was the Spaniards' last ploy, a kamikaze mission to immolate Hawkins with every sailor's worst nightmare: a fire at sea.

Now it was his crew's turn to panic. With shouts of "Make off!" men began scrambling to escape, dropping wounded comrades overboard and leaping for the *Minion*. Job Hartop watched as two men jumped and missed, plunging into the water to be crushed between the two hulls.

Francis Drake did not hesitate. He cut the lashings that bound him to the *Minion* and *Jesus* and moved out of harm's way. Hawkins could not control his men, even though he shouted to them that the unmanned fire ship, which was already drifting off course, was less of a threat than the guns on shore. Finally he ordered everyone to abandon ship and joined the scramble onto the *Minion*. He was the last man off the *Jesus* (in those days, no captain in his right mind went down with his ship)—or thought he was, when he turned back to see his eleven-year-old nephew, Paul Horsewell, still on deck with another sailor. In the boy's hand were a crystal plate and goblet which he had tried to rescue from his uncle's cabin at the last minute.

Everyone now turned to the boy as the *Minion* began to move away. "Jump! Jump!" they shouted. Young Horsewell was about to obey when a stray shot suddenly struck the man next to him, who fell overboard. Shaken, the boy threw the goblet and plate into the sea and silently watched as the *Minion* sailed out of range. He would never see his uncle, or England, again.

Whatever Hawkins's feelings at that moment, he and his men had to move quickly. Shot was still falling fast around his new flagship, the *Minion,* as he signaled Drake and the *Judith* to join him out of range. As they sailed into the gathering dusk, the sound of gunshots died away, while the burning fire ship lit up the western sky behind them. No other Spaniards followed them: they had clearly had enough of battle with

Hawkins. And so, finally out of sight of San Juan de Ulloa, Hawkins and Drake were able to drop anchor in the dark and assess their losses.

Hawkins had begun the day with six ships; he now had two. Of his three hundred men, he had lost more than a third. It was true that he had given nearly as well as he had gotten, and sent the Spaniards' two proud flagships to the bottom. He had escaped the trap they had elaborately set for him, including the fireship. But escape had cost him dearly, in blood, ships, and, thinking of the silver he had been forced to abandon on the *Jesus,* treasure. Yet no grief at his losses could equal the rage he felt at having been deceived and betrayed. The Spaniards had given their word and then played him false. Somehow, someway, he would make them pay.

In the morning, he had one more nasty shock. The *Judith* was gone. A few hours before dawn, Drake had raised anchor and set sail, taking with him the bulk of the gold and silver his cousin had transferred to him and leaving Hawkins and his overloaded, undersupplied ship to their fate. A heartless and selfish move, no doubt—but also a clear-eyed one. The *Judith* escorting the wounded and clumsy *Minion* might make it home to England: the *Judith* alone almost certainly would. Here in 1568, on his first command, Francis Drake revealed himself as he would be for the rest of his career: a smart, bold, ruthless bastard.

Hawkins may have cursed Drake's name and his own bad luck, but he also knew that, whatever had befallen him and his men up to this point, worse was almost certainly going to come. No coastline, port, or island in the Caribbean was now safe. The *Minion* would have to sail directly for Europe without stopping for supplies, even though she was woefully short of food and water.

When they learned this, almost half his crew, including Job Hartop, told him they wanted to be left behind on the coast to take their chances with the Spanish or the natives, rather than live on boiled leather on the voyage home. Hawkins did not mind; it lessened the number of men he would have to feed. And contemplating the coming trip, he could hardly blame them.

The Atlantic crossing took three months. Hawkins had to deal with starvation, storms, and mutiny. His men ate every living thing they could find on the ship—pigs, dogs, rats, and parrots, until they got down to chewing on pieces of oxhide and leather gloves. Halfway through, the dread of every long-distance ocean voyager struck: scurvy. Men's gums bled, their teeth fell out, and their legs and fingers turned black. Finally the *Minion* made landfall in northwest Spain. Hawkins entered the port of

Vigo to beg for food before all his men died. A Spanish eyewitness caught sight of him there: gaunt and haggard, but with the same crimson velvet breeches and a scarlet leather jacket trimmed with silver braid, and the same air of self-assured command.

The *Minion* left Vigo on January 20, 1569, and reached Plymouth Sound on January 25. Of the one hundred men he sailed from America with, there were fifteen survivors. When he came ashore, he learned that Drake and the *Judith* had arrived in Plymouth three days earlier.

But Hawkins was too preoccupied for recriminations. For one thing, there was still business to be done. Even after all that they had been through, Hawkins was able to send to his partners in London more than 25,000 golden pesos, on four packhorses. As for what he had lost at San Juan, he and his syndicate filed a lawsuit with the Court of Admiralty with a claim for £28,000 in damages, including the cost of the *Jesus* and its guns, arms, equipment, and Hawkins's shipboard wardrobe.

Then he tried to find out what happened to his men who were still in Spanish hands. News was hard and slow to come by, but what did trickle in for the next couple of years was not good. Most of those taken at San Juan de Ulloa had been killed out of hand; the few survivors, like Robert Barrett, were held for trial in Spain. The men Hawkins had left behind on the Mexican coast fared no better. They had originally split into two groups. The smaller group headed north, and although they managed to evade the Spanish, only three of the twenty-three ever found their way back to England. The larger group had headed south for Tampico. They were quickly caught and forced on a death march to Mexico City without food or water, on which many died. When the survivors reached the capital, Don Martín Enríquez wanted to hang them all but was persuaded to wait for a proper investigation. Some were sent to be tried in Spain. The rest had to wait until 1571 when a special board of the Mexican Inquisition convened to consider their cases—not as pirates but as Protestant heretics.

The Inquisition tried thirty men. Eleven had been sixteen or younger in 1568 (which shows how young sailors were in Hawkins's day) and were given relatively light sentences. Miles Phillips, who was just fourteen when he sailed with Hawkins, went to prison for three years. Hawkins's nephew, Paul Horsewell, who had chosen to remain on the *Jesus* rather than jump, was given a flogging and even less prison time. Eventually, Horsewell was released, converted to Catholicism, and married a half-caste Mexican woman. His descendants were still living in Mexico a century later.

The remaining nineteen were not so lucky. Almost all received a back-breaking flogging and then were condemned to serve in the floating prisons of His Catholic Majesty's galleys. William Griffin of Bristol was sentenced to two hundred lashes and eight years in the galleys; John Williams of Cornwall and Robert Plinton of Plymouth, the same. Thomas Goodal of London got three hundred lashes and ten years. The Mexican Inquisition decided George Ribsey of Gravesend was not sufficiently repentant of his Protestant views and that he should be burned at the stake—although it graciously allowed him to be strangled before being put to the fire. Of the rest, only Miles Philips would live to return to England.

As for the prisoners shipped to Spain, most died in captivity (one, George Fitzwilliam, managed to escape and get a letter to John Hawkins to give him some idea of what was happening to his former men). Robert Barrett and Job Hartop were put on a ship for Havana in 1571, with a final destination in Spain. As they entered the Florida Channel late that night, Barrett noticed that they were sailing too close to the point of land known as Cape Cañaveral, and shouted in Spanish to the crew to open sail and to the helmsman to bear away. Barrett had saved the Spanish ship and crew, as the captain profusely admitted. The Spanish repaid him by shipping him across the Atlantic to prison at Terceira in the Azores, where he tried to escape but failed.

Barrett arrived in Seville in chains and was incarcerated in the Casa de Contratación, the headquarters of Spain's New World trade monopoly, which Hawkins had tried to break in vain. Inquisitors condemned Barrett's fellow prisoner Job Hartop to ten years in the galleys and then life imprisonment in an inquisitorial prison. Barrett and another Englishman, John Gilbert, were burned at the stake, this time without the mercy of being strangled first.

Hartop would end up serving twelve years as a rower in the Spanish galleys—the equivalent of a death sentence for most men, including every one of his fellow English prisoners. Hartop, however, survived, although "hunger, thirst, and stripes we lacked none," he wrote later, "til our several times expired." In 1585 Hartop came back to Seville to turn in his rower's loincloth for a penitent's robes and to begin his life sentence.

For the next four years, Hartop languished in a Spanish prison. In the meantime John Hawkins redesigned the English navy, drawing on his own experience at San Juan de Ulloa; Francis Drake captured Cartagena and destroyed the Spanish fleet at Cádiz; Queen Elizabeth ordered the beheading of Mary Queen of Scots; the Armada sailed and was beaten in the English Channel; Sir Walter Raleigh set up his ill-fated colony in America; and Hawkins and Martin Frobisher began a series of regular English patrols off the Azores in hopes of capturing the Spanish treasure fleet.

Then, in 1590, the Inquisition allowed Hartop to begin a prison work-release program as a servant for a merchant family in Seville. One day in October, he saw his chance and escaped. He made it to the port of San Lucar, where he caught a ride on a Flemish coastal vessel. Off Cape St. Vincent, the southwestern tip of Spain, they were intercepted by the *Dudley*, one of the new English warships on its way to patrol the Azores. Hartop was free at last. He finally returned to England on December 2, 1590.

It was just a little more than twenty-three years since he had left home.

CHAPTER TWO

Beginnings

O What a Thing had been then,
If that they that be Englishmen
Might have been the first of all.
—JOHN RASTELL, 1517

HY DO MEN go down to the sea in ships?
Juan Escalante de Mendoza, a Spanish nautical expert in
the sixteenth century, argued that two classes of men spent
their lives at sea. The first kind did so because they had no choice. As
poor men raised near a harbor or port, Mendoza said, they became fishermen or sailors because no other way of life was open to them. And what a
way of life! The dangers of their occupation—of death by drowning,
storms, shipwrecks, mutiny, and piracy (which persisted in the English
Channel until well into the seventeenth century)—made it the most hazardous in a hazardous world. The Elizabethan writer Richard Hakluyt
admitted that most sailors were young men because few lived long enough
to grow old. To quote the proverb: "Those who would go to sea for pleasure would go to hell for pasttime."

But Mendoza said there was a second group of mariners who did just
that, men "whose nature inclines them toward the restlessness and the art
of sailing." Far from being repelled by the sea's perils, they are drawn to it.
Instead of being vexed by its unpredictable ways, they find in it a kind of
freedom. Many of these men enjoy the advantages of wealth and education. Yet "something else appeals to them so that they abandon their
studies to follow their natural inclinations" and go to sea.

It is easy to see John Hawkins as belonging to that second group; likewise his cousin Francis Drake. Although in the minority, it is men like
them who have been the hard core of seafaring communities throughout
history, from the Phoenicians and Greeks to the Vikings and Christopher
Columbus. Men who go to sea because in the final analysis they like it;
men who want to make it clear to the universe that they are not intimi-

dated by it and will not be shaken by it, no matter what it has in store. In Hawkins's part of the world, the West Country—Cornwall, Devon, Somerset, and Dorset—such men were plentiful. That fact made the West Country the original nursery of England's overseas empire and the British navy.

Of course, there are other maritime communities in Britain. There are the so-called Cinque (or Five) Ports of the eastern English Channel—Hastings, New Romney, Hythe, Dover, and Sandwich—which were so important to English trade in the Middle Ages. There are the North Sea coastal cities like Great Yarmouth in Norfolk, less than fifty miles from where Horatio Nelson was born, and Whitby in Yorkshire, where Captain James Cook grew up and apprenticed as a common seaman. There are the towns of the North Foreland and the Downs like Sandwich and Deale and those on the Clyde estuary in western Scotland. But the West Country enjoys a geographic advantage over them all. Jutting into the Irish Sea like an extended foot, it looks out on the world in four directions at once.

It faces north to Wales and Scotland, and west toward Ireland and the Atlantic, the route to the great codfish banks off Iceland and Newfoundland. It also faces south to the French coast of Brittany, where Cornish sailors traded with their Celtic Breton cousins for centuries, and then down to the Bay of Biscay and the Iberian peninsula. But a ship from ports like Falmouth in Cornwall or Dartmouth and Plymouth in Devon could also enter the English Channel, follow the prevailing winds eastward through the Straits of Dover, with Dover and Sandwich on one side and Boulogne and Calais on the other, and fish for herring in the North Sea or trade for timber or furs in the Baltic. In short, almost anywhere an Englishman would want to go by sea, he could reach with fair ease and speed from the West Country.

Although it is open to the world, it is also a bastion. The ragged, jagged coastline of Cornwall and Devon face the Bristol Channel to the north with limestone and shale cliffs rising some four hundred to six hundred feet above sea level, and the English Channel to the south with forbidding headlands alternating with twisting treacherous shoals. It offers many harbors but no large beaches for a foreign attacker. Julius Caesar, William the Conqueror, Philip II, Napoleon, Hitler—all of England's invaders and would-be invaders have had to look farther east for a place to land their armies.

Yet the same coast is the perfect haven for seafarers. From Land's End at its westernmost tip, Cornwall is dotted with ancient harbors—

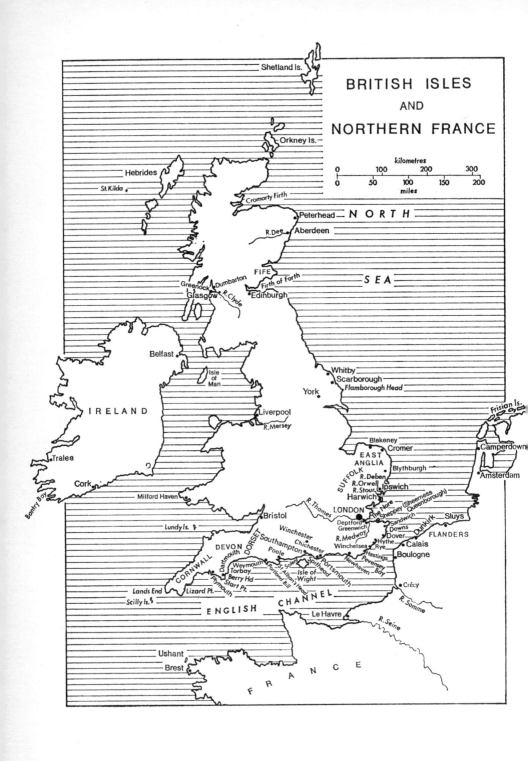

BRITISH ISLES
AND
NORTHERN FRANCE

kilometres
0   100   200   300
0   50   100   150   200
miles

Shetland Is.

Orkney Is.

Hebrides

St.Kilda

Cromarty Firth

N O R T H

Peterhead

R.Dee   Aberdeen

FIFE

Greenock   Dumbarton
Glasgow   R.Clyde
Firth of Forth
Edinburgh

S E A

Belfast

Isle
of
Man

Whitby
Scarborough
Flamborough Head

York

I R E L A N D

Liverpool
R.Mersey

Frisian Is.

Blakeney
Cromer

Camperdown

EAST
ANGLIA

Blythburgh

Amsterdam

Tralee

SUFFOLK
R.Deben
R.Orwell
R.Stour
Ipswich
Harwich

Cork

Milford Haven

R.Thames
LONDON
The Nore
Sheppey (Sheerness)
Queenborough)

Bristol

Deptford
Greenwich

Sandwich
Downs
Dover
Hythe
Rye

Dunkirk

Sluys

FLANDERS

Bomtry Bay

Lundy Is.

Winchester
Southampton
Chichester
Poole

R.Medway
Winchelsea

Calais

DEVON
DORSET

Boulogne

CORNWALL

Dartmouth
Weymouth
Torbay
Berry Hd.
Plymouth
Start Pt.

St.Catherines
Portland Bill
St.Alban's Head
Isle of
Wight
Spithead
Portsmouth

Hastings
Pevensey
Newhaven
Rye

Crécy

R.Somme

Lands End
Lizard Pt.
Scilly Is.

E N G L I S H   C H A N N E L

Le Havre

R.Seine

Ushant

Brest

F R A N C E

Penzance, St. Ives, Falmouth, Truro—where for a thousand years Scandinavians, Romans, Irish, Saxons, and perhaps even the occasional adventurous Phoenician, landed to trade for the products of Cornwall's interior, tin, copper, and gold. The landmass of Devon, about twice the size of Cornwall, is covered by two great granite moors, Dartmoor and Exmoor, and crisscrossed by a complicated network of rivers. Some flow north, forming inland ports west of the Bristol Channel like Barnstaple and Bridgewater. The others run south, creating a series of shipping ports facing on the English Channel: Exeter on the Exe, Totnes and Dartmouth on the Dart, and Plymouth on three at once, the Plym, the Tavy, and the Tamar, forming the most extensive deep-water anchorage in southwest England.

Exeter, Barnstaple, and Totnes date back to Anglo-Saxon times. Totnes was where the mythical founder of Britain, Brutus of Troy, was supposed to have landed and where English knights left for the Second Crusade. However, the advent of King Henry II and Queen Eleanor of Aquitaine, with their extensive interests in France, gave birth to Dartmouth and Plymouth. Plymouth quickly became a favorite launching point for military expeditions across the Channel. The Black Prince assembled three hundred ships there for his invasion of France in 1356. Plymouth and Dartmouth offered good shelter for large numbers of ships—although the entrance to Plymouth Harbor could be a death trap in stormy weather—but also towns large enough to quarter an army. And, of course, they supplied a labor force who knew boats and knew the sea.

The West Country bred a distinctive kind of mariner. They were men and sometimes women (when Lord John Russell visited Devon in the 1540s he found fishing boats with female crews) who were not only skilled in handling a boat but in farming, herding, and in the case of Cornwall, mining. They were inured to the dangers the sea offered, and resourceful, able to replace a sail or repair a boat at sea—or build one from scratch on land if they had to. A lifetime of navigating Devon and Cornwall's treacherous coastal waters, of judging the unpredictable Atlantic weather, and having to choose a safe sea route or landfall before sailing, gave them the kind of independent intelligence their land-bound cousins never had the chance to acquire.

But their dangerous life also taught them the importance of discipline and teamwork, the cumulative cooperative effort that every ship needs to survive its voyage. That explained the importance of having as many family members on board as possible. West Country sailors like Hawkins were notably clannish, and suspicious of strangers. Yet the need for teamwork also encouraged them to think of all their crewmen as to some degree equal partners in running and handling the ship. It bred a rough shipboard egalitarianism that would be passed on to the British navy and persist through centuries of the navy's harsh martial law and discipline at sea.

For whether he was rich or poor, fisherman or pirate, every West Country man shared a distinct maritime culture, a world strikingly different from that which arises from the routines of the land. It had its own values, its own outlook on life, even its own language—as sailors still do today. For landlubbers thrown into this peculiar world, the effect could be disconcerting. Ancient philosophers believed seafarers formed their own category of beings, distinct from either the living or the dead. A recruit for the British navy in the eighteenth century who had never been to sea thought much the same thing: "Nor could I think what world I was in, whether among spirits or devils. All seemed strange; different language and strange expressions of tongue, that I thought myself always asleep or in a dream, and never properly awake."

Even among the English, the seamen bred in the harsh, primitive landscape of the West Country stood out. "Fouler ways," Sir Robert Cecil wrote when he visited Dartmouth, "more desperate ways nor more obstinate people did I never meet with." Geoffrey Chaucer also met them when he came to Dartmouth as a customs official almost two hundred years earlier in 1373, just as Devon was beginning to replace the Cinque Ports as the center of English seafaring. He summarized their character with his Shipman in *The Canterbury Tales,* who was drawn from a Dartmouth captain Chaucer knew named George Hawley:

> *Hardy he was, a way to undertake;*
> *with many a tempest hadde his beard to shake.*

Chaucer adds that his Shipman was a "good fellow," meaning a tough customer, "and of nyce conscience took he no keep." For good reason. Although a bastion, the West Country was always vulnerable to attacks from the sea. Viking marauders had preyed on the ancient monasteries of Cornwall. During the Hundred Years' War, Genoese mercenaries rowed their war galleys west through the Channel, sank ships in Plymouth Harbor, and made it almost all the way to Bristol. French fleets returned to burn Plymouth in 1377, and again in 1403, when six hundred houses were destroyed and most of the inhabitants were killed or taken prisoner. In 1595 the Spanish pillaged and burned Penzance. A hundred years later the French navy attacked Teignmouth.

The perpetual threat of violence and pillage turned West Country men into warriors, and pillagers in their own turn. In the sixteenth century, the Spanish ambassador dubbed them "savages." They had a Europe-wide reputation for being "the most infamous for outrageous, common, and daily piracies."

Yet it was out of this rough, undisciplined, but fearless and resourceful population that the Elizabethan age would find its greatest sailors (a word just coming into use when Elizabeth took the throne in 1558). John Hawkins, Francis Drake, Walter Raleigh, Humphrey Gilbert and John Davis, explorer of the Northwest Passage, were all from Devon. They were also related to one other by blood or marriage. Cornwall produced many great families of sailors including the Killigrews, Eriseys, and Trelawneys (Hawkins's mother was a Trelawney), but one name would out above the rest: Richard Grenville, whose father was captain of Henry VIII's *Mary Rose* and drowned when it capsized. The vice admiral on board at the time, Sir George Carew, was from Devon.

Somerset would have to wait until the next century to generate naval heroes like Robert Blake and William Dampier. Bristol's heyday belonged to an earlier Tudor era. But even with the rise of London as England's maritime capital, the West Country remained at the core of the English seafaring tradition—and the Royal Navy. It was as much the nursery of the navy in the age of Nelson as in the age of Hawkins and Drake. The notorious Captain Bligh was a Cornishman; so was Nelson's signal lieutenant at the Battle of Trafalgar. Nelson's mentor, Admiral Hood, came from Dorset; the officer who sailed back to England with the news of Nelson's death was born in Tavistock. Even in the nineteenth century Devonshire supplied the navy with more officers than any other county in England.

A good example is Robert Falcon Scott. He grew up at Outlands near Milehouse, a rise of ground overlooking Plymouth Sound. As a boy he watched the great navy ships plying in and out of harbor, their white sails spread before the breeze or leaving a wispy trail of gray smoke, if they were under steam. Scott's greatest dream was to join the British navy; in 1881 he got his wish when, as a cadet, he boarded the training ship HMS *Britannia* at its moorings on the river Dart. In twenty years he would become a captain and the most famous of all British polar explorers, perishing with the rest of his party on his way to the South Pole in 1912.*

The West Country tradition continued into the Second World War. Plymouth's naval base at Devonport remained a crucial manning depot for Royal Navy ships. In fact, when the battle cruiser HMS *Repulse* arrived in Singapore in 1941, it was known as a "Guz ship" because so many of her crew were "Guzzlers" or West Country men—so called for their love of Devonshire cream and Cornish pasties.

In the sixteenth century, the typical Guzzler was tough, resourceful, independent, and ready for a fight. Hawkins's betrayal at San Juan de Ulloa was the excuse they needed. The incident made Spain, once England's main ally in continental politics, Public Enemy Number One in the West Country. A new chapter in English history was about to open, with three decades of war, raids, and reprisals in the farthest reaches of Asia and the New World. England was moving decisively away from Europe, toward the Atlantic and the sea.

. . .

On the morning of Friday, October 12, 1492, Christopher Columbus, resplendent in a scarlet velvet doublet and holding the royal banner of Spain in his hand, knelt on the shore of the island of San Salvador and kissed the ground. From that moment, the Atlantic sailor became the new Indispensable Man in history.

The Mediterranean was the ancient heart of European seafaring, just as it was the core of Europe's economy. In the Middle Ages Mediterranean sailors taught the rest of Europe how to sail more efficiently with the triangular lateen (or Latin) sail mounted parallel with the keel, for greater maneuverability in all kinds of weather. They gave their northern counterparts the compass and the first navigational charts. But the conditions sailors met in waters facing onto the Atlantic—powerful tides (rare in the Mediterranean), rocky and treacherous shoals, violent storms alternating with dense fogs—created a different kind of sailing culture. The Atlantic sailor demanded sturdy ships with a deep draft to take the

---

*Britain's other great polar explorer of the twentieth century, Robert Shackleton, was neither a Royal Navy officer nor from the West Country. But the naturalist on his *Endurance* expedition, T. V. Hodgson, was, having been curator of the Plymouth Museum.

buffeting of heavy seas and violent weather. He took frequent soundings to test water depth as he approached shore. He learned how to pick out safe harbors by sight along an unfamiliar coast. Finally, he learned to rely on skill and luck when faced with the unknown.

These were the same harsh and unforgiving conditions sailors would find when they ventured along the coasts of Africa and America, as the age of European exploration got under way. Likewise in the Indian Ocean and Pacific. Even Columbus, who was Genoese by birth, had learned after years of living in Portugal to set aside the sailing habits of his native Mediterranean for those of his adopted Atlantic home. Without them, he probably would never have reached America.

So after centuries of obscurity, Atlantic man's moment had arrived. It took the English some time to realize this, and how they were uniquely situated—geographically, politically, culturally—to take advantage of it. This, in spite of the fact that they had already been to the New World well before Columbus.

On July 15, 1480, John Lloyd sailed his ship of 80 tons out of Bristol harbor. Lloyd was a sailing master and pilot, some said the best in England. He belonged to a select group of Bristol merchants who specialized in the long-distance carrying trade to Spain and Portugal: Thomas Croft, John Jay, Robert Strange, William Spencer, and Robert Thorne. Lloyd regularly made the run from Bristol to Lisbon and Huelva, carrying wool and dried cod in exchange for goods from Portugal and Spain's imperial possessions: sugar, wine, olive oil, and oranges.

But this time Lloyd's destination was exploration, not trade. He was going to try to find what the Portuguese chart maker Andrea Bianco called the Ylha de Brasil or the "Isle of the Blessed," which according to long-standing legend among seafarers, lay due west from Lisbon. The Portuguese had looked for Brazil and assumed they found it when they discovered the Azores. Lloyd had other ideas. Unfortunately, storms off the coast of Ireland drove him back. But the following July, two other ships, the *George* and the 100-ton *Trinity,* set off again. They belonged to Thomas Croft, William Spencer, and William de la Fount, who had a license to send ships into the Atlantic for unknown destinations. The *George* and *Trinity* returned weeks later—and refused to say where they had been. But the rumor around Bristol was that they had found the greatest fishing grounds of all time.

Codfish was an essential part of the medieval European diet. Bristol fishermen had been visiting the busy cod banks off Iceland for years.

Then they began to look farther west. Since the farther out fishermen went the more likely it was their catch would spoil, the Bristol cod fleets learned to take their catches ashore and dry the fish on the beach (it also saved them the cost of salt for preservation). If Bristol fishermen had found the Grand Banks, then it is also likely they would have looked for land nearby to dry their fish.

But did they land in North America? Two tantalizing bits of evidence suggest they did. The first is a letter Bristol sea captain Robert Thorne wrote to King Henry VIII in 1527, stating that his father and another Bristol merchant named Hugh Elliott "were the discoverers of the New Found Lands, of which there is no doubt." Thorne certainly knew that in 1497 John Cabot arrived on the North American coast, and named it Newfoundland. So his remark had to refer to an earlier voyage, and indicates that Cabot's name for that rocky shore was already known to Bristol sailors. Thorne offered no direct proof for his claim, but it certainly suggests someone from Bristol had been to America before 1497.

But before 1492? In 1956 a Spanish archivist discovered a letter from John Day, yet another Bristol merchant, to Christopher Columbus. The letter is undated but must have been written before March 1498. It mentions past voyages by Bristol seamen "who found Brasil, *as your Lordship knows. It was called the Isle of Brasil and it is assumed and believed to be the mainland that the Bristol men found*." The main subject of Day's letter was John Cabot's voyage the year earlier: he even sent Columbus a copy of Cabot's map of the Newfoundland coast. So Day's reference to earlier trips to America "many years before" (*en autros tiempos*) means Columbus has stiff competition for his claim to have discovered the New World, to say the least.

That makes geographic sense as well. Bristol sits much closer to the American continent than either Spain or Portugal. Although the prevailing winds come out of the west, it was a logical place to start for sailors looking for routes across the Atlantic. Columbus himself almost certainly visited Bristol in 1477 and may have sailed out as far as the Grand Banks with one of its fishing fleets, although the evidence is not conclusive. When Columbus was looking for backers for his original idea for sailing west to reach India and China, the English were on his short list. In 1488, after being turned down by the Portuguese and then Spain (four years later, Ferdinand and Isabella would change their minds), Columbus sent his brother to London to put their plan to the new king of England, Henry Tudor.

Henry had just won a civil war, defeating Richard III at the Battle of
Bosworth three years earlier and crowning himself Henry VII. He was
preoccupied with the problems of establishing order in a kingdom
wracked by decades of violence and turmoil. He had no attention, let
alone money, for the Columbus venture. But Henry may have had other
reasons for turning them down. One of his closest backers was none
other than Bristol merchant Thomas Croft, whose brother was treasurer
of the king's household. They may have warned him off the Genoese
sailor's plan because they had already been there. Columbus was not
going to reach China, they would have said; all he would find would be
the rocky, barren shores of New Found Land.

So Henry Tudor turned Columbus down, and missed a vital moment
in world history. But when Columbus found not rocks and fog but the
natives and gold of the Caribbean, Henry and his entourage were more
receptive toward John Cabot in 1497. Like Columbus, Cabot was Italian
(from Venice, not Genoa); like Columbus, he was loyal to an idea, and
did not care which king he served as long as he got ships and money.
Cabot also wanted to reach China, but this time from Bristol. That would
shorten his trip; rumors about Bristol merchants sponsoring trips to
"Brasil" for more than a decade must have confirmed his hunch. He
would sail west across the Atlantic, then steer north, not south as Columbus had. In no time Asia would appear on the horizon.

This time Henry Tudor agreed. He gave Cabot permission to claim
for England "whatsoever lands, countries, regions, or provinces of heathens or infidels" he might find that other Christian powers had not discovered before. In May 1497 Cabot left Bristol on the *Matthew,* a ship of
50 tons with a crew of only twenty men. It took them less than half the
time it had taken Columbus to cross the Atlantic, and in little more than
thirty days they spotted land. Cabot rowed a small boat ashore and
planted three flags: England's, the pope's, and the banner of St. Mark's for
his native Venice. He and his men could see signs of recent human activity: a notched tree, an abandoned fire, even some wooden tools. But no
one came out to meet them. There was only an eerie stillness, broken only
by the roar of the surf. So Cabot and his men filled their water casks and
"being in doubt, he returned to his ship."

Cabot and the *Matthew* explored the coast of what it is now Newfoundland for a month. They visited the Grand Banks, but no one was
especially impressed by this discovery—almost certainly because the Bristol men already knew about them. He returned to England on August 6,

bringing back some of the crude tools he had found to prove that the New Found Land really existed.

John Cabot received a honorific title and more money, but the wealth of Asia had eluded him, just as it had Columbus. He set off again the next year with four ships but Cabot's own disappeared in a storm off the west coast of Ireland. His son Sebastian then took up the cause, organizing a syndicate of Bristol merchants calling themselves "The Company Adventurers of the New Found Lands." He visited the coast of North America several times, explored the waters between Greenland and the Arctic, and discovered the entrance to Hudson's Bay. He even brought back three live Eskimos, who became wards of the king, acquired European clothes, and settled down to live in Westminster Palace.

But England was already too late in the race to discover and exploit new worlds. Spain and Portugal had established an early and seemingly insurmountable lead. In 1489 Bartolomeo Diaz reached the southern tip of Africa and the Cape of Good Hope. Columbus continued to explore the Caribbean on his voyages after 1492 until his death in 1506. In 1494 the Pope had issued an executive order which in effect divided the non-European world between the two Iberian kingdoms, giving America to the Spanish and Asia to the Portuguese (an earlier pope, Eugenius IV, had felt free to give Portugal the right to conquer and enslave all of Sub-Saharan Africa). In 1498 Vasco da Gama sailed the Indian Ocean and reached India.

The Spanish and Portuguese literally encircled the Eurasian landmass with new sea routes. They had turned the tables on western Christendom's traditional enemies, Islam and the Ottoman Empire, and opened a previously unknown continent to European penetration. Over the next three decades Spanish conquerors Hernán Cortés and Francisco Pizarro would topple the Aztecs and Incas, making South America and the Caribbean the core of a Spanish empire in the New World. Portugal would make good its claim to eastern sections of that continent, which it would call Brazil, just as Ferdinand Magellan would establish Spain's foothold in Asia by landing in the Philippines. Spain would begin extracting gold and silver from Mexico and Peru, and extend its reach northward across the Rio Grande River and into Florida. Portugal would trade for pepper and spices in Asia, making Lisbon the emporium of the world.

England's opportunity to play any part in this had long passed. The Cabots did fix the northern coast of North America in the European imagination. Sebastian Cabot drew up elaborate maps and charts establishing England's claim to it. But compared to the bullion from New Spain and Peru, the claim seemed worthless. Cabot himself was convinced that he had found a sea route through the American continent to Asia, a "northwest passage," but no one would give him money to explore it. Finally, in 1512 he gave up and left to serve the king of Spain for the next thirty-five years.

In the meantime, the king of England's attention was finally being drawn to the sea. But what was attracting him was not visions of gold but the sound of guns.

*   *   *

Generations of naval historians have taught us to think of Britain's destiny as linked to the sea. After all, no place in Britain is more than sixty-five miles from the coast. But this was not how medieval English kings saw their realm. They focused on their rich and populous hereditary lands in France. They did not see the English Channel as the first line of defense of Fortress Britain. Instead, it was an inconvenient interruption of travel and communication between the two halves of their domain. English ships that sailed under the royal banner served merely to minimize that inconvenience, by ferrying messengers, supplies, and the occasional army back and forth between France and the British Isles.

For five hundred years England had no permanent navy. The "Navy Royal" was not a thing but an event, an assemblage of ships, soldiers, and sailors for a specific military expedition. When King Edward III organized his great flotilla to invade France in 1347, barely thirty of seven hundred ships actually belonged to the king. All the rest were borrowed from private merchants and fishermen. Once the army landed, the fleet broke up and individual ships sailed away to resume their normal trade or fishing schedules. They only met again if there was another army to ferry or loot to be carried home.

The man in charge of assembling these temporary fleets and outfitting and manning them was the Lord Admiral. *Admiral,* a word with Arab origins, and borrowed from the more advanced seafaring world of the Mediterranean, first appears in English in 1295. In England, the admiral's job was largely administrative. He shared it with the Clerks of the King's Ships and only commanded the Navy Royal in the sense that he organized the resources of the kingdom necessary to raise a fleet.

In fact, the most important task the Lord Admiral of England performed in the Middle Ages was not military at all, but judicial. Every week disputes between ships or merchants at sea came to his various Admiralty courts, set up in every major port in England and supervised by his vice admirals. Litigants paid hefty fees for a swift hearing, and fat bribes for a favorable judgment. The Lord Admiral's share of that money, and his share from the salvage of abandoned wrecks and captured enemy merchant ships, or "prizes," usually made him a rich man. The office became an object of political competition and intrigue. Personal influence at court, rather than military experience at sea, was the primary qualification. It was never quite the case, in Gilbert and Sullivan's phrase, of "Never go to sea and some day you may be ruler of the King's Navy," but it could come close. For a time in Henry VIII's reign, the Lord Admiral was a boy of seven.

Since the Lord Admiral was usually busy with duties on land or counting his money, actual command of the Navy Royal at sea fell to the king himself, or some other great noble he selected to command. Such a figure was called a captain, a term borrowed from land warfare. This was not surprising since medieval war at sea looked very much like war on land. Ships fought each other in much the same way they had since Greek and Roman times. After coming alongside each other to trade volleys of arrows or crossbow darts (or later, stones or lead shot from primitive firearms), soldiers and knights then scrambled on board the enemy's deck to kill the crew and capture the ship. The fighting was hand-to-hand, with the same weapons as on land and just as savage. The longbow, crossbow, sword, and pike were the crucial equipment on a Navy Royal ship in the Middle Ages, along with the men who used them. Those who actually handled the ship itself, its master and his crew, counted for very little.

Since virtually any large craft could do the navy's primary job, transporting soldiers into battle, ships completely dedicated to warfare were rare. Those that were followed the pattern of the classic warship of the Mediterranean, the multi-oared galley. Their open decks and shallow draft made them useless for long-distance travel in northern European waters, let alone on the open ocean. But for fighting in the Irish or English Channels, or what was called "the narrow seas," their light construction, speed, and superb maneuverability easily outclassed heavier, clumsier northern sailing vessels such as the cog, the potbellied freighter of northern medieval trade, or even that Mediterranean hybrid, the caravel. By the fifteenth century galleys also began carrying cannon. Crammed with one hundred to two hundred soldiers and archers, and outfitted with multiple guns sweeping in all directions, the Mediter-ranean war galley remained a formidable fighting machine.

Unfortunately, English kings never could afford enough of them. After a brief and glorious interlude under King Henry V, war and civil war in the fifteenth century sapped the resources of the English monar-chy and its maritime enterprise. Not a single new ship was built at royal command for almost half a century. All through the Hundred Years' War, English ports lay open to attack from the galleys of its rival, the French. During the War of the Roses, the Crown became so enfeebled it could not stop pirates from operating in its own waters. At one point Edward IV had to pay 11,000 crowns to Basque shipowners for the losses they suffered at the hands of pirates from the West Country.

At the same time, English seafarers were falling behind the latest technological changes pioneered by other Atlantic-based maritime coun-tries like Spain and Portugal. Merchants who wanted the latest ship designs, such as the three-masted caravel, which Columbus used for his *Niña* and *Pinta* in 1492, or the big carrack, which carried Ferdinand Magellan around the tip of South America into the Pacific in 1520, had to buy them from foreign builders. It was not until the 1420s that English sailors even began using a compass.

Under these conditions, any thought of the English controlling their own coastline, let alone access to the Channel, seemed far-fetched. In 1485 Henry Tudor was able to sail his tiny invasion force from France into Milford Haven in Wales with no interference from Richard III and then beat him at Bosworth Field. Once he took the throne as Henry VII, he followed the lead of his more prudent predecessors. He decided the only way to guarantee England's security was to cultivate powerful friends abroad, in particular Ferdinand and Isabella's Spain.

Henry VII did not ignore England's need for its own access to the ocean and the wider world. Besides encouraging the Cabots, he pro-moted the merchant dynasties of Bristol like the Crofts and decreed that all wine coming into England had to be carried in English ships. He pur-chased a warehouse for royal naval provisions at Greenwich, just east of London on the Thames, and fortified Dartmouth, pioneering the use of cannon for defending forts from attacks from the sea. He even commis-sioned two large armed naval vessels, the *Regent* and the *Sovereign*—the first the English Crown had built in fifty years.

But when the king of France married the heiress of the kingdom of

Brittany, exposing the whole of England's southern coast to French fleets operating out of Breton ports like Brest and Saint-Malo, Henry understood he could not face the French threat alone. He cemented his alliance with Spain by marrying Princess Catherine of Aragon to his son and heir. Bride-to-be Catherine and her ladies-in-waiting arrived at Plymouth on October 2, 1501. Little did she realize that she would soon be a pawn in the power struggle of the English Reformation, and only the first of the six wives of Henry Tudor's son, Henry VIII.

Prudence and circumspection, the hallmarks of Henry Tudor's regime, enabled him to keep the peace and build a large royal surplus before he died in 1509. His son Henry VIII had other plans. The hallmarks of his thirty-seven-year reign were impatience and greed. Greed for food, which soon affected his figure; greed for sex and for an heir, which led him to divorce Catherine of Aragon and marry first Anne Boleyn and then a string of successive queens. Greed, too, for absolute control over his kingdom, which was the real cause of his break with the Roman Catholic Church and the creation of a separate Church of England, with Henry as Supreme Head, in its place.

Greed, finally, for power and glory. Henry dreamed of making England a great empire—he was in fact the first English ruler to use the term *empire* to describe his realm. He wanted England to take its rightful place as a great continental power. Yet of all its former French possessions, only Calais and the Channel Islands were still left. So empire building meant war with France, and that in turn meant a large and effective navy as well as an army.

For his new Royal Navy his model was, ironically enough, his neighbor to the north and France's ally, Scotland. Its king, James IV, was obsessed with the new bronze artillery of the age, which could fire farther and more accurately than any guns forged before. James not only used them on land, as powerful siege artillery, but also at sea—in fact, he was probably the first monarch to put large siege-style cannon on ship, in his war with clan chieftain Donald Dubh MacDonald for control of Scotland's Western Isles in 1504. The king of Scotland built for his purpose a big oceangoing vessel, not a war galley at all but a massive three-masted carrack of 700 tons, which he dubbed the *Margaret,* after his wife and Henry VIII's sister.

Henry may have been recklessly ambitious in military matters, but he was also a skillful copycat. He built three massive war vessels, floating fortresses of the *Margaret* model, with towering castles in the fore and aft and large gun decks below. The first was called the *Henry Grace à Dieu* (later the *Great Harry*). The second took the delightful name of the *Peter Pomegranate*, while the third was literally the sister ship of James IV's *Margaret*, and named for Henry's other sister, the *Mary Rose*.

The *Mary Rose* remains the most famous ship of the Tudor navy, largely because her remains now have their own museum in Portsmouth after marine archaeologists pulled them up from the deep in the 1960s. When she was originally built in 1509–10, the *Mary Rose* was a state-of-the art Renaissance warship. Her designers had finally and definitively abandoned the old clinker style of constructing hulls, the bolted overlapping planking that had characterized ships for northern waters since Viking times, and adapted the smooth close-fitting caravel style planking, permitting a much bigger and stronger construction—strong enough to carry big, ship-cracking guns.

The *Mary Rose* had seven of them, their great bronze muzzles poking out of gunports (which a Frenchman had invented in 1501) cut in the ship's sides, front, and stern, and thirty-four other lighter iron cannon. In 1536 she was rebuilt again, with no less than ninety-six guns, the heaviest weighing more than a ton. The *Mary Rose* was the first English ship to carry cannon in her waist, where the heavier timbers could absorb the shock, and to have two continuous gun decks. No war galley dared approach her. The age of big guns at sea had arrived.

Yet for all her advanced design, the *Mary Rose* remained a prisoner of the conventional thinking of the age. She had a crew of two hundred, including officers whose titles would endure throughout the age of sailing navies. She officially had a captain, since she was large and important enough to rate a commander with that prestigious title; a master in charge of handling and steering the ship and a master's mate; a purser in charge of the ship's supplies and cargo; a boatswain or bosun who looked after the ship's rigging and a bosun's mate; and then gunners, stewards, quartermasters, a cook, a carpenter, and even a surgeon.

But the *Mary Rose* also carried an equal number of infantry along with their infantry weapons: pikes, longbows, and more than two hundred suits of armor. Her guns were not set up to fire the classic "broadside" of later naval battles but to repel boarders coming from every direction. Some even faced out over her own deck. The heaviest were designed to pound an enemy vessel into immobility before *Mary Rose*'s soldiers got on with the important job of taking the ship by storm. In the hold the ship even carried two hundred of the long pointed stakes that archers inserted in the ground to protect against cavalry attacks.

As long as the Atlantic world continued to take its military cues from the Mediterranean and land warfare, it could not find the same competitive edge it already enjoyed in the sphere of exploration. In that regard, Henry VIII was no different than other European rulers, or his medieval predecessors. But his determination to spend money to get the navy he wanted did have important unforeseen consequences.

First, he expanded the number of royal ships from twelve to eighty-four. To build and service them he had new shipyards constructed on the Thames at Deptford, Erith, and Woolwich, just above and below his palace at Greenwich so that he could visit the docks himself. He also took the first tentative steps toward building Fortress Britain by putting up extensive fortifications along the southern English coast, including twenty new forts to defend the Kentish coast and the mouth of the Thames. Henry would spend almost one-third of his annual revenues on fortifications—most of it paid for by the sales of land from his dissolution of England's monasteries.

Henry also built new ship facilities at Portsmouth, where King John had first built a dock in the thirteenth century and which was an important assembly point for fleets of the "Navy Royal." But the real headquarters of Henry's navy was Deptford. By the time of his death more than six hundred shipwrights and laborers were working there or at Woolwich and Portsmouth. Engineers were kept busy digging out Deptford Pond, "wherein shall ride at all times and float those ships ensuing, that is to say the *Great Galley,* the *Mary Rose,* the *Peter Pomegranate,* the *Great Bark* and the *Lesser Bark.*" Warehouses, docks, building-yards, and workshops sprang up in abundance.

The man in charge of all this was William Gonson, Keeper of the King's Ordnance and then Paymaster of the Fleet. Gonson was so good, in fact, that his sudden death in 1545 forced a crisis. Since there was no one competent enough, or equipped with the right political connections to do everything Gonson had managed on his own, his duties had to be split up into seven separate offices with seven separate officers. Taking Gonson's place were a Master of Naval Ordnance, a Treasurer, a Surveyor and Rigger in charge of all the king's ships' rigging and sails, a Lieutenant or Vice Admiral (abolished in 1565), a Clerk Controller, a Clerk of the Ships, and finally a Keeper of the Storehouse.

The old Keepers of the King's Ships disappeared. Now a single body, the Navy Board, assumed responsibility for the king's navy as a whole, answering to the Lord Admiral himself. Each official had specific duties and considerable autonomy in dealing with them. Each was an experienced seaman, and each was well paid—the Lieutenant alone drew down a salary of one hundred pounds a year.

No such corporate body controlled any other navy in Europe, and none ever would. The Navy Board represented a managerial revolution in government, based on a formal division of labor combined with collective responsibility. Over time it gave the Royal Navy a competitive edge over every other navy, indeed over every other government, in Europe.

For Henry himself, it came just in time. The summer of 1545 saw renewed war against both Scotland and France. A fleet under Lord Admiral Lisle sailed into action in the Firth of Forth and struck at Edinburgh and Leith. Lisle then had to return quickly to England to deal with a threatening French invasion. On July 19, 1545, he and his ships, including the magnificently rebuilt *Mary Rose*, floated out of Portsmouth with banners and streamers flying to meet a French fleet carrying almost 30,000 men.

A large crowd gathered on shore to watch the battle in the summer sunshine, including the king himself and the *Mary Rose*'s commander's wife, Lady Carew. Battle was joined in the choppy water, with the *Mary Rose* in the center of the fight. As the ship discharged her guns at the attacking French galleys, Carew ordered his men to bring the ship around to fire from the other side. However, as they did so, the new lower gunports (which had been cut only sixteen inches above the waterline) let the water pour in; the *Mary Rose* listed heavily, rolled over, and then sank like a stone.

"A long wailing cry" went up on shore as the crowd saw her go under; Lady Carew watched her husband vanish beneath the waves and fainted into King Henry's arms. Only a handful of heads eventually bobbed to the surface. George Carew, his co-commander Richard Grenville, and nearly two hundred men were gone forever. Henry could only offer Lady Carew the comforting thought that Lord George's brother was still alive to carry on the Carew line, "hoping that of a hard beginning, there would follow a better ending."

He might have wished the same for himself. Even with the loss of his best ship before his eyes, Henry managed to win the battle of Portsmouth and stave off a French invasion. Two years later he died, leaving behind a sickly son, Edward VI, who soon became the pawn of competing political factions. Henry VIII's wars had cost more than three million pounds, including half a million for his navy. They had failed to gain an inch of territory in France although they had made Channel travel safer for English ships—not at all the results Henry had intended. They also bankrupted the treasury and left the economy in a shambles. When peace with France finally came in 1550, England's fortunes were at a new low ebb.

The man who arranged peace was also the man of the hour, nautically speaking, Lord Admiral Lisle. He was a Dudley, from an active and ambitious Sussex family, and the best Lord Admiral England had yet had. The creation of the Navy Board in 1545 may even have been his idea. After Henry VIII's death, the Lord Admiral's close relationship with the new young king won him the titles of Duke of Northumberland and then Lord President of the Royal Council.

Northumberland understood that England needed to reach for broader horizons if it was going to survive as an independent power. He struggled to keep the navy strong and encouraged overseas voyages and trade. He met Sebastian Cabot, who had returned to England in 1548 after a successful career in Spain and was advising a syndicate of London merchants who wanted to find a northeast sea route to Asia. Theirs was the first merchant venture to get direct Crown support, almost certainly at Northumberland's urging.

Unfortunately, the Lord President's virtues were muddled by his insatiable ambition. After defeating his political rival, Lord Protector Somerset, Northumberland cultivated support among Protestant extremists and pushed the English Church in directions that even its most reform-minded clerics came to resent. As that resentment spread and solidified, Northumberland's prestige ebbed.

Then in the spring of 1553 young King Edward began coughing blood and lost strength—he was dying of tuberculosis. Northumberland made one last desperate play to keep power by putting Henry VIII's grand-niece Lady Jane Grey on the throne to succeed Edward and marrying her to his son, Guildford Dudley. The plot fizzled and all the participants were caught and imprisoned in the Tower of London, as Edward's Catholic sister Mary became queen with broad popular acclaim. England's best Lord Admiral went to the execution block, just as his father Edmund Dudley had forty-three years earlier. His own son and the hapless Lady Jane soon followed.

Mary now ruled a kingdom on the brink of religious anarchy. Henry

VIII's breakup of the English Church had set off a firestorm of religious conflict and controversy, which would sear the reigns of all his children, Edward, Mary, and Elizabeth. Men and women paid for their beliefs with their lives. Many Protestant clerics, including the former Archbishop of Canterbury, were burned at the stake under Queen Mary, thus earning her the sobriquet of Bloody Mary. Later, Jesuits and Catholic conspirators would go to the execution block under her sister Elizabeth, earning her an excommunication from the pope.

That firestorm swept over England's West Country as well. At one extreme, the traditional Catholic gentry of Cornwall led a rebellion against the radical Protestant Prayer Book in 1549 and besieged Exeter (one of the refugees who found shelter behind its walls was the father of Francis Drake). Suppressing the Prayer Book Rebellion required thousands of troops and cost many more lives. At the other extreme, Protestant gentlemen in Devon joined Wyatt's rebellion in 1554 to prevent Queen Mary's marriage to Prince Philip of Spain—the man who would later be Hawkins's and Drake's nemesis—and to put her sister Elizabeth on the throne instead.

Sir Peter Courtenay and Sir Gawain Carew, cousin of the commander of the ill-fated *Mary Rose,* tried to raise the country with the rumor that Philip was coming to make the kingdom submit to his rule. In fact, that was just what Philip would try to do with his armada thirty-four years later, but in 1554 no one cared. With no support, and with the gates of Exeter shut in their face, the rebels fled to France on a ship belonging to one Walter Raleigh, along with their cousins Peter Killigrew and Edmund Tremayne. Another Protestant naval officer, William Wynter of Bristol, wound up spending several months in the Tower, as did Princess Elizabeth—although in the end Mary decided to spare her sister's life.

However, Mary's disastrous marriage to Philip soon dissipated whatever political support she had enjoyed. In June 1557 she declared war on France at Philip's behest, although her treasury was empty and her Parliament deeply disapproving (Philip meanwhile was furious that Parliament refused to give him full powers as king). Peter Killigrew returned from exile to take a navy commission and William Wynter was given back his command. But the navy they served was largely reduced to escorting English and Spanish troop ships. It was so ineffective it could not even force foreign ships to lower their flags as they passed through the Channel, as it had in the days of Mary's father and grandfather.

Then on New Year's Day 1558, French troops stormed the English base at Calais, which fell in less than a week. The last English possession on the Continent had been lost. National humiliation was added to Mary's woes.

Queen Mary is supposed to have said that when she died, they would find "Calais" engraved on her heart. Certainly she felt its loss personally: her health began to decline irrevocably soon afterward. But the loss of Calais also marked the end of an era—in one sense, the end of the Middle Ages for England. The door to the medieval vision of continental dominion had slammed shut. Which doorway now led to the future was still not obvious. But when it did open, it would swing decisively to the west.

CHAPTER THREE

Unknown Limits

*The rude Indian canoa haileth those seas, the Portingals, the Saracens
and Moors travaile continually up and down that reach from Japan to
China, from China to Malacca, from Malacca to the Moluccas; and
shall an Englishman better appointed than any of them all (that I say no
more of our Navie) fear to sail in that Ocean?*
—RICHARD HAKLUYT THE YOUNGER, 1589

GEOGRAPHY, SOME HISTORIANS argue, is destiny. If that is
true, then the accession of the Tudors already gave England a distinctive westward thrust. They were a Welsh dynasty. Henry
Tudor had grown up in South Wales and bore the nickname of the Black
Bull of Anglesey. "When wilt thou, Black Bull, come to land? How long
shall we wait?" Welsh poets sang on the eve of Bosworth. Henry's battle
standards at Bosworth included the red dragon of Cadwaladr, the national
symbol of Wales, and his victory there was also a victory for the Welsh.
Many became part of the new royal court and government. Their wild,
beautiful, underpopulated country, which had lived in almost perpetual
revolt against the English Crown in the Middle Ages, would become a
bulwark of the new dynasty. Like Devon and Cornwall, Wales would play
a crucial role in the emergence of an outward-looking maritime Britain.

Henry VIII carried out the legal union of England with Wales in
1536. When his daughter Elizabeth came to the throne in 1558, what had
been a steady stream of Welshmen into London and the government
became a flood. Her closest advisor was William Cecil, whose grandfather had come from Wales to London to serve Henry VII. Two great
Welsh families, the Herberts and the Sidneys, supplied her with courtiers
and privy councillors, including the Earl of Pembroke; her Lord Deputy
of Ireland, Henry Sidney; and his son the soldier-poet, Sir Philip Sidney.
The Devereux family from the Welsh borders became her trusted Earls
of Essex, father and son.

Meanwhile, the intellectual ferment in Tudor Wales would create much of what we call the Elizabethan Renaissance. One Herbert son would be the patron of Shakespeare; another would send a fellow Welshman, the architect Inigo Jones, to study in Italy. Sir Philip Sidney's circle included the dramatist Ben Jonson and another Welsh intellectual, John Dee. Later, England's literary heritage would be decisively shaped by two other figures of Welsh descent, Lord Herbert of Cherbury and John Donne.

Queen Elizabeth's west-leaning bias also extended to Wales's neighbors in the West Country. It included important women as well as men. Blanche Perry, who had been Elizabeth's nurse and taught her Welsh, became Keeper of the Queen's Books and Chief Gentlewoman of the Privy Chamber. Katherine Ashley, who had been Elizabeth's governess and had gone with her to the Tower in the dark days after Wyatt's rebellion, was rewarded with the posts of Mistress of the Robes and First Lady of the Bedchamber.

Kat Ashley was a Champernowne, a Devonshire family that had been in the thick of Wyatt's rebellion; her sisters married into two other leading Devon families, the Raleighs and Gilberts. Arthur Champernowne, vice admiral of Devon, then married the widow of the *Mary Rose*'s captain, George Carew—thus rolling Champernownes, Raleighs, Carews, Gilberts, and Grenvilles (they were cousins from Cornwall) all into one active, politically connected clan. Young Walter Raleigh became their point man at court after 1575, along with his brother Carew, his half brother Humphrey Gilbert, and his cousin, Richard Grenville. All four would end up with knighthoods. Restless, ambitious, and intellectually alert, this circle of young Devonians would link up the energies of the West Country with the expansive cultural horizons of Elizabeth's Welsh courtiers.

Those horizons also had a strong religious tincture. The reign of Queen Elizabeth saw the rise of an English Protestantism more confident and purposeful than its predecessor under Edward VI. It would give an aggressive jolt to England's dealings with the outside world. So it has an important place in our story, as does the man who launched it.

John Foxe was not from the West Country but from the port city of Boston in Lincolnshire. He had been tutor to the sons of the Duke of Surrey and fled abroad to escape the persecutions of Mary's reign. He had avoided being burned at the stake like so many of his Protestant friends and mentors, but when he returned to England, he was determined that their memory not be forgotten. In 1563 he published in English his account of their persecution and martyrdom, entitled *The Acts and Mon-*

uments of the English Church. It very quickly went into multiple abridged editions, many with sensational woodcut illustrations. As *Foxe's Book of Martyrs,* it became the most widely read book in England, even more than the Bible. Copies of it and its illustrations were displayed in virtually every church in England. It would shape the thinking of English men and women from Shakespeare and Edmund Spenser to Charles Dickens and Cardinal Newman.

Foxe's most sensational chapters detailed the violent deaths of Protestants during the reign of Mary and Philip; in fact, it was Foxe who turned Queen Mary into "Blood Mary" of English legend. But Foxe also asserted that England, not Martin Luther's Germany, was the true home of the Protestant Reformation. His history showed that from the Emperor Constantine* and John Wyclif to Henry VIII, Englishmen had always upheld the Gospel of Christ against the forces of evil, and especially against the pope in Rome. The accession of Elizabeth, "our noble and worthy queen," crowned that achievement. Foxe saw her as the new Constantine, sent by God to protect the True Religion and bring peace and harmony to the world: "It cannot be sufficiently expressed what blessed happiness this realm received in receiving her at the Lord's gracious hand."

All this was a travesty of the historical facts, of course, although very flattering for the new queen; but Foxe's message went beyond mere political propaganda. He had deliberately recast the history of England by turning it into a religious community embarked on a sacred mission. *The Book of Martyrs* was filled with the stories of not only queens and bishops but ordinary men and women, whom God had chosen to spread His Gospel and carry out His will. Those who read it or had it read to them, or just looked at the plates, learned that being English meant enjoying a privileged relationship with God, much as the Jews had enjoyed before the coming of Christ. Foxe had set in motion the idea of England as God's Elect Nation, and a view of the cosmos summed up by Elizabeth's Bishop of London, John Aylmer: "God is English."

The impact of this Protestant patriotism on the Elizabethan age, particularly on its seafarers, would be hard to exaggerate. John Foxe died in 1587, before the Spanish Armada was launched. But the man who defeated it, Lord Admiral Howard of Effingham, was his former pupil. Walter Raleigh's mother appears in *The Book of Martyrs,* where Foxe praises

---

*Constantine, who gave Christianity its official status in the empire, was born in the Roman province of Britain.

her as "a woman of noble wit and of good and godly opinions." Francis
Drake took a copy of the book with him on his voyage around the world
and spent his idle moments coloring in the pictures. He even wrote to
Foxe, calling him "my very good friend" and thanking him for his prayers
of support. And when John Hawkins reflected on the disasters that befell
him and his men at San Juan de Ulloa, he was moved to say, "If all these
miseries and troublesome affairs of this Sorrowful Voyage should be perfectly and thoroughly written," there could be only one man who to do it:
"he that wrote the Lives and Deaths of the Martyrs," meaning John Foxe.

Hawkins's debacle also echoed Foxe's message in another way. Foxe's
evangelical Protestantism charged England's relationships with other
European powers with a new apocalyptic significance. The Spanish had
been England's sometime allies; now Foxe showed them working hand in
glove with the pope and Antichrist. France had once been the main
enemy; now it paled by comparison with the Spanish threat, especially
since France hosted its own large Protestant minority. And Spain's
empire in the New World, which had once been only a regrettable
inconvenience, was now the unwarranted possession of the "children of
darkness."

As Hawkins's exhausted survivors spread the story of their betrayal
and suffering, it only confirmed what readers of *The Book of Martyrs* were
already thinking. Taken together with stories of the Spaniards' mistreat-
ment of the native Americans, and the horrors and tortures of the
Inquisition, the disaster at San Juan de Ulloa confirmed the picture of a
Spanish empire as evil as it was powerful. And this evil empire loomed
not just over England but—thanks to Columbus and Magellan—the
entire world.

Something had to be done, English Protestants kept telling themselves. But what? Elizabeth's councillors were reluctant to do anything to
provoke Spanish wrath. They knew England was isolated and militarily
weak, while Spain had the best navy and biggest army in the world. A hostile Spain could cut England off from Europe, sever her vital trade links
with the Netherlands and Germany, and upset the delicate balance
between Protestant and Catholic powers on the continent. Men like
William Cecil and Francis Walsingham might be admirers of Foxe and
believers in the Protestant cause, but they also understood the realities of
power and the limits of England's strength.

John Hawkins, still smarting from what he saw as Spanish treachery,
did what he could. He pursued his claims in the Admiralty Court; he

hounded the Spanish ambassador to release his captured men. In June 1570 he sent the Earl of Leicester a daring plan for attacking the Spanish silver fleet in the Azores—the first of many such plans. But Cecil and the royal council turned it down. They knew a bigger crisis was developing. The pope had just excommunicated Queen Elizabeth and a major Catholic rebellion had broken out in northern England. A large Spanish fleet of ninety ships was gathering near Antwerp, which might be aimed at England. In fact, it turned out to be an escort to Spain for King Philip's new German bride, and so the crisis passed. But Hawkins was still intent on building up his own private navy of armed ships in Plymouth, which he could mobilize at a moment's notice. By 1571 it had grown to sixteen ships and by his own count over four hundred cannon and 1,500 men. It would be the core of England's first overseas fighting fleet.

Some of the money for this probably came from Hawkins's other project: his work as England's first secret double agent. During one of his visits with the Spanish ambassador, Hawkins had dropped hints that he was unhappy with Elizabeth's government and its failure to support his claims for damages. Over the next several months, and in league with William Cecil's secret service, the sea captain from Plymouth steadily led the credulous man on. He even convinced the ambassador that in the event of a Spanish invasion, he would use his private fleet to help them topple Elizabeth and put the Catholic Mary Queen of Scots on the throne.

With the king of Spain's approval, the ambassador laid out an elaborate plot based on Hawkins's deceptions. He even accepted a secret code cipher from Hawkins with which to write clandestine letters—all of which Cecil read, since his agents had devised the code. The ambassador also gave Hawkins large sums of money, which he apparently pocketed as his just due for what the Spanish had cost him at San Juan de Ulloa.

By September 1571, John Hawkins was hip-deep in the unfolding Spanish conspiracy. He wrote a note to Cecil (now Lord Burghley), in which we can almost hear his indignant West Country accent: "Their practices be very mischievous, and they be never idle, but God, I hope, will confound them and turn their devices upon their own necks." A few weeks later, Burghley finally sprang the trap on the so-called Ridolfi Plot.* Hawkins had not only helped to foil Spain's plans but sealed the

---

*So called because Roberto Ridolfi, a Florentine banker, was one of the key participants in the plot.

fate of Mary Queen of Scots: one of the letters he had carried to the Spanish ambassador was from Mary herself, consenting to the plan. Even more important, Hawkins had established beyond doubt that King Philip was Elizabeth's mortal enemy—and England's.

Still, Elizabeth could do nothing. She sent some help to French Huguenots at La Rochelle, under Hawkins's command. She allowed Huguenot nobles in London to hand out commissions to sailors to attack Spanish shipping and volunteers to go fight alongside the Huguenots in France (one of them was fifteen-year-old Walter Raleigh). She encouraged the Dutch Protestants in their war with Philip whenever she dared. But a direct confrontation with Spain, a war she could not afford and which she could not win, was out of the question.

But Queen Elizabeth and her councillors did realize that if war came, the sea was their first line of defense. They did nothing to discourage Hawkins's assembling of ships. They organized England's first maritime survey in 1570, and another in 1572. They even established Wednesday as well as the traditional Friday as national fish-eating day, "to encourage ship-building and to increase the breed of mariners" who "by God's grace [would be] able to defend the Realm against all Foreign Powers"—thus linking England's security quite literally to the price of fish.

And if they could not wage overt war against Spain, they could sponsor a covert war, thanks to one of the oldest traditions of life at sea: piracy.

• • •

"Who are you?" Cyclops asks Odysseus and his men in Homer's *Odyssey.* "Do you wander about as traders or risk your necks as pirates?" It was a normal question in the ancient world, where pirates were as much a part of the seagoing economy as regular merchants. Often they were one and the same. Roman law established the principle that the seas were open and belonged to no one. But this also meant that those who sailed them did so at their own risk. The Romans themselves had to invest huge resources to protect their merchants from pirates in the very heart of their empire, the Mediterranean. They soon discovered, however, what every other government in the premodern world learned to its chagrin: as soon as one nest of pirates was dispersed or destroyed, another took its place. Before the rise of the British navy, brigandage at sea was simply too easy, too profitable, and too difficult for those who made the laws to catch and punish, to disappear completely.

So governments did the next best thing. Like terrorism in our own day, they learned to control piracy by making it an instrument of their will, instead of an obstacle to it. Medieval kings issued "letters of marque," licenses permitting mariners to attack ships of other countries based on a private claim for damages. These would also be called letters of reprisal: by the 1290s English kings were routinely signing them and then claiming a share of the money made from selling off captured ships and goods or prize money. During the fourteenth century, the Crown's Admiralty courts normally assigned one-quarter of all prize money from letters of marque to the king, while the pirate ship's owners received another quarter, and the pirates themselves the other half.

This was during peacetime. In a war the result was a virtual free-for-all against enemy merchants. This government-sponsored thievery could backfire, of course, since it encouraged the enemy to retaliate in kind, and it never stopped the pirate outlaw from operating on his own. But it made money for the king literally at the stroke of a pen, which sharply defrayed the costs of war at sea. It thus became a general rule that as a government's resources for a navy declined, its reliance on piracy increased—and vice versa.

Henry VIII, as usual, raised things to a new level. When war broke out against France in 1544 he authorized English sea captains to attack not just French merchants but any merchants doing business with them, including those from France's new partner Spain. In March 1545 Southampton merchant Robert Reneger hijacked a Spanish galleon loaded with gold, pearls, and sugar off Cape St. Vincent, which brought nearly 20,000 ducats in prize money—over 7,000 English pounds. The Spanish made a furious outcry, calling the English sailors "savages," but once Henry had pocketed his share of the loot, he ignored their complaints.

Reneger's success made privateering a boom industry for West Country captains and shipowners. Walter Raleigh's father, who was also vice admiral of Devon, profited handsomely from it. Even old William Hawkins gave up the uncertain dangers of the African trade for the certain profits of government-approved piracy. In September 1545 he asked for and got letters authorizing him "to annoy the king's enemies." In fact, he annoyed them and everyone else so much that the Admiralty Court had to lock him in prison temporarily to prevent an international outcry.

This was because once set in motion, privateering proved hard to stop. Even after peace was signed, letters of reprisals continued to be issued—sometimes by the Crown itself, as Northumberland did in 1550, but more often by local officials who saw that allowing others to steal at sea was a sure way to get rich themselves. Of course, this wealth came at a price. It regularly hurt relations with otherwise friendly or neutral countries, as with Spain in 1545, and it bred a broader indifference to the law in maritime communities like Cornwall and Devon. But under the right circumstances, privateering allowed the Crown to conduct a covert war on its enemies on the cheap. Northumberland had used it to harass the Spanish and Portuguese in the New World; now Queen Elizabeth would do the same.

John Hawkins was, of course, the perfect candidate for such "letters of reprisal." The queen had taken a keen interest in his earlier slaving voyages, in spite of their occasional turn to violence. She was reportedly upset about the loss of the *Jesus*. But Hawkins was over forty and less willing to spend long stretches of time at sea. However, there was nothing to prevent his young cousin Francis Drake from taking his place.

For all his spectacular exploits and brilliant personality, Francis Drake remains an enigma. The Victorian view of Drake as a dashing and valiant knight-errant nobly serving queen and country was largely a myth. The new version, that he was nothing more than a lying and bloodthirsty self-serving pirate, has the danger of becoming a countermyth in its place.

The truth probably lies somewhere in between. Certainly like the other West Country "sea dogs," he was unafraid of violence and used to living one step ahead of the law. But the fact remains we know almost nothing about his early life. His father was a minister, who probably had strong evangelical opinions (although one of Drake's most recent biographers has cast doubt on this), but who also seems to have had his own troubles with the law. The traditional stories of Edmund Drake serving as a navy chaplain and raising his family on a disused ship hulk anchored in the Thames seem to be largely untrue. Instead, young Francis Drake was probably raised by his Hawkins cousins in Plymouth before he sailed as purser on one of their ships in 1558.

At eighteen, Francis Drake was short, stocky, and cocksure, a genuine sailor of fortune. He already understood that the real law of the sea was the law of the jungle—as his actions at San Juan and afterward showed. Far more than John Hawkins, Drake was temperamentally suited for the life of a privateer. As he himself said in one of his early letters, "If there be cause, we will be devils rather than men."

Drake was thus the perfect instrument for Elizabeth and Burghley's covert war. He thirsted for revenge for what had happened in San Juan harbor. He told friends, "I am not going to stop until I have collected the two million that my cousin John Hawkins lost"—two million being the money Drake believed they might have taken from the treasure *flota*. An image of great rows of silver bars neatly piled on shore, waiting for the Spanish fleet, burned in his brain. The queen's covert war against Spain would be his excuse for going after them, at Nombre de Dios.

It was a daunting task. The Spanish empire at that time was the largest and wealthiest in the world. When he came to the throne in 1558, Philip II had inherited from his father a collection of territories that spanned the globe from Manila to Tunisia. He was sole master of North and South America, with the exception of Portuguese Brazil, as well as of Spain, the Low Countries, a large part of Italy, and a long stretch of cities and fortresses along the coast of North Africa. He had at his disposal not only the wealth of the New World, including the great silver mine of Potosí in Peru but also the Netherlands, the financial and industrial heart of Europe.

Philip commanded the best and most professional army since the Roman legions. Spain's ships and sailors cruised every ocean; its merchants visited every port; Spain's war galleys completely dominated the western Mediterranean; Philip's victory over the Turks at Lepanto in 1571 made Spain the dominant power in the eastern Mediterranean as well. No surprise, then, that the Spanish saw themselves as a race destined to rule the world, as the heirs to the Roman Empire, Persia, and Egypt of the Pharoahs. They assumed they were God's chosen people as much as Foxe's Englishman—and with infinitely more reason. The globe itself was theirs to conquer and rule:

> *Con l'espada y el compás*
> *Más y más y más y más.*

> With the sword and the compass
> More and more and more and more.

Yet this multicontinent empire, for all its vast territories, diverse resources, and awesome power, increasingly depended on a single slender thread to survive. This was a thread of silver, which led from the mines of Peru and Mexico to the warehouses of the Casa de Contratación in Seville (and then later in Cádiz). The annual royal share, or *quinto*, had grown from two million ducats—almost 650,000 pounds*—in 1560 to

---

*In other words, more than three times Queen Elizabeth's entire annual budget.

almost twice that by 1570. It was the envy of every other ruler on the planet.

But even this was not enough. Almost every silver bar or coin of the royal *quinto* went directly to Philip's bankers in Antwerp and Genoa, who advanced him the even larger sums he needed to keep his empire going. Their confidence in Philip depended on that steady flow of silver; so the future of his entire empire hinged on the annual arrival of the American silver fleet.

And yet, incredibly, Spain had no full-time fleet to protect this vital lifeline. Instead, Philip had devised an elaborate convoy system, or *flota,* with armed merchantmen providing their own protection. Spanish ships sailed for America in two groups, one bound for the viceroyalty of New Spain (Mexico) and the other for Peru. Once they arrived off Hispaniola, the South American–bound section sailed to Cartagena (now the capital of Venezuela) to drop off goods and supplies, and then headed to Panama, where they picked up the ton or so of Peruvian silver mule trains had carried up from Panama City on the Pacific coast through the jungle to a tiny depot on the Caribbean: Nombre de Dios.

The Mexican-bound fleet, meanwhile, made its way to San Juan de Ulloa (the scene of Hawkins's recent debacle), to pick up the treasure from Mexican mines. Then, loaded down with their precious cargo, the two fleets made their final rendezvous at the most important port city in all of Spanish America, Havana. From there they would make their long slow way back across the Atlantic, arriving after several months in the Azores to take on supplies, drop off their sick and dead, and to pick up fresh armed escorts for the rest of the way home.

The convoy system developed around the time of Hawkins's first voyage to America in 1565, in order to ward off French Huguenot privateers. But Hawkins and Drake realized that the *flotas* were the true lifeline of Philip's empire. If they could cut that silver cord, they could bring that mighty empire to its knees, and with it the Antichrist. Hawkins had first proposed doing it in 1570, and had been turned down. Now it was Drake's turn to have a try.

Drake knew the convoys were too powerful to be attacked directly. But Spain's lack of a permanent naval presence in the New World was a fatal blunder. It had allowed John Hawkins to travel freely through the Caribbean on his three slaving voyages. Now it would allow Drake to pursue his target and strike at Spanish American ports with impunity. Over the next five years he would make the lives of the colonists intolerable. He replaced Hawkins as the most feared figure in the New World; the dreaded El Draque, who came and went as he pleased.

In this he had another unexpected ally: Philip II. Surrounded by piles of papers and documents at his desk in the palace at El Escorial, Philip's attention was focused on Europe. He wanted his territories in Italy secure and the Protestant rebellion in his Netherlands suppressed. The New World and its silver, like the black and Indian slaves who dug it out of the ground, were merely means to an end. Other than that, he hardly gave it a thought.

Yet every decision, every piece of news had to pass through his hands and required his authorization and signature. A letter from Mexico written to sail with the *flota* took four months to reach Madrid. A letter from Manila could take up to two years. Getting a response from El Escorial meant another four to six months. Distance, not privateers, was the real enemy of the Spanish empire in the New World. As one colonial official put it, "If death came from Madrid, we should all live to a very old age." So by the time Philip learned of trouble in the Carribean, decided on a course of action, and sent his orders, it would be already too late.

Drake made a series of hit-and-run reconnaissance voyages to the Caribbean in 1570 and 1571, with a single ship of only 25 tons, the *Swan*. These trips revealed to him all he needed to know: the Spanish Main was his for the taking. At the end of May 1572 he got down to business. He took two ships out of Plymouth, the *Pascoe* (a Cornish name) which he borrowed from John Hawkins and redubbed the *Pasha,* and the *Swan,* now commanded by his brother John and another Devon sailor from South Tawton, John Oxenham. They took on board three disassembled pinnaces for service along the coast and headed for Guadeloupe.

Drake's real destination, however, was Panama. He planned to take Nombre de Dios by surprise, just as Hawkins had taken San Juan de Ulloa, but this time before the Spanish convoy arrived from Cartagena and after the Panama City mule trains had unloaded their silver. He and his men would grab the waiting bullion and get out before the Spanish could catch him.

However, Nombre de Dios was a real port, not just a shingle of sand like San Juan. Drake could only guess at how many soldiers, or what kind of fortifications, he would have to deal with. It was a daring plan for a commander with only two ships and less than a hundred men: but Drake trusted to surprise, luck, and Spanish incompetence.

The *Pasha* and *Swan* reached Port Pheasant, a sheltered harbor just east of Nombre de Dios, on July 12. A day or so later they were joined by another English ship, commanded by an old comrade from the San Juan voyage, James Raunce of the *William and John*. Drake loaded seventy-three men, armed only with twenty-four muskets and sixteen crossbows, into his three oared pinnaces and another small boat. At three o'clock in the morning, as the moon rose, Drake and his men rowed silently into Nombre de Dios harbor.

Unfortunately, a lookout on a Spanish ship at the entrance spotted them almost at once, and by the time Drake's men were scrambling onto the beach, church bells were ringing the alarm. They raced up the main street where they met a hail of gunfire from a group of thirty or forty aroused citizens (luckily, it turned out the town had no professional garrison, only amateur militiamen). Drake returned fire, and when John Drake and a party of English suddenly appeared from a side street, the Spaniards broke and fled.

Still, there was no time to lose. Drake led his men to the governor's house, where informants had told him the silver was stored before being loaded on the ships. There, Drake claimed later, they found on the ground floor a pile of silver bars seventy feet long and twelve feet high. However, Drake stopped his men before they could begin carrying the thirty- and forty-pound bars outside. There was even more, he told them, in the treasure house around the corner, in addition to gold, gems, and pearls.

A predawn thunderstorm broke suddenly overhead, dousing the scene in a violent downpour, as the men scrambled to the great stone building. At the doorway, with the rain and thunder whipping around them, Drake proclaimed, "I have brought you to the mouth of the treasure of the world," and ordered his men to break down the door. But just as they were hammering on the panels, Drake slumped against the wall and collapsed. He had been wounded during the fight in the street; his men had not noticed the stream of blood flowing from his leg in the dark. Now, at the moment of triumph, Drake lay semiconscious at their feet.

With their leader fallen and the sounds of the Spanish militia regrouping coming from all sides, Drake's men panicked. They scooped him up, tied a tourniquet around his leg, and scrambled back to their boats, leaving the treasure doors unopened and the pile of silver in the governor's house untouched. Dawn was breaking as they frantically rowed out of the harbor. The Spanish chose not to follow. The English were safe and not entirely empty-handed: they managed to grab the

Spanish vessel that had given the original alarm on the way back to Port Pheasant. It turned out to be full of wine from the Canary Island, a welcome cure for dry mouths and empty stomachs after their raid. But the original mission had failed.*

Yet as he lay recuperating from his wound, Drake decided there was no reason to head back to England. Instead, he would stay in the Caribbean until the next mule train of silver arrived in Panama, in four months' time. James Rance evidently balked at this audacious plan and set sail for home. Drake did not miss him. He decided he actually needed fewer, not more ships, so that he had more hands for his raiding-parties. So he scuttled the Swan, took his brother and his men on board the Pasha, and for the next three months sailed leisurely up and down the coast, attacking vessels and gathering loot and supplies—while the Spanish proved unable to do a thing to stop him. These successes came at the price of the deaths of his brothers John and Joseph: one of wounds, the other of yellow fever.

When Drake sailed back to the Panama coast in December 1572, he had hatched a new plan. Instead of meeting the silver at its destination in Nombre de Dios, he would intercept it mid-trail. To do this he made allies with the community of escaped slaves who lived in the jungle, the cimmaroons. They hated the Spanish, who loathed and feared them, but they were receptive to Drake's extended hand of friendship. He was probably the first white man who treated them as equals—never mentioning that he shipped hundreds of slaves to America with John Hawkins just four years earlier.

The cimmaroons became Drake's eyes and ears on the ground. Together they set out across the isthmus for Panama City, looking for a spot for the perfect ambush. Day after day they passed through the thick jungle, with the cimmaroons building palm-thatch huts each night for themselves and the Englishmen, until they came to the foothills of the Cordilleras. As they scaled higher and higher, the cimmaroons pointed out a tree at the top of the rise, with steps cut in it leading to a wooden platform. Drake climbed up and gazed out. A shimmering blue ribbon of water stretched out far below him.

He was the first Englishman to see the Pacific Ocean. John Oxenham

---

*It is also more than likely that the treasure house was empty. Drake's informants had been wrong and the silver fleet had been to Nombre de Dios and sailed days before Drake arrived.

joined him and heard Drake remark, "God of His goodness give me leave and life to sail once in an English ship in that sea." Oxenham swore that unless Drake drove him from his company he would follow him there "by God's grace." They shook hands on their deal and climbed back down to rejoin their comrades.

It took them three more days to descend down to within sight of Panama City. Drake had only eighteen men with him, and thirty cimmaroons, but a spy told him that a mule train loaded with gold and jewels was leaving that night. Drake ordered his men to put on their white linen shirts over their doublets so that they could recognize one another in the dark. Then he distributed them and the cimmaroons in the long grass on either side of the road, and waited as the sun fell beyond the trees and the horizon.

Finally, in the inky darkness they could hear the faint tinkling of bells: the silver bells the pack mules wore as they wound their way along the trail. However, once again, at the crucial moment Drake's luck ran out. One of his men panicked and fired his pistol. The Spanish guards yelled and opened fire, and the entire raiding party had to hightail it into the jungle. There they blundered into another party of Spaniards, who sprayed them with musket fire, grazing Drake in the face and wounding another man. The group finally eluded their pursuers but the mule train was long gone.

But Drake still refused to give up. This time he would intercept the train closer to Nombre de Dios, with the help of French volunteers who had arrived on a cruising privateer and more cimmaroons. They sailed to the mouth of the Francesca River, left their ships behind, and then followed the river up to the trail by foot. On the night of April 29, 1573, they arrived and once again sank down into the grass to wait. They were so close to the town that Drake could hear the hammers of the Spanish shipwrights still working in the harbor.

Then the hammers faded and the sound of the mule train bells coming closer and closer took their place. For once, Drake's men held their fire until the ambush was sprung. The guards put up a brief fight and the French captain, Le Testu, was badly wounded. However, once the fighting was done and they opened the packs, they found that each of the two hundred mules was carrying more than three hundred pounds of silver and gold. Drake had his treasure at last. It was far more than his men could carry, so they buried most of the silver in a series of land-crab

burrows, jammed the gold into their doublets, wished the stricken Le
Testu good luck and Godspeed, and fled into the thicket.

The Spaniards rallied troops from Nombre de Dios and followed
Drake's trail as best they could. They found Le Testu and killed him,
along with another Frenchman who had lost his way and fallen behind.
Their severed heads and that of a cimmaroon killed in the raid went on
display in the marketplace in Nombre de Dios. But the Englishmen and
the rest of their allies had gotten away, with a treasure worth almost one-
fifth of the queen's annual revenue.

Drake and his men followed their way downriver to the shore, where
Oxenham and the others were to pick them up. When they reached the
rendezvous, however, they found no one—only a trio of Spanish galleons
patrolling far offshore. The men were aghast, but Drake wasted no time
worrying about what had happened to their comrades. Instead, he immediately asked for volunteers to help him build a boat. "I will be one," he
said. "Who will be the other?"

Within two days they had lashed together a raft of tree trunks and
fitted it with a crude mast and sail made from an empty biscuit sack.
Setting off at night, they managed to evade the Spanish patrols and finally
found Oxenham and the *Pasha* sheltering behind one of the small islands.
As the *Pasha*'s men pulled him on board, they asked with anxious faces
how the raid had gone.

Drake, exhausted but exultant, at first said nothing. "Well," he began
in sorrowful tones, but then with a grin, he pulled out an enormous gold
bar from his doublet and cried, "Our voyage is made!"

Yet Drake was still not finished. Despite the obvious danger, he was
still determined to get at least some of the treasure they had buried in the
jungle—and find out what happened to the Frenchmen they had left
behind. After a day or two they returned to the coast once again, with
Drake dispatching Oxenham and an armed party back to the trail where,
virtually under the noses of the Spanish patrols, they learned of Le Testu's
fate and extracted a dozen or so of the large silver bars (the Spaniards
eventually found the rest). After giving the French crew their share of the
treasure, and allowing the cimmaroons to help themselves to whatever
tools, weapons, or gifts they wanted, Drake finally set sail for home—
almost a year from the day he had left.

On his way back, Drake allowed himself one final gesture of defiance.
As the *Pasha* passed Cartagena, he could see the great Spanish *flota* drawn

up in harbor. Drake insisted on sailing past the entire fleet with the English flag of St. George flying from his mainmast and pennants and other flags streaming behind.

Heavy rains off Florida allowed Drake to return to England without stopping to replenish his water casks. On August 9, 1573, he dropped anchor in Plymouth. It was a Sunday and most inhabitants were in church. But "the news of the captain's return . . . did so speedily pass over all the church . . . that few or none remained with the preacher" as the crowds poured down to the quay to welcome Drake and to "see the evidence of God's love and blessing towards our Gracious Queene and Country."

God's blessing, and Drake's, was indeed bounteous. The total haul for his investors came to more than 20,000 pounds—a mere fraction of the annual Spanish shipments of bullion, but more than twice what Hawkins had brought back from his fateful voyage in 1569. Drake's share made him a rich man. But the success of his raid involved more than just money. He had proved that the Spanish empire in America was vulnerable. A daring and ruthless man could go and steal what he liked. A new window onto the world had suddenly been pried open for England.

Yet for four years, no one followed up on Drake's success. Relations with Spain were beginning to thaw. There were to be no more official raids in the Caribbean. So Drake took himself to Ireland to join the fighting there, and the charting of England's future shifted briefly from men of action to men of ideas.

• • •

The same year as Hawkins's voyage to San Juan de Ulloa, young Richard Hakluyt was visiting his cousin and namesake in his chambers at the old Middle Temple in London. The elder Richard Hakluyt was a rich Welsh lawyer with close connections at court (he was friends to both Lord Burghley and Sir Philip Sidney), but his first love was geography. His cousin found his room strewn with "certain books of Cosmography, with a universal map," he remembered. "Seeing me somewhat curious in the view thereof," the older man "began to instruct my ignorance. . . . He pointed with his wand to all the known Seas, Gulfs, Bays, Straights, Capes, Rivers, Empires, Kingdoms, Dukedoms and Territories." Hakluyt then described to the fascinated boy the variety of commodities each produced, "and their particular wants, which by the benefit of traffic and intercourse of merchants, are plentifully supplied."

Then, to complete the picture, Hakluyt led him to a copy of the Bible and opened it to the 107th Psalm, "where I read that they which go down to the sea in ships, and occupy by the great waters, they see the works of the Lord, and his wonders in the deep." In short, those who traveled the world's oceans, and the geographers and navigators who guided them, were as much servants of the Lord's will as Foxe's godly Englishmen.

The teenager was hooked. The geography the elder Richard Hakluyt pursued as a hobby, the younger Hakluyt would organize and deliver as regent master lecturer at Christ Church, Oxford. He became the close friend of Drake and Sir Walter Raleigh. Together with his famous *Voyages,* Hakluyt's lectures gave Elizabethan England its first understanding of the new picture of the world that had emerged since Columbus, and its first full appreciation of the importance of seapower.

The English had been slow to turn to "the new geography," at which the Spanish, Portuguese, Dutch, and French had excelled for decades. But with the tide of Spain's empire rising on all sides, the anxiety about what England's place might be in any future global order triggered a new and intense interest in geography among scholars and politicians. The advantage the new geography offered was not just pointing out where previously unknown places were, like America and the Philippines and the Pacific Ocean (also known as the Great South Sea), but also how to get there by following the new sea routes. Practical navigation, along with related sciences such as astronomy and geometry, went hand in hand with remapping the surface of the world. The Hakluyts were only two of a group of men whose fascination with maps, charts, and globes suddenly seemed relevant to England's political and economic future.

Sebastian Cabot, a living link to the age of Columbus, had been bribed to return to England in 1548 to teach the art of navigation. His maps of the coast of Newfoundland and Labrador were still hanging in Whitehall Palace thirty years later, to be studied and restudied by budding explorers. In 1561 Richard Eden published the first book in English on navigation, translated from a treatise a Devonshire pilot, Stephen Borough, brought back with him from Spain. It would remain a standard work on oceangoing travel until the 1630s.

John Dee was a Welshman (the Hakluyts were Welsh as well) and a mathematician, astronomer, astrologer, and sometime alchemist and magician. He had studied abroad with the greatest mapmaker of the age, Gerard Mercator. Dee advised the first great English overseas venture, the Muscovy Company expedition of 1553. Dee had laid out for the expedition's sailing master, Richard Chancellor, a journey into completely unknown waters, running north and east to the White Sea and Russia. Chancellor would have little to help him beyond his own homemade quadrant and Dee's charts. But his confidence had been bolstered by the new geography's most startling proposition: that all the world was connected by the sea.

This was not an entirely novel idea. The Greek philosopher Aristotle had guessed that the three continents known to the ancient world, Africa, Asia, and Europe, were encompassed by a great ocean. But Aristotle's theory remained only a theory. The waters ancient and medieval mariners knew were either landlocked or land-surrounded: the Mediterranean, the Baltic and North seas, and the Black Sea. Few saw any point in sailing through the Straits of Gibraltar into the vast and remote Atlantic. The only other large ocean medieval geographers knew was the Indian Ocean, and even that was believed to be hemmed in by great continents and landmasses.

But Columbus and then Magellan had shown that it was the other way around: the earth's landmasses were all surrounded by great interconnecting oceans. Navigable water links allowed sailors to pass from the Atlantic to the Indian Ocean via the Cape of Good Hope, or to the Pacific through the Strait of Magellan, and then across the Indian Ocean back to the Cape of Good Hope. A sailor could set out in one direction and return home from the other—just as Magellan's ships had done in 1520. The new geography encouraged the notion that once you chose a destination, it no longer mattered which way you went, but rather which route got you there the quickest.

For generations, the destination of choice for Europeans had been Asia, the source of spices, silks, and seemingly unimaginable wealth. Since 1498 the Portuguese controlled the principal eastern sea route running around Africa and the Cape of Good Hope, and had regular trading posts in India (Goa and Calicut), China (Macao), and the Moluccas, the islands between Sulawesi and New Guinea which are now part of Indonesia. Columbus and John Cabot had tried an alternative western route and failed, although in the process they had found a continent new to Europeans and, for the Spanish at least, a major source of wealth.

Now, by examining a globe crisscrossed by new sea routes, Dee, Hakluyt, and other English geographers believed the odds were good for finding yet another sea link to Asia. This involved going north, and then either west or east over the top of the world—or as close to it as one dared. It would dramatically shorten the distance and coincidentally short-circuit the Portuguese and Spanish. It would also make England, with its easy access to points north and west, a key player in world trade. And so the search for the Northwest Passage, as well as a northeast one, was on.

It was a plan born of economic desperation as much as geographic daring. For centuries England's wealth had depended on its sheep. Wool and woolen cloth were its one important commercial export, while virtually everything else England needed had to be imported from Flanders, Germany, France, and Spain. The wars of Henry VIII had put the wool trade into a tailspin, made worse by the religious wars of the 1560s and tensions with Spain, which controlled Antwerp, the main port of access for London wool merchants. The drastic interruptions of trade in 1562–64 and then in 1569–73, as the Spanish Netherlands plunged into civil war, left London high and dry. Starved for business, London's merchants were forced to look elsewhere for markets. Forty years earlier, when times were good, they had been content to leave the exploration of the Atlantic to Bristol and the West Country. Now, faced by bankruptcy, they too began to turn west—one reason why John Hawkins found so many eager London investors for his slaving voyages—and began to dream of a miraculous passage to Asia.

It was the route to the northeast that yielded the first results. Chancellor's two ships set out from London on May 10, 1553. Although one ship was lost in a storm with all hands, Dee's charts enabled Chancellor to be the first Englishman to cross the Arctic Circle, then find his way through the ice to the White Sea and then travel by sledge to Moscow, where he was graciously received by Czar Ivan the Terrible. Chancellor's successors created a modest trade link leading south through Russia to the Caspian Sea and the camel caravans of Bokhara. Later, they reached the court of Persia.

By 1568 there was a permanent English ambassador in Moscow. Relations were so good that Czar Ivan even toyed with proposing marriage to one of Elizabeth's ladies-in-waiting. The Muscovy Company's connections in central Asia would eventually lead English merchants to India and to the creation of the East India Company, although China and the fabled wealth of Cathay still eluded them.

For that, Richard Grenville told the queen's Privy Council, one needed an Atlantic route. Grenville was a hardy seaworthy Cornishman, son of the Richard Grenville who had gone down with the *Mary Rose.* In

1574 he and a group of fellow West Country sailors believed their home counties offered a prime starting point for a sea route to Asia, and that they had "ships of our own well prepared" for such a venture. Grenville envisioned a bold strategy of armed English convoys, the Protestant equivalent of Spain's annual *flota,* carrying English goods to China right under the noses of the Spanish and Portuguese. If they resisted, "our strength shall be such as we fear it not," Grenville confidently proclaimed. Armed English merchants regularly cruising the Pacific would be both a bitter blow to Spanish "Papistry" and an economic coup for England.

Even after Drake's raid on Nombre de Dios, Grenville's plan seemed far too bold and dangerous. Under pressure from the London wool lobby, Elizabeth was working to patch up relations with Spain and Antwerp. With the queen's latest peace offensive under way, Grenville's ideas met a cold reception. But the search for a westward passage soon found a new and more convincing advocate, one who combined the principles of the new geography with appeals to English patriotism.

Humphrey Gilbert was one of Kat Ashley's bright young cousins from Devon and half brother to Walter Raleigh. He had been brought up at court, and educated at Eton and Oxford. But he was equally at home in the violent maritime culture of the West Country. Physically and mentally tough, Humphrey Gilbert was an enthusiastic sailor—his last words were "We are as near to heaven by sea as by land"—and a violent and brutal soldier. He had fought in Ireland alongside Richard Grenville, and crushed an Irish rebellion in 1569 with terrible ferocity. It earned him the permanent hatred of the natives, who called him "more devil than man." The motto on his coat of arms was *Quid non?* (Why not?).

Gilbert was a passionate student of the new geography. His brother Adrian was Richard Hakluyt's best friend and shared an interest in alchemy with John Dee. Humphrey Gilbert even wrote a book insisting that navigation should be part of the education of every gentleman. But the most important principle Humphrey learned from his brother's friends was that North and South America were really one great island. The Strait of Magellan bounded its southern tip, the South Sea or Pacific its western side. The Atlantic formed its eastern edge, but then also flowed up around its northern boundaries, as the Cabots had discovered. That northern sea, which "severeth it from Grondland [Greenland]," had to connect with the sea that separated America from Asia on the Pacific side. It was that connection, Gilbert proclaimed, "which I take now in hand to discover."

A northwest passage from England to Asia. John Rastell, brother-in-law of Thomas More, had yearned for it 1517. Robert Thorne of Bristol had invested money in finding it, and together with John Barlowe put a plan to get there before Henry VIII's Privy Council in 1541 (they were turned down). Sebastian Cabot even claimed to have found it during one of his trips, while Jacques Cartier, the French explorer, believed the strong west-to-east ocean current he had found off Labrador must lead to it. Gerard Mercator was so convinced it must exist that he put it on his famous map of the world in 1569—even though no one had actually seen it.

Gilbert believed a trip through the passage would take a third of the time required by sailing to Asia via the Cape of Good Hope and would cut the distance to China via Russia by half. Since it was far from Mexico or Peru, there was no threat of a war with Spain. "By the Northwest," he wrote, "we may safely trade without danger, or annoyance, of any Prince living, Christian or heathen." He recited his evidence for the existence of the passage, including Cartier's mysterious currents, and explained how England was uniquely located to take advantage of this new route.

In fact, Gilbert said, that was what frightened the Spanish and Portuguese so much. He asserted that the King of Portugal knew of the passage but had ordered his geographers to keep it a secret, "for that (said the king) if England had knowledge and experience thereof, it would greatly hinder the king of Spain, and me." According to an English merchant in Seville, the Spanish themselves were frantically searching for a northwest passage at its western or Pacific end. And the name they gave it? The Englishman's Strait.

Gilbert's manuscript circulated for several years without result. Then on a cold winter's day in 1576 the poet George Gascoigne was visiting Gilbert's house in Limehouse near the London River, and found it among the papers heaped on Gilbert's desk. Gascoigne asked to borrow it and showed it to his cousin Martin Frobisher. Frobisher was not from the West Country but Yorkshire and had settled in London to become a merchant seafarer. But the lean years of the 1560s had driven him to Devon-style piracy to make ends meet.

Until 1576 his life had been a failure. He had no real experience with long-distance ocean navigation and no interest in large-scale commercial enterprise. Like Drake and Gilbert, he had an amoral violent streak. But Frobisher was a man with big dreams and even bigger imagination—"Such a monstrous mind," said one member of the Privy Council who met

him, "that a whole kingdom cannot contain it." Indeed, not even a continent, and Humphrey Gilbert's notion of a northwest passage now filled
Frobisher with a sense of purpose and resolve.

His enthusiasm carried everyone away. He found a prosperous London merchant as partner, who convinced his fellow merchants to sink
their money in Frobisher's projected Cathay Company. In the words of
Frobisher's latest biographer, a man whose "reputation was one of almost
unremitting blackguardry" for attacking merchants at sea, now had a distinguished number of them as his investors. Other investors in the
Cathay Company included Lord Burghley and the Earl of Leicester. Even
Elizabeth gave him her blessing, if not her money.

John Dee was talked into teaching Frobisher the rules of geography
and how to use navigational instruments. Stephen Borough, the distinguished pilot from Devon, agreed to act as master of one of Frobisher's
three tiny ships. They set off from Deptford on June 7, 1576, loaded with
a cargo for trade with the Chinese: woolen sweaters from Devonshire and
Hampshire, linens, ribbons, lace, children's straw hats, silk purses, looking
glasses, spectacles, and dog collars. A great crowd gathered to see them
off. As they sailed down the Thames past Greenwich Palace, the queen
waved her handkerchief from her window.

It was a wild and ill-considered enterprise from the start. Richard
Grenville branded it "utterly impossible." Frobisher's ships were not
equipped to deal with hull-cracking icebergs, his men were not prepared
for the freezing cold, and navigation in northern waters was made more
difficult, as John Dee knew, by the fact that lines of longitude tended to
converge as one approached the North Pole, making it hard to measure
one's exact position. One ship was lost off Greenland; another turned
back. But with only eighteen men left, Frobisher pushed on. He found
landfall on July 28, on what is today Resolution Island in Canada, just off
Baffin Island, and claimed it for England and his queen.

Although he did not know it, Frobisher had found the entrance to
Hudson's Strait. However, he then veered north into a dead-end gulf,
which is now Frobisher Bay. There the English made camp. Huddled and
shivering around their fires, they made their first encounter with a moose
and with local Eskimos. They were Inuits, who were easily enticed into
doing some trade with the strange Englishmen. "They exchanged coats of
seal, and bear skins, and such like, with our men," wrote one of Frobisher's
men, "and received bells, looking glasses, and other toys in recompense"
(no record of what the Inuits made of the spectacles and dog collars).

Frobisher stayed for almost a month without finding his passage and lost five more men in the process. Then one morning in August he awoke to find a blanket of snow on his ship deck. The Arctic winter was coming, and so Frobisher and his remaining thirteen men set off for home. All they had to show for their stay were an Inuit captive whom Frobisher had tricked into coming back with them (he died before they reached England) and a mysterious black stone his men had found on one of the desolate islands. It was the size of a loaf of bread and contained particles of a sparkling substance. To Frobisher it was just a strange rock, but when he got back to England his partner Michael Lok knew what it was at once: gold.

The wife of one of his partners tried putting some in the fire, and when it was taken out and a drop of vinegar added, "it glistened with a bright marquesset of gold." A wave of speculation fever hit London. The rumor spread that Frobisher had discovered the new Peru, a land where precious metals were just waiting to be dug out of the frozen tundra. There was only one objection. Most mineral experts, including John Dee, believed that gold was a "hot metal," native to warm climates like Mexico and South America, and not the frozen North. But these doubts were soon swept aside. America, everyone knew, was where the gold was; so why not on the shores of Englishman's Strait as well as in Peru or New Spain?

Frobisher was warmly received by the queen, who dubbed the new lands he had found *Meta Incognita*—"the Unknown Limit." Given his discovery of these gold-laden islands, the future for England seemed limitless. The Northwest Passage was forgotten in the frenzy to get more samples of Frobisher's exciting black gold. He had no trouble raising money for a second expedition in 1577 and came back with more than 140 tons of it. It was unloaded, with great secrecy and ceremony, in Bristol and secured in Bristol Castle under four separate locks. One of the keys went to William Wynter, a member of the Navy Board.

The first experts brought in to examine the sparkling black rock pronounced it worthless. But Frobisher persisted until he found assayers who would give a favorable opinion, including the master assayer of the Tower of London. Their experiments were not quite finished before Frobisher launched a third even bigger expedition, with fifteen ships. This time he intended to establish a permanent mining camp on Countess of Warwick Island. He also made one last attempt to find his northwest passage but found every direction blocked by ice. Once again, the intense cold made staying impossible and so Frobisher struck camp and brought back nearly 1,150 tons of his black gold.

He returned to England to hear the terrible news. The huge sample he brought to the assayers had reduced down to a few tiny gold specks. What Frobisher had found what not a new form of gold but a mineral scientists now call pyrite. We have another name for it: fool's gold.

There would be no more trips to the Unknown Limit. The Cathay Company collapsed. Frobisher furiously blamed it all on his partner, calling him a "bankrupt knave." His partner ended up in Fleet Prison. Frobisher himself escaped with only the loss of his reputation and his dreams. But the fiasco also left him without a ship, without a command, nothing.

It was in many ways a classic story, an English version of the Legend of El Dorado or the Seven Cities of Cibola, or even Ponce de Leon's search for a Fountain of Youth. It was by no means the last one, as Walter Raleigh's ventures into the jungle of Guyana proved twenty years later. But it underlined one basic point: the new geography had taught Englishmen how to get to remote places, but not what to do once they got there. The dream of instant wealth and power acquired simply by sailing in the right direction remained just that—a dream.

So attention shifted back to where the real wealth was, the silver and gold of Spain, and to Francis Drake.

CHAPTER FOUR

"Incomparable Empyre"

The English are the greatest murderers and proudest people in all
Europe and I am surprised that God tolerates them so long in power.
—ANONYMOUS IRISH WRITER, 1578

Such that seek for fame in foreign places, forsake Great ease, and wealth
where they were bred are special men, and do deserve more grace than
all the rest.
—THOMAS CHURCHYARD, 1579

D RAKE WANTED TO be the first Englishman to sail the Pacific
Ocean. However, his lieutenant from the Nombre de Dios raid,
John Oxenham, beat him to it. He would also be the first
Englishmen to bid for a foothold in the South Seas.

Oxenham returned to Panama in 1575 with seventy men and a ship of
140 tons, to reestablish contact with the ex-slave cimmaroons. After
beaching his ship, Oxenham took two cannon and started south across
the isthmus. With the typical resourcefulness of Devon sailors, they built
themselves a 45-foot pinnace out of cedar logs and began a series of raids
along the Pacific coast.

For two or three weeks Oxenham was the master of the sea routes to
Panama, striking at Spanish towns and settlements, freeing slaves, and
hijacking and looting ships, including a coastal vessel from Lima carrying
more than 100,000 pesos in silver. Oxenham was a skilled sailor, an
enterprising officer, and a passionate Protestant. He and his men left a
trail of vandalized Catholic churches and smashed altars. But he lacked
Drake's discretion and ability to command—and his good luck. Oxenham
quarreled with his crew and antagonized the cimmaroons, who turned
against him and even handed some of his men over to the Spanish. On his
route back from the coast, his Spanish pursuers easily followed his trail
and caught him and his men in an ambush. They massacred everyone
except Oxenham, his ship's master, his pilot, and five young boys, so that
they could be brought back in chains to Lima to face the Inquisition.

It was not often that the inquisitors had a well-connected English sea captain, a comrade of Drake and Hawkins, at their disposal. They ranged far and wide in their interrogation. Oxenham confessed that the queen had not authorized his voyage, but he did reveal that the English were interested in routes to the South Seas and in South America in general. He told them of Richard Grenville's 1574 plan for a reconnaissance in force into the Pacific, and of his own hopes for a reward from the queen if he had been able to establish a permanent English base in Panama.

Then they asked him about Francis Drake.

"Yes," Oxenham said, "he is a very good mariner and pilot. There is no man in England better equipped to do this."

"Will the queen grant Drake a license for privateering?" they asked.

"I don't think so, but Drake has told me that if the queen would give him leave he would sail through the Strait of Magellan and set up a colony." Oxenham told them others wanted to do the same, and that if Queen Elizabeth died many Englishmen would come to settle in America.

The inquisitors paused. "So it is only your queen who prevents Drake coming back to raid our settlements?"

"Yes."

Oxenham lay in prison another fourteen months until he and his two officers were dragged from their cells and thrown into penitents' robes. They were paraded barefoot across Lima's central square as part of the Inquisition's public condemnation of heretics, its ritual "act of faith" or *auto-da-fé*. Then the ecstatic crowd watched as they were hanged one by one.

. . .

So where was Drake? His take from the Nombre de Dios raid had made him rich, but by 1575 most of his money was gone. He had spent it on clothes and a house and furnishings, but also on three ships. They were his investment in a new sphere of activity, a place that would become the "hard school" for a generation of English soldiers and sailors, and England's dress rehearsal for empire: Ireland.

Almost all the leading figures of Elizabeth's navy—Drake, Grenville, Gilbert, Frobisher, Raleigh—ended up serving in Ireland at one time or another. It was in Ireland that Humphrey Gilbert first wrote down his idea for a northwest passage to Asia. It was there that Walter Raleigh first conceived of founding an English colony in America. And it was in

Ireland that Francis Drake first formulated his plan for his expedition into the Spanish Pacific, the expedition that would eventually take him around the world.

Ireland's role as the catalyst for English ambitions sprang from its recent history. English kings had enjoyed formal lordship control over Ireland since the twelfth century, but over the centuries they had lost control to independent Irish chieftains and feudal princes. Beyond the Pale, that slender belt of territory around Dublin that was under direct English rule, lay a wilderness of bog, forest, and violent Celtic tribes who practiced a rough-hewn form of Catholicism and lived in a state of constant internecine warfare. Henry VIII had crowned himself king of Ireland and broke up the ancient Irish monasteries and seized their property. But it was his daughter Elizabeth, and her Lord Deputy, Sir Henry Sidney, who took on the task of reducing Ireland to obedience and turned their restless Welsh and West Country compatriots loose to do it.

To Sidney, the Irish were savages, almost less than human. He said his goal was to "make the name of an Englishman more terrible now to them than the sight of a hundred was before." The plan was to establish a series of fortified settlements in the most dangerous part of Ireland, northeast Ulster, and to steadily drive the Irish out. Arthur Champernowne, vice admiral of Devon, was one who volunteered for this free land grab; he brought in his relatives, including Humphrey Gilbert, to help. Later the Devonians switched their efforts to Munster and were joined by Cornishmen Edmund Tremayne and Richard Grenville. Another nobleman from the Welsh borders, Walter Devereux, Earl of Essex, created another settlement, or "plantation" as they were called, as did London merchant Thomas Smith.

The English plantations in Ireland were the single largest movement of population in Europe in the sixteenth century. Their goal may have been strategic: keeping hostile Scots out of northeast Ulster, and keeping Spanish ships from landing in Munster. But the real impulse was profit. They became the original model for all future English colonial settlements. They were also, like the voyages of exploration, backed by private investors, and the results were something akin to genocide.

Irish chieftain James Fitzmaurice Fitzgerald led the first revolt against the settlers in 1569, burning Grenville's house at Tracton Abbey and massacring entire families. Sidney gave Humphrey Gilbert full powers as military governor to crush the rebellion. Gilbert slaughtered the Irish "man, woman, and child," wrote his biographer Thomas Church-

yard, "and spoiled, wasted, and burned by the ground all that he might."
Those he spared he forced to crawl on their bellies to his tent, passing a
long line of severed heads set on the ground on either side, so that, as
Churchyard said admiringly, "it did bring great terror to the people when
they saw the heads of their dead fathers, brothers, children, kinfolk, and
friends" as they begged for their lives and promised to obey the English
in the future.

As far as Gilbert and his fellow conquerors were concerned, it was all
the Irish deserved. They did not even see them as Catholics but as pure
heathens—as savage as any tribesman in Africa or America. Cultivated
English visitors like Walter Raleigh and Edmund Spenser found the
chiefs of Ulster, like Jamie Fitzgerald and Turloch Luineach O'Neill,
"proud, valiant, miserable, tyrannous, unmeasurably covetous, without
any knowledge of God or almost any civility," and were shocked at the
poverty and chaotic violence that seemed to reign everywhere. Thomas
Smith, founder of a plantation on Ardo peninsula in County Down, said
God had made the English fit "to inhabit and reform so barbarous a
nation . . . and to teach them our English laws and civility and leave robbing and stealing and killing each other."

The Irish thought otherwise. Smith's son was murdered by his own
servants and the settlement had to be abandoned. But the sense of a
civilizing mission, and with it a sense of innate superiority, remained.
John Foxe may have taught his contemporaries that they were God's
Englishmen. But it was in Ireland that they first learned to see themselves
as the natural rulers of others. Spain might have America and the
Caribbean to exploit, and Portugal Brazil and the markets of Asia. But at
least the English had Ireland. That translated into a license to rule and
colonize—and a license to kill.

The Earl of Essex got letters patent from Elizabeth authorizing him
to ethnically cleanse large portions of Antrim. Essex spent the next two
years waging a brutal war against the O'Neills of Tyrone and their ally
from western Scotland, Sorley Boy MacDonnell, son of the Lord of Islay
and Kintyre. The next step was to take Sorley Boy's stout fortress on
Rathlin Island, a craggy weather-swept chunk of rock three miles from
the Irish coast and only thirteen from Scotland. To do this he needed
ships, and the man he found to supply them was Francis Drake.

Drake jumped at the chance. Within a few months he had assembled
the ships he had captured in the Indies into a little naval force, along with
two transports for three hundred soldiers and eighty horses under the

command of John Norris. They sailed across to Rathlin Island on July 22, 1575, and stormed the fortress for four days until the Scots, including large numbers of women and children Sorley Boy had moved there for safety, surrendered. The Scots commander was able to arrange for himself and his wife and child to be spared. But the rest, Norris insisted, would have to "stand on the courtesy" of his troops.

As the gaunt and wretched Scots filed out of the castle gate, the English fell on them with swords and pikes. Almost six hundred people were butchered, as for the next two days Norris's men hunted down and killed every man, woman, and child they found on the island and picked it clean. What role Drake played in the massacre is unknown. One recent biographer argues that he regularly led armed parties into battle on shore, and so must have been present when the slaughter began. Another points out Drake always spared his Spanish captives and treated them well; he would have little reason to break that rule on Rathlin Island. But if he did, no one in England condemned him or Norris for their butchery.

In financial terms, however, the expedition to Rathlin Island cost Drake heavily. He had paid for the ships out of his own pocket and probably invested a large sum in Essex's colonization scheme. The English garrison soon abandoned Rathlin, and within a year not only had Essex's little colony at Clandeboy been massacred by avenging MacDonnells, but most of the other Elizabethan plantations had either been abandoned, destroyed, or were sinking under the weight of perpetual poverty and strife.

The English attempt to colonize Ireland had failed. But some wondered whether what had proved so difficult in Ireland might not succeed somewhere else. The question was where. Richard Grenville in 1574 had suggested Australia—or rather Terra Australis, the great undiscovered continent that geographers believed had to exist on the Pacific side of the southern tip of South America. His application for letters patent was supported by West Country worthies like William Hawkins, Edmund Tremayne, and Plymouth merchant Martin Dare (ancestor of the first English child born in the New World, Virginia Dare). However, since no one had seen Terra Australis, no one was particularly keen on leaving England to move there. Grenville's proposal found no takers.

Others proposed a continent they did know existed: North America. Richard Hakluyt the lawyer concluded that, for whatever reason, God had seen fit to let the Spanish and Portuguese establish their empires in the southern half of America. However, the northern, more temperate part, remained unexploited. He argued that English colonies there could become rich with agricultural products, including grain, wine, and olive oil, and supply the raw materials, such as timber, hemp, and tar, needed to maintain English ships and her navy.

Hakluyt also believed colonization did not necessarily mean war and genocide on an Irish scale. He believed there was another, easier way, involving cooperation not extermination of the natives: namely, trade, or as the Elizabethans called it, traffic. "To plant the Christian religion without conquest, will be hard," he wrote. "Traffic easily followeth conquest, [but] conquest is not easy." But "traffic without conquest seemeth possible, and not uneasy."

Hakluyt's ideas were too farsighted for his contemporaries. Hardened by the Irish experience, they found conquest a more attractive option. But their imaginations still ran westward, including Humphrey Gilbert's. His last idea, finding the Northwest Passage, had brought Martin Frobisher humiliation and bankruptcy. Undismayed, Gilbert sent the royal council a new proposal tantalizingly titled, "How Her Majesty May Annoy the King of Spain." It involved a naval raid on the French, Portuguese, and Spanish fishing fleets off the Grand Banks, then sailing down to the West Indies to attack Santo Domingo and Cuba. There Gilbert and his men would establish fortified English bases for raids on the rest of the Spanish Empire, and also claim and occupy land for English colonies.

Gilbert got the council's reluctant approval and began raising, money, men, and ships in Devon and Cornwall. They were a rough crowd. Some were pirating in the Channel even before they left on November 18, 1578. Then three ships broke off to take up pirating full-time—the temptation was too much—while Gilbert and the other six ships sailed on, including the 100-ton *Falcon,* commanded by Gilbert's twenty-four-year-old cousin Walter Raleigh, who flew a banner with the motto, "I seek not death, nor flee the end."

The expedition was probably bound for what is today the coast of the Carolinas and Virginia, but storms and bad weather forced them back to Ireland. Only one ship, Raleigh's, got as far as the tropics (exactly how far no one knew, least of all Raleigh) before having to head back. Gilbert and one of his fellow captains stopped on the way home to attack and pillage a French merchantman. The other ship, the *Red Lion,* went down in a storm; Gilbert sold his share of the loot in Cornwall. The ensuing uproar was tremendous, and by the time Humphrey Gilbert was back in England in

April 1579, he was facing charges of piracy. So he, like the rest, beat a hasty retreat to Ireland, where he commanded ships against the joint Irish-Scottish fleet of the Fitzgeralds.

Hakluyt and others were disappointed that the first English voyage to colonize North America had degenerated into marauding and thievery. But Gilbert, as usual, was undeterred. Soon he would be back at the royal council with a proposal for another expedition to America. But this time he found the council happy, even eager, to hear his ideas. Something had happened to change their attitude, and it had to do with Francis Drake.

* * *

Fifteen hundred and seventy-six found Drake still in Ireland and still broke. The support and patronage of the Earl of Essex had proved a dead end; that year the earl suddenly died, some said poisoned. However, Drake's future also looked brighter, thanks to the friendship he had struck up with a young gentleman in Essex's entourage named Thomas Doughty.

Doughty was everything Drake was not. He was wealthy and well-born, educated at Cambridge and friend to intellectuals at court like the queen's geographer and astrologer John Dee. Doughty was a genuine soldier as well as a scholar, while Drake still had never held a queen's commission either on land or at sea. Doughty was also a strong Protestant: "He feared God," remembered one friend. "He loved His Word, and was always desirous to edify others and confirm himself in the faith of Christ."

However, from Drake's point of view Doughty's chief virtue was his connections at court. In 1576 he landed a job as private secretary to Sir Christopher Hatton, Elizabeth's spokesman in the House of Commons and a member of the Privy Council. This access allowed Doughty to discreetly mention to Hatton and his fellow councillors an idea he and Drake had hatched in idle moments in Ireland. This was a major raid on the Spanish settlements on the Pacific coast of South America, including Lima, the home of the Spanish viceroy and the gateway to the silver mines of Peru.

It was a daring idea, staggering in its implications and problems. It might even lead to war with Spain. But Hatton and the others seized on it at once. Its evolution after it was taken up by the Privy Council is unclear. It is possible its backers never completely agreed on what its objectives were, even as Drake was setting sail in November 1577. In any case, Drake was summoned to a private interview with the queen, who, according to

Drake, told him, "I would gladly be revenged on the King of Spain for divers injuries that I have received." After years of trying to avoid confrontation with Spain, she was signing on to Drake's plan.

What had changed her mind? Perhaps the uneasy awareness that avoiding conflict with Philip had made her position less, not more, secure. One by one her allies against Spain had dropped out. France's Protestants had suffered a permanent blow from the Saint Bartholomew's Day Massacre and by 1576 their access to the sea was reduced to a single fortress, La Rochelle. Meanwhile the Dutch had concluded a peace with Philip's governor in February 1577, which promised a withdrawal of all Spanish troops. Elizabeth had helped to promote the treaty; but in June the Spanish governor staged a coup d'état, recalling his top commander, the Duke of Parma, and seizing the key fortress at Namur. The coup split the Dutch and pushed them to the point of collapse. That summer, Elizabeth learned that the Spanish governor was directly involved in another assassination plot against her. Still, Elizabeth dithered on what to do. In September she offered money and support to the Dutch; in December she withdrew it again.

Her royal council had always been divided between hawks and doves. But now the leading dove, Lord Burghley, was ill and away. Hawks like Hatton, Walsingham, Leicester, and the Earl of Lincoln, Elizabeth's Lord High Admiral, were in the ascendant. They sensed that the mantle of empire might be passing from Spain and Portugal, and that Drake might be their instrument for acquiring it. They became his principal sponsors, along with Sir William and John Wynter, who were both on the Navy Board, and John Hawkins, who was about to become navy treasurer. No voyage had ever had such extensive backing from the English political establishment or from official representatives of the Royal Navy—which meant Drake would have the use of the queen's ships, and the commission he yearned for.

Yet the plan remained shrouded in secrecy. The queen told Drake anyone who let Spain know what was happening would lose his head. The official destination was listed as Alexandria and the eastern Mediterranean. Almost nothing survives of the royal council's discussion about the plan, while the only copy of the final proposal has been badly damaged by fire and is almost illegible. However, what survives gives a fairly clear picture of what Hatton and Walsingham had in mind.

Drake was to assemble six ships for a voyage across the Atlantic and then head south toward the pole and the Strait of Magellan. From there he would pass into "the south sea then ... far to the northwards as" the 30th parallel or the northern end of Mexico's Baja peninsula. He was to travel along "said coast," meaning the Pacific coast of South America, for five months, looking for opportunities for trade and obtaining "special commodities," while claiming for England such lands as did not already belong to another Christian prince. It was expected that he would return to England in thirteen months, and by the Strait of Magellan. There was no thought of Drake finding a northwest passage—let alone sailing around the world.

As for "special commodities," Drake at least had no doubts about what that meant: loot from Spanish ships, perhaps even silver treasure. For him, the voyage was from first to last a pirating expedition, a chance to recoup his personal fortunes at King Philip's expense. The other backers, including Elizabeth, were careful not to give Drake that license explicitly, but they understood what he was up to. They doubtless saw his piracy as the key to the return on their investment—although none could have guessed how large that would really be.

The document ended by urging speedy approval of the plan. "Otherwise the voyage cannot take that good effect, as is hoped for"—meaning, the Spanish would find out. By September preparations were under way. William Wynter's son John brought the new royal warship *Elizabeth* of 80 tons down from London to Plymouth, along with the 15-ton pinnace *Benedict*. John Wynter was to share command with Drake, as would Drake's friend Thomas Doughty. Another of the queen's ships, the *Swallow;* the little *Marigold* with six guns; and the provision ship *Swan,* soon joined them. Drake himself provided the principal ship for the voyage, a 150-ton vessel he had built to his specifications in 1574. The queen named it the *Pelican,* but it is better known today as the *Golden Hind.*

The *Pelican* belonged to a new generation of oceangoing ships, which the Spanish called *galeons* or galleons, and which the English had only just begun building. They were slimmer than their predecessors like Hawkins's *Jesus* and more seaworthy. They also had lower fore- and aftcastles, which made them more stable and maneuverable in rough weather. Galleons generally came with four masts of sails: foremast and mainmast with two or three square sails each (mainsail, topsail, and sometimes a "top gallant"); a rear or mizzenmast with a pair of triangular lateen sails hung "fore and aft," meaning parallel with the ship's center line, and a "bona-venture" mizzen mounted on the aftercastle. A bowsprit with a square-rigged spritsail in the front of the ship completed its rigging.

The galleon combined the seaworthiness of Atlantic ships with the battle-worthiness of Mediterranean galleys. They were the first ocean-going ships meant to carry heavy armament. Although the *Pelican* was a small galleon, she carried a full complement of guns: seven on each side with gun ports, and the four heaviest in the bow. The *Pelican* may have been only sixty-eight feet in length with an eighteen-foot beam or width—not much larger than a wide-load semitrailer truck—but a Portuguese pilot who saw her pronounced her "staunch" and fit for transoceanic travel.

This was the ship with which Drake and his crew of seventy was to cross the Atlantic and sail the Pacific. As was typical of the age, that crew was very young—perhaps a third were only teenagers—and included lots of relatives: Drake's brother Thomas, "not the wisest man in Christendom," his young cousin John, John Hawkins's nephew William, and Thomas Doughty's brother. They also included a number of non-seamen, well-born friends of Doughty's who volunteered for what they saw as a glorious adventure. They would turn out to be the bane of Drake's existence.

There was one other aspect of the *Pelican*'s crew worth noting, since it carried implications for the future: its international flavor. Although most came from Devon like their captain, there was also a Danish gunner, two Dutchmen, and a "black Moor" who had been Drake's servant on his Nombre de Dios raid. As time went on, Drake would add a Greek, another Dutchman, numerous Spanish and Portuguese sailors, as well as blacks and even a South American Indian—not to mention a series of Hispanic pilots who guided Drake's course along every coast, from Brazil to California.

The *Pelican* and the other ships were soon loaded with the usual supplies for a long-distance voyage: biscuit, beer, wine, salted beef and pork, dried codfish, oil, and salt. After a false start on November 22, the fleet finally left England on December 13, 1577, and made Cape Cantine on the African coast on Christmas morning. Even at this point, no one except Drake, Doughty, and Wynter knew their exact destination, although many had begun to guess that they were not going to Alexandria and that they had a long voyage ahead, possibly as far as the West Indies. Doughty had even hinted as much to one of the crew, remarking prophetically, "If we bring home gold, we should be the better welcome."

But Drake was in no hurry. He raided along the African coast and hijacked several Spanish vessels (one of which he swapped for the *Benedict*), until he reached the Cape Verde Islands on January 28. There he had a stroke of good fortune that transformed the voyage: he captured an experienced Portuguese pilot named Nuño da Silva, who knew the coast of South America and, even better, had excellent charts. Drake decided to wait no longer; he made Doughty captain of the captured Portuguese vessel, renamed it the *Mary*, and set out on his 3,000-mile trek across the Atlantic.

Finding their way with a map posed no difficulty for Drake or any other Elizabethan seaman, even when those maps were, as Drake would soon discover, incomplete or inaccurate. The ancient Greek astronomer Ptolemy was the first to crisscross his map of the world with a grid of lines of latitude and longitude, with the equator cutting across the center, and the first to pinpoint cities and landmarks by their degrees north or south of the equator, and east and west of a zero line of longitude (medieval geographers ran it through the city of Jerusalem, for them the center of the world). Mapmakers of the Renaissance copied the same pattern, but also crisscrossed them with lines running diagonally from various points of reference, so that a mariner could plot his courses running north, south, east, or west with relative ease.

The great difficulty in all navigation at sea is not deciding where you are going, but finding out where you are. Sailors had had the compass since the twelfth century, but that only told them their relative bearing. Getting a real fix required some outside point of reference. For centuries sailors had relied on landmarks to tell them where they were, but in the midst of the Atlantic or Pacific or Indian Oceans there were none. In fact, since so many voyages, including Drake's, involved travel to places no European had been before, even other ways of judging one's position, such as certain ocean currents or familiar islands on the horizon, could provide no help. So the age of exploration compelled sailors and navigators to become creative about finding ways to keep their ships on course.

Fortunately for them, there was the sun.* At the equator, zero latitude, the sun passes directly overhead. Depending on whether one is north or south of that line, the sun follows a course closer to the horizon. If a sailor could figure out exactly how far the sun was from the zenith point, or where it would be if he were sailing on the equator, then he would have a way to calculate his latitude—the first half of his exact position.

---

*Or the stars. Celestial navigation posed its own set of problems, but otherwise it followed the same principles described here.

Hence the astrolabe. The Portuguese developed it in the fifteenth century from the mariner's quadrant; the earliest book on navigation in English had a picture of an astrolabe; Drake almost certainly had one on the *Pelican*. It was made of cast brass and was held waist high on the deck of the ship, suspended by a piece of rope, and then slowly turned until it was facing the sun. Then the ship's master turned the astrolabe's upper arm until a tiny spot of sunlight passed through the pin-hole sized aperture and fell on the pin hole of the lower arm. A scale allowed him to read the sun's altitude at its highest point, at noon. He wrote this down on his slate and then consulted an astronomical table, which gave the sun's declination on that day, so that he could calculate the true elevation of the sun. By subtracting that number from ninety degrees, he had his measure of latitude—or so he hoped.

The astrolabe, although convenient to use, was not always accurate. The pitching of the ship and the swaying of the device could make reading difficult. Sixteenth-century sailors came to prefer the cross staff, a piece of wood thirty inches long with a sliding crosspiece. By placing it up against the eye and sliding the crosspiece back and forth, until its lower edge aligned with the horizon and the upper edge with the rim of the sun, one could read the angular height of the sun. Then it was back to the declination tables, and by adding or subtracting that number from the cross staff reading, one's latitude position was determined.

The cross staff was an improvement over the astrolabe, but it had its own headaches—quite literally, since getting an accurate reading meant staring directly into the sun for minutes at a time. Like the astrolabe, it also demanded a sailor who knew how to read.

But calculating latitude was child's play compared to figuring out the second half of the equation, one's longitude position. Sun and stars provided no help at all, unless one knew exactly what time they were passing overhead or at the horizon—and this was information no clock of the age could provide.* In fact, until the eighteenth century, determining longitude was the greatest obstacle to transoceanic navigation, and its greatest peril. No sailor, no matter how skilled, ever knew exactly how far east or west he was traveling until his ship actually arrived at his destination—or, as happened almost as often, ran aground on some unexpected reef or shoal.

---

*This was because no pendulum or similar mechanism could keep accurate time on a moving, swaying ship.

It was like finding one's way around a foreign city in which all the east-west streets have street signs but the north-south ones, although named on the map, do not. The only way to figure out how far east or west one has gone is to count—city blocks on land, or miles traveled at sea.

That meant using the log and line. The first mention of it comes in *A Regiment for the Sea,* written in 1567 by Devonshire sailor William Bourne, and the first English book on navigation ever published. The log was a piece of wood to which a rope was attached, with knots tied at intervals to mark out a series of fathom lengths of six feet. The sailor heaved the log overboard, letting it stream behind; measured the distance covered by timing the number of knots with a half-minute hourglass; and then worked out his average speed—which is why nautical speeds are measured in knots to this day, and why the record of the ship's speed and distance is still called the ship's log. That average speed gave him a rough distance from his last position, and by checking with his compass and his map, a way to judge his longitude as well.

This technique was called "dead reckoning"—with no particular irony attached to the word *dead.* It was only a rough guide to one's position; it made it easy to overestimate one's speed and needed to be supplemented with constant soundings of water depth, so that shoals or shallows did not come up sooner than expected. But for all the uncertainty and danger, dead reckoning worked pretty well, especially if one's captain was particularly experienced and skilled—and very lucky.

Fortunately for his men, Drake was all three. Every day he carefully pricked out his course on his chart (Sebastian Cabot had introduced the first marine charts to English sailors) with a pair of compass dividers. Then he scrupulously wrote down the results in his journal, along with illustrations of the coastline, landmarks, and the approaches to harbors. Drake also consulted rutters, handwritten pilot manuals with valuable information about tides, water depths, and landmarks along specific trade routes. One existed for the routes along the Guinea coast as well as Brazil. A copy sits today in the British Museum, and Drake may have had a copy, too. He also kept a world map at hand, probably Ortelius's, executed in Antwerp in 1564 but circulating in London by the time Drake left England. Flat maps were not as good for measuring latitude and longitude as globes, but globes were too expensive and valuable to be risked at sea.

The only other navigational help Drake had was a book on Magellan's original voyage around the world, and an English translation of a Spanish traveler's guide to America. Otherwise Drake was on his own, on a trip that was a plunge into the complete unknown—the equivalent today of an expedition to Jupiter. This was why the capture of da Silva was such a godsend: he was just the experienced pilot Drake needed in unknown American waters. Drake made sure da Silva was comfortable, inviting him to dine at his table and to bunk in the gentlemen's sleeping quarters. They spent long hours together poring over the charts and rutters, and translating into English the pilot's charts of the Brazil coast and the Plate River delta. Da Silva became fluent in English and Drake's devoted friend. Without the Portuguese captain's help, Drake later told the queen, he could never have completed the voyage.

• • •

But if Drake's navigation worries were receding (although da Silva noted that the first thing Drake took from every ship he captured were its charts, astrolabes, and compasses), his problems with his crew were just beginning. At the center of the trouble was his old friend Thomas Doughty and the young gentlemen volunteers who looked upon him, not Drake, as the real leader of the expedition. The friendship that had blossomed on land turned sour at sea during the sixty-three days of the Atlantic crossing, thanks to Francis's brother, Tom Drake.

Doughty had accused him of stealing cargo from the Portuguese prize, which da Silva had piloted and Doughty now commanded. Blood being thicker than honor, Drake lost his temper with Doughty, not his brother, and put himself in charge of the prize, ordering Doughty back on the *Pelican*. Tom Drake continued to poison relations between his brother and Doughty, telling Francis how Doughty had complained at having to serve under a mere commoner and those "who took upon them[selves] to be masters." Francis Drake knew Doughty outranked him by social status and connections, if not by the queen's orders; the gossip touched a raw nerve with the poor parson's son. So when he heard that Doughty had had a run-in with Drake's trumpeter on board the *Pelican*, he ordered him stripped of command and relegated him to the *Swan*, their diminutive supply ship.

On February 20 the expedition crossed the equator, and on April 5 they finally had their first sight of the coast of Brazil. They failed to find safe anchorage and a series of storms scattered the fleet in all directions. The Portuguese prize, the *Mary*, and its crew vanished—foundered or run onto the rocks.

Meanwhile, on the *Swan* a storm of another kind was brewing. Although commander of the ship by virtue of his rank, Doughty was deeply offended by his demotion. He needled the former captain, John Chester, and quarreled with the ship's master. "Let us not be thus used at these knaves' hands," he exclaimed to Chester at one point, "if you will, we will put the sword again into your hands, and you shall have the government [of the ship]."

All this made Drake even angrier. To him, Doughty's words sounded like a call for armed mutiny. He decided that the *Swan* had to go and ordered its cargo transferred and the ship destroyed. Doughty had lost his command and his one remaining shred of dignity; he screamed at Drake that he no longer trusted him. Drake struck him across the face and ordered him lashed to the mast, an order the *Swan*'s crew carried out with pleasure. Doughty and his brother John were then rowed out to the *Christopher,* and then later the *Elizabeth,* where they were held incommunicado.

The ships stayed for two weeks off Brazil's Cape Tres Puntas, killing seals for meat and fraternizing with the natives. After they set sail again, Drake told Wynter and the *Elizabeth*'s crew that Thomas Doughty was a "seditious fellow" and a conjuror, and that his brother was worse: a witch and a poisoner. "I can not tell from whence he came," he said, "but from the devil I think." Drake even hinted that the bad weather they were experiencing was the result of the Doughtys' baleful influence.

But the real issue between them was not witchcraft but social class— and Drake's obsession with having total authority. He intended to punish Doughty for his presumption, and to make it clear that it was the up-from-nothing Devonshire seafarer, not the well-born courtier, who was really in charge. On June 19 they made anchorage at San Juan, almost 50 degrees south latitude, and on the last day of the month Drake ordered everyone ashore. He sat as judge, and Thomas Doughty was summoned before him. Drake said he was going to empanel a jury to try Doughty for mutiny and sedition.

Doughty asked what power Drake had for holding such a trial. Drake ignored him and proceeded with the reading of the charges, which included poisoning the Earl of Essex in Ireland and saying the royal council had been corrupt when it approved Drake's voyage. Doughty, his hands tied behind his back, defended himself as best he could, insisting that even Lord Burghley had known about and approved the expedition.

"No, that hath he not," Drake answered.

"He hath it from me," Doughty replied.

That sent Drake into a frenzy. "What this fellow hath done!" he bellowed to the assembled crew. "His own mouth hath betrayed him!" He insisted his hand-picked jury vote guilty. One of the gentleman on it, a lawyer by training, protested, "This is not law nor agreeable to justice." Drake lashed back, "I have not to do with you crafty lawyers, neither care I for the law, but I know what I will do."

The jury, properly intimidated, voted Doughty guilty. With Doughty now at his mercy, the triumphant Drake now spoke to the throng on the beach. Now, and only now, did he reveal to them their final destination. He produced a sheaf of documents* signed by the various members of the royal council which he claimed gave him full command of the voyage and the power to punish any offenders with death. By getting rid of Doughty, Drake told them, their success would be assured. The poorest sailor would be a rich man and "the worst in this fleet shall be a gentleman." Then he demanded a show of hands of those who thought "this man worthy to die." Most did as he demanded—although many, according to one eyewitness, silently prayed that they be delivered from Francis Drake as well.

John Wynter, the other commander of the expedition, had remained silent through the whole proceeding: he said later he was afraid Drake would kill him, too. Drake did not care. He finally had the complete authority he wanted. He gave Doughty two days in which to prepare himself for death. Doughty asked to be put ashore and allowed to take his chances with the Spanish rather than be executed. Drake refused but allowed him to be beheaded, as befitted his social rank, rather than hanged or shot. Doughty asked Drake to spare another of the young gentlemen, Hugh Smith, whom Drake also suspected of conspiring against him. "Well, Smith," Drake said, "I forgive thee, but by the life of God I was determined to have thy ears nailed to the pillory." Doughty thanked Drake, embraced him and called him "my good Captain," and put his head on the block. In a second it was over. Drake held the severed head up in front of his crew and exclaimed, "This is the end of traitors."

The whole episode shows Drake at his worst. Cruel, vindictive, distrustful to the point of paranoia, manipulative, deceitful (the queen's commission that Drake claimed he left in his cabin and promised to show his men never turned up). Yet it also marked a turning point for the future.

---

*These included everything except the queen's commission, which the sailors naturally clamored to see but Drake claimed he had left in his cabin.

Drake had established one of the key principles for English maritime life and the British navy: unity of command. The captain of the ship, and the captain alone, holds complete authority, including the power of life and death over his crew. He and he alone decides what is to be done, no matter how arbitrary or unfair it may seem. And no one, regardless of title or social rank, may challenge him on his ship.

Drake drove that point home when he reassembled his crew one last time on Sunday August 11, before they set off for the Strait of Magellan. He had Fletcher administer Communion and then in a famous speech told them that "these mutinies and discords that are grown amongst us" had to stop, particularly any discord between gentlemen and sailors.

> I must have it left, for I must have the gentleman to haul and draw with the mariner, and the mariner with the gentleman. What, let us show our selves all to be of a company, and let us not give occasion to the enemy to rejoice at our decay and overthrow. . . . If this voyage shall not have good success, we shall not only be a scorning unto our enemies, but also a great blot to our country for ever; and what a triumph that would be for Spain and Portugal!

Calm had been restored; his men would now obey Drake without question. And future generations of sea captains, in the British as well as foreign navies, could thank Drake for establishing their absolute authority—and thank the blood of Thomas Doughty.

However, the most dangerous part of the voyage still lay ahead: passing the southern tip of South America through the Strait of Magellan. The three remaining ships* ran down the coast until they found the mouth of the strait, but contrary winds kept them from entering until August 23. When they did, they found themselves where no non-Spanish sailor had ever gone. It was a twisting, winding channel, battered by turbulent winds and flanked by distant ranges of mountains covered with snow and ice, with the occasional volcano poking up into the clouds. At times the steep tree-covered hills on either side acted like a wind tunnel,

---

*It was just before they left that Drake is supposed to have rechristened the *Pelican* as the *Golden Hind* in honor of his patron Sir Christopher Hatton (the *hind,* or female red deer, was part of Hatton's coat of arms). No contemporary English document backs up this story; but Drake's ship has been known ever after as the *Golden Hind,* and so *Golden Hind* it shall be here.

bringing sudden dangerous gusts that would nearly hurl them into the
cliffs. At other times they seemed to have reached a dead end, only to
have the channel sharply twist away to the next turning. Islands appeared
of which the principal inhabitants were armies of penguins; on one island
Drake's men killed more than three thousand and salted and dried the
flesh for food.

On September 6, nearly two weeks after they had entered the strait,
they found themselves in the Pacific—and sailed directly into the teeth of
a storm that threatened to blow them back into the channel. They tried
to find shelter to their northwest but discovered only open sea. Once
again, Drake's maps had misled him. Meanwhile, the storm grew in intensity and the ships became separated for good.

It was as if the ghost of Thomas Doughty really had bewitched
them. No one saw the *Marigold* again. Wynter on the *Elizabeth* managed
to gain the shelter of the strait, and after the storm abated remained
there for nearly three weeks. His men watched the coast and lit daily
signal fires, but there was no sign of Drake. Their prearranged rendezvous, in case they were separated, was to be on the South American
coast, near Valparaiso. But Wynter had had enough, and decided to
head back through the strait and go home. Later, his crew would accuse
him of cowardice; when he arrived back in England, the government's
first act was to throw him in prison. However, Wynter could give them
sobering news: Francis Drake was certainly dead, lost with his ship and
all hands.

But Drake, of course, was not dead. He had been blown far to the
south and southwest, and there accidentally made the voyage's first major
discovery. The mountains and hills that lined the southern side of the
Strait of Magellan were not part of another vast new southern continent,
Terra Australis, but were part of a series of islands called Tierra del Fuego,
which were surrounded by open water running all the way to the Atlantic
at Cape Horn—although evidence suggests Drake himself did not get
that far. But he did see enough to guess the rest: the Atlantic and Pacific
did meet in open water. The seas of the world really were one.

The storms finally let up and Drake could make landfall on October
28, 1579. He had less than eighty men, out of the one hundred and seventy who started the trip. He was down to one ship—and that one battered and badly in need of repair. But it was the most heavily armed ship
in the Pacific Ocean. At a single stroke, England enjoyed, however briefly,

naval supremacy in that ocean. And the entire coast of South America, from Valdivia to Acapulco, was open to him.

With the exception of Lima, the Spanish settlements along the Pacific coast were pitifully small. Most had less than one hundred fifty inhabitants, and they were poorly defended, for good reason. They never had any need for it. No one but fellow Spaniards ever sailed this ocean. The appearance of Drake and his *Golden Hind* with its menacing open gun ports bristling with cannon and his fierce ragged men was more startling and frightening than a spaceship full of armed aliens turning up at Martha's Vineyard. Thanks to another captured pilot and his charts, Drake was able to make his way confidently up the coast. For three months Drake looted the defenseless towns, taking food and everything of value—and, of course, vandalizing their churches.

Those who were encountered him were invariably impressed. They noted his sumptuously furnished cabin and his splendid dinner table, with its silver dishes bearing a noble coat of arms etched in gold that Drake claimed was his own (it was not). Trumpeters and violinists performed while Drake wined and dined his guests, including the pilot da Silva, a glum John Doughty (Drake watched his every move), and a steady succession of Spanish prisoners, whom he regaled with stories and peppered with questions in his pidgin Spanish.

Drake told them that "there was no one in the world who understood the art of navigation better than he" (da Silva must have smiled at that one). He showed them his copy of Foxe's *Book of Martyrs* and relished their Catholic reaction to the illustrations of monks and bishops burning victims at the stake and kings prostrating themselves before the pope— "There is an evil man," Drake would add. He also asked for news of the fate of John Oxenham: he did not know that he had been executed shortly before Drake arrived. He also asked if anyone had news of Viceroy Enríquez, the man who betrayed him and John Hawkins at San Juan Ulloa. Finding him "would give me a greater joy than finding all the gold and silver of the Indies," he told one prisoner. "I would soon show him how gentlemen keep their word."

This was sheer bravado. Drake's real goal was treasure; it had been from the start. He and his men picked up a few gold coins and silver bars from the towns and coastal vessels they looted. But it was not until he reached the southern coast of Peru in February that he learned of a ship owned by a merchant named Sant Juan de Anton, which had left Callao de Lima with a load of silver bullion bound for Panama. The *Nuestra Señora de la Concepción** was almost a week ahead of him, with several ports to visit on the way. If Drake was to catch her, he would have to hurry.

Yet another captured pilot guided Drake into Callao, the port city of Lima. There he seized several vessels, although he found very little worth taking, and learned that Oxenham was indeed dead. Now all his attention was on the prize of the *Nuestra Señora*. Farther north, off Malabrigo, he captured yet another pilot who had seen the treasure ship just a couple of days earlier; at Paita he was told it was only forty-eight hours ahead of him. Drake ordered his men to press on more sail and offered a prize to the first man to see the Spanish galleon.

At three o'clock in the afternoon of March 1, young John Drake was aloft in the maintop when he spotted the white sails of a large ship off Cape San Francisco. Drake reefed sail to slow his progress and not alarm the *Nuestra Señora,* and gradually made for her. For six hours the chase went on in slow motion. As Drake grew closer, the *Nuestra Señora* gradually appeared in full view to starboard, and Drake could see she had no guns or armaments. Not until nine o'clock, as dusk was falling, were the English close enough to hail. Drake stood on his poop deck in his helmet and breastplate and called out to the *Nuestra Señora*'s owner and master, San Juan de Anton, that he was an English ship and ordered him to strike his sails. Anton answered, "What English demands I strike sail? Come do it yourself!"

Drake obliged by opening fire. The first cannon shot brought down the mizzenmast, as English sailors on deck and on the masts' fighting platforms delivered a rain of arrows, one of which wounded Anton. Drake's nimble pinnace ran around the Spaniard's stern and a party of forty men were soon clambering up her sides. Anton saw that it was hopeless, and surrendered.

Drake found on board the largest treasure anyone had ever taken from a Spanish ship. It came to more than 360,000 pesos, with over thirteen hundred silver bars and fourteen chests stuffed with reales and gold coins. It was, almost literally, the mother lode. Drake was exultant. He clapped Anton on the shoulder, told him to cheer up, that these things happen in war, and left orders that his prisoner was to be fed as an honored guest at his own table. He gave John Drake his reward for spotting

---

*Sometimes called the *Cácafuego*—literally the "shitfire," or depending on the placement of the accents, "spitfire."

the ship first, a gold chain, then put thirty men on board the *Nuestra Señora* and kept it and Anton under guard.

It took six days to transfer the twenty-five tons of silver bars and the massive chests of gold into the hold of his ship. Drake was in an excellent mood. He dined with the usual trumpet and viol accompaniment, chatted with Anton, and had the news of Oxenham's death confirmed. Before he let Anton go, he gave him and his men presents from the booty he had taken on earlier raids: a German matchlock musket, a silver gilt bowl, a sword and shield, some mirrored ladies' fans, and thirty pesos in coin for each man. As a Drake biographer puts it, "It is easy to be generous with someone else's money."

The *Pelican's* hold was crammed with Spanish treasure. Drake's fortune was made—as was that of his investors. Only one problem remained: how to get home with the loot. Drake guessed that the way he had come was now blocked. By now the Spanish, fully alerted, would have the Strait of Magellan swarming with warships. He mulled over the problem with Anton, and even described his options. He could head across the Pacific to Indonesia, and then find his way home via the Indian Ocean and the Cape of Good Hope. Or he could continue north up the American coast and hope to find that elusive northwest passage that might bring him home by an Atlantic route. Drake was careful to keep Anton guessing, but by the time he released him and the now empty *Nuestra Señora,* Drake seems to have opted for the northern route. Only if that failed, would he go for the much longer route that would take him literally around the world.

Meanwhile, Drake continued his forays along the coast of Ecuador, Panama, and Mexico. On a deserted island he beached and "careened" his ship, hauling it up out of the water and tipping it on its side so its bottom could be cleaned of barnacles and recaulked to seal the leaks. Barnacles, weed, and wood-boring worms were the plague of every ship that sailed in the South Seas or Caribbean; most rarely lasted more than seven years in the tropics before the hull fell apart. Even when his men had finished and plugged the leaking timbers, Drake knew he would have to careen his ship again before he headed home.

Drake skirted Acapulco, where heavily armed Spanish galleons from the Philippines stopped on their way south. Instead, he made his way steadily up the coast of California, as he left the last Spanish settlements far behind.

How far did he get? The sources clash, as do the interpretations of historians. A leading expert has argued the evidence suggests he got as far north as 48 degrees north, or roughly where Seattle sits today. Drake's most recent biographer, Harry Kelsey, doubts he got farther than modern-day Catalina Island, or 33 degrees north. Certainly the notion that Drake, who was sailing a leaky ship laden with treasure, would push his luck on an unfamiliar coast without a pilot or charts, does seem far-fetched.

But legend, supported by at least some evidence, suggests he landed somewhere near the 38th parallel, near San Francisco Bay (the ship needed careening again). There he met the local Indians—although Drake's story that they believed him to be a god and made him their king, or at least an honorary chief of the tribe, sounds like pure moonshine. There, it seems, he also decided he was far enough away from Spanish America to establish a claim for Queen Elizabeth to the land he called Nova Albion, or "New England"—in imitation of the Spanish, who had taken possession of Mexico as New Spain. He erected a brass plaque in the name of the queen, with a picture of her and the arms of England taken from a sixpence piece, and assured his native audience that "so tractable and loving a people" deserved "to be ruled by her and brought by her to the Gospel and true knowledge of God."

Queen Elizabeth's newest subjects could not have understood what Drake was saying, and they must have been puzzled when he and his crewmen knelt and performed the first church service in English in America. But they may have been interested enough to watch as Drake finally set his sails west on the twenty-third of July, and might have lingered on the headlands to see his ship slowly disappear over the horizon.

. . .

Drake's departure from Plymouth in November 1577 had originally been overshadowed by another event, one that galvanized the attention of the nation. A large comet appeared in the sky, with a long flaming tail that was visible even at midday. The celestial apparition "bred great fear and doubt in many of the Court." So Elizabeth sent for her court astrologer John Dee to explain what was happening.

Dee was not only a master of navigation and geography but a brilliant astronomer. He told Elizabeth the comet did not foretell disaster but something hugely positive, a major cosmic realignment. On November 28 just as Drake was about to set sail, Dee arrived at Windsor Castle with news that left her and her court thunderstruck. He said that he could now prove that the New World belonged to England, not Spain, and that Elizabeth should lay formal claim to it.

John Dee remains one of the most mysterious but fascinating figures of the Elizabethan age. He was a Welshman born in 1527, skilled in everything having to do with mathematics, from astronomy and geography (he drew the first serious map of America in 1580) to helping Lord Burghley's secret service with its cryptography and codes. He had learned his mapmaking from the Dutch master himself, Gerard Mercator. After Sebastian Cabot's death, Dee became the Crown's principal advisor on navigation and was the first Englishman to reveal how mathematics was crucial to its study. He even claimed to have discovered a way to calculate longitude exactly, although no one ever learned what it was. He did advise Chancellor and Frobisher on their searches for northern seaward passages, and he became a mentor to Humphrey Gilbert and Walter Raleigh—and to Thomas Doughty.

But Dee's influence and interests went far beyond matters of sea and sky. He also dabbled in alchemy and, even more discreetly, in the arts of black magic, including telepathy and demonology. When a mysterious effigy of the queen had been found in the quarters of a Catholic conspirator, a sort of Elizabethan voodoo doll, Dee was the man brought in to "defuse" it. He was also something of a historian and antiquary. There in his rambling house at Mortlake on the Thames, among books, maps, herbs, alchemical apparatus, globes and navigational instruments, and mechanical devices (including a mechanical bird that sang a variety of tunes), he had assembled various documents relating to the history of early Britain and King Arthur.

King Arthur was a national hero to Welshmen like Dee, and to the Cornish, who claimed him as one of their own. Henry Tudor tried to trace his descent directly to King Arthur; he had named his first son Arthur and had him baptized at Winchester, which was supposed to be the site of the original Camelot. For the Tudors, Arthur and his Knights of the Round Table were not so much symbols of chivalry but conquest. According to his great medieval chronicler Geoffrey of Monmouth (also a Welshman), King Arthur had not only ruled the British Isles, but France and most of western Europe after the fall of the Roman Empire. He was advancing on the gates of Rome itself, it was said, when treachery called him home to be killed by his nephew Modred.

Humanist-trained historians like Polydore Vergil mocked the whole story and lambasted Geoffrey of Monmouth as an ignorant faker. But Welsh and West Country scholars clung fiercely to the source of their national pride. In 1572 Humphrey Lloyd published in Latin his *Breviary of*

Britain, which described Arthur's ancient dominion over England, Scotland, and Wales as a *Britannicum imperium,* or British empire. A new term and a new concept were born, which Lloyd and others saw as the key to England's role in future history.

John Dee went further. He extended Arthur's empire to anywhere he could find an ancient British connection. When he finished, it embraced Ireland, Scotland, Iceland (Arthurian Britons apparently having gotten there before Leif Erickson), Greenland, the Orkneys, Norway, Denmark, and Gaul, and all the seas connecting them. And since Dee had found a story that King Arthur had once sponsored an expedition to visit lands west of the Atlantic, the "British empire" now also had to include North America.

It was a brilliant ploy. At one stroke, Dee made nonsense of Spain's claim to legitimate rule in America and invalidated the papal Treaty of Tordesillas, which had divided the non-European world between Spain and Portugal, on the grounds that no Christian nation had prior title to them. Now one had—and dominion of the oceans in between.

Dee had opened a way for the English to lawfully contest the Spanish and Portuguese for the empire, and much more. Dee saw Britain sitting in the cockpit of a new world system. Back in 1570, in his *Elements of Geometry,* he had exclaimed, "What a privilege God had endowed this island with by reason of situation, most commodious for navigation, to places most famous and rich." Now, in 1577, in light of the comet and other world events, he prepared a master brief on the subject for the queen entitled, *General and Rare Memorials Pertaining to the Perfect Art of Navigation.*

"No King, No Kingdom," Dee proclaimed, "hath by Nature and Human Industry" a more perfect right to world empire than Elizabethan England. At the helm of "this Imperial Monarchy," which she had inherited from King Arthur, Elizabeth was free to establish the kind of universal rule that John Foxe had foreseen for her and that had eluded every other great empire in history, from Alexander the Great and ancient Rome to even mighty Portugal and Spain. How could she accomplish all this from her tiny island kingdom? All she needed, Dee said, was a navy "of three score tall ships or more, but in no case fewer," well appointed with guns and supplies and fully manned by men like Gilbert, Hawkins, and Drake.

Such a navy could first of all guarantee that "henceforth neither France, Denmark, Scotland, Spain, or any other country can have such liberty for invasion or . . . annoy the blessed state of our tranquility." It would protect the English coasts and the western approaches to the Channel, wipe out piracy, and drive out foreign fishing fleets from the North Sea and the Grand Banks, which rightfully belonged to England. It would expand English shipping and dispense with the need for large expensive armies. No foreign prince could contemplate invading Britain without confronting this terror of the seas.

A permanent navy, Dee concluded, was "the Master Key wherewith to open all locks that keep out or hinder this incomparable British Empire" from expanding its share of global trade and the discovery of new lands. The resulting inflow of treasure would make England the richest nation in the world, and more than pay for the navy. A new world order would arise, Dee predicted, one in which all foreign princes would bow to Britain's will. "God's glory, the wealth public, and the honorable renown of this Island Empire" would embrace the globe.

In the context of world history, we can call Dee prophetic. In the context of 1577, he was an idle dreamer. He imagined the annual cost of such a navy at something like 200,000 pounds, the equivalent of Elizabeth's entire annual budget. But Elizabeth was still excited when she heard about it and even drove down to Mortlake to hear more. She brought him back to Richmond Palace to discuss his plan with Lord Burghley. Burghley, like any sensible statesman and administrator, killed it on the spot. Dee's brief career as policy wonk was over; he went back to his maps and magical diagrams. But his place as the original prophet of the British navy was secure.

That was on September, 17, 1580. Little more than a week later, Burghley had more pressing news, this time from Plymouth. Drake was home.

Compared to the drama and dangers of his South American passage, the rest of Drake's voyage was almost anticlimax. Crossing the Pacific had taken two months—it was a bigger ocean than non-Spanish geographers had imagined and, as Drake showed them, almost 10 degrees of longitude bigger. It was not until the middle of November 1579 that he finally touched down on an island in the Moluccas. This was the center of Europe's spice trade with Asia, and although Drake had arrived in the middle of Ramadan, the sultan of the island, who hated the Portuguese, feted Drake in style and gave him monopoly rights for dealing in pepper on his island—the first faint flickers of England's future presence east of Suez.

There was a sticky moment on the voyage to Java, when the *Pelican* got stuck on a reef and they had to throw cannon and bales of spices overboard before the ship righted herself and slid back into deep water. But the trip across the Indian Ocean was uneventful, and they did not see land again until June 18, 1580, when Table Mountain came rising up over the Cape of Good Hope, at the southern tip of Africa: "The fairest cape we saw in the whole circumference of the earth." They reached Sierra Leone on July 22, and were off the Canary Islands a month later.

Oddly, no one knows the exact date a tired but triumphant Drake and his remaining crew of fifty-eight men made it into Plymouth harbor. But as the bells of St. Andrew's rang out in celebration and the crowds swarmed onto the ship, including Drake's wife, Drake must have had some concern about what his reception from the queen would be. His famous first question on arriving back in England—"Is the queen alive and well?"—reflected not just his concern for her, but for himself. If she were dead and Spain's ally Mary Queen of Scots was on the throne, he might just as well sail back to the Moluccas. Even if she were alive, stories of his depredations in South America, including Doughty's death, might lead her and her councillors to disavow him and any knowledge of his actions.

But Drake need not have worried. When the queen and Burghley got wind of the size of the take from the *Nuestra Señora,* any misgivings they had vanished. Drake went to London with seven packhorses loaded with gold and silver, and six magnificent emeralds for the queen. They met and spoke for six hours. The next time she appeared in public, she wore the emeralds. Her share alone of Drake's treasure came to almost 160,000 pounds, enough to pay off her entire foreign debt and still have 40,000 pounds left over to invest in a new trading company for the Levant. Her return and that of other investors came to 47 pounds of every 1 pound invested, or a total return of 4,700 percent.

The following January Drake sailed up the Thames to Deptford, where the queen met him and knighted him on board the *Golden Hind.* He was now a gentleman—his final revenge on Thomas Doughty—and had his own coat of arms, with a ship resting on the globe as his crest. He was also immensely rich. The royal council allowed him to keep over 10,000 pounds as his own private share. That was the official figure: the real figure, together with all the other booty he had taken from Spanish churches, ships, and their passengers, probably came to much more. The richest pirate in the world was now able to buy a country estate, Buckland Abbey, from Richard Grenville.

But the real achievements of his trip and the fact that Drake had sailed around the world were still a secret. Drake's men were sworn to secrecy on the route he had taken back to England on pain of death. The Spanish ambassador still believed he had returned via the Strait of Magellan as late as April 1582. The map Drake had drawn, including the corrections he made of the coast of South America, remained under lock and key. Even his ship's journal became a state secret; once Drake handed it over, even he was not allowed to see it again.

It would be nearly a decade before all the details of Drake's voyage were finally published. Yet it already had set off a national sensation. Ballads and broadsides appeared, celebrating Drake as the queen's intrepid knight-errant: the beginning of the Drake legend. Drake's voyage, and its spectacular success, also sparked imitators. Drake and the queen were already planning a second expedition to leave in December. It fell through, but another was planned for 1581 and still another for 1582, which actually did sail. For every official expedition planned, there were dozen private ones. As the Spanish ambassador noted morosely, "At present there is hardly an Englishman who is not talking of undertaking the voyage, so encouraged are they by Drake's return."

England's reputation as a seafaring nation also took an enormous leap forward. In a single trip, Drake had done what Magellan, da Gama, and Diaz had taken decades to do separately. He had moved his countrymen to the forefront of overseas exploration. When Thomas Cavendish repeated the same circumnavigation in 1586–88, this time without the help of Portuguese pilots, English voyages around the world were beginning to seem old hat.

The effect on England itself was no less startling. One witness noted Drake's success "inflameth the whole country with a desire to adventure unto the seas." According to historian Theodore Rabb, the voyage played a vital role in spurring English interest "in the possibilities for personal and national profit in faraway lands." It also spurred England's first major step toward becoming a maritime commercial nation—and in taking control of its own economic destiny.

Even as late as 1570, England's trade was still largely in the hands of foreigners: Italians, Germans, and Flemings. England was their market for raw materials. Bankers in Hamburg and Antwerp, wool merchants in

Genoa and Lübeck, and fish wholesalers in Stockholm and Lisbon made the key decisions affecting the English economy. The Tudors set to work to change this. In fact, the founding of the Muscovy Company in 1553 marked the first time English merchants systematically organized an overseas business enterprise.

Now Drake showed them just how far their horizons could reach. Over the next four decades more than thirty new trading companies would spring up. The Levant Company, the Virginia Company, the East India and Massachusetts Bay companies were only the most famous. Their model was the joint-stock investment schemes of the Irish plantations, but their inspiration was Sir Francis Drake.

The dim outlines of the elder Hakluyt's dream of colonies organized to promote trade, not conquest, and Dee's "Incomparable Empyre," were beginning to take shape. But all that lay in the future. Now, in 1580, the celebrations of Drake's return were tempered by a sense of foreboding. Things were heating up with Spain.

CHAPTER FIVE

The World Is Not Enough

ON AUGUST 4, 1578, King Sebastian of Portugal perished with his army at the battle of Alcazar-Kebir, near the Atlantic shore of Morocco. The Battle of the Three Kings (so called because his enemy, the sharif of Tangier, also died in the battle, as did the former sharif, who was serving in Sebastian's army) brought Portugal's long tradition of crusading against the Moors to a sudden disastrous end. It also left the country without a ruler.

Sebastian had no children. His elderly uncle, Cardinal Enrico, deaf and nearly blind, reluctantly assumed the throne, but the better claim belonged to Philip II of Spain, whose mother had been the cardinal's elder sister. When the news of Alcazar-Kebir reached Philip, he told his courtiers and his generals he wanted the situation handled "very delicately." He even waited until Cardinal Enrico died in January 1580 before sending an army under the Duke of Alba across the Spanish-Portuguese border. Most Portuguese offered no resistance. Lisbon did hold out for the cardinal's bastard nephew, Don Antonio, and had to be taken by Alba's veterans fighting house to house. However, by the end of August, Philip's Iberian *Anschluss* was over. On September 12, 1580, he was declared king of Portugal. Philip wrote a glowing letter to Alba, "I don't know how to express the gratitude that I owe you for this."

Philip II had reason to be happy. He already ruled the largest empire in the world. Now he possessed the second largest as well. The extensive Portuguese possessions in Africa, Asia, and Brazil were entirely at his disposal, as was Lisbon, the richest, busiest and best-fortified port on the Atlantic. In its shipyards Spanish naval officers were delighted to find ten newly built fighting galleons, the latest in military design and technology and ready to serve what was now the world's lone superpower.

Philip sent the new galleons into action to crush insurgent support for Don Antonio in the Azores, Portugal's key link to America. His best admiral, the Marquis of Santa Cruz, led a naval assault under heavy fire on the central island of São Miguel in August 1582. Exactly a year later, an even larger fleet, or *armada,* of 98 ships and 15,000 men arrived in the Azores at Terceira. In the first naval battle in history decided by gunfire, Santa Cruz overwhelmed the insurgents' fleet and that of their French allies. Don Antonio was finished; the Spanish conquest of Portugal was complete. Flushed with victory, Santa Cruz wrote to Philip urging him not to sit on his laurels. "You should follow up this victory," Santa Cruz exclaimed, "by making arrangements for the invasion of England."

With the French bogged down in civil war, and the Dutch rebels on the run (the Duke of Parma's army was already pounding on the gates of Antwerp), England was the last puny obstacle to Philip's vision of world empire. Philip was not keen on war with the island kingdom. He preferred to keep it and its heretic queen at arm's length, while he consolidated his grasp on the mainland of Europe. The raids by Hawkins, Drake, and England's other privateers had been annoyances and embarrassments rather than a serious threat: mere pinpricks compared to the vital stakes on the Continent. And since Elizabeth would die without heirs, her successor Mary Queen of Scots or Mary's son James would be his ally, anyway. So Philip shelved Santa Cruz's idea for now. But with his hand so much stronger, the opportunity to keep Elizabeth off balance was irresistible.

The logical place to do it was Ireland. Within days of the fall of Lisbon, Philip dispatched a small Spanish expeditionary force to join the native Irish army Jamie Fitzgerald had scratched together at Smerwick, for a full-scale rebellion. It landed at Dingle Bay on the west coast and for a moment it looked as if Ireland would flare up in a massive revolt. However, William Wynter swooped in with four warships, including one commanded by Walter Raleigh, and cut off and destroyed Fitzgerald's ships. The rebels were surrounded, while siege guns landed from Wynter's ships hammered them mercilessly. Finally, the Spanish troops were induced to surrender. When they did, the English massacred them in cold blood. This was Ireland, after all—as the English commander, Martin Frobisher, an old Irish hand, might have warned them.

Philip could shrug off the defeat. He knew time was on his side. But for Elizabeth and her advisors it was a serious wake-up call. Drake's raids in the Caribbean had provoked the world's lone superpower into permanent hostility, and now they faced it alone. England had no allies anywhere; she was vulnerable from every direction and coast. England was more isolated than she would be in 1940 against Hitler. Round-the-world voyages and dreams of empire were one thing; war with Spain was quite another.

England had not fought a major war for 150 years. It had no standing army. There was no royal financial mechanism to pay for one or economic infrastructure to support it. Elizabeth's royal councillors knew next to nothing about conducting modern military operations, and she had no generals or admirals of the outstanding caliber of Alba, Parma, or Santa Cruz. All she had were ships and a handful of sailors and captains, who believed they could make up for experience and discipline with their belligerent Protestant spirit. As Drake told John Foxe, "Our enemies are many but Our Protector commandeth the world."

Still, on sober days, it must have looked pretty hopeless. Yet events over the next decade would forge this motley collection of pirates, adventurers, and courtiers into an efficient fighting force, the best navy in the world. They would militarize English society to a degree it had never known before, and direct its national energies toward waging war at sea.

. . .

Defense of Elizabeth's realm against Spain would depend on her navy—frankly and simply because she had nothing else. But what had happened to it since the death of her sister Mary?

Outwardly, very little. It comes as a shock to realize that all the voyages, raids, and seafaring ventures of the age, including the conquest of Ireland, were all conducted by private hands and investors, not the Royal Navy at all. Hawkins and Drake and Humphrey Gilbert were never professional naval officers; in a strict sense, no one was. The "Queen's Navy" was still just a collection of ships, built and kept at her expense, for which her Lord High Admiral found captains when they needed to be sent to sea. Hawkins and the others had borrowed her ships, like the *Jesus* and the *Elizabeth,* for their own purposes; they had proved they could handle single ships in battle. Hawkins and Gilbert had even had the heady experience of holding the "queen's commission" (in Gilbert's case, on land not at sea). But before 1588 no one except William Wynter had experience serving in, let alone commanding, a fleet of true warships. The men from Devon were merchants first, pirates and seafighters second—and private entrepreneurs from start to finish. As an institution, the Royal Navy had played as yet little part in their lives, and almost none in the shaping of England's global future.

Still, in this case appearances deceive. Henry VIII's administrative revolution in creating the Navy Board had put Elizabeth's navy into experienced, capable hands like those of William and John Wynter, who served as Elizabeth's Master of Ordnance and Clerk of the Ships, respectively. Navy treasurer Benjamin Gonson had maintained an orderly house for more than twenty years, with some help from his son-in-law, who happened to be John Hawkins. There were still not as many ships as there had been under Henry VIII, but they were in better shape than under Edward or Mary. When Elizabeth came to the throne in 1558, an official "book for sea causes" listed twenty-one naval ships in service, with another ten too worn-out to be any further use.* Her officials estimated there were a further forty-five merchantmen that could be converted in time of war—a standard practice. This was not a bad turnout; probably enough to hold the English Channel against a French invasion. But against the Spanish threat to come, and a combined Spanish-Portuguese fleet, the Royal Navy was going to have to rise to a higher level.

The man who accomplished that was John Hawkins. When Benjamin Gonson died in January 1577, son-in-law Hawkins took his place. Forty-eight years old, as active and ambitious as ever, he would use his experience as oceanic slave trader and privateer to shake things up at the Navy Board.

On any given day, Hawkins could travel from his headquarters at Tower Hill in London down the Thames to see for himself the state of his new charge. His boat would drift past the docks Henry VIII had built at Deptford, which was no longer a major anchorage but where new ships were still being built; then past Greenwich Palace and Woolwich, where William Wynter's men oversaw the navy's guns and ammunition. At the mouth of the Thames past Gravesend and Tilbury—where Queen Elizabeth would greet her troops assembled to oppose the Armada ten years later—he would steer south around the Isle of Grain and then up the Medway to just below Rochester bridge, where the river formed a U-shaped bend at Chatham. There a new dockyard had been built under Edward VI, guarded by a fort at the top of the right arm of the bend at Upnor, and another at the mouth of the Medway called Sheerness. This would be the main anchorage of the Royal Navy for the next 150 years.

At Chatham Hawkins could see the queen's ships moored in two large groups. They were stripped and empty, as was the custom, with all their

---

*One of them the ill-fated *Jesus of Lübeck*.

rigging, sails, and masts taken down and stored on shore. They floated high on their anchorage, since they were empty and carried no ballast. All around them a small army of clerks, shipwrights, and workmen went through the routine of rummaging, painting, cleaning, replacing timbers and deck planks, making sails, spars, and rigging, exterminating vermin in the holds (Chatham had a professional rat catcher on its staff), and hauling ships into dry dock in order to check for wear and tear below the waterline.

Hawkins would also meet his shipwrights Philip Pett and Matthew Baker. In 1578 they were putting finishing touches on two new ships, the *Revenge* and the *Scout,* which had been built according to the new galleon design they first tried out on another ship sitting nearby, as workmen repaired and repainted its beakhead prow. It bore a name that would become immortal in the Royal Navy: *Dreadnought.*

All these new ships (*Dreadnought* had been finished in 1573) had a longer keel, relative to their width or beam, than their predecessors, even more than Drake's *Golden Hind.* This gave them a serviceable, sleek look— "the head of a cod and the tail of a mackerel," as their builders liked to say—and a longer gun deck. Hawkins would note with approval the trimmed-down fore- and after-castles, the structures that had made his old *Jesus* so top-heavy and unsteady. And like their Portuguese and Spanish galleon counterparts, these were ships built specifically to carry heavy guns, although the best and longest still sat in the bows facing front.

Still, the *Dreadnought* and the *Revenge* were a major breakthrough in warship design. They were called race-built, because of their "raced" or razed fore- and after-castles, which at least one old captain complained took away their "majesty and terror." But what they lacked in size and impressive appearance, they made up for in speed, maneuverability, and above all firepower. John Hawkins may not have inspired the race-built galleon, as used to be claimed, but he did make sure they were the principal ship built in the queen's dockyards.

He also encouraged another innovation: the use of plans and drawings for building a ship, which could allow a vessel to be constructed without its designer, Matthew Baker, being physically present. Hawkins brought another experienced captain from Devon, William Borough, to serve as Clerk of the Ships and reorganize the navy's system of outfitting. He set up a relief fund for sick and wounded common sailors, the Chatham Chest, and gave them their first pay raise since Henry VIII. He also built at Deptford the first true drydock in history, with massive gates that could shut out the river at will, permitting routine below-waterline work for minor as well as major repair. It gave the English navy an edge in dockyard technology over other nations that it would never entirely lose.

But all this was nothing compared with the English advances in guns and gunnery. Cannon had been going to sea since the fourteenth century, and not just on European ships, but Chinese, Turkish, and Arab ships as well. However, in the fifteenth century Europeans discovered that it was not just the number of guns that mattered, or even their size, but how they were made. The old forged-iron cannon were unsafe (they tended to blow up when the charge was too large), inaccurate, and clumsy to use, since they had to be enormous in order to fire a stone or ball of any appreciable weight (the classic siege gun or bombard might weigh as much as seven tons and have a bore diameter of twenty inches). So bronze began to replace iron, as a more flexible, durable, and more reliable metal.

Cast bronze was expensive; the work also demanded highly skilled labor. Although Spain and Portugal both needed large numbers of guns to defend their empire by land as well as at sea, neither developed a proper gun-making industry. Instead, they imported what they needed from Germany and the Netherlands—which made Philip's possession of the Netherlands even more of a strategic asset.

Spain and Portugal had plenty of money to spend on imported bronze cannon. England, especially in the later years of Henry VIII, did not. So Henry began to look for an alternative. He found it in the Weald iron range of Sussex and Kent, where, beginning in 1543, a team of iron-masters began to experiment with cast-iron artillery pieces. They were inferior to bronze, especially at the larger calibers; if the gunner did not watch for overheating, they also tended to explode without warning. But they were a lot cheaper to make and easier to produce—less than a fifth the cost of bronze. And so out of the smoke and heat of their cramped stone foundries, Sussex artisans like Ralph Hogge turned out inexpensive, highly serviceable, and ready-made cast-iron guns, which soon became famous across Europe.*

It was England's first major homegrown industry, ancestor of the iron

---

*What made the English cast-iron gun so effective? Although no one realized it at the time, the key was English iron ore, which was filled with millions of microscopic fossilized sea creatures, called the Greys. They permitted the "flux" necessary for a superior purification of the ore. The sea had come to England's rescue again—this time, the primeval sea.

foundries that would launch the Industrial Revolution. The cast-iron gun allowed sailors like Hawkins and Drake to arm their ships cheaply and plentifully: more than half of the guns on the *Jesus* were iron. Hawkins had seen the devastating effect they could have when he sank the Spanish flagships at San Juan de Ulloa; he made sure the queen's other ships were outfitted the same way. Although he and others still preferred their heaviest guns, the culverins, to be made from bronze (produced at the royal foundry at Houndsditch), a cast-iron demi-culverin could still smash a wooden ship or galley at 350 to 400 yards.

The result was a revolution in sea fighting. The 750-ton *Mary Rose* carried more than ninety-six guns, but only six could be classified as heavy ordnance. By contrast, the *Revenge* carried twenty-two heavy guns out of her total of forty-six, giving her four times the firepower of the *Mary Rose.* Mounted on wheeled gun carriages that could be easily maneuvered from one side of the ship to the other, Hawkins's culverins and demi-culverins were to be the direct ancestors of the guns of Nelson's navy. Some would remain in service for a century or more. When a British navy squadron took the French fort at Goree in West Africa in 1758, they would find on its ramparts a bronze culverin still in use, inscribed, "Thomas Pitt made this piece, 1582."

That same year, John Hawkins's ambitious plans ran afoul of his rival, William Wynter, who accused him of administrative malfeasance as treasurer. The queen ordered an official investigation under the supervision of Burghley, Walsingham, and her Lord Admiral. Drake, Frobisher, and Walter Raleigh were brought in as experts. They discovered that not only had Hawkins run his office with no undue corruption (in that era, an achievement in itself) but that he had also built a navy second to none in the world. Its fast, light ships were more heavily armed than anyone else's; they carried more shot and gunpowder; and, thanks to the Navy Board, could mobilize faster and more efficiently than any other force in Europe. Elizabeth's Lord Admiral, Lord Howard of Effingham, enthused, "I protest it before God, were it not for Her Majesty's presence I had rather live in the company of these noble ships than in any place."

Elizabeth took small comfort from all this. She was still distracted by events on the Continent. The Protestant Dutch cause was collapsing; their leader, William of Orange, was dead and their greatest city, Antwerp, had fallen to the Spanish. Parma's troops also controlled the port of Dunkirk, less than fifty miles from the English coast, and possible launching point for an invasion of England. She had also learned of the most serious assassination plot against her yet, organized by the English Catholic Francis Throckmorton with the connivance of the Spanish ambassador himself. Elizabeth ordered the ambassador expelled, and began considering sending what little support she could to the desperate Dutch. But she urgently needed an equalizer in this unequal contest with Philip of Spain, one that could offset his huge advantage in soldiers, arms, allies, and strategic position.

Hawkins gave her the answer. He had proposed intercepting Philip's silver fleet as early as 1570, and even assembled a dozen ships at his own expense to carry it out. He renewed the offer again in 1579. The basic lesson of Drake's circumnavigation was that even a small force could turn the Spanish empire in America upside down, and perhaps even take the *flota* by surprise. But Hawkins was now thinking in larger strategic terms. He pointed out to Lord Burghley that Spain's power depended on sea links it could not protect. "The greatest traffic of all King Philip's dominions must pass to and fro by sea," he wrote, "which will hardly escape intercepting." Cut off that traffic, particularly the links to America and its silver, and you could bring the entire structure crashing down. The truth was beginning to dawn, just as John Dee had predicted. Command of the sea, not land or continents, was what counted.

In July 1584 Hawkins presented his plan once more, and this time Elizabeth was desperate enough to accept. He and his brother had just launched their own successful and lucrative raid in the West Indies in 1583, with John's son Richard, aged twenty-one, making his privateering debut. A steady drumbeat of raids like this, he told Elizabeth and Burghley, would cripple Spain's ability to make war, and all without risking a general conflict. They "would not by any means," he assured them (wrongly, as it turned out), "draw the King of Spain to offer a war."

Whether they believed Hawkins or not, they authorized him to prepare an expedition—either to the West Indies or the Moluccas, to encourage the Portuguese colonies there to revolt against Spain; no one could quite decide. But everyone agreed who should command it: Francis Drake.

The former boy pirate was now forty-four years old. He had grown round and stout since his triumphant voyage around the world. Like Hawkins, he had served Plymouth as a member of Parliament; he had a second wife from a distinguished Somerset family and played the country squire at Buckland Abbey. But he was still full of fight and eager to return to sea.

This raid would be classic Drake, with a difference. This time he would be going not as an independent privateer but with the queen's commission, and the title of Admiral.* Instead of a handful of undersized ships, he commanded twenty-two fighting vessels, the largest being the 600-ton race-built galleon, *Elizabeth Bonaventure,* and 2,300 men, with Martin Frobisher as his vice admiral. The money to pay for the ships still came from private investors, including Hawkins and Drake himself. They would expect Drake to spend his time grabbing Spanish treasure. Yet this was more than just a plundering raid. This was war on the king of Spain. The Royal Navy was about to prove its strategic worth for the first time.

It almost failed the test. Long delays and Elizabeth's hesitation delayed its departure and ruined the element of surprise. Philip, alarmed at the rumors that Drake was aiming for his treasure fleet, ordered the immediate seizure of all English ships and goods in Spanish or Portuguese ports. That finally prompted Elizabeth into action. She ordered a counter-embargo, dispatched Drake's brother Bernard to attack the Spanish fishing fleet off the Grand Banks, and gave the go-ahead to Francis Drake to set out on September 14, 1585.

When Drake unexpectedly turned up at Vigo on the coast of Galicia a month later, on October 11, the result was panic and frantic dispatches to Madrid. Drake easily took the town and sacked it but found little plunder worth taking. He stayed on for more than a week, hoping to catch the silver fleet as it made its way home to Spain (in fact, he had just missed it). Then Drake, Frobisher, and the rest spread their sails for the by-now-familiar route to the Indies, threading their way through the Canaries to the Cape Verde Islands, and catching the prevailing northeast trade winds to take them across the Atlantic.

It was a brutal trip. Disease broke out on the ships, probably a strain of pneumonic plague, which decimated Drake's crew and soldiers. By the time they reached Dominica in the lesser Antilles, he had lost nearly five hundred men. But he and his infantry commander, a burly old captain from the Irish wars named Carleille, were thirsting for battle. On New Year's Day 1586 they swooped into Santo Domingo harbor, taking the garrison and the townspeople by complete surprise. Drake forced them to pay 25,000 pesos, or nearly 8,000 pounds, to spare their town, then

---

*Although Elizabeth was still prepared to disavow him if he did something truly awful or provocative.

stayed for a month to replenish his ships' stores and his men's health. At the end of January, they were off again, with their eyes on the big prize: Cartagena.

Cartagena was one of the biggest and wealthiest cities in Spanish America. But it proved incapable of defending itself against its English attackers. The Spanish even enlisted local Indian tribesmen to help out with volleys of poison darts, but all to no avail. Drake landed Carleille's men four miles down the beach from Cartagena to take the city from the flank, while Drake and Frobisher led storming parties into the harbor under withering fire. Arrows and darts swept off hats but bounced off armor breastplates, while Drake was drenched with blood when four men in his pinnace were dismembered by chain-shot. Within an hour the battle was over. Cartagena surrendered, paid the usual ransom (Drake demanded 100,000 pounds but had to settle for a third of that), and then breathed a sigh of relief when Drake left the harbor and sailed north. The plague was still with him; Spanish prisoners later remembered bodies being cast overboard almost every day. The three hundred black slaves Drake had freed in Cartagena came in handy for fleshing out his dwindling crews.

Drake toyed with the idea of attacking Havana, and anchored west of the city at Cape St. Antonio to mull it over. His presence threw its citizens into a frenzy of fear that they would be the next victims of "El Draque," who (it was rumored) murdered priests and friars and tortured well-to-do settlers to find their gold. But in the end Drake decided to save Havana for another day. Instead, he swung north again to Florida, where he raided the tiny settlement at Saint Augustine. The Spanish fled into the bushes; all Drake found was a lone French prisoner, a Huguenot, who greeted his liberators by playing a well-known Protestant tune on his flute. The English burned the stockade, cut down the trees, and carted away what little of value they could find. They made one more stop on the Atlantic coast,* then headed for home, with the royal Spanish banner Drake had captured at Santo Domingo now hanging in his cabin, on which was stitched the motto Philip II had adopted since his annexation of Portugal: *Non sufficit orbis*—The world is not enough.

Yet the raid itself had been a flop. Instead of getting holds full of captured silver, his investors lost money—a return of not much more than

---

*The stop was in Virginia; for details, see chapter 7.

fifteen shillings on the pound. Drake had quarreled constantly with his subordinates. After watching Drake at work, Frobisher swore point-blank he would never serve under him again. Even worse, the raid stirred Philip II into action. His oldest and most trusted advisor, Cardinal Granvelle, wrote a furious letter: "I keenly regret that the Queen of England makes war on us so boldly and dishonestly, and that we cannot get our own back."

In July 1585 the pope had called on Spain to launch some "outstanding enterprise" in support of the faith. Just two weeks after Drake struck at Vigo, Philip wrote a favorable response to the pope, and even before the English had arrived home in Plymouth, Philip was asking the Duke of Parma to draw up formal plans for an invasion of England.

* * *

Philip II rose every morning at his palace at the Escorial before dawn and attended Holy Mass. Then he went to his office, where the windows looked out on the royal chapel. Besides being the center of government, the Escorial was a Hieronymite monastery, and like his monks, Philip kept a strict schedule. Two illuminated clocks ticked past the minutes and hours as he sat at his desk. He rarely left before both had struck nine o'clock at night.

Philip kept this brutal schedule because he insisted on supervising every aspect of his global empire himself. He relied on each department and every royal councillor to give him the information and documents he needed to accomplish this feat of direct personal control. His Council of War regularly met nearly three hours a day, as did his Council of the Indies (although after Drake's depredations, they added three afternoons a week). These two councils produced nearly three hundred documents at each session. Other departments produced nearly as much.

The result was that Philip was drowning in paper. The French ambassador, watching him at work, figured he handled close to two thousand separate pieces of paper a day. Philip read every report, every outgoing letter—when he found a grammatical error in one, he crossed the whole thing out and told his secretary, "Do it over"—and every royal order that required his signature. An English spy said he did more work than three full-time secretaries: "In this manner his pen and purse governeth the world."

Philip rarely lost his temper. Once a nervous clerk, instead of sprinkling sand to dry the signatures, poured out a bottle of ink, ruining an entire day's work. Philip never raised his voice; he merely explained to the boy, "This is the sand; this is the ink." Yet now, surrounded by stacks of paper and bundles of reports, measuring his life out minute by minute, he somehow had to fit in time to plan the momentous project of his life, the launching of an invasion fleet, an armada, to topple Elizabeth of England.

It is true that Spain's power seemed overwhelming and England deeply vulnerable. But it is also worth remembering that in 1588 Philip was faced with a war he did not want, a military campaign he could not afford, and an invasion plan no one except Philip thought could succeed.

For one thing, Philip had seriously underestimated Elizabeth's determination to resist his will, and the skill of English privateers in threatening his vital lifeline to the Indies. Drake's raid had meant the silver fleets could not sail in 1586, and Spanish merchants in Seville and Cádiz were facing bankruptcy. For another, England's most potent weapon, its navy, owed some of its prowess to Philip himself. When he became prince consort to Queen Mary in 1555, he found his wife's navy in pitiful shape. Prince Philip had insisted she begin building new ships immediately and refurbish the navy's logistical base, moving the bulk of the fleet to Portsmouth to command the English Channel. He had even written: "Since England's chief defense depends upon its navy being always in good order to serve for the defense of the kingdom against all invasion, it is right that the ships should not only be fit for sea, but instantly available." How Philip must have regretted those words three decades later, and the efficiency with which the English had followed his advice!

Nonetheless, there were good grounds for optimism. After examining maps and surveys of the English coastline, and the history of every invasion of England since Julius Caesar, Philip and his advisors came up with three different plans. The first was the brainchild of the Marquis of Santa Cruz. It involved a massive invasion fleet of 510 ships and more than 55,000 infantry and 1,600 cavalry, which would force its way through the Channel and descend on London with irresistible force. If Philip agreed to his plan, Santa Cruz promised him in February of 1586, "I will emerge victorious from it as in the other things I have done for you."

However, even as master of the world, Philip knew he could not begin to pay for an invasion on this scale. So he turned to the plan put forward by his commander in the Netherlands and his nephew, the Duke of Parma. Parma envisaged a surprise strike across the Channel with 30,000 of his seasoned veterans transported on barges at night. The crossing would take only ten or twelve hours, Parma guessed, eight if they found a favorable wind. They would land at either Dover or Margate, quickly overwhelm any puny English resistance (both he and Philip knew Elizabeth had no standing army) and take London before the navy, Drake, or anyone else had time to react. All Parma needed was enough barges to carry his men, and enough men to leave behind to deal with the Dutch. But he also warned Philip that his opportunity for a surprise attack was fading: already ordinary citizens in the streets of Antwerp were arguing about which plan Spain would use for its invasion of England.

Philip worried that Parma's scheme left too much to chance. If the English caught on to what was happening (a strong possibility), they could intercept Parma's defenseless troop transports in mid-Channel and blast them out of the water—a scene too horrible to contemplate. So his chief naval advisor, Bernardino de Escalante, came up with an ingenious counterplan, which combined the best features of Santa Cruz's and Parma's.

Santa Cruz would indeed sail from Lisbon with a large invasion force, only with 150 ships instead of 500. His destination, however, would not be London but Ireland, specifically Waterford harbor (another possibility Escalante weighed was Milford Haven in Wales). The movement of this large armada would draw the main English fleet west out of the Channel, allowing Parma to dash across and march on London unopposed. Philip liked the plan: diversion and surprise, and all within a reasonable budget. But he insisted on one proviso: instead of Santa Cruz's galleons remaining in Ireland, to cover landings along the southwest coast of England and cut off Bristol and Plymouth, Philip said he must sail back up the Channel to meet Parma's barges and escort them across. Whatever their misgivings about this clumsy modification to the plan, Escalante and Santa Cruz agreed and immediately set to work building the invasion fleet.

This was not easy. There was no efficient administrative body like the English Navy Board to oversee the project and delegate authority and tasks. Everything had to be done virtually from scratch—and all with Philip's written approval, which meant lengthy delays. But even if there had been a Spanish Navy Board, the ships, supplies, and men needed strained the ordinary resources of Philip's empire. Biscuits, rice, beans, bacon, and salt fish for the armada had to be measured in the thousands of bushels, and water and wine in quantities that emptied the vineyards and cellars of Spain; 123,000 rounds of great shot were needed for the fleet and 2,500 artillery pieces, including siege guns for the assault on London. Twelve thousand sailors had to be recruited, and more than eighteen thousand soldiers, plus thousands of horses and mules.

Then there were the logistical headaches confronting Parma's army in Flanders: building the transport barges, finding sailors and pilots to man them, equipping and feeding the soldiers as they concentrated at Dunkirk. As they waited, Parma's troops consumed upward of 50,000 loaves of bread a day each day, week by week, month by month, as the imperial machinery ground slowly on and ships, supplies, and men assembled eleven hundred miles away in the port of Lisbon.

Santa Cruz had estimated his original plan would cost Spain 3.8 million ducats. By 1587, it was apparent this "slimmed down" plan was going to top ten million. Every month the armada sat idle in port getting manned and outfitted, it was draining out of Philip's treasury more than 700,000 ducats—almost six times what it cost Elizabeth to maintain her own navy. Even with the silver convoys from America back in service and more bountiful than ever, Philip was at the end of his financial tether. He confessed to his advisors: "This is the matter which gives [me] the most anxiety." He told them, "Finding money is so important that all of us must concentrate on that and nothing else." If he could not pay for the ships and men, Philip said gloomily, "I don't know what will become of them."

Philip tried every desperate measure. He borrowed against future tax revenues; he sold his late wife's jewels. He sold off titles of nobility, trading privileges and monopolies, powers of lordship in towns and villages. The power and authority of the Spanish monarchy, carefully accumulated over a century since Ferdinand and Isabella, was dispersed and sold off in order to fund his armada. When nothing else would work, Philip simply confiscated the ships of foreign merchants and turned them into transports and escort vessels.

So, slowly and painfully, the resources of his global empire began to come together in Lisbon harbor. Salt meat and lard from Galicia and Malaga, salt anchovies and sardines from Galicia and Andalusia, cheese from Sardinia, rice from Valencia and Lombardy; 56,000 bushels of biscuit flour from Burgos and Castile, another 40,000 from Naples, and 12,000 more from the Canary Islands. Wine came from as near as the commander's own estate in western Andalusia, and as far away as Crete. Merchant haulers from Hanseatic League cities like Hamburg, Rostock, and Danzig brought naval stores and timber, and Flemish traders gunpowder and cannon.

Diplomatically, things were coming together as well. In February 1587 came the news that Mary Queen of Scots had been executed. Far from posing a problem for Philip, it simplified his plans: after deposing Elizabeth, he would assume the throne of England himself. It also made the English wildly unpopular in France, where Mary had grown up and had been married to their king. Riots broke out and English merchants were stoned. Philip added to the English sense of isolation by encouraging Elizabeth to believe he wanted to negotiate a separate peace without her Dutch allies, and when she jumped at the chance, leaking the news to the Dutch, who were furious. But then two major blows fell on Philip, which forced him to modify radically his plans. The first came in May, when Philip arrived at his desk to learn that Francis Drake had just taken Cádiz.

. . .

The English had not been since idle since his preparations were under way. They knew what they were up against: in a gesture of misplaced pride, Philip had published the entire fleet list of the armada, which circulated across Europe and of course in London. By the time Drake returned from his Caribbean raid, Hawkins and the Navy Board were building nine new ships and rebuilding others. Taking a page from Philip, the Privy Council ordered an embargo of foreign shipping and took over sixty-four merchantmen, thirty-three supply ships, and forty-three privately owned pinnaces to enhance the fleet (among them were seven ships Richard Grenville had assembled for his own raid on the West Indies). In the end, the English would have more ships than the Spanish Armada.

Plans for defense on land got under way as well. Lord Burghley had built up an emergency reserve of 300,000 pounds, made possible at least in part by the queen's profits from the capture of the *Nuestra Señora.* That money now went to double the navy's budget and to pay for a mobilization of able-bodied men, trained or untrained, to defend the realm. In March 1587 the summons went out to every county in England to raise soldiers, cavalry, weapons, and cannon. The Earl of Leicester was appointed Lieutenant-General of Her Majesty's Forces in southern England, with a force of 23,000 infantry, 2,756 cavalry, along with 4,892 pioneers armed with scythes, billhooks, and pitchforks.

But Burghley and the queen understood they would never be enough. England had a population less than half of Spain's, and a quarter of

France's. Even if it were possible to call up everyone included in a general muster, which was supposed to be a third of a million men, only a fraction of that number had any military training, not to mention adequate weapons. No one knew where the Spanish might land; Leicester's army had to watch the entire southern coast (three thousand men alone were needed for the Isle of Wight). If the Spanish did land, what chance did these amateurs have against Parma's veterans, who had conquered half the Low Countries and were "the best soldiers at this day in Christendom," in the estimation of Leicester himself? Admiral Howard, who had every faith in his ships and sailors, wrote, "God send us the happiness to meet with them [the Spanish] before our men on land discover them, for I fear me a little sight of the enemy will fear the landmen much." The navy really was England's only hope.

However, Hawkins and Drake saw the real dilemma. The queen's ships could husband their resources, patrol the Channel, remain close to harbor, and wait for the Spanish to come; or they could take more decisive action. Drake in particular was eager to get another crack at the Spanish, as were his men: "I thank God," he wrote to Francis Walsingham, "I find no man but as all members of one body to stand for our gracious Queen and our country against Antichrist and his members." Either he or Hawkins persuaded the queen to sponsor one more foray to break up Spanish shipping and divert the king of Spain's resources away from his "great enterprise." In March Elizabeth agreed, and by the end of the month Drake had assembled in Plymouth a force of sixteen ships, including the *Elizabeth Bonaventure,* the formidable *Dreadnought,* and the Lord Admiral's own *White Lion.* Drake's preparations were fast and furious. "The wind commands me away," he wrote to Walsingham, and sailed on April 2.

On April 5 he was off Cape Finisterre and by the sixteenth he was in sight of Lisbon itself. There he learned from a captured coastal craft that a very large merchant fleet was assembled at Cádiz, the second largest port in Spain, loading supplies for the armada and having no armed escorts. Drake canceled plans for a West Indies raid and decided to make for Cádiz, arriving there late in the day on April 19. After a violent argument with his second-in-command, William Borough, over whether the port's defenses were too strong to permit an attack, Drake charged into Cádiz Bay, furling all English banners and standards so that no one would know who they were until it was too late.

It was the trick he had learned from Hawkins at San Juan Ulloa. Once again it achieved complete surprise. The populace of Cádiz was watching an acrobatic display in the main square when the dreaded El Draque suddenly appeared, with guns blazing and pinnaces loaded with English soldiers rowing toward the helpless ships in the harbor. Drake burned and sank thirty merchant vessels, including a magnificent galleon belonging to Santa Cruz himself. The English warships demonstrated their superior firepower, sweeping away the heavily armed galleys supposed to defend the harbor, and sailing away without losing a single ship.

Drake then made for Sagres, a massive 200-foot-high headland near Cape St. Vincent, which sheltered merchantmen on their way to Lisbon and Seville. For nearly a month Drake sat astride the main shipping lane between Spain and the East and West Indies, capturing and destroying cargoes destined for the armada, and triggering a national panic in Spain. Finally, Drake leisurely made his way off, making a final sweep of the Azores where he captured an inbound Portuguese carrack heavily laden with china, velvet, silk, gold, and precious gems from Asia, as well as black slaves. Even after he and his men had stripped it of its most valuable cargo, the prize brought nearly 140,000 pounds in profit when he returned in triumph to Plymouth—with the hapless Spanish still fumbling to follow his trail of looting and destruction.

The delay to Philip's material preparations for the armada was negligible.* Supplies, even ships, could be replaced. But Drake's raid did force the king into a fateful decision. It was now crucial to get the armada out of Lisbon as soon as possible and joined up with Parma's expeditionary force. There would be no diversion to Ireland. The entire force—galleons, supply ships, soldier transports, and all—were to sail directly into the Channel to meet Parma. Everything now depended on the landing in England.

Then, on February 9, 1588, Philip received the second blow. The Marquis of Santa Cruz, Philip's best admiral and the man who had originally proposed the invasion of England, was dead. He had been killed by the same typhus epidemic that was decimating the soldiers and sailors sitting idle at the Lisbon docks. This was a major setback. Santa Cruz's replacement, the Duke of Medina Sidonia, was neither as incompetent nor reluctant to command as English historians used to imply. He was in

*The old story, often repeated by historians, that Drake had permanently crippled the Spanish Armada by destroying its supplies of seasoned barrel staves, thus forcing it to draw its drinking water from green and leaky casks, finds no support from Spanish documents.

fact a first-rate administrator, just the man to head a Spanish Navy Board
if one had existed, and in the event, Medina Sidonia proved himself a
capable and fearless admiral. He may have owed his command to his
noble titles rather than his experience at sea, but that was also true of
Elizabeth's Lord Admiral, Charles Howard of Effingham.

But Santa Cruz had been a brilliant fleet commander, a man of
supreme self-confidence and overreaching ego. If the situation war-
ranted, he did not hesitate to disobey Philip himself. Medina Sidonia
lacked that one essential quality of leadership in battle: the willingness to
jettison the plan and rely on the killer instinct instead. All the great Royal
Navy commanders had it, from Drake and Blake to Hawke and Nelson.
Medina Sidonia's biggest mistake in the summer of 1588 was to insist on
following Philip's orders to the letter, even when they guaranteed defeat.

He did command a fleet that was, at first sight, very impressive. By
May Philip had assembled a fighting force more than twenty times the size
of the armadas that guarded the Indies *flota* and more than two and a half
times the firepower of his entire navy in the Mediterranean. It consisted of
more than 130 ships and 30,000 men, of whom 18,000 were foot soldiers.
The ships included 35 first-class warships, 20 of them galleons, including
the 10 state-of-the-art fighting galleons Philip had acquired when he
annexed Portugal. The rest were armed merchantmen, supply ships, hulks,
and transports assembled from all over Europe. There were heavily armed
merchantmen from Galicia and the Basque seaports, like the 46-gun
Nuestra Señora del Rosario and the 47-gun *Santa Ana* from Guipúzcoan. But
only about half the fleet was Spanish- or Portuguese-built. Carracks from
Dubrovnik, slowing moving hulks or *urcas* from Venice, Genoa, Hamburg,
and Danzig, and galleys from Sicily and Naples, made up the rest. In fact,
the biggest and best fighting ship in the armada, the *San Francesco,* with 52
bronze guns, actually belonged to the Grand Duke of Tuscany, Cosimo de
Medici.

To his credit, Medina Sidonia saw the problems the moment he
assumed command. He lacked enough experienced sailors, enough skilled
pilots who could guide a fleet so large and diverse through the English
Channel, and enough supplies. Originally loaded with eight months' supplies, the armada was down to only four months' by May. When the fleet
finally sailed on the twenty-eighth, some ships were already running out
of food and water.

But the most serious shortage was guns. Medina Sidonia knew that
the converted merchantmen in Elizabeth's fleet were heavily armed,

thanks to the cast-iron English gun. He scrounged up cannon wherever he could find them. Forts around Lisbon were stripped of their artillery. Pieces used as trophies from the wars of Philip's father, Charles V, were pressed into service. The seven bronze foundries in Lisbon worked round the clock. When Medina Sidonia arrived to visit his fleet, he found forty brand-new pieces waiting for him. By clandestine means, even one hundred cast-iron Sussex guns ended up in the Spanish fleet.

These were not nearly enough. Medina Sidonia was not only short on guns—only six ships in the entire fleet carried more than forty, whereas every English ship over 250 tons had at least that number—but shot, gunpowder, and trained gunners. And Elizabeth had by now assembled a fleet of 140, ten more than his armada.

Medina Sidonia's confidence plummeted. He might get his large unwieldy force safely out of Lisbon and Spanish waters and into the Bay of Biscay. But how he was going to rendezvous with Parma and his 27,000 soldiers and 300 vessels of all kinds in mid-Channel was still unclear. Parma himself had decided the attack was going to be a failure. He was already preparing arguments as to why his men should never leave Flanders.

Only one man believed the invasion of England would succeed: Philip II. He never visited the armada or inspected its ships; he never took steps to learn firsthand what huge problems his commanders were facing. But he convinced himself that whatever problems did exist would be solved by God. Philip believed as intensely in the righteousness of his cause in the eyes of God as any English reader of John Foxe. He had seen the hand of God in the death of King Sebastian of Portugal at Alcazar-Kebir in 1578, and again in Santa Cruz's victory at Terceira in 1582. God had miraculously advanced the Spanish Empire before; he would again now. When one of his councillors asked what the armada was to do if it ran into storms in the Channel, Philip said: "Since it is all for His cause, God will send us good weather."

One hundred and ninety-eight priests said mass on board the ships as the armada readied to sail. The pope declared a special indulgence for everyone who sailed with it, up to and including everyone who prayed for its success. The entire royal family spent three hours a day on their knees in the chapel before the Holy Eucharist. Religious processions were held in Madrid every Sunday and holiday in its support. On April 25 the archbishop of Lisbon led a special ceremony consecrating the banner that would fly from Medina Sidonia's flagship. It bore the arms of Spain and the image of the crucified Christ. Underneath it read: "Rise up, Lord, and vindicate Thy cause."

On May 28, 1588, the Armada finally, slowly, slid out of Lisbon harbor. Philip was tense but confident. He wrote: "Things hang in the balance. Please God, let the events [in the north] be for His Cause, and may He assist us," adding, "as is so necessary."

At least one unidentified officer in the fleet agreed. At the consecration ceremony, the papal nuncio had asked him how he thought the battle would go. The soldier's mood was grim. He answered bluntly, "The English, who have faster and handier ships than ours, and many more long-range guns, and who know their advantage just as well as we do, will never close with us at all, but stand aloof and knock us to pieces with their culverins, without our being able to do them any serious hurt." When the nuncio asked him what the Spanish needed to win, the officer answered, "A miracle."

His prediction was about to be put to the test.

CHAPTER SIX

Armada:
The Victory That Never Was

They came, they saw, they fled.
—ANONYMOUS, 1588

ON JULY 29, 1588, Thomas Fleming was patrolling in his large oared pinnace off the Scilly Isles, at the far western entrance or "Western Approaches," to the English Channel, when he spotted a cluster of white sails set against the horizon. There were too many for a fishing fleet, he decided. As he looked closer, he realized they were what his superiors had expected: the Spanish Armada's advance squadron, waiting for the rest to catch up. Fleming gave the order to his men to turn about and set them at their oars as he raced to bring the news to the Lord Admiral and his vice admiral Francis Drake, in Plymouth harbor.

The fact that they were in Plymouth and not farther up the Channel was a tribute to the character and judgment of the Lord Admiral, Charles Howard of Effingham. He had taken office in 1585, when he was just under fifty and just as the Spanish crisis was building to its climax. He was the fourth generation of his family to hold the title Lord Admiral. A contemporary judged him "a hearty Gentleman, and cordial to his sovereign, and of a most proper person." He also loved his ships, especially his flagship, the 500-ton *Ark Royal*, which he had bought from Walter Raleigh, who had built it to race-built galleon specifications and had originally dubbed it *Ark Raleigh*.

Howard described with touching pride how it drew crowds of five thousand a day when he docked during a visit to Flushing in Holland. He thought her the best ship in the world "for all conditions. We can see no sail, great or small, but how far soever off they be we fetch them and speak with them." As for the other race-built galleons under his command, "I have been aboard of every ship . . . and in every place where any may creep, and I do thank God that they be in the estate they be in, and there is not a one of them that knows what a leak means."*

Howard was the ideal Lord Admiral for the Elizabethan navy. He was a former pupil of John Foxe, and hid behind his aristocratic reserve a staunch Protestantism and a shrewd ability to handle men. His principal job as Lord Admiral was procuring and outfitting ships, but he was determined to command the fleet himself. What he did not know about fighting at sea, he made up for by trusting the judgment of those who did. "My Lord," he told Burghley in May as the fleet began to gather, "here is the gallantest company of captains, soldiers, and mariners that I think ever was seen in England."

The one he trusted most was his navy's treasurer, John Hawkins. Howard had accomplished the amazing feat of getting Hawkins and old William Wynter to work together, and admired Hawkins's success with the race-built galleons. He also understood that Hawkins and his West Country colleagues had grasped the seriousness of the impending conflict with Spain long before the government did. When Philip's false peace maneuvers were under way, Howard grimly wrote, "There was never, since England was England, such a stratagem and mask made to deceive England withal as this . . . treaty of peace." Howard repeatedly reminded Elizabeth that the best defense was a good offense, and urged her to put her ships to sea and harass the armada before it set sail—advice that met deaf ears until Drake's raid on Cádiz in March 1587.

Drake was his other professional confidant. Francis Drake was not pleased that Howard was in command of the queen's ships and not himself; but as a commoner, he naturally had to yield place to the son of one of the greatest families in England. But Drake told Howard bluntly that to wait for the Spanish in the English Channel was suicide. If the English fleet was not going to tackle the armada in its home waters, the least it could do was head down to Plymouth, where it could be quickly outfitted and victualed, and guard the "western approaches," the Atlantic waters between Cornwall and Brittany at the mouth of the Channel. By waiting for the Spanish there, Drake argued, the English would also gain the advantage of the weather gauge.

To appreciate Drake's strategy, we need to remember that all ships with sails must sail with the wind, whether it blows north, south, east, or

---

*An understandable exaggeration: the *Dreadnought* had leaked so badly during Drake's raid on Cádiz that it delayed his arrival off Lisbon by almost two weeks.

west. In battle, being upwind or "to windward" means having the initiative, as long as the wind holds. It allows a captain to decide whether to close and fight, and how fast to do so, depending how much sail he puts out or hauls up; or whether to turn away and wait. He can also bring more ships to bear when and where he wants, even when his enemy outnumbers him.

By contrast, the leeward captain's options are necessarily more limited. He can tack or "beat to windward" and thus lose speed and position; he can "close haul" and shorten his sails to stand and meet the threat; or he can run before the wind. If his windward enemy is faster and stronger, even that becomes a hopeless cause. In any case, it is the man to windward who holds the "weather gauge" and who controls the tempo of action, and in a fight at sea, as in most fights, that means half the battle.

Hence Drake's plan: to beat the Spanish by slipping behind them as the prevailing westerly winds blew them up the English Channel. Then the English could choose their moment to strike. "The advantage of time and place in all martial actions is half the victory," he told the queen and his colleagues. In February he brought his flagship, the *Revenge*, and a detachment of his ships down to Plymouth to prove his point.

By June 3, most of the rest arrived. The first was Howard in his *Ark Royal*; then came John Hawkins in the *Victory*; finally Martin Frobisher in the *Triumph*. All but the *Triumph* were race-built or rebuilt galleons. The other captains from Devon were also there. Walter Raleigh was ashore in Plymouth as vice admiral of Devon, supervising the elaborate system of fire beacons that would pass the news of the arrival of the armada up along the English coast. Richard Grenville had delivered his ships into Plymouth harbor in early May, but he was needed on land, to organize soldiers and supplies in Cornwall. Only Raleigh's half brother Humphrey Gilbert was absent:* although whether anyone really missed that headstrong and sadistic ruffian is hard to judge. Another fifteen ships under Lord Henry Seymour guarded the eastern approaches of the Channel and kept an eye out for Parma

The fleet sat for a month in Plymouth, although its officers were not idle. They continued to pester the queen to let them try to catch the armada as it sailed into the Atlantic. For once, she relented, and Howard, Hawkins, and Drake eagerly set out west beyond the Lizard Point of Cornwall and the Scillies, getting as far as the Bay of Biscay before storms

---

*For the reason, see chapter 7.

drove them back. Now, two weeks later, Fleming breathlessly arrived with the news they had been waiting for and dreading. Howard's response was: "The southerly wind that brought us back from the coast of Spain brought them out. God blessed us with turning us back." Legend has it Fleming found Drake high on the Hoe overlooking Plymouth Sound, leisurely playing bowls. He heard the news without turning his head. "Time enough to finish the game," he is supposed to have said, "and beat the Spanish after."

The story may be true—there is no evidence that it is not. However, true or untrue, Drake was right: the tide was running high into the Sound and no English ships could leave harbor. They would have to wait until evening, before dropping their kedge anchors and warping out, one by one, to meet the Spanish threat.

As night fell, Drake was everywhere on board the *Revenge,* inspecting his ten culverins and six massive demi-cannons and cannon perriers in his lower gun deck, and the four semi-culverins and eighteen other guns on the upper deck. An eyewitness watched Lord Howard with his sailors on the *Ark Royal,* "making enquiry how they did, and calling to them by name to know in what case they stood, and what they did lack." This was an advantage that all the English ships had over their Spanish opponents: their captains knew their ship and their men and passed among them with an almost democratic familiarity by sixteenth-century standards. Howard prided himself in knowing how to raise sails and being able to lay a gun himself.

Also, Spanish ships invariably included an infantry commander, who demanded precedence over the captain of the ship. Disagreements between them were common, with the infantry officer ordering the ship to do things it could not do, and bad feeling was the result. Such a division of command could infect the entire ship, with quarrels over precedence and honor breaking out below decks as well as above; faction competed with faction, while soldiers and crew were often at odds, as were their commanders—with, as we shall soon see, fateful consequences for one ship, the *San Salvador.*

The English ships, by contrast, enjoyed unity of command, and not necessarily the ferocious sort Drake had demonstrated with Thomas Doughty ten years earlier. There was only one captain, a seaman, and since the ships were smaller, they carried few soldiers and even fewer army officers for him to quarrel with. The principle Drake had laid down, that gentlemen must "haul and draw with the mariner, and the mariner with the gentleman," made for a more efficient, better organized, and often even a cleaner ship than its Spanish counterpart. Similarly, years of West Country privateering guaranteed a regular supply of experienced fighting sailors and Navy Board gunpowder, shot, and supplies. It had taken Philip two years to assemble and outfit his armada. Elizabeth, by contrast, was able to mobilize hers in less than six months. Now they were ready, as Howard confidently put it, to "make sport" with the Spanish fleet.

Meanwhile, Medina Sidonia was still reassembling his armada off the Scillies. It had been a rough trip. Bad weather out of Lisbon had slowed his advance to five miles in three days. Then a series of summer squalls—the same ones that had kept Howard and Drake from leaving Plymouth— pummeled his fleet, springing timbers and snapping off masts and rigging, and forced him into Corunna in Spain to refit and resupply. His water had been almost gone, and disease had broken out: soldiers and sailors were dying even as their officers despaired of keeping everyone fed. Medina Sidonia had spent six weeks in Corunna and, after examining the state of his forces and the options open to him, wrote a long letter on June 24 to Philip asking him to abandon the whole enterprise. Philip refused, and so Medina Sidonia gloomily sailed on.

Yet another storm disrupted the armada, and only on July 29 was Medina Sidonia able to reunite his fleet, in time to find himself in sight of land off Lizard Point. There the clear weather offered the Spanish a brief but golden opportunity. Four captured fishermen from Falmouth told them that Howard and his warships were already in Plymouth. Medina Sidonia held a war council with his chief officers. They strongly urged a surprise attack, to catch Howard helpless in his harbor—just as Drake had caught the Spanish at Cádiz. But Medina Sidonia demurred. His orders were not to enter any English port before he had succeeded in meeting up with Parma. So they passed Plymouth by and proceeded up the Channel, not realizing what an opportunity they had thrown away.

This was because the Spanish still did not believe the bulk of the English fleet was so far west. They assumed it would be somewhere near the Straits of Dover. So when they caught the first sight of enemy sails, they assumed it was just Drake's squadron. That night Howard was able to slip around and gain his weather gauge. It was a nasty shock for Medina Sidonia the next morning to emerge from his cabin and see the English fleet arrayed not in front of him, as he expected, but behind.

Howard's shock was only slightly less. "All the world never saw such a force as their was," he admitted later, as it spread out before him in a great dense forest of masts and sails. Nonetheless, Howard sent a small pinnace, aptly named the *Disdain,* to fire a charge at Medina Sidonia's flagship in a gesture of formal challenge, and so like medieval knights jousting at the tilt, the two fleets closed for battle.

Medina Sidonia had drawn up his armada in four dense-packed squadrons, arranged in parallel columns or line abreast, with his slowest hulks in the center and his fighting galleons and galleasses on either flank and in his rear. The English rushed forward with gun ports open and as many guns wheeled and lashed pointing forward as possible. This was no classic battle of broadsides: each gun was aimed on its own, while the master gunner himself gave orders to the helm. Bow chasers fired first; then the guns on the leeward side as the ship turned; then the guns in the stern as the bosun shouted to his men aloft to luff sails and brought the ship to a halt. Then, as the ship turned back, the guns on the other broadside opened up, as the ship completed its stately pirouette past its target. Wreathed in smoke, the *Revenge* or *Bear* or *Vanguard* then tacked back to windward to reload, as gunners clamored over the side or squeezed through the gun port to swab their pieces (Elizabethan guns had to be lashed in place because the ships were too narrow to allow for recoil). In this way, the English guns got off on average a shot an hour; whereas the Spanish, keeping to their tight box formation, were sometimes lucky if their guns could fire back one shot a *day.*

But as the afternoon wore on, this was all they needed. The English galleons raced and danced in a confusing melee, "their ships so fast and quick they can do anything they like with them," firing and crews cheering when occasionally a shot struck home. But they did not dare get too close, because the Spanish were ready to throw their grappling irons and board in a flash. Knowing the Spanish carried more infantry, and realizing they could not force their way between ships that were often only fifty paces apart, the English had to keep outside the box and out of grappling-hook range. Instead, they blasted away at long distance with little effect.

Medina Sidonia's second-in-command, Juan Martínez de Recalde, and his big galleon *San Juan de Portugal,* came under fire from Frobisher, Drake, and Hawkins all at once, yet suffered only minor damage. Lord Admiral Howard, watching the action from his *Ark Royal,* declared, "We durst not adventure to put in among them, their fleet being so strong." Medina Sidonia, while impressed with the English ships' speed and quick handling, was pleased that his armada had kept its order and emerged almost unscathed.

In fact, it was only after the battle was finished for the day that disaster struck. The flagship of the Andalusian squadron, the 1,150-ton, 46-gun *Nuestra Señora del Rosario*, was accidently rammed by another Spanish ship, losing her bowsprit and then mizzenmast and mainyard. As the helpless ship struggled to clear the debris, an enormous explosion shattered the evening calm. It was the *San Salvador*, another flagship, carrying 64 sailors and 319 troops, as well as most of the pay for the armada's crews. Its entire powder magazine had exploded, much as the *Almirante* had during the battle in San Juan harbor. But no English shot had touched her and no one ever discovered why she blew up. But there were rumors had it that one of its German-born gunners was furious at the ship's captain for making passes at his wife, who was actually on board, and so had torched the powder magazine himself (when the English examined the burned-out hulk, they did find a woman still alive inside). But the loss of life was catastrophic, and the sight of the *San Salvador*'s smoldering hulk and the sound of the screams of the burned and wounded meant a discouraging end to the day's otherwise satisfactory proceedings.

Night had fallen. The stricken *Rosario*, left behind by its fellow Spaniards at Medina Sidonia's orders (which infuriated many of the Spanish commanders, who believed the *Rosario* was worth a fight), now lay helpless in the path of the English fleet, which surged forward to catch up with the receding armada. Howard assigned Drake to take the lead, with a lantern on his stern to guide the rest through the gloom. Then, at around midnight, Drake came in sight of the *Rosario* and made a fateful decision. Later he would claim he broke formation because he thought the *Rosario* was leading other Spanish vessels in a feint around the English landward flank. But the wretched truth was, Drake saw an opportunity for some easy thievery and took it. By dawn he had the *Rosario* under his control, and found in its hold more than 55,000 golden ducats, which he sent along with the *Rosario* to Torbay, under the escort of one his ships, the *Roebuck*. But by deserting his post, Drake had left the rest of the English fleet literally in the dark. Howard had almost sailed into the rearmost ships of the armada before he realized his mistake and turned back.

An entire day was lost reassembling the scattered ships, thanks to Drake's misconduct. Martin Frobisher on the *Triumph* was also furious that Drake had taken the entire treasure for himself. "Like a coward he kept by her all night, because he would have the spoil," Frobisher raged, "but we will have our shares, or I will make him spend the best blood in his belly!"

In fact, Frobisher's real test was coming that same day, when battle was renewed off Portland Bill. Once again, the wind took a capricious hand, for the first (and only) time in the Spaniards' favor. It shifted from the west to the northeast; suddenly it was the armada that had the weather gauge. Realizing what was happening, Howard and the *Ark Royal* veered north to catch the wind; Medina Sidonia's most powerful squadron turned to follow on a convergent course. Howard might have been trapped if the wind had not shifted once again, back to the southeast and then south-southeast. That enabled Drake, Hawkins, and fifty other vessels to rush to their leader's rescue.

Frobisher's *Triumph* also ran into trouble and found itself surrounded by four great oared galleasses, heavily armed and teeming with soldiers. Medina Sidonia eagerly ordered them to get close enough to grapple and board. The *Triumph* was an older ship, "high charged" with old-style fore- and after-castles, and slow to respond to the helm. But Frobisher's heavy guns saved him, as the galleasser's commanders warily stayed out of their range. With difficulty, the *Triumph* escaped her would-be boarders, even as Howard's ships came up in support.

For the next three days the chase proceeded up the Channel in this same fashion. Medina Sidonia estimated the two sides exchanged more than four thousand shots, all to little or no effect. The English were dismayed that the Spanish had kept their formation and remained untouched. Even more worrying, they still had no idea where the armada were going. They knew it was part of an invasion force; but they were clueless about where, or how, it was planning to land. On July 31 they had guessed Portland; now they thought possibly the Isle of Wight. So on Wednesday August 3, as the two fleets approached Wight, Howard decided to change his tactics. Until now the English had attacked individually, with no formal order or formation. Howard decided to divide his fleet into four squadrons, each commanded by one of his leading officers: Drake, Hawkins, Frobisher, and himself. That set one precedent: from then on, all important Royal Navy operations would follow the basic squadron organization.

Then Howard set another. Instead of attacking pell-mell in individual pirouettes, each commander was to lead his squadron into action in single file, firing on his opponent and then turning away to allow the next ship to fire, and then the next. Born in a moment of frustration, Howard's single-file "line ahead" formation would dominate naval warfare for the next three centuries.

The results were still mixed, in part because a dead calm on Thursday took away the Englishmen's advantage in speed. Hawkins had to order his men into their boats to tow the *Victory* in range of two Spanish stragglers, a Portuguese galleon and an armed West Indies merchantman. The Spanish galleasses again showed their worth as fighting vessels, as they rowed up to drive off the *Victory* and *Ark Royal*. Frobisher again was almost caught until the breeze suddenly freshened and allowed him to escape unharmed. Meanwhile, Drake's attack had nearly driven the Spaniards' left flank onto the Owers, a stretch of shallow water or shoals. At the last minute, however, Medina Sidonia steered them clear and put the Isle of Wight and the English coast behind him.

The English had yet to sink or capture a single Spanish ship in battle. But they were euphoric that the armada had not managed to land in England (they did not know that that was never part of the plan). Howard declared Thursday's action a success and generously knighted Hawkins, Frobisher, and several other English officers on board the *Ark Royal*—including his nephew Thomas Howard. His dispatch describing his thrilling "victory" set off across the water to the queen.

The queen was getting ready to go to Tilbury camp to greet its soldiers and their lieutenant-general, the Earl of Leicester. On August 18 she arrived at her makeshift "Camp Royal" resplendent in white velvet with an embossed silver breastplate, and carrying a silver captain's baton chased in gold. Her dyed red wig was decorated with pearls and diamonds, as she rode around the camp to meet her soldiers. Her famous speech, in which "I know I have the body of a weak and feeble woman, but I have the heart and stomach of a king, and of a king of England, too," may have stirred some patriotic hearts. But anyone with any military training would have realized that Camp Royal could not have withstood five minutes of a determined assault by Parma's troops, if they had advanced up the Thames.

But where were Parma's troops? That was the question Medina Sidonia himself was asking as Friday, August 6, dawned. The French coast was coming into sight and there was no sign of the Army of Flanders's transports or their escort vessels. By four o'clock the armada was just outside the port of Calais. The English were only two miles behind as the afternoon's light breezes barely stirred their sails. Howard had been joined by Lord Seymour and now had his entire force at his disposal.

Aware he was in a sticky situation, Medina Sidonia decided to drop anchor in Calais and send word to Parma at Dunkirk to hurry up.

The answer he got back was disturbing. His messenger returned on Sunday with news that Dunkirk was virtually deserted. The boats there were not loaded, no soldiers were on board, the cannon were still drawn up on shore. Even more disturbing was the letter he received from Parma, stating flatly that it was impossible to meet Medina Sidonia in anything less than six days. Medina Sidonia's messenger guessed sourly it would be more like two weeks.

The fact was Parma had given up on the whole enterprise. He was still angry that Philip intended to keep the kingdom of England for himself, instead of giving it to his favorite nephew, Parma. He also appreciated the real difficulties of getting his soldiers out to sea and into deep water where the armada could protect them from marauding Dutch attacks. It was too great a risk; in his own mind Parma was pulling out. Medina Sidonia was going to have to shift for himself.

Even as this news was sinking in and Medina Sidonia summoned a Sunday night war council to discuss what to do next, the English intervened in a decisive way. It is not clear who came up with the idea of sending fireships into the armada's moorings in Calais. One version says old William Wynter, who had joined Howard along with Seymour's squadron, first suggested it. Certainly Hawkins and Drake could draw on their firsthand experience at San Juan, of how fireships could push an enemy into panic even if they did not set a single ship alight.

Eight of the smaller English vessels were jammed with barrels of tar and pitch, old hemp, anything that would burn, with their guns charged to the muzzles so that they would combust with a mighty roar when the flames got to them. It was a bright and warm moon-filled night. The Spanish ships were swinging silently on their anchor chains when the eight fireships came in riding the midnight tide at a brisk two and a half knots. On each was a single man, whose job was to spread the tar and pitch, set the fire, and steer the creaking vessel into the Spanish line before jumping into a small boat to row back to the English fleet.

One by one they came alight; Spanish lookouts spotted them, and shouted the alarm. Rushing up on deck, Medina Sidonia ordered all ships to cut their cables and drift clear of the danger. All except one, the galleass *San Lorenzo,* did so without incident; the fireships slid past without harming a single ship and without so much as an explosion.

But for the first time, the Armada had lost its formation. As dawn came up on Monday August 9, Howard and the English fleet moved in on the scattered Spanish ships. Howard himself veered off to take the stranded *San Lorenzo;* Drake led the rest of the English fleet into battle off Gravelines. This time they decided to draw in closer—"within musket shot of the enemy," or 300 yards, which henceforth became standard fighting range in the Royal Navy. This time their shots began to tell. Drake steered directly for Medina Sidonia's flagship, the *San Martin,* and pounded it with shot. Then Frobisher came up in the *Triumph,* with the rest of his squadron firing away across the *San Martin's* bow and stern, smashing her upper works. Hawkins and his squadron took their deadly turn next.

One by one the other Spanish warships came to support their belea-guered admiral. More than 260 ships were locked in mortal combat, in the first great naval engagement in modern history. The Spanish fought with reckless bravery, but their shortage of ship-killing guns, and particu-larly their shortage of ammunition, shifted the tide of battle to the English. By late afternoon, when the Spanish managed to re-form them-selves and the English drew off, almost every one of the armada's first-class warships were badly damaged and leaking. Dead sailors and body parts littered their upper decks; spewed gore and smashed timbers filled the lower ones. The *San Mateo,* a powerful galleon that had been sur-rounded twice and fought itself clear with horrific casualties, left a wake red with blood as it ran itself aground to avoid sinking; so did the *San Felipe.* The *Maria Juan,* pride of the Biscayan squadron, was not so lucky. It sank beneath the waves, taking 259 men with it.

A sudden storm and heavy rain obscured the scene as Medina Sidonia counted his losses and pondered what to do. "Not a man among us slept that night," recalled a Spanish chaplain on one of the ships. A miraculous shift of wind enabled Medina Sidonia to steer his damaged fleet clear of the dangerous Zeeland Banks off the coast of Holland. The prevailing westerly winds were propelling him into the North Sea; the prospects for an invasion of England lay far astern. His armada had suf-fered more than six hundred killed and eight hundred wounded in the action off Gravelines. His own flagship had been riddled with 107 sepa-rate shots.

Yet battered as the armada was, it was still intact and able to keep for-mation. The duke and his officers now decided that their top priority was to get it home intact. That meant only one thing: "obeying the wind" to their southwest by steering north along the east coast of Britain and then around the northern tip of Scotland into the north Atlantic. The Spanish dumped the remaining horses and mules overboard to save on water; rations were cut to eight ounces of biscuit, half a pint of water, and half a pint of wine per man (the rest of their food was either gone or spoiled). Then, after hanging a wretched galleon captain convicted of quitting his post and parading his body through the fleet as an example—"to encourage the others," as Voltaire would say of a similar execution of a British admiral one hundred and fifty years later—the armada set off into seas only a handful of its ships' pilots had ever seen.

Their English pursuers, meanwhile, had no idea the battle was over. They lost sight of the Armada on the fourteenth and worried that Medina Sidonia would still try to land on England's North Sea coast or take refuge in Hamburg or some neutral Scottish or Danish port. "Their force is wonderful great and strong," Howard told Francis Walsingham, adding hopefully, "and yet we pluck their feathers little by little." But there was no disguising the fact that the armada had emerged from the great battle largely unscathed. Some complained that a great opportunity had been lost thanks to Howard's cautious tactics. Walsingham was thrust into a deep gloom: "So our half-doing doth breed dishonor and leaves the disease uncured."

Then, as if on cue, typhus broke out on board the English ships just as they ran out of food. They could not have followed the Armada even if they had wanted to. The *Elizabeth Jonas* lost two hundred of her five hundred crewmen. Some ships did not even have enough fit men to weigh anchor. Soon sick and starving English sailors and soldiers lay helpless in the streets of Dover and Rochester. And then there was still the threat of Parma, waiting in his lair at Dunkirk to strike.

It was not until August 30, almost two weeks after Elizabeth had appeared at Tilbury, that she felt confident enough to plan a victory celebration at St Paul's Cathedral in London. Lord Admiral Howard received the queen's official thanks and a pension of 200 pounds a year. But Elizabeth recognized who her real savior had been in a hymn of praise to the Lord God she composed herself:

> *He made the winds and water rise*
> *To scatter all mine Enemies.*

Indeed, the armada's troubles with the weather were just beginning. It rounded the tip of Scotland still in good shape: Medina Sidonia had

110 of the 117 ships with which he had started the campaign. But every stage of the voyage along the western Scottish and Irish coasts became a station of the cross in a monstrous maritime Passion Play.

Storms blew some helpless ships, with their sick and wounded crews, onto the rocks and cliffs, and others out of sight. Twenty-eight ships went down as Atlantic gales took a heavy toll of the big Mediterranean merchantmen and freighters. The Spanish had no charts of the waters they were in; only one captain, Vice Admiral Recalde, had ever been to the Irish coast. The map of Ireland on which the others relied showed the western Erris Peninsula as forty miles shorter than it actually was: as many as ten ships and their crews slammed into it and paid with their lives for that simple cartographic mistake.

Meanwhile, the sight of dozens of Spanish ships hauling and tossing off the Irish coast sent its English masters into a panic. They suspected the Spanish might try to land, as they had eight years earlier in Smerwick, and raise a native rebellion. As wrecked ships and sailors began washing ashore, the Lord Deputy, Sir William Fitzwilliam, was convinced a full-scale invasion was under way. His answer was characteristic: kill them all.

He found help from the Irish themselves. Some, like the McSweeneys of Tirconnell and the McDonnells of Antrim, did help shipwrecked refugees. But many others looted and often killed the stricken men as they were swept ashore. A Spanish captain described what happened to his crew when his ship smashed up on the rocks near Sligo:

> Many were drowning. . . . Others, casting themselves into the water, sank to the bottom without returning to the surface; others, on rafts, and barrels, and gentlemen on pieces of timber; others cried out aloud inside the ships, calling upon God; captains threw away their chains and crown pieces into the sea, the waves swept others away, washing them out of the ships.

Helpless, he watched the fate of his crew:

> I did not know what to do, nor what means to adopt, as I did not know how to swim, and the waves and storm were very great; on the other hand, the land and shore were full of savages [i.e., the native Irish], who went about jumping and dancing with delight at our misfortunes; and when anyone of our people reached the beach 200 savages and other enemies fell upon him and stripped him of what he had on him until he was left in his naked skin.

More than six thousand Spaniards died on the Irish coast. Most died from drowning; some were killed by locals (one, Melaghlin McCabb, claimed to have killed eighty with his battle-ax), but the rest were massacred by the English militias. The governor of Connaught reported gleefully to the queen, "Thus was all the province quickly rid of those distressed enemies." In Galway at St. Augustine's monastery, which is now Fort Hill, three hundred prisoners alone were murdered in cold blood. When Fitzwilliam learned that the Connaught governor had set aside fifty more to be held for ransom, he furiously ordered them killed as well. To this day Spanish fishermen stopping in Ireland will come to pray at the cemetery at Fort Hill, where thirty-seven bodies had been thrown into a mass grave.

On September 21 Medina Sidonia limped into Santander harbor with only eleven ships still with him. Some crews were so exhausted that they could not even lower anchor and simply ran aground. Medina Sidonia, who was himself desperately ill and had been confined to bed rest, wrote a note to Philip: "The troubles and miseries we have suffered cannot be described to Your Majesty." Philip II was as usual at his desk at the Escorial when news came of the disaster that had befallen his armada. He listened without emotion, then (according to one witness) said simply, "I sent my ships to fight against men and not against the winds and waves of God," and then went back to his correspondence.

Still, the news was not as bad as it first appeared. Over the next few days another thirty ships returned; by the end of the month sixty-five of Medina Sidonia's fleet had made it home. In the end, probably a third of the armada never returned to Spain. But less than 20 percent of those were actually Spanish—most were larger and clumsier foreign vessels, not seaworthy Iberian galleons. As Philip is supposed to have remarked, these were losses, like the loss of life (almost two-thirds of the armada's soldiers and sailors), he could replace. The Invincible Armada had failed, but it had not been defeated: the English had been almost helpless to stop it. With Parma's troops still assembled at Dunkirk, it was conceivable another try might have better luck. Philip was certainly undeterred: he even gave orders for building another armada for 1589. In fact, he would build three more armadas before he died in 1598, although none would ever come as close to England, or to success, as the first.

Yet even as trees as far away as Yugoslavia were being cut down for new masts and timbers, and shipyards in Lisbon, Cádiz, and San Sebastian were laying the keels for new galleons, something was missing.

The failure of the Armada shattered Spain's imperial self-confidence. Its own officers felt it. Vice Admiral Recalde died less than three weeks after returning home; Medina Sidonia swore he would never have anything to do with the sea again. Rumors swirled around Parma that he had turned coward by abandoning the invasion, rumors so persistent that finally he spent an entire day in the main square of Dunkirk with his sword offering to fight anyone who would repeat them to his face (none did). As for Philip, everyone noted the change that came over him: his beard turned gradually white, his skin a sickly pallor, as a series of health problems began that would hound him to his grave ten years later.

It was Spain's first major setback in the eyes of the world. At the crucial moment, it seemed, God had abandoned the people He had designated to govern the world. The once bright Spanish future became streaked with a new pessimism, from which it would never recover. One of Philip's friars wrote privately: "It lost us the respect and good reputation that we used to have among warlike people." For the first time, Europeans sensed that the future might not depend on the will and might of Spain. The crack of doom had sounded over the global system it had built and exploited; a new one would begin to take its place.

If the defeat of the Armada shattered Spain's sense of divine mission, it had the opposite effect in England. In a strict sense, the English had accomplished nothing. Bad luck, bad planning, and bad weather had doomed the enterprise, not the Royal Navy. But the English insisted on acting as if they had scored a great victory. Even the bad weather became a Protestant "divine wind," with God miraculously foiling the evil designs of the Antichrist. Commemorative medals were struck with the motto *Flevit Deus et inimici dissaparunt* (God breathed upon the waters and His enemies were dispersed). Portraits of Elizabeth appeared showing the queen in her glorious regalia and lace, with the Spanish fleet scattering and sinking behind her, as she rested her hand confidently on a terrestrial globe.

Elizabeth's victory over the Spanish Armada confirmed her status as the monarch uniquely chosen to defend the Protestant faith and God's divine order on earth. John Foxe had compared her to Constantine; John Dee to King Arthur. Dee's friend, the Italian astronomer and mystagogue Giordano Bruno, predicted she would "enlarge the circumference of her dominion to include not only Britain and Ireland but some new world, as vast as the universal frame." The Virgin Queen became a heaven-sent sovereign who would create a new golden age for God's Englishmen. Indeed, the age of Edmund Spenser (whose Protestant epic *The Faerie*

Queen was written shortly after the events of the Armada), William Shakespeare, Christopher Marlowe, Ben Jonson, Inigo Jones, and Francis Bacon would soon follow on the heels of the age of Hawkins and Drake.

So the Armada confirmed one powerful myth, that of the English as Chosen People, but it also launched another. That would be the work of young Richard Hakluyt, the Oxford geographer who had discovered his life's calling among the charts and maps in his cousin's chambers in the Middle Temple.

The younger Hakluyt had been serving as chaplain to the English embassy in Paris during the events of the Armada, and after the battle he escorted Lord Admiral Howard's sister home to England. During his stay in France, he had been forced to listen to foreigners who slighted the English efforts at oceanic discovery and exploration, compared to their own. In order to "stop the mouths of the reproachers," as he put it, Hakluyt decided to put together a complete collection of "the maritime records of our own men, which are hitherto scattered and buried in dust," which would prove that the English were second to none in the transformation of the globe.

At great personal labor and all at his own cost, Hakluyt painstakingly assembled whatever materials he could find to document a century of English overseas ventures. The result was *The Principal Voyages, Traffics, and Discoveries of the English Nation,* which first appeared in 1589 and then in an expanded edition ten years later. Hakluyt put himself into the role not of historian but archivist, selecting and editing documents that would tell the story on their own. But the selection itself was significant.

Hakluyt went back as far as the legends of King Arthur (shades of John Dee) and the expeditions of medieval English kings to the Holy Land to show that the English had always been a voyaging and expansive nation. He wanted to prove that the English "in searching the most opposite corners and quarters of the world . . . have excelled all the nations and peoples of the earth." As for non-English voyages, Hakluyt had almost nothing to say. The doings of Sebastian Cabot, Richard Chancellor, Robert Thorne, Frobisher, Drake, and Hawkins swell the volumes of the *Principal Voyages;* the names of Columbus, Magellan, and Vasco de Gama appear hardly at all. Anyone reading the book might assume the discovery of the New World and the opening of Asia to European trade was due to Englishmen and Englishmen alone.

This was pure propaganda, of course. But no one could deny the remarkable change that had taken place in English seafaring. In 1538 one lone merchant from Plymouth, old William Hawkins, was making trips across the Atlantic. By 1588 English sailors were making regular runs to America, Russia, Asia, around the Cape of Africa, and above the Arctic Circle—even around the world. On the heels of the defeat of the Spanish Armada William Cavendish came into Plymouth harbor on September 9, 1588, after completing the second English circumnavigation of the globe. No place on earth seemed beyond their reach. The historian J. A. Froude once called Hakluyt's *Voyages* the prose epic of the modern English nation. However, it was an epic that specifically linked England's past and future to the sea and to empire. Richard Hakluyt did for English seafaring what John Foxe had done for English Protestantism: he made it seem an essential part of the national character.

Hakluyt's friend John Davis, a Devonshire sailor who would spend his life looking for the Northwest Passage and also invented the most valuable navigation instrument of the next era of oceanic discovery, the backstaff,* expressed it perfectly: "There is no doubt that we of England are this saved people by the infallible presence of the Lord, predestined to be sent into these Gentiles in the sea, to those Isles and famous kingdoms. . . . It is only we, therefore, that must be these shining messengers of the Lord, and none but we!"

The second expanded edition of Hakluyt's *Voyages* appeared in 1598. It became particularly celebrated (the queen herself read it) because it included a detailed map of the world by famed mapmaker Edward Wright. Wright, an associate of John Dee, was the first cartographer to discover how to use the method Mercator had developed for showing the globe's lines of latitude and longitude accurately on a flat surface. The result was a map unlike any that had appeared in England or anywhere else. It became the most famous English map of the sixteenth century, and certainly the most accurate. Later, some English scholars would argue it was the best ever made.

Well they should. Because Wright's portrayal of the world, besides achieving a breathtaking accuracy of longitude and latitude and size of continents, also placed Great Britain at the dead center. The very points and lines of the compass seemed to connect it to every part of the globe, across the Atlantic and from all sides. It was a vivid emblem of his friend John Dee's words: "What a privilege God had endowed this island with

---

*A huge improvement on the cross staff, it allowed the navigator to get a fix on the sun's position by measuring the shadow it cast rather than staring directly into its rays.

Edward Wright's Map of the World, 1598

by reason of situation, most commodious for navigation, to places most famous and rich."

The new geography, like the Spanish Armada's defeat, had cast England's maritime destiny, or so it seemed. The only limit it and its navy faced was the extent of the oceans themselves.

CHAPTER SEVEN

Pirates

The Spaniard shall have no peace beyond the line.
—SIR FRANCIS DRAKE, 1579

*The wealth of both Indies seems in great part but an accessory to the
command of the seas.*
—SIR FRANCIS BACON, 1625

THE ROYAL NAVY'S "victory" over the Spanish Armada had
breathed a new self-confidence into the English nation. There
was a sense of divine chosenness, of new possibilities, even of
being at the center of the world—as Edward Wright's new map so
graphically implied. The only question was what the English would do
with it.

The answer was, not much. Unbroken lines of historical development
come rarely. Progress moves in fits and starts, with almost as many backward steps as forward ones. This was the case of the Royal Navy after the
Armada. Following an initial burst of enthusiasm and creativity, resources
that had been activated were squandered, and lessons forgotten. It would
take sixty years before the navy would find itself fully back on track, and
back on the world stage.

Yet it was precisely during those years that England became a key
player in the new Atlantic-based world economy, and that Englishmen
came to see sea power as essential to their future. As a result, the Royal
Navy would become a major bone of contention in national politics, and
central to the nation's life and institutions. In fact, the navy would shape
the history of England in the fifty years after the death of Queen
Elizabeth as powerfully as it would shape the history of Europe in the
fifty years leading to the death of Louis XIV.

None who watched the Spanish Armada pass harmlessly into the
North Sea in the first weeks of September 1588 would have been surprised by this—but for almost all the wrong reasons. In the euphoric
aftermath of victory, the vulnerabilities the campaign had exposed were

overlooked. It was wind and weather, not English gunnery or seamanship, that wrecked Spain's chances. A more resolute or resourceful commander than Medina Sidonia might have trapped the English fleet at Plymouth, or landed his troops in England without waiting for Parma and used his ships to cover their advance on London. Elizabeth's navy proved it could supply and maintain its ships quickly but not for long periods of time. After a summer at sea, English ships found themselves without shot, without food or water, with hulls and masts severely battered, and sailors sick and dying—and without pay.

For all its skill and bravado, this was not a navy prepared for a long and serious overseas campaign. Yet this was precisely what Elizabeth ordered it to do next. She decided she would launch her own armada: a fleet of ships and men under Francis Drake to destroy what was left of the Spanish navy, to capture that year's silver fleet, and incidentally, raise all of Portugal in revolt against its Spanish masters. Naturally there was no money to pay for this huge effort. The bulk had to come, as usual, from private investors, who expected to get their profits from the captured *flota*. So at great expense a fleet of over one hundred vessels and nearly 20,000 men set sail from Plymouth on April 18, 1589, under the command of Drake and his old partner in crime from Rathlin Island, Sir John Norris.

The English armada was almost as much a fiasco as the Spanish had been the year before. Drake proved that while he was a brave seafighter and daring privateer, he was incapable of planning a large strategic operation. He and Norris wasted valuable time trying to take Corunna, where Medina Sidonia had initially taken shelter the previous June. They sank three battered Armada survivors but failed to capture the town—and lost all element of surprise in the process. They finally reached the coast of Portugal and their troops disembarked. Norris marched to the gates of Lisbon without serious resistance, but could not invest the city, as pestilence broke out in his camp and forced him to retreat. Reembarked, Drake and Norris spent weeks in a fruitless search for the elusive *flota*. Finally, they gave up and returned to England without fighting a major battle but losing half their force to disease and spending 100,000 pounds for nothing. A furious queen ordered Drake from her sight.

The disgrace of Drake was a harbinger of a decade of failure and frustration. In addition, the heroic age of Elizabethan statesmen and sailors was fading fast. The queen's closest friend and keen supporter of war with Spain, the Earl of Leicester, died only days after the Spanish Armada left the Channel in 1588. The other pillar of an aggressive anti-Spanish policy, Francis Walsingham, followed in 1590, along with Drake's old benefactor, Christopher Hatton, in 1591. That same year Richard Grenville was cruising the race-built *Revenge* off the Azores when he allowed himself to be trapped by a flotilla of Spanish galleons. After a nearly twenty-hour gun duel with fifteen enemy ships, which left the *Revenge* smashed and sinking and Grenville dying from multiple wounds, the man the Spanish called "*el gran corsario*" went out in a blaze of glory but to no larger purpose.

Then came Martin Frobisher's turn, killed leading an attack on the Spanish garrison at Blavet in Brittany in 1594. Although he prevented the Spanish from establishing a permanent base on the English Channel, their raiding galleys still managed to get to Cornwall. Just six years after the Armada, Spanish soldiers were landing on English soil and burning Penzance, Newlyn, and Mousehole.

The truth was that English policy was floundering. Philip II, meanwhile, was building ships, strengthening garrisons and bases in the West Indies, and reinforcing his armies in Flanders. He even launched another armada in October 1596, but storms off the Portuguese coast scattered and destroyed it. He tried again in 1597: a fleet of at least two hundred ships with eight thousand men got as far as the Lizard Point in Cornwall before, once again, violent storms sent it reeling back to Spain. That was Philip's last attempt before his death in 1598; but the English fear of Spanish invasion, and sense of vulnerability, remained. Rumors that Spaniards were coming set off a national panic in 1598 and again in 1599, with citizens of London closing off streets and rushing to Tilbury with 30,000 militiamen to repel the imagined attackers.

At the same time, Elizabeth and her advisors became obsessed with intercepting the Spanish treasure fleet, what John Hawkins called "the method of Jason," and defeating Philip "by fetching away his golden fleece." Hawkins wanted regular English patrols off the Azores for that purpose. A sound enough idea; but without money, resources, or a regular base with which to rest and refit, he could not keep ships at sea long enough to catch the silver fleet except by chance.

Above all, he had no money. The navy's share of the budget shrank, as England's land operations on the Continent grew. Seven thousand English soldiers were now in France helping the new king, Henry IV, against Spanish-backed Catholic extremists; another seven thousand fought alongside the Dutch. Soon there would be a large army in Ireland.

Meanwhile, every Spanish treasure convoy from 1588 to 1595 was able to get through without incident. About the only things the Azores patrols had to show for their efforts were freeing Job Hartop,* and the loss of Grenville and the *Revenge*.

So Elizabeth reverted to a previous strategy and ordered her two aging sea dogs, Drake and Hawkins, to the West Indies one last time, in hopes they could recapture the old magic. It should have been a spectacular finish to their careers. Instead, Drake and Hawkins quarreled incessantly. The hero of Cádiz found the man who had rebuilt the Royal Navy too timid, and the former slave trader from Plymouth found the cousin who had abandoned him at San Juan de Ulloa too bold. Part of Hawkins's caution was also due to the fact that he was desperately sick, and worried about his son Richard, who had been captured by the Spanish two years earlier. On November 12, 1595, the day they landed at San Juan harbor, Puerto Rico, to take a crippled treasure galleon, Hawkins lost his fight for life and died.

The assault on San Juan failed, so Drake sailed on to his old haunt, the Spanish Main. "God hath many things in store for us," he told his crew, "and I know many things to do her Majesty service, and to make us rich." He revisited the places that had made his reputation a quarter-century before: Riohacha, where he and Hawkins had sold slaves to local planters at gunpoint; Santa Marta; and finally Nombre de Dios. But now the Spanish had fortified the Panama isthmus and crushed his ex-slave cimmaroon allies. Instead of a quick march through the jungle and mountains, Drake's soldiers were repulsed and Drake came down with dysentery.

As the expeditionary force neared Portobello, Drake's condition grew worse. He drew up his will and asked to leave his bed to don his old helmet and breastplate to meet death, as he said, "like a soldier." On January 28, 1596, the last pioneer of English sea power passed on to his Maker. His crew laid him in a lead coffin and lowered it into the sea, to the sound of cannon salutes and trumpets "echoing our . . . lamentation for so great a loss."

Of the two, the loss of John Hawkins was greater. He had built a Royal Navy that, whatever its shortcomings, was equal to any in the world. He showed how it could be an offensive strategic weapon, not just the defender of the "Narrow Seas." He also gave it the first modern global

---

*See chapter I.

strategy: severing the trade links between an enemy and its colonies. It
would become the primary mission of all European navies for the next
two centuries.

But in the short run, Drake's legacy was more crucial. It was epitomized by a sentence he had uttered during his trip around the world in
1579: "The Spanish shall have no peace beyond the line"—meaning the
line of longitude just west of the Azores that the papal bull of 1494 had
used to divide the unknown world between Spain and Portugal. Since
1559, it had marked the outside limit of all peace treaties signed by
European powers. For the next century and a half, there would indeed be
no peace "beyond the tropic line," as white Europeans of all nations
turned the Caribbean and South Atlantic into a permanent war zone, a
perpetual struggle for treasure, trade, colonies, and dominion.

Drake had launched the golden age of European piracy, an era still
remembered for its swashbuckling buccaneers, bloodthirsty corsairs,
sunken Spanish galleons—and slave traders in the Middle Passage. Henry
Morgan, Captain Kidd, and their French, Dutch, and Spanish counterparts learned to raid where they pleased under the flag but outside the
control of their national governments. By triggering the collapse of the
Spanish and Portuguese empires in the New World, Drake had opened a
"war of all against all," in Thomas Hobbes's immortal phrase, in which life
is "nasty, brutish, and short." Yet out of this anarchy would eventually
come Europe's new colonial empires, including England's, and a new
world order.

Drake's example was instantly taken up by a rising generation of
English seamen. From 1589 to 1591 no less than 235 privateering vessels
sallied forth from English ports. Their excuse was the war with Spain;
their declared mission was capturing Spanish treasure galleons, although
few were courageous enough to sail as far as the West Indies. Instead, they
preyed on the unarmed international shipping in the English Channel and
its western approaches. Many ventured south to Cape Finisterre and the
Bay of Biscay, and farther south to Cape St. Vincent near Cádiz. One
Dutch expert estimated that in March 1590 alone there were more than
twenty English pirates hovering off Cape St. Vincent, and another forty
off Corvo in the Azores.

Some hunted in packs, but most preferred to work alone so that they
would not have to share their booty: Scandinavian furs from a Dutch *fluyt*
ship, Madeira wine from a Portuguese coaster, or even bolts of wool from
a fellow Englishman. They included ranking English naval officers, such

as Sir Richard Leveson, the Lord Admiral's son-in-law, and Sir Walter Raleigh. They included many of the English nobility, who were beginning to take a keen interest in things nautical as well as piratical. One was the late Earl of Leicester's son, Robert Dudley, who had taken up the study of navigation at age seventeen, as well as "marine discipline and war," and was the first English navigator to plot a great-circle course. The Earl of Warwick kept his pirate ships busy in the Caribbean, while the elegant and cultivated aristocrat Sir Kenelm Digby (he would introduce the painter Anthony Van Dyck to the English court) wreaked havoc in the Mediterranean.

The third Earl of Cumberland, George Clifford, sank his entire family fortune into piracy. In 1598 he managed to do what Drake could not, and took and looted San Juan, Puerto Rico. But Cumberland's greatest moment came in 1592 when he caught a massive Portuguese carrack in from Asia, the *Madre de Díos,* off the Azores. In her hold were more than 537 tons of pepper, cloves, cinnamon, mace, and nutmeg; fifteen tons of ebony; and chests overflowing with gold, silver, pearls, and ivory. His jubilant crew brought the *Madre de Díos* into Dartmouth harbor, where the locals swarmed over the ship and stripped it of everything they could carry. Walter Raleigh had to be released from the Tower of London to restore order.* Even after the vandalism and looting, the *Madre de Díos* brought in more than half a million pounds in prize money: the greatest single capture of the Elizabethan age.

Few English pirates ever got prizes worth even a fraction of that amount. But they did effectively destroy Spain and Portugal's commercial shipping, while transferring more than 400,000 pounds into the English economy—even before the capture of the *Madre de Díos.* Merchant investors of the East India Company (founded in 1600) and Levant Company quickly learned to use piracy to pad their profits when business was slack.

But the spirit of piracy could not sustain serious military operations against Spain. The proof came with the last great campaign of the Elizabethan war, the attack on Cádiz on 1596. Lord Admiral Howard, now nearly sixty, assumed formal command; but as his squadrons assembled at Plymouth, real leadership passed to a pair of daredevil courtiers, Raleigh and the Earl of Essex. More than a thousand gentleman adven-

---

*A jealous Queen Elizabeth had sent him to the Tower for marrying one of her ladies-in-waiting.

turers eager for combat and loot joined the party, including the poet John Donne, who offered his services to Essex and won a berth on one of his ships. The Earl of Cumberland was keen to command one of the squadrons but backed out when he learned he had been superseded by Sir Thomas Howard. Seventeen royal warships, forty-seven armed merchantmen and pinnaces, along with eighteen ships on loan from the Dutch United Provinces, left Plymouth on June 1.

Howard's tight security kept the Spanish from discovering the fleet's destination until it dropped anchor outside Cádiz on June 19. The harbor was crammed with shipping, including the Golden Fleece itself, the treasure fleet. As English guns smashed the Spanish galleys standing in their way, proving once and for all that the era of the Mediterranean war galley was over, English troops landed and looted the town. However, battle order soon broke down as captains scrambled for individual prizes. The desperate Spanish were able to burn their treasure galleons before the English could grab them. More than 12 million ducats went to the bottom. Yet Philip still had enough cash left to launch armadas that year and the next, while Howard, Essex, and Raleigh had to return home empty-handed.

They tried for the treasure fleet again in 1597, this time off the Azores, but the expedition ran into devastating storms. The rivalry between Raleigh and Essex flared into open hostility—at one point their ships nearly fired on each other. As they quarreled, their subordinates watched helplessly as the treasure fleet sailed into Terceira and safely unloaded the treasure under the fortress guns. Essex managed to bag a brace of prizes to pay for his end of the venture; but the fleet returned to England in a sad state, with broken masts and spars, water and supplies gone, and having narrowly missed an encounter with Philip's own armada on its way to Cornwall. If storms had not dispersed the Spanish fleet, the English might have lost their navy and the war.

The pattern of failure was becoming clear. The old Elizabethan idea that the navy could make up for money and numbers by relying on the ships of courtiers and private investors earning their return through prize money no longer worked. The Royal Navy now faced strategic missions the old methods could not support. Any chance of correcting the problem disappeared under Elizabeth's successor, James I. Naval decline and the spirit of piracy took over.

Queen Elizabeth died on March 24, 1603. Her commitments to war on land, like those of her father Henry VIII, had brought the country to the brink of bankruptcy. Her navy had maintained its strength on a shoe-string budget, and was actually larger and stronger than it had been in 1588. But 2 million pounds had gone into the war in the Netherlands; the Dutch owed her 800,000 pounds they never paid back, Henry IV of France another 300,000. More than 4 million pounds had gone into defeating the revolt of the Catholic Earl of Tyrone in Ireland, which had secured English rule but left the country a shambles.

The new king was determined to avoid the same mistake. James I was a Scot (crowned James VI in Scotland), a theologian and scholar (as evinced by the King James Bible), and totally innocent of any idea of how England's experiment in aggressive sea power had brought it to the brink of dominance in the Atlantic. He fancied himself the peacemaker of Europe, the man who would eventually lead Protestants and Catholics to a reunion of Christendom. The first step had to be peace with Spain. James signed the final treaty in 1604, earning the undying enmity of the Dutch who were still fighting for their lives. Then, despite howls of protest from the West Country ports, he banned letters of marque to privateers against Spanish shipping. The most vocal exponent of war with Spain, Walter Raleigh, went back into the Tower.

Peace did ease the budget, allow the army to come home, the merchants to return to Spanish ports, and the navy to sit idle at Chatham. Its ships were the first to fly the king's new flag with the English cross of Saint George superimposed on the Scottish cross of Saint Andrew: the Union Jack.* But James's high-minded treaty left the status of territories "beyond the line," including America, unresolved. Legal privateering may have ended, but illegal piracy quickly took its place. Even James's closest advisor, Robert Cecil, son of the deceased Lord Burghley and now secretary of state, was up to his neck in it, as was Lord Admiral Howard.

Meanwhile, peace crippled the navy. Lord Howard (now Earl of Nottingham), once a galvanizing force, was too old to keep his grip. Even as he profited from pirates' prizes in his Admiralty courts, he allowed the same greed to take over the Navy Board. For three years after John Hawkins's death, there had been no Treasurer of the Navy, as the rest of the administration sank into incompetence and corruption.

None of this was entirely new. Even Hawkins had had a private stake in the granting of contracts and victualing and fitting of ships: it was part

---

*First adopted by the Royal Navy in 1606, it took decades before it became the national flag.

of his so-called Great Bargain with the Crown that made him treasurer in the first place. But Sir Robert Mansell, who became treasurer in 1604, regularly sold supplies to the navy at double the price he paid for them, while bureaucratic crooks like victualer Thomas Bludder, Sir Thomas Button, and the vice admiral of Cornwall, Sir James Bagg (known to his victims as "Bottomless Bagg") bred a regime of kickbacks, skimming, embezzlement, and outright thievery. Everyone pitched in. Bosuns regularly cut lengths of anchor cable and sold them, so that cables listed as ninety fathoms long (540 feet) were actually only sixty. Clerks padded accounts; pursers bought their offices and looted their ships to pay for it; captains and lieutenants (the new word coming into use for the captain's second-in-command) sold their ship's stores in foreign ports. One even sold the guns from his own command, the *Resistance*.

By 1608 the reign of men like Mansell, Bludder, Button, and Bagg forced the king to call a board of inquiry. It found ships rotting in their docks, bribes the rule of the day, and "everyone practiceth to accomplish his own end of profit, not caring how he hath it as long as he may come by it." The navy was, the board concluded, "for the greatest part manned with aged, impotent, vagrant, lewd, and disorderly companions."

Yet James did nothing. A second board had to be summoned ten years later, which found that out of forty-three navy ships on the books, no less than twenty-one did not exist or were too decayed to go to sea. Nottingham was finally retired, his office reorganized—the old hero of 1588 was the last Lord Admiral to depend on privateering prize money for his income—and even the Navy Board was temporarily replaced with a new naval commission. It proposed capital improvements for Deptford, which got new docks, and Chatham, which got a face-lift and eventually its first mechanical clock.

But the damage was done. Disgruntled officers and common seamen, who had not seen a pay raise since 1588, preferred piracy or sailing on a Levant or East India Company merchantmen, to serving on the king's ships. Many even preferred service with the Dutch (one was the ill-fated explorer Henry Hudson). England's ability to defend its home waters steadily declined. Spanish corsairs found haven in Dunkirk for raids in the English Channel; English pirate chieftain Peter Easton set up in Irish waters with a fleet of twenty ships. When the king offered him a pardon in 1612, Easton blithely refused: "I am, in a way, a king myself." On a visit to England in 1614, even James's brother-in-law King Christian of Denmark was robbed by pirates.

The worst were the corsairs from North Africa and Algiers. Renegade English pirates expelled by the peace of 1604 taught Moslem sailors how to navigate the Atlantic with race-built galleons. They now regularly preyed in the Western Approaches looking for captives to sell as slaves. They attacked West Country fishing fleets, raided the Cornish coast and snatched merchant ships in Plymouth harbor. Some ranged as far as Newfoundland. Between 1609 and 1616 turbaned Moslem pirates took more than 446 English prizes and sold more than seven thousand English captives into slavery.

King James was finally goaded into action. In 1620 he ordered two aging Elizabethan veterans, navy treasurer Mansell and John Hawkins's son Richard, to take six warships and twelve armed merchantmen to suppress the corsair nest at Algiers. Mansell had not been to sea since 1604; Hawkins, who was nearly sixty, had not been since ten years before that. They had too puny a force to enter that heavily fortified harbor; for diplomatic reasons, James forbade them to attack Algiers itself; after two ineffectual attempts, Mansell and Hawkins returned, humiliated. The first foray of English seapower into the Mediterranean had been a farce.

The North African corsairs posed one kind of challenge to England's maritime security. A more serious one came from England's fellow Protestants and former protégés, the Dutch.

* * *

The Dutch were the real beneficiaries of the victory over the Armada in 1588. Parma's distractions with the English invasion had given the rebellious Dutch provinces breathing space to reorganize their defenses and gain naval control over the continental coast of the English Channel. Although Spain would not formally recognize Dutch independence until 1648, the Calvinist republic's future was secure. The English privateering wars helped also, by crippling Spanish commercial shipping, thus opening the way for the Dutch to go on the offensive around the world. They would prove themselves to be Drake's apt pupils in the art of hit-and-run piracy and terror. They were also the world's best businessmen.

With the new Dutch oceangoing *fluyt* ship—twice as long as a standard galleon with a flat bottom to provide a large, square cargo hold— merchants from Amsterdam, Rotterdam, and Haarlem could transport goods cheaper and faster than anyone else. In an age when overseas trade consisted of those countries with access to the sea buying and reexporting goods to those who did not, this cheap freight service made the Dutch the arbiters of world trade. Even Philip II had realized that Spain's empire could not operate without their help, and in the midst of their revolt against him allowed them to bring grain, timber, and naval stores into Lisbon and Cádiz.

By 1600 Dutch merchants were everywhere. They completely dominated the Baltic and North Sea, controlling three-quarters of the grain and timber trade and squeezing out English fishing fleets. The Dutch were also taking over the carrying trade in the Mediterranean, from Barcelona to Constantinople. Then in 1602 their East India Company punctured the Portuguese spice monopoly in Asia by arming their merchantmen in the English manner, and swooping down and capturing key Portuguese forts in the Moluccas.

Dutch merchants seized control of the African gold and ivory market. They forced their way into the West Indies as well, where Dutch privateers disrupted the *flota* system, colonized northern Brazil at Pernambuco, established a settlement on Curaçao for growing sugar, and made themselves masters of the flourishing slave trade. The Spanish were helpless to prevent it; too late they realized, as one diplomat put it, "He who possesses the sea will have dominion over the land." Within two decades, the Dutch West Indies Company turned the Caribbean into a virtual Dutch lake. Then in 1628 one of its captains, Piet Hein, realized the dream of every pirate and privateer since Drake: he captured the entire Spanish treasure fleet, worth nearly one and a half million pounds, allowing the company to declare a dividend that year of 75 percent.

The Dutch Republic was the first maritime power in modern history. Its seaborne merchants took advantage of the wars raging across the rest of Europe to become the middlemen of world trade, doing business with both sides. They enjoyed access to more capital and liquidity than those of any other country, thanks to the creation of the Bank of Amsterdam and the Amsterdam stock exchange. Smart, innovative, and opportunistic, Dutch traders also backed their business deals with private military muscle. The East India Company was able to raise troops, build forts, assemble fleets, and wage war at will around the Pacific. When Philip III of Spain put together a fleet of galleons in the Straits of Gibraltar to sail east and drive them out of Asia, the East India Company sent a force of twenty-six warships into the Straits and sank them all.

Piracy and trade made Holland the most affluent society on the planet. Even in the midst of war, its citizens enjoyed their fabled "embarrassment of riches" that overflowed with abundant food, drink, tobacco, books (it was the most literate society in Europe and an international publishing center), flowers, art, and architecture. A golden age of Dutch culture flourished, the age of Rembrandt and Vermeer, of thinkers and scientists like René Descartes, Hugh Grotius, and Anton van Leeuwenhoek, inventor of the microscope. In 1669 Amsterdam got the world's first public street lighting. The Dutch style of life was the envy of Europe and they knew it. Their portraits by Rembrandt and Frans Hals show us a nation of smiling, well-fed, alert men and women, with immaculate white ruffs and a self-confidence bordering on self-satisfaction.

The English watched the 1600s turn into "the Dutch century" with a particular envy and resentment. They puzzled over why the success and power their fellow Protestants and former protégés enjoyed, seemed to have passed them by. Yet the meteoric rise of the Dutch seaborne empire also obscured basic weaknesses of Dutch society and its governing institutions—and important lessons for the future of England's own maritime power.

The first was the fact that Holland's freewheeling business ethos, which encouraged an unprecedented degree of personal liberty and freedom of conscience, also undercut every attempt to create a strong unified state. This had a decisive impact on the future state of the Dutch navy. In truth, there was no Dutch navy. Five separate admiralties, including one each for Amsterdam and Rotterdam, were each responsible for arming and maintaining its own fleet, appointing its own admirals and officers, collecting customs and prize money, and providing armed convoys for shipping. Unity of command was hard to come by except in a crisis and demanded careful cooperation and negotiation. No wonder that the governing body of the Netherlands, the Estates General, preferred to let their Indies companies maintain private fleets and do the fighting themselves.

The same problem haunted the Dutch army. Unlike Britain, Holland was not an island: it had to fight for its existence by land as well as by sea. To meet the challenge, the Dutch had by 1600 created the most efficient and modern army in Europe. But eighty years of constant war against Spain and then forty against France meant constantly mounting taxes, managed again by each separate province. By 1670 the republic was fielding an army equal in size to that of Louis XIV, more than 100,000 men, even though France had ten times the population. Dutch ranks had be filled with expensive foreign mercenaries, just as most of its navy were actually German, Scandinavian, and even English sailors.

By the end of the century the average Dutch burgher was paying three times the taxes of a French- or Englishman. Holland's unprecedented wealth enabled it to bear the burden, but a run of bad luck in a naval or ground war always threatened to push this fragile polity over the edge.

In the end, it was love of wealth, rather than love of religion or country, that turned the Dutch into efficient warriors by land and sea. In fact, love of wealth trumped everything. "Jesus Christ is good," the Dutch liked to say, "but trade is better." A refreshing attitude in an age of religious wars, but the decay of the old Calvinist faith in the atmosphere of laissez-faire profiteering created a moral vacuum, which opened the way to an amorality and a libertarian indifference in their dealings with others.

It was not for nothing that the Dutch proved adept masters of the slave trade. After John Hawkins's last voyage in 1568, the English had largely dropped out of the business. When they returned to it in the 1620s, it had grown in volume and ruthlessness, with thousands of Africans dying in the dreadful trip across the Atlantic and thousands more worked to death in the plantations in Brazil and the Caribbean islands. The brutality never bothered the Dutch, the industry's leaders, any more than they were bothered by the genocidal campaigns the East India Company conducted against recalcitrant tribes in the Indonesian Spice Islands. Of course, the English did no less in Ireland. They would become skilled and efficient in the slave trade, but they would also take the lead in abolishing it, and then the evil of slavery itself. No abolitionist sentiment ever interfered with the Dutch desire to turn a profit.

The same was true of another notorious Dutch practice, trading with the enemy. This constantly undermined Dutch war efforts, as their own merchants continued to do business with their sworn enemies—even selling them cannon and shot. Trading with the enemy was not unknown among the English: at the height of war Sir Walter Raleigh allowed timber from his Irish estates to be sold to Spanish shipbuilders. But English patriotism and anti-Catholicism gave it the stigma of treason and dishonor that it never had among the Dutch. They sold rope and sailcloth to the Royal Navy on the very eve of its war against the Dutch Republic in 1652 and offered insurance policies for its ships; some Amsterdam merchants even invested in the Dunkirk privateers who preyed on their own city's shipping.

Most galling to the English, however, was the hypocritical Dutch position on "freedom of the seas." Their great apostle of international law, Hugo Groot or Hugh Grotius, had enunciated this principle in his treatise *Mare Liberum* (*The Free Seas*). The world's oceans belonged to all humanity, Grotius declared, and no political state could deny its use to the merchants or sailors of another. It was a high-minded ideal, one that John Hawkins had anticipated in his voyages in the Spanish Caribbean and which stands as the original formula for the idea of "free trade." But the Dutch were the first to violate it themselves. They routinely excluded competitors from their markets in Indonesia and Japan and did not hesitate to shoot their way into markets that tried to exclude them.*

In 1618 Dutch fishing fleets descended on the whale-hunting grounds around Spitzbergen, which English fishermen claimed as theirs by exclusive royal right. A full-scale battle resulted. James I was outraged: this was piracy no less than the depredations of the Algiers or the Dunkirk corsairs. Characteristically, he chose a scholarly rather than a military response. He turned to lawyer John Selden to refute Dutch pretensions and defend his royal prerogative.

Selden was not just a great legal mind. He was an intimate of literary men like Ben Jonson and Michael Drayton, a historian of Britain and its peoples, and in the judgment of one modern historian, "the greatest scholar in the country." Selden drew on his historical knowledge to construct a very different view of the relationship between the state and the sea from Grotius's *Mare Liberum,* which he believed was merely a pretext and license for Dutch piracy.†

Instead, Selden titled his work *Mare Clausum,* or *The Closed Sea.* It argued that James I's titles as king of Scotland, England, and Ireland made him in fact ruler of Great Britain, and that by law "the King of Great Britain is Lord of the Sea flowing about" his domains, including the Channel, the North Sea, and Irish Sea. Echoing John Dee and Humphrey Lloyd of an earlier generation, Selden insisted that the ancient Britons possessed this title before they had been conquered by the Romans, and that this "Empire of the Waters" had been passed down to their medieval successors, the Tudors and Elizabeth, and now to James. The King of England was free to exclude whomever he wished from his watery dominion, and claim it exclusively for his own fishermen and sailors. "The Sea and the Land were made one entire Body of the British Empire," Selden con-

---

*The Dutch remained the only foreign merchants allowed to trade in Japan until 1854.
†In fact, *Mare Liberum* was originally published as part of a larger work, *De Jure Praedae* or *The Law of Prey,* on taking prizes at sea.

cluded, and rule over the seas that touch Great Britain is part and parcel of "the Dominion of the Island."

It was an important moment, even though James never published *The Closed Sea* and the Dutch continued to venture into waters the English claimed as their own. Yet for the first time, England's destiny as a maritime nation was stated as a matter of law, an inviolable principle linked directly to royal prerogative. Possessing the seas became one of the most conspicuous, and according to Selden most venerable, symbols of British monarchical rule—and of Great Britain as a community.

None of this, of course, hindered the course of Holland's seaborne empire, which continued to expand at English expense. Languishing in his cell in the Tower of London, Walter Raleigh could write, "Whosoever commands the sea, commands the trade; whosoever commands the trade of the world, commands the riches of the world, and consequently the world itself," but no one in the government listened. Even when the Dutch East India Company captured, tortured, and executed a score of English merchants in 1623, driving the English out of the Moluccas, James I refused to allow the national uproar to disturb his policy of peace and accommodation.

Yet had he known it, he had inherited from his predecessor a naval strategy that would eventually make England the dominant player in the Atlantic-based world system: the colonization of America.

• • •

When Francis Drake sailed away from the smoldering ruins of Saint Augustine in Florida in June 1586, he made one more stop before heading home. It was Croatan Island in the outer banks of what is today North Carolina, where English settlers from the tiny colony of Roanoke had set a signal fire. They were happy to see Drake. After enduring a year in America, they were ready to leave. Hungry, sick, and exhausted, they convinced Drake that instead of just dropping off supplies, he should take them all back to England. As they sailed away, their handful of pitiful abandoned huts was all that remained of the misbegotten scheme of that other Devonshire adventurer, Walter Raleigh, to found the first permanent colony in America.

Later, a variety of motives would inspire English colonies in America: trade, fishing, escaping religious persecution, the desire to start life over as part of a new society, in "New England." But the original impetus was naval and strategic. From the start, Raleigh sold Queen Elizabeth on the idea of a North American settlement as a base for her war against Spain in the Carribean, and attacks on the Spanish treasure fleet.

In 1584 Raleigh inherited the letters patent the queen had given his half brother Humphrey Gilbert, to plant a settlement in America anywhere on the coast north of Florida. Gilbert had had grandiose plans which, like so much in his life, were never realized. He had envisaged confiscating land from the native Americans, just as he had taken it from the native Irish, and giving it to English settlers in exchange for military service. An ideal society would arise, of sturdy yeomen, obedient servants, leisured aristocrats, and brilliant scholars like his brother Adrian and his friend John Dee. It was all drawn from Gilbert's reading of Thomas More's *Utopia,* and Gilbert intended to preside over this real-life utopia as its philosopher-ruler. He even had a copy of *Utopia* with him when he set sail in June 1583 to explore the coast of Newfoundland and Labrador in his small pinnace the *Squirrel* and two other ships, and was reading it on the way home when a set of storms off the Azores struck his tiny fleet. The last words anyone heard him utter—"We are as near heaven by sea as by land"—were read aloud from *Utopia* to his crew, even as their ship foundered and sank: "Devoured and swallowed up of the Sea," as an eyewitness said, just like his plans for a perfect America.

When he learned of his half brother's death, Walter Raleigh wasted no time in grief. He won the inheritance of Gilbert's letters patent and set to work fitting the American project to his own character and ambition.

We are still stuck with the image of Sir Walter Raleigh crafted after his death, as the gallant knight spreading his cloak at Queen Elizabeth's feet and introducing tobacco to England from the New World (in fact, it was either Drake or Hawkins). The real Raleigh was a typical West Country adventurer, a predator on the herd. Thanks to his aunt Kat Ashley, however, he had grown up at court, which gave him a veneer of sophistication and culture a Drake or Grenville never had. A poet as well as a soldier, classically tall, dark, and handsome, his good looks and charm had won him the favor of Queen Elizabeth, who promoted him to Lord Lieutenant of Cornwall, Vice Admiral of Devon, and captain of her bodyguard. However, his contemporaries noted only two things about him: his complete lack of integrity or scruples and his abiding hatred of Spain. The first earned him the nickname "Walter Raw Lie"; the second sent him to sea as a privateer and then as the architect of an English empire in America.

Raleigh set up his headquarters at Durham House in London, sur-rounding himself with books, maps, and a team of experts. One was Richard Hariot, navigator and friend to John Dee, who would join the first group of Roanoke colonists in 1584. Another was the younger Hakluyt, whose *Discourse on a Western Planting* couched Raleigh's colonial venture in familiar terms of expanding agriculture and trade, spreading the Protestant faith, and the Englishman's civilizing mission, of which "nothing [is] more glorious or honorable."

But Hakluyt also stressed the need to break the back of Spain's empire. Once a secure base had been established in America, Hakluyt assured prospective investors, English ships would venture out to raid King Philip's fishing fleets in the Atlantic to the north and his treasure ships in the Caribbean to the south. Spain's empire would collapse; Raleigh and his investors would become rich and the queen would reign supreme in the New World. With these goals in mind, Raleigh fixed the site of his colony far south of Newfoundland along the coast of North Carolina, within striking distance of the Caribbean, and named it Vir-ginia, after Elizabeth the Virgin Queen (that gesture earned him his knighthood).

Raleigh saw Roanoke as a base not just for the Royal Navy but for his own pirating activities. Piracy was in Raleigh's blood. His father had been in and out of Admiralty courts on charges of piracy; in his part of the world, robbing other ships was a natural part of going to sea. Over his life, it became Raleigh's primary source of income, and years later he would reminisce fondly of those "journeys of pickery . . . to run from cape to cape, for the pillage of ordinary prizes." Born in the spirit of piracy, his colony at Roanoke would ultimately be destroyed by it.

His cousin Richard Grenville took a Royal Navy ship to escort the first boatloads of settlers there in 1585. He stopped on the way at Puerto Rico to plunder a pair of Spanish vessels—Raleigh expected such raids to pay for the costs of the colony—and grabbed another on the way back to Plymouth. However, Grenville had run his first ship onto a sandbar on the Carolina coast, sinking it and most of the settlers' supplies for the winter. Facing starvation, the settlers begged Raleigh to send Grenville back with fresh supplies. He never arrived—almost certainly because he was too busy chasing Spanish prizes. When Drake unexpectedly showed up, belatedly offering supplies at Raleigh's request, those still alive at Roanoke, chose to go home instead. Three days after they left with

Drake, Grenville showed up at last to find an empty beach and a deserted village. Grenville consoled himself for his tardiness by taking some more prizes and burning towns in the Azores before returning home.

Raleigh used Thomas Hariot's highly varnished account of the Roanoke settlement, *A Brief and True Report of the New Found Land of Virginia,* to drown out the critics and raise money for a second try. This time the colony was not supposed to be at Roanoke but on Chesapeake Bay, where a deepwater port could be established for English shipping. However, by a navigational error (proving once again the perils of longitude) the second expedition found itself back at Roanoke. Impatient to get on with his "pickery," Raleigh's captain refused to carry them farther north. He dumped the colonists there and sailed off in search of prizes.

At tremendous hardship, the colonists managed to hold on. Virginia Dare, descended from a Plymouth family, was the first English child born in America. Roanoke's governor John White returned to England to try to raise more help. Two pinnaces set off in 1588 but never arrived—too busy plundering unarmed Spanish merchantmen. The armada prevented another relief expedition. When John White finally did return in 1590, as part of yet another privateering force, he discovered the settlers gone, with no trace of their fate except the word *Croatan* mysteriously carved on a tree.

Too little, too late. Raleigh shrugged and went back to piracy and another fruitless get-rich-quick scheme, a search for lost gold mines in Guyana. But the idea of a naval base in America did not die. It survived the queen's death in 1603 and James I's Spanish appeasement policy, which went so far as locking Raleigh in the Tower and condemning him to death on trumped-up charges of treason. But when Robert Cecil (who had been Raleigh's silent partner in several privateering raids) leaked to Parliament that the peace treaty with Spain signed in 1604 did not extend to the Americas, a new crop of investors and naval strategists quickly appeared.

On March 9, 1606, James I appointed a board of merchants and government officials to establish a royal colony in America. They included the treasurer of the navy, Sir Robert Mansell, and a future one, Sir Fulke Greville; John Hawkins's son Richard; parliamentarian Sir Edwin Sandys; Thomas Smith, London's leading overseas merchant and a key figure in Raleigh's original Virginia Company; and a wealthy landowner of Welsh descent from Huntingdonshire, whose namesake nephew would make the family famous: Sir Oliver Cromwell.

There was a clear naval and anti-Spanish bias to the group, and a clear sense of historic mission along the lines of Hakluyt and Foxe. Sir Edwin Sandys lamented that the Protestant peoples of northern Europe, "for all their multitude and strength," never "had the honor of being founders or possessors of any Great Empire." Now they would, he believed, in America. Two companies were set up, one made up of Plymouth investors and the other of London merchants. The London Company managed to get its settlers across the Atlantic first, landing in 1607 just south of Raleigh's original destination of Chesapeake Bay, at a settlement they named Jamestown after their new king.

Within a year three-quarters of its settlers were dead. But unlike Roanoke, the Jamestown colony survived. This was due in large part to the extraordinary character of its military governor, Captain John Smith. Smith had long experience as a soldier on land, but he had also been a privateer in the Mediterranean and fought the Spanish at sea. He was a skilled sailor and navigator who charted the waters around Chesapeake Bay and in 1627 published a book, *A Sea Grammar,* which gave an entire generation of English seagoing soldiers a basic knowledge of ships, sails, navigation, and naval discipline. It was that same discipline that Smith introduced to the Jamestown colony. Applying the principle of "the gentleman must haul with the mariner, and the mariner with the gentleman," Smith forced all the settlers to work and share the burden of defending the homes and fields. Smith saved Jamestown, and with it the English presence in America.

Another discipline then intervened, the religious kind. By 1609 the London Company learned to appeal to a very different kind of settler, evangelical patriotic Protestants whom contemporaries called Puritans. "The eyes of all Europe," one of their circulars proclaimed, "are looking upon our endeavours to spread the Gospel among the Heathen people of Virginia [and] to plant an English nation there." The same appeal worked for its western twin, the Plymouth Company, who recruited a band of sturdy religious dissidents, the Pilgrims, to act as guinea pigs in establishing another Virginia colony. They set off in 1620 and once again fell prey to a trick of navigation, and landed far north instead, in the bay the natives called Massachusetts. There the Pilgrims found the most famous of all the English North American settlements, which they named after their home port: Plymouth.

Puritanism combined a strict religiosity with a keen sense of English chosenness. It proved indispensable in bearing up under the hardships and rigors of creating a settlement where there were only trees and a strip of beach or shore. By the 1620s the success of Jamestown and Plymouth inspired another group of West Country Puritans to launch a third settlement in New England, which became Massachusetts Bay Colony. They would name their capital Boston, the original home of John Foxe.

At the same time, the Virginia colony was sprouting seaborne off-shoots. Bermuda was the first, when the lead ship of the 1609 expedition for Jamestown, the *Sea Adventure*, was driven by a storm on the shore. Its West Country commander, Sir George Somers, pulled together the one hundred and fifty survivors, built a camp and organized a community, which after ten months built its own pinnace and set out for Virginia (their story would inspire William Shakespeare's play *The Tempest*). Later, they returned to Bermuda to create a tobacco-growing colony, which by 1615 had more than six hundred settlers, while Virginia shifted to the same crop. Other settlers pushed farther south into the Caribbean, to St. Christopher, or St. Kitts, in 1624, Barbados in 1627, and Nevis in 1628.

The lands "beyond the line" were suddenly filling up with English-speaking colonists. When Hawkins first arrived in the Caribbean in 1564, there were probably less than 70,000 Spanish inhabitants in the entire New World. Between 1620 and 1642 close to 60,000 Englishmen, almost 1.5 percent of the nation's population, left Britain for North America. Virginia and the colonies in the West Indies drew the majority, including thousands of Irish, who came willingly or unwillingly to be servants for the English planters (by 1650 they outnumbered the English). Boston alone enjoyed a population of more than eight thousand, with thousands more on the way.

The old idea of establishing a permanent naval base had been forgotten. But many who came still dreamed of rich Spanish prizes. Sir Ferdinando Gorges was a Raleigh cousin and well schooled in the art of piracy. He also enabled the Pilgrims to get their official land grant for their settlement in Massachusetts. Christopher Newport had lost his right arm in a battle with a treasure galleon, and sacked towns and took prizes all across the Caribbean. But he was also the man who led the original Virginia expedition in 1607, and his timely arrival with supplies saved the colony from disaster more than once (the town of Newport News is named after him).

Yet many more were coming to America for more urgent, and disturbing, reasons. They came not to become rich but to escape a growing political and religious crisis at home. England was about to undergo an upheaval like no other in its history, which the Royal Navy had helped to set in motion and which would propel the navy itself into the modern age.

CHAPTER EIGHT

Rock the Nations

The Lord hath done such things amongst us as have not been known in
this world in a thousand years.
—OLIVER CROMWELL, 1654

ON NOVEMBER 19, 1630, a group of noblemen, landed gentlemen, and London businessmen gathered at Brooke House in Holborne. At their head was Robert Rich, Earl of Warwick, whose Puritan convictions had diverted his attention away from the rewards of the Stuart court toward those offered by the sea. He was active with the East India Company; he was on the board of the colonies in Virginia and Bermuda; and helped the Pilgrims emigrate to America. He also commanded a fleet of privateering vessels he inherited from his father.

Beside him sat Lord Brooke, whose stepfather Fulke Greville had been navy treasurer; Viscount Say and Seele, another Puritan nobleman; Gray's Inn lawyer Oliver St. John; and a Cornish landlord and member of Parliament named John Pym. They and fourteen other investors were about to create a new joint stock corporation to colonize two tiny islands off the coast of Nicaragua, Henrietta (named after Charles I's queen) and Providence.

More than thirty English overseas trading companies were set up between 1575 and 1630. What made the Providence Island Company different was not its social mix, since England's nobility and gentry had long found common cause with its merchant class in seaborne enterprise. Nor its geographic mix: the fact that many board members came from East Anglia and the East Midlands simply reflected that region's growing importance in English maritime trade, second only to London. Nor was it even its Puritan religious connections, which spanned both sides of the ocean. Indeed, one of Warwick's friends and neighbors was John Winthrop, founder of the Puritan commonwealth in Massachusetts, while Lord Brooke's wife's niece would marry the founder of the one in Connecticut, Roger Williams.

What made the Providence Island Company unusual was that it was set up to pursue privateering as well as trade. Henrietta and Providence were to serve as bases for plundering Spanish shipping. Stressing "the extraordinary importance of the place" for making England "a great power in the West Indian Sea," the investors in the Providence Company would carry the tradition of Drake and Hawkins directly into the new century—and use it to topple the English monarchy.

In 1641, Spanish warships would finally overrun the colony, and the sailors, pirates, and ships it sheltered dispersed to other parts of the Caribbean. But the Providence Company's directors would become the core of the parliamentary opposition to the Stuart throne, and lead their country into civil war in a little more than a year. Fully two-thirds of the Providence Company's directors would sit in the parliament that would declare war against Charles I in 1642. Oliver St. John would be John Hampden's lawyer in the celebrated Ship Money case; John Pym would become "King Pym," leader of the House of Commons during the civil war; the Earl of Warwick would serve as Parliament's Lord Admiral. And St. John's cousin, Oliver Cromwell, who had contemplated emigrating to New England in the 1630s, would eventually become the new English Commonwealth's Lord Protector.

These men would also be the architects of a new English navy, one suited to England's emerging role as a player in the high-stakes game of international trade and seaborne empire. What drove them initially was a hatred of Spain and international Catholicism inherited from their English Protestant forebears, and a belief that it was England and no one else whom God had decreed to inherit Spain's empire—and the profits thereof. But they also brought a new spirit of nationalism, discipline, and energy to the English scene, and to a navy badly in need of both. In fact, it was precisely the navy's problems that brought the Stuart monarchy to the point of crisis, and would lead directly to its downfall.

• • •

"War with Spain is England's best prosperity," declared Sir Edward Coke, England's leading judge and legal mind, to the assembled members of the House of Commons in 1624. Benjamin Rudyerd, member for Plymouth and a director of the Providence Company, agreed. He pointed out that Spain's American silver was fueling the resurgence of Catholic Habsburg power on the Continent, as Europe was embroiled in the Thirty Years' War. The way to foil the King of Spain's ambitions was "to cut him up at root," Rudyerd exclaimed, "and seek to impeach, or supplant him in the West Indies." Queen Elizabeth and her sailors had almost done it through raids and privateering. A new generation must do it through war, "which is the manlier and more English way." Sir John Elliott, member for Devon and its vice admiral, also weighed in: "Spain is rich. Let her be our Indies, our storehouse of treasure."

Until now, Elizabeth's successor remained deaf to this constant clamor for war. James I's closest friend was Spain's ambassador, Count Gondomar, who for nearly two decades enjoyed virtual veto power over English foreign policy. Gondomar had goaded James into arresting and then executing Sir Walter Raleigh for treason, and convinced him to offer Prince Charles as a suitor for the hand of the Spanish infanta (although the marriage never took place). He even persuaded the king to do nothing when Spanish forces invaded the German Palatinate in 1618 and drove James's own son-in-law into exile; and then when the English Parliament protested, to have it dissolved. By 1624, however, Parliament had had enough. They wanted war, and nothing but war. "Spain must be the enemy," said Sir Robert Phelips, and he and his allies intended to force the issue.

Yet James had good reasons for avoiding the religious conflicts raging on the Continent. His reign had seen a massive expansion in England's overseas trade and shipping—largely because it remained neutral while the Spanish, Dutch, Swedes,* French, and Germans were at each other's throats. When he came to the throne in 1603, the annual tonnage of English shipping was 60,000 tons; by 1629, it was more than 115,000 tons. Even with the constant plague of foreign piracy, business had never been better. North American colonies had taken root, if not blossomed. London had become an international emporium handling tobacco, sugar, and indigo from America and spices and cloth from Asia. English merchants were discovering that peaceful commerce was preferable to high seas "pickery."

James could also point out that war had become a vastly more expensive enterprise, including war at sea. Warships were getting larger and their armaments more extensive and sophisticated, just as land armies were. The race-built galleon was no longer enough. The Danes had introduced a warship, the *Tre Kroner,* with two full gun decks instead of the *Ark Royal*'s or *Dreadnought*'s one. It had been designed by a Scottish shipbuilder

---

*King Gustavus Adolphus would enter the Thirty Years' War in 1630.

who had studied with English shipwrights and now surpassed them. The Royal Navy responded with a similar two-decker with additional guns on the upper deck, the *Royal Prince*. It was one of the few ships built during James's reign, but which carried fifty guns and displaced 1,900 tons—almost four times the size of Lord Admiral Howard's *Ark Royal*. The French in turn launched the *St. Louis,* a 1,400-ton monster with sixty guns; the Swedes the *Vasa,* with sixty-four. Spanish shipyards were busy turning out their versions of what they called *galeones gruesos,* or "grand galleons," as were the Dutch. In 1637 England would top them all with the *Sovereign of the Seas,* the ancestor of Nelson's *Victory,* displacing 2,700 tons and with no fewer than one hundred guns on three separate decks.

All these formidable fighting machines required money: money to build, money to man, money to supply and keep in fighting shape. Far more, certainly, than anyone in England was willing to pay, even as large standing armies in the field and fighting navies at sea strained the resources of its neighbors, including Holland, to the breaking point.

One that did break was Spain. Sir John Eliot had called Spain rich. In fact, under Philip II's successors it was well on the way to becoming poor, and the most important reason was its huge military commitments, above all its land forces. The army devoured Spain's dwindling supply of bullion, it drove the government to mortgage its tax receipts three to four years out, sent Spain's economy into freefall and the government spinning into bankruptcy every twenty years: in 1607, in 1627, in 1647. Its merchants had been chased from the oceans; its silver fleet became increasingly easy prey for privateers; its navy would be decisively beaten in 1639, and its once invincible army four years later. When the Spanish Crown tried to revamp and restructure its military obligations, the result was armed revolt, first in Catalonia, and then in Portugal, which finally regained its independence in 1664. The crushing cost of war turned the world's lone superpower into the "sick man of Europe" before the century was out.

Spain's fate was a useful cautionary tale about the dangers of an aggressive war policy. The opposition in Parliament, however, ignored it. On the contrary, they argued that a naval war could pay for itself through privateering, as it had in Elizabeth's day (which was largely a myth). They worshiped at the shrine of Sir Walter Raleigh, who became a virtual Protestant martyr after his execution in 1618 and who had argued, "We must not look to maintain war upon the revenues of England" but rather upon high seas piracy. Their other hero became Francis Drake, whose son John published a glowing biography of his father, entitled *Francis Drake*

Revived, which dwelt on his lucrative treasure raids in the West Indies and berated the Englishmen of his own generation for their effeminacy in not following his father's lead.

Members of the House of Commons heatedly debated whether England should send an army into Germany to fight the Habsburg menace, or join hands with the Dutch to shut down the Channel to Spanish troop ships and army pay ships. In either case, they asserted, there was no need to increase England's defense budget or provide additional "supply" through taxes. The Crown's obligation was to take up the Protestant cause, not ask for the funds with which to do it.

The result was a permanent political impasse, and a growing crisis. Parliament wanted a naval war with Spain, but did not want to pay for it. If James did not pursue war, he was attacked as being "soft" on Spain and international Catholicism. If he hinted he was willing to fight, as he did in 1624, and demanded money with no strings attached as a matter of royal prerogative, Parliament invariably refused, believing (rightly) that he was not serious and would only use the money to enrich and reward his followers, and (wrongly) that war should pay for itself.

It was James's court favorite, George Villiers, Duke of Buckingham, who tried to use the Royal Navy to break that impasse—although in the end it would destroy him and James's successor, Charles I. Villiers was the handsome "royal pet" for both father and son; like Elizabeth's Raleigh, he combined devastating good looks with a shrewd intelligence and ruthless ambition. The infatuated James I promoted him to earl, then Duke of Buckingham, and then to a seat on the Privy Council.

But Buckingham's real ascent to power began when he set his sights on becoming Lord Admiral. It was at his instigation that the 1618 naval board of inquiry was launched, which pushed the Earl of Nottingham out and brought Buckingham in. It was not all for show. The board did suggest some real reforms, and as Lord High Admiral, Buckingham tried to carry some of them out. But he also saw that the only way the Royal Navy could get the funds it desperately needed was to go to war, and that by overturning James's policy of peace with Spain he could break the logjam between Crown and Parliament—and make himself the most important power broker in England.

He got his chance when James I died in 1625. As Prince of Wales, Charles I had relied on Buckingham as his closest friend, and obediently followed his advice to turn the Puritan anti-Spanish sentiment in the country to his benefit. Together they asked Parliament for money for a naval expedition against Spain along the lines of Drake and Raleigh. Still distrustful, Parliament voted only 140,000 pounds before hastily adjourning as the plague broke out in London.

It was not nearly enough. The years of neglect and mismanagement of the navy now demanded a reckoning—and no one paid for it more than the common English seaman.

• • •

He was probably around 40,000 strong in 1625. On shipboard he and his mates were divided into two shifts or watches, the starboard watch, named after the right or "steerboard" side of the ship, where in medieval times the steering oar had lain, and the *larboard* watch, named after the left or "ladboard" side, where goods were loaded while in port (the word would eventually replace "landboard"). He worked on deck three shifts a day of four hours each,* under the command of the captain, the lieutenant, both of whom held royal commissions, and the ship's master in charge of sailing and navigation. He also answered to the warrant officers, sailors authorized by Admiralty warrant to supervise the rest of the crew: the bosun in charge of sails and rigging; the master gunner, who aimed and fired the ship's cannon; the quartermaster, in charge of keeping the guns supplied and armed; the purser, in charge of ship's victuals; and the trumpeter, whose clarion notes blared from the poop deck gave the important signals in battle and to other ships.

Naval commanders had paid little attention to their ordinary crewmen (John Hawkins was an exception), partly because they were of such low social station, "this intolerable scum of rascals, whom the land hath ejected for their wicked lives and ungodly behavior," partly because they were overwhelmingly part-timers, and partly because officers knew how few would be left alive at the end of the voyage.

Indeed, in 1625 there was no such thing as a Royal Navy seaman (or indeed a Royal Navy officer). In 1625, and right up until the nineteenth century, the Royal Navy was about *ships,* not men. The Navy Board built and outfitted them, and kept them supplied when they were in port; the Admiralty commissioned their captains and officers, who in turn had to find the crews to man them. Sailors were sailors, as far as the authorities

---

*Except the two so-called dog watches of two hours each, at four o'clock to six in the evening, and six to eight o'clock, which prevented the same men from keeping the same watch every day.

and most captains were concerned, and very few cared where a seaman came from or where he went once his temporary service on a royal ship was done. After all, the navy was still part-time: its ships were kept empty and in storage at Chatham unless they were needed, while the fact that so many merchant ships had to be well armed meant that most sailors had some experience of handling a ship during a seafight.

The growth of trade and shipping during James's reign kept England's employed and busy, but it also stretched the manpower very thin—too thin for the navy to keep up. So to man its vessels, it came increasingly to rely on impressing or drafting sailors on shore or from merchant ships, often by force. The brutal navy press gang would become notorious in the age of Nelson and Captain Bligh. But Tudor and Stuart captains relied on it far more, and the resentment it aroused was much stronger, since most sailors knew serving on a king's ship was a virtual death sentence.

"We are used like dogs," a group of navy sailors once complained to Sir Ferdinando Gorges, "we had as lief be hanged as dealt with as we are." One reason was pay. In 1585 John Hawkins had raised it to ten shillings a month (it had been five under Henry VIII), and there it stayed for forty years, even as prices and the cost of living rose, including the competing pay from merchant service. The Duke of Buckingham ordered it raised to fourteen shillings in 1625, and fifteen the next year. But since the Stuart navy was chronically short of funds, common sailors were the last to be paid, if at all. In August 1626 a mob of unpaid sailors stormed the Duke of Buckingham's carriage and refused to let him go until he promised to give them their backpay. In October another group attacked his carriage again while he was in the Privy Council and smashed it to pieces. Crews often would strike or take down the ship's sails so that it could not leave port until they were paid—so that even today, any kind of organized work stoppage is known as a "strike."

Of course, collecting their pay also required surviving the voyage. Seafaring was a young man's job and already dangerous enough. Few sailors were over forty, and almost none lived past fifty. But the prospects on a king's ship were even worse. Captains could count on perhaps a third of their crews dying on a voyage, even without a shot being fired.

One reason was scurvy, the result of a diet without adequate sources of vitamin C. The food on ship was pretty much the same as it would be a century later: salt fish with biscuit, oil, and mustard on Wednesdays and Fridays (or fish days); salt beef or pork, dried peas and beans, and beer the rest of the week—all foods that could be preserved for long periods of time. The preparation of food was rarely hygienic and the navy's corrupt victualing system meant that the food was usually short or going bad. The ship's own victualer or purser often cheated his men unmercifully. But even when food was plentiful, the lack of fresh fruit and vegetables with vitamin C meant outbreaks of scurvy, which in a month or two could decimate a crew and leave a ship incapacitated. One historian has estimated that as many as one-half of all shipwrecks in the Atlantic and Pacific may have been caused by crews too weak from scurvy to manage their ships.

Even worse, however, was typhus. Crowded unsanitary conditions, with soldiers, sailors, and gunners all jammed together below decks* made warships floating incubators of the disease. It was probably typhus that devastated Drake's expeditionary force to Lisbon in 1589, and it was typhus now that overwhelmed Buckingham's ill-fated attack on Cádiz in 1625.

The fleet already had enough problems. There were not enough experienced naval officers—the admiral in charge, Viscount Wimbledon, had never been to sea before—and not enough ships: out of one hundred vessels, only thirteen belonged to the navy, and twenty had to be borrowed from the Dutch. As the ships gathered in Plymouth harbor, the best sailors simply slipped over the side and ran away. The supply system broke down; like the Spanish Armada thirty-seven years earlier, some ships had consumed all their food and water even before the fleet finally sailed on October 8. Viscount Wimbledon (whom the sailors dubbed Viscount Sitstill) had to be goaded into issuing sailing orders, and the choice of Cádiz as their destination was made at the last minute.

The result when they arrived was entirely predictable. Wimbledon decided to split his fleet into three: while his second in command or vice admiral took charge of the leading ships, he as admiral commanded the middle squadron, and a rear admiral brought up the hindmost. It was the chain of command every fleet after him would follow. But in the event the merchantmen in his squadrons refused to fight. Even the king's ships took no action; after a couple of days some ragged and ill-fed soldiers did manage to land but got so drunk on casks of captured wine that all discipline broke down. Giving up, the fleet reembarked only to encounter severe storms, even as typhus was spreading through the ships. By the

*Although sailors were now sleeping off the floor in rope hammocks, an invention from the West Indies introduced in Drake's time.

time they limped into Kinsale harbor in Ireland, Wimbledon's flagship was leaking so badly that mariners below decks were working knee-deep in water, and only thirty men were well enough to work the sails.

It was probably the lowest point in the history of the Royal Navy. The fiasco had cost more than half a million pounds, twelve times the annual naval budget, and left Buckingham's reputation in shreds. When Parliament met again in 1626, Sir John Eliot rose to his feet. Eliot had been Buckingham's protégé; he owed him his office as vice admiral. But the Cádiz disaster changed him from friend to foe. He had seen the fleet sail, and watched it return to Plymouth a shambles, with sick and dying sailors lying helpless in the streets.

Now he spoke angrily to the assembled members: "Our honor is ruined, our ships are sunk, our men perished, not by the sword, not by an enemy, not by chance but . . . by those we trust." The time had come to force Buckingham from office, he said, and for Parliament to take command of the navy's finances and those of the government itself. The years of struggling to force the Crown to face up to its responsibilities had to come to end: "Without some reformation in these things," Eliot concluded, Parliament should not give Charles a single penny.

Together with his fellow West Country member, John Pym, Eliot began drafting a bill of impeachment against Buckingham. King Charles refused to consider removing his friend and scolded the members: "Remember that Parliaments are altogether in my power for calling, sitting, and dissolution." When the House of Commons called on the House of Lords to remove Buckingham, Charles exercised that power on June 15 by ordering Parliament to dissolve.

But the battle lines had been drawn. The controversy had turned Buckingham into a symbol of the corruption and venality not only of the navy but of the Stuart court. Buckingham got his revenge by forcing Eliot out of his post as vice admiral on corruption charges (brought by none other than the vice admiral of Cornwall, James "Bottomless" Bagg). But meanwhile, "the ships are unprovided," Buckingham's treasurer told him, "and the whole service [is] at stand." The king tried to get a forced loan from various English counties and communities, and threw into prison sheriffs and landowners who refused to collect it. One of them was Eliot.

Desperate to ingratiate himself with Parliament's anti-Catholic majority, Buckingham ordered the fleet back to sea to protect the French Protestant fortress of La Rochelle, which was under siege by the French king Louis XIII. Yet another expedition without funds or proper supplies; yet another expensive failure. A navy officer tried to report the pathetic scene in the streets of Plymouth afterward, as discharged sailors lay sick and dying in droves. "I vow to God I cannot deliver it in words," he wrote to Buckingham, "unless my Lord take it speedily into consideration, the king will have more ships than men." Faced by mutiny, parliamentary attacks, new depredations by pirates in the Channel, and whispers that he was a crypto-Catholic and in the pay of the French, Buckingham rushed down to Portsmouth to assemble a new expedition himself. When a disgruntled army officer stabbed him to death there in August 1628, the former glamour boy of Stuart politics had become the most hated man in England.

However, Buckingham's death could not save Charles from his next humiliation. Parliament had already reassembled in a foul mood, and once again said it would not give the king money until its demands were met. Eliot, Pym, Sir Edward Coke, and a young Huntingdonshire squire named Oliver Cromwell wanted a bill that confirmed the rights of all Englishmen against the kind of illegal imprisonment used in the forced loan case and against seizure of property—the first bill of rights in English history since Magna Carta. John Eliot had turned what was a dispute over funding the navy into a general struggle for the liberty of the nation and Parliament—"that which is more than our lives," he said, "[more] than all our goods, all our interests and faculties." The bill did not pass, but a Petition of Right did in June, which the king again refused to sign.

Charles still needed money so Parliament continued to sit until February the next year. Then, in a furious and hysterical session, the House of Commons passed a resolution against unlawful taxation and pro-Catholic trends in the Church of England while two members held the house speaker in his seat by force, so that he could not close debate. Equally furious, King Charles vowed he would never call another Parliament again. John Eliot was thrown into the Tower, where he died in 1633—a martyr to the Protestant cause and to the defense of the rule of law and English liberty.

But the money problem remained, especially for the navy. So in 1633 Charles and his councillors came up with the idea of ship money. At a single stroke, it would both save the Royal Navy and doom the Stuart monarchy.

The idea of creating a national tax to support the navy was not entirely new. By law, "ship money" was a traditional tax on coastal towns and counties like Plymouth and Cornwall, and used to pay for the royal ships that defended them in time of war. Medieval and Tudor monarchs had collected it regularly. But one of Queen Elizabeth's last acts was a plan to organize a separate naval squadron for escorting unarmed merchant ships, to be paid for by voluntary contributions from across the nation. She died before it could be implemented, but the government revived the idea in 1618 and again in 1628—before dropping it in fear that Parliament would protest.

But in 1633 there was no longer any Parliament, and so Charles felt free to impose his demand for money for his navy not just on coastal communities but on inland counties as well. His lawyers argued that it was a natural extension of his sovereign powers as "lord of the sea"; they even published John Selden's 1618 tract on *The Closed Sea* to back up their arguments—ironically so, since Selden was now one of Charles's most tireless opponents.

The result was a national uproar. But the effect on the Royal Navy was instantaneous. The first levy in 1634 netted almost 80,000 pounds (London and some other port cities were allowed to contribute ships instead of cash). Buckingham had dreamed hopelessly of one day having a navy of seventy large ships—ten more than John Dee had deemed necessary to rule the waves—and thirty fast pinnaces. Now Charles had the resources to make the dream come true. Ship money made it possible to build new ships like the superheavy *Sovereign of the Seas*. In the summer of 1635 the tax paid for a squadron of twenty-four ships to set out on a cruise of English waters to face down pirates and offer protection to the fishing fleets. None of the ships was fast enough to catch any of the sleek Algerian corsairs, but a system of regular patrols around the British Isles was under way: the first full-time employment for the Royal Navy.

As the money increased, so did morale. Sailors still struggled to get their pay, but their discomfort was eased somewhat by the permanent presence of shipboard surgeons and chaplains (first introduced by Buckingham in 1627). New full-time duties demanded experienced officers rather than just gentlemen adventurers or independent entrepreneurs (the only way England was able to fight its war with Spain after the Cádiz fiasco was with the Earl of Warwick's private fleet). Ship money created a new class of professional naval officers, men with obscure backgrounds who rose from being a ship's master or even lower rank. Hence their nickname, "tarpaulin" officers, after the oilcloth foul-weather gear sailors wore on deck.

Captain William Rainsborough was one. Born in Whitechapel in London, he served for years as a sailing master in the Levant trade before becoming Lord Admiral Northumberland's flag captain. In 1637 Rainsborough and three other "tarpaulins" took their ships into the pirates' nest at Salee in North Africa. They managed to blockade the port for more than five months, seize its fortress and ships, and free more than three hundred English captives. It was the only successful raid against the Barbary pirates the Stuarts ever made and proof of what even a small force led by skilled and disciplined officers could do.

However, the success at Sallee was overshadowed by the growing national protest over the ship money levies. The Earl of Warwick warned the king he would not raise a finger to make his tenants pay a tax he and thousands of others considered illegal. Oliver Cromwell's cousin, John Hampden, decided to make a test case of it in the Exchequer Court, hiring as his lawyer another Cromwell cousin and fellow investor in the Providence Island Company, Oliver St. John. In *Rex v. Hampden* St. John argued that imposing a tax without consent constituted an illegal seizure of property and contrary to English law. The king's attorney general argued that a national tax for a national navy protected private property, instead of injuring it, and was part of the king's prerogative as sovereign of the seas.

By a narrow three-to-two vote, the court agreed with him. Writing for the majority, Justice Lord Coventry wrote:

> For safety's sake . . . the Wooden Walls are the best walls of the kingdom, and if the riches and wealth of the kingdom be respected for that cause, the Dominion of the Sea ought to be respected.

Wooden walls—yet that was precisely how the English political nation did *not* see the Ship Money fleet, especially after the disaster off the Downs two years later in October 1639.

The Downs were the sheltered waters inside the Goodwin Sands, between Sandwich and Walmer Castle, a favorite rendezvous point for Channel shipping. In October a Spanish fleet commanded by Don Antonio Oquendo dropped anchor there to escape the beating it had taken from a Dutch fleet for the past three days. Oquendo, whose father had commanded a division of the first great Spanish Armada, now led the last, a desperate attempt to reverse Spain's flagging fortunes in the war against the Dutch United Provinces. However, a Dutch fleet had caught up with it off Beachy Head and raked it over, using the technique the English had pioneered in 1588, the line ahead attack. It allowed the Dutch commander, Maarten van Tromp, to dominate the battle, even though the Spanish outnumbered him fifty ships to sixteen, or more than three to one. Seeking to escape the pounding, Oquendo took refuge in the Downs, where an English squadron under Sir John Pennington was already anchored.

Pennington sent notes to the flagships of both Oquendo and Tromp warning them to cease and desist their fight in neutral English waters. Tromp, a tough Dutch tarpaulin in his own right, grimly replied, "No one can command at sea farther than his guns can reach." He continued blockading the northern entrance to the Downs, as day by day more Dutch ships arrived for the final showdown. By the fifteenth Tromp had assembled more than one hundred ships and sixteen fireships, and launched his attack on the helpless Spanish fleet. Pennington fired a few token shots to protest the slaughter and then discreetly withdrew, as the Dutch ships knocked Oquendo's fleet to pieces. Oquendo's flagship alone took 1,700 cannon shots. The Spanish lost over forty ships and more than seven thousand men, while only one Dutch ship was sunk and casualties came to less than a hundred. Spain's reputation as an effective super-power was broken forever.

So was the reputation of the Ship Money fleet. The destruction of the last Spanish Armada caused celebration in Puritan circles, but the fact that it had taken place in formally neutral waters with a royal squadron, including the all-powerful *Sovereign of the Seas,* watching impotently nearby, was a blow to royal pride. Sixteen hundred and thirty-nine was a grim year for Charles I. He was facing a looming war with rebels in Scotland, growing discontent over his religious policies, and now a national protest against paying ship money for a fleet that seemed useless anyway. Almost one-third of the 1638 levy remained uncollected, while 1639 promised to be worse, even as the costs of preparing for war in Scotland skyrocketed. Charles was forced to swallow his pride and summoned another Parliament in December, the first in almost twelve years. But the clamor from Pym, Warwick, and the rest for radical reform of government and church was so intense he dissolved it again on May 5, 1640.

With the abrupt dismissal of the so-called Short Parliament, the king's situation was desperate. His ill-paid army had been routed in Scotland; another Ship Money fleet had cruised the Firth of Forth around Leith and Edinburgh with no effect. Yet the afternoon of the fifth the Spanish ambassador came with a miraculous offer. The disaster in the Downs led Spain to offer Charles I a secret subsidy of 4 million ducats if he would lend them the Ship Money fleet to escort their vessels through the English Channel.

Charles was jubilant. Here was the financial independence he had been looking for; a way to pay for his war and make himself master of the situation. Within twenty-four hours he had rounded up the ringleaders of the parliamentary opposition: Warwick, Pym, Hampden, Lords Brooke and Say and Sele, and Sir Walter Earle were thrown in prison— significantly, all except Earle were members of the board of the Providence Company. When the news spread, riots broke out in London, with dockworkers, apprentices, and mariners rallying to Warwick, their favorite captain. Nineteen-year-old seaman Thomas Bensted would be tried and executed for treason for his role in the riot.

Charles was eventually forced to release his prisoners, but the break between the Crown and the political nation was complete. Facing disaster in Scotland, the king was forced to summon yet another Parliament, which Pym would dominate. Parliament's first act was to outlaw ship money; two years later they and Charles were at war.

A conflict over the navy had propelled England into civil war. As it happened, the navy would also provide the key to victory—and its global aftermath.

. . .

When the civil war broke out in 1642, the Royal Navy split across the bow. Its tarpaulin captains and sailors, who were furious at years of royal neglect and lack of pay, became almost to a man supporters of Parliament; with a single exception, its well-born officers joined the royalist side.* But they could not command their ships and crews to go with them. Although royalist captains found privateering vessels to serve Charles I, except for a pro-royalist mutiny in the Downs in 1648, the bulk of the fleet was against him from the start.

This meant that as the war on land raged from 1642 to 1648, Parliament's navy was able to cut off royalist bases, support parliamentary siege operations like that of Plymouth in 1643, and prevent foreign monarchs from sending help and supplies to Charles's forces. Even more

---

*The exception was Sir George Ayscue, later to be one of the stars of the Restoration navy.

important, the navy kept London's international trade networks open, and its warehouses in Wapping and Limehouse full. That trade was crucial for Parliament's revenues and its credit with investors in the City of London: without it, the rebellion would have collapsed. More than anything else, this proved to be the navy's decisive role in the war. It enabled Parliament's forces to reorganize as the New Model Army under Oliver Cromwell, score a decisive victory at Naseby in 1645, and establish an English republic, the Commonwealth, after Charles I's trial and execution in 1649.

The war years also returned control of the navy to men experienced in handling money, warfare, and the sea. Power passed to tarpaulin officers like William Rainsborough and William Penn; Puritan merchants from London; members of the shipmasters' guild at Trinity House in Deptford; sea captains and former privateers from Providence Island and other outposts; and the parliamentary friends of the Earl of Warwick, who became Lord Admiral. These men were true believers in England's Protestant destiny, in its overseas trade and colonies, and in the righteousness of liberty and property—as well as balancing the books. Together they would solve the problems that had plagued the navy for more than four decades and retarded England's emergence as a maritime power.

The first was money. At the end of the first year's fighting in 1643, Parliament faced a fiscal crisis. John Pym decided something drastic had to be done, and proposed an excise or "value-added" tax on salt and meat, which would be paid directly to the navy. It was precisely the sort of regressive national tax Parliament had objected to with ship money, but this time it was Parliament itself which was proposing and consenting to it—a crucial difference. Although unpopular, the excise was a huge success. Before the war was over it was paying for the army as well; by 1649 it was drawing in more than 380,000 pounds a year, all of it to support England's military. The navy also got the lion's share of customs duties, which were collected and counted by the same parliamentary committee that oversaw the navy. Taken together, excise and customs enabled England to maintain the largest armed forces it had ever known—more than 100,000 men in arms—without having to resort to the sort of long-term borrowing that crippled its old enemy Spain, and later France. It constituted a fiscal revolution that would survive the Restoration, and gave the Royal Navy its first permanent financial base.

The second was ships. Warwick launched a navy building program that the Commonwealth expanded, as it discovered that armed merchantmen were no longer adequate for the complex and far-flung operations of

the republican navy: cruising the Channel, siege support and troop transport in the Irish Sea, eventually campaigns in North Africa and off the
coast of Portugal. By 1649 there were forty-five navy warships; in 1650
there were seventy-two. Buckingham's dream had finally come true, but
thanks to Parliament, not the Crown.

Just four years later under Oliver Cromwell, the navy numbered
more than one hundred and thirty-three ships, the largest full-time navy
in the world. It included not just large heavily armed ships like the 100-
gun *Sovereign,* the 1,200-ton *Naseby* with eighty guns, and the *Swiftsure* and
Dragon with sixty, but smaller faster vessels modeled on the new ship the
Spanish first introduced in their privateering havens at Dunkirk: the *fre-
gata* or frigate. Lightly armed but festooned with multiple sails, the frigate
was ideal for swift privateering—or defending against it.

Six new frigates came out of English shipyards in 1649, and another
ten in 1650. The navy could now deal with the privateer threat, whether
from royalist bases in Ireland, or from Dunkirk, or from North Africa.
Long-distance merchant ships for the Levant or East India companies
continued to travel armed, but the navy no longer needed them to make
up its numbers. The distinction between merchant and navy ships was
becoming permanent, as was the division of labor within the navy itself,
between larger "battle ships" for fleet-size actions and smaller frigates for
cruising and patrols.

All this construction and supplying took place with a new atmosphere of efficiency and (relative) incorruptibility. The old royalist Navy
Board gave way to naval commissioners appointed by Parliament itself,
with Pym's Puritan friend from Massachusetts Harry Vane as navy treasurer watching every penny. Ironically, Vane worked best with the former
Admiralty administrators of the Ship Money fleet. They found their skill
and experience complemented by Vane's drive and dedication, as he
never tired of reminding his subordinates that they were "not placed in
employment to serve themselves but to serve the public."

The third and final issue was men. Parliament raised the pay of seamen to nineteen shillings in 1643, and in 1653 to twenty-four for those it
deemed "able-bodied seamen," meaning "fit for helm, lead [measuring
water depth], top [handling sails in the fore- and maintops], or yards." It
also gave its seamen a direct interest in the taking of prizes, with each
sailor collecting ten shillings for every ton taken or sunk. In addition, the
navy's tarpaulin captains enjoyed a sense of democratic solidarity with
their men and crews that had not existed even in Elizabethan times.

Some, like Captain Christopher Myngs, had been ordinary seamen themselves and took a keen interest in making sure their men were well fed, well paid, and happy. One declared the beer his men had been given so foul he ordered it dumped overboard, to great cheers and applause. Another, Jonathan Taylor, used to bring fresh food himself to men who were sick; in the summer of 1653 George Monck paid out of his own pocket for lodging for wounded men on shore at Southwold.

The greatest naval commander of the age, Robert Blake, said of his sailors, "The meanest of them are free-born Englishmen as well as myself." The crews reciprocated their captains' devotion. Seamen often requested to serve with a favorite captain, just as captains asked that their officers switch with them when they changed commands. Common sailors stoutly defended their officers when they were criticized or slandered. Ninety-seven of them signed depositions in support of Captain John Pearce when he was dismissed for cowardice. Caught up by the egalitarian spirit of the new Commonwealth, some captains even addressed their men by their Christian names. Although food often remained bad and pay irregular, a habit of trust and solidarity grew between captain and crew, a sense of community on shipboard, which the Restoration navy and the return of gentlemen and courtiers to command was never able to erase.*

The result by 1653 was a new kind of navy, one ready to serve the agenda of England's new ruler, Lord Protector Oliver Cromwell. Although he never actually served at sea, Cromwell was the crucial link between the English navy's past and its future. Generalissimo of the New Model Army, he was a cousin of many of the Providence Company investors who had built the parliamentary and Commonwealth navy. Having united England, Scotland (defeated at Worcester in 1651), and Ireland (beaten into submission by 1652) into a single political entity, Cromwell also revived the Providence Company's vision of a great Protestant English empire in America. Cromwell proclaimed that his fellow Englishmen must "not let slip out of their hands the most noble opportunities of promoting the glory of God and enlarging the bounds of Christ's kingdom." Thanks to Parliament, he had by 1654 the means to do it, a navy with "160 sail of brave ships well appointed [to] swimming at sea." However, before Cromwell could implement his plan to drive the Spanish out of America, he first had to deal with Holland.

---

*In the entire Commonwealth period (1649 to 1660), only one sailor was hanged for a crime on shipboard.

He had no particular quarrel with the Dutch. At one point he even hoped for a political union between the two Protestant nations (that would have to wait until 1688 under William of Orange). But another crucial issue drove a wedge between them: trade. Parliament had passed two so-called Navigation Acts in 1650 and 1651, forbidding all foreign ships from trading with English colonies, and prohibiting the importing of goods from Asia, Africa, or America except on English ships with English crews. Both acts were pointed directly at the Dutch, who since their final peace with Spain in 1648 were rapidly reclaiming the markets they had lost. In the wake of defeating Charles I, Englishmen decided they were tired of being a second-rate economic power. The feelings in Whitehall and in the City were summed up by General Monck: "The Dutch have too much trade, and the English are resolved to take it from them."

The Navigation Acts created for the first time a seaborne English economy geared toward a single national interest, with Parliament and businessmen in London joining hands to promote profits and grow the system—the system later to be called mercantilism. John Selden's *Closed Sea* had found a new generation of readers in the English Commonwealth, who republicanized the arguments for the king as "lord of the seas" by bestowing that power on the English nation itself and its navy. In fact, the very first English translation of Selden's seminal work appeared in 1652, with a frontispiece showing the allegorical figure of Britannia wielding her scepter over her watery dominion—the first explicit reference to Britannia ruling the waves.

For that reason, Parliament required Dutch ships to lower their flag in the presence of English warships and to submit to a search for any royalist contraband. In May 1652, Admiral Tromp, the grizzled victor of the Battle of the Downs, was passing with his squadron through the Dover Straits when an English squadron under Robert Blake ordered him to dip his colors. Tromp refused, Blake opened fire, and the first Anglo-Dutch war was on.

Fortunately, England now had a navy ready for the task and a set of commanders to match. In 1648 Parliament had removed Warwick as Lord Admiral for suspected royalist sympathies* and installed in his

---

*Not as far-fetched as it seemed: his brother the Earl of Holland had been implicated in a royalist plot and executed.

place a trio of generals from the New Model Army whose loyalty and discipline were unquestioned. They were given the title of Generals at Sea, but they were hardly landlocked soldiers. One, Alexander Popham, had commanded privateers in the 1630s; the second, Richard Deane, was a former shipmaster; the third, Robert Blake, had sailed as a merchant trader. A fourth, George Monck, would rise to equal brilliance as a sea commander. But the one who stood above the rest, the one who used the first Dutch war to launch the English navy into the modern age, the one of whom Horatio Nelson said, "I do not reckon myself his equal," was Blake.

Like the sailors of the Elizabethan age, he came from the West Country, growing up in Bridgewater where his father had been a merchant and where the young Blake watched ships ply in and out of the Bristol Channel. Blake sat for Bridgewater in the Short Parliament, and joined the parliamentary army during the civil war. He was a Puritan and profoundly Protestant; whenever he could, he avoided fighting on the Sabbath. But by 1644 he had become one of the New Model Army's ablest officers, working with Warwick's naval squadron to lift the siege of Lyme Regis. Four years later he was a General at Sea and chasing royalist privateers. In 1650 he blockaded one of their principal nests, the city of Lisbon, for more than five months—a brilliant feat of logistics and planning and a foretaste of the kind of long-term operations the new English navy could carry out.

It was Blake who confronted Admiral Tromp over lowering his flag on May 12, 1652, and the General at Sea to whom Cromwell entrusted overall command of the war—the first ever fought completely at sea. Blake's encounter with Tromp in May, and later against another Dutch fleet off Kentish Knock in September, gave him keen insight into the new kind of naval tactic, the line ahead battle.

This was a major step forward from the pell-mell scramble of sea fighting in Elizabethan times. Even organizing ships and squadrons into a line ahead formation demanded careful preparation and discipline, to prevent faster-moving ships from overtaking slower ones, or ships drifting apart with every subtle shift of wind. But once that line reached the enemy, its steady volleys of flying shot, with one ship emptying its guns and then the next, could be overwhelming. Since the Spanish Armada, grappling and boarding ceased to play any significant part in battle plans. Victory now belonged the side with the most firepower, meaning the one with the most ships—one reason European navies would grow larger and larger—and the most guns.

Hence the appeal of the broadside. No one planned to make the guns facing out on either side of the hull the ship's main battery: Drake and Raleigh had carried their best guns pointing forward. But as ships like the *Prince Royal* grew in size and gun decks, there was no place to put the extra cannon except along the sides. The first recorded use of the broadside might be in 1625, when a Royal Navy ship and an East Indiaman commanded by Richard Swaley, ran into a Portuguese squadron and employed a broadside attack with devastating effect. At the Battle of the Downs, Admiral Tromp had demonstrated how effective it could be in a major engagement; since Swaley became a leading parliamentary admiral he probably passed the knowledge on to the new republican navy. By 1650 it was said no foreign vessel would face an English warship in equal combat, almost certainly because of the English broadside.

In addition, the new generation of English warships were well suited to the line ahead formation. They tended to be large and slow-moving, very different from the quick-maneuvering, race-built galleons of Hawkins and Drake's day. But a line ahead commander wanted ships that went "steady as she goes," and could throw quantities of shot with its fifty or sixty guns. And here the traditional English truck carriage proved a blessing. English gunsmiths were making their cannon shorter with wider muzzles for more punch, while the movable carriage allowed these to recoil, reload, and fire again with relative speed. Never again would gunners crawl out of their gun ports to swab down their charges. The standard English warship made a superb "ship of the line," once it was used in the right way.

The first real test came at Dungeness on November 30, when Blake and a mixed fleet of navy ships and merchantmen tried to intercept a large Dutch convoy led by Tromp himself. Outnumbered and outfought, Blake was furious that so many of his captains broke formation and turned and fled. Many were merchantmen who were afraid of losing or damaging their cargoes; but some were regular officers, who refused to give up their right to go into action as they, not their commander, saw fit, and their right to take prizes if they could get away with it. Blake railed to the navy commissioners about "the baseness of spirit, not among the merchantmen only, but many of the State's ships," and threatened to resign unless they did something drastic.

The commissioners did. They fired six navy captains, including Blake's own brother. They ordered that henceforth every merchant ship pressed into navy duty had to have a captain appointed by the navy, not the ship's owners. Also henceforth, the fleet would be divided into squadrons commanded by junior flag officers, to enforce order and discipline. And the commissioners drew up a disciplinary code for ships in battle, which would become the Articles of War, and which would, with minor changes, govern the behavior of the British navy right up to 1860.

Of the thirty-nine rules, violation of no fewer than twenty-five carried the death penalty (although only after a court-martial). Many later rules and penalties were aimed at the ship's crew, but the crucial ones imposed after Dungeness concerned their captains and officers. They curtailed their independence to question orders, take prizes, or take on commercial cargo for their own profit. Above all, the Articles of War made it impossible for a would-be Francis Drake or Walter Raleigh to disregard orders and act on his own once the admiral gave the signal for battle.

An admiral now enjoyed the same unquestioned authority over his fleet that a general enjoyed over his army, or indeed a captain over his ship. A new era of naval warfare was about to dawn: the age of the all-powerful sea commander, who, like his counterpart on land, directed his forces like pieces on a chessboard—playthings of his authority and his strategic sense.

To make the point the navy commissioners appointed two other Generals at Sea, Richard Deane and George Monck, to serve beside Blake. They caught up with Tromp again twenty miles south of Portland Bill on February 18, 1653, as he was again escorting merchant ships through the Channel. The two fleets were roughly equal, but the English were fresher and better equipped. They fought a running battle over the next three days: by the end, Blake had been badly wounded and the captain and master of his flagship *Triumph* were dead, but he had lost only one ship while Tromp had lost at least twenty. The English captured more than fifty merchant ships, although the new rules also allowed crews to claim prize money for ships they sank as well as those they captured—an incentive to see the battle to the finish, rather than just grab and run.

The Battle of Portland turned the tide of the war. As the Dutch prizes were towed into harbor, eyewitnesses could see the devastating impact of the English guns, with decks "much dyed in blood, their masts and tackle being moiled with brains, hair, pieces of skulls." More lightly armed and smaller, with a shallower draught to navigate in home waters, Dutch warships were finding themselves outmatched and unable to fight while protecting the merchant convoys. Blake's strategy of choking off Dutch shipping in the Channel, the lifeline of the United Provinces, was working. "Why should I keep silence any longer," one of Tromp's fellow admirals angrily exclaimed to the Dutch States General, "the English are at present masters both of us and of the seas."

Desperate to break the stranglehold, the Dutch fleet forced another battle off the Gabbard shoals east of Harwich on June 2. After the chaos and confusion of Portland, Blake and his fellow generals had carefully drawn up a set of instructions for "better ordering of the fleet." These made sure the fleet performed as a unit, with flag signals from the commander in chief indicating when to carry them out. When he finally raised his red flag, signaling battle, "Then each squadron," the instructions read, "shall take the best advantage they can to engage with the enemy next unto them, and in order hereunto *all ships of every squadron shall endeavor to keep in line with their chief.*"

These words are usually celebrated as the first explicit orders for a line ahead battle. But the line Blake, Deane, and Monck wanted was not a line of battle but a line of bearing, so that the fleet moved in unison in single file leeward toward the enemy until the signal was given to fight. Then the ships would join up line-abreast and sail in with guns blazing, trapping each enemy ship between two simultaneous broadsides.

This is what they hoped to do at the Gabbard. But just as the three English squadrons moved in for the kill, the wind suddenly dropped. Unable to tack into the wind to form up, the English did the next best thing and kept their line formation, while pounding away at the Dutch. The effect was spectacular: another twenty Dutch ships sunk or captured, and hundreds of dead and wounded, while not a single English ship was lost. The only serious casualty was Blake's colleague Deane, killed by a stray shot. So with Blake still incapacitated and Deane gone, the fleet now belonged to General George Monck.

Monck, as it happened, was also from the West Country, the son of a Devonshire landowner and a cousin of the Grenvilles. He had been a volunteer in the Cádiz expedition of 1625 under Sir Richard Grenville and although his military career was built on land not at sea, he would prove more than a match for Holland's greatest admiral, Martin Tromp. The two met at Texel Island near Scheveningen on July 31, 1653. After the disaster at the Gabbard, Tromp was determined to fight only when he had

the weather gauge and could control the pace of battle. But as his fleet
bore down on the English line, Monck suddenly gave the signal for his
ships to turn and meet the Dutch while remaining in line ahead. It took
the Dutch completely by surprise; a lucky musket shot killed Tromp just
as the battle began, creating more confusion.

The English ships crashed through the Dutch line, guns blazing, and
then picked up the wind to crash through again from the other direction,
severing the two lead Dutch squadrons from the rest of the fleet. Then
Monck gave the order to tack back to windward. In unison the English
turned and charged through a third time, smashing the hapless Dutch
ships with one broadside after another. The Dutch fleet disintegrated, as
"their ships which had all their masts gone struck their colors," said an
eyewitness, "and put out a white handkerchief on a staff." The rearmost
Dutch squadron turned and fled, while the rest struggled on until
evening, by which time thirty ships had been sunk or crippled.

The Dutch had had enough. Their navy had been ravaged and their
best admiral killed. The English blockade had captured more than 1,500
Dutch merchant and fishing vessels. The once bustling streets of Amsterdam were empty. Riots broke out in the nation's seaports. Desperate, the
once all-powerful republic sued for peace. The treaty it signed at
Westminster the following April was more conciliatory than it might
have expected: Cromwell was eager for peace in order to pursue his war
with Spain. But the Navigation Acts remained in force; Dutch fishermen
had to pay for the right to fish in English waters, and Dutch captains had
to dip their colors in the Channel. Amsterdam would be active and prosperous again; its bank vaults, taverns, and dinner tables would be full to
overflowing again; ten years later its navy would even beat an English
fleet in battle. But the once-invincible Dutch Republic had been hum-
bled, and the English had finally arrived.

The next step was for Blake to take his fleet into the Mediterranean
to deal with the pirates of North Africa. With his hard-hitting ships of
the line and fast-running frigates, he was able to sail into their principal
nest at Porto Farina on the west coast of the Gulf of Tunis, silence its
powerful shore batteries, and chase down fugitive corsairs as they tried to
escape without losing a single ship. His presence in the Mediterranean
prevented France from seizing Naples, and convinced Portugal to sign a
treaty giving the English the monopoly of trade with its empire in Brazil,
Bengal, and West Africa. Like everyone else, the Portuguese sensed the
scales of power were shifting toward the English.

Indeed, everything seemed to be falling into place for God's Chosen People. "Most men cry up war with Spain, saying that the fleet and the army must be kept in employment." Founder of the Quakers George Fox urged Cromwell to "rock the nations as a cradle." Cromwell swore he "would not desist until he came to the gates of Rome." In December, with Blake still in the Mediterranean, he ordered Admiral William Penn to assemble a fleet of thirty-eight ships and 3,000 soldiers for an expedition to the West Indies. Penn and his army counterpart, General Robert Venables, were to pick up 5,000 more volunteers in Barbados and St. Kitts—proof of how much those colonies had now grown—and turn the island of Hispaniola, where Christopher Columbus first launched Spain's New World empire and where John Hawkins sold his first slaves to Spanish colonists almost a century before, into a permanent English naval base.

It would have been a great irony and indicator of how much historical fortunes had reversed, if they had succeeded. But the attack failed, as Venable's volunteers came down with dysentery, yellow fever, and cowardice. On their way back from Hispaniola, however, Penn and the navy took the lead and conquered Jamaica in less than a week. By the end of the century it would be the center of the English slave trade in the Caribbean.

One great dream had been realized: a secure English base in the West Indies. Another came the next year, in September 1656, as Blake was blockading the coastline of Spain and dispatched Captain Richard Stayner with a team of frigates to capture the Spanish silver fleet on its way in from Havana. Stayner sank three ships and captured two, while three of the smaller vessels escaped. But when he dragged the haul into Portsmouth, his two prizes disgorged more than 700,000 pounds sterling, which went to London in thirty-eight massive wagons. Seven months later, Blake repeated the same feat himself in the Azores, although this time he did not bother taking any of the ships. Instead, he sent them all to the bottom of Santa Cruz harbor. He had proved that English navy could now cut Spain's silver thread to America at will. Spain's doom as a world power was now complete.

However, Blake would not live to enjoy his triumph. Keeping the blockade of Spain through the winter of 1656–57—a feat of seamanship and logistics unmatched until the Napoleonic Wars—destroyed his health, which had not recovered from his wounds at Portland. Robert Blake died just as his ship arrived in Plymouth Sound and his command ended. "As he lived," said one of his officers, "so he continued to the death, faithful."

Cromwell ordered a massive state funeral, and the Bridgewater merchant's son was laid to rest in Westminster Abbey. Yet Cromwell's own days were numbered. He had made England a world power. But there was growing discontent with his heavy-handed dictatorial rule and the cost of endless war. Eleven months later the Lord Protector would be dead of pneumonia and would join Blake in Westminster Abbey. A new round of sweeping political changes was in the offing.

Yet during his five-year reign, Oliver Cromwell had done what no other ruler in English history had done. He had secured the British Isles as a single state, including Scotland and Ireland, and secured England's future as a colonial trading empire. Above all, he had built an English navy which in number and quality of ships, in its finances and administration, in its officers and men, and in its global reach, was superior to any in the world.

Everything now depended on how that navy would fare under his successors.

CHAPTER NINE

Mr. Pepys's Navy

Abroad your empire shall no limits know,
But, like the sea, in boundless circles flow.
Your much-loved fleet shall, with a wide command,
Besiege the petty monarchs of the land.
—JOHN DRYDEN, ASTRAEA REDUX, 1660

ALL THE WORLD IS now at a loss to think what Monck will do now," wrote Samuel Pepys, an obscure clerk for the Exchequer, in his diary for January 18, 1660. In fact, General at Sea Samuel Monck was back on land and taking his army on a slow march from Scotland for London. The victor of Scheveningen was fed up with the chaos and confusion reigning in England since Cromwell's death two years earlier. Many, including Pepys, hoped he would now kick out the remaining radicals in the army and Parliament and pave the way for a return of the monarchy.

The decade-long experiment in republicanism had failed. The Commonwealth had saved England from Charles I's absolute rule and had given the nation a strong and effective navy. But idealism and high hopes had, by Cromwell's death, dissolved into chaos. Only a king, it seemed, could bring back a sense of law and order, and offer a stable framework around which the other institutions of the country could rally. To those who controlled the nation's destiny, the question was not if the exiled Charles II should return to England, but when.

At the center of the intrigue was commander in chief of the fleet, Edward Montagu, who also happened to be Samuel Pepys's cousin. Montagu had served with Blake at Cádiz, then replaced him as Cromwell's most trusted admiral. Now his support steeled Monck's resolve. On February 3, his troops entered London to loud cheers and glowing bonfires. "The common joy," wrote Pepys, who came up from Whitehall to see the spectacle, "was everywhere to be seen." On the sixteenth Monck ordered Parliament to dissolve itself and allow the election of a new Parliament, to invite Charles II back from exile in Holland.

Ten days earlier Pepys had received a note from Montagu asking to meet in the garden adjoining Whitehall Palace. As they strolled, Montagu told his cousin that "he would use all his own and the interest of his friends that he hath in England to do me good" and then "asked me whether I could without too much inconvenience go to sea as his Secretary." Pepys jumped at the chance. It not only rescued him from his deadend job at the Exchequer and secured his place in the new government; it also gave him the opportunity to meet the new king when Montagu set out to pick him up at the Hague.

They left the Tower of London by barge on February 23 to board the *Swiftsure,* a 900-ton ship with sixty guns, lying at anchor at Greenhithe. Pepys made himself as comfortable as he could in his tiny cabin, set up his writing materials, and managed to sleep through the night. "The weather being good, I was not sick at all," he confided to his diary, "yet I know not when I shall be."

This was Pepys's first trip at sea, and after they transferred to Montagu's old flagship, the 80-gun *Naseby,* and made for open sea he started to feel "dizzy and squeamish." But he soon forgot his discomfort in the excitement of watching the rest of the fleet greet the *Naseby* as it arrived off Deale, with the blue waters of the Channel flashing in the sunlight. "Great was the shot of guns from the castles and ships and our answers," Pepys wrote, "I never heard yet so great rattling of guns." As billows of smoke swept over the deck and through the *Naseby*'s towering masts and rigging, Pepys watched boats launched from the other warships to bring their commanders and officers to Montagu's cabin.

Pepys's connection with Montagu now put him on intimate terms with the men who made England a naval power: Vice Admiral John Lawson ("a very good natured man," Pepys enthused); William Penn, who had taken Jamaica five years earlier; and Captain Richard Stayner, who had captured the silver fleet off Cádiz. When Pepys was sitting alone in his cabin playing on his violin "in a melancholy fit," he was thrilled when Stayner and Montagu invited him to dine with them in the admiral's cabin.

Learning to be at home with his superiors, Pepys was also learning the pleasure of making his inferiors jump. "I was infinitely pleased," he told the diary, "to see what a command I have to have everyone ready to come and go." But none of this matched the thrill of arriving at the Hague and watching the thirty-year-old king and his brother, the Duke of York, come on board on May 22 in their flowing periwigs and broad-brimmed hats. Pepys had the honor of firing the gun above his cabin to salute the king—"which was the first time that he hath been saluted by his own ship since the change"—although Pepys stuck his head too close to the blast and nearly lost an eye. Later, he listened with great emotion as Charles paced the quarterdeck of the *Naseby* (soon to be renamed the *Royal Charles*) and described his painful years as a fugitive and exile. Pepys also met the Duke of York, "who called me Pepys by name, and upon my desire did promise me his future favour"—a promise he would keep, both as Lord High Admiral and as King James II.

The royal party finally arrived at Dover on the twenty-sixth where it was announced that Charles had signed a general amnesty for the nation that had overthrown his father and for nearly eleven years had excluded him from the throne.* "The shouting and joy expressed by all," Pepys wrote, "was past all imagination." On leaving ship, Charles struck his head on one of the low beams in his cabin, as non-sailors often do, and good-naturedly marked the spot with his knife (Montagu ordered Pepys to go back later and gild the spot with gold paint). Then Pepys had the special honor of escorting one of the king's famous spaniels to shore, "which shit in the boat, which made us laugh and me think that a King and all that belong to him are but just as others are."

Pepys's first trip at sea had been momentous enough. But what of the future? His cousin told him, "We must have a little patience and we will rise together." Rise they did. A month later Montagu, now the Earl of Sandwich, gave him the post of Clerk of the Acts for the new Navy Board. To Pepys it meant primarily a pay raise to 350 pounds a year and a house adjoining his new offices, in Seething Lane west of Tower Hill. He was not yet thirty. He had no clear idea what his new job was, or even what the title meant. Yet it would change him, and with him the history of England.

Samuel Pepys was a bureaucrat, not a warrior; a landlubber, not a sailor. He would go to sea exactly five times in his entire life. But he would do more to transform the Royal Navy than any figure since John Hawkins.

---

*Although Charles did put to death a dozen of the men directly responsible for his father's execution. One of them was Harry Vane, the former navy treasurer: poor recompense for one of the two men who left him a navy second to none in the world. The other, John Pym, died in 1644, long before Charles I went to the scaffold.

His famous diaries reveal the foibles, weaknesses, and self-doubts of the private man: the son of a London tailor, an amateur musician with a taste for literature and stylish furniture, an upwardly mobile overgrown adolescent who got drunk with his friends and slept with the maid, even after his wife found out. Yet the public Pepys stands as a towering, almost heroic figure, someone whose name would be hallowed in the halls of the Admiralty long after the rest of England had forgotten him.

Pepys was not perfect. He was never as selfless and unbiased as he liked to portray himself. Many of the crucial decisions for which he would be given credit originally came from his masters, Charles II and James II. Still, as Clerk and then Surveyor of the Navy Board, Pepys would keep the Royal Navy going during some of its darkest days. Later, as first secretary of the Admiralty, he would make it into a permanent professional fighting force and instrument of empire. Monck, who originally opposed Pepys's appointment, would later call him "the right hand of the Navy." Certainly without him, it might never had emerged in the next century as the most dominant military force in the world.

. . .

Of course, it started in 1660 as a navy second to none. Charles II inherited more than one hundred and twenty warships from his predecessors. Blake and Monck had made England a major player on the world stage. The Dutch had turned themselves into a formidable naval power in order to keep their overseas trade. The English did the opposite. It was their rise as a naval power, driven by the discipline of the New Model Army and militant Protestantism, that allowed them to become a major trading nation.

The proof comes in the explosive growth of English shipping. In 1629 it came to 115,000 tons a year; the decades of turmoil and civil war dipped those numbers to less than 95,000 by 1670. But the Royal Navy's budget had grown more than four times over the same period, from 138,000 pounds a year on average in 1644 to 600,000 pounds by 1660. As the navy became the largest in Europe, the trade numbers rebounded: by 1676 they reached more than half a million tons. For the rest of the century, despite systematic French campaigns to intercept English shipping, it never dropped below 350,000 tons. Meanwhile, the Navigation Acts fostered a merchant marine ready to supply skilled seamen for the navy, and vice versa. As the navy grew, England's trade grew with it and so did England's wealth, just as John Dee had predicted a century before.

Indeed, the navy itself was now a crucial part of the kingdom's economy. The four royal dockyards were the largest single employer in England.
They consumed timber, hemp, tar, and resin; flax for canvas, iron for nails,
fittings, anchors, and cannon; food, beer, and wine in quantities that
demanded the labor and effort of thousands of workmen across England.

England's entire forest industry was in the hands of the navy. Only
English oak, *quercus robus,* was considered good enough for the making of
one of the king's ships. But building one required nearly three thousand
trees. As a result, the ancient oak forests of Sussex, Surrey, Kent, and
Hampshire shrank alarmingly, so much so that the wood supply for other
purposes, such construction and charcoal burning, had to suffer. The
navy's demand became so great that iron manufacturers had to turn to
burnt coal, or coke, as a substitute for the dwindling supply of charcoal.
This in turn would transform the English iron industry, and started a
sequence of technological improvements in iron production that would
last through the Industrial Revolution.

The demand for mast timber also drove England's North Sea and
Baltic trade with Scandinavia. When the Dutch wars interrupted the
flow of Norway spruce from this crucial source, the dockyards turned to
New England. The virgin forests of Maine and New Hampshire yielded
the sort of trees the Royal Navy needed for its mainmasts: one hundred
feet tall and almost three feet in diameter at the base. The Maine colony
grew up around supplying Royal Navy timber: by law every tree more
than twenty-four inches in diameter became navy property. Without the
demand for what were called "naval stores," the merchants of New
England would have been far less prosperous—and England's economic
future far more in doubt.

Charles II had no desire to interrupt this flow of prosperity. He cut
and dismantled Cromwell's army: never again would it be allowed to
direct the fortunes or devour the resources of the kingdom. But Charles
was deeply committed to the navy and eager to show the London business
community that he believed in England's maritime future. As he told his
sister, "England can only be considerable by our trade and power by sea."
He appointed his brother, the Duke of York, as Lord High Admiral and
passed his own version of the Navigation Acts.

But danger loomed on the horizon. The success of Cromwell's navy
had launched an expensive naval arms race across Europe. Every power,
from the Netherlands and France to Denmark, Sweden, and soon Peter
the Great's Russia, was pushing to catch up, even as Portugal and Spain

dropped behind. The struggle for control of the Atlantic, and with it the Baltic and North seas, was just beginning: who would win depended on who could afford to build the most powerful ships the fastest.

To keep track of what it had and what it needed, the Commonwealth used a system for classifying or rating ships by size and armament. "First-rate" ships were the largest, like the 172-foot-long *Naseby*, now the *Royal Charles*. Displacing more than 1,200 tons* each, these seagoing monsters required a full-time crew of seven or eight hundred men. They carried anywhere from eighty guns in the case of the *Royal Charles*, with the largest able to fling a 42-pound cannonball nearly a mile, up to a hundred guns in the case of Charles I's *Sovereign of the Seas*, now the *Royal Sovereign*. Since they were virtually unsinkable, first-rates usually served as flagships for admirals. Their magnificent and ornate decorations with crests, lions, unicorns, sea gods, and sea nymphs, "head, waist, quarter, and stern so largely enriched with carved work overlaid with gold," gave them the appearance of floating palaces. Too expensive to risk at sea except in national emergencies, they were also formidable fighting machines. These were the ships, as Pepys learned, "that do the business."

Second-rates like the *Swiftsure*, with sixty to eighty guns, and third-rates with fifty-four to sixty-four guns, made up the bulk of the ships in the line ahead fighting formation on which English admirals increasingly relied. Then there were fourth-rates mounting thirty-four to fifty-four guns and weighing in at around 500 tons, and fifth-rates, frigates with twenty or thirty guns, which patrolled and hunted privateers rather than serving as "ships of the line."

These ships established the basic design of warships until the age of steam. They were almost three times longer than their beam or width, compared to two times for a Tudor ship like the *Mary Rose*. Getting rid of the bonaventure mizzen, and adding a topsail on the bowsprit's rigging, made ships easier to handle, while adding a sail above the topsail, the "top gallant," gave them more speed. This made even the largest maneuverable and fast for its size: the *Royal Charles*, when all additional stay and studding sails were spread, could make 12 knots, although five or six was more usual. For speed mattered far less than firepower.

---

*The word "ton" comes from "tun," the medieval English term for barrel or wine cask, which shipwrights used to measure the cargo capacity of the ships they built. As such, it is not a measure of weight but volume, which Parliament first tried to standardize in 1694.

As the rating system itself indicated, the guns dominated the life of the ship and the navy. The names they had carried since Henry VIII's time, like culverin and saker, disappeared: from now on, they would simply be known by the weight of the shot they threw—and the heavier and the more of them the better, for the line ahead battle.

Shipwrights Peter Pett and Anthony Deane were constantly devising ways to cram as many on a ship as possible without sending it to the bottom. They also made the gun deck floors with as few joints as possible, to prevent the constant firing of broadsides from shaking the ship to pieces. These ships had to be solid and impervious, not just to take hits but to take the strain of being a floating artillery battery, firing volley after volley in a sea battle that could rage for hours or even days.

Building and outfitting these seagoing fortresses at the yards at Deptford, Woolwich, and Chatham cost enormous sums of money: the *Sovereign of the Seas* alone ran to more than 60,000 pounds. And since nearly half the navy was now on permanent duty, supplying and maintaining them also cost more than ever. More, in fact, as Samuel Pepys discovered when he arrived for work in July 1660, than the Crown could afford.

Pepys was part of a newly overhauled Navy Board, which reflected the changes made during the Commonwealth. Its four officials—treasurer, surveyor, comptroller, and clerk—were now supplemented by three commissioners from the Treasury, including one, William Coventry, who would become Pepys's friend and mentor. The Navy Board's job was to supervise the construction, outfitting, and maintaining of the navy's ships until they went to sea, when the Admiralty took over. The board met twice a week in its offices at Seething Lane, and Pepys soon discovered that his colleagues saw their jobs primarily as a way to enrich themselves and their friends. Surveyor Sir William Batten had even helped himself to the disabled seamen's fund, the Chatham Chest, to pay for his magnificent estate at Walthamstow. Pepys decided it was time to change how things were done, and launched a new standard of bureaucratic efficiency for the navy and for English government as a whole.

He bought two books to guide him. One was Captain John Smith's classic *Sea Grammar,* and the other John Selden's *Closed Sea*—the notion of England's natural sovereignty over the seas was now standard operating procedure for the Royal Navy. Pepys learned about navigation charts and tide tables, Davis's backstaff and telescopes. He bought several slide rules for measuring timber in cubic feet and learned how to use them (his friendship with nautical instrument maker Ralph Greatorex led him to join the Royal Society and eventually become its president). He went on board every vessel he could find, learned the names for every part of the ship, and even took lessons on how to draw them.

His new job turned Pepys into a happy workaholic. In the summer he would rise at four o'clock to walk down to Deptford or Woolwich, or take a boat around to Chatham to visit the stores and see the ships. He became friends with designers Pett and Deane, and was fascinated with the arduous process of shipbuilding. He would watch as more than a hundred men would labor twelve hours a day for eight months, cutting and fitting each mammoth beam, timber, and joint with their handmade tools. The finished hull would be launched in a "spring tide" to allow plenty of water under the keel while the builders and visiting notables toasted themselves from a bowl they would then toss overboard—the origin of the modern christening ceremony.

Then would come the masts, some rising as high as 130 feet, and the twenty or so miles of rope hemp twisted into 6- and 3-inch-thick stays and shrouds to prop them up. Then the rest of the rigging: halyards, sheets, and braces to raise, lower, and turn the sails to the wind, and scores of great wooden tackle-blocks connecting each to the yardarms and spars. Finally, the anchors—often a dozen at a time, since anchors were often fouled or lost—with massive eight-inch-diameter cables folded and stowed on the lower deck. Then, and only then, would come the guns. Each weighing two or three tons, they would be distributed on the main deck and the heaviest, the 42- and 32-pounders, in the two lower decks of a first-rate or second-rate like the eighty-gun *Victory*, launched in 1666.

Every ship was only as good as the quality and quantity of the materials used to build it. Realizing this, Pepys met with anyone who could help him to save money while improving quality. He questioned Dutch rope makers when he encountered them at a tavern, and arranged for a series of demonstrations of the differing strengths of rope hemp. He did the same for the navy's supply of timber. He traveled to Wapping to learn about the different kinds of lumber used for shipbuilding, and to Epping Forest to see for himself "the whole abuse His Majesty suffers in the measuring of timber." Pepys broke the contract with Batten's favorite timber supplier when he discovered one who offered a better product for less. He even forced flag makers to lower their prices by threepence a yard.

Pepys found it hard to change the system and did not hesitate to take kickbacks himself from his suppliers—but only, as he took pride in point-ing out, *after* the contract was signed. But he did demand careful account-ing for every penny spent. "My delight is in the neatness of everything," he confessed, and that included the account books of the victualers, sup-pliers, and dockyard managers. His self-confidence soared. When Batten and his minions objected to the new standards, Pepys put them in their place. "I was in the right," he remembered after one argument, "and was the willinger to do so before them, that they might see *I am somebody*."

His hard work won him promotion to Surveyor General of the Navy Board in 1665. He resolved "never to baulk taking notice of anything that is to the king's prejudice, let it fall where it will." Armed with numbers and statistics, he defended the navy's budget against all challengers, including Parliament, and made the navy's welfare the touchstone for all his decisions. Coming home late at night to sit with his wife or play the violin, he admitted his greatest vexation was that "I do not find other people as willing to do business as myself when I have taken pains to find out what in the yards is wanting and fitting to be done."

Yet as Pepys examined his accounts, walked the docks, and talked to officials in the Treasury, grim reality set in. Even in peacetime the navy cost an average of more than 450,000 pounds a year, with another million in debt outstanding. Yet the king's entire annual grant from Parliament came to only 1.2 million—and as Pepys discovered, the actual sum was less than two-thirds of that. No king, no matter how committed he was to sea power, was going to let the navy consume more than half his income. "The want of money," Pepys wrote after only a year on the job, "puts . . . the navy out of order." Inevitably, it faced a slow starvation unless some radical solution was found for its funding. And given Parliament's unending hos-tility to new taxes, that seemed unlikely.

In short, England had created a navy that outstripped the ability of its political institutions to maintain it. That point came home with a vengeance in 1664, when war with the Dutch flared up again.

As in so many wars, the cause was greed and bad economics. Con-ventional wisdom held that markets were finite things and trade a zero-sum game: it could only be shared between competing nations like England and Holland, never expanded. As one sea captain put it to Pepys, "The trade of the world is too little for us two, therefore one must down." Charles II and his brother James believed destroying the Dutch trading empire would not only help English merchants, they hoped it would increase the Crown's revenues from trade regulation and free the monarchy of Parliament's tight purse strings forever. In short, "We all seem to desire" war, Pepys wrote in his diary. "For my part," he added, looking over the expense sheets and supply lists for the fleet, "I dread it."

To incite the Dutch, the Admiralty sent Captain Robert Holmes and a squadron of fast ships to the coast of Africa to attack and burn the Dutch bases for the slave trade. Then Holmes crossed the Atlantic and seized Holland's principal settlement in North America, New Amsterdam, which he renamed New York, after the Lord Admiral. The Dutch responded by declaring war and in the early months of 1665 the English fleet gathered in the icy waters around Portsmouth.

It was a strong and confident force: one hundred and thirty ships and more than 21,000 men, with a brace of skilled and experienced commanders. Montagu, now Earl of Sandwich, commanded the rearmost Blue Squadron, while Prince Rupert, commander of Charles I's navy during the civil war and a brilliant sea tactician, led the leading White Squadron from the *Royal Charles*. The central squadron, the Red, was led by the Lord Admiral himself, with William Penn acting as captain of the fleet with a new body of troops for maritime service, the Admiral's Regiment— ancestor of the Royal Marines. After setting sail, they caught sight of the Dutch fleet off Lowestoft on the English east coast on June 3, and after two days of maneuvering closed for battle.

This took time. Organizing and sailing a fleet in line ahead formation was a slow, tedious process and required careful discipline and an admiral with a alert mind and an iron will. The entire line could extend more than five miles, with each ship barely one hundred yards apart. As half of each watch went aloft to set or furl sails, the other half hauled on the lines operating the yards and sails, the halyards, braces, and sheets in order to hold the ship as near to the wind as possible, so that barely enough breeze passed over the back end of the sail to keep the ship moving without luffing the canvas. This was sailing "close hauled": it was hard work, especially since the ships of the era had few fore-and-aft sails for adjusting course to the vagaries of the wind. It demanded constant attention from the captain, crew, and helmsman to keep their place in line, and from the commanding admiral.

As he paced the quarterdeck of his flagship, the admiral had to anticipate any problem and signal the other ships in this long ungainly formation when and which way to turn. This was impossible without written instructions issued beforehand. Admiral Blake had issued the first set during the first Dutch war with signal flags to match, although most

admirals still liked to send officers by boat through the fleet to shout the
order to each ship. In 1672–73 the Duke of York authorized a single standard set of fighting and sailing orders, so that an admiral could count on
his ships following each other in line for combat even if they missed the
crucial signal to attack.

Naval combat was becoming a mammoth game of Follow the Leader,
or even Crack the Whip. An admiral from the next age, Cloudsley
Shovell, succinctly said of the line ahead battle, "Without a miracle 'tis
numbers that gain the victory." Everyone had to move in concert in order
to bring those numbers to bear. Any mistake might open a gap, allowing
the enemy to bring his broadsides to bear and rake exposed sterns and
bows, or to send ships through to double-team his opponent and pound
him from both sides at once. In short, captains who tried to act on their
own could disrupt everything—and doom the fleet. James's instructions
even made firing on the enemy too soon a court-martial offense, to prevent captains from hitting a friendly ship.

So battle came slowly, with each fleet moving at little more than two
knots—no faster than a running tide. They passed each other in parallel
lines but in opposite directions, with ships banging away at each other
without hitting a thing. Then they turned and passed again, the whole
slow-motion parade taking more than five hours as captains watched
their ammunition dwindle away to no purpose. It was only on the third
turn that James finally gave the signal for his fleet to turn to meet the
Dutch on the same tack at which point all order broke down and all hell
broke loose.

Many miles away the poet John Dryden was quietly rowing down the
Thames toward Greenwich with a group of literary friends when they
could faintly hear the guns at Lowestoft "like the noise of distant thunder." The boat drifted along as "they had attentively listened till such time
as the sound by little and little went from them." Then one of the poets
lifted his head and proclaimed the day a success: the receding sound had
to mean the Dutch were fleeing.

He was right. As the two lines of ships crashed into each other, with
shot flying in all directions and shattered masts, rigging, and bodies tum-
bling into the sea, James's *Royal Charles* swung into action alongside the
Dutch admiral's flagship, the 76-gun *Eendracht*. They exchanged punishing
broadsides: shots swept away four of the Duke's companions, as James
was bathed in blood and knocked to the deck by a severed head. Then a
lucky English shot split open the *Eendracht*'s powder magazine and the

mighty ship exploded in a blast they plainly heard in the Hague sixty miles away, killing the admiral and all but five of his 400-man crew.

Leaderless, the rest of the Dutch fleet began to slacken fire. With ships from five separate admiralties and under twenty-one separate admirals, there was no one to take charge. Instead, the Dutch turned to flee as the English dispatched fireships to complete their rout. Four Dutch ships collided as a fireship set them alight and burned them to the waterline; six more perished the same way. In all, the Dutch lost more than thirty ships and five thousand men, and would have lost more if one of James's courtiers, Lord William Brouckner, had not told Admiral Penn that the Lord Admiral wanted to cease pursuit and disengage for the night. When James returned to deck and found the sails slackened, he was furious and said his orders had been misunderstood. But it was too late; the Dutch retreated to safe haven and the English fleet returned home disappointed but triumphant, having lost only two ships and fewer than eight hundred sailors.

Pepys declared Lowestoft "a great victory, never known in the world," but as soon as the fleet was back at Portsmouth the recriminations began. The commanders did not just fight over who was to blame for the Dutch escape, Penn or Brouckner. Prince Rupert and Sandwich fought over the future of the fleet and who should advise James; James clashed with his political enemies, including Albemarle; former royalists accused former republicans of trying to take advantage of the confusion of battle to defect to the enemy.

Underlying all the rancor was an issue that had raised its head before in the Royal Navy, that of social class. The navy's command was now divided between its new gentlemen officers like Brouckner, pillars of the Restoration, and tarpaulins like Penn and Sandwich who had earned their ranks during a decade of active service under the Commonwealth. Well-born courtiers assumed their social status entitled them to command; tarpaulins resented the way a coat of arms or coronet could trump experience in the distribution of rewards and promotions. Distrust and jealousy came to infect every squadron and flagship, and sometimes the quarterdeck of individual ships. The split between gentlemen and tarpaulins was "a distinction I am both ashamed and afflicted to mention," Pepys wrote in a memorandum. "Among other good ends of what I am now doing the removing of that distinction will be one."

However, the bitterness flared again after Sandwich's disastrous attempt to catch the Dutch East India Company's fleet in the harbor in

Bergen, Norway, when Dutch and Danish guns drove the English off even as Sandwich's sailors were ransacking local Lutheran churches. Then in the spring of 1666, Prince Rupert and Albemarle allowed their squadrons to become separated and chased around the eastern end of the Channel by Dutch admiral de Ruyter for four days, losing ten ships (including the great *Royal Prince*), two admirals, and one of their best tarpaulin captains, Christopher Myngs. Officers close to the Duke of York blamed Albemarle for the debacle; he in turn accused them of cowardice, and demanded that five of them be dismissed.

And through it all the perennial problems were lurking below decks, with common seamen unhappy about their pay, or lack of it, and their victuals, which were usually unfit to eat. Unrest and desertion became rampant. Almost every ship went into battle at Lowestoft seriously undermanned, and mutinies had broken out in the Portsmouth dockyards after the fleet's return, just as the Great Plague was breaking out in London.

Pepys watched it happen, helpless to do anything. "The lamentable moans of the poor seamen that lie starving in the streets for lack of money," he admitted, "do trouble and perplex me to the heart." But there was no money to pay anyone, only paper IOUs. Even when there was, the navy treasurer refused to pay sailors their full wages, reasoning that this would encourage them to desert. In 1667 a hundred or so besieged the Navy Board's offices in Seething Lane, yelling curses and throwing stones. Yet when Pepys attended the funeral of Captain Myngs, Myngs's heartbroken crew gathered around Pepys's carriage with tears in their eyes, and said that "having now done the last office of laying him in the ground, we would be glad we had any other to offer after him, and in revenge of him." They even volunteered to take a fireship into the heart of the Dutch fleet in a final suicide mission, to "show our memory of our dead commander, and our revenge." But Pepys could offer them nothing but words of condolence and drove on.

Events were building to a crisis. A belated victory over de Ruyter on July 28, St James's Day, earned praise from poets like Dryden—"*It seemed as there the British Neptune stood/With all his hosts of water at command*"—but changed nothing. The Great Fire burned out the heart of London in September 1666 and threw the government into turmoil. With no money forthcoming, a massive strike broke out across the docks while suppliers stopped deliveries. With no sailors or supplies, the fleet was laid up at Chatham, unable to sail.

De Ruyter saw his chance. In June 1667 he took his fleet to sea and moored it at the mouth of the Thames, prompting the commissioner of the yards at Chatham, Peter Pett, to write to Seething Lane asking for "help for God and the King and the kingdom's sake." It was too late. On the twenty-second a Dutch squadron swung up the Medway, and around the bend at Upnor to Chatham. The English fleet was caught completely unprepared. The guns on Upnor Castle could not fire: the cannonballs did not fit the guns. Albemarle frantically ordered his men to scuttle their ships to keep them out of Dutch hands. The Dutch, meanwhile, took their time, setting three great ships ablaze and taking the pride of the English fleet, the *Royal Charles,* under tow. Ironically, many of the Dutch ships were manned by English sailors, who jubilantly shouted to onlookers on shore, "We were paid with tickets [i.e., written IOUs], now we are paid with dollars!" An eyewitness called the sight of the 96-gun *Loyal London* and second-rates *Royal Oak* and *Royal James* slowly burning down to the waterline "the most dismal spectacle my eyes ever beheld." Ruyter then leisurely returned home, leaving behind a scene of pandemonium and devastation, with the *Royal Charles* as the spoil of victory.*

The Medway raid was a national humiliation. Six great ships had been lost and two captured: total losses came to 200,000 pounds. It set off a panic in the capital and prompted Pepys to put his father and wife on a coach for the country. Sailors' wives roamed the streets, screeching, "This is what comes of not paying our husbands!" Naturally, Parliament demanded scapegoats. There were arrests, even an execution, and Peter Pett was sent to the Tower. Charles's first minister, Lord Clarendon, was impeached and fled into exile. Rupert and Albemarle testified to Parliament about the "intolerable neglect" the navy had suffered at the hands of the Navy Board, and the failure to keep it supplied and outfitted. The Duke of York and his secretary and navy commissioner William Coventry were Parliament's primary targets and could say nothing in their own defense; so the job of protecting the navy's reputation fell to Samuel Pepys. On Thursday, March 5, 1668, he was summoned to speak before the House of Commons.

He gathered together his facts and figures, drank a half-pint of mulled sherry and a glass of brandy to steady his nerves, and then made

---

*The *Royal Charles*'s magnificent stern piece, with its painted lion, unicorn, and royal coat of arms, is still on display at the Rijksmuseum in Amsterdam.

his entrance into the House just before midday. He sensed the hostility of the members the moment he entered. First he had to listen to the damning report of the committee on the state of the navy. Then Pepys began to speak. To his own amazement he spoke for three and a half hours, almost all without notes, "as if I had been at my own table," calmly defending himself, his colleagues, and the navy's system of expenditure. The House of Commons sat stunned, as it realized its attack had misfired: members who had been the most hostile now proposed postponing any vote and moving on to other matters. Pepys's colleagues were relieved and overjoyed. The next day, Coventry greeted him with the words: "Good morrow, Mr. Pepys, that must be Speaker of the Parliament!" Others called him another Cicero; the Solicitor General told Pepys "he thought I spoke the best of any man in England," and everyone agreed "that I have done myself right for my whole life."

Even more important, Pepys had done the navy right. More than any admiral or sea officer, he had saved its reputation and honor. James, Rupert, Sandwich, and the rest were too embroiled in their own interminable quarrels over precedent and promotion to notice, any more than the politicians. But for a brief moment Pepys had shown how a skilled bureaucrat could subdue critics with a relentless barrage of facts and figures, and how a commitment to efficiency and excellence—for in truth, as he put it, "the whole business of the office was done by me"—could put the navy beyond the reach of contending political factions. It was a happy harbinger for the future, despite the disaster in the Medway.

And the war did not end so badly. Despite their victories at sea, the Dutch had lost huge sums of money and trade revenue (Robert Holmes's lightning raid on the harbor at Vlieland the previous year had cost them more than one hundred and fifty merchant vessels). They were as eager for peace as their opponents. The final treaty signed at Breda in July 1667 represented a fair balance of interests. The Dutch won concessions on the Navigation Acts and got back their outposts in the West Indies. The English, however, kept New York, closing the strategic gap between their New England colonies and those of the Middle Atlantic and South. A continuous coastline of English colonies would soon sprout thriving ports: Boston, Newport, New York, Philadelphia, Baltimore, and Charleston.

The Breda treaty also made the Dutch secure in the East Indies. The Moluccas, Java, and Surinam would remain the cornerstone of their overseas empire until World War II. The English East India Company, foisted permanently out of the Spice Islands, found a new base of operations in the port Charles II received as part of his dowry from the Portuguese princess Catherine of Braganza: Bombay.

However, English interest in Asia was being overshadowed by the growing importance of America. Besides, there was a new distraction. Even before the second war with the Dutch was over, an even larger threat had appeared, with the rise of the Sun King, Louis XIV of France.

* * *

The story of the Royal Navy as an agent of change is not just about how it set in motion or sustained certain trends that shaped the future of the world: the end of Iberian hegemony, the rise of Atlantic trading economies, the colonization of North America, the making of an English-speaking overseas empire. It is also about how it prevented things from happening that might have shaped the world differently.

The most important was having all Europe ruled by a single man or power. The possibility that a single individual might have at his command all the resources, economies, and technologies of that powerful continent, and use them to dominate the rest of the world, would haunt the course of modern history right through the twentieth century. It would inspire a series of megalomaniacs, from Louis XIV and Napoleon to Adolf Hitler and Stalin. Indeed, a good deal of modern history has been about trying to stop them from succeeding, including the history of the British navy. Louis XIV was the first and came the closest, in part because he saw the real significance of the Royal Navy almost before anyone else did: how a large standing navy opened the path to power and empire.

France had been an important naval power in the Renaissance: Henry VIII was barely able to beat back its invasion fleet at the Battle of Portsmouth in 1545. But then decades of religious wars and political anarchy threw the French kingdom into chaos, and destroyed its maritime presence in the Atlantic and the Channel, a fact of which the Elizabethans took full advantage. As a result, crucial years were lost. Although France had active seafaring communities, including in Brittany, the French version of the West Country, its sailors, privateers, and oceangoing merchants never played the same crucial role in shaping French policy as they did in Elizabethan England.

Instead, the rebirth of the French navy depended on a land-bound bureaucrat, Louis XIII's first minister, Cardinal Richelieu. His great-grandfather had helped to found the Channel port at Le Havre in Normandy, and his father had been a sea captain there. France's weakness at sea, Richlieu stated in his *Political Testament,* "pierced the heart of a good Frenchman." He devoted serious sums of money to building an effective navy as well as a powerful army. By the time Richelieu died in 1642, France had a fleet of sixty sailing warships, with twenty-five royal galleys plying the Mediterranean.

All this was possible because France was the most populous kingdom in Europe, and its tax base the richest. When Louis XIV took over the reins of the kingdom in 1661, he was able to convert the taxes and rents wrung from France's peasantry into the sinews of a powerful bureaucratic state. He mobilized France's aristocracy to serve him in his armies—the largest in the world, with over 120,000 men—and at his palace at Versailles, also the largest in the world, with over 10,000 full-time residents, hundreds of miles of gardens, fountains, and more than 3500 marble statues. He recruited a cadre of middle-class administrators to collect his taxes and run his government. All classes of French society came to serve Louis's personal glory, which was, as Louis himself put it, "the worthiest and most beautiful aim of the prince." He had dubbed himself the Sun King for more reasons than one. Everything that happened in France was to revolve around him and his divinely ordained authority; everything was to reflect his absolute power and self-regarding *gloire.*

That included his navy. His chief finance minister, Jean-Baptiste Colbert, personally directed a massive French naval buildup. Colbert deployed an elaborate administrative hierarchy, with eight separate navy bureaus (there would be ten by 1712), each with its own first secretary in Paris taking Colbert's orders and passing them on to their subordinates in the provinces. He ordered a registry of every seaman and sailor in France and set up a rotating system so that they spent one year out of three serving in the Sun King's navy. France's greatest military engineer, Sebastien de Vauban, rebuilt the navy's main Mediterranean base at Toulon, while the royal dockyards at its Atlantic bases, Brest and Rochefort, turned out a steady stream of new warships.

The results were astonishing. Colbert built more than eighty ships between 1666 and 1670. The navy grew from twenty-five active ships in 1661 to one hundred and forty in 1671, of which twelve were new first-rate (or *premier rang*) ships of the line, and thirty new *deuxième rangs.* Colbert borrowed the English rating system to organize his fleet, just as his shipbuilders followed English models in their ship designs. The biggest was the *Soleil Royal,* a 120-gun behemoth of more than 2,400 tons. Completed in the Brest yards in 1671, it was the biggest warship in the world, just as France now had the biggest navy: the obedient instrument of its monarch's will and ambition.

Colbert accepted the standard notion that naval wars opened the way to overseas wealth. He saw trade itself as a form of warfare, "a perpetual and peaceful war of intelligence and industry between nations." Although he came from a merchant family from Nantes, he looked down on merchants themselves as greedy profiteers, who thought "only of their own interests" instead of "the general welfare of the state," meaning the power and glory of Louis XIV. But their business did bring wealth into the kingdom, which Louis would need to sustain his coming wars of conquest. Therefore, France had a stake in destroying the Dutch Republic and taking over its seaborne empire. Doing this would require help, and to Louis and Colbert England seemed the logical ally.

Colbert recognized that the English had "a natural hatred" of the French, going back to the Hundred Years' War. They were more like the Dutch than they cared to admit. But Colbert knew they coveted the Dutch markets as well; they had just fought two wars over them. He and Louis also knew that Charles II needed money. Therefore, through a series of secret diplomatic maneuvers, they presented him with a deal. They would supply Charles with an annual subsidy of 200,000 sterling—almost half his naval budget—and a squadron of thirty warships if he would join with him against the Dutch. They were also prepared to offer him an additional bonus of 100,000 pounds if he converted to Roman Catholicism.

Like his father thirty years earlier, Charles jumped at the offer of foreign money. He and his brother had admired and envied Louis for years: a sovereign monarch whose will was absolute with no pesky parliaments to deal with, a court awash in money and glamour. On May 22, 1670, Charles signed a secret treaty at Dover that promised him certain ports in Zeeland and Flanders* in exchange for a joint declaration of war against the Dutch Republic and a declaration of religious freedom for all English Catholics. He promised to convert to collect his bonus, but never did. His brother James, however, had already crossed over to the Catholic Church—a fateful move, and one which the Lord High Admiral labored to disguise, unsuccessfully, from his Protestant officers and fleet.

Since his famous diary stops in 1669, it is not clear what Pepys knew of the secret provisions, if anything. Whatever reservations he had about

---

*These were Brill, Flushing, Sluys, and Cadsand.

the character of his sovereign (and the diary shows he had many), Pepys worked devotedly to get the king's ships ready for yet another war against the Dutch, the third in less than two decades. He fended off the accusations of the parliamentary commission set up to investigate the Navy Board, arguing powerfully that the Royal Navy's problems were not about corruption or poor leadership or creeping Popery but a lack of parliamentary support, what Pepys dubbed "the costliness of poverty." The navy was still in debt to the tune of half a million pounds, with almost all of it coming due before the fleet could go to sea in 1670.

The Crown was in fact drowning in debt, more than two and a half million pounds' worth as 1671 ended. Meanwhile, war was in the offing. Colbert had imposed a punishing tariff on the importation of Dutch goods, while the Dutch responded with one of their own on French goods. Louis and Colbert urgently needed the English fleet at sea. Yet even with his secret subsidy, Charles was strapped for cash. So he decided on a simple but disastrous expedient: he stopped all payments to the Crown's creditors on January 2, 1672, and turned his debts into "loans" to be paid back at some future date with interest. The result was financial panic, as many leading merchants who owned Crown debt were ruined and others thrown into bankruptcy. The Stop of the Exchequer ruined the monarchy's credibility with London's financial community; the public Declaration of Indulgence in March permitting Catholic worship in England completed the job. But it did give Charles the breathing space to get his brother and his fleet to sea.

Charles declared war on the Dutch Republic on March 27. Louis did the same on April 6, as his 140,000 man army swept over the Flemish-Dutch border to encircle and destroy the frontier fortresses on the Rhine. On May 7 the Lord High Admiral and Lord Sandwich rendezvoused with the French fleet from Brest, commanded by the Comte d'Estrées. They greeted each other with volleys of salutes and cheers, as the English commanders had the opportunity to check out their new allies and their magnificent new ships. Eight carried 70 guns or more, and another sixteen between 50 and 68 guns; d'Estrées's flagship, the *St. Philippe,* impressed everyone with its broad clean lines, as did the 70-gun *Superbe*—so much so that King Charles ordered shipmaker Anthony Deane to use it as the model for the next generation of English warships.

Yet this magnificent fleet was about to run afoul of that grizzled veteran of both previous wars against the English, the marauder of the Medway, Admiral de Ruyter. He caught them as they anchored in Sole

Bay on the Suffolk coast. In the scramble to cut cables and get off the shore, Admiral d'Estrées missed a crucial signal from James's *Royal Prince* and sailed away from the battle, even as James and Sandwich engaged the Dutch fleet head-on. It was another confusing and bloody melee: afterward, de Ruyter called Sole Bay the longest and most desperate battle he ever fought. James had to transfer his flag twice, first from the *Royal Prince* when its captain was killed and the main-topmast shot down, smothering the mainsail, and then from the *Saint Michael,* commanded by the intrepid Robert Holmes, when it had taken so many hits below the waterline it could no longer be steered. The Duke's bravery under constant withering fire became legendary; an admiring sailor called him "General, Soldier, Pilot, Master, Seaman; to say all, he is everything that man can be, and most pleasant when the great shot are thundering about his ears."

But bravery could not save the day for the English. The Earl of Sandwich fought until his *Royal James* was ablaze from stem to stern, before ordering his men to abandon ship. As his own boat was being lowered into the water, panicky sailors leaped aboard and capsized it, and Sandwich disappeared beneath the waves. The only way his body could be identified when it washed ashore twelve days later was by its Order of the Garter ribbon and star.

Sole Bay saved the Dutch Republic. Only three ships were lost on either side, although more than four thousand sailors died in the battle. But de Ruyter's victory stopped the English fleet from blockading the Dutch coast or landing support for Louis's invading armies. A few weeks later a twenty-one-year-old Prince William of Orange—whom Pepys had met on his visit in 1660 and remembered as a "very pretty boy"—was elected as captain and admiral general for all the Dutch provinces. On June 22 he ordered the dykes opened, as southern Holland from the river Maas to the Zuider Zee became a massive sheet of water and Amsterdam an impregnable island citadel. The Sun King's blitzkrieg was halted in its tracks at the water's edge. Although the war would drag on another five years, its final outcome was never in doubt.

Sole Bay also doomed the Franco-English alliance—and changed English politics forever. D'Estrées's innocent mistake was seen as a deliberate act of French betrayal. When a combined French and English fleet again met defeat at de Ruyter's hands at the battle of Texel on August 11, 1673, commander Prince Rupert accused the French again of abandoning the English in the hour of peril. He even quoted a Dutch prisoner saying that the French were a bunch of "damned cowards." Meanwhile, the young Prince of Orange had become an overnight Protestant hero in a nation that still saw the world in terms of Foxe's *Book of Martyrs.*

In October Charles made one more attempt to raise funds for his failing war. His Lord Chancellor, the Earl of Shaftesbury, made a rousing speech, calling on the House of Commons to crush their Dutch rivals once and for all. He even quoted the ancient Roman senator Cato, *Carthago delenda est,* "Carthage must be destroyed," and told the members, especially those representing London's mercantile interests, "this is *your* war." But they were fed up and made their displeasure known in Parliament. Catholic France, not Protestant Holland, now seemed the greater threat. Pepys's friend William Coventry, made the point: "The interest of the king of England is to keep France from being too great on the Continent, and the French interest is to keep us from being masters of the sea." The result was no money. Charles had no choice but to drop out of the war.

Pepys's cousin and patron was dead; his navy's fleet and morale in tatters. Yet Pepys was more indispensable than ever to the Stuarts—"I see that on all these occasions," Pepys wrote, "they seem to rely most on me." He had become their shield in dealing with Parliament; his eloquence— the French ambassador pronounced Pepys one of the best public speakers in England—his reputation for probity, but above all his command of facts and figures, preserved the Royal Navy as an institution. During the navy's darkest days, Pepys kept it afloat in more ways than one.

Meanwhile, a Protestant backlash was in the offing. In June 1673 Parliament passed a new Test Act, forcing James to resign as Lord High Admiral because of his Catholic connections. Charles decided to appoint Pepys as first secretary of the new board that would replace his brother. This proved to be a stroke of good luck, since Pepys would now bring the same energy and drive he had used to shake up the Navy Board to transform the Admiralty.

First he moved its offices to Derby House, located midway between Westminster and Whitehall Palace, to reflect the navy's new relationship with both king and Parliament. From his sunlit office and lodgings overlooking the Thames, Pepys would oversee three major changes in the way the navy worked, changes with huge implications for the future.

The first was a new shipbuilding program. "The French and the Dutch are daily building," he warned Parliament in a speech on February 21, 1677, and to meet that threat he proposed launching thirty new warships, including ten of no less than eighty guns each and twenty third-rates.

These involved nothing less than a revolution in ship design, since they would all be built according to a single set of specifications worked out by Pepys, shipwright Anthony Deane, and Charles II himself. For the first time a "class" of warships would meet a uniform standard of tonnage, guns, and overall design, even though half the ships were to be built at private shipyards. Even more remarkably, Pepys's eloquence opened Parliament's purse strings, to the order of more than 600,000 pounds. The result was one of the most successful class of ships of the line ever launched. Nine hundred tons each, and 151 feet long on the gun deck and 40 feet wide in the beam, the 1,677 third-rates would be the backbone of the English line of battle for the next two decades.*

The second involved the royal palace at Greenwich, which Henry VIII had used to visit his royal dockyards at Deptford and Woolwich. Pepys kept his office there during the latter half of 1665 for the same reason. With its open green meadows and splendid view of the Thames, Greenwich was a wonderful escape from the grim hurly-burly of London, especially during the Great Plague. It was during walks there that Pepys met the mathematician Jonas Moore, who talked to Pepys about the ways in which the new advances in astronomy could improve long-distance navigation. With Pepys's help, Moore became a prime mover behind the creation of a Royal Observatory at Greenwich; its first Astronomer Royal, John Flamsteed, would be a Moore protégé. However, the observatory never lost its original links to the navy and became a thriving center for studying navigation as well as the stars.

His other Greenwich contact was John Evelyn. Like Pepys, he was a member of the Royal Society and avid diary keeper; he was Charles II's Commissioner for the Sick and Wounded and Prisoners of War.† He and Pepys struck up a lifelong friendship and between them laid out the first plans for creating a royal hospital for wounded and injured seamen. The original idea belonged to the Duke of York, who was moved by the suffering of his sailors at Sole Bay; but the creation of Greenwich Seamen's

---

*For the first time, all thirty ships, even the first-rates, were equipped with guns made of iron, marking the Royal Navy cast-iron gun's final victory over its brass rival.

†He was also an avid horticulturalist who launched a national campaign to replant England's dwindling oak forests for navy timber. Evelyn later boasted he had inspired the planting of more than a million trees. It was Evelyn's campaign that allowed the Royal Navy to meet its tremendous need for new ships during the eighteenth century.

Hospital would have to wait until the reign of William and Mary. By then, Pepys's fellow Royal Society member Christopher Wren would be its architect and Evelyn its first Treasurer.

The Seamen's Hospital was an attempt to deal with the problems faced by those at the low end of the navy's ranks. Pepys's third great reform addressed the problems at the top. The rivalry between gentlemen and tarpaulins was undermining the navy's effectiveness. Being a commoner himself, Pepys naturally sympathized with the tarpaulins. He understood that they were too often squeezed by poor pay and poor prospects for promotion. But being a royal servant, he was also convinced that "gentlemen ought to be brought into the Navy," since they were "men that are more sensible of honour than a man of meaner birth." Pepys added, "No man living can be more inclined than myself to favor a gentleman that is a true seaman." What was needed was a system by which the tarpaulin officers could get the rewards and job security they deserved, while the gentlemen could ballast their elevated social status with some real experience at sea.

The volunteer per order system, introduced in 1661, had tried to address this problem, by giving an adolescent nobleman a ship's berth in order to get the training he needed for a career in the Royal Navy. It was the first step toward creating a program of navy midshipmen, or "young gentlemen" as they were called as late as Nelson's day—even though the era when they were all scions of aristocratic houses was long gone.

Then in 1668 came the half-pay system for unemployed flag officers, which Pepys extended to captains of first- and second-rates. Half-pay established the principle, if not always the practice, that experienced sea officers without ships to command should remain in reserve on shore, in case they were needed in the outbreak of war—which, in the coming century, was more a matter of *when* than *if*. It was a huge step toward a professionalization of the naval officer corps and created a standard with which all Royal Navy officers, noble and commoner alike, could live and be judged.

In 1677 Pepys oversaw the next huge step, the mandatory examination for admission to the rank of lieutenant—the first and most important rung on the ladder to captain and admiral. The exam was comprehensive, ranging from navigation and astronomy to gunnery and signaling; it was rigorous, and compulsory for everyone, however rich or well-connected—or alternately, however hardened by a lifetime of war at sea. The candidate for lieutenant had to be at least twenty years of age, have spent three years at sea including one as a midshipman, and had to produce references to his "sobriety, diligence, obedience to order and application to the study and practice of the art of navigation." Everything reflected Pepys's ideal of the perfect officer for the Royal Navy, a man "sober, discreet, and experienced," who admired and obeyed authority but could also think and act on his own—much like Pepys himself.

Inequities and abuses remained, much as they did in the royal dockyards; the tension between tarpaulins and gentlemen would continue to haunt the navy into the next century. But Pepys had done more than anyone before to create a single professional standard for service and promotion. His reforms pointed the way to the Navy List, introduced in 1700: they made the Royal Navy a model of bureaucratic, as well as military, efficiency.

Yet Pepys's most desperate personal crisis, and the monarchy's, was still ahead. It started, improbably enough, with a personal triumph. In February 1674 he was elected a member of Parliament for Castle Rising in Norfolk. But one of his Admiralty commissioners, the Earl of Shaftesbury, watched his success with barely stifled rage. Shaftesbury was a cunning political animal; as Lord Chancellor and part of the government's inner circle, he had been prime mover behind the war with the Dutch. He was a keen advocate for London's mercantile lobby and for expanding England's overseas trade and colonies.* The anti-Dutch sentiments of his *Carthago delendo est* speech had been perfectly sincere. But Shaftesbury sensed the political winds were shifting, and he intended to ride them into power.

He hated James—they had a long-standing quarrel over how to manage the fleet—and he dreaded the growing Catholic influence at court. His doctor and friend John Locke encouraged him to believe that the power of the Stuart monarchy needed to be curtailed, for the sake of England's liberty, prosperity, and religion. So the sight of James securing a seat in the House of Commons for one of his protégés in order to vote the royal line, spurred Shaftesbury into action. He tried to overturn the election, on the grounds that Pepys was a closet Papist (untrue). Then Shaftesbury turned to other discontents in Parliament—Sir William Coventry, William Lord Cavendish, Lord Russell—and became their leader and patron. An organized opposition party began to take shape,

---

*The most famous were the settlements he sponsored in the Carolinas south of Cape Fear, for which John Locke wrote a brilliant but unusable constitution and whose capital Charles Town, or Charleston, would become a leading Atlantic port.

the Whig Party. Their cause was parliamentary control of government and religious liberty for Protestants, but their method in the 1670s was anti-Catholic bigotry and the politics of personal destruction.

To avoid charges of treason, Shaftesbury and his allies directed their attack not on the king but his brother. They mobilized militant Protestant feeling behind a campaign to exclude the former Lord High Admiral from succession to the throne, and to destroy his political influence. Exclusion became the first great constitutional crisis since the English civil war: it would consume two Parliaments, inspire John Locke's *Two Treatises on Government,* cause the arrest and execution of James's personal secretary and several Jesuit priests, and unleash a wave of hysteria across England, epitomized by the sensational claims by a former navy chaplain, Titus Oates, about a vast Catholic conspiracy to murder King Charles.

Guilt by association during the Popish Plot hysteria of 1678–79 was enough to ruin public reputations and even threaten lives. One of those was Pepys's. Everyone knew his close relationship with James: in the hysterical anti-Catholic atmosphere, with Oates claiming that Catholics were planning take over the fleet, fingers began to point at Pepys. In the election of 1679 the Whigs won a large majority of seats and Shaftesbury became president of the Privy Council. He relaunched his attack on Pepys, including the charge that he was a secret Catholic. There was even testimony from a renegade sea captain named John Scott that Pepys had sponsored a secret privateering ring to attack English shipping. Pepys's reign at the Admiralty had been one of "Plot, Popery, and Piracy," his enemies in Parliament said, and now he had to pay for his crimes.

This brought Pepys to his feet, in a blaze of indignation. "Mr. Speaker," he sputtered, "it must be a great misfortune to have so many things cast upon me at once, and all by surprise." But this time Pepys's eloquence could not save him. On May 22 he was sent to the Tower of London to stand trial for treason.

Fortunately, it never took place. His friends, including John Evelyn and William Coventry, rallied around him, while the Duke of York scoured every embassy in Europe to find information to discredit Scott and Pepys's other accusers. The tide of public opinion had also begun to turn against the Whigs, as their efforts to exclude James from the throne threatened the country with civil war. Members of Parliament loyal to the Stuarts rallied around a former prime minister who had began his career as a navy commissioner, Sir Thomas Osborne. They would accuse the

Whigs of attacking the principle of hereditary right and the sacred foundations of the monarchy. Just as Shaftesbury, Locke, and their friends became the first Whigs, so Danby and his followers became the first Tories, defenders of "throne and altar" and enemies of Protestant radicalism. England was getting its first taste of party politics—the unintended fruits of a failed naval war and a failed Stuart foreign policy.

But what ultimately saved Pepys was the absurdity of the accusations against him and his own reputation for probity and integrity. He had built a Royal Navy that was rapidly preparing for the future, with a total tonnage nearly equal to that of France* and more than 12,000 men. It was a navy that could now account for every penny it spent; a navy that was increasingly being seen as above politics, too vital to the nation to become the plaything of plot and faction.

Finally, in June 1680, the last charges were dismissed. Eventually, Shaftesbury took Pepys's place in the Tower (he was released by a Whig grand jury and fled to Holland in 1682) and the political atmosphere changed enough for Charles II to restore his loyal servant to his offices at Derby House.

In 1684 Pepys, now fifty-one years old, accepted two great honors. In May he was appointed first secretary for the Affairs of the Admiralty, with a generous salary of 22,000 pounds a year and letters patent under the Privy Seal. He now had sole authority over both the Admiralty and the Navy Board; in effect, he was now as much an all-powerful Secretary of the Marine as his rival Colbert. Then, in December, he was elected president of the Royal Society. It was as president that Pepys would grant approval of the publication of Isaac Newton's *Principia Mathematica,* with his name appearing on the title page of a work by a scientist as well known to mariners and hydrographers for his analysis of tides as he was to physicists and astronomers.

Pepys's legacy was nearly complete. In the next three years, the political atmosphere in England would undergo another rapid change of front. But thanks to Pepys, the Royal Navy would never again face penury at home or humiliation at sea.

---

*The Royal Navy tonnage was 132,000 (compared to 88,000 in 1660) versus France's 135,000.

CHAPTER TEN

Revolution

It is from England that the salvation of Europe must come.
—WILLIAM, PRINCE OF ORANGE

I N THE AUTUMN of 1687, the Netherlands' Prince William of Orange was watching events across the Channel with increasing disquiet. England's king, James II, the former Duke of York and Lord High Admiral, was systematically undermining his own ability to rule. James's open Catholicism, including publicly attending mass, and his pro-Catholic policies were alienating Whigs and Tories, Anglicans and Dissenters alike. Having destroyed his credibility at home, the danger was that James might turn to another Roman Catholic monarch for support, Louis XIV of France—the king whose army and navy was poised like a dagger at the Dutch Republic's heart.

Louis and his ambassador had encouraged such an alliance ever since James had come to the throne in 1685. James's brother Charles II had taken up a similar offer in 1670, and that alliance had nearly crushed Holland out of existence. If it happened again, the consequences could be even worse. France not only had the largest army in the world, but now the largest navy. England had the second largest. The two together could control the Channel from the western tip of Brittany to the North Sea; they would put the Dutch Republic in a permanent stranglehold that it could never hope to break.

As Captain-General of the Dutch Republic, Prince William could not let that happen. William understood little of English politics, still less its navy. But he did understand power, and how it could be used for good or evil. So to prevent a union of the French and English fleets, and to keep Louis XIV at bay, he began to conceive a plan so audacious and daring that he dared not mention it even to his closest political allies. He would launch a preemptive invasion of England itself, in order to knock James out of the French orbit and bring the country on board as Holland's ally, not its enemy, as it had been in the last three wars.

In November 1688, one hundred years after the Spanish Armada, William of Orange would launch another invasion of the British Isles. However, this invasion was aimed not at crushing England, but forcing it to assume the leadership of Europe. It would trigger the so-called Glorious Revolution and lay the political foundations of modern Britain. But it should be remembered that what prompted the invasion were the new challenges and realities of sea power. In the late autumn of 1688 the fate of Europe hung in the balance, and the Royal Navy found itself holding the scales.

* * *

It seems strange that the navy, which owed so much to James, would end up playing so prominent part in bringing him down. As Lord High Admiral, he had been a favorite of its seamen and captains. They admired his bravery—"General, Soldier, Pilot, Master, Seaman; . . . he is everything that man can be," they said after Sole Bay—and they knew that he fought to get them the ships and resources they needed. Indeed, at his accession the money flowed as never before. In addition, James's handpicked Admiralty secretary, Samuel Pepys, worked to make the navy a tough and lean fighting force, with an important role in the wider world.

The Royal Navy still had no permanent squadron in the West Indies, despite that region's growing importance to English trade. But in the Mediterranean, it had acquired a base by dynastic accident. Tangier came as part of the dowry of Charles II's Portuguese bride in 1662. It was a bustling but squalid sun-baked port at the northwestern tip of Africa almost in sight of the great rock of Gibraltar, the gateway of the Pillars of Hercules. Pepys was one of its commissioners and his brother-in-law ran its naval stores. The hope that Tangier would become a base for ending piracy through the Straits of Gibraltar never came about: its harbor was never large or deep enough to maintain more than a few frigates. But it did become the navy's first home away from England.

Pepys's brother-in-law described it as "this hell of brimstone and fire and Egypt's plagues," but navy officers liked serving in Tangier. Their anticorsair patrols brought combat experience and promotion, as well as prize money; they also enjoyed carrying cargoes for English merchants trading in the Mediterranean, in exchange for a share of the profits (a practice Pepys tried to ban but with little result). Their commander was an ambitious and thoroughly unscrupulous officer named Arthur Herbert, who used his success in suppressing the corsairs around Algiers to get himself promoted back to England as Admiral of the Fleet in 1683.

Albemarle and Prince Rupert were gone, and the other admirals of the Dutch wars either dead or retired. So Herbert and his protégés from Tangier, like John Benbow, George Rooke, and Cloudsley Shovell, were the rising generation of Royal Navy leadership. Most counted as gentlemen rather than tarpaulins (Benbow was an exception); most were heavily involved in politics and various factional intrigues, including against one another. Herbert was Master of the Robes as well as admiral; his rival Admiral Edward Russell ran his own faction in Parliament and eventually became secretary of state. But events in March of 1687 were about to draw them together, as the king summoned Admiral Herbert into his presence for a private chat.

James had made himself unpopular with those who counted in English politics: the landed class and their merchant allies who dominated Parliament and local government. He had not started that way. Although he was known to be a Roman Catholic, he began his reign with strong burst of public support. The failed Rye House plot of 1683, which sent leading Whig radicals Algernon Sidney and Admiral Russell's cousin William Russell to the scaffold, and the bloody Monmouth uprising in 1685, had both tried to replace James with Charles II's illegitimate but Protestant son the Duke of Monmouth. However, they only made James seem sympathetic to most law-and-order-loving Englishmen, if not exactly popular.

But James's obsession with promoting the interests of his fellow English Catholics, even in the teeth of law, custom, and public opinion, squandered whatever political capital he had. James may have had a dream of one day bringing England back into the arms of Rome: his more zealous Catholic courtiers certainly talked that way, which added to the apprehension the rest of the nation felt about him.

But James's fatal error was to insist that the 40,000 man army he had raised to defeat Monmouth become permanent, and that the many Catholic officers he had recruited for it remain under commission. Fears of a permanent standing army in England, vivid since the dictatorship of Oliver Cromwell, now joined up with the usual anti-Catholic fears. Men asked themselves if James intended to use his army to impose Catholicism on England, just as Louis XIV had used his army to destroy the Protestant Huguenot community from France just three years earlier.

By contrast, the navy had very few Catholic officers, even among James's own protégés. Those who were, like Sir Roger Strickland, had so obviously converted for political reasons that no one took them very seriously. But now the king revealed to Herbert his next move. He was going to lift the Test Acts and grant full religious toleration to all Roman Catholics and Protestant Dissenters in England. James wanted all his major officeholders to support his Declaration of Indulgence, as it was called, and he wanted Herbert's active support—and the support of the navy.

Arthur Herbert was a hard man. He had commanded a ship at Sole Bay and lost an eye to an Algerian corsair during his Tangier command. He had a reputation for being a hard-drinking, hard-gambling, hard-wenching cynical bastard—in Pepys's words, "Of all the worst men living, Herbert is the only man that I do not know to have any one virtue to compound for all his vices." But James's proposal left him aghast. The olive branch offered to dissenting groups was an obvious attempt to out-flank Anglican resistance to toleration for Catholics. Dissenters had been the strongest supporters of the Monmouth rebellion; most would not be fooled by James's offer of full religious and civil liberty.* Herbert also realized that this meant Catholic officers like Strickland, officers he despised, would enjoy royal favor more than ever.

But above all Herbert was offended because James assumed he would have no scruples about such a radical assault on the political and religious foundations of England. Herbert angrily refused to have anything to do with it. James was surprised and just as angry: "A man who lives as you do ought not to talk about his conscience," the king said.

"I have my faults, sir," cried Herbert, glaring at a king notorious for his adultery, "but I could name people who talk much more about conscience than I am in the habit of doing, and yet lead lives as loose as mine." In a rage, James dismissed him from his posts, including commander in chief. A Pepys favorite, Lord Dartmouth, took Herbert's place. But the reverberations of Herbert's dismissal were felt all through the navy and even in Westminster, as James's stock continued to plummet and the atmosphere of crisis grew.

---

*An exception was William Penn, leader of the Quakers and son of Admiral William Penn. He would later name the American colony the Crown permitted him to create after his father: Pennsylvania.

In April the Declaration of Indulgence was published, and met an angry backlash across England. Over the summer many of Roger Strickland's Catholic protégés were promoted over the heads of more experienced officers; Strickland himself, in spite of Pepys's bitter objections, became rear admiral. An attempt to install Catholic chaplains in the fleet set off a near mutiny. In July James dissolved Parliament.

Meanwhile, powerful events were stirring on the other side of the Channel. In August Louis imposed a trade ban on herring from the Dutch Republic, followed by stiff new tariffs on Dutch textiles. Holland's position in world trade was on a long slow decline, even as England's merchant fleet had grown by more than 50 percent in the last three decades. Any attack on its vulnerable balance of trade was a serious matter; so serious that William of Orange's warnings about Louis over the past decade finally began finally to sink home.

Like Winston Churchill in a later century, Prince William had to push hard to convince his fellow countrymen that they had to act against an implacable enemy bent on their destruction before it was too late. And like Churchill, William understood that even when he convinced them to fight, they could not fight alone. The Dutch Republic would need allies on land. William turned to the German princes in the League of Augsburg, who had organized to prevent Louis XIV's aggression along the Rhine frontier. He would also need an ally at sea, and that meant England. William's plans for a preemptive invasion got under way in deathly secret; he even kept his own government in the dark until a month before he sailed. But he knew the Royal Navy was all that stood between success and failure, survival and destruction.

The reality of modern sea power was beginning to sink in. Even without leaving port, a large powerful fleet like that of France posed a potential threat to its neighbors' sea routes and access to markets. The Dutch navy, or rather navies, had declined to barely half the tonnage of the French navy; the heroic age of Tromp and de Ruyter was definitively over. Only the Royal Navy, with more than one hundred and seventy ships, including nearly as many first-rates as the French, could make up the difference; only England could exert enough control over the Channel to offset Louis's massive advantage in land forces. And only extreme action, in effect a coup d'état with English support, had any chance of compelling James to join forces against France. "It is now or never," William told a confidant, as he put his bold plan in motion.

It was not quite as far-fetched as it might have seemed. William was, after all, heir to the throne of England, since James had no sons and William was married to his eldest daughter, Mary. He was a Stuart himself on his mother's side. He had kept close tabs on English politics and kept a network of influential contacts and supporters in the kingdom. They too feared Louis: "The nation cannot be beaten at sea by the Dutch," said one back in 1675, "but may be by the French." Given the choice between submitting to a Dutch invasion or France and the Roman Catholic Church, they would not hesitate. William was already a hero for having stood up to Louis XIV and was widely seen as the champion of international Protestantism. All he would need was a valid excuse for putting his plans into high gear, and he would find plenty of collaborators once he reached the shores of England.

If he *could* reach the shores of England. For that, too, depended on the navy. Without its cooperation, or at least acquiescence, his plan was useless. So among the first secret contacts he made in England were Admirals Herbert and Russell. Russell, whose cousin had been executed for plotting against James, made numerous trips to Holland from the beginning of 1687 until the following spring. Then in November came rumors that James's queen was pregnant. The prospect of a Catholic Stuart dynasty stretching on long after James had departed the scene, now gave everything an additional urgency.

In April 1688 William told Russell of his worries. However, he would not move on his own, he said; he needed an invitation from a sufficient number of leading aristocrats and notables to come to England to protect the Protestant faith and restore Parliament. On June 30 Russell and six other worthies, including the Tory Earl of Danby and the bishop of London, signed such a letter. The next day Arthur Herbert left London disguised as a common seaman with the letter in his baggage, along with a verbal assurance that both the navy, army, and 95 percent of the population, would rally to William. The next time Herbert would see England would be at the head of William's invasion fleet four months later: the largest invasion fleet to cross the Channel until D-Day in 1944.

James never grasped what was happening until too late. The French ambassador in the Hague had learned what was up and Louis warned James several times, but James refused to believe his own daughter and son-in-law could be actively plotting his downfall. In September Louis invaded the German Palatinate, the first step toward encircling and destroying the Netherlands. By the end of the month William was assembling his armada in the shallow waters of the Maas estuary, with fifty warships and more than four hundred transport under Herbert's command. It was only then that James made his first countermove: he authorized the impressment of sailors to man the fleet and told Lord Dartmouth to prepare for a "great and sudden invasion from Holland."

Dartmouth was in a difficult position. He was close friends with his second-in-command, the hated Catholic Roger Strickland. He also despised Herbert: if any English admiral was likely to take Herbert on in a full-scale engagement, it was he. But many of Dartmouth's best officers were Herbert protégés; his rear admiral, Sir John Berry, vigorously opposed Catholic influence in the fleet. Besides, Herbert had secretly circulated a letter among the fleet's commanders and captains, warning them that an English "victory" would really mean the ruin of Protestantism and the nation. "The kingdom has always depended on the navy for its defense," he wrote, "so you will go farther by making it the protector of her religion and liberties." Nonetheless, following James's orders, Dartmouth took his bitterly divided force of sixty sail down to the Gunfleet in the Thames estuary in mid-October, to wait for battle.

On October 29 William walked on board his flagship, the Brill, with his banner flapping in the freshening breeze. Quartered with the arms of the house of Nassau and of England, it displayed the Orange family motto, "I will maintain," to which were added in three-foot-high letters, "the liberties of England and the Protestant religion." However, by the time this Dutch armada set sail the wind was shifting to the west, and blowing harder, so hard that they had to bear up and ride the storm out along the shore before returning to harbor. On the first of November they tried again, as the wind shifted around to the east and carried them well into the Channel.

William had intended to land in Yorkshire, far from James's army assembled on the southern coast, but the fickle wind again forced a change of plans. During the night it began to barrel out of the northeast, barring entry into the North Sea; instead, he was forced to turn into the Channel and toward the waiting English fleet. But the same wind now trapped Dartmouth and his ships in their shelter in the Downs. They had to sit by impotently as the 1688 invasion fleet swung past them in the exact reverse course of its 1588 predecessor: through the Straits of Dover, where huge crowds turned out on the chalk cliffs to watch, past the Portland Bill and Isle of Wight, past Portsmouth and on into the West Country.

It was a strange moment. No one had planned to come back to this part of England, although the anti-Catholic feeling of Drake and Hawkins and Raleigh lived on in their descendants. Devon and Somerset had been at the center of the Monmouth uprising. But in the early morning of the fifth the fleet found itself being pushed along toward Plymouth, with Dartmouth's ships in hot pursuit, when the wind reversed itself again, allowing William to make safe harbor at Torbay, opposite Exeter. The same westerly gales now also forced Dartmouth, who was actually in sight of Torbay and the Dutch fleet, back up the Channel into the Downs. The Orange forces could now make their landing with no interference.

In 1588, a "Protestant wind" had prevented the invasion of English shores. In 1688, one saved it. It was also November 5, anniversary of the Gunpowder Plot.* William, the committed Calvinist, turned to his Anglican chaplain, Gilbert Burnet, with a grim smile: "Well, Doctor, what do you think of predestination now?" They leaned over the side and watched as William's army—English, Dutch, and German troops, French Huguenots, even Swedes in black armor and fur cloaks—began to disembark, while local fishermen rowed boats out to take them to shore. On the ninth Exeter threw open its gates to the invaders, as townspeople, farmers, and West Country gentry gathered around his standard.

Even before William began his march on London on November 21, it was clear he had won without firing a shot. The same westerly winds kept Dartmouth pinned down in the Downs and then at Spithead; James's army was paralyzed by indecision until on the twenty-third James decided to retreat rather than fight. That night his best general, John Churchill (later to be the Duke of Marlborough), deserted to the Orange cause, followed by James's other daughter, Anne. James returned to a silent and hostile London, which was impatiently waiting to surrender to its Dutch conqueror. On December 11, James packed his remaining bags, threw the Great Seal of State into the Thames, and fled. The next day Dartmouth surrendered the fleet.

It was a great and bloodless victory, but James's flight caught everyone by surprise. William and his supporters had expected him to become their unwilling accomplice, signing on to their reforms as the price for keeping his throne. At Sheerness James had boarded a vessel, still hoping

---

*This was the 1605 Catholic plot to blow up James I and Parliament, which was foiled and which remains an English national holiday (with strong anti-Catholic overtones) until today.

to contact Dartmouth, when local fishermen intercepted him at Faversham; troops returned him to London shortly before William arrived. William, however, had changed his mind: better to let the king "escape" again without any embarrassing meetings or scenes before Parliament. So it was not until Christmas Day 1688, that James finally reached the French coast near Calais to begin his life as an exile under the personal protection of Louis XIV.

The Glorious Revolution, therefore, had accomplished what William most feared, although only after he had won: James was now Louis XIV's committed ally. This meant two things for the future. First, it effectively destroyed any credibility James still had. William and Mary now took his place as the legitimate monarchs of England. They would preside over the sweeping constitutional changes that followed in the next year: the Convention Parliament, the passing of the Bill of Rights, the Toleration Act, the Mutiny Act—all under the aegis of a regime that, however popular, was in the final uncomfortable analysis imposed by force of arms rather than legitimate succession (although a series of Succession Acts would try to take care of that). Only James's heir, born the previous July, enjoyed that claim: an irrelevant point perhaps to a triumphant English Parliament, but important anywhere that Roman Catholics lived in large numbers, such as Ireland or Scotland.

Second, it meant Dutch and English interests were now firmly one. Their future as free peoples depended on stopping Louis XIV. "France is at the bottom of all Slavery," exclaimed John Evelyn, "and that was to be brought upon us" if James returned. But England had no army: James's 40,000-man establishment had scattered to the wind with the end of his regime. Raising another would take time and money. The only tool William had at hand was the Royal Navy.

Fortunately, it emerged from the revolution in good shape and more united than ever. The vacillating Dartmouth was dismissed; Strickland and other Catholic officers resigned. Pepys believed he could not serve the new regime in good conscience and quit the Admiralty, choosing permanent retirement after nearly twenty-two years of matchless service. Everyone else was relieved at the regime change: some captains would even claim it was their secret agreement to ignore James's orders, rather than any "Protestant wind," that kept them out of William's way and allowed the revolution to succeed. The victorious leader of the Dutch expedition, Arthur Herbert, reclaimed his post as commander in chief, with the new title of Earl of Torrington. He was still getting his fleet ready when William declared war on France in April 1689.

This was a naval war by default, but one unlike any the Royal Navy had fought before. Its series of wars against the Dutch did nothing to prepare it for the long, bitter conflict ahead, which would drag on more than two decades and on three continents—its first brush with the experience of world war. The constant threat of invasion, the need to support land operations in Ireland and the Continent and protect convoys in the Atlantic and Mediterranean, would demand full-time, year-round service from a navy still used to mothballing the bulk of its fleet between December and April.

Above all, it faced an enemy unlike any other. The Dutch, like the Spanish before them, had fought primarily defensive wars, struggling to keep their seaborne empires from the encroaching English. The new French enemy was tough, aggressive, and more organized, with a centralized bureaucracy and a powerful economy at his fingertips.

The French navy reflected the same virtues. Although Colbert had died in 1683, his son, the Count of Seignelay, had continued his father's system of rigorous organization, meticulous attention to detail, and aggressive buildup of naval power. In 1689, the French navy had more ships, better-armed and faster ships, and for the first and only time in its century-long conflict with its British rival, better and more experienced admirals.

The French formula for success was simple. Build the best ships, train the best officers and seamen, drill to perfection, and you will win the day. They turned the demanding art of sailing close-hauled in line ahead into an exact science. French admirals' sailing instructions were all written on neatly printed forms. Their leading naval theorist was a Jesuit mathematician named La Hoste, who devised precise balletic maneuvers for fleets, which even he admitted had little practical value but remained valuable for study and training. French shipmasters learned to hold their ships "six points of the compass"* to the wind, while the English navy could ask only seven, since few of its ships were seaworthy enough to keep on that rigorous tack for long (since sailing so close to the wind ran the risk of drifting to leeward and "missing stays," or failing to shift back on the other tack).

"By the book" became the standard for the French navy, just as trusting one's instincts and "muddling through" remained typical of the Royal

---

*Or roughly at an angle of 70 degrees from the wind.

Navy, especially at sea. The one made a navy skillfully precise and beautiful to watch, but with a tendency to be overorganized and needlessly rigid. The other made a military service able to respond quickly to crisis, but subject to breakdown at unexpected moments.

One such moment came now, at the very beginning of the war. As usual, no one had thought to pay the navy's sailors, in spite of William's new government, and so they refused to board their ships. The fleet sat idle, unable to sail, while Louis took the opportunity to land James with a small French force in Ireland, to raise its Catholic population against the new regime. James was suddenly back in the picture, with only the Irish Channel keeping him from returning to England—and with an army of only nine thousand men to stop him.

The Royal Navy was all that kept England from being plunged into a French-backed civil war. Herbert managed to get a few ships out in time to stop a second and larger French fleet from landing at Kinsale (they landed instead at Bantry Bay), and another six thousand French troops reached Ireland the following year. Yet Louis held his navy back. His attention was focused on the land war, where his armies were fighting the combined forces of the League of Augsburg, including Holland and Spain, in a bloody series of sieges and fortress battles. This allowed Herbert to land William and a small army in northern Ireland and relieve the siege of Londonderry. It was not until June 1690 that Louis finally authorized his admiral, the Count of Tourville, to take the fleet out of Brest harbor to engage the Anglo-Dutch fleet in a showdown for control of the waters around Britain.

Tourville's appearance off the Isle of Wight on June 23, 1689, caught Herbert, now Lord Torrington, by surprise. Some of his most trusted officers, like Cloudsley Shovell, were away with their ships; he had only fifty-eighty ships of the line, against Tourville's seventy-five. He wanted to avoid battle and withdraw up the Thames, where the French could not bring their greater numbers to bear. But Queen Mary (now in charge with William in Ireland) and her advisors were horrified and ordered him to attack at once. And so, with the fate of kingdoms and dynasties and Europe itself at stake, Torrington had no choice but to raise anchor off Beachy Head and carry out their order.

He was outnumbered but had the wind at his back, with Tourville lying dead ahead perpendicular to his advance. His Dutch allies led him in, turning to starboard to engage the leading French squadrons on a parallel course, while Torrington aimed his own fleet for the French center. His plan was to spread his ships as thinly as he could, so that the French could not overlap his shorter line of battle and "double" him at either end.

The plan might have worked if Tourville had been less alert and his men less skilled and disciplined. Counting the allied ships as they made their turn in a slow column of billowing white sails, Tourville realized how few they were and what they were trying to do. He ordered his center to surge ahead, opening a gap in his line but allowing him to overtake the Dutch as they came onto his course. What Torrington most feared now happened: the French had caught his van in a vise, with the lighter-armed Dutch ships pinned between double lines of French broadsides. Torrington signaled his lead admiral, John Ashby, to rush to their rescue but Tourville's magnificent 104-gun flagship, the *Soleil Royal,* poured out a devastating fire that crippled Ashby's ship as she drifted out of line and his squadron dropped back.

The Dutch fought on bravely but hopelessly for another five hours. By noon the battle of Beachy Head was essentially decided and everyone knew who had won. The next day five disabled allied ships, including the English 70-gun *Anne,* were set ablaze by their own crews while the rest of Torrington's fleet escaped on the morning tide to safety. Tourville might have pursued more forcefully, but he had decided to keep his fleet together and relish his victory.

And a major victory it was. The allies had lost fifteen vessels while Tourville had lost none. Holland was effectively finished as a major naval power and the French were now masters of the English Channel. Panic set in all along the coast and in London. People expected the French to sail up the Medway to burn Chatham, as de Ruyter had done just twenty years earlier, or to land troops in Kent. Torrington was rewarded for following orders against his better judgment by being thrown in the Tower. Queen Mary wrote a humiliating letter to the Dutch States General, apologizing for Torrington's "abandonment" of the Dutch squadron and offering 10,000 gulden for the widows of Dutch sailors killed in the action.

Then just as suddenly the mood changed. News had come from Ireland. The day after Beachy Head, William had routed James and his army at the Battle of the Boyne and was advancing on Dublin. Then, after anchoring briefly at Torbay and sacking the village of Teignmouth, the French fleet had returned to Brest with sick crews, depleted stores, and nothing to show for their success. Even more amazingly, news arrived that Louis had dismissed Tourville in a fit of pique, for failing to crush the English fleet.

The French learned a sobering lesson at Beachy Head. Victory might make them masters of the Channel, free to enter it when they pleased and leave when they wished. But they could not stay there. There was not a single deepwater harbor between Brest and Dunkirk they could use as a base for major fleet operations. The English coast, by contrast, offered a series of well-protected ports and harbors—Plymouth, Exeter, Torbay, Southampton, Portsmouth, Spithead—from which its navy could regroup, outfit and maintain its vessels, and strike at its enemies from any direction. Geography had given the English a permanent advantage in a war for control of its seaways. French sea power would struggle against it for the next century, to no avail.

Geography deterred the French, but so did the presence of the main royal fleet, even in defeat. Certainly that was Torrington's argument when his court-martial got under way in December 1690. He would claim that he had avoided an all-or-nothing battle at Beachy Head in order to make sure the fleet remained intact. "Whilst we had a fleet in being," he said, he was sure "they [the French] would not make the attempt" to invade England. Torrington was acquitted and a new concept in naval strategy was born, that of a "fleet in being" whose simple existence would be enough to deter an opponent from acting offensively. It would become a hallmark of the British navy for more than two hundred years, and the justification for maintaining a large and powerful battle fleet in peacetime as well as at war.

But how to pay for it? That was the problem that had beaten every naval administrator in the seventeenth century, from Buckingham to Pepys. The Glorious Revolution had reaffirmed Parliament's power over the purse. It still hated standing armies, but standing navies were another matter. After Beachy Head its members said, "They dare not go back into the country if they do not give money liberally." The House of Commons voted to build twenty-seven new warships and new docks at Plymouth. But even this was not going to be enough to sustain a navy that would more than double in size, cost more nearly two million pounds a year, and have to fight constantly on three fronts at once—the Channel, the Irish Sea and Atlantic, and the Mediterranean.

Events at sea forced the issue. On June 17, 1693, the French fleet attacked a huge convoy of four hundred merchant ships bound for the

Mediterranean port of Smyrna. Despite the best efforts of Admiral George Rooke's puny escort, Tourville captured almost a hundred ships and trapped the rest in Spanish ports, making it too dangerous for them to leave. The lost convoy cost upward of a million pounds, and set off a financial panic in England. The lost money and coin forced William's government to pay their bills that year with paper instead and organize a subscription loan based on future tax revenues—a loan that would become the basis for the Bank of England.

It was the first of a series of fiscal expedients with which the new regime kept the war going, and which historians now call the Financial Revolution—the second revolution to transform England after 1688. Some expedients, like the national bank and a national lottery, came from Dutch practice. But the most important came from the Royal Navy. Since the Stop of the Exchequer in 1672 the navy had handled its pressing debt problems by issuing tallies, or "navy bills," secured by future tax revenues from the Exchequer, and paying 10 percent interest. London speculators regularly traded discounted navy bills in an ongoing market, making investors comfortable with the idea of buying and selling pieces of government debt as government bonds.

In 1689 the government took over the navy's debt, paying off suppliers and victualers and shipbuilders with bills issued by the Exchequer and crediting the amount to the navy's account. What had once been the king's problem, how to pay for "his" navy, now became the nation's and Parliament's responsibility. Exchequer bills or bonds would allow the government to spend more than 42 million pounds on the wars of the League of Augsburg. It expanded the army to 75,000 men and the navy from 109 ships in 1690 to 176 ten years later—and all without prompting a political crisis. Since customs and excise taxes paid the bulk of the bills over the long haul,* creditors could see that a growing economy meant flowing revenues, which was precisely what a strong navy guaranteed. It was an early and unforgettable lesson in supply-side economics: from that point of view, the navy was more than paying for itself. The modern English state had arrived, with powerful fiscal and military instruments at its disposal. These would be the powerhouse of modern Great Britain.

It did not come without a struggle. Some in Parliament fumed about the growth of state power and a large standing army—just what they had

---

*Excise alone brought in more than a third of state revenue after 1689, and customs another fifth.

wanted the Glorious Revolution to prevent. The storms of party politics swirled back and forth throughout William's reign and beyond. Whigs supported his efforts to build up an army to fight Louis XIV on the continent and saw the navy primarily as a way to secure Ireland and defend the British Isles. Tories like Pepys's friend Thomas Sprat believed, "The English greatness will never be supported or increased in this age by any other wars but those at sea." They insisted the navy was all that was needed to stop Louis XIV, by crippling France's trade and taking away its colonies. "I am for . . . His Majesty to take care of the sea," said one MP, "and let your confederates [i.e., the Dutch and Germans] take care of the land." Whigs and Tories clashed on every issue, from religion to the monarchy to foreign policy. But everyone was united on one thing: the need for a strong navy. It was now a sacrosanct institution, crucial to the future of the nation. "The Navy is of so great importance," wrote the marquis of Halifax in 1693, "that it would be disparaged by calling it less than the life and soul of government."

Louis, meanwhile, was growing frustrated with the course of his war, both on land and at sea. The Jacobite revolt in Ireland had collapsed. Static siege warfare along the Dutch frontier frustrated his desire to secure a port on the Maas or Scheldt estuaries for invading England. His minister Seignelay died in 1690, leaving the French naval administration in inexperienced and uncertain hands while costs continued to mount. Tourville was back, engaged in a series of complicated maneuvers in the western entrance to the Channel designed to disrupt English and Dutch trade, which would culminate in the capture of the Smyrna convoy. But he was also avoiding any direct confrontation with the English fleet, now under Sir Edward Russell, which was getting stronger by the month. The king became fed up with Tourville's cautious approach and ordered a new strategy for victory in 1692, one more fitting to Louis's sense of *gloire*.

He decided that Tourville and the French fleet must spearhead an immediate invasion of England. James II and his advisors had convinced Louis that even a small landing would set off a revolt against William and Mary. Louis ordered twenty regiments of Irish and French infantry to assemble at Saint-Vaast-la-Hougue on the Cherbourg peninsula. Tourville was to gather up the different squadrons at Brest and Rochefort in Brittany and Toulon on the Mediterranean, and then escort the invaders across the Channel in time to defeat the English as they sortied out to meet it and before the Dutch could join them.

Everything depended on speed of execution and surprise. Louis lost the first due to the problem he and his ministers had ignored for too long: the French navy's crippling lack of manpower. For all its impressive size, magnificent ships, and complicated bureaucratic rules, it could never find enough sailors. Manning ninety-three ships of the line and thirty-eight frigates demanded 45,000 men out of a total seafaring population of 55,000. Even more than their English counterparts, French sailors evaded navy service whenever they could. But the Royal Navy's seafaring population would grow steadily in the new century with the expansion of its merchant fleet. By contrast, the French would eventually be forced to draft soldiers, even peasants, to fill the lower decks.

Shortage of sailors delayed Tourville's departure by almost a month. By then, Louis had lost his second advantage. News of his invasion prepa-rations had inevitably leaked to William and his government. They moved soldiers to Portsmouth, mobilized the militia, arrested Jacobite and Catholic dissidents,* and ordered Russell to get his fleet up and ready to meet the threat. Nonetheless, Louis refused to alter his plans, even though he knew Tourville would never have time to assemble all his squadrons. He ordered him to go to La Hougue at once with whatever ships he could find and attack the English fleet, whatever its strength. This is my direct order, Louis XIV told Tourville, "and I wish it to be exactly followed."

One can only sympathize with Tourville—a better admiral than his master deserved. As he entered the Channel on May 15 he had only forty-four ships of the line, while Russell would have as many as ninety. The sit-uation was in fact the exact reverse of Beachy Head: a commander in chief ordered against his will to fight a numerically superior opponent. On the eve of battle, knowing he had no hope of success, Tourville sum-moned his officers to the magnificent admiral's cabin of the *Soleil Royal,* and showed them the king's note. They had already been accused of cow-ardice, he told them; at least they would not be accused of disobedience. He shook hands with each, and then ordered them to their ships.

Meanwhile, Admiral Russell was on his flagship, the 100-gun *Britannia,* when the first Dutch ships joined him in the Downs. He commanded the most powerful military force ever assembled in the English Channel:

---

*Two of those arrested were Pepys and Lord Dartmouth; Pepys was soon released, but the unfortunate Dartmouth died in the Tower.

eighty-two ships of the line and seventeen frigates, more than 7,000 guns and 40,000 officers and sailors. Russell himself commanded the Red Squadron in the center, with Cloudsley Shovell as his rear admiral. The Dutch in the White Squadron would lead the line of battle when the fleet was on the starboard tack, and the English Blue Squadron under Vice Admiral Rooke in the 96-gun *Neptune* and Rear Admiral Richard Carter in the 90-gun *Duke,* on the port tack. Russell read to his officers a letter from Nottingham and the queen: "God preserve your person, direct your counsels, and prosper your arms: and let all your people say Amen." To his sailors, he was more blunt: "If your commanders play you false, overboard with them, and with myself the first."

The fleet stood out to sea on May 17 in a long winding line more than five miles long, with frigates deployed in front and on the flanks. On May 19 Tourville caught his first sight of the allies on his eastern horizon as he came to up to Barfleur, only a few miles from La Hougue. With his heart in his mouth, he gave the signal for combat.

Like Torrington at Beachy Head, Tourville had the wind behind him: but then so did his opponent. Like Torrington, he also hoped to spread his line thin to protect his smaller force, and ordered his rearmost ships to stay out of gun range in order not to be doubled. Instead, the real fighting came in the center, as the *Soleil Royal,* flanked by three first-rates with three gun decks each, engaged the 100-gun *Britannia,* the 96-gun *Neptune,* and 96-gun *St. Andrew,* commanded by George Churchill, brother of the future Duke of Marlborough, in a violent, ear-splitting clash of the titans at less than two hundred yards.

Cannon roared out broadsides of fire and iron; volley after volley crashed through sails, rigging, and timber, with shot and splinters tearing men limb from limb.* "In a trice we were so buried in fire and smoke, and had such hot service ourselves, that we could not see or mind what others did." By noon the *Soleil Royal* had taken so many hits it had to be towed out of line to make repairs. Then the wind changed: the great clouds of gun smoke began to drift over the English ships as the breeze blew out of the northwest. Shovell saw his chance. He luffed sails and put his helm down away from the wind, so that he and his squadron glided through the French line in the rear. At almost the same time, the leading Dutch ships

---

*One of the *St. Andrew*'s crewmen also happened to be a woman. She survived the battle, was invited to meet the queen, and won a certificate of good conduct from Captain Churchill.

broke the French line in the front, cutting off the 68-gun *Bourbon* and turning the rest back to windward.

"At that moment," Shovell wrote afterward, "they began to run." Caught between fire on two sides, the French had no choice but to beat to windward to escape the pounding. Then the wind almost died and a late afternoon mist began to descend. The *Soleil Royal,* its battered companion the *Admirable,* and the other French ships had to tow themselves away in painful slow motion, the gunfire never stopping. Carter's squadron was next to drift through the gap in the thickening mist and past the French guns. Carter himself was pierced by a splinter from his own yardarm, and lay dying on the deck. "Fight the ship," he gasped to his men, "Fight the ship as long as she swims."

Shovell was also hit by flying debris and taken below. By now almost all order had been lost, as ships and squadrons fought piecemeal in a confused melee until evening, when fog engulfed the entire scene. Tourville used it to make his escape to La Hougue.

He had taken a terrible beating but, incredibly, still had not lost a single ship. In fact, a standard ship of the line, with its two-foot-thick timbers, could take literally hundreds of shots without sinking. Even hull shots close to the waterline only left holes eight or nine inches in diameter, quickly patched by the ship's carpenters. The one mortal enemy a ship like the *Soleil Royal* faced was fire, and this is what the English now brought to Tourville's battered and exhausted fleet as it lay at various anchorages around La Hougue and the Cherbourg peninsula. On May 21 and 22 fireships swept in, while Shovell's squadron, now under Rooke's command, blasted the French shore batteries. In the confusion, boatloads of English sailors rowed up to individual French ships and set them alight. The *Soleil Royal,* the *Admirable,* and the 76-gun *Triomphant* had all run aground; they went up in a great holocaust of fire and smoke. Squadrons of French cavalry desperately charged the beach, as the seamen fought them off with boathooks. By evening fifteen French ships of the line were blazing hulks, including the greatest battleship in the world, the *Soleil Royal,* along with almost all of James II's transports. James, the former Lord Admiral, watched the scene from the cliffs above and, in spite of himself, exclaimed: "Ah, none but my brave English could do so brave an action!"

Yet what he had witnessed was the end of his last hope of regaining his kingdom. Russell's victory at Barfleur and La Hougue not only stopped any invasion of England; it also gave the Royal Navy its first taste of naval supremacy. Shaken by defeat, Louis shelved any plans for more major fleet actions. Despite his recent victories on land, including the capture of the great fortress at Namur, his money was running out. The royal treasury was swamped with debt, which, unlike the debt of William's government, he could not hope to pay back. Famine would break out the next year, ruining the French peasantry on whom ultimately Louis's wealth depended. Although the dockyards at Rochefort and Brest continued to turn out new ships, and although Tourville would take the Smyrna convoy in 1693, La Hougue marked the high-tide mark for the French navy. Never again would it come so close to dominating the European high seas. After 1692 it was Britannia who would rule the waves.

La Hougue marked a watershed for the Royal Navy as well. Russell was an overnight national hero. His written sailing and fighting instructions for the battle formalized the line ahead formation and would dictate British naval tactics right through the American Revolution. In gratitude for the sacrifice at La Hougue, Queen Mary ordered ground broken for the Seaman's Hospital at Greenwich—ironically, her father's project. Wren's and Vanbrugh's magnificent design would dominate the Greenwich skyline, a palace built not for an absolute monarch, like Versailles, but for the common English seaman. "If you take this same blunt sea-animal in his tar jacket and wide-kneed trousers," enthused one author, "you'll find him of more intrinsic value to the nation than the most fluttering beau in it."

The new hospital would join the Royal Observatory and the school of navigation Pepys had set up there in 1685. From now on the navy would be in the forefront of almost every maritime technical, medical, and scientific development—usually twenty years ahead of the merchant marine. The year 1693 saw the first coastal survey of Britain by Captain Grenville Collins; seven years later the navy began experiments with a new, more efficient way to steer the rudder: the ship's wheel.

Yet the war of the League of Augsburg was far from over. Louis was as firmly entrenched in his fortresses as ever. Mary and her advisors clashed with Russell on whether to capitalize on his success by invading France. When Russell demurred, fearing the risks involved, they relieved him of command. Meanwhile, Louis and his advisors were devising a new strategy for the war at sea, a strategy that would also change the meaning of modern naval warfare and very nearly succeeded.

Louis's principal military advisor, the siege expert Vauban, came up with the idea in 1695 after watching Tourville's successful interception of the Smyrna convoy, and following the debacle at Barfleur and La Hougue. Vauban noted that both England and Holland depended on the sea for their wealth as well as their ability to pay for the war effort—now dragging into its sixth year. He also noted that Brest, the principal French naval base, "is so placed as though God had made it expressly for the purpose of the destruction of the commerce of these two nations." Therefore, he concluded, since the Royal Navy now had the upper hand at sea, the best policy Louis could pursue "is the shaking of the buttresses of the League [of Augsburg] by means of a subtle and widespread war" against their merchant shipping. Instead of risking everything in large line ahead fleet actions, what the admirals termed a *guerre d'escadre,* the French navy could break up into small privateering expeditions hit-and-run raids, a *guerre de course,* that would bring England and Holland to their knees.

Hawkins and Drake, of course, had pioneered the *guerre de course* concept with their privateering wars against Spain. But this would be a massive systematic campaign, operating out of secure naval bases—Brest, Rochefort, Toulon—and involving hundreds of heavily armed navy ships, in addition to individual privateers. Louis himself liked the idea. It would save him money—the navy budget would be cut by half by 1695—and still allow him to keep his main fleet "in being" for another great battle, if opportunity arose. Like other forms of officially sanctioned piracy, it might even make money: the vision of French ports packed with fat English and Dutch prizes made Vauban's strategy irresistible.

The results were spectacular. There would be nothing like it again until the German unrestricted submarine campaign of World War I. The French took over *four thousand* Dutch and English merchant prizes, all but five hundred after 1695. Swashbuckling privateers like Jean Bart and Claude de Forbin sailed out from harbors like Saint-Malo and Dunkirk, and roamed up and down the Channel, bagging unsuspecting ships or even entire convoys. In the Caribbean, one French privateer burned and looted Cartagena, another Rio de Janeiro. Others raided the scattered islands of the English and Dutch Antilles and made life miserable for merchants and planters alike. English trade in the Mediterranean virtually came to a halt.

The City of London screamed for something to be done. Parliament passed a Cruiser Act, authorizing money for new navy ships to hunt down the privateers, and set up a commission to advise the Admiralty how to protect merchants and trade—what would eventually become the Board of Trade. The Admiralty was beside itself. It brought Russell back to command a navy now with a budget of more than two and a half million pounds but helpless to stop the French attacks. It ordered Anthony Deane and other shipbuilders to turn out faster, lighter-armed frigates. It tried to cut off the *guerre de course* at the source with attacks on Brest and Saint-Malo, both of which failed miserably. It was not until the war was nearly over that the Royal Navy realized it had had the solution all along: a permanent fleet in the Mediterranean.

In 1694 Russell had brought his fleet, including eight three-deckers, through the Straits of Gibraltar in response to the loss of the Smyrna convoy. Since Tangier had been evacuated since 1683, his principal base became Cádiz, lent to the English by their Spanish allies. The city Drake and Raleigh had once terrorized now gave English warships docks and supplies, as Russell shut down the *guerre de course* in the Mediterranean, choked off France's own trade, and kept a large part of the French fleet trapped at Toulon.

Unfortunately, Russell failed to follow through with his Mediterranean strategy. The fleet pulled out in the late autumn of 1695; the Toulon squadron was free to join Vauban's *guerre de course*. With the English pressure gone, the Duke of Savoy decided to sign a separate peace with Louis XIV for 1696. At the same time, the Emperor Leopold began pulling his troops out of Italy. The allied cause began to unravel, and in less than a year a final peace treaty was signed at Ryswick. Louis's ambitions had been blunted, not beaten, but the worst crisis English commercial shipping had ever faced was over.

However, Cádiz and the Mediterranean remained the new focus of attention for the Royal Navy. The reason was geopolitical. Spain's last Habsburg king, Carlos II, was dying.

Diplomats had been waiting for him to die for decades. Severely retarded at birth and deeply emotionally disturbed, "Carlos the Bewitched" was the last grotesque heir to the dying empire of Philip II. Since he had no children, the issue of what would happen to Spain and its still-valuable overseas possessions, especially America, haunted the halls of power even as the war against Louis XIV ground to an end. Unfortunately for the rest of Europe, the best claim belonged to a grandson of Louis XIV, Prince Philip of Bourbon. By gaining control over the Spanish empire by proxy, Louis would gain a more sweeping victory than the one he had just been denied. "If the world are unable to master

France and tear Spain out of its hands," said one English statesman, "France must be master of the world."

So following Ryswick, the allies dealt with the Spanish succession question by negotiating two formal treaties to put a German Habsburg on the Spanish throne and give France Naples, Sicily, and Milan in exchange for renouncing the Bourbon claim. Louis, however, refused to endorse any partition of the Spanish empire: he wanted it all. So as Carlos the Bewitched lay dying in the fall of 1700, William and his allies had to be ready for war again. This time the Royal Navy would not make the same mistake: as soon as war broke out, a squadron would enter the Mediterranean and secure the allies' southern flank.

Then Carlos gave the tense international situation a last bizarre twist. From his deathbed he renounced the 1699 treaty and named Philip Bourbon his formal heir. The Spanish ambassador rushed to Versailles, where he breathlessly told Louis: "Sire, the Pyrenees no longer exist!" With Carlos's will in hand, Louis moved his armies into the Spanish Netherlands to disarm the Dutch garrisons there, and forced Spain and Portugal to sign an agreement closing all ports, including Cádiz, to English and Dutch warships. As war broke out in September 1701, the navy found the gateway to the strategic heart of Europe slammed shut in its face.

The war of the Spanish Succession would last almost twelve years. It would put the Royal Navy to its ultimate test in blocking Louis XIV's conquest of Europe. It had to be virtually everywhere at once. It had to protect convoys in the Atlantic against privateers; it had to try to keep the French fleet bottled up at Brest; it sent patrols into the Azores to prevent the Spanish silver fleet from falling into French hands; it sent six frigates into the West Indies to protect Jamaica and the other English islands; it supported operations in Canada and Nova Scotia; and finally, it had to fight a major campaign to force its way into the Mediterranean. Indeed, the first serious operation of the war was Admiral Rooke's attempt to retake Cádiz in 1702, which fizzled and forced him to pull back into the Atlantic. The next year English statesmen managed to pry Portugal loose from Louis's diplomatic grip, and Lisbon was the base for another unsuccessful attempt in 1703.

Finally, in May 1704, Rooke along with his colleagues Shovell, George Byng, and Sir John Leake, organized one final push. They took with them thirty English and nineteen Dutch ships of the line, and a force of 2,400

seagoing soldiers, whom the Dutch and English called marines, commanded by the new queen's cousin, Prince George von Hesse-Darmstadt.

They started out badly. They intended to make for Nice but decided
instead to take Barcelona, which they did but then abandoned. Then
Rooke and his colleagues heard more menacing news: the Brest fleet had
passed through the Straits of Gibraltar and was joining the squadron at
Toulon, creating a powerful force of more than ninety-five warships.
They themselves had only sixty-eight; they needed a safe and secure
anchorage west of Toulon in which to plan their next move. Once again,
the admirals talked about taking Cádiz, when young Hesse-Darmstadt
spoke up: Why not take Gibraltar instead?

It was not an entirely novel idea. Gibraltar was a small anchorage, but
profoundly safe under the shadow of the great rock rising six hundred
feet from the shore and connected to the mainland by a narrow, barren
isthmus. Oliver Cromwell had thought of taking it in 1656; others had
brought it up as a possible English station in the Mediterranean. Rooke
even had in his pocket a proclamation from the Allies' candidate for the
Spanish throne, Prince Charles, asking his subjects in Gibraltar to welcome the fleet when it stopped there. So although Byng and others
expressed their doubts, Rooke liked the plan. He knew the Spanish had a
garrison and batteries there but far fewer than at Cádiz; besides, time was
running out and they could not afford another failure.

On August 1, 1704, Rooke and Shovell took their fleet into Gibraltar
Bay. The Spanish governor could look out on a long line of sails stretching
across the horizon, and watch as boats rowed squads of red-coated
marines for the shore. With Hesse-Darmstadt at their head, they quickly
scrambled up the rocky shore and seized the isthmus, cutting Gibraltar
off from the land. A note arrived from Rooke's flagship, asking the governor to surrender. Honor, rather than any hope of success, required him to
refuse. So Rooke ordered Rear Admiral George Byng to make his preparations and on August 3 the bombardment began.

The thunderous sheet of flame that erupted from every porthole
revealed what these ships of the line really were: floating mass artillery
batteries, far more dangerous and destructive than any artillery battery
on land. The Spanish positions fell silent one by one, as the marines and
sailors from the English ships swarmed over the abandoned rubble. By
evening the governor had surrendered the city, after negotiating a three-
day grace period. And so it was not until August 6 that Prince George von
Hesse-Darmstadt took formal possession of Gibraltar—not for England,

of course, but for the Austrian prince Charles of Habsburg, as Charles III of Spain.

Yet the real battle was still to come. Rooke and Shovell stood out to sea to deal with the French fleet. On August 24 they joined battle off Malaga, with Shovell leading in the van and Leake bringing up the rear. Although the French had more ships, the two fleets were almost equal in ships of the line, thanks to the Dutch contingent. The two opponents slogged away at each other in line ahead from ten in the morning until evening. Again, no ship was sunk, although the casualties were terrible— more than 2,500 on each side. The fight ended just as the English, who had been at sea for more than six months, were running out of ammunition. Shovell noted that some of his captains had less than ten cannonballs left when the two sides broke off.

Malaga ended in a draw. But it sealed the fate of Louis XIV just as decisively as the land battle fought, as it happened, that very same day: the duke of Marlborough's crushing victory at Blenheim. The war of the Spanish Succession would drag on for another eight years. But Louis would never again have the chance to bring the full strength of his army or navy to bear on his enemies. His fleet returned to Toulon, where it remained laid up for the rest of the war. Mounting debts would cripple the French state and the economy as his enemies's armies encircled France and forced Louis to accept a peace settlement.

The peace treaty signed at Utrecht in 1713 confirmed his grandson Philip as king of Spain, with the proviso that he could never be king of France as well. But it also deprived Philip of key parts of the Spanish empire. One was the Spanish Netherlands, so that the Dutch Republic would enjoy a permanent buffer of safety against future French aggression—and England against future invasion. The other, even more important, was Gibraltar. Together with the island of Minorca, captured in 1708, it would become the linchpin of the British Empire in the western Mediterranean and the British navy's presence in the region right down to the present.

Here was a third revolution for the emerging Britain, a geopolitical one.* Possession of Gibraltar meant that the European continent was bounded by British sea power on two sides. It could now divide its enemies and their forces, while the Royal Navy's supremacy at sea gave

---

*Including in 1707 England's merger with Scotland, creating the United Kingdom of Great Britain—as it has remained to this day.

Britain unprecedented opportunities for maneuver on land. The pattern of the future was fixed, with the British enjoying a geopolitical advantage no other European power could match.

The pattern of future sea warfare was fixed, too. The line ahead formation guaranteed the Royal Navy's "fleet in being" could never be beaten in battle. Tested and perfected by a series of fighting admirals—Torrington, Russell, Shovell, Rooke, and Leake—it enshrined British naval supremacy. The line ahead battle, as Shovell had observed, was a numbers game. By keeping the French fleet split between its Mediterranean and its Atlantic bases, which thanks to Gibraltar and Minorca the Royal Navy could now do, the British home fleet held a permanent numerical advantage over its archrival. Never again would the French navy come as close to challenging that supremacy as they did in 1690–92; after Malaga it would be another hundred years before the French would risk everything in another all-out fleet fight with the Royal Navy. When they did, they would meet their enemy in very different circumstances, yet strangely enough in almost the same place: this time on the other side of the Straits, between Cádiz and the Rock of Gibraltar, in the windswept waters off Cape Trafalgar.

CHAPTER ELEVEN

Going Global

To thee belongs the rural reign
Thy cities shall with commerce shine;
All thine shall be the subject main,
And every shore it circles thine.
—JAMES THOMSON, *RULE BRITANNIA* (1740)

THEY CALLED THEMSELVES buccaneers, or *boucaniers,* after the wooden rack or *boucan* they used for drying meat from the wild pig herds on the Caribbean islands of Hispaniola and Tortuga. Others simply called them freebooters, or in French *filibustiers*—and many of them were French. They were smugglers, hijackers, robbers, kidnappers, and soldiers of fortune, the original pirates of myth and legend, although few ever flew the Jolly Roger and most spent their stolen treasure instead of burying it.

They were also the direct heirs of Drake's war "beyond the line." For more than a century they lived by picking the bones of the Spanish empire in the West Indies and Caribbean. When the European powers were at war, they offered their services to anyone who needed privateers: the English, starting with the Providence Island Company; the French, Dutch, even the Spanish. When Europe was at peace, the buccaneers returned to plunder and murder, making life for all except the most fortified port and most heavily armed merchantman a constant torment.

By 1641 the Spanish had overrun Providence and Tortuga, and the buccaneers moved to the deserted northern coast of Hispaniola. But when the Royal Navy drove the Spanish out of Jamaica in 1655, it became the favorite haunt for Drake's successors. Wild and freewheeling Port Royal became their base, and Henry Morgan their leader.

Morgan was a tall, dark, violent Welshman, nephew of a revolutionary Major General and privateering protégé of the Royal Navy's Christopher Myngs. In the spring of 1668, as Samuel Pepys was defending the navy's honor before Parliament, Morgan conceived a scheme worthy of an Elizabethan seadog. He assembled a fleet of twelve ships and five hundred men for an attack on Portobello on the Panama coast, where Drake had fought his last battle and which had replaced Nombre de Dios as the assembly point for the Spanish *flota*'s bullion. On July 10, 1668, Morgan and his buccaneers landed at Boca del Toro Bay, and transferred to canoes for a surprise attack at dawn on the eleventh.

Like Drake at Nombre de Dios, they were soon spotted and lost the element of surprise. But with a blood-chilling yell the pirates poured out of the jungle and swept past the castle defending the town. They herded the terrified townspeople into the church. When the castle defenders refused to surrender, Morgan dragged out some of the women and several friars and nuns and used them as a human shield to rush the fort, while other buccaneers scaled the castle walls on the seaward side. After taking the castle and putting many of the garrison to the sword, Morgan spent the rest of the day looting, drinking, and raping.

The next day Portobello's remaining fort surrendered and Morgan set an English flag on its flagstaff. He then sent a letter to the governor of Panama, saying he would burn the city to the ground unless the governor paid 350,000 pesos. After three weeks of negotiations, and after routing a Spanish force sent to relieve the town, Morgan got his ransom. He arrived back in Port Royal a hero, as he and his men spent nearly a month carousing in its streets and bars.

The capture of Portobello was the sort of exploit a Drake or a Raleigh would have envied and admired. By the standards of Elizabethan Ireland, it was almost humane. There was only one problem. Spain was now England's ally, thanks to a treaty signed almost a year earlier. In London the Spanish ambassador vigorously protested Morgan's actions; but the old idea that European treaties did not apply beyond "the tropic line" allowed Charles II to shrug the protests aside.

But they did lead to a new Anglo-Spanish treaty signed in Madrid in 1670—one that marked a genuine watershed. For the first time, Spain formally recognized the existence of England's colonies in the New World, and for the first time England agreed to rein in its privateers in the Caribbean. Morgan and Jamaica's governor, Thomas Modyford, paid no attention. In January 1671 they organized an even more ambitious attack on Panama City itself, the main bullion portal on the Pacific.

Morgan and his men threaded their way across the jungle-covered isthmus, just as Drake and Oxenham had a century earlier. But this was a force of more than two thousand, while thirty-eight ships waited offshore to fend off the Spanish West Indies fleet. Morgan completely routed Panama City's defenders, while the Spanish commandant put his own city to the torch to keep it from falling into the pirates' hands. Morgan found little bullion—his take came to less than half the Portobello ransom—but "the famous and ancient city of Panama," as Morgan wrote, "the greatest mart for silver and gold in the whole world," was completely destroyed.

This time London had to act. A new royal governor was sent out to arrest Modyford and send him back to London, where he wound up in the Tower of London. Morgan himself was arrested in April 1672 and shipped home in the Royal Navy frigate *Welcome.* What saved him was his connection to the second duke of Albemarle, whose father, Samuel Monck, had been the friend of old General Morgan. Morgan convinced Albemarle that he and he alone could control the buccaneers and turn Jamaica into a safe and secure fortress in the Caribbean. Albemarle persuaded Charles to give Morgan a knighthood and send him back as lieutenant governor of Jamaica.

It was a classic case of poacher turned gamekeeper. When he returned in 1675, Morgan turned on some, if not all,* of his former colleagues and imposed a rough-and-ready law and order, while becoming a wealthy landowner himself. By 1680 he was even urging London to stamp out buccaneering for good, in order to protect England's trade with Spain. He would serve only two more years before internal squabbles forced him out and a new governor took his place. But the end of the golden age of piracy was in sight.

The Jamaica Act of 1683 made it illegal for Englishmen to fight under any flag except that of the king, on the principle that the king's sovereignty over the seas extended to the behavior of his subjects who sailed them. Feeling the shift in the wind, most of the remaining buccaneers left for the Bahamas or the Carolina coast, while peace and quiet drove Morgan to drink. On August 24, 1688, just as William III was preparing his invasion of England, Sir Harry Morgan died. The navy ships in Port Royal harbor fired a twenty-two-gun salute in tribute—one of them, appropriately enough, the frigate *Drake.*

Morgan left behind a comfortable estate, with more than six thousand acres of sugar cane, the crop that would soon transform Jamaica. His

---

*Bartholomew Sharp still managed to conduct raids on Portobello and the Panama coast; one of his crewmen was twenty-seven-year-old William Dampier.

piratical successors, like William Kidd and Blackbeard, would not be so lucky. The Royal Navy was about to return to its modern birthplace, the Caribbean and Spanish Main, to wipe out Drake's ugly legacy. In the next century *privateers* would still get their official letters of marque; some would even be navy officers. But *piracy*, private war for private gain in defiance of public law, lost its appeal to the rulers of Great Britain and its emerging mercantile empire. From the Caribbean to the Indian Ocean and Barbary Coast, the buccaneer and the corsair found an implacable new enemy in the British navy.

Because, irony of ironies, Great Britain was coming to enjoy the kind of hegemony Spain enjoyed in Drake's day. The Treaty of Utrecht in 1713 created the "Incomparable Empyre" John Dee had prophesied. Besides Scotland and Ireland, England now possessed Gibraltar and Minorca in the Mediterranean, controlling southern Europe's access to the Atlantic; it secured all of Hudson's Bay, Newfoundland, and Nova Scotia in North America, and the waters dominating the Grand Banks and great fisheries of America and Europe. Together with its colonies in America, Jamaica, and other islands in the Caribbean, and the East India Company's growing base at Bombay, this seaborne British empire was about to become the centrifuge of a new world economic system centering in the Atlantic, and on a single product: sugar.

The story of sugar is the story of the great economic shift that underlies so much of modern history, namely the rise of capitalism and its geopolitical consequences. It began as a product of the old world system. Imported from the Mediterranean in the fifteenth century, sugarcane found a home first in the Portuguese Azores, then on land hacked out from the Brazilian rain forest. The Dutch soon learned how to process and refine it, and although they never became large producers, they were important carriers for a growing European market. It was the English and French who turned sugar cane into an immense agribusiness industry; by the 1660s it covered every acre of islands like Barbados and Martinique. All across the Antilles chain, from Santo Domingo and Cuba to Jamaica, earlier white immigrants and landholders gave way to massive sugar cane plantations, and a colonial society of masters and slaves.

For black slaves, it was a living hell. For the whites (and some non-whites) who guarded the slaves or loaded them on slave ships, it was a life of constant danger, even a death sentence—the death toll for crews in the Middle Passage was almost as high as that of their slave cargo. But for planters who could stand the heat, disease, and brutality, this one crop brought them a windfall far surpassing any captured galleon. Sugar replaced gold and silver as the wealth of the Indies, and English and French colonies Spanish ones, as the economic heart of the New World.

These windswept tropical islands—Martinique and Guadeloupe for the French, Curaçao and Aruba for the Dutch; Barbados, St. Kitts, Nevis, Antigua, and Jamaica for the English—with their endless vistas of sugar-cane fields and the smoking chimneys of sugar refineries, represented the first large-scale British investment overseas. Merchants from Boston and New York carried away molasses and rum, while bringing in slaves, dried cod from the northern fisheries, lumber, pork, and other foodstuffs. By 1700 the West Indies replaced Mother England as the biggest market for American colonial merchants, thanks to the demand for sugar.

And for those living in London or Bristol or Liverpool, or indeed anywhere in Britain, it became literally the sugar in their coffee and tea— and the sweetener of their cakes and fruit preserves, the rum in their bellies, and the profits on their balance sheet. As early as 1660 English imports of sugar were larger than all other colonial imports combined. By 1700 the average Britisher was consuming four pounds of sugar a day; by 1720 it was twelve pounds a day. Sugar became the cornerstone of the economy and the British way of life.

Bristol was the first port outside London to reorganize itself on the basis of the sugar trade. The city of Robert Thorne and John Lloyd, the original home of English overseas ventures, got a new lease on economic life. The docks where generations of Bristol fishermen had set out for the Grand Banks gave way to sugar refineries—twenty-five by 1750, more than any other British port. For sugar was the first colonial import to be processed into new products rather than just re-exported: the first "value added" export commodity. It gave Bristol a flourishing distilling industry, and a glass industry to make the bottles for the thousands of gallons of rum shipped around the world and to the Royal Navy. London would remain the queen of outports for British sugar—more than three-quarters of the total—and Liverpool would become number two by the 1790s. But Bristol and Liverpool ran the other component of the sugar boom, its uglier and nastier side, the slave trade.

The Treaty of Utrecht had finally ratified John Hawkins's great ambition by giving British merchants an annual license or *asiento* to sell slaves in Spanish America. But the Spanish demand for African slaves was soon outstripped by the demand from the sugar plantations in Brazil and on the French and English islands. The brutal conditions there created an insatiable need for more and more human chattel: sometimes it was cheaper to buy new slaves than to feed the old. When the Royal African Company lost its monopoly in 1697, dozens of new merchants swept in to reap the fantastic profits the slave trade now offered. Bristol was first, managing one-fifth of all slaving voyages, but then in 1740 Liverpool took over.

In the last years of the slave trade, more than a hundred slave ships a year would leave Liverpool for the West African coast. There they sold iron goods, rum, and other commodities to their African counterparts, packed their human cargo under unimaginable conditions of heat, disease, brutality, and squalor, and set out across the Atlantic for Jamaica and the other islands. Jamaica, being the biggest, had the biggest demand: by 1713 there were eight black slaves for every white person. Without the demand for sugar, the African slave trade would have languished and withered away; instead, it expanded it from barely 7,000 persons in 1650 to almost 70,000 a year by 1750—half of them in British ships. It also grew a lucrative export business to Africa, including a market for cheap cotton goods from India and Asia.

A complex and profitable economic network had come to rest on the West Indies sugar connection. It involved the investment of millions of pounds and a network of merchants, shipowners, traders, wholesalers, and retailers that stretched around the world. It promised quick fortunes: many planters only had to work their slave plantations for a few years to retire back in England, sunburned and hoarse-voiced, with an immense income. The new economy also brought sickening bankruptcies, which could plunge an entire sector of the industry into ruin—even the government itself.

The South Sea Company got its infamous start by converting outstanding navy bills into capital for investing in the *asiento* slave trade. Soon it was involved in a host of other activities, including exchanging long-term government debt for company shares. Promises of huge profits in the West Indies markets drove a frenzied London Exchange to dizzying heights: the crash and bursting of the South Sea "Bubble" in 1721, toppled the ruling Whig ministry and threw the nation's fiscal resources into a panic. The new prime minister, Robert Walpole, managed to restore order. But the episode showed that financial disaster could shake the foundations of the British state just as severely as any French invasion or Jacobite menace.

People were learning the downside of economic "interdependence." Any failure of public confidence; any threat to these far-flung and brittle trading networks; any wrench in the works, such as a war or swarms of privateers shutting off access to markets, could set off a chain reaction. "No African Trade, no Negroes; no Negroes, no Sugars, Ginger, Indicos, &c.," Daniel Defoe, spokesman for the South Seas Company, pointed out, "no Sugars &c., no Islands; no Islands, no Continent; no Continent, no Trade." So all eyes began to turn anxiously to the one institution they believed could prevent such a disaster and protect their fortunes: the Royal Navy.

Despite some hesitations, it was a navy ready to rise to the challenge. It was now twice the size of any other fleet in the world: one hundred and nineteen ships of the line, and sixty-three frigates and sloops of war. It had learned some hard lessons on how to deal with a war on merchant trade, a *guerre de course,* during the War of Spanish Succession. Louis XIV had tried to repeat his success in the earlier war against William and Mary, but the navy had learned how to limit the damage. Total merchant losses for the entire war, 1702–12, were half of what they had been in the previous war. Convoys with navy ships allowed ships to travel through the Channel, or into the North Sea, or into the Atlantic. Other ships kept constant patrol in the Western Approaches and off Dunkirk, as much to safeguard merchant traffic as to prevent an attack or fleet action.

The navy was also building more frigates and other lighter, faster vessels, brigs and sloops, to sweep the seas clean of pirates and privateers. It had only twenty-six in 1690, as the first war against the French began. That number had doubled by 1710, and nearly doubled again by 1750, when one hundred and eight kept constant patrols in virtually every sea British merchants did business.

It also learned to use the methods of *guerre de course* as effectively as the French. Royal Navy ships attacked enemy merchant vessels in both wars, of course, but private investors took an increasing hand. Fast and well-armed privateers conducted sorties from Bristol and Whitehaven; Plymouth and the Channel Islands; and New York and Baltimore, not to mention Port Royal in Jamaica. By the end of the Spanish succession war they were outstripping the navy in prizes by almost three to one. Some of the privateers' ventures were spectacular, almost epic in their ambitions. William Dampier had been both a naval officer and a buccaneer when he set off in 1703 to capture the last great prize of the Spanish *flota* system, "the prize of all the oceans," the Manila galleon. Although he missed his galleon, Dampier did manage to be the first Englishman to see the west coast of Australia.

A year after his return, Dampier joined Captain Woodes Rogers on a three-year privateering cruise around the world. This one did catch the Manila galleon, and netted its private backers almost 150,000 pounds. Both Dampier and Rogers also wrote books on their adventures, best-sellers that habituated the British reading public to the idea of their war-ships roaming remote parts of the globe and prepared the way for the voyages of Captain Cook.

Not everything in the war against privateers went well, by any means. In 1708 the French attacks grew so bad Parliament demanded a revision of the 1694 Convoys and Cruisers Act, so that the navy devoted more of its resources to protecting the English coastal trade, the most politically sensitive part of the British merchant marine. But in success or failure, these years taught the Admiralty how to deal with what was now the most important political institution in Britain, Parliament. The very thing that drove Admiralty officials crazy, the rage of party politics over naval policy and questions in the House of Commons about defeats and blunders at sea, also made them cognizant of the needs of the nation at large and sen-sitive to public opinion. The Admiralty would end up controlling no less than ten parliamentary boroughs. Thirty-eight naval officers were also members of Parliament. At the same time, the war of words in the Commons and on the street in books, broadsides, and pamphlets, some of which were written by the admirals themselves, made the British public better informed on naval matters than any other nation.

The mercantile interests of the Board of Trade all recognized that their future depended on the success and strength of the Royal Navy. Britons, wrote one commentator in 1708, had "no ways of making ourselves consid-erable in the World, but by our Fleets; and of supporting them, but by our Trade, which breeds Seamen; and brings in Wealth to maintain them." While budgets of other nations' navies in the eighteenth century, including France, rose and fell according to shifts in the political wind, spending on the British navy rose steadily in peacetime as well as in war.

Spending that money still depended on the Navy Board and its com-missioners. They now presided over the largest industrial organization in the world, with its sprawling complex of dockyards and warehouses and hospitals. The Navy Board had five clerks in 1694; by 1704 it employed sixty-three, who also audited the accounts of the two other bodies administering the navy's needs, the Boards of Victualing and of Sick and Wounded.

But all three had to answer to the Board of Admiralty, now housed in its new building at Whitehall. There a solid corps of experienced administrators and admirals, or "sea lords," grew up over the decades, men with unprecedented continuity of office and responsibility. Josiah Burchett began his career as one of Pepys's clerks; appointed secretary of the Admiralty in 1694, he remained in office until 1742. His successor had served almost three decades in the Admiralty, as well eleven years at sea. Philip Stephens then took the office in 1763 and held it for the next thirty years. When he retired, he continued as Lord Commissioner until after Trafalgar. Two generations of civil servants, and two only, would link the navy of Pepys and Monck with the navy of Nelson.

The navy also found a new social equilibrium. The tug of war between gentlemen and tarpaulins gradually gave way to a naval officer corps in which it became difficult to tell them apart. Socially speaking, the quarterdeck belonged to Britain's ruling class: sprigs of gentry and nobility, sons of the "respectable" professions, including, significantly, sons of the Royal Navy itself. But snobbery and political connections had their distinct limits. The nephew of a popular captain or of an Admiralty official might find the climb from midshipman to command of one of His Britannic Majesty's ships relatively easy, as young Horatio Nelson did. But when the well-born George Rodney wanted a post, he was told the support of the senior admiral on the Board of Admiralty counted for more than that of the prime minister himself.

Candidates and patrons were many; the posts, determined by the Navy List introduced in 1700, were few; the most desirable, such as an admiral's flagship, fewer still. Thanks to the Restoration's reforms, no one could get a lieutenancy without sea service, no matter how well connected; and recognized ability generally had an edge in the fierce competition for commands. The eighteenth-century navy was never a true meritocracy. But it was the one profession in Georgian Britain in which men with no money or education could enter and succeed by sheer talent, and did.

William Bligh's father was a customs clerk; James Cook was a common merchant seaman. John Pasco was the son of a Plymouth dockyard caulker: he became Nelson's signal lieutenant at Trafalgar and died a rear admiral. Justinian Nutt sailed on George Anson's *Centurion* as an officer's servant. During their voyage around the world he became ship's master, then acting third lieutenant; eventually he would be a post captain. James Almes's father was a menial servant to the Duke of Richmond. Almes rose to be post captain; his son became a vice admiral.

Even more remarkable was John Parkins, the pilot seaman who ended up commanding the brig *Endeavor* as lieutenant and then the frigates *Turk* and *Arab* as post captain, until ill health forced him out in 1805. Remarkable enough because Parkins spent his entire career as a Royal Navy officer in the West Indies, without once visiting England. But remarkable, too, because Parkins was black, the son of a slave and very probably a former slave himself.

Yet everyone recognized that, in an age of social deference when workingmen were supposed to doff their hats to gentlemen and address them as "sir" or "milord," social rank enhanced the professional one. A well-born or wealthy captain could provide clothes, food, and supplies, even extra ammunition for his ship and men out of his own pocket. His social distinction was balanced by his midshipman training. It taught him how to navigate and how to command, but it also forced him to haul the sails, man the guns, spread his hammock, and share the same hardships and even the same punishments (except flogging) as his future crew. "When a Gentleman hath learnt how to obey," the marquis of Halifax wrote in 1693, "he will grow very much fitter to command."

Halifax saw that a gentleman with true experience at sea, one that "smelleth as much of pitch and tar as those there were swaddled in a sail cloth," will enjoy "an Influence and an Authority, infinitely superior to that which the mere seaman can ever pretend to." Halifax the politician even compared the presence of gentlemen on shipboard to the role of the peerage in a constitutional monarchy, leading the commons by precedence and example but also balancing the absolute all-powerful authority of the captain—an unspoken social compact to soften the one imposed by the Articles of War.

For navy ships were still manned by sailors who saw themselves as civilians. Many were not English at all, or even Britons. The crew of a ship like Nelson's *Victory*, like that of Drake's *Golden Hind*, was a hodgepodge of different nations (twelve, in the *Victory*'s case) and races. Any loyalty they felt was to the captain and his officers, not the service; many did not hesitate to challenge the authority of a man whom they considered no better than themselves. George Shelvocke joined the

Royal Navy as a common seaman and rose to ship's master and then second lieutenant. After the Utrecht treaty, he turned to privateering: when war flared briefly with Spain in 1719, he took his ship the *Speedwell* to the South America west coast to raid Spanish shipping—a replay of Drake's expedition of 1579. Instead he ran into a "a great variety of inexpressible troubles and hardships both by land and by sea." He quarreled with the captain of his accompanying ship, the *Success*; he quarreled with his crew, and when the *Speedwell* ran on the rocks off Más a Tierra four hundred miles west of Valparaiso in Chile, his men voted to strip him of command and cut his share of prize money to that of a common sailor.

Shelvocke complained, "They will never rest until they have made themselves entirely their own masters by making away with us." Bad luck (his superstitious crew blamed it on an enormous black albatross that stalked their ship at the Cape Horn, which they finally killed*), bad weather, and the spitefulness of others (when he finally got home to England in 1723, his owners had him thrown in prison for piracy and fraud) all played their part in Shelvocke's ordeal. But in the end his problems with command had class roots. In extreme situations, a captain's social authority might be his last redoubt against mutiny, as William Bligh would one day find out.

Breeding, education, experience, and "interest," meaning political connections, all helped an aspiring navy officer—but nothing helped so much as success in battle. A reputation as a fighting captain and admiral certainly earned respect and admiration, but winning in combat earned more, while also earning prize money for himself and his men. George Anson, who owed his promotion to First Sea Lord (the senior admiral on the Board of Admiralty) to his victories at sea, always told his admirals that "if they would have a fleet to depend on," that they should promote "the lieutenants to command whose ships have been successfully engaged upon equal terms with the enemy."

For whatever else it was, the eighteenth-century navy was a fighting navy. The Admiralty had no staff or time for thinking about sophisticated strategy. Its approach to its job was still to defeat the enemy fleet in time of war and defend the British Isles against invasion. Protecting British merchants was only a secondary goal, and one some thought a distraction.

---

*A century later, Samuel Coleridge would turn this incident into *The Rime of the Ancient Mariner.*

But to keep up with any of these tasks in a more complex world, the navy also needed a bigger physical infrastructure, with modern docks in England and permanent bases overseas.

The Royal Navy already enjoyed the best naval facilities in Europe, and the most drydocks for refitting its warships—Chatham alone had four. But Chatham, like the other yards of the Tudor era, Deptford and Woolwich, sat in the Thames basin, far away from what was now the main theater of operations, the Atlantic and western Channel. The wars of Louis XIV made Portsmouth a more convenient home port for the fleet. There ships could refit in the fourteen-week process of cleaning and replacing worn masts and rigging, essential for keeping a fleet of wooden warships afloat, and conduct repairs close to their main anchorage for guarding the Channel, at Spithead opposite the Isle of Wight. Chatham, Deptford, and Woolwich became the places for storing ships not in use and building new ones (although most of the new frigates and sloops for the navy were built in private shipyards). By 1718 there were more than 1,700 men working at Portsmouth, with its two drydocks and two wet docks, as well as slipways, storehouses, blacksmith shops, rope yard, and mast pond, where the massive fir timbers used for masts were stacked to season underwater for as long as twenty or thirty years.

But the dockyard that grew the fastest during the eighteenth century was Plymouth. Curiously, the navy never considered using the home port of Drake, Hawkins, and Raleigh until the need for a place to supply and refit ships while watching French moves in the western Channel brought Plymouth into its own. In 1691 work began on two large new docks, the first ones ever built in England entirely of stone, and a thousand-foot rope walk. By the 1720s the Plymouth yards covered more than forty acres and employed five hundred men. When Daniel Defoe visited it, he also found "a very handsome street, spacious and large . . . and so many houses are since added, that it has become a considerable town"—the town that would eventually be christened Devonport, a community created entirely by the needs of the Royal Navy, which would grow to dwarf Plymouth itself.

Gibraltar and the island of Minorca, with its long, deep, sheltered harbor at Port Mahon, offered the Royal Navy a commanding presence in the Mediterranean. A fleet under George Byng stationed there was able to intervene and prevent Spain from reclaiming its possessions in Italy, with a crushing defeat of the French- built and -trained Spanish fleet at Cape Passaro in Sicily on August 11, 1718—putting the seal on British naval supremacy in that ancient sea. Leith in Scotland and Great Yarmouth in Norfolk allowed navy ships to conduct merchant convoys through the Baltic during the Great Northern War between Sweden and Russia, and made the Royal Navy a powerful instrument of policy in a part of the world where vital English, Dutch, and German interests all coincided.

In North America, Royal Navy ships at first used Port Royal in Nova Scotia, but the threat of French privateers operating out of Louisbourg at Cape Breton led the navy to turn to the old fishing harbor at Chebuco, which would eventually be rebuilt and renamed Halifax. The ten or so ships stationed there every year guarded the approaches to the New England fisheries, as well as the navy's access to the forests of Maine and New Hampshire. The government-built port of Savannah in Georgia hosted navy warships to patrol the southern colonies. By 1735 it had a sloop of war on permanent station.

Most vital of all, of course, was the base protecting the West Indies. The East Indies remained the private province of the East India Company, which had reorganized and expanded in 1698. It maintained its own armed ships to guard its interests, just as its Dutch rival had, and felt no need of Royal Navy support. But the West Indies sugar islands were more vulnerable, as well as more valuable, and exposed to attack by enemies both public, like the French and Spanish, and private, like the buccaneers.

Admiralty plans proceeded, as usual, in fits and starts, although the stakes were huge. Vice Admiral John Benbow led the first squadron assigned there in 1701, with four ships of the line, to protect merchants from French privateers and to prevent the *flota* from reaching Spain to fill Louis XIV's coffers. Benbow was one of the last tarpaulin captains of the old school, an "honest rough seaman" who served under Admiral Herbert in scouring out corsairs' nests along the Algerian coast. After a raid on Salee, he had returned to Cádiz with thirteen pirates' heads, which he deposited at the feet of the royal governor. He seemed the perfect man to deal with the French marauders along the Spanish Main, and on August 19, 1702, his flagship, the *Breda* of seventy guns, and five others caught up with a flotilla of nine French ships off Santa Marta.

What followed would make Benbow the first popular hero of the eighteenth-century navy. He would pursue the French for the next three days virtually single-handed, while the rest of his squadron hung back. Only the smaller *Falmouth* and *Ruby* offered help, even when the *Breda* was fighting the French flagship virtually yardarm to yardarm, and chain shot had shattered Benbow's leg. Benbow was still ready to go on fighting when the captains of the other ships, led by Richard Kirkby of the *Defiant*, begged him to stop. Together they signed a letter stating that "we think it not fit to engage the enemy at this time." Benbow dismissed their views as "all a vision false and cowardice" and refused to shake Kirkby's hand as the captain left the *Breda*. But with his right leg gone and his ship a shambles, Benbow had no choice but to break off.

He got his revenge when they returned to port. Benbow court-martialed his disobedient officers. Kirkby and the captain of the *Greenwich* were both found guilty and shot; the others had their careers ruined. Ironically, they had been right. Benbow's continued attack on a superior foe would have been suicide. But the Admiralty upheld the convictions. No council of captains, no matter how sensible, would ever be allowed again to challenge an admiral's orders, now matter how rash. The iron rule of law, discipline, and obedience governed this new Royal Navy, and violators would face death—even if they were admirals themselves.

As for Benbow, he died of his wounds but would become immortal, in popular song—

> Brave Benbow he set sail
> For to fight, for to fight
> Brave Benbow he set sail to fight.
> Brave Benbow he set sail
> with a fine and pleasant gale
> But his captains they turn'd tail
> in a fright, in a fright.

and on tavern signs across England.* When peace came, his naval successors in Jamaica would join in another campaign, to wipe out the remaining pirates of the Caribbean.

What forced them to act were the depredations of Captain William Kidd. Born in Greenock in Scotland and son of a minister, his story was the opposite of Henry Morgan's. He started as a legitimate privateer, with a license to hunt French prizes during the war against Louis XIV and then roust out pirates along the coast of New York and New Jersey. But in early 1698 he attacked an English ship in the Indian Ocean, the *Quedagh*

---

*Including the fictional Benbow Inn in Robert Louis Stevenson's *Treasure Island*.

Merchant, claiming it was flying a French flag and then seized its cargo of silk, calico, sugar, and opium for his investors. By the time he sailed the *Merchant* back into the Caribbean, the word was out to have him arrested for piracy. The newly arrived Admiral Benbow had told his officers to "take particular care for apprehending the said Kidd and his accomplices wherever they shall arrive."

Kidd returned to New York to prove his innocence to the governor, Lord Bellomont, who also happened to be chief investor in the voyage. Bellomont solved any awkwardness this revelation might have caused by having Kidd arrested, while the East India Company demanded Kidd's head. The Royal Navy frigate *Advice* brought him back to England in chains for trial. He went to the gallows on May 23, 1701, still protesting his innocence in front of an enormous crowd. Kidd willed his black slave to his jailor and with his last shilling he bought enough rum to get roaring drunk. The rope broke on the first try, but the hangman managed to find another as the mob surged around and the second time the noose held. Three days later the Admiralty ordered his body cut down and taken to Tilbury Point twenty-five miles downstream on the Thames. In short, the place where Elizabeth had learned her gang of pirates had beaten the Spanish Armada would now be famous for the iron cage dangling Kidd's body over the water, to warn passing mariners of the penalty for piracy.

For Kidd had fallen victim to a new, less tolerant attitude toward the time-honored tradition of theft at sea. A few years earlier, Kidd's exploits would have been business as usual. His investors included not just governor Bellomont, but the victor of La Hougue, Edward Russell, now Lord Orford, along with three other Whig peers—and even, for a 10 percent cut, King William III. No wonder Kidd protested, "I am the innocentest person of all": he had done nothing more than Drake had done for Robert Dudley or Christopher Hatton. But the Crown could now afford to stand by the law, and with the Royal Navy it had the instrument to enforce it.

The Kidd case forced Parliament to take the issue of American piracy seriously (he had even been brought into the House of Commons to testify). The first tentative step, ironically enough, had been the appointment of Bellomont, whom William had given special powers to put down pirates in the region—a warrant Bellomont had discharged by hiring Kidd. More lasting change came with a new Piracy Act, which for the first time established vice-admiralty courts in the colonies, so that seagoing thieves could be tried quickly instead of waiting to be hauled back to

England. In 1718 a proclamation offered rewards of 100 pounds for the arrest of a pirate leader, 40 pounds for his officers, and 20 pounds for a pirate seaman. The next year the government offered amnesty for buccaneers who turned themselves in before September 1718. More than six hundred took up the offer—although that still left more than fifteen hundred scattered across the Bahamas, Florida, and the Carolina coast.

By then, Jamaica itself was largely free of pirates. But the governor still complained, "There is hardly one ship or vessel coming in or going out of this island that is not plundered." The reason was clear: "the neglect of the Commanders of His Majesty's ships of war." So even before the September deadline ran out, the Board of Trade sent Captain Woodes Rogers, naval hero and former privateer himself, as governor of the Bahamas to clean out the remaining buccaneers. He arrived in July at Nassau with four navy ships, the frigates *Milford* and *Rose,* and sloops *Buck* and *Shark*. News of his coming had already led many to scatter for the Carolina coast, including the one who would become the most famous pirate of them all, Edward Teach, known to posterity as Blackbeard.

Teach came from Bristol (so did Rogers). He had served on English privateers during the War of the Spanish Succession, learning his trade from the buccaneer Benjamin Hornigold, before setting up in the piracy business for himself. His enormous black beard "covered his whole face and frightened America more than any Comet that has appeared there for a long time." Teach found his new home in North Carolina's Outer Banks—right where Walter Raleigh first planned to set up his privateering colony. They offered a crooked maze of islands, coves, sandbanks, and inlets, from which a ship could emerge to strike and then hide for months without detection. The man his own men called "the devil incarnate" turned Ocracoke Island on Pimlico Sound into his private pirate lair and took more than twenty prizes. Teach terrorized the port of Charleston, seizing eight vessels in its harbor, and openly careened his ship the *Adventure* at Cape Fear.

It was Virginia's governor Alexander Spottiswood who finally summoned the Royal Navy to "extirpate this nest of vipers" and deal with Blackbeard. Two sloops of war, *Pearle* and *Lyme,* were stationed at the mouth of Virginia's James River; but they drew too much draught to enter the shoals and shallows around Pimlico Sound. So *Pearle*'s captain dispatched one of his lieutenants, Robert Maynard, with sixty men on a still smaller sloop to follow Blackbeard's trail to Ocracoke.

At dawn on November 21 they spotted Teach's *Adventure* moored on

the inner side of the island. With almost no wind, Maynard let the flowing tide carry him toward the island, when shots suddenly rang out from
the *Adventure*. "Damn you for Villains," Teach shouted, "who are you and
from whence came you?" Maynard shouted back, "You may see by our colors we are no pirates," and ran up the Union Jack. At this, Teach cut his
ancho cable and rode the tide into a narrow channel. Maynard followed,
only to run aground and catch a broadside of bird shot, iron bits, and
nails, which killed his midshipman second-in-command and wounded
twenty others.

As the smoke settled, Teach believed he had wiped out Maynard and
led his men to board the vessel—only to realize his mistake when the rest
of the sailors scrambled up to engage the pirates hand to hand. Maynard
and Teach exchanged sword cuts; Maynard tried to run him through but
struck his cartridge box instead. Teach broke Maynard's sword hilt, while
Maynard pulled a pistol and shot the pirate through. But Teach refused to
go down, as the other British sailors now closed on the flailing desperate
figure.

Shots struck home, as did sword thrusts, but Teach, bleeding and
roaring, fought on. Then one of Maynard's men, a Scottish Highlander,
brandished his claymore and laid Teach a tremendous blow across the
neck. Teach dropped to his knees on the deck with an exclamation; then
with a single stroke (it is said) the Highland sailor struck his head off. As
Maynard's men threw the headless body over the side, they found
Blackbeard had taken no less than five gunshot and twenty-five sword
wounds. Maynard ordered the head stuck out on the bowsprit, a grisly
trophy to lead their way back to Virginia.

Blackbeard's death, and that of his henchman, Stede Bonnet, hanged
in Charleston, spelled the beginning of the end of the buccaneers. They
had confidently assumed Woodes Rogers would fail to reform the
Bahamas, or even turn to piracy himself. But instead he convinced
Blackbeard's own mentor Hornigold to accept an amnesty and help
arrest ten other pirates for trial before a vice-admiralty court in Nassau
in December. All but one were hanged: another pirate leader, Charles
Vane, went to the gallows in Jamaica the next year. Pirates began leaving
the Americas for more remote places like the West African coast,
Madagascar, and the southern Indian Ocean. Pirate attacks in the
Caribbean dropped from fifty in 1718 to only six by 1726. Soon, Royal
Navy expeditions would drive the remainder out of Madagascar and kill
their last leader, Bartholomew Roberts, off the coast of Sierra Leone. By

1730, the navy was effectively ending the scourge of piracy in the Atlantic.

Ending smuggling was another matter. Most merchants appreciated the end of violence and pillaging on the high seas. But evading the restrictions of the Navigation Acts on what goods could be bought and sold where, and avoiding paying the hated customs and excise duties, was normal business practice in British America—and indeed in Britain itself. Scotland and the West Country turned their pirates' havens into smuggling coves within a couple of generations. Respectable merchants from Boston and New York and Charleston regularly ran contraband goods to colonists in Jamaica or Barbados in exchange for sugar, molasses, and rum; many more did the same for the French planters on Martinique and Guadeloupe.*

But this was nothing compared to the profits in illicit trading with Spanish America. The *asiento* contracts allowing English merchants to sell slaves to the Spanish colonists only permitted one ship a year to trade in other goods, but no one paid any attention, least of all the colonists. As in Hawkins's day, government-sponsored monopolies left the colonists hungry for goods only smugglers could supply. Virtually any price they paid for manufactured iron products like pots, nails, and guns or cotton cloth was lower than the one the official Spanish merchants offered. In exchange, English entrepreneurs left with indigo, cocoa, logwood, doubloons, and chests of pieces of eight.

The center of contraband trading was those same ports where John Hawkins found his best customers one hundred and sixty years earlier: Riohacha, Santa Marta, and Cartagena. Between 1713 and 1763, not a single registered Spanish trading vessel called at Riohacha; by contrast, more than 155 smugglers were spotted there in the same period (many more probably arrived undetected). The losses to the Spanish Crown were running toward a million pesos. So the Spanish government organized a coast guard, or *guarda costa,* of armed ships from local ports, with orders to stop and arrest any Englishman carrying contraband cargo.

The Spanish coast guard, some of them ex-pirates themselves, could be brutal. Most did not care whether they terrorized smugglers or respectable merchants. Then, in April 1731, they stopped one of the latter, Robert Jenkins, on his way back from Havana. Although the Spaniards

---

*They were helped by the fact that the French government forbade planters to sell rum in France, for fear it would ruin the brandy makers.

found no contraband, they ransacked Jenkin's cargo, stole his navigation instruments, roughed up his crew, and as a final gesture of contempt, sliced off Jenkin's ear. Seven years later Captain Jenkins told his story in front of an outraged House of Commons, showing his severed ear, still preserved in a ball of cotton. The story (and it was not the only one Parliament heard) conjured up vivid memories of the Spanish Inquisition and of Elizabethan seamen like Job Hartop being tortured and sent to the galleys. When asked how he felt at that desperate moment, Jenkins answered, "I recommended my soul to God, and my cause to my Country." The public demanded that this outrage be punished and an avenging fleet be sent to sea. Even more, its mercantile lobby demanded that Spain's resistance to "free trade," meaning trade with English businessmen, come to an end.

The official declaration of war against Spain came in October 1739, with cheering crowds lining the London streets and bells ringing from church steeples. The "War of Jenkins' Ear" marked a new public confidence in the Royal Navy, which would last through the end of the century and beyond. The nation could now look forward to war as never before, because they assumed the navy would keep the fighting far from British shores. Any expense involved, they assumed, would be easily made up by the expansion of trade or the capture of treasure. Besides, everyone knew that the British navy, "as essential to our Safety and Wealth as Parliament or Magna Charta," was going to win.

This faith in the navy's invincibility was of recent vintage. It defied logic and even, given the navy's sometimes dismal history, experience. But it would become an unshakable part of the Royal Navy's national image, and no one was more responsible for spreading it among the British public than the West Country's leading number of Parliament, Admiral Sir Edward Vernon.

Vernon reflected the dual nature of the new breed of Royal Navy officer. He was on one side a gentleman with strong Whig political connections (his father was secretary of state under William III) and a cultivated education (he went to Westminster School and knew both Latin and Greek). He had been a member of Parliament since 1722. But he also had strong sea credentials, reflecting the navy's new global responsibilities. He served as a lieutenant on Shovell's flagship at the battle of Malaga; he had served with Admiral Byng in the Baltic, and with Admiral Sir Charles Wager in the West Indies. Eventually he took over the West Indies squadron, harrying smugglers and Spanish privateers until he returned home in 1721. He knew the Caribbean intimately and believed that it represented an opportunity for Britain no one had realized before. Using his seat for Penrym in Cornwall as his pulpit, Vernon preached a doctrine of naval strategy that envisioned using the Royal Navy not just as a defensive shield but a weapon for offense. His dramatic and sometimes violent speeches were heavily publicized in the press, and they made the public see naval warfare as the way Britain could become the most powerful nation on earth.

As Vernon pointed out, the Caribbean had become the cockpit of world power. It was still the soft underbelly of the Spanish empire, thanks to the continuing flow of American bullion—Spain's most valuable and most vulnerable possession. But it was also important to France, with its growing share of the sugar and slave trades. By "keeping a superiority at sea" in the West Indies, Vernon argued, Britain could break the power of one empire, and forestall the rise of another. "Destroy their settlements in America," Vernon said, "and Spain falls." He had seen the decrepit Spanish naval presence across the Caribbean; he believed they had little fight left. In 1729, Vernon told Parliament he could take Portobello with three hundred men. Now, ten years later, he believed the British navy could crack the Caribbean wide open, if it acted at once. "Let who will possess the country," Vernon said, "our Royal Master may command the wealth of it," through control of the seas.

Even before war broke out, the navy had wanted to send a second squadron to Jamaica. When he heard this, Vernon rushed down to the Admiralty to see his old mentor, First Sea Lord Sir Charles Wager, and ask to command it. Although Vernon had never commanded a squadron in battle, Wager gave him the office in early July. "His appointment will be good news to the seamen and to the City," Vernon's brother wrote in his diary.

As the last English captain to capture a Spanish treasure galleon in the Caribbean in 1709, Wager had been thinking along the same lines as Vernon. Wager had spent half a century in the Royal Navy and his vision was even more ambitious. As he dispatched Vernon to the West Indies "to commit all hostilities against the Spaniards in such manner as you shall judge the most proper," he was also sending another contingent into the Pacific, to disrupt trade along the coast of Chile and Peru and then push on to Manila, gateway to the East Indies. Squeezed from both ends, Wager believed, the Spanish Empire would be doomed. He even foresaw a great revolt against the Spanish Crown spreading across Latin America, led by colonists eager for free trade with Britain—exactly what would happen a hundred years later.

Meanwhile, Vernon, who was now vice admiral of the Blue,* sailed for Jamaica with four ships of the line and a frigate, the *Norwich*. He arrived in October, just in time to learn of the declaration of war and plan his campaign. The government had been keen on an attack on Havana, Spain's biggest port in America, but Vernon feared an attack there would tie up too many ships and troops. "Lay aside all thoughts of such expensive land expeditions," he told the government. Instead, he would strike the same target that had attracted Drake and Morgan: Portobello on the Panama coast, "the only mart for all the wealth of Peru to come to Europe."

The plan worked perfectly. On November his six ships† dropped anchor in Portobello harbor to bombard the forts guarding the city. They had been built and reinforced since Morgan's raid seventy years earlier, but could not stand up to the disciplined salvoes from Vernon's battleships, as marines and seamen scrambled ashore and overran the Spanish batteries. Vernon repeated the successful amphibious formula that took Gibraltar, but against greater odds. The next day the city was his.

Unlike Morgan, Vernon permitted no rape or plundering. His goal was not to destroy the city, or even loot it: it was to open it up to British merchants. So after demolishing the remaining fortifications and spiking his enemy's guns, and giving his men 10,000 Spanish dollars in bullion as lawful prize money, Vernon treated Portobello with a humanity and justice even Spanish authorities had to acknowledge. For Vernon despised the wanton violence of pirates and privateers, as much as he despised indiscipline, both on his ships and ashore. The source of much of it in the West Indies, he had learned prowling the streets and taverns of Port Royal, was drink—"the formidable Dragon," as he put it, that stood in the way of an orderly ship. Drunkenness, he told his army counterpart, would in the long run "cost us, as great a loss of men, as a General [fleet] action."

So Vernon figured if he could not have his men completely sober he would have them half-sober by issuing a concoction of his own: a half-pint of rum mixed with one quart of water. It had an instant effect. The

---

*Although the Royal Navy had expanded far beyond the bounds of the old battle fleet and its Red, White, and Blue squadrons in 1739, its flag officers were still assigned the original nine titles, namely, Admiral of the Fleet, Admiral of the White, and Admiral of the Blue; Vice Admirals of Red, White, and Blue; and Rear Admirals of the same.
†Including a ship from the Jamaica squadron, the *Hampton Court*, with seventy guns.

success Vernon had in raising the spirits (literally) of his crew without
intoxicating them, transformed life on shipboard for the Royal Navy. For
the average seaman, his half-pint of rum (later a full pint) became the
center of his daily routine. He and his officers would name it after its cre-
ator, "Old Grog," the nickname Vernon carried because of the program or
heavy silk cloak he wore on the quarterdeck in dirty weather. And since
rum kept better than beer, grog was the perfect drink for long voyages
and the navy's new overseas profile.* Nor did distillers complain about a
navy that would by the end of the century consume thousands of gallons
of rum a day.

When news of Vernon's victory at Portobello reached England in the
early spring of 1740, it set off a national sensation. Songs and broadsides
celebrated "Admiral Vernon, the scourge of Spain," and compared him to
Drake and Raleigh.† His plump face and periwig stared out confidently
from engravings and tavern signs. His birthday became a virtual national
holiday. A leading West Indies merchant threw a banquet at Drapers' Hall,
with a huge dessert cake in the shape of Portobello with Vernon's sugar-
cake ships anchored in front of it. Both houses of Parliament voted
Vernon thanks and sent him an inscribed gold box. The city of London
turned one of its principal market streets into Portobello Road. Poet
James Thomson composed a poem to celebrate the victory, which Thomas
Arne would set to music, and it would become a paean to the renewed
sense of national destiny:

> When Britain first at Heaven's Command,
> Arose from out the azure main,
> This was the charter of the land,
> And guardian angels sang this strain:
>
> Rule, Britannia! Britannia, rule the waves!
> Britons never will be slaves.

Having succeeded with one prong of his planned attack on Spanish
America, Wager now launched the other. In the end, Prime Minister

---

*British sailors in home waters were stuck with a beer ration until the end of the cen-
tury, although it too was generous: a gallon a day.
†One of those who served with Vernon of Portobello was an officer born in America
named Lawrence Washington. Washington admired him so much he named his
Virginia estate which was later inherited by his brother, George Washington, Mount
Vernon.

Walpole vetoed an attack on the Philippines, but he did authorize a smaller force to round Cape Horn and raid the Pacific coast of Chile and Peru, in hopes it might somehow link up across the Panama isthmus with Vernon's forces in the Caribbean. Wager had his doubts about the plan, and the resources assigned to do it; but he had none about the man he picked to lead it, the thirty-seven-year-old commander of the 60-gun *Centurion* just back from the West Indies, Captain George Anson.

If Vernon is the Abraham of the navy of Nelson and Hood, Anson is its Moses. Tall, dark, taciturn, he had been at sea since he was fourteen. Like Vernon, Anson had learned his business under fighting admirals like George Byng and John Norris; like Vernon, he had strong Whig political connections which secured him command of ships even when the navy was not fighting wars. Some of the ships were small—the sloop *Weasel* carried only eight guns—and the duties tedious: one was command of a small frigate out of Charleston harbor for chasing down the few remaining post-Blackbeard pirates, giving him plenty of time to live ashore and even buy property around Charleston.* But the assignments kept him in the eye of the Admiralty. When trouble loomed with Spain in 1737 and the sixty-gun *Centurion* needed a captain, it chose Anson and dispatched him to patrol the West African coast. After a cruise to the West Indies, he returned to Spithead to learn of his new mission.

Cloudsley Shovell had once said, "The misfortune and vice of our country is to believe ourselves better than other men, which I take to be the reason that generally we send too small a force to execute our designs." Shovell was now dead, but his words rang true as Anson watched the expedition being fitted out in the docks at Portsmouth. He had six warships, including the *Centurion,* and two merchant vessels to carry supplies. But the scramble to reinforce Vernon's coming attack on Cartagena and the fleet in the Mediterranean took away the most experienced seamen, leaving him with too many novices and wastrels brought in by the inevitable press gangs. Even worse, the soldiers he was to take with him turned out to be largely pensioners from the Chelsea military hospital. Some were in their sixties, a few in their seventies, and many crippled and lame. Eighty vanished into the streets of Portsmouth on the night they were supposed to sail. Most of the rest died before they reached South America; only four on the *Centurion* were still alive when they cleared Cape Horn.

That itself would be an ordeal of epic proportions. It took a year to

---

*Part of his 12,000 acres would become Charleston's first suburb, Ansonborough.

get enough supplies and sailors to leave Portsmouth, and six weeks to get to Madeira instead of the usual two. Flies from the rotting stores swarmed over the ships as they left Madeira on November 5, 1741, and within two weeks typhus and dysentery had swept through the crews. By the time Anson reached the coast of Brazil, more than eighty men had to be sent ashore to recuperate from the *Centurion* alone. The rats were then smoked out of the ships and the lower decks scrubbed out with vinegar— the navy's cure-all for epidemic disease. But when the sick returned on board, they brought along malaria as well.

As they made for Cape Horn, they passed the Island of True Justice, where Drake had beheaded Thomas Doughty more than one hundred and seventy years before, and a set of bleak islands at 51° south latitude and 60° west longitude. Anson marked them down as a possible base for future South Atlantic operations; later they would be dubbed the Falklands. Anson's passage was far more arduous than Drake's—and more dangerous, because he knew a large Spanish squadron was looking for him. The storms that swept up from the Antarctic hid him from the Spanish but kept him trapped off the tip of Tierra del Fuego for three months. Ice continually froze on rigging and sails; the 24-gun *Wager,* named after the admiral, lost its starboard chain plates that held its shrouds and stays in place, and its mizzenmast.

Anson had to rely on dead reckoning to try to steer north into the calmer waters of the Pacific. It was not until mid-April, when the moon finally peeked through the clouds, that Anson realized that the entire time he had been steering the wrong direction. With no sure way to calculate his longitude, he had worked his way back east, not west, by more than four hundred miles. Cloudsley Shovell had made a similar navigational error on his return to England from the Mediterranean in 1702, running onto the Gilstone Rocks of the Isles of Scilly days before he expected to find them. That mistake cost him his life, and all but one of the 1,315 officers and men on his flagship *Royal Anne,* the 70-gun *Eagle,* and 50-gun *Romney.*

Anson's error proved nearly as fatal. As he grimly beat back to windward, the great scourge of long-distance voyages broke out: scurvy. Although no one knew the cause of this deadly vitamin-deficency disease, they did know that if a ship on a long voyage went without fresh food and vegetables for more than six weeks, its crew was doomed. Anson's overcrowded ships had even fewer fresh supplies than usual because of the extra men; now these men began to grow sick and die. As the ships continued to beat against the storms, they died in the hundreds, while those still able to go aloft lost fingers and toes to frostbite.

Examining the log of the *Centurion* today at Greenwich's National Maritime Museum is a moving experience. Its stained cover and blotched daily entries betray the terrible ordeal Anson and his men suffered—as does the daily list of dead and dying men. On April 24 the *Centurion* lost sight of the other ships. On May 3 it lost its main topsail. When it finally sighted the Island of Juan Fernandez (or Más a Tierra) on June 10, meaning their ordeal was over, it found itself alone. As Anson dropped anchor, more than a third of his crew were dead; another one hundred and eighty sick men had to be carried out in their hammocks. Anson worked stripped to his shirt to carry them on shore. "To so wretched a condition," wrote an eyewitness, "was a sixty-gun ship reduced."

Then, one by one, the other straggler ships appeared: the fourth-rate *Gloucester*; the merchant *Anna*; even the tiny sloop *Tryal,* commanded by a young lieutenant named Philip Saumarez. But even after staying on Juan Fernandez for three months to eat, recover their health, and mend their ships, the picture was grim. Two-thirds of their men were dead, and their other ships were gone for good.

The *Wager* suffered worst. After being helplessly lost in the violent storms, the *Severn* and *Pearl* had turned back for Rio de Janeiro (the Spanish were themselves too storm-tossed to follow). But the *Wager,* minus her mizzen and half her chain plates, tried to stay with Anson, only to run onto the rocks of a barren island off the coast of Chile between 47 and 48 degrees south, at a place still called Wager Island. There was no food except what Captain Cheap and his men could salvage from the wreck: a half-pound of flour and one slice of salt pork a day. One of the crewmen had a pet dog; they killed it and ate everything except the paws. Three weeks later they dug up the paws and ate them. One boy had to be forcibly stopped from eating a dead body on the beach.

Facing either cannibalism or death, the ship's lieutenant and a group of sailors chose to set out in the ship's fifty-foot longboat, which they named the *Speedwell,* to thread their way 350 miles through the treacherous Magellan Straits back to Brazil. With unbelievable courage and tenacity, Lieutenant Bulkeley and thirty other survivors navigated their open boat back through the Straits of Magellan all the way to the mouth

of the La Plata on January 28, 1742, a journey of 2,500 miles—a feat of
endurance unequaled until Captain Bligh navigated an even smaller craft
from the *Bounty* to Australia.

Meanwhile, the loss of the *Wager* had forced Anson to alter his own
plans. It had carried his field artillery, as well as most of the squadron's
wine and rum. Given his battered ships, thinned crews, and the loss of the
Severn and *Pearl*'s combined ninety guns, this projection of British power
into the Pacific was beginning to look hopeless. So for the next several
months Anson was reduced to Drake's strategy: hit-and-run raids along
the Chilean coast. They brought loot for his men and refits for his vessels,
but hardly shifted the strategic balance. Only one thing could turn the
trip into a success: capture of the Manila galleon.

The Manila galleon was a nautical legend. It was rumored to be the
largest ship in the world, as large as 2,000 tons, and once a year it made
the world's longest unbroken voyage, three thousand miles from Manila
to Acapulco on the coast of Mexico. Loaded to the gunwales with the
fabled riches of the east—gold, silk, damask, spices, pearls—it returned to
the Philippines with great chests of silver bullion. Thomas Cavendish was
the first to capture one during his global circumnavigation in 1587. When
he returned to Greenwich, he was able to deck out his ship with sails of
blue damask and a great blue and gold silk banner, and each of his sailors
with a chain of gold around his neck. Woodes Rogers was the second.
Anson was now determined to be the third. He knew the galleon was due
in at Acapulco in March. So on March 1, 1742, he dropped anchor near
Acapulco and fanned out his ships to keep watch forty miles off the coast.

They waited three weeks. Nothing. With his water running out
Anson gave up: either the galleon had arrived early, or the governor of
Acapulco, learning of Anson's presence, had canceled the return voyage.
So, putting all his surviving men on the *Centurion* and *Gloucester* and scuttling his remaining ships, Anson set off across the Pacific. Scurvy cut
them down again as the ships made their way along 13 degrees north latitude. Ultimately, the *Gloucester* had to be abandoned, too; it had seven feet
of water in its hold, and only sixteen men and eleven ship's boys to handle
its sails. When the *Centurion* finally reached the island of Tinian, north of
Guam, she was losing eight men a day to scurvy. Anson himself had come
down with scurvy, although he continued to help out at the pumps.

After lying up at Tinian (which including a harrowing nineteen days
when storms drove the *Centurion* far out to sea, leaving Anson and his crew
on shore convinced they had been abandoned), Anson set out for Macao,

Portugal's main port in China. There he stayed for six months, refitting and careening his battered vessel, as his thoughts once again turned to the Manila galleon. Where could he find her? Finally, an English merchant captain told him the best bet was Cape Espiritu Santo in the eastern Philippines, the first landfall of the west-bound galleon. So on April 19, 1743, Anson set sail from Macao and arrived at the cape on May 20. There Anson waited, tacking back and forth before the shore, training the new Chinese and Malay crewmen he had hired in Macao to handle the guns, while lookouts searched the eastern horizon for a foreign sail.

They waited three weeks. At first light on the morning of June 20 a sail appeared to the southeast. It was a Spanish galleon; at first it looked as if it might be a pair. Anson was unperturbed. "My lads, we'll fight them both." But as the crew slung their hammocks and cleared the deck for action, lookouts realized it was only one, the *Nuestra Señora de Covadonga*. It was actually one of the smaller galleons: at 700 tons, smaller and more lightly armed than the *Centurion*. Anson gave chase as the weather turned to squalls and rain; at half past noon he raised the British colors and twenty minutes later came alongside.

Anson did not have enough men to fire a broadside. Instead, his gunners had to run from gun to gun along the lower deck, loading and firing each in turn. The two ships fought for an hour, as Anson's men peppered the Spaniards with grapeshot and volleys from marksmen in the tops.

Then the Spanish fire slackened and stopped. Anson, his face "black as a Mulatto with the Smoke of the Powder," ordered Lieutenant Saumarez to take a party aboard. Saumarez found a slaughterhouse, the deck "covered with carcasses, entrails, and dismembered limbs," and the survivors huddled below decks. The Portuguese captain had been too badly wounded to give the order to surrender. But in the *Cavadonga*'s hold Saumarez discovered 1.3 million pieces of eight and 35,000 ounces of Peruvian and Mexican silver, a treasure worth almost a million pounds. It took a week to get it all loaded on the *Centurion*, so that Anson could set sail for Canton, and then make his way across the Indian Ocean and around the world back home.

Anson had left Spithead on September 18, 1740, an unknown captain. He returned on June 15, 1744, a national hero. His story was harrowing. Of 1,900 men who had left with him four years earlier, more than 1,400 were dead—and only four of them from enemy action, against the *Cavadonga*. But the British public and the government were eager for a success. Vernon's attempt to follow up his capture of Portobello by taking Cartagena had been a dismal flop. Even with more than one hundred ves-

sels and 14,000 troops, his efforts had bogged down, as Vernon quarreled
with his fellow officers and 10,000 men died of yellow fever. A disastrous
defeat off Toulon in February had blotted the Mediterranean fleet's reputation, and put its admiral before a court-martial.

Now Anson's last-minute success was magnified into a major triumph. Thirty-three great wagons bore the treasure through the streets of
London, guarded by the *Centurion's* sailors—barely a quarter still alive
from her original crew. A military band marched them up to Pall Mall,
where Anson met the Prince and Princess of Wales. The press compared
"our immortal Anson" to Drake, and (perhaps more appropriately) to
Ulysses; the capture of the *Cavadonga* to the feats of ancient Rome. On
June 18 he was received by the king at Kensington Palace, and made Rear
Admiral of the Blue. A year later he was on the Admiralty board. His personal share of the prize money—three-eighths of more than 350,000
pounds—would make him a rich man. Many of the men who fought
beside him at Cap Espiritu Santo became rich, too. Lieutenant Saumarez
would get more than 7,000 pounds for his share, and even the common
seaman's tiny fraction came to 300 pounds: more than twenty years' regular pay.

In a strategic sense, Anson's voyage had been a failure. But for the
navy, it marked a crucial turning point. For the first time, the Royal Navy
had run the kind of long-distance operation in the Pacific once left to privateers like Dampier, Rogers, Shelvocke, and Drake. Like Vernon's failed
attempt to capture Cartagena, the cost in human lives had been terrible,
but not because of enemy resistance. They were instead the costs of an
institution that was trying to do too much too soon. Failure would force
the navy to confront the problems inherent in its new global responsibilities, both in peacetime and in war, and to make far-reaching changes.

For example, the voyage's high death toll from scurvy would inspire
the surgeon of the fourth-rate *Salisbury,* James Lind, to start to make a
series of clinical trials to find an antidote. Lind's experiments—the first
controlled experiments in medical history—would lead him to conclude
that lemon or lime juice most effectively prevented the disease's outbreak. By 1757 Lind published his findings and dedicated them to Anson;
by the end of the century, British navy sailors were regularly taking lime
juice with their grog, finally dispelling one of the greatest obstacles to
long-distance sea travel.

The other great obstacle was the longitude problem. Anson's brutal
experience at Cape Horn intensified efforts to find a way to accurately

calculate longitude at sea.* Parliament's Longitude Act of 1714 had offered a hefty prize for the man who arrived at the solution. Clockmaker John Harrison had been working for years on an accurate chronometer, to allow a ship's navigator to plot his longitude by the course of the sun or stars in relation to the time he left port. But even before Harrison developed a prototype that satisfied him, a German mathematician named Tobias Mayer solved the problem.

He painstakingly drew up a set of lunar tables allowing the calculation of longitude by the movements of the moon. In 1757 he sent them to the First Lord of the British Admiralty, who just happened to be George Anson. The navy's tests proved their accuracy; officers like James Cook were using them years before Harrison's chronometer was finished. Harrison may be a more heroic figure than the pedestrian Mayer, and his story more deserving of bestsellerdom. But it was Mayer, not Harrison, who first got the Longitude Board's prize money in 1767, and Mayer's tables, not Harrison's chronometer, that made the Greenwich meridian the zero point for all oceangoing navigators.

Anson's final contribution may have been a matter of vanity rather than saving lives and ships, but its effects were to be just as far-reaching. It happened in Macao in December 1742 when he was refitting the *Centurion* and learned that a high-ranking Chinese mandarin was coming to inspect his ship. Anson knew it was the first time a British naval vessel had ever appeared in Asia, and he was determined to make a good impression. So he ordered one hundred of "the most sightly" of his crew to shed their usual shabby and motley seagoing garments and put on the uniforms of his dead marines. This impromptu honor guard, complete with a 15-gun salute, so impressed the Chinese that Anson used them again when he towed the *Cavadonga* into Canton harbor.

The Royal Navy had never bothered with uniforms. Common seamen and officers, even admirals like Vernon, wore whatever clothes suited them regardless of rank or appearance. But the idea was now fixed in the minds of a group of Anson's officers "that a uniform dress is useful and necessary for the commissioned officers." In 1747 a group of them met at Will's Coffee House to push their cause. Philip Saumarez came up with the basic design, a dark blue coat with buff waistcoat and gold trim.

---

*John Hadley's reflecting octant, developed in 1732, had solved the problem for latitude, replacing the old backstaff and Davis quadrant sailors had been using since Elizabethan days.

A year later, it was formally adopted as the dress uniform for all admirals, captains, and commissioned officers. It was a major step in the professionalization of the British navy. It made the separation between navy officers and those of merchantmen or privateers, once so blurred, virtually complete. Royal Navy officers had become a distinct body, with their own identity, their own rules and standards, and now their own unique look.

Yet Philip Saumarez would never wear the uniform he designed. He had died the year before, commanding his ship the *Nottingham* in a furious gun duel off Cape Finisterre against a more heavily armed ship of the line, a French ship this time not Spanish, the 74-gun *Intrépide*. For the Royal Navy was about to face its grimmest challenge yet: a sixty-year struggle with France for the empire of the oceans.

CHAPTER TWELVE

Divide and Conquer

*I flatter myself that the great advantages Britain has, by being entirely
Mistress of the Sea, will come to be better understood, and used
with much more advantage than it has been hitherto.*
—EARL OF STAIR, 1743

I know that I can save this country, and I know no other man can.
—WILLIAM PITT, 1757

*What has exalted Britain to its present power and glory?
Its naval strength duly employed.*
—The Daily Monitor, 1759

FOR A CENTURY the maritime nations had been hard-wiring a new world system, based on trade, colonies, and navies, inside the decaying shell of the old. The question in the minds of European statesmen now was: who would dominate it?

Clearly not Spain. Even though its new Bourbon dynasty had refurbished the decrepit Spanish empire, including building a new navy; even though the outflows of silver from its American mines were more than double what they had been in the age of Philip II, its will in international affairs had ceased to matter. It was trade, not empire, that mattered now, and Spain's business outlook remained chained to a Casa de Contratación mentality and the imperial past. For all his overconfidence, Admiral Vernon had been right: those who controlled the sea lanes, through navies and a merchant marine, did control the destiny of those who controlled the land. So like the Portuguese, the Spanish knew the security of their once-great empire depended on stronger allies, who could project the modern sea power they could not.

Nor was the Dutch Republic in the running. They were no longer the aggressive maritime power of a century ago. If the Spanish had sacrificed business for empire, the Dutch had done the opposite. They were still active middlemen in international business and finance; and still a pros-

perous country. But the forty-year desperate struggle against Louis XIV
had killed the will for war. The Treaty of Utrecht had given the Dutch the
security guarantees they needed. Their armies were demobilized; their
navy shrank to second-class status. By 1740 the Dutch were content to
enjoy the fruits of their merchant fleets, still the largest in the world (the
British did not pass them as the leading trading nation until the 1770s),
their lucrative trading posts in the East Indies, and leave the struggle for
dominion to others.

That left Britain and France. The rest of the eighteenth century
would see these two powers locked in a more or less continuous naval
rivalry for control of the new world system. That rivalry would shape the
future of Europe and the globe down to Waterloo and Trafalgar. Both
nations would fight fierce, even important battles on land, but the truly
decisive ones would take place at sea. In the end, Britain would win. But
that outcome was never predetermined. The central issue was not who
had the largest fleet, the best admirals, or the most bases, but who could
use them effectively. Vision, intelligence, and the will to win counted as
much as men, ships, and guns.

In that respect the British started with no special advantage. The
War of Jenkins' Ear proved that even if they had the best navy in Europe,
they still did not understand how to use it. The British public had
expected an easy victory over the Spanish, "mere poltroons" who "durst
not look our squadrons in the face at sea." The colonies in America would
rise up to welcome their British liberators: "Millions of miserable People
wou'd bless their Deliverers: their Heart and their Minds wou'd be open
to us."

But instead of giving up at the first sight of British warships, the
Spanish reverted to a French-style *guerre de course* while concentrating all
their resources to defend their most important bases, Cartagena and
Havana. Privateers from Spanish ports scored success after success against
British shipping, which the navy seemed unable to prevent, even as the
Spanish *flota* evaded their attempts to stop it. Ten thousand British soldiers and sailors would die at the gates of Cartagena of malaria and yellow
fever, while Vernon and his subordinates argued and quarreled. The admiral's stock in the public mind shrank away, to the point where Horace
Walpole remarked that just two years after the capture of Portobello, no
one even spoke of Vernon or the Spanish war: "One would think they had
both been taken by a privateer," he joked.

Disaster in the Caribbean was followed by humiliation in the Mediterranean, where the Spanish fleet neatly slipped through the Gibraltar squadron's attempt to blockade Cádiz. When the navy's commander in chief refused to go after Spanish privateering ports on the Channel for fear it would divide his fleet, Prime Minister Newcastle burst out: "For God's sake, if he can't do this, what can he do?"

The point was, no one knew. Strategic thinking at the Admiralty and in the government was still primitive. The assumption that having the largest navy in the world, more than one hundred ships of the line and fifty-eight frigates and sloops of war, would be enough to overawe any opponent, proved unfounded. In fact, the tradition of keeping the "fleet in being" to deter an enemy limited the navy's range of action and made it less effective, rather than more. Then in October 1743 came the worst news of all when France, alarmed by British aggression in the West Indies, signed an alliance with Spain, while backing Prussia under its new king, Frederick the Great, against Britain's embattled ally, Austria. Thanks to its overambitious and incompetent masters, the British navy was back at war with its most formidable foe.

Louis XIV had died bankrupt and decrepit in 1715, his dreams of imperial *gloire* in ruins. But the French belief that they were destined to dominate Europe and the world remained undimmed. Ironically, it was an alliance with Britain signed in 1718 that gave them breathing space to rebuild and restore their power—just as it gave Britain freedom of maneuver in the Mediterranean and the Baltic in the two decades after Utrecht. By the 1730s France's economy was growing even faster than Britain's. French merchants plunged into the new markets in sugar, rum, and slaves in America with gusto, benefitting, like everyone else, from the British navy's suppression of piracy in the region. The same was true of the textile trade in Asia. By 1735 France's East India Company was outstripping both the Dutch and English in value of sales.

As France's army remained second to none, its navy steadily rebuilt. By 1740 France had more than fifty-three ships of the line, including the magnificent new 74-gun two-deck battleship, the best and most modern warship afloat. Fifty-three was still less than half the total British strength, but once it joined up with Spain's fifty battleships, Britain's naval supremacy looked very precarious indeed.

As these grim facts sank in, the British public's mood plummeted. Bumptious overconfidence gave way to pessimism and panic. Rumors that France was preparing for a major invasion of England rippled through Parliament and the cabinet as early as 1740. Now, as war approached, far from keeping any invasion plans secret, the French deliberately leaked them through spies and diplomats. Facing an enemy more and more governed by public opinion, the French figured the rumors would make Parliament demand that the main fleet—"without which force," the navy's own commander in chief Sir John Norris had said, "this nation will ever be in great danger"—remain at Portsmouth, thus paralyzing the navy.

It was a master stroke of psychological warfare, especially since it was followed up with real action. In February combined Spanish and French squadrons set sail from Toulon to cruise the Mediterranean, while the French squadron from Brest dropped anchor off Dunkirk, where the government was assembling transports to take the son of the Jacobite pretender, Prince Charles Stuart, and a French army across the Channel. Prime Minister Newcastle was in a frenzy. "If Norris can get time enough, to put himself between Dunkirk and us, all is safe," he said, "but if our heavy arsed sailor does not come up. . . . God knows what will come of this affair."

What came was only a temporary reprieve, which did little credit to the navy. Storms off the Channel wrecked the French transports and left Charles Stuart stranded on the beach. Furious at the delay, Prince Charles set off anyway with a small band of followers to raise the revolt in western Scotland. His two ships managed to slip past the British fleet in the Straits of Dover, and would have made it easily if the third-rate *Lion* had not spotted them off the Lizard and forced one of them, the *Elisabeth,* to turn back. As it happened, the *Elisabeth* was carrying the bulk of Charles's men and his armaments, including his artillery. The *Lion's* alert reaction had doomed the revolt. But enough Scottish clans did rally around Bonnie Prince Charlie to set off a major crisis.

Events in the Mediterranean barely turned out better. The British squadron under Admiral Mathews managed to intercept the Franco-Spanish fleet in the waters off Toulon on February 11. The resulting battle was, in the words of one historian, "the greatest example of tactical disorder in British naval history." Mathews scored some early hits, but failed to follow his retreating enemy to leeward, for fear it would break up his line ahead formation. One of his officers, Edward Hawke, commanding the old 70-gun *Berwick* with an inexperienced crew, disobeyed and rushed in alone to engage and capture the formidable Spanish vessel *Poder.* The rest hung back, allowing the French and Spanish to slip safely back to Toulon. Afterward, Mathews accused his second-in-command of misunderstanding his signals and letting them escape; the second-in-command replied in kind; both ended up in very public and ugly courts-martial. It was a humiliation for the navy. The only person to emerge with any credit was the disobedient Hawke.

After Toulon, the mood was bleak. Yet in December 1744, the man who would turn the situation around was already on the job. George Anson was still only a captain and still recovering from his bouts with scurvy from his voyage around the world when the government put him on the Admiralty Board. Over the next decade, Anson would bring about the most important and far-reaching reform of the British navy since Pepys. He would not only save its reputation but give it its first modern strategic doctrine, one that would eventually deliver Britain its empire, Europe its security, and, incidentally, America its freedom.

When Anson arrived at the Admiralty, Pepys's memory still haunted its halls and offices. The most recent Admiralty secretary, Sir Josiah Burchett, had started as a clerk under Pepys; Admiralty staff were still quoting Pepys's minutes and memos written sixty years ago. And by coincidence, Anson's closest collaborator on the board was the great-grandson of Pepys's patron, Lord Sandwich. John Montagu, fourth earl of Sandwich, was only twenty-seven; Anson was forty-eight. But the two worked wonderfully together, and with the support of their First Lord, the Duke of Bedford, they would run the Admiralty and the British navy for almost twenty years.

Anson's starting point was challenging what he called the "tyranny of custom" in the navy, which "is often very troublesome to those who oppose it" but which was no longer relevant to the navy's changing role in a changing world. Sandwich backed him completely: when he became First Lord himself in 1748, he told Anson, "I would not lose a moment to desire that you would consider yourself as in effect the head of the Admiralty."

Anson shook up the service from top to bottom. He brought the Navy Board to heel, making it submit finally to the Admiralty's authority and instructions. He insisted on personally reviewing ship designs and revised the system of ship ratings, so that each class reflected a uniform tonnage and firepower.* In 1748 he authorized the introduction of uniforms for commissioned officers based on Lieutenant Saumarez's original design.

---

*From now on, all first-, second-, and third-rate ships of sixty guns or more were designated as battleships, "fit to stand in the line," and all fourth-, fifth-, and six-rate frigates and sloops, as cruisers, fit for patrol and convoy work. Anson's classification was soon adopted by all other navies, and lasted for nearly two hundred years.

He also supported the momentous step of removing the obstreperous Vernon from command of Channel forces in December 1745 and court-martialing Admiral Mathews. For Anson realized the navy faced a basic problem at the top: too few good officers were becoming admirals because there were too few admirals. Since the Commonwealth the navy had maintained only nine: the two admirals of the White and Blue, the six rear and vice admirals of the Red, White, and Blue, the commander in chief, or Admiral of the Fleet. Most were elderly—Norris, the commander in chief in 1744, was in his mid-seventies—and owed their promotion from the captain's list to seniority not ability.

Anson decided to overhaul the system, although even he never managed to expand the official number of admiral flags or force old admirals to retire (the fiction of only nine flag officers in the British navy persisted until 1805, by which time there were more than 160). But he could weed out superannuated captains by giving them the title "Rear-Admiral without distinction of Squadron," in effect taking them out of the service but with an admiral's status and half-pay. It was a radical but brilliant idea, and the growing number of what came to be called Rear Admirals of the Yellow (after their nonexistent squadron) allowed the Admiralty to decide which able captains made it to the top of the ladder, and which incompetent ones did not.

Anson also took on, although even he could not solve, the most serious personnel problem the navy faced: finding more sailors. Simply put, the navy now had more than 150 warships scattered around the seas but still no systematic way of getting crews to man them. "The tyranny of custom" dictated that sailors still signed on to a specific ship and left when its voyage or their duties were done. In an age when more than half the fleet was stripped and stored at Chatham or Deptford every winter, it almost worked. With a navy on full-time duty, facing the constant threat of war, the obstacles in trying to round up the 40,000 seamen to get the fleet to sea could be overwhelming.

Anson had experienced it firsthand, when he was unable to find crewmen for the Pacific expedition, and he knew the dilemma the navy faced. In its old-fashioned way, Parliament would not permit any draft or conscription, which it believed smacked of military dictatorship. So without enough volunteers, the only alternative was the press gang and its routine roundup of unwilling and often inexperienced recruits.

Anson did what he could. He took over the Royal Marines from the army, hoping to use them as a permanent source of unskilled labor for manning the fleet. More important, he changed the Articles of War to reflect the stark fact that nearly every navy ship would be going to sea with a large number of untrained, unwilling, and even criminal-minded "newly raised men." The new articles tightened and harshened discipline, making even half-pay officers subject to court-martial and making "cowardice, negligence, or disaffection" a compulsory death sentence offense. The result was a navy justice system that, for the average sailor, was swift and physically punishing, but rarely arbitrary. Its principal brutalities, like the bosun's lash and cat-o'-nine-tails, were offset by the better food and the grog ration (also mentioned in Anson's 1756 regulations). Above all, it was a system that routinely took on a shipful of human debris and in a few months turned them into efficient, obedient sailors, and in so doing, taught them a trade that would last them a lifetime.

But Anson's biggest contribution to the navy's future was a strategic one, the establishment of a permanent Western Squadron. Ironically, the original idea belonged to Vernon. "The surest means" for the "defense for the kingdom [and] security of our commerce," he wrote from Portsmouth in August 1745, was "keeping a strong squadron in the Soundings," meaning the Western Approaches to the Channel. But Vernon was removed before he had a chance to try it. Now it was Anson, promoted to vice admiral in July 1746, who took the steps to create one and then, with characteristic forthrightness, to command it himself.

The prevailing winds in the English Channel are southwesterly ones, blowing west to east. Any French or Spanish fleet would have to enter the Channel from the Western Approaches, since neither country had an adequate deepwater port on the Channel itself. And since Anson knew no invasion force could embark from Normandy or Calais or Dunkirk without a strong naval escort, he realized a British fleet stationed permanently in the Western Approaches could block any enemy fleet coming to help. A permanent Western Squadron standing to windward could also keep watch on Brest and bottle up French warships there; it could also protect the coasts of Ireland and western Scotland. Just as important, it could protect British convoys going to and coming from the East and West Indies and pounce on French ones from the same places.

In short, it was a strategic breakthrough whose time had come. What was needed was a base from which to operate—Plymouth was the obvious choice—and the logistics necessary to keep a squadron roaming the tens of thousands of square miles from Cape Clear to Finisterre, for months at a time. In July, with Bedford's permission, Anson pulled together the various ships and squadrons in the Channel into a single force of six battleships and nine cruisers under his new rating system. Originally Anson chose the 64-gun *Yarmouth* for his flag. But as April began in 1747, he shifted to the 90-gun *Prince George* after learning that a French expedition was setting out from La Rochelle to retake Cape Breton in Canada. On the ninth Anson and his squadron, including his old *Centurion,* left Plymouth to intercept them.

They cruised the Soundings for almost a month. When Anson finally caught sight of the French off Cape Finisterre on May 3, he found a smaller armed force than he had expected: only five ships of the line and four frigates escorting twenty-eight merchantmen bound for Canada and the East Indies. He prepared to attack at one o'clock; by seven o'clock it was all over. Six French warships had struck their colors; three East Indiamen were captured on the spot, and the next day the *Yarmouth* and the *Nottingham,* commanded by his protégé Philip Saumarez, rounded up most of the rest. In a single afternoon, Anson had proved the value of his Western Squadron—what would come to be called the Channel Fleet.

Most surprising, however, was how Anson won his battle. Although he had started in classic line ahead formation, when he saw the French were tacking away to escape, he ordered a general chase, allowing his captains to break formation and choose their targets. For Anson had made it clear how he intended to fight beforehand, "having called them all on board the morning before the action, and given them directions which he believed would be right for them to do, supposing they should not be able to see, or he to change his signals."

This, too, was a Vernon innovation. On his outward-bound voyage for the West Indies in late July 1739, he had drawn up a series of orders to supplement the "permanent" Sailing and Fighting Instructions, now more than forty years old. Vernon felt they used the line ahead formation as a way to avoid rather than trigger a decisive engagement—perfectly understandable in the perilous aftermath of Beachy Head. But Vernon wanted a strategic approach more suited to offense, one that gave his captains freedom to "come to a closer engagement" under all conditions, even when they could not see his signal flags. So in addition to giving his officers room to choose how and when to attack, he also briefed them carefully before the battle, to make sure they understood his strategy as well as he did.

The old fighting admirals of Queen Anne's navy probably did the same—Vernon may have learned the technique from his old patron

Rooke—but Vernon, and now Anson, made the pre-battle briefing standard practice. The line ahead was becoming a more flexible, and a more aggressive battle formation, and no officer would exploit it better than the man who took over the Western Squadron in August that year, Edward Hawke.

Hawke's career is a good example of the problems, as well as opportunities, an able sea officer faced in the eighteenth-century navy. Unlike Vernon and Anson, he had no political connections; his father was an undistinguished Lincoln's Inn barrister. Hawke came aboard the 20-gun sloop *Seahorse* as a volunteer by warrant at age fifteen. His first trip to sea carried him from the Medway to New York City in 1720. It took four uneventful years of service to make midshipman; almost four more to get his first commission as lieutenant, although he passed the necessary exam much earlier. He was cruising the Caribbean on a small sloop of only ten guns, the *Wolf,* when its captain died and he took over as master and commander. After two years, Hawke lost his temporary commission and became a half-pay retiree, eking out a living on fivepence a day.

The coming of war in 1739 brought him back for convoy duty until an army officer uncle with a friend at the Admiralty arranged for his first real commission, the 70-gun *Berwick* on June 14, 1743—just as war was breaking out with France. Hawke ended up in the Mediterranean squadron; his intrepid capture of the *Poder* was the one bright spot in the Toulon battle debacle. He continued to serve in the Mediterranean with skill and competence, even becoming a commodore, but no one noticed. His uncle died in 1746. Hawke lost his commodore's pennant. New Year's Day, 1747, found him a captain without a ship at age forty-two, and back on half-pay.

In fact, he narrowly missed being pushed out of the navy altogether. That month King George II got the list of captains due for promotion to "Rear Admiral without Distinction of Squadron"—the kiss of career death. One of them was Hawke. But King George remembered Hawke's name from the Toulon battle dispatches; he told the startled Anson he would not allow such a brave and intrepid officer to be "yellowed" out of the service. So Hawke became a Rear Admiral of the White on July 15, 1747, and headed down to Plymouth to take up his new duties as port admiral.

It was essentially a desk job, helping the new commander of the Western Squadron, Vice Admiral Peter Warren, deal with the problems of refitting and victualing ships heavily buffeted by weeks at sea in the western Atlantic. The constant wear and tear meant there were always fewer ships ready for action than any admiral liked, and fewer sailors thanks to the inevitable scurvy. In August Warren came down with scurvy himself. He requested leave and suggested that Hawke temporarily replace him until he felt better. At first Anson hesitated to put so valuable a post in the hands of "so young an officer." But Warren reassured him, adding that there was "no immediate service of great importance," anyway, and none in the offing.

Warren could not have been more wrong. Desperate to break the Western Squadron's strangehold on its Atlantic trade, the French government was ordering every warship in Brest harbor it could spare to be fitted out and ready to escort more than 250 merchantmen to the West Indies. The result was a small but impressive force: a 60-gun East Indiaman and eight ships of the line, including three of the new French 74s: *Intrépide,* *Terrible,* and *Monarque.* The escort's commander, De l'Etrenduère, had the 80-gun *Tonnant* as his flagship. All were well manned, and faster and stronger than any of Hawke's ships with the same number of guns.

Hawke meanwhile had set sail from Plymouth on August 10 and got word from a Dutch trading vessel of what was up in Brest harbor. How many ships he could bring to bear against Etrenduère's convoy depended on how long he would be at sea waiting for them. Every week of patrol was a race against outbreaks of scurvy, or running low on food and water, or having hulls so fouled with weeds that ships had to be sent back to Plymouth. After two months at sea, from mid-August to mid-October, with lookouts scanning the horizon every day for enemy sail, Hawke had two ships too riddled with scurvy to continue. That left him only fourteen, all low on water and badly needing cleaning, when on the morning of October 14 a lookout spotted the French convoy.

"I immediately made the signal for all the fleet to chase," Hawke wrote. "About 8, saw a great number of ships, but so crowded together that we could not count them." Hawke had more fighting ships but none with more than seventy guns. But he had told his captains to fight the enemy aggressively and as closely as possible: "at pistol shot," he liked to say. So when the effort to form up in line ahead took so long that it seemed the French were getting away, Hawke gave them the signal to renew the chase and the British flung themselves on their prey.

The *Princess Louisa* was the first to hit Etrenduère's line. The others followed in obedience to Hawke's other key instruction: once a ship had crippled an enemy vessel, it moved on the next, leaving slower comrades to finish the job. One by one the French warships took a punishing fire, as three of Hawke's ships moved on the starboard tack to squeeze the French line from windward while the rest attacked from leeward. As they closed to pistol range, less than fifty yards, they poured out volley after volley of case shot that tore down French masts and rigging and swept the upper decks clear. By one-thirty the first French ships began to surrender. Hawke even tried to engage his 66-gun *Devonshire* with Etrenduère's 80-gun *Tonnant* but ran afoul of the shot-up *Eagle*, commanded by a young officer named George Rodney, which had lost its ship's wheel and could no longer steer. But Hawke did take three prizes himself: *Séverne*, *Trident*, and the 74-gun *Terrible*, which fought on until seven at night before "she called for quarter." The *Tonnant* herself was so badly damaged that the *Intrépide* had to tow her away into the darkness.

Every other French warship surrendered. Only two still had a mast standing; more than 4,000 French sailors were killed, wounded, or captured. Their brave sacrifice—"no ships behaved better than the enemy's," wrote one British captain after the fight, "or sold their liberties dearer"—had allowed the merchant convoy to escape. But the British had only 170 killed (the saddest loss being *Nottingham*'s Philip Saumarez, killed in the fruitless chase after the *Tonnant* and *Intrépide*) and did not lose a single ship. Hawke could write in his dispatch, "Commanders, officers, and companies behaved with the greatest spirit and resolution, in every respect like Englishmen." The very next day Hawke sent the sloop *Weasel* off to Jamaica to alert the commander of the West Indies squadron, George Pocock, of what had happened. A month later Pocock caught the defenseless convoy and took more than forty prizes. Another one hundred French merchantmen remained holed up in Martinique, unable to sail because Hawke had captured the warships that were supposed to escort them back to France.

The second Battle of Finisterre established Edward Hawke as the master of the new flexible line ahead battle pioneered by Vernon and Anson, and as the greatest fighting admiral of his day. It also left the French fleet divided and the French Atlantic trade at a standstill. Louis XV and his ministers lost heart as they realized how vulnerable this British superiority at sea really made them. British ships at Gibraltar were keeping half the French fleet stuck at Toulon, while Hawke kept the other half pinned down at Brest. Although the occasional ship got through to Bonnie Prince Charlie (including the one that would eventually take him away), no large-scale help could reach him as the Jacobite revolt was crushed at the battle of Culloden and Scotland secured. In 1744 a British squadron had entered the Indian Ocean for the first time; by July 1748 Admiral Edward Boscawen had ten warships to control the coast of India. The French were losing the privateering war as well: British captains with letters of marque, many sailing from North American ports, had taken more than 1,200 French and Spanish prizes, while the French caught less than half that number. With its rapidly expanding merchant marine, the British hardly missed their losses; for the French, the losses spelled economic disaster unless the war stopped.

The peace signed at Aix-la-Chapelle in 1748 was more a truce than a treaty. It settled nothing. But it did give the nations of Europe a decade in which to regroup and digest the new geopolitical realities. The Spanish had lost all economic control over their empire as British merchants now traded openly in every Latin American port except Havana. The Portuguese kept theirs only because of their alliance with Britain. The Dutch were finished as an important power and retreated further into apathy and neutrality. Meanwhile, a new land power had emerged in central Europe, Frederick the Great's Prussia, just as an old one had survived France's and Prussia's efforts to break it up, namely Habsburg Austria.

The French had seen their bid to dominate Europe checkmated once again by the British: on land at the battle of Dettingen in Germany and at sea by the twin defeats at Finisterre. As for the British, they now completely dominated the seas surrounding western Europe and held the reins of power in America and the Western Hemisphere. Thanks to Anson and Hawke, they were finally learning how to use their naval strength effectively.

In less than a decade they would be put to an even more severe test. The ink on the Aix-la-Chapelle was hardly dry before the French were rebuilding their fleet and plotting their revenge. War was coming again, to be fought not just in Europe but across the globe. Fortunately, at the critical juncture, Britain would find a politician who finally understood how to use the navy Anson and the Admiralty had built, as a decisive instrument of power in history's first true world war.

He was the grandson of Thomas "Diamond" Pitt, a flamboyant Dorsetshire merchant who had ruthlessly used the reorganized East India Company and a crumbling Moghul empire to make a fortune in India and become governor of Madras.* Thomas Pitt returned to England in

---

*Including acquiring a fabulous diamond worth almost 25,000 pounds, which he eventually sold to the Duke of Burgundy for almost three times that amount.

1710 an immensely rich man, and bought himself a seat in Parliament for Old Sarum, the most notorious "rotten borough" in Britain, with only seven voters. Old Pitt passed it on his son, and his grandson William, who took it over in 1735. So William Pitt, the politician who would proclaim that Parliament's duty was to carry out "the will of the people," started his career by sitting for the borough that epitomized what his followers would call Old Corruption.

From his maiden speech in the House of Commons on April 22, 1735, to his fatal seizure on the floor of the House of Lords on April 7, 1778, everything William Pitt did marked him as the most extraordinary politician of his age. He was larger than life in ways that revealed his West Country origins. His impatience had no limits and his ambition no bounds. He could stomach no authority except his own: Pitt said himself, "I cannot bear the least touch of command." He drove himself so mercilessly it repeatedly broke his health, both mentally and physically. He would plunge into depressions so deep he would lock himself in his room and trays of food had to be passed through the door. He would rise to oratorical heights that literally terrified his audiences. As an admirer put it, "He slaved like a clerk and spoke like a God." Comparison with Churchill is inevitable.

Pitt's detractors, like Churchill's, dismissed him as a "wicked madman" and a demagogue. Lord Perceval accused him of "a self-conceit and an arrogance of nature beyond all parallel." But even Perceval admitted William Pitt "possessed a wonderful power of words," a power that would bring him a passionate following far beyond Parliament. Pitt was the first prime minister to mobilize public opinion "out of doors," in the coy contemporary phrase, to the cause of empire, trade, and sea power.

As a young politician he had heard the Jenkins case and joined Vernon and the others in their attacks on the Walpole administration for letting it happen. "Is this any longer a nation?" Pitt declaimed. "Is this any longer an English Parliament, if with more ships in your harbors than all the navies of Europe, with above two millions of people in your American colonies" the government refused to go to war with Spain? "Sir, Spain knows the consequence of a war in America," he added, "whoever gains, it must prove fatal to her." It was a classic statement of the view of naval power popular among parliamentary Tories and anti-government Whigs, the so-called blue water school.

"All the maxims of British policy" dictate waging war by sea not land, wrote its founder Jonathan Swift, "the sea being the element where we

might most probably carry on the war with any advantage to our selves."
This was why Tories like Swift so bitterly opposed Britain's involvement
in the land campaigns of the War of the Spanish Succession, and why
opposition Whigs like Vernon and Pitt expected an easy victory over
Spain in the War of Jenkins' Ear. Events proved them wrong, but the
"blue water" strategists did grasp an essential point about British naval
power: without it, Britain's overseas trade could not grow. And it was "the
vastness and extensiveness of our trade," said a writer as early as 1718, that
made Britain "the most considerable of any nation in the world."

As member of Parliament in the 1730s William Pitt understood the
importance of trade to Britain's future and to Britain's emerging identity
as a commercial, as well as religious, Elect Nation. "When trade is at
stake," he argued, "it is your last entrenchment; you must defend it or per-
ish." But as a statesman in the 1750s, Pitt would turn the standard formula of seapower and trade inside out. Instead of seeing the navy as a
weapon for getting and defending overseas empire, he saw overseas
empire as a tool for the navy, giving it the bases it needed to defend
British mercantile interests and to increase its own global reach.

John Oldmixon may have been the first to point out, back in 1708,
that what really made Britain great was not trade but its fleets. Trade was
merely a way to pay for them. But Pitt saw even deeper and clearer. The
old view of seaborne empire, going back to Hawkins and Philip II, was of
a mother country connected to its various colonies by trade routes, a network of long delicate filaments stretching out over vast empty oceans.
Pitt showed that instead of the oceans dividing Britain's empire, they
united them. The fact that the seas were all one could enable a powerful
navy to consolidate Britain's imperial possessions and divide and distract
those of its enemies. Pitt turned Britain's supposed weakness, its far-
flung global trading networks, into a strategic strength. In fact, the more
far-flung, the better. Viewed in this way, the Royal Navy gave Britain's
maritime empire a vibrancy and dynamism none of its predecessors, not
even the Dutch, ever had. For Pitt himself, that dynamism needed to be
directed to a single urgent task: crushing France's ambitions for world
hegemony.

The threat was certainly real enough. Historians often portray
eighteenth-century France as a world of enlightened salons and cos-
mopolitan minds like Voltaire and Montesquieu. In fact, it was a deeply
militarized society, with a ruling class that thirsted for war and a bureau-

cracy dedicated to finding ways to pay for it. Its powerful army and navy had once served the *gloire* of Louis XIV. Now they served the self-interest of the French aristocracy, which formed in effect a military caste. Any involvement in trade or the professions brought *dérogeance* and loss of noble status; positions in the Church or at Court were limited to a tiny few. For all but the richest or most intellectually gifted, the army or navy was their one outlet, and war their one chance at fame. "Kingdoms are not conquered, and an empire is not obtained without fighting battles," said Louis XV's war minister, the Count of Belle-Isle, as he built an army of more than 200,000 soldiers (compared to 30,000 British soldiers in all of England, Scotland, and Ireland) and as France's always competitive navy was on the rebound.

It had modernized itself by abolishing the last of its galley fleet in 1748, and concentrated on building its fast and powerful 74s and 64s, the core of a fighting fleet of sixty ships of the line and thirty frigates. By 1756 the rebuilding was nearly complete, and the new Académie de la Marine at Brest was turning out officers to command its ships and squadrons. Minister of the Marine Maurepas was ready to mobilize his fleet behind an ambitious plan to shatter Britain's world position once and for all.

What set it off, and thus lit the fuse for world war, was the British Admiralty's decision in 1749 to build a new naval base at Halifax in Nova Scotia. The French worried that it would serve to cut off its own vital naval base at Louisbourg, and thus isolate Canada from France. So they countered by reinforcing the series of forts reaching down the St. Lawrence River to the Great Lakes, from Quebec to Detroit and Michilimackinac, and then extending into the Ohio River Valley with Fort Duquesne in 1753. This strategic barrier would, they hoped, block English settlers from pushing their way beyond the Alleghenies into the French Louisiana Territory and secure France's American empire before it was too late.

The American colonists in turn felt cut off and demanded that London act. It sent out General Braddock with an army the same year to take Fort Duquesne, and so the struggle for control of the interior river valleys of North America, from the Mohawk to the Mississippi and the Ohio, was on. Braddock was defeated and killed; Admiral Boscawen's squadron failed to stop French reinforcements; another British force failed to take Fort Niagra, while a third succeeded to taking Beauséjour on the Bay of Fundy. All of this was before any formal declaration of war between France and Britain. Yet the same "tail wags the dog" colonial struggle was taking place in India, where the French East India Company's general the Marquis Dupleix and his English counterpart Robert Clive had been waging a covert war against each other for almost two years.

With war already under way on two continents, the French government turned to a new ally—Austria—for the last leg of their plan. Together they would thrust deep into Germany, to threaten Hanover, King George II's German principality and home. This in turn would force the British to withdraw troops from North America—Then another French army would stage invasion maneuvers along the western coast, forcing the British to concentrate naval forces in the Channel to prevent any attack. This would allow the French squadron at Toulon to regain control of the Mediterranean and convince Spain to throw in their lot with its Bourbon cousin.

It was a complicated but well-thought-out global strategy—the first of its kind for the French, and one that took full advantage of their chief strength, their invincible army. War came to Europe at the end of August 1756, when Prussia struck at Austria's ally Saxony. The French army drove King George's Hanoverian troops back to the North Sea and on April 19 French forces from Toulon launched a surprise attack on the British base at Port Mahon on Minorca. The Admiralty ordered John Byng to take a detachment of ships to reinforce Gibraltar and relieve the siege. He encountered the French fleet off Minorca but refused to fight a decisive battle. Only half the British ships fired a shot, while the French gleefully broke off and secured their position around Port Mahon. After four days, Byng held a dispirited council of war and decided to return to Gibraltar. On June 29, Port Mahon surrendered. Only complicated diplomatic maneuvering from Westminster and the presence of Byng's fleet at Gibraltar kept Spain from joining the victorious French. If it had, Britain's numerical superiority at sea would have vanished overnight.

As it was, its position in the Mediterranean looked increasingly untenable. So did its positions elsewhere. The French in Canada under Montcalm were pressing toward the Hudson River Valley and threatening to cut the American colonies in two; French forces in India were closing on Madras; Admiral Hawke's attempt to keep a continuous watch on goings-on at Brest had failed, as scurvy once again broke out among his exhausted men. "Had I stayed out a week longer," he told Anson, "there would not have been men enough to have worked the larger ships, they fell down so fast."

It was a summer of discontent in London, bordering on despair.

"Distress, infinite distress seems to hem us in on all quarters," William Pitt wrote. He blamed the Newcastle ministry's "weak infatuated conduct" for the string of failures, for remaining on the defensive instead of taking forthright action. Many, particularly in the business community, were now saying Pitt was the man to turn things around. Newcastle had already offered Pitt a place in the cabinet in 1755, but Pitt refused unless he were also given the leadership of the House of Commons and Britain stopped trying to bring Russia in as its ally against France. Newcastle refused; even when in 1756 Russia decided to join France and Austria instead, he would not budge. It was Byng's abject performance at Minorca that finally convinced the king that Newcastle had to go, and in December Pitt became part of a new cabinet as one of its secretaries of state. As such he would organize the war's strategy over the next four years.

Pitt saw at once what had been holding Britain back: it had no strong ally on the Continent to balance French power. He decided that should be Prussia. Frederick the Great had already signed an alliance with Great Britain, but fierce fighting in the east against Austria and Saxony tied up Frederick's resources. Now Pitt convinced the king to give Prussia, "the last bulwark of the liberties of Europe," the one resource Britain had in abundance, money. For four years Pitt would pay paid Frederick an annual subsidy equal to the entire Prussian budget. Pitt's strategy proved its value when Frederick's troops scored a brilliant victory at Rossbach in November 5, 1757, neutralizing the French threat to Germany and shattering the myth that the French army was invincible.

A new vista for British diplomacy had opened. For decades its statesmen had talked about establishing a "balance of power" in Europe, meaning a permanent diplomatic check on France's ambitions and on any invasion from the continent. Now Pitt discovered how to make that balance of power a reality. The combination of Britain's superior naval strength *plus* a strong continental ally or allies would stop France, or indeed any other European power, from invading or making trouble for Britain's imperial ambitions. Now Britain could quit playing defense and go on the offensive. "We shall conquer America through Germany," Pitt said.

In this Pitt found an indispensable ally in George Anson. Pitt appointed him First Lord of the Admiralty on July 2, 1757. It was Anson, not Pitt, who organized the new offensive strategy and became the real architect of final victory. Its linchpin, he argued, had to be a permanent Western Squadron. "Our Colonies are so numerous and so extensive that to keep a naval force at each equal to the united force of France would . . . double our navy," he warned Pitt. "The best defense, therefore, for our colonies as well as our coasts, is to have such a squadron always to the westward . . . either [to] keep the French in port, or give them battle with advantage if they come out."

In charge of this powerful force, christened the Channel Fleet and eventually numbering thirty ships of the line, would be Admiral Hawke. Hawke was working out a plan with Anson whereby supply ships could out from Plymouth and reprovision his ships with fresh food directly at sea. It beat the scurvy for the first time, and Hawke's mania for cleanliness on shipboard fended off other diseases like typhus and prison fever. After three continuous months at sea, Hawke could report, "Except for one or two ships, the squadron is very healthy, and for the sake of our Country at this critical juncture, I hope it will continue."

Anson's strategy at sea, like Pitt's on land, was classic divide and conquer. The Channel Fleet's presence divided the French navy between Brest and Toulon; neither force could join the other without fighting Hawke on less than equal terms. It also divided France from its trade and colonies, just as Pitt's alliance with Prussia divided France's armies and forestalled any attack on England—especially since there could be no united French fleet to support it. Now the rest of British naval and military might could roll up France's overextended empire like a Persian carpet. Anson and Pitt had reversed the war's controls and were poised for victory.

First, however, they had to deal with Admiral Byng. To this day historians debate the pros and cons of the case. Byng was a fine and respected officer, son of the victor at Cape Passaro, and his failure at Minorca was as much a matter of following the official orders for line ahead battles too literally as it was a failure of nerve. Anson (who was not blameless himself for the loss of Minorca) had ordered Byng brought back to England for court-martial. The court of twelve naval officers had to find him guilty for avoiding battle: under Anson's own revisions to the Articles of War, they had no choice but to sentence Byng to death.

No one imagined it would be carried out. The king's pardon was expected every day. But the British public demanded a scapegoat for the string of recent defeats; Pitt was either unwilling or unable to intervene to save the hapless Byng. So despite public pleas for mercy from Horace Walpole, Samuel Johnson, Voltaire, and even the French commander at Toulon, John Byng was executed by firing squad on the quarterdeck of the captured French warship *Monarque* in Portsmouth Harbor, on March 14, 1757—the first and only British admiral ever executed for cowardice.

Afterward, Walpole wrote of Byng, "The persecution of his enemies, who sacrifice him for their own guilt and the rage of a blind nation, have called forth all my pity for him." Byng pleaded that he was merely following the fighting instructions to the letter, to avoid losing formation when in the presence of the enemy. But that was just the problem. The Royal Navy could not afford officers who just stuck to the letter: it needed men who acted boldly, who were willing to take risks, even break the rules in order to bring about a decisive engagement. The execution of Byng was not the result of the navy's hidebound rigidity: just the opposite. Voltaire made a famous scathing remark about Byng being executed "in order to encourage the others." But a year later Edward Hawke would alter the standard fighting instructions for his Western Squadron, crossing out the line about engaging the enemy "in the Order the Admiral has proscribed" and writing in instead, "as close as possible, and therefore on no account to fire until they shall be within pistol shot." Bold action, taking the initiative, hard close combat, were the hallmarks of the new navy Anson and Hawke were creating. It was the legacy they would leave to Horatio Nelson, and Byng's sacrifice was a sad but necessary part of securing it.

A new fighting spirit, and a new fighting ship: the 74-gun third-rate. It was based on the revolutionary French design, taken from the examples Hawke had captured at Finisterre in 1748. Anson had to bring in a whole new Navy Board to get the surveyors to accept working on a "foreign" design, no matter how patently superior. The design itself remained so secret that even the shipwrights were told they were still building 70s until the number of gunports made the issue plain. The first came down the slipways in 1755 as the *Dublin* class. Each carried twenty-eight guns on two decks on either side: the quarterdeck carried fourteen instead of the old 70s' twelve, and four bow chasers in the forecastle instead of the usual two. The extra firepower was less important than the higher firing platform, with two decks instead of three, and the superior sailing.

The arrival of the 74 marked, as one historian has said, "the greatest breakthrough of British naval shipbuilding of the eighteenth century." The *Dublin* class was followed by the *Hero, Hercules,* and *Thunderer;* then in early 1757 came the *Bellona* class, with gun decks 168 feet long, the standard for the next two decades. By 1759 there were fourteen 74s in active service. They would be the backbone of the British battle fleet until

Trafalgar, and the backbone of Anson's campaign to smash the French with a series of sharp, bold naval strikes. Combined with amphibious landings and British land forces well supplied and protected by sea, they would deliver a collective blow from which the French Empire would never recover.

India was the first to fall. Thanks to George Pocock's Bombay squadron, Robert Clive now had command of the sea at his back. The closest base for French warships, by contrast, was Mauritius, far to the south and west near Madagascar. Pocock kept Clive's mixed army of native and British regiments supplied and cut off French reinforcements, frustrating every French attempt to regain control of India's eastern coast and the heart of Bengal. The British navy enabled Clive to beat his rival Dupleix at the battle of Plassey in 1757, lift the siege of Madras in 1759, and allowed Eyre Coote to crush the main French army at Wandiwash in 1760. The victories made the East India Company the most powerful political player Southeast Asia and English, not French, the language of imperialism in India. They also secured Britain's growing trade with that part of the world. For the first time, India became an important and valuable part of its mercantile empire.

Meanwhile, the Western Squadron's blockade of the French coast starved French forces in North America of the men and supplies they needed to follow up their earlier success. Then in 1758 Admiral Boscawen and General Amherst ran a joint army-navy siege of Louisbourg, forcing the city to surrender and thus cutting off the French army in Canada. British armies could now begin pushing the French out of the Great Lakes and Ohio Valley. Fort Duquesne fell in the autumn, which the victors renamed Pittsburgh after the new prime minister. Ticonderoga and Fort Niagara fell next. That left only Quebec.

In the summer of 1759 a fleet of twenty-two ships of the line and twenty-seven frigates under Admiral Sir Charles Saunders arrived at the mouth of the St. Lawrence with a 9,000-man army commanded by General Wolfe. With the help of ship's master James Cook, who carefully charted the river's many unpredictable shallows, Saunders successfully got his fleet up the St. Lawrence and past Quebec's guns to disembark Wolfe's men just south of the city—a feat army officers watching thought impossible. For two months, Saunders kept Wolfe's men supplied while fending off every attempt to attack his vulnerable ships. Then, on a crisp September morning, British troops stormed the Heights of Abraham and took Quebec. The battle cost Wolfe his life, as well as that of his opponent,

Montcalm. But it decided the fate of North America just as Plassey decided the fate of India, another tribute to the reach and skill of the British navy.

In the West Indies, Anson sent amphibious forces to scoop up Martinique and Guadeloupe, along with St. Lucia and Grenada. In West Africa, Senegal fell, the hub of the French slave trade, and the fortress at Goree. In the Mediterranean, the Gibraltar squadron blockaded part of the Toulon fleet in Cartagena on the coast of Spain, and then defeated the ships sent to break the deadlock. Toulon itself remained in a chokehold until the French commander tried to break out in late July 1759, only to meet the Gibraltar force, now under the tough Cornishman Edward Boscawen, off Lagos on the Portuguese coast. Boscawen, "Old Dreadnought" to his men,* sank two French warships, captured another three, and then bottled up the remainder in Lisbon. With the French navy driven from the Mediterranean, retaking Minorca was clearly only a matter of time.

"Our bells are threadbare with ringing of victories," Horace Walpole wrote that autumn. "In short, Mr. Pitt and this little island appear of some consequence even in the map of the world." Walpole had once sneered at Pitt as a demagogue and charlatan. Now, he confessed, "I give him all the honor he deserves."

The French, by contrast, were desperate. One by one, they were watching their overseas possessions disappear. Their armies were stalled in Flanders and Germany. Almost two thousand British privateers and more than seventy Royal Navy frigates had stripped them of their overseas trade, from the Caribbean to the Indian Ocean. British merchant trade, by contrast, actually *increased* during the war, despite the hundreds of ships taken by French privateers. Even more important, the French navy was not replacing its lost ships. Both sides had been building ships furiously since 1750, but when the war started, the money for new French construction dried up while the British shipyards got even busier. By December 1758 the Royal Navy had 276 warships in commission, with over ninety ships of the line, and was still growing. The French could not show more than a third of that number.

Earlier that summer, the French ambassador in Vienna despairingly

---

*The nickname was the name of the 60-gun fourth-rate he had commanded, but it also fit his personality. Once he was called on deck in the middle of the night: "Sir, there are two large ships, which look like Frenchmen, bearing down on us; what are we to do?" "Do?" Boscowan in his nightshirt answered. "Do? Damn 'em, fight 'em!"

wrote, "No trade left, consequently no money. . . . No navy, consequently no strength to resist England. The navy has no more sailors, and having no money cannot hope to procure them." The same shortage of money, supplies, and seamen had hamstrung the French navy in wars before; it would in wars after. In the final analysis, for all its skill and brilliance, the French navy had no staying power. French governments simply were never under the same political pressures, the same passionate public dedication, to having a navy second to none that British governments faced. "The moment we lose our Dominion of the Sea," an English author wrote in 1756, "we cease to exist." For the Frenchman, sea power was merely a useful adjunct to land power. For the Briton, sea power already enjoyed the status of national mission and myth—not to say survival.

However, that did not stop the French government from asking its navy to do the impossible. In 1759 the war minister Belle-Isle and the new foreign minister, Choiseul, came up with a last reckless gamble to force Britain out of the war with a sudden invasion of Scotland. Belle-Isle's plan called for the Toulon and Brest squadrons to somehow break their blockades and unite on the coast of Brittany, at Quiberon Bay one hundred miles south of Brest. There they would pick up army transports and escort an invasion force past the British fleet and land them somewhere north in the Clyde estuary, for a march on Edinburgh. Then the two squadrons were to navigate around the northern tip of Scotland—the 1588 Spanish Armada's course in reverse—and enter the North Sea to pick up French troops in Flanders at Ostend, to escort them for an invasion of the Essex coast. Even if the invasion failed, Choiseul hoped it would trigger a panic in the London Exchange and collapse Britain's fiscal structure. With no money, he reasoned, Pitt would have to quit.

The plan was drawn up by ex-generals with no understanding of sea operations; it completely ignored the fact of British naval superiority. It made Philip II's plan for the Armada look straightforward and sane. The wretched man they chose as their Medina Sidonia was the sixty-four-year-old commander of the Brest squadron, Vice Admiral and Count de Conflans-Brienne.

He was typical of the French naval officer corps: a skilled seaman, a competent administrator, scion of two ancient noble houses. He combined personal bravery with a deep sense of honor. But like all his fellow French admirals, his confidence had been shaken by Britain's string of naval successes. Ever since the defeat at La Hougue sixty years before, French naval thinking had been largely defensive. The habit of defeat

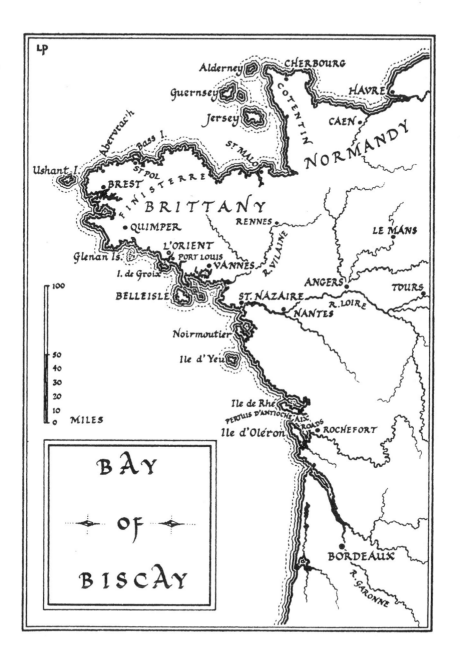

LP

Alderney
CHERBOURG
Guernsey
HAVRE
Jersey
COTENTIN
CAEN
ST MALO
NORMANDY

Ushant I.
Abervrac'h
Bass I.
ST POL
BREST
FINISTERRE
BRITTANY
RENNES
LE MANS
QUIMPER
L'ORIENT
PORT LOUIS
R. VILAINE
Glenan Is.
VANNES
I. de Groix
ANGERS
TOURS
BELLEISLE
ST. NAZAIRE
R. LOIRE
NANTES
Noirmoutier

Ile d'Yeu

100

50
40
30
20
10
0   MILES

Ile de Rhé
PERTUIS D'ANTIOCHE AIX
ROADS
ROCHEFORT
Ile d'Oléron

BAY

of

BISCAY

BORDEAUX
R. GARONNE

bred a caution, a timidity, that contrasted sharply with the boldness and daring of an Anson or a Hawke. So it was Hawke who felt free to bottle up Conflans in Brest harbor for six months, with British frigates brazenly keeping station at its entrance every day while the French sat and did nothing.

This was Hawke's system of close blockade. It was the result of the British navy's excellent seamanship and its new logistics at sea. Hawke had started in May with twenty-five ships of the line. They included seven of the new 74s and the 100-gun *Royal George,* which had taken ten years to build, needed 880 men to man, and represented a major step forward in the design of first-rate battleships. Hawke kept a small offshore squadron under Augustus Hervey to watch the comings and goings at Brest, then deployed his main force near the island of Ushant. From there he could cruise the entire Biscay coast as far as Rochefort, intercepting any ship that tried to enter a French port.

The result was that nothing got in or out of Brest. Every new piece of rigging, every cannon ball, every sack of flour or cask of wine the French fleet needed, had to be brought overland or landed farther down the coast. Hawke's blockade prevented the French from reinforcing Canada, and thus secured Wolfe's victory at Quebec. It kept them from saving Guadeloupe and Martinique. It allowed Pitt to devote all his resources to his campaign of global conquest even when he and Anson knew that a French invasion was coming and that the battleships at home were seriously undermanned. The close blockade had become a new strategic weapon in modern warfare and a hallmark of British naval dominance.

None of it would have worked without Hawke's system of victualing at sea. When Dr. James Lind studied the results, he found them "perfect and unparalleled." Hawke had kept more than fourteen thousand men at sea for six months. Yet only one man on his flagship *Ramillies* was too sick to perform his duties, and only twenty in the entire fleet. Fresh provisioning and scrupulously clean ships had kept scurvy and typhus away from Hawke's crews.

The one thing Hawke could not control, however, was the weather. Autumn gales came slashing out of the west, threatening to push him off the French coast and into the Channel. In early November he had no choice but to put into Torbay to find shelter. The blockade was broken. Conflans saw his chance and made for open sea. There would be no Toulon squadron to join him; Boscawen had taken care of that with his victory at Lagos. Yet the war minister told Conflans to press on with the invasion, anyway. Conflans glumly obeyed. Even if he could not beat Hawke, he said, "at least I will have fought for glory."

Conflans managed to beat his way out of Brest harbor on the four-teenth. That same day Hawke transferred his flag to the *Royal George* and set out from Torbay. He had twenty-three ships of the line against Conflans's twenty-one; the rest, like the *Ramillies,* were too battered to sail. But at least he knew where Conflans was heading: Quiberon Bay, where the French invasion troops had been waiting for an escort for months.

Quiberon Bay lies nestled between the rugged coast of Brittany and the island of Belle Isle, with a row of small islands, called the Cardinals, guarding the entrance from the south. As Constans approached in the early hours of the twentieth, the British frigates stationed there fled north. The weather was fierce, as a constant gale blew out of the west-northwest. A storm was coming, which would make entering the bay, with its rocks and unexpected shoals, dangerous. Conflans was still chasing the frigates away, and wondering how he would get his ships, with their undermanned and untrained crews (one, the *Thésée,* had a large draft of peasant conscripts), safely into harbor when a lookout spotted a line of unknown sails astern on the darkening horizon. Conflans called off the chase and watched with his telescope until the truth finally sank in.

It was Hawke. "At first the wind blowing hard at South by East and South drove us considerably to the westward," he wrote afterward to the Admiralty, "but on the 18th and 19th it proved more favorable." He had picked up two additional frigates, the *Maidstone* and *Coventry,* before con-verging on Quiberon Bay, only a few hours behind Conflans. "At about half past eight o'clock on the morning of the 20th . . . the *Maidstone* made the signal for seeing the fleet. I immediately spread aboard the signal for the line abreast, in order to draw all the ships of the squadron up with me."

Conflans had two choices. He could rally his ships and try to fight Hawke at the very entrance of the bay on a "lee shore," with the violent winds threatening to drive them both onto the rocks of the Cardinals, or he could pass into the bay itself and take shelter, gambling that the British would not dare to follow. A unknown lee shore was every sailor's night-mare. Hawke had no French pilots or charts. Surely he would not put his entire squadron at needless risk, Conflans thought, especially with a storm coming.

But Conflans did not know Hawke. "Monsieur Conflans kept going off under such sail as all his squadron could carry, and at the same time keep together," Hawke wrote, "while we crowded after him with every sail engaging." In contrast to his French counterpart, Hawke had confidence in his sailors and their seamanship. He had confidence that his officers— captains like Richard Howe of the *Magnanime*, a French-built 74 now in the lead of Hawke's force; Charles Hardy in the *Union* and George Gambier in the *Burford;* Augustus Keppel in the *Torbay* and Samuel Hood in the 32-gun *Minerva*—would fight the way Hawke liked—as quickly and as closely as possible. Above all, he was confident that if he fought the French, regardless of the weather, he would win. So Hawke ran up his white flag with a red cross on the *Royal George*'s fore topmast head and fired his signal gun three times: the order for general chase.

It was certainly the worst conditions under which a major naval engagement was ever fought. One violent squall after another descended on the two fleets. Huge waves rose, their crests breaking with a thick misty foam against a darkening sky, and then violently dropped away, making it almost impossible for ships to avoid colliding as they lost their wind and steerage way in the trough of the swell. Yet even as the wind howled and ships' wheel chains shuddered and waves slammed against rudders with a dismal clang, the leading British ships got within range of the rearmost French.

"At half-past two p.m. the fire beginning ahead, I made the signal for engaging." Howe's *Magnanime* was the first to get in close range. As they came astern of the 80-gun *Formidable,* he ordered his men to "hold their fire until they put their hands on their enemy's guns." Their broadside ripped into the Frenchmen's hull and "pierced [it] like a cullender," remembered an eyewitness, as the *Formidable* reeled and dropped back. The 74-gun *Torbay* and *Devonshire* took on the *Magnifique* as the wind and rain intensified, while the *Magnanime, Montagu,* and *Warspite* had a violent collision. Howe somehow managed to steer his ship clear and continue after the *Formidable*. Other British ships were now catching up, firing at the bucketing rearmost Frenchmen.

At 3:30 the storm reached its height. The seas were so high that ships opening their lowest deck of gun portals threatened to heel over and founder. Hawke spotted Conflans's flagship, the *Soleil Royal,* through the gusting mist and turned to the *Royal George*'s master, Thomas Conway. "I say," he shouted against the wind, "lay me alongside the French admiral." Conway, his face dripping with rain and sea spray, bellowed they might run aground. "You have now done your duty in appraising me of the danger," Hawke bellowed back, "let us now see how well you can comply with my orders."

The *Royal George* surged forward. The first French ship Hawke encountered was the *Superbe,* with seventy guns and 800 men. The *Royal George*'s second broadside sank her with all hands. A similar disaster overtook the *Thésée,* now heavily engaged with Keppel's *Torbay.* A heavy sea smashed into both, flooding their lower gun ports. Keppel shouted to the wheel to turn the *Torbay* into the wind, to bring her upright, but the *Thésée* with her peasant crew was not quick enough. The green water rushed in and, as with the *Mary Rose* two hundred years earlier, drove her to the bottom. Keppel immediately ordered his men into the boats and, in spite of the danger, broke off the battle to look for survivors. The *Torbay*'s crew only managed to save nine out of the *Thésée*'s 650 men.

"At about four o'clock the *Formidable* struck," Hawke wrote, "and a little after, the *Thésée* and *Superbe* were sunk. About five, the *Héros* struck, and came to anchor, but it blowing hard, no boat could be sent to board her." It was now almost dark, the weather as brutal as ever, but Hawke still refused to give up the chase. He closed on the *Soleil Royal* for a broadside but Conflans managed to get his violently pitching ship away. As Hawke tried to steer across the Frenchman's wake to rake its stern, another French ship* lurched between them and Conflans again escaped, close-hauling his sails to try to escape northward.

By now almost every French ship was running away as fast as she could. "The confusion was awful," wrote a French officer afterward. "We were in a funnel, as it were, all top of each other, with rocks on one side of us and ships on the other." Only total darkness prevented the panic from becoming a slaughter. That night eight French ships managed to work their way out of the bay. Conflans himself tried, but after colliding with two of his consorts, he gave up and dropped anchor to ride out the night and the storm. Hawke did the same: "I made the signal to anchor, and come-to in fifteen feet of water." The gales continued without letup, as the French and British ships tossed on their anchor cables all night and through the dawn.

"As soon as it was broad daylight," Hawke reported, "I discovered seven or eight of the enemy's line-of-battle ships at anchor between Point Penris and the river Vilaine, on which I made the signal to weigh in order to work up and attack them. But it blowed so hard from the NW. that

---

*Ironically, it was the *Intrépide,* the French ship that had escaped Hawke fifteen years earlier at Finisterre.

instead of daring to cast the squadron loose, I was obliged to strike top-gallant masts. Most of the [French] ships appeared to be aground at low water." Indeed, two of them were, including the *Soleil Royal*, which Conflans finally had to abandon and order his crew to set alight. The other, the *Héros*, suffered the same fate at the hands of a British boarding crew. All the rest, ships of the line and frigates, were desperately throwing overboard everything they could find—casks of food and water, spare anchors, cannonballs, the cannons themselves—in order to float up over the sandbar into the river and escape. All except one did, although four broke their keels going over the top of the bar, and later had to be scuttled. Meanwhile, their wretched admiral remained stranded on shore, watching his fleet disintegrate before his eyes.

For Conflans, it was a disaster and a humiliation. He had lost his flagship and four more ships of the line. The rest were either trapped at Rochefort or up the Vilaine river. Defeat did not destroy his career: in 1761 he became Minister of the Marine. But the defeat at Quiberon Bay ended the French navy as an effective fighting force for the rest of the war. Conflans himself admitted, "The morale of the fighting and civil officers was at the lowest ebb."

As for Hawke, he had given the Royal Navy its most decisive victory until Trafalgar. He had suffered only one officer and fifty seamen and marines killed, and 250 wounded. Only two ships were lost, thanks to the storm not enemy action. Quiberon Bay not only erased any chance of a French invasion, it eliminated the French navy as a strategic threat. "When I consider the season of the year, the hard gales on the day of action, a flying enemy, the shortness of the day, and the coast we were on," he told the Admiralty, "I can boldly affirm that all that could possibly be done has been done."

The Admiralty and the British public agreed. Quiberon Bay was hailed as a major triumph, and the House of Commons voted Hawke a pension of 2,000 pounds a year. Actor David Garrick thrilled London audiences with his recitation of his poem "Hearts of Oak," which became the Royal Navy's unofficial anthem.

> *Come cheer up my lads, 'tis to glory we steer,*
> *To add something more to this wonderful year,*
> *To honour we call you, not press you like slaves,*
> *For who are so free as the sons of the waves?*

In the navy, November 20 would be remembered in every captain's cabin and officers' gun room with a toast: "May all our commanders have the eye of a Hawke and the heart of a Wolfe."

It took time for the French to grasp the true dimensions of their defeat. Too late, France had convinced Spain to join their coalition. Instead of strengthening the French fleet, the declaration only exposed Spain's overseas empire to the implacable British war machine. A joint army-navy expedition took the crown jewel of Spanish America, Havana, in 1762; Admiral Draper sailed with a squadron from Madras and took Manila in 1763. French statesmen might have paid more attention to the warning of the Duke of Choiseul after his defeats in the 1740s: "There is an extraordinary blindness in all the great projects which are made in Versailles, which consists in making the Realm run the dangers of war and pay all the costs without stipulating any advantages for the Crown"— words that would ring true in the future as well.

Eventually Havana and Manila were returned to Spain in the final peace treaty, signed in Paris the next year. To the fury of Pitt and the British public, France would get back Martinique and Guadeloupe in the same deal. But in India and North America British hegemony was secure and permanent. The restoration of Minorca secured the Mediterranean. Britain was also now the dominant power in West Africa and in the Caribbean, as it added Grenada, Dominica, St. Vincent, and Tobago to its sugar colonies. And Britain's navy, grown to over three hundred vessels and 60,000 officers and seamen, enjoyed naval supremacy around the globe. Its victories had laid the foundation for a British Empire on which the sun would not set until the mid-twentieth century, an empire without precedent in its wealth, population, and its capacity for economic growth.

Yet the man most responsible for the navy's success, George Anson, did not live to see the final victory. His position and power in the Pitt administration was unshakable: a model for all future First Lords of the Admiralty. But his health never completely recovered from the ordeal of his circumnavigation in 1740–44 and plagued him throughout the war. Despite the successes, he was unhappy for another reason: he had to command his navy from behind a desk instead of from a quarterdeck. After reviewing the Western Squadron at Spithead, he told Lord Holderness how "it gave me great pleasure to see them . . . and would have given me much more to have gone to sea with them." The answer came from the Duke of Newcastle: "What was then to become of the Admiralty?" But fate did not refuse him his last wish. Very briefly, when Hawke was temporarily out of action in 1761, Anson did take over the fleet, hoisting his flag both as First Lord of the Admiralty and as commander in chief at sea—a unique honor in the history of the Royal Navy.

A year later in June he was dead. On the floor of the House of Lords, Pitt, now Lord Chatham, said of him, "To his wisdom, to his experience and care the nation owes its glorious successes of the last war." Anson had turned the strategically effective navy that Admiral Vernon envisioned more than a quarter-century earlier into a reality, just as Hawke had used it to achieve decisive victory. He left behind a phalanx of brilliant subordinates—Hawke, Boscawen, Pocock, and Saunders (who had sailed with him on the *Centurion*)—and a rising generation of equally capable captains: Hervey, Keppel, Rodney, Gambier, Hood, and Howe. The year 1763 saw Britain at a new apogee of power. Britain and its navy now had to adjust to the new responsibilities, and perils, of global empire.

CHAPTER THIRTEEN

Close Encounters

I had ambition not only to go further than any one had been before,
but as far as it was possible for man to go.
—CAPTAIN JAMES COOK

Have we not been treated with abominable insolence,
by officers of the navy?
—JOHN ADAMS

I am in hell!
—FLETCHER CHRISTIAN

I
T IS ONLY when we look backward that history assumes a predictable pattern. Viewed the other way around, as it is lived, it
abounds in inexplicable turns and strange surprises.

James Cook was the son of Scottish farmworkers who had settled in
Yorkshire. He worked for his father from the age of eight cutting hedges
and digging ditches until he was apprenticed to a shopkeeper in the
nearby village of Staiths. It was 1744; James Cook Jr. was sixteen. Apart
from a smattering of education at the village school, nothing distinguished him from the thousands of other poor day laborers eking out a
living across northern England. Nothing certainly to indicate that he was
going to become the greatest navigator and explorer of his age, the dar-
ling of the British Admiralty and Royal Society, the man who would add
more territory to the British Empire than any other Royal Navy officer in
history.

Yet it was in Staiths, a busy fishing port on the North Sea, that James
Cook caught that same bug Escalante de Mendoza had described so many
years before, the young man's "natural inclination" for an adventurous life
at sea. The old story that he was inspired by a shilling piece bearing the
mint mark of the South Sea Company may or may not be true. Anson
returned from his voyage around the world in 1744; some word of his
adventures must have reached the fishing trawlers and boatyards of

Staithes. But whatever the reason, Cook decided to set off for the seaport of Whitby the same year to sign on with a North Sea collier.

The East Coast coal business was a humble but crucial part of England's maritime trade. Specially designed freighters called "cats" regularly set out from Whitby, Hull, Grimsby, or Hartlepool with loads of coal for London (almost a million tons a year); others made the trip across the North Sea to Scandinavia and Germany. Seamen in the coal trade were skilled coasters, able to spot their way through dangerous shoals and along unknown shores in any kind of weather. It was an unromantic but valuable introduction to the world of seafaring; certainly Cook learned enough about navigation and pilotage to be offered a ship of his own in 1755. But his employer was disappointed when Cook turned him down and announced he was going to London instead. He was going to sign on with the Royal Navy.

Given the usual myths about the eighteenth-century navy and Winston Churchill's notorious remark about it being ruled by "rum, sodomy, and the lash," it seems amazing that anyone them would have actually volunteered for one of His Britannic Majesty's ships. In fact, navy ships had plenty of willing recruits, particularly skilled seamen like Cook. They understood that work on a naval vessel was actually easier than on a merchantman. A typical man-of-war of 1,200 tons divided its daily workload among 400 sailors, while the same size merchant ship bound for the West Indies might have only 120 men on board (on East Coast colliers even fewer). Also contrary to myth, a navy able seaman's pay of 22 shillings and sixpence a month was largely competitive with that of most merchantmen, and it was guaranteed, which was not the case with an unscrupulous or bankrupt merchant shipper. Volunteers for the king's service also often collected a bounty, sometimes as much as five pounds—more than James Cook Sr. could earn as a farmworker in a year.

And no merchantman ever paid out prize money, which could make even the youngest and least experienced hand on a navy ship suddenly, often disastrously, rich. The all-time record was 485 pounds, paid in 1762 to each sailor on the *Active* and *Favourite* for their joint capture of the Spanish galleon *Hermione*: enough to let men buy gold watches on Portsmouth Hoe and cook them in frying pans for fun. But sailors who were part of less spectacular catches still made tidy sums. One sailor from Anson's *Centurion*, who was paid only the first portion of his prize money, was able to get so drunk that he fell into the Thames and drowned with fifteen guineas still in his pocket. Even a sailor paid off from a long voyage could end up with a purse jammed with thirty or even forty guineas. No wonder the girls of Gosport used to sing:

Sailors, they get all the money,
Soldiers they get none but brass,
I do love a jolly sailor,
Soldiers they may kiss my arse.

However, in wartime, and in the ramp-up for war, these skilled volunteers, however eager, were no longer enough. The navy in 1755 numbered around 10,000 sailors; by 1760, in the midst of the Seven Years' War, it needed 85,000. Since the total active seamen in Britain outside the navy was probably around 80,000, that meant gathering in men from anywhere, and by any means, it could. And that meant relying on the institution as well known to Buckingham and Pepys, as it would be to Nelson: the press gang.

Again, the myths about press gangs overshadow the historical truth. The navy relied on them not because it was a cruel taskmaster but because British society gave it no other option for manning its ships. Far from being an abuse of authority, the Impress Service's powers were entirely legal and carefully circumscribed. Entire categories of seamen were officially exempt, including sailors like Cook in the collier trade, fishermen, whalers, and apprentices in their first three years at sea. But these restrictions (amounting to almost half the seafaring population) made the job of finding enough skilled men for the navy even harder, and made the efforts to round them up more drastic and intrusive.

It was a classic vicious circle. Resentment and resistance compelled the navy to resort to force, which bred still more resistance. Local magistrates tried to frustrate the press gang's work whenever it could: in the West Indies and America they claimed the right to ban them altogether. It was local governments, not the Impress Service, that tried to pawn criminals, drunks, and mentally retarded off on the navy; riots against press gangs, often provoked by navy deserters, broke out frequently in British ports. Impress officers were regularly arrested and thrown into prison, their sailors assaulted and sometimes killed.*

For this reason most ships preferred to press sailors themselves,

---

*In one notorious case in 1743, a judge even ruled that killing a press gang member was a legitimate act of self-defense, and could be done with immunity from the law.

rather than rely on the Impress Service. They also preferred taking them at sea, where the unwilling could not escape and local townspeople could not interfere. Still, violent resistance from merchant ships was not unknown, especially from sailors anxious to reach port and get their pay. In 1760 some of them took over the navy tender that had picked them up, the *Tasker,* beat up her lieutenant, and escaped to shore. But most pressed men already knew the drill and accepted the situation.* Life on a navy ship was never so bad, and life on a merchantman or on shore never so good, that seamen automatically tried to avoid taking "the King's shilling."

Yet even as Cook signed on to the 60-gun *Eagle* in June 1755 with war clouds looming, the navy already found itself with too few sailors and too many pressed men. "I do not believe there is a worse mann'd ship in the navy," its captain complained, so he was on the lookout for experienced and intelligent new recruits. Interviewing them to determine their fitness was the duty of a ship's first lieutenant. If he found a sailor like Cook who knew how to handle sails and rigging; who could tie twenty or thirty different kinds of knots and knew the hundreds of parts of the ship by name; who could balance himself on a foot-rope one hundred feet in the air and furl a wind-buffeted sail in the rain or in the dark, and who could even take his turn at the ship's wheel—in other words, a sailor who could "hand, reef, and steer"—the lieutenant would rate him "able seaman." He would get the higher monthly pay of 22s. 6d., and if he did his duty and avoided being drunk, he was a prime candidate for captain of the top for his watch, or captain of the forecastle, or any one of the other petty officer posts.

If the man had at least been to sea before and "can make himself useful on board, but is not an expert or skillful sailor," the lieutenant rated him ordinary seaman. Those who could not even do that were "landsmen": they worked on deck as "waisters," hauling the sheets, braces, and halyards, or as "idlers," helping the carpenter or cook or sailmaker with non-nautical tasks. No captain liked to sail with less than a third of his crew as able seaman or more than a third as landsmen. Yet a navy ship like the *Eagle,* with its careful discipline and organization, could turn a man who had never been to sea in his life into an able seaman in just two years. As for able seaman James Cook, he became master's mate in less than a month.

The four hundred or so crewmen on the *Eagle,* petty officers and all,

---

*In the *Tasker* case, some forty sailors actually refused to escape and remained on board.

slept on the lower gun deck, suspending their hammocks between the
24-pounders that made up her main armament. Royal Navy regulations
gave each sailor a total width of fourteen inches in which to sling his hammock but since half the crew was on watch at any given hour, in practice
that opened up to a capacious twenty-eight. Like the men on Grenville's
Revenge or Montagu's *Naseby*, they were divided into two watches, "larboard" and "starboard," working four-hour shifts on deck and then getting four hours rest below.* But unlike their Elizabethan or Stuart
ancestors, they benefitted from better pay, better food (taken together
three times a day on the same gun deck on wooden trestles and with
square wooden plates—hence the expression "three square meals a day"),
and a more attentive support staff, including the ship's surgeon and chaplain. Many ships even had a schoolmaster who taught the illiterates on
board and the dozens of ship's boys, some as young as eight or ten, who
were part of life on every navy ship.

They also benefitted from a reform which was just coming in as Cook
was volunteering, the new system of divisions. Pioneered by Vice Admiral
Thomas Smith in 1755, it gave each ship's lieutenant personal charge of a
division of the ship's company, with midshipmen in charge of each subdi-
vision. They became directly responsible for the discipline and health of
the men under them. They had to make sure every sailor had proper
clothes and a change of linen at least twice a week, that his hammock was
washed and stowed, and that he knew his duties and was not drunk or
disorderly. The divisional system dramatically improved life on Royal
Navy ships. It forced officers to get to know their men as individuals; it
taught the midshipmen to handle their future crewmen with humanity
and understanding, as well as firmness and discipline. It taught every navy
officer what conscientious officers like Captain Hugh Palliser of the *Eagle*
already knew, "that [the] confidence and affection of the people I have
under my command" was an essential part of captaining a ship at sea.

Palliser recognized James Cook's abilities at once and gave him lessons
not only in navigation but trigonometry and mathematics. He promoted
him to master's mate and then to master, putting Cook fully in charge of
sailing and navigating the ship. As war approached that next spring, Cook
learned the tedious routine of a Royal Navy ship on Channel blockade

---

*The exception were the so-called dog watches of two hours each between four and
eight in the evening, which created an odd number of watch shifts and kept men from
having to do the same tasks at the same time every day.

duty. Weeks at sea watching for strange sails in all weather and sharing patrols with frigates like the *Falkland* and *Swan*; weeks in Plymouth replenishing stores and cleaning ship's hulls, and replacing damaged masts and rigging; then back to sea for another spell of boredom and isolation (it was only from a Spanish snow* out of Bristol that the *Eagle's* crew learned that war had been declared against France). Then the excitement of chasing and catching a 50-gun French fourth-rate, the *Duc d'Acquitaine,* in a violent gun duel at point-blank range for forty-five minutes until the *Acquitaine* struck, followed by a jubilant return to Plymouth and a first taste of prize money.

On October 18, 1757, Cook turned twenty-nine. On the same day he received his new warrant as ship's master for the 60-gun *Pembroke,* part of the expedition "Old Dreadnought" Boscawen was mounting for the capture of Louisbourg in Canada. It was on that expedition that Cook first learned from a British army officer how to make maps. They would become Cook's fascination, as he mastered the technique of translating the three dimensions of landmarks, shores, rocks, and shoals precisely and exactly onto two dimensional charts. After Louisbourg, his meticulous correction of existing charts of the St. Lawrence River, and creation of new ones where none existed, saved Saunders and Wolfe's expedition to Quebec, and won him the reputation as one of the navy's finest navigators. No surprise, then, that with the coming of peace, the Admiralty put him in charge of charting the coastline of Britain's new Canadian possessions. Or that in November 1767 his name should come up when the Royal Society announced it wanted a navy ship for an expedition into the Pacific Ocean.

It is easy to see why the Royal Society wanted a navy ship. The navy was after all on the cutting edge of nautical technology and navigation: if anyone could get them there safely and back, it was a Royal Navy vessel. But there were reasons why the Admiralty was interested in the Royal Society's proposal, as well. A voyage to do a parallax measurement of the transit of Venus from a point in the Pacific Ocean was more than just a crucial step for measuring the size of the solar system. It was also a crucial step in opening up the last unknown ocean.

Except for the narrow track across the Equator crossed each year by the Manila galleons and occasional foreign interlopers like Drake and Anson,

---

*A large two-masted and square-rigged sailing vessel.

the Pacific was still for Europeans an unexplored void. On maps it was sprinkled with vaguely identified islands and continents, some very real, such as New Holland and New Zealand, which Dutchman Abel Tasman had explored in the 1640s, and others wholly theoretical and imaginary. As in Grenville and Drake's day, many still believed there was a vast populous continent to the south, Terra Australis Incognita, just waiting to be discovered. Scientific societies clashed over where to find the great Northwest Passage, repeating the same arguments that engaged Humphrey Gilbert and John Dee two centuries earlier. For understanding the Pacific as part of the globe, there were still more theories than facts, and more hopes and ambitions than means to carry them out.

So the British Admiralty, spurred on by the government, decided to dispel the mystery—and also lay claim to any Great Southern Continent before a European rival did. In 1764 it sent one of Anson's former officers, John Byron, on one expedition; in 1766 it sent Samuel Wallis on another. Wallis found no Great Southern Continent, but he did discover Tahiti; his second-in-command, Philip Carteret in the sloop *Swallow*, found Pitcairn Island and passed through the Solomons and the Admiralty Islands north of New Guinea. By the time he returned the Admiralty knew they were also facing French competition in the race for the Pacific, under Louis Antoine de Bougainville.

Bougainville was not the first European to reach Tahiti—Samuel Wallis had that honor—but his descriptions of the island and its people would make it a permanent part of the Western imagination. A soldier, not a sailor (he had been aide-de-camp to General Montcalm at the battle of Quebec, which might have allowed him to meet Cook, although he never did), Bougainville had to teach himself navigation and raise the money for his first voyage from wealthy relatives. He himself had been inspired by Anson's voyage around the world: like Anson, he had a strategic vision of using the Falkland Islands as the stepping-stone to the Pacific. His first voyage was an attempt to colonize the Falklands, unaware that Captain Wallis was doing the same thing. The result was a three-way international tiff, with France, Britain, and Spain each pressing their respective claims—not the last time Britain would fight to hold on those bleak, forlorn islands.

It was Bougainville's second voyage that made him internationally famous. Equipped this time with a 26-gun frigate and with two distinguished scientists on board, Bougainville reached Tahiti on April 2, 1768. Wallis's visit had been prosaic, even violent; he had fired on Tahitian canoes that seemed to threaten his cutter. But Bougainville found in Tahiti a tropical paradise, with an idyllic landscape, gentle generous people, and willing native girls as amorous as Venus with "the goddess's celestial form." A modern myth was born, that of the "noble savage," who is "born essentially good, free of every prejudice, and who follows . . . the gentle impulses of instinct not yet corrupted by reason." Bougainville's voyage would spread this sentimental view of non-Western cultures across Enlightenment Europe. It would set the stage for the revolutionary Romanticism of the coming century. But it also raised the stakes in the race to see who would open up the Pacific first.

Even as Bougainville was arriving in Tahiti, the Royal Society was arguing that their project for tracking the transit of Venus would be a vital contribution to the science of navigation as well as astronomy. It wanted Alexander Dalrymple to lead the expedition, a Scot who had sailed for the East India Company and who was an enthusiastic believer in the Great Southern Continent. But the First Lord of the Admiralty, who was none other than Sir Edward Hawke, balked. He declared "he would rather cut off his right hand than permit anyone but a King's Officer to command one of the ships of His Majesty's Navy." So when Admiralty secretary Stephens, who knew all about Cook's brilliant work in Canada, mentioned his name, Hawke agreed. There was only problem. Cook was still just a ship's master, a warrant not a commissioned officer. So Hawke generously raised his rank—to first lieutenant. And so James Cook became "First Lieutenant Cook of His Majesty's Bark *Endeavour*," which was now being outfitted at Deptford for its foray into the unknown.

With his command of astronomy (he had even published a paper on solar eclipses) and his navigational expertise, Cook was the perfect man for the job, just as the *Endeavour* was the perfect vessel. Like Cook himself, she came from the Whitby coal trade, a converted cat 106 feet long and 29 feet across the beam—just the kind of sturdy broad-bottomed ship (it drew only fourteen feet of water when fully loaded) Cook would need to explore unknown inlets and coastlines. Cook packed her with everything he required for a long-distance voyage with a crew of eighty-four (including the inevitable number of pressed men). Eight tons of ballast went into the hold, along with twenty tons of ship's biscuits and flour, 1,500 pounds of sugar, oatmeal, raisins, vinegar, oil, and malt; 1,200 gallons of beer, 1,600 gallons of brandy and rum, 4,000 pieces of salt beef and 6,000 of salt pork; along with spare timber and planking, sailcloth, barrels of tar, and powder and shot for the *Endeavour*'s ten carriage guns and twelve swivel guns mounted fore and aft.

In addition, Cook brought on board almost four tons of a high-smelling pickled cabbage that the Germans called sauerkraut. Cook was determined to avoid any outbreak of scurvy—he had seen twenty-two men die of it during the *Eagle*'s blockading patrols, and twenty-nine on the *Pembroke*—and believed the sauerkraut could serve in the place of fresh vegetables. His sailors hated the stuff, although they were allotted 80 pounds each for the duration of the trip. Cook had to flog some of them into eating it.

He also brought along the latest instruments of navigational science. The kind of haphazard dead reckoning voyage Francis Drake had made, or even George Anson, had become a thing of the past. Cook had an improved azimuth compass, developed by Goodwin Knight in 1751, which lessened distortions of the magnetic field for a more accurate directional reading. One was mounted in his cabin directly over his head, and another installed in the ship's binnacle, the enclosed and illuminated box on the quarterdeck that allowed those at the ship's wheel, with its new helm indicator,* to check their direction in all weather and at night. Latitude could now be measured down to a minute of a degree thanks to Hadley's sextant, which used movable mirrors to fix the angle of celestial bodies against the horizon more accurately than ever before.

For measuring longitude, Cook could turn to the Royal Society's lunar tables. Their complicated calculations posed no problems for a mathematically inclined navigator like Cook. Barometers, now standard issue on all navy ships, would allow him to anticipate drastic changes in the weather; an achromatic lens telescope, developed by Peter Dollond of London, gave him a long-distance view of the world free from color distortion. The one navigational aid he lacked were adequate charts. But then Cook was completely equipped to create his own—charts so accurate and meticulous that to this day modern hydrographers have found little room for improvement.

At Plymouth on August 26 Cook picked up one last unexpected piece of cargo: naturalist Sir Joseph Banks and his baggage of eight servants, two dogs, and a heap of trunks and scientific equipment. Banks had con-

---

*Developed in the 1750s from the one on the French 74 *Invincible,* captured in the first battle of Finnisterre—yet another of Anson's contributions to the welfare of the Royal Navy.

vinced his friend First Lord of the Admiralty Lord Sandwich to let him and his entourage* join the Royal Society's astronomer as the *Endeavour's* scientific team. The one problem was where to put them. The ship was already to full that Cook had ordered his men to leave their sea chests behind and take their belongings in large canvas bags (the ancestor of the sailor's duffel still in use today). Cook's own so-called great cabin at the stern was only 14 by 18 feet, and had to serve as office and public dining room as well as sleeping quarters. In the end, Cook moved six of his officers out of their tiny aft cabins into even smaller ones on the below deck to make room. Banks, who was almost half the age of his captain, was largely unconcerned about the trouble he had caused. Wealthy and arrogant, he was the spoiled child of privilege. After they returned to England, he would even grab the lion's share of credit for the voyage.

But Joseph Banks was also a brilliant and tireless naturalist, and skillful organizer of the zoological, botanical, and even anthropological data that poured in daily from every side. His presence on the *Endeavour* marked a turning point in the history of Western exploration: a shift from forays of conquest, plunder, and profit to a genuine effort at expanding the boundaries of human knowledge. He is the direct forerunner of Charles Darwin on the HMS *Beagle*. The friendship he and Cook struck up on the voyage would forge a permanent link between the Royal Navy and modern science.

Banks himself was deeply impressed by Cook's conscientious and precise approach to his job. "He was never afraid of approaching an unknown coast," Banks would remember, "and would for weeks and months together persevere to sail amongst sands and shoals, the very appearance of which would have been thought by most seamen a sufficient reason for leaving them." Cook came off the Cape Horn into the Pacific in a direct northwestern course, allowing him to prove that there was no Great Southern Continent anywhere west of the island of Juan Fernandez or the coast of Chile. He and the *Endeavour's* crew were to spend three months in Tahiti building the Royal Society's observatory, more than enough time to dispel any notion that his was a tropical utopia of "noble savages." The weather was warm and clear, but the flies flew so thick that Banks's naturalist painter Sidney Parkinson found they would literally eat the paint off the paper. Although the Tahitians were cheerful

---

*They included the botanist Daniel Solander, a student of the great Linneas himself, two "natural history painters," and Banks's secretary.

and easygoing and free with sexual favors—one chieftainness tried to have sex with Banks in her boat as he was being rowed to shore—they seemed to be also shameless thieves, stealing everything that was not guarded or tied down. Their behavior could swing without warning from touchingly open to aggressively hostile. They largely saw Cook, with his muskets and cannon, as a potential ally in their own interminable and bloody intertribal wars.

The Admiralty had told Cook to handle any indigenous peoples with "every kind of Civility and Regard"; Cook told his men to treat the Tahitians "with all imaginable humanity." But the wanton thievery broke Cook's patience, to the point that he ordered some of the offenders flogged, as if they had been navy seamen. There was even gunfire and death. Parkinson bitterly exclaimed, "What a pity that such brutality should be exercised by civilised people upon unarmed ignorant Indians!" The *Endeavour*'s sailors had fewer compunctions. When they discovered Tahitian maidens were willing to exchange sex for ship's nails, one man broke into the ship's stores and stole 120 pounds of them.*

As for Cook, he had no illusions about what the future held for the Tahitians, "the most obliging and benevolent people I ever met with," and their fragile culture. "We introduce among them wants and perhaps diseases which they never before knew," he wrote sadly, "and which serve only to disturb that happy tranquility they and their forefathers enjoyed." Better, he decided, that Europeans had never appeared at all.

When they finally left Tahiti on July 13, Banks brought along a native youngster to act as the *Endeavour*'s interpreter in their next round of stops. Some islands were overtly friendly (such as Bora Bora), others violently hostile (Rurutu); some were both (Raiatai). But the most important part of the voyage was still ahead: Cook was under secret orders to sail south to 40 degrees latitude to find the great continental peaks Wallis had spotted south of Tahiti. What the Admiralty and many of his officers hoped Cook would find was the leading edge of the Great Southern Continent; what he found instead was the eastern coast of New Zealand. He began at once a detailed coastal survey, covering more than two thousand miles of coastline, which proved once and for all that New Zealand was really two separate islands, and not a peninsula attached to some larger continent.

From there Cook headed west and found the northern tip of Van

---

*Cook gave the enterprising thief two-dozen lashes, the worst punishment during the whole voyage.

Diemen's Land* and then swung north to the southeastern coast of New
Holland. Seventy years earlier, William Dampier had charted the west
coast for the navy, and found nothing but mountains and desert. But no
European had ever seen the eastern side until on April 19, 1770, the
Endeavour reached the southeastern tip of what Cook would dub New
South Wales. He proceeded with the same meticulous surveying and
charting, after reaching a bay large enough to let him anchor and reprovi-
sion. The *Endeavour* stayed for nine days. Banks was so delighted with the
new botanical specimens he found that Cook named the anchorage
Botanist Harbor, which he later changed to Botany Bay—ground zero for
Britain's new empire in the Pacific.

The *Endeavour* continued up the Australian coast and then through
the Great Barrier Reef (which twice nearly doomed the ship) and the
Torres Strait separating New Holland and New Guinea. Through it all
the *Endeavour* remained scurvy-free thanks, at least in part, to the sauerkraut: only four cases in two years at sea, an unheard-of record. It was
only when they reached Batavia, the first outpost of European civilization
and capital of the Dutch East Indies, that disease struck the ship in the
form of malaria and dysentery. Cook himself fell ill. But when he finally
arrived home in June 1771 his voyage had completely changed the known
geography of the Pacific. He had been gone for nearly three years, yet the
Admiralty was anxious to send him off again.

Cook's second voyage is famous not so much for the purpose of the
trip—looking for the ever-elusive Great Southern Continent by going
east not west, passing the higher latitudes of the South Atlantic and the
Cape of Good Hope into the Indian Ocean and Pacific—as for the means
he used to do it. Cook had on board his new ship, the *Resolution,* an exact
model of John Harrison's chronometer for calculating longitude, the
H-4. The H-4 had actually failed its ten-month trial at the Royal
Observatory between May 1766 and March 1767. Cook was severely
doubtful about the utility of Larkum Kendall's copy, K-1, compared to
lunar tables. But in the end K-1's success in keeping an exact Greenwich
time with which to do celestial observations won Cook over. He called it
"our trusty friend the Watch" which "exceeded the expectations of its
most zealous advocate." The longitude problem had been solved for good.
The great distances that had cut Europeans off from remote parts of the

---

*Later renamed Tasmania after its original Dutch discoverer.

globe no longer looked so forbidding—the first tentative steps toward envisioning the global village. The chronometer became only the latest tool in securing the British navy's dominion over the waves.

But the voyage of 1772–75 was also full of important discoveries, or at least confirmation of previous European finds. Cook passed through Polynesia into Melanesia; he fixed the location of Tonga and Easter Island, and found a chain of southern Pacific islands he dubbed the New Hebrides. Above all, he established there was no Great Southern Continent. There was only Antarctica, presenting the outer rim of its vast ice sheets to the *Resolution* at 71 degrees south latitude, the highest latitude any mariner would reach for another half century.

His third voyage in 1776 would bring him north, to solve the last remaining geographic mystery, the existence of the northwest passage. By then his work had won him international fame. Although the Royal Navy was now at war with the Americans, and soon would be with the French, both countries told their navies that Cook and the *Resolution* were to pass unmolested. He journeyed up the North American coast to 70 degrees north, finding no possible passage from Pacific to the Atlantic that was not blocked by miles of ice. He returned to reprovision in Hawaii, the last major archipelago he discovered, naming them after the First Lord of the Admiralty as the Sandwich Islands. Here was another idyllic paradise inhabited by a people as open and friendly, but as culturally unpredictable, as the Tahitians. Cook became embroiled in an argument over a stolen boat, and was killed.

"Thus fell our great and excellent Commander!" wrote his first lieutenant James King, who had been with him on the second and third voyages. "How sincerely his loss was lamented, by those who had so long found their general security in his skill and conduct." Joseph Banks wrote, "His paternal courage was undaunted. His patience and perseverance not be fatigued. . . . His diligence and application were beyond example." The Royal Society struck a commemorative medal in his honor. Cook was a new kind of naval hero, one who earned public acclaim not in battle but in research and exploration. His former officers George Vancouver and William Bligh would extend that tradition: Bligh in the South Pacific, Vancouver in the north by surveying the Pacific coast above California, including Puget Sound (named after one of his lieutenants), and by making the Sandwich Islands a formal part of the British Empire.

Then, nine years after Cook's death, the first ships of transported criminals would arrive from England at Botany Bay. His voyages had laid the foundation for a new British Empire in the Pacific even as the old Atlantic one was, thanks to the Royal Navy, falling apart.

* * *

It was the navy's own strength that was the source of the problem. The coming of peace in 1763 had left the British government with a massive debt of over 140 million pounds. Pitt had borrowed heavily to build an empire; now the new prime minister, Pitt's brother-in-law, George Grenville, wanted the empire to pay the bill. Above all, he wanted the colonies in North America, which had benefitted so much from the war, to pay some share of the cost of the navy and army that protected them. Direct taxation was not possible; no colonial legislature would stand for it. But Grenville was determined to have them pay the customs duties imposed by those mainstays of British overseas trade, the Navigation Acts, which colonial merchants had ignored or flouted for far too long. And Grenville saw the means to do it: by using the Royal Navy to crack down on the smuggling industry in North America.

By 1763 the New England founded by the twin legacies of West Country entrepreneurship and the Protestantism of John Foxe, was probably the wealthiest per capita society in the world. Part of the reason was their trade in contraband. Every year merchants set out from Boston and Newport and New York for the West Indies with shiploads of lumber or dried codfish, which they exchanged for hogsheads of sugar, rum, and molasses. The richest part of their West Indies trade was with the French islands like Guadeloupe and Martinique, in blatant defiance of British law, but the economy of New England came to depend on it.

Virtually every wealthy American merchant involved in the rum trade, the wine trade, or even tea trade, was to one degree or another a smuggler. For decades, fast-running New England schooners, sleek two-masted fishing boats with fore-and-aft sails for quick handling, allowed the lawless Americans to thumb their noses at an overextended Customs Service. Even in the midst of the war with France, they kept up a brisk trade with the enemy, buying illegal French trading licenses for two hundred dollars. In 1760 William Carlisle, master of the *Dove,* sailed out of New York City with one sewn into his breeches. Once at sea, Carlisle flew either a French or British flag whenever it suited, and when he reached Martinique, French merchants there greeted him as an old friend as he moved freely from island to island. All of this was according to the

Dove's first mate, who quickly turned king's evidence when Carlisle was finally caught.

The Royal Navy had cracked down hard on the illegal trafficking as part of its war on French trade—cracked down so successfully, in fact, that Grenville decided to keep up the vigilance after the war. In 1764, the Royal Navy became in effect the largest law enforcement agency in the world, with more than forty warships mobilized to enforce Parliament's new Sugar Act. The Sugar Act actually cut the import duty on foreign molasses, to encourage Americans to do their business under the law; but it also brought elaborate new regulations and warrants for determining what a ship was carrying and at what port she previously called. Even a ship of less than 50 tons caught loitering two leagues from the coast without a regular port destination could be seized on suspicion of smuggling.

The man in charge of the North American squadron at Halifax was Alexander Colville, Rear Admiral of the White. A crusty and cantankerous Scot, Colville had done two previous tours of duty in America. He was convinced all American merchants were smugglers at heart if not in fact, and that the "well-known mobbish Disposition of the Inhabitants" of cities like Boston and New York meant that any smugglers his men caught would be set free from the courts there unless he could try them directly in Halifax. He had many of his captains and lieutenants actually sworn in as customs officers; and to encourage them in their work, ships' officers and men were to collect half the value of the captured vessel and contraband cargo as prize money, just as in wartime. Enforcing the Sugar Act was to be a self-evidently lucrative proposition: Colville made no secret of his hopes of building a comfortable retirement from the seizures.

As navy frigates and sloops swept down on American trading vessels from every side, the colonists seethed with rage. Most accepted the principle of the Crown regulating colonial trade; they just assumed the regulations did not apply to them. The new rigid enforcement "has caused a greater alarm in this country" than the French advance into the Hudson River Valley during the Seven Years' War, the governor of Massachusetts reported. "The Merchants say, There is an end of the trade in this Province." Feeling against the Royal Navy ran high. Instead of being the colonies' protectors, it was becoming their persecutors. Philadelphia merchant Benjamin Franklin explained the general outrage:

> By posting Frigates all along the coast, with armed tenders and cutters to run into every river and creek, the officers of which were all vested with

Custom-House powers, and who, especially in the lower Rank, executed their Commissions with great Rudeness and Insolence, all Trade and Commerce, even the most legal, between Colony and Colony, was harassed, vexed, Interrupted.

When the navy schooner *St. John* cruised Narragansett Bay looking for contraband molasses, the citizens of Newport, Rhode Island, took matters into their own hands. The *St. John* had already made them testy by impressing sailors from local vessels; they had responded by bombarding British sailors with bricks and stones. Then, when the *St. John's* captain refused to let the sheriff arrest three of his men accused of theft, gunners at the fort overlooking Newport harbor were told not to let the sloop get away. As the *St. John* stood out to sea in the late afternoon, the fort hailed her and then opened fire. Eight cannonballs dropped fore and aft of the hapless *St. John* as she fled for the shelter of the man-of-war *Squirrel* waiting at the edge of the harbor. Eventually tempers cooled and the three men were put in the sheriff's custody, but the relations between colonists and the Royal Navy were now on the knife edge in every port on the eastern seaboard.

The whole experience, according to Massachusetts assemblyman James Otis, "set people a thinking, in six months, more than they had done in their whole lives before." What they were thinking was that this new Sugar Act and its enforcement were frontal assaults on their rights as Englishmen. They violated the principle for which the English civil war had been fought, which was enshrined in the Revolution of 1688, and which Otis summed up in a single phrase: No taxation without representation. Yet here was Parliament using its power over the purse, and its navy, to tyrannize Englishmen living on the other side of the Atlantic.

Then came the next stage of Grenville's revenue-raising program, the Stamp Act. Grenville may have imposed this new tax on paper products and official documents, including college diplomas, as a way to force the thirteen colonies to come up with a plan for taxing themselves instead. If so, it failed disastrously. Instead, the resentment and suspicion growing in the colonies, exploded into a firestorm.

Nine of the thirteen colonies, including Massachusetts and Virginia, banded together in a Stamp Act Congress to protest the new measure—a harbinger of colonial congresses to come. "Taxation without representation is tyranny" became the rallying cry for groups of well-to-do American merchants calling themselves the Sons of Liberty. Many, like Sam Adams and John Hancock of Boston, had grievances against British customs officials already; in fact, in cities like Boston the Sons of Liberty became in effect a smugglers' lobby. Their agitation spilled out into the streets. The objects of their wrath were customs officials and navy vessels, in that order. In Boston a mob sacked and burned the home of royal governor Thomas Hutchinson. In others cities, customs officials fled for their lives to the safety of Royal Navy ships.

Navy officers were puzzled and dismayed. Like the Tahitians, the Americans seemed to obey no rules they could identify. Yet these Stamp Act riots were merely reflections of the same mobile British maritime culture, the same aggressive self-assured individualism of Hawkins and Drake. An Englishman's "inherent rights and liberties" were supposed to include carrying his property where he pleased and charging the price he wanted. The Royal Navy's job was to protect his seagoing trade, not harass it. In fact, most naval officers hated playing customs inspector. The riches they had been promised for catching smugglers never materialized; morale in the North American squadron was sinking fast. So Halifax greeted with relief the news that a new government in London had repealed the Stamp Act and that the crisis was finally over.

But it was not. The new chancellor of the exchequer Charles Townshend was about to unleash a fresh wave of import duties. He intended to show once and for all that Parliament would regulate trade as it, not the colonists, saw fit. Meanwhile, customs officials in Boston aimed to get their revenge by targeting one of the leading Sons of Liberty, merchant John Hancock.

At twenty-seven, Hancock was perhaps the wealthiest man in America. He had inherited a business from his uncle built on sweetheart government contracts, and was heavily involved in the whale oil business, the tea and Madeira wine trade—and like his late uncle, in illegal smuggling. In April 1768 customs agents boarded and searched his brig *Lydia*. Then on May 9 they seized another of his ships, the *Liberty*, in from Portugal with a cargo of Madeira they claimed was contraband. As the warship *Romney* appeared in Boston harbor to tow her away, a mob swarmed onto Hancock Wharf and attacked the *Romney*'s jolly boat and its crew. Then they turned on harbor official Benjamin Hallowell and customs agent Joseph Harrison, who fled for their lives. Within hours Boston's streets were under mob rule. Hallowell and Harrison escaped to the *Romney*, as the governor pleaded with London for help.

It arrived on October 1. It was two British regiments of foot, with

two Irish regiments on the way. The sight of red-coated soldiers marching up King Street with fixed bayonets and navy warships lining the harbor with their gun ports open, provoked cold silent rage and defiance.
Silversmith and Son of Liberty Paul Revere depicted the scene in an
engraving that vividly spread the message to the other colonies: armed
tyranny had come to Boston.

"There seems to be a direct and formal design on foot to enslave all
America," Hancock's friend John Adams wrote in the Boston Gazette. To
make his point, he added: "Have we not been treated, formerly, with abominable insolence, by officers of the navy?" Protests against the Townshend
Acts, dubbed the Intolerable Acts, broke out across the colonies. When
British soldiers actually fired on rioters the next year in the so-called Boston
massacre, killing five and wounding a half dozen more, Adams's baleful
warning seemed confirmed.

In fact, the government in London was desperate to find a way out of
the crisis. It repealed the Townshend Acts; it slashed the import duties on
tea, again hoping this would encourage Americans to trade within the
law. But it was too late. In 1772 the navy sloop Gaspée was chasing a merchantman near Providence, Rhode Island, when it ran aground. Citizens
of Providence, led by merchant John Brown,* stormed aboard, screaming:
"God damn your blood, we have you now!" They shot her lieutenant,
routed her crew, and then set the Gaspée ablaze.

The next year came the most notorious of all acts of American uncivil
disobedience. A gang of rowdies dressed as native Indians stormed the
ships of the East India Company in Boston harbor and heaved its chests of
tea overboard. The Boston Tea Party had been organized by Hancock and
Samuel Adams: they and their smuggler friends were fearful that the new
lower duties on tea would cut into their own illegal traffic. In response, the
authorities closed the port of Boston and appointed General Thomas
Gage as emergency governor. Although neither side knew it yet, the war
for American independence had begun.

In 1775 Britain confronted a situation no nation had ever faced
before: a major land war against a transoceanic enemy, who could and did
deny the British army any secure base for support or supplies. The result
was a logistical nightmare. Every bit of powder, shot, and equipment for
the 50,000-man army had to be brought in by sea at a distance of more

---

*A prosperous Providence merchant and active slave trader. Brown's descendants
would be the founders of Brown University.

than three thousand miles. Every year each British regular or Hessian mercenary on the ground consumed one-third of a ton of food, which also had to be shipped in. Besides the enormous cost—more than 12 million pounds a year or 12.5 percent of national income by 1780—the nature of the American war stretched the Royal Navy's resources to the breaking point. Nor did it have the ships to blockade the two thousand miles of American coastline. Instead, the Admiralty's Lord Sandwich insisted in keeping the bulk of the fleet at home to face what he saw as the real threat: France and Spain allying with America to attack the rest of the British Empire.

The Americans did what they could to exacerbate the situation. Their fledgling Continental Navy waged its own *guerre de course* against British shipping. They had proved to be daring and resourceful privateers during the last two wars; now their frigates and sloops turned that daring against Britain itself. In 1777 alone they captured more than 300 merchantmen, while the Royal Navy only managed to catch fifteen of the American raiders. The most famous of all, John Paul Jones, was a sea-hardened, emotionally volatile, English-hating Scot. The cruises of John Paul (the Jones was a pseudonym) in the brig *Ranger* and then in the French-built *Bonhomme Richard* never affected the course of the war in any strategic sense. But they were an acute embarrassment to the British navy, especially when he outfought the 44-gun frigate *Serapis* in a bloody gun duel off Flamborough Head.

That was how Captain Jones wanted it. He never forgave the British navy for refusing him a midshipman's berth as a young man. Instead, he nursed his grievance until it turned into an obsession: he pursued the enemy with a hatred bordering on self-destruction. Taking on the heavier-gunned *Serapis* cost him his own ship and half his crew; in fact, he never fought the British navy again. But his long-term vision for the future United States Navy, which the American Congress turned down, arose from the same love-hate obsession. Even the uniform he first chose to wear in battle was not his country's own, but his personal take—dark blue with buff waistcoat and facings—on that of a Royal Navy captain.

Jones and fellow American privateers used French ports as safe havens for their forays. They and their patron, ambassador Benjamin Franklin, hoped to provoke the British into inciting a war with France. The French, it must be said, were ready to rise to the bait. After the humiliating Treaty of Paris in 1763, a thirst for revenge swept through corridors of Versailles and the Ministry of Marine. Minister Choiseul brought this revanchist zeal to rebuilding the French fleet. By 1770 Choiseul had regrown the French navy to 35 frigates and 65 ships of the line, including the 110-gun *Ville de Paris,* which outclassed the biggest British first-rates by more than a thousand tons. He pressed his Spanish counterparts to do the same: the result was a revived Spanish navy with 55 modern battleships. For the first time, and at huge expense, a combined French-Spanish fleet outweighed the British in total tonnage, if not in actual number of ships.

The French then took another page out of the British book in rethinking their global strategy. The British are "a restless and greedy nation," foreign minister Vergennes pointed out, "powerfully armed and ready to strike at the moment [they] shall find it expedient." By bogging them down in a land war in North America, the French could keep them weak on the Continent and in the West Indies. An independent America would cripple Britain's colonial trade and secure American markets for the French. And if the French could convince their Spanish Bourbon cousins to join them, and avoided any conflict with potential British allies in Europe, they would have Great Britain isolated and divided. Divide and conquer had worked for Pitt; now it could work for France.

In February 1778, Louis XVI put his seal to the alliance with the Americans. Fourteen months later, Spain joined in. No one in London was too surprised. Since 1763 every British government had assumed that its navy might have to fight a joint French-Spanish fleet. It was just that no one had envisaged fighting a protracted land war on the other side of the Atlantic at the same time. Suddenly and ironically, Britain found itself in the same position France had been in during the last war: pinned down by a war on land, while an enemy's naval strength cut its colonial links by sea. Lord North's leadership had been indecisive at best; now he became almost paralyzed as his government's North American strategy unraveled and bad news began to arrive by every dispatch packet.

In 1777 General Burgoyne, marching south from Canada, was trapped at Saratoga and forced to surrender. In 1778 the French Toulon squadron broke out to cruise the American coast, compelling the British to abandon Philadelphia; when it returned the next year, they gave up Newport. As a French army landed in America, the Dutch Republic declared a policy of armed neutrality, meaning it would fire on any British warship trying to seize its cargoes bound for France or America. Within a year the Dutch were also at war with Britain, potentially adding another thirty-one ships of the line to the French-Spanish total.

By the end of 1780 the British were facing not just the loss of their American colonies but Gibraltar (under siege by the Spanish), Minorca (the same), and the West Indies. The Admiralty's Lord Sandwich told his colleagues that when he thought of the fate of Jamaica, he spoke "with trembling. . . . Indeed, I am in constant apprehension of hearing that the blow is already struck." The French and Spanish even felt strong enough to launch a combined fleet to occupy the Isle of Wight and besiege Portsmouth. At the end of July 1779 it left Brest for the Western Approaches, a latter-day armada with 63 ships of the line and admirals in epauletted uniforms and periwigs instead of doublets and morion helmets. Bad weather and disease doomed the enterprise; but a French contingent did get close enough to Plymouth to force a closing of the harbor and set off a panic until the French withdrew.

The episode proved that Britain had lost control of the seas, and with it the power to control events. Lord Sandwich admitted as much in September, when he told the Cabinet, "It will be asked why, when we have as great if not a greater force than ever we had, the enemy are superior to us." The answer was, he said, "England until this time was never engaged in a sea war with the House of Bourbon thoroughly united . . . and having no other war or object to draw off their attention." But England was now stuck with such a war, in America, "which essentially drains our finances and employs a very considerable part of our Army and Navy." The war against George Washington and the Continental Army had become the least of it. Unless the Royal Navy could reassert its dominance, Britain's own future looked bleak.

In the end, it was Sandwich who turned the situation around, and saved the British Empire. He did not save it by some brilliant military master stroke. Like Lord North's other ministers, he remained trapped by an unworkable strategy. He did it by keeping his mind on what was really at stake, and by turning the navy from a transatlantic shuttle service for the British army into once again an instrument for decisive victory.

The position of First Lord of the Admiralty was now, thanks to George Anson, one of awesome power and responsibility. The First Lord sat in the cabinet; one could say it was the most important cabinet post of all, since it demanded so much skill and expertise. "Capacity is so little necessary for most employments," Henry Fox once said, talking about ministerial posts, "that you seem to forget that there is one where it is absolutely so—viz. the Admiralty." John Montagu, Fourth Earl of Sandwich, had sat on the Admiralty Board since his mid-twenties; he had learned the business of managing the largest industrial enterprise in the world, with its fleets, dockyards, bases, recalcitrant admirals, and importunate Navy Board officials, from the great Anson himself. He was also Cook's great patron, and recognized the lasting value of his achievements when the rest of British society was lionizing Sir Joseph Banks.

Sandwich was a linguist and art connoisseur, a pillar of high society, and the leading cricketeer of his day. But when it came to his beloved navy, he committed himself with a seriousness of purpose that impressed everyone who met him.* At fifty-four, Sandwich was at the height of his powers. "A tall stout man," as Fanny Burney described him, "and looks as furrowed and weather-proof as any sailor in the Navy; and like most of the old set of that brave tribe, he has good nature and joviality marked in every feature."

These were certainly years to try anyone's good nature. Despite the setbacks in the privateering war and clamor for warships for America, Sandwich had fought hard to keep the fleet from being dispersed on urgent but trivial missions and to keep it concentrated against any French or Spanish attack. He also took two major steps that had long-lasting consequences for the future of the British fleet. The first was adopting a new cannon being forged by the Carron Iron Works in Scotland, a squat, stout but powerful gun, light enough to be mounted on the upper deck or forecastle but with a devastating 32-pound punch. In a yardarm to yardarm fight, the carronade could turn the tide of combat. Yet the second step was even more important: Sandwich's decision to copper the fleet.

The hulls of wooden sailing ships had always been their Achilles' heel. The constant soaking of seawater left them caked with barnacles, seaweed, and, in the tropics, vulnerable to the *teredos* shipworm. Since Odysseus' time, the only remedy was constant careening and cleaning—a time-consuming and hazardous operation, especially for large ships since their weight put a strain on the outer hull and bulwarks. Even so, even the best-built wooden vessel rarely lasted fourteen years; in the tropics, even less.

Mariners did what they could to slow the decay. They tried coating their ships' bottoms with "white stuff," a mixture of whale or seal oil, rosin, and sulfur, to retard the weeds, and tallowing—but these washed

---

*He even invented the meal that is named after him, a piece of salt beef wedged between two pieces of bread, not in order to stay at the gambling table through dinner, as legend suggests, but to sustain himself during his long hours at his desk at Admiralty House.

away. John Hawkins was the first to try sheathing his ships with fir plank-ing, but that too eventually had to be replaced. Attempts at lead sheathing set off an electrolytic reaction with the ship's iron fittings, which pulled the planks and rudder apart. It was not until 1762 that a method was found to bolt sheets of copper to the hull, which not only protected it from weed and shipworm, but gave it a durable smooth surface.

In 1775 the sloop *Hawke,* fitted with copper plates attached by lead-capped iron bolts, returned after five years in the West Indies. Dockworkers were astonished to find it needed no cleaning and was ready to go to sea again. Sandwich was impressed, and although the copper was expensive (1,500 pounds sterling for a 74-gun third-rate) and the process demanded extensive time in dry dock, he ordered the coppering of the entire navy. In 1779 the first ships of the line, *Invincible* and *Russell,* got their copper bottoms. By 1781 Sandwich had coppered 82 battleships and 115 frigates—more than half the fleet.

The result was a seagoing revolution. No longer did warships have to interrupt naval operations for cleaning. Coppered ships spent a third less time in the dockyards than other ships did. The slick copper bottom also gave square-rigged vessels a new burst of speed and lightness of han-dling—so light that some captains had trouble keeping their ships in the standard line of battle. A British squadron of older ships could now out-race and outchase a new French or Spanish squadron, bring its guns (including the new devastating carronades) to bear faster and leave the scene quicker. The superiority the Bourbon fleets had enjoyed in weight and ship design vanished in a blaze of copper.

This new sheathing was particularly crucial because the pivot point of the war had shifted to warmer climes. A British army under General Cornwallis had been driven back across Virginia to Yorktown at the mouth of the James River. A French squadron of twenty-six ships of the line under Admiral de Grasse had cut off Cornwallis. The North American squadron under its new commander Thomas Graves had come down into the Chesapeake Bay to drive de Grasse away; at Virginia's Cape Henry the fleets joined battle on September 5, 1781.

It was a fight the British should have won. Grave's subordinate, Samuel Hood, wrote to Sandwich, "Yesterday the British fleet had a rich and most delightful harvest of glory presented to it, but omitted to gather it." Instead, a confusion of signals (Graves had run up the signal for close action at the same time as the flag for keeping line of battle), and de Grasse's skill in avoiding a more decisive engagement cost Graves the battle and sent him back to New York. By the time he returned, Cornwallis had surrendered. The American War of Independence had been won and lost. Now it was a question of whether de Grasse and the French would make it a clean sweep, by taking the British West Indies. Only one man now had the brilliance, nerve, and, thanks to the carronade and the coppered fleet, the fighting tools to save the day: George Rodney, commander in chief of the Leeward squadron and Rear Admiral of the Blue.

Of all the unlikely British naval heroes, from Francis Drake to Horatio Nelson and Jack Fisher, Rodney remains the most morally ambiguous. He was a dazzling sea officer, with an incisive grasp of the tactical situation and strategic moment. His skills made him post captain at age twenty-three and rear admiral at forty-one. But Rodney also had an unquenchable greed for money that corrupted everything he touched. He stole from captured prizes (which was illegal and especially shameful for a flag officer) and cheated other officers out of prize money. He treated everyone with a high-handed arrogance, alternating angry outbursts with wheedling self-pity. He was also a degenerate gambler, and the outbreak of war found him in France, hiding from debtors' prison.

Yet Sandwich had the insight to bring Rodney back to England to take over the Leeward Islands station—even though it had been seventeen years since Rodney had officered a ship in wartime, and he had never commanded a fleet in action. Sandwich and Comptroller of the Navy Charles Middleton knew the risk they were taking. They assigned Rodney a reliable flag captain to keep an eye on him, and a special commissioner to keep his books. Sandwich even specifically warned him not to interfere with other admirals' commands or officers—a request Rodney would blithely ignore.

But in the crucial matter, their trust in him was well placed. In late December 1779, Rodney set sail with twenty-two ships of the line, his first duty being to reinforce the besieged Gibraltar garrison. Late on January 16 he surprised a Spanish blockading squadron on the other side of Cape St. Vincent. The Spanish admiral lay to Rodney's windward side, and the treacherous cape to his lee. However, Rodney had prepared for this with a brand-new battle signal for his captains: engage the enemy from the lee side.

It caught the Spanish completely off guard. In the fast-growing winter darkness Rodney's copper-bottomed fleet beat swiftly to windward while the Spanish line collapsed. Rodney captured six out of eleven ships of the line, including the Spaniards' flagship. He had scored Britain's first clear victory of the war. The "Moonlight Battle" relieved the siege of

Gibraltar, made Rodney a national hero, and established the attack from leeward as a viable tactical principle. Since the sixteenth century every battle fleet had twisted and turned, sometimes for hours, to gain the weather gauge. But Rodney had seen smaller French forces use their position downwind to turn away from certain defeat. Pressing an inferior foe from the leeward side left him nowhere to run. Perhaps slowly but always inevitably, he would come under Rodney's guns. As he put it to Sandwich, "When the British fleet take the lee gauge, the enemy cannot escape."

Rodney would use the same tactics when he reached the West Indies, to prevent the French from taking Barbados and checkmate their fleet in the waters around Martinique. He could not prevent Grave's defeat in the Chesapeake the next year; but when de Grasse established himself with thirty-six ships of the line at Martinique's Fort Royal in February 1782, Rodney was at Barbados with thirty-seven. De Grasse was under orders to sail for Santo Domingo to rendezvous with the Spanish fleet for the attack on Jamaica. As his ships set sail on the night of April 6, they were spotted by the frigate *Endymion,* which rushed back to alert Rodney. Five days later, on Friday April 12, the British under Rodney and Admirals Samuel Hood and Samuel Drake, caught up with them.

De Grasse drew up his line in the waters between the northern end of Dominica and a group of small islands called *Îles des Saintes* or the Saintes, and steered south to engage Rodney—keeping, as always, safely to the windward side. But his plans were disrupted as Rodney pressed him hard from the lee position as the two fleets passed in opposite directions. The carronades, and a new flintlock firing system for the main guns, gave the British an almost two-to-one advantage in broadside firepower: the French took a terrible pounding. When de Grasse tried to escape by signaling his fleet to "wear"—to bring their sterns through the wind in order to reverse direction—the English ships were too close to allow the French captains to maneuver and had to ignore his order.

Then came a sudden subtle wind shift, from southeast-south to southeast, which threw the French line into confusion as Rodney pressed closer still. Through the clouds of gunsmoke his flag captain Sir Charles Douglas saw what was happening and rushed up to Rodney: "Break the line, Sir George, and the day is your own."

Rodney angrily replied, "No I will not break my line," thinking Douglas meant the British line of battle. But Douglas meant the *French* line, which was now drifting apart, leaving ships vulnerable to double-team attacks from every side. After a sharp argument, Rodney realized what he meant, and said, "Very well, Sir Charles, you may do as you please," as their 90-gun flagship *Formidable* led the way through de Grasse's line.

The *Formidable* gave two broadsides to the French 74 *Glorieux,* leaving her masts and sails in a helpless tangle; salvos from the next British ships moving through the gap dismasted her completely. One by one the French ships were raked from head to stern, as the British poured out simultaneous broadsides from port and starboard, "one peal of thunder and blaze of fire from one end of the line to the other." The last French ship to strike colors was de Grasse's flagship, the mighty *Ville de Paris:* only three men were still left on the upper deck when the ship surrendered. Four other ships were shattered hulks, including the *Glorieux;* total French casualties came to more than three thousand. British losses were less than a third of that. The *Marlborough,* which had led the British line and engaged twenty-two enemy ships in succession, suffered only three men killed and sixteen wounded. Rodney's success was a tribute to the superiority of British gunnery and to the new strategy for victory in a line ahead battle: break the enemy's line before he breaks yours.

The battle of the Saintes expunged Graves's defeat the year before and restored Britain's naval supremacy. It came too late to prevent American independence, or to save Sandwich's tenure at the Admiralty: he had resigned with the rest of North's ministry in March. But it did limit the terms the French and Spanish could dictate in the final peace treaty signed in 1783. Britain kept Gibraltar and all its West Indies possessions except Tobago and relinquished Florida and Minorca to Spain, and Ceylon and the Dutch Antilles to Holland. But otherwise the British Empire remained intact, especially in Canada and India, where the French had to accept permanent British control.

The biggest loss, of course, was the thirteen American colonies, but even here the battle of the Saintes guaranteed that while Britain had lost the war, she had won the future. France's confidence in its navy quickly collapsed; it seemed pointless to continue the struggle against Britain's maritime hegemony. "That nation," Vergennes wrote gloomily, "has in its constitution and the establishments which it has permitted her to form, resources which are lacking to us." It was a telling admission: the war effort had saddled the French Crown with an insurmountable debt. Less than six years after France's "victory" in the American Revolution the country was on the brink of bankruptcy. Louis XVI would be forced to a drastic measure, the summoning of an Estates General, which would lead to his overthrow and the French Revolution.

So France never benefitted economically from its support for America, as it had planned—quite the opposite. Economically speaking, the real winner was, ironically enough, Great Britain. The victory at the Saintes secured its maritime power and command over the Atlantic: the United States would become as dependent on their trade with Great Britain as they had been before independence. America became a crucial market for the new manufactured goods produced in Britain's growing Industrial Revolution: by 1789, the value of British exports to the former colonies already exceeded prewar levels. Before his death, William Pitt had warned that if America won its independence, he would advise every gentleman in England to sell his lands and move there: the greater partner, he said, must ever control the lesser. The Saintes had prevented that from happening. The navy had ensured that it was America that was in Britain's economic back pocket, not the other way around—at least for the foreseeable future.

* * *

The experience of the American war had enabled some young naval officers to shine. Twenty-year-old Horatio Nelson rose from lieutenant to post captain in less than a year, although he joined his frigate to Samuel Hood's squadron too late in take part in the Saintes victory. Lieutenant William Bligh, on the other hand, found only frustration and disappointment. He did get combat experience and even command of his own ship, the captured French frigate *Belle Poule*. But for an accomplished seaman who had been James Cook's navigator on his last voyage, being put on the beach and on half-pay with the coming of peace was discouraging. He took up merchant sailing to make ends meet and would have to wait four years until he had another navy command, the HMS *Bounty*—the one that would make him the most notorious naval officer in history, fiction, and film, and besmirch the Royal Navy's reputation for two hundred years. Yet the true story of the mutiny on the *Bounty* reveals more about the strengths and virtues of the British navy than its abuses—as well as the virtues of Bligh himself.

Compared to the myth, the facts are quite plain. Unlike Cook and unlike John Paul Jones, the gardener's son from Kirkcudbright, the sea was in Bligh's blood. He was descended from an old Cornish family and baptized in Plymouth. His father was a customs officer and knew many navy officers. They got his son William a berth as a captain's servant at age seven on HMS *Monmouth,* where his half brother was a surgeon. The boy probably never went to sea: putting one's infant relatives on the muster roll in order to collect their pay was a typical navy fiddle. Even James Cook did it with his two sons on the *Endeavour*.

William Bligh definitely did go to sea in 1770 on the *Hunter*, a 10-gun navy sloop. Six months later, he became a midshipman and transferred to the frigate *Crescent*, where he learned his basic sea trade. Like his hero Cook, he became a skilled navigator and displayed a rare gift for mathematics. So much so that just six years later, Cook chose the twenty-one-year-old Bligh to be master of the *Resolution* for his third and last voyage.

Bligh did many of the voyage's charts and most of the navigating. He watched grief-stricken as Cook was cut down and murdered by the Hawaiians, and as the *Resolution*'s crew went on a vengeful rampage, killing natives and burning their village. Bligh did nothing to stop them—in fact, it may have been Bligh's decision to open fire on a native canoe that incited the crowd around Cook to attack and kill him. Certainly it was an early example of the rash impetuous Bligh of legend: second-in-command Lieutenant King even said the shooting gave "a fatal turn to the affair." Bligh and King quarreled the entire way home and when promotions were handed out in 1780, Bligh was passed over. Not for the first time, his temper and rude tongue made others forget that he was a dutiful and often considerate officer and a brilliant seaman.

One who did remember, however, was Duncan Campbell, who ran a small merchant fleet from the Isle of Man. After the peace in 1783, when Bligh was on half-pay and had no prospects for post or promotion, Campbell (who had learned about Bligh from his friend Joseph Banks) gave him a job. Bligh did this for four years, making several trips across the Atlantic and marrying Campbell's niece. Campbell's help did not stop there. He knew Banks and the government were organizing a new expedition into the Pacific to transplant breadfruit trees in the West Indies, as a source of cheap food now that the Americans had severed the supply of dried codfish from New England. He knew Banks needed a navy captain who had navigated the central Pacific—there were not many at this date. Campbell suggested Bligh. Banks, of course, knew Bligh's reputation; he made the offer and in the first week of August 1787 Bligh enthusiastically accepted. "I can only assure you," he wrote to Banks, "I shall endeavour, and I hope succeed, in deserving such a trust."

The *Bounty* myth-makers often present the breadfruit voyage as a harebrained scheme. In fact, it was a conscientious effort to find not just a cheaper food staple for the slaves in the West Indies but a more nutritious one, and one that would grow all year-round. It was an early example of how the British navy's closing of transoceanic distances made it possible to move natural species from one part of the globe to another: in effect, globalizing the plant kingdom. The *Bounty* mutiny cut the project short, but Bligh would complete the transplantation on a second trip ten years later—only to discover that the slaves hated the taste of breadfruit and refused to eat it.

Certainly Bligh was jubilant with the voyage's prospects—that is, until he saw his ship. The *Bounty* (originally the *Bethia*) was a small ship, even smaller than the *Endeavour,* and only twenty-four feet ten inches across the beam. Almost the entire lower deck between the main and mizzenmasts and the stern—the deck where all Bligh's officers usually had their separate cabins—would be taken over to provide a greenhouse for the transplanted breadfruits and workspace for the *Bounty*'s botanist David Nelson. This meant very cramped quarters even for a crew of only forty-six. Although he was able to handpick his crew himself and exclude any inexperienced or unwilling pressed men, Bligh saw the problems at once. Besides the overcrowding, he would also be the only commissioned officer on board; all the rest, almost half the complement, were warrant officers and midshipmen. Since there was no room for a complement of Royal Marines to help maintain order, the only way Bligh could enforce any discipline would be by flogging—and midshipmen could not be flogged.

This again flies in the face of the myths about the *Bounty,* which reinforce Winston Churchill's misleading remark about "rum, sodomy, and the lash." The truth was the rum ration was never seen as a way to quell resentment against intolerable conditions or inedible food. Food on navy ships was remarkably good by the standards of the day, and certainly plentiful, even on the *Bounty.* A seaman could count on three hot meals a day, with salt beef or pork, beer (in the tropics, brandy or grog), biscuit or baked bread, cheese, and usually some fruit or vegetables—and in the *Bounty*'s case, plenty of Cook's standby anti-scorbutic, sauerkraut. It was only on very long voyages without landfall for gathering fresh food or in unpredictable disasters at sea that men were thrown back on decaying rotting provisions, or even no provisions at all—and those on a merchant ship were usually in worse shape than those on a well-stocked navy one.*

As for "sodomy," the careful research of N. A. M. Rodger and other

*Since Bligh was his own purser, he was able to make sure that his men got the best available food in large quantities and protect against shipboard theft.

scholars indicates that homosexuality was no more prevalent in the navy than anywhere else in British society, and probably a good deal less.* "A ship at sea was about the most difficult possible place to commit sodomy," writes Rodger, "and moreover it was almost the only crime in the Navy for which the death penalty was often awarded." The reason for the severity was not far to seek: few things could undermine the solidarity of a ship's company faster than suspicion of a "bugger" on board, especially with teenagers and even preteens a regular part of the crew.

In fact, it was the relative youth of a ship's crew that made "the lash" so necessary. Since the Elizabethans, seafaring had been a young man's profession: in 1780 probably 80 percent of the navy's sailors were twenty-five years old or younger. Many, but not most, were functionally illiterate; at least some had been pressed and were not happy about being there (although none, of course, on the *Bounty*). Every workingman had grown up in a society in which physical violence was an accepted part of life, and beatings, kicks, and blows a common way to punish even minor transgressions. So a bosun's mate using a rope's end to "start" a slow-moving sailor might come as an unpleasant humiliation, but hardly an outrage. By and large, crews supported flogging as the best way to punish the wrongdoers among them. When the sailors on strike at Spithead in 1797 presented their list of grievances against the navy, flogging was not among them.

Books and movies have made the ritual all too familiar. All hands summoned aft to "witness punishment," the miscreant stripped to the waist and tied to the rigging or a grating propped against the ship's gunwale; the captain reading the pertinent passage from the Articles of War and ordering a dozen lashes; the bosun taking the cat-o'-nine-tails out of its red baize bag (hence the expression "letting the cat out of the bag") and laying it on with a will; then the unfortunate taken below to have salt rubbed into his wounds (actually in order to prevent infection) while the captain tells the lieutenant, "Dismiss all hands."

What is missing from the Hollywood version is the crucial fact that a dozen lashes was all a Royal Navy captain could order on his own authority for any single offense. Any punishment more severe required a formal court-martial, a cumbersome and time-consuming affair, not to say unpredictable: his fellow sea captains might dismiss even serious charges,

*During the Seven Years' War, authorities prosecuted exactly eleven cases of sodomy of a total naval population of seventy thousand men—and four of these ended in acquittals.

including striking an officer, to avoid imposing the mandatory death penalty.

The truth was that a captain's authority was far less godlike than the hair-raising formulas of the Articles of War implied, and that of his officers even less. The articles did not even extend to offenses committed on shore until 1749: even then, any officer who trifled with his men would find them ready to settle scores when they reached harbor. In 1762 Lieutenant Ralph Dundas of the *Coventry* was severely beaten by a gang of resentful sailors led by his own gunner's mate. In another case, an unpopular lieutenant from the *Maidstone* was knifed outside Sheerness yard. That did lead to a court-martial, but the only one of its kind for an offshore assault. In general, as far as the Admiralty was concerned, a captain or officer away from his ship was on his own

Even on shipboard, a captain was in a difficult position. There was no navy legal code, no shore patrol or police, and no navy judicial system. Apart from the offenses bringing a mandatory death sentence (in 1787 there were eight, compared with more than two hundred capital offenses in the British civil code), the only authorized tool he had for punishing crime was the dozen lashes—or whatever else he might think up *and* what the rest of the ship's company would accept as fair and just. That even included punishing "mutiny," which technically meant refusing to obey an officer's orders, something which on a ship full of hyperactive, physically aggressive, and sometimes drunken young men, happened all too often.

For at the end of the day, the captain's authority rested on the consent of his crew. That was usually forthcoming, even if he was not a "gentleman," since sailors understood that for the safety of the ship someone had to have final say, and that he should expect swift obedience for the same reason. But a captain who overstepped those accepted bounds, or lost the trust of his men, would soon find himself alone and "naked unto his enemies."

Bligh understood this. This was why he desperately wanted to have his authority strengthened by being made a real post captain, not just master and commander. The Admiralty refused—just as they had refused to promote James Cook. So the infamous Captain Bligh was not a captain at all when the *Bounty* set sail on December 23, 1787, but still merely a lieutenant. And although Bligh liked his new crew, finding them "all in good order" as they made their way for Tenerife, there was only one person on board he knew he could completely trust. That was the man who had served him as midshipman on one of his merchant ships, and who had been with him twice in the West Indies. Indeed, they were such close friends Bligh had made him master's mate. His name was Fletcher Christian.

Although Christian would be at the center of the drama about to unfold, in the end we do not know much about him. The closest thing to a personal account comes from his brother, long after the mutiny. But everything suggests he was an obliging, intelligent sailor but essentially a man out of his element. He came from a family from Cumberland who were well-to-do—rare for a rating turned warrant officer. Two of his brothers even went to Cambridge. Fletcher Christian was supposed to do the same, but then the family went bankrupt and ended up on the Isle of Man to live with relatives. So instead of being launched for a career in the law or at the university, eighteen year-old Fletcher found himself a Royal Navy midshipman, then ended up with Bligh—besides George Courtenay, commander of HMS *Eurydice,* the only captain he ever served.

We can never know what resentment may have lingered over having to serve as master's mate for a man who was a friend and mentor but, in the final analysis, below Christian's social class. He may have had his doubts even after Bligh promoted him to first lieutenant over the head of ship's master John Fryer. Fryer was a hard taskmaster, far harder than Bligh: the one sentence for flogging on the entire trip out was at Fryer's instigation, not Bligh's. Bligh took good care of his men. He divided the crew into three watches instead of two, just as Cook had done, in order to give his men eight hours' rest between four-hour bouts aloft and on deck: "It adds much to their content and cheerfulness," he wrote in his journal.

He organized dancing every evening on deck, complete with a fiddler. When the *Bounty* hit bad weather off Cape Horn and fought the southerly gales for a month, Bligh opened up the great cabin for his men to sleep at night; he ordered rations of straight grog to warm them as the yards and sails became caked with ice. When he finally gave up and told his crew they were sailing eastward for the cape of southern Africa, he thanked them all for their courage and endurance. The Bounties cheered loudly, Fletcher Christian included: they had survived the ordeal without losing a single man, spar, or sail. Proof indeed that their captain was an extraordinary officer and the *Bounty* a lucky ship.

The trouble began when they finally reached Tahiti on October 26, 1788. Their assignment of gathering breadfruit kept them there for nearly six months: as always, it was when a ship was in port, not at sea, that regular discipline suffered—especially with the idyllic temptations of an island that had beguiled the crews of Cook's *Endeavour* and Bougainville's *Boudeuse.* Bligh admired the Tahitians, despite their open sexual practices (including publicly deflowering virgins as young as seven years old), but resented the steady rise of venereal disease among his crew and growing laxness among officers who were supposed to keep order. He lashed out at them all—"Such neglectful and worthless petty officers I believe never were in a ship as are in this"—but especially at Fletcher Christian. It was becoming apparent his first lieutenant barely knew his business, and when three men deserted in early January, Bligh blamed Christian as much as he blamed the men. Hayward, the midshipman in charge of the watch, was thrown in irons, and Bligh made it clear to Christian he was no longer second-in-command.

Day after day, Bligh was seething and made the mistake of letting everyone know it. "I am having great difficulty carrying out my duties, sir," complained Christian. Bligh struck back: "You damned cowardly rascal! Are you afraid of a set of natives while you have arms to defend yourselves?" Bligh went out on the quarterdeck: "You are all a parcel of lubbery rascals," he bawled out at all and sundry. "With four more men, and all of us armed with broomsticks, I could disarm the lot of you."

Fletcher Christian confided to the ship's carpenter, "Flesh and blood cannot bear this treatment any longer." In fact, it was the inconsistency between Bligh's harsh language and his relatively lax maintenance of order—two of the three deserters received forty-eight lashes (or twelve each for four offenses), when another captain would certainly have hanged them—that disconcerted and bewildered his crew.

By the time they left Tahiti on April 6, 1789, the Bounty was an emotional powder keg ready to blow. The detonation came over the issue of stolen coconuts. Bligh found that the fresh supply they had taken from the island had unaccountably dwindled, and he turned on his first officer, Fletcher Christian, while the rest of the Bounties listened aghast.

"Damn your blood," he boiled, "you have stolen my coconuts!"

Christian confessed to taking one but denied he had helped himself to more.

"You lie, you scoundrel," Bligh went on in a blind rage, "you have stolen one-half!"

"Why do you treat me thus, Captain Bligh?" Christian exclaimed, almost in tears. "I hope you do not think me so mean as to be guilty of stealing half your coconuts."

"Yes, you damned hound, I do." Then he turned around and accused the rest of the Bounties of the same thing: "There never was such a set of damned thieving rascals under any man's command before. God damn you, you scoundrels, you are all thieves alike and combine with the men to rob me!" Bligh ordered the men's grog stopped, and stormed below.

For Christian, the incident was the last straw—especially when the captain's servant came to his berth that evening asking him to join Bligh for supper, as if nothing had happened. The captain's behavior no longer obeyed rhyme or reason and Christian knew what he had to do: he would desert the ship and make back for Tahiti or one of the other islands. He confided his plan to midshipman Edward Young, who pointed out the dangers of trying to leave the ship in uncertain and shark-infested waters. Young had a better idea: why not take over the *Bounty* himself? The men still trusted and admired Christian; he was after all a true gentleman as well as an officer. They would stand with him if he removed Bligh as captain.

This conversation, or something like it, turned Fletcher Christian from potential deserter to conspirator and mutineer. Mutiny, real mutiny with sailors overpowering their officers and seizing the ship, was almost unheard of in the Royal Navy—although not infrequent in the merchant service. The reason was simple: most navy officers worked to keep good relations with their ratings, often cultivating ties with the lower deck that lasted a lifetime. Anson and Hawke took a close personal interest in former crewmen even as they sat in the Admiralty; even crusty old Admiral Colvill made sure a sailor who had been with him almost twenty years got his promotion to bosun. Hugh Palliser had supported seaman James Cook in the same way, just as Cook supported William Bligh. Bligh neglected to follow the navy's own example. His words had alienated his crew, and his actions bewildered them. Now he was about to pay the price.

Just before dawn on April 28, Bligh was shaken out of his sleep and pulled from his bunk. In his tiny six- by seven-foot cabin loomed five armed men, including Fletcher Christian. "What is the meaning of this violence?" Bligh demanded. "Hold your tongue, sir," Christian curtly replied. By the time they brought him up on deck, other mutineers had taken Fryer and the other officers prisoner. With no marines to stop them, they had found it ridiculously easy to seize the ship. The realization that they had just made the mistake of their lives took somewhat longer.

As for Bligh, he was a different man. Instead of the snarling irrational tyrant, he remained calm and collected, even with his hands awkwardly tied behind his back (in tying the knot the sailor had inadvertently tied up his nightshirt, leaving his buttocks exposed) and with shouting men brandishing muskets and cutlasses all around him. He calmly reproached Christian for his treachery, and reminded him that Bligh's own infant daughter had once sat on Christian's knee. "Do you consider this treatment a proper return for all the friendship I have given you in the past?"

Now it was Christian's turn to explode. "That—Captain Bligh—that is the thing," he stuttered wildly over and over again. "I am in hell—I am in hell!"

The mutineers' plan was to put Bligh, his clerk, and two midshipmen, John Hallett and Thomas Hayward, in the longboat and set them adrift with five days' supplies. Instead, thirty men—more than two-thirds of the crew—volunteered to go with Bligh, even though he faced almost certain starvation and death. However, there was room for only eighteen: as they clambered aboard and the boat swung past the Bounty's stern, there were cries of "Don't forget I have had no hand in this!" and "I wish I could go with you to see my wife and family!" as well as "You'll never reach the shore!"

Paradoxically, the mutiny had put Bligh at the top of his form. "I felt an inward happiness which prevented any depression of my spirits," he wrote afterward. He took charge of dividing up the boat's meager supplies, and single-handedly navigated the 23-foot longboat almost four thousand miles, from the uncharted waters of the Coral Sea through the Great Barrier Reef and Torres Strait to the Dutch colony of Timor, where they made landfall after a harrowing forty-eight days. He had done it thanks to his sextant and his lunar tables, and without losing a single man*—and with a homemade Union Jack, sewn together from scraps of clothing and signal flags, hanging proudly from the boat's mizzen shroud. Bligh was weak and sick, sicker than he revealed in his first letter to his wife in two years ("What an emotion does my heart and soul feel that I have once more an opportunity of writing to you and my little angels"); but he was anxious to return to England, to set in motion the wheels of justice—and get his revenge on Fletcher Christian.

Christian himself would never be caught. He and the other twenty-four men on the Bounty, of whom only a dozen or so were genuine mutineers, sailed back to Tahiti. There several wanted to settle down and marry native women; Christian, however, knew that Tahiti was now a regular lay-by for the Royal Navy and feared lingering there for long. So he decided they would settle in the nearby island of Tubuai—thus setting up the very first English colony in the South Pacific. However, their dreams of paradise soon dissolved into a series of bloody shootouts with local natives: Christian agreed to return to Tahiti and let those who wished to

*Although two died shortly after they were safely on shore at Timor.

stay, stay. Sixteen did; the other nine, including three of the men who had joined him in Bligh's cabin the night of the mutiny—John Mills, Matthew Quintal, and John Adams—sailed away in the *Bounty*.*

The others soon wished they had sailed with them. On March 23, 1791, the HMS *Pandora* arrived at Tahiti looking for the renegade Bounties. Bligh's story had been a national sensation: he had been triumphantly acquitted in his court-martial (the Articles of War required every captain who lost his ship, for whatever reason, to face a court-martial) and the Admiralty dispatched Captain Edward Edwards to round up the mutineers for trial in England. By every account, Edwards was a stupid, brutal officer and an even worse sailor. He caught fourteen of the men he was after, including some, like Peter Heywood, who had resisted the mutiny, and imprisoned them in a closed iron cage on the *Pandora*'s deck—what became known inevitably as Pandora's Box. There they stayed in irons under oppressively brutal conditions until Edwards managed to run his ship onto the Great Barrier Reef. Four were still manacled inside when the *Pandora* broke up and died; the rest joined the shipwrecked crew on a tiny sandback Edwards named Wreck Island. They would set out in four homemade boats for Timor, a thousand miles away. For two of *Pandora*'s midshipmen, Thomas Hayward and John Hallett, it was a painful irony, since they had made almost the same voyage in Bligh's longboat as *Bounty* midshipmen just two years before.

In the end, the Admiralty was able to assemble ten men for trial in September 1792. By then, public opinion had swung against Bligh and toward the mutineers—much as it has ever since. Christian's lawyer brother had painstakingly put together the whole story of the *Bounty* voyage from testimony of the eyewitnesses and written an account placing the blame squarely on Bligh. However, the job of a navy court-martial was to punish mutiny, no matter how justified or provoked; and it found six men guilty, even though there were considerable doubts about the role of two of them, John Morrison and Peter Heywood, in the revolt itself. However, the court did recommend mercy and both would receive full pardons; the

---

*They would eventually reach Pitcairn Island, where Christian ordered the *Bounty* scuttled and burned and where the men made their permanent homes. The navy never found them until 1825, by which time the *Bounty* mutiny was more a matter of curiosity than judicial vengeance, and only one was still alive: John Adams. Adams himself died in 1829 at age sixty-five. Ironically, Fletcher Christian had survived only two years before the local natives of Pitcairn, whom he and his men had tried to enslave, rose up and killed him. Strange indeed that the man whose name was a byword for rebellion should die at the hands of his own slaves.

president of the court, Admiral Samuel Hood, even took Heywood on as a midshipman on his flagship HMS *Victory*. Only three men would ever hang for their role in the mutiny—proof not just of how slowly and inefficiently the wheels of navy justice turned but also that no one, except Bligh and perhaps Edwards, cared all that much about catching the criminals. Far from being terrified by the *Bounty* mutiny, the Admiralty had understood what an extraordinary event it really was.

Bligh's reputation would be tarnished forever, although the Royal Society recognized his achievements as a cartographer and navigator by presenting him with a gold medal, just as they had James Cook. He had more personal problems with officers on subsequent commands, leading to not one but two courts-martial: one against his ship's master on the *Director,* the other against his first lieutenant on the *Warrior,* in a case that eerily parallels his quarrel with Fletcher Christian. Then at the very end of his career, thanks again to Sir Joseph Banks, he became governor of the colony founded on the shore Cook had first discovered, on Botany Bay. There Bligh would face yet another uprising against his authority, this time by a cabal of local farmers and British army officers. As soldiers marched him off to jail past a jeering, cheering crowd and with his daughter Betty in tears, Bligh might well have reflected on the words of Fletcher Christian: "I am in hell."

That was in 1808. By then the world had changed irrevocably, and with it the British Navy. On July 14, 1789—exactly one month after Bligh had steered his battered boat into Timor harbor—events in Paris were propelling Europe into a conflagration without parallel in its history. The struggle for the soul of the global system had begun.

CHAPTER FOURTEEN

The Elephant and the Whale

"Well then," I exclaimed, "I will be a hero."
—HORATIO NELSON

ADMIRAL SIR SAMUEL HOOD, commander in chief of the Mediterranean squadron, paced the quarter deck of his flagship HMS *Victory* in disbelief. He had never heard of such a thing. Accept the surrender of an entire French fleet! Yet this is what its commander, Admiral Turgoff, and the citizens of Toulon wanted him to do. Two men had rowed out to where Hood was blockading the harbor entrance and offered to deliver him all twenty French battleships and frigates. All they wanted in exchange was British protection against their own government. It was September 1793. After a year of the new French Republic, the people of Toulon had had enough.

Just four years earlier, on July 14, 1789, crowds in Paris had stormed the royal fortress of the Bastille, setting in motion's the world's first democratic revolution. The pattern it set soon become all too familiar: a vast social upheaval launched in the name of liberty and "the rights of man," ending in dictatorship, terror, and a despotic police state. The original proponents planned for something very different. They had confronted a king and government at Versailles paralyzed by debts from the American war and from trying to build a navy to compete with Britain. The men of 1789, whom the people of Paris had attacked the Bastille to protect, intended a British-style revolution along the lines of 1776 or even 1688: a constitutional monarchy guaranteeing the liberty of individuals and rights of property under law, and answering to a representative but narrow franchise of property owners.

By the spring of 1792, however, their hopes and those of well-wishers, including many in Britain, had withered away. France had no politically active business class that could rally around these liberal changes: there was no French equivalent of the City of London or Board of Trade. Instead, power passed to radical lawyers and disgruntled intellectuals:

Robespierre, Marat, Danton, St. Just. They would ruthlessly sweep aside every institution of the old regime in France: monarchy, aristocracy, the Church, even the calendar and the seven-day week. In its place they set up a radical republic, based on abstract ideals of equality, justice, and the General Will. For the first time, terms like *comunisme, idéologie,* and *terreuriste* became part of the political vocabulary. And for those unwilling to submit to the Republic of Virtue, there was the guillotine.

Britain was slow to react to the changes taking place across the Channel. Prime Minister William Pitt, son of the Earl of Chatham, had hoped for trade links with the new French government. As late as February 1792, he was predicting Europe would enjoy peace for the next decade and a half. But then French radicals began preaching a "crusade of liberty" against their neighbors. Prussia declared war, as did Austria, while the French radicals formally abolished the monarchy in August. In September, thousands of political prisoners were massacred in Paris and French armies crossed the Rhine. Yet Britain refused to stir.

In January 1793, France's former king Louis XVI went to the guillotine. Pitt condemned it in Parliament as a "dreadful outrage." Yet it was only after French revolutionary troops pushed into the Austrian Netherlands and broke the long-standing treaty with Britain closing the Scheldt estuary to maritime traffic, that Pitt was finally moved to say that "France has trampled under foot every law, human and divine" and that England must prepare for war. The revolution had its eye on Britain, however, and declared war on February 1, promising that angry mobs would topple the Tower of London just as they had the Bastille. Fortunately, Pitt and the nation were ready, as was the Royal Navy.

History is made by those daring enough to respond to the challenges circumstance sets before them. Five times Britain's navy had fought France in the last century—from 1689 to 1697, 1701 to 1713, 1744 to 1748, 1756 to 1763, and 1778 to 1783—and five times it had ultimately won. Each time it had faced unprecedented obstacles, and each time it found the strategy and the men to overcome them—Russell at La Hougue, Rooke at Gibraltar and Malaga, Anson at Finisterre, Hawke at Quiberon Bay, Rodney at the Saintes. Each time, victory had had enormous consequences for Britain and the world. The wars against Louis XIV had created the modern British state and its parliamentary politics; the wars against Louis XV had created the British Empire and made it the major player in the new global system. In the last round, Britain had lost a portion of that empire, but also secured its grip on the world's economic future.

Dealing with the old French challenge had consumed Britain's geopolitical attention for more than a century. Pitt himself was born while his father was grappling with it. But this was a different kind of enemy. This was a revolutionary dictatorship, prepared to bring terror against its own people and total war against the rest of Europe. Indeed, fighting this spirit of radical revolution, "that ungovernable, that intolerable and destroying spirit," as Pitt called it, which "threatened to overwhelm all civilized society," and "carries ruin and desolation wherever it goes," would give Britons a new self-awareness. They would realize that this time their navy was defending more than just imperial possessions or lucrative trade routes. Something much deeper was at stake.

On February 1, the day war was declared, Pitt told Parliament this new war was "not a contest for acquisition of territory. It is a contest for the security, tranquility, and the very existence of Great Britain, connected with every established government, and every country in Europe." Britain now stood for a way of life in sharp contrast to the totalitarian values arising out of revolutionary France. "The equity of our laws . . . and the freedom of our political system," Pitt said, "have been the envy of every surrounding nation." Yet this was precisely why Robespierre and his radical allies hated Britain so much and were determined to destroy her. They saw this war as a struggle for the future, not just of Europe but the world. It was time Britons did, too.

For the first time in their history, Englishmen were coming to see their nation, "our laws, our liberty, and our religion," as Pitt put it, as representing a powerful moral force in European civilization. Defending that civilization had become an imperative that even transcended national interest. Since John Foxe and Francis Drake, the English had enjoyed a sense of *superiority* to other European nations, especially Catholic ones. Now they recognized their *solidarity* with them, the existence of shared values and institutions—and a shared danger. It would make Britain the only country to remain continuously at war with France right down to the fall of Napoleon, even when peace might have preserved its security and its empire. It would be why Horatio Nelson would say, "Although we might one day hope to be at peace with France, we must ever be at war with French principles"—meaning the principles of violence and terror, the abolition of individual liberty and the extinction of spiritual man.

Great Britain as a moral force—given the way it had acquired its empire, and was still working to exploit and maintain it, this may seem hypocritical, even ludicrous. It did to many at the time.* But it is not coincidence that in five years Pitt would bring forward a bill banning the slave trade and take the first tentative steps toward Catholic emancipation. The winds of change that brought radical revolution to France would bring liberal reform to Britain—and within four years, even to the Royal Navy.

The navy, as always, was considered the first line of defense in any conflict with France, and the strategy in 1793 was no different. Hood and the other admirals had put to sea to impose the usual blockade on French ports and naval bases, and to prevent any union of the various French fleets. But now the Union Jack, flying on frigates at the edge of Toulon or Brest harbor or on ships at sea, represented something else to millions of unhappy Frenchmen: a sane alternative to revolutionary upheaval and terror. By that summer, many, indeed the majority, had turned their backs against the government in Paris. Spontaneous uprisings spread across the country. One seized control of Marseilles, France's principal southern port, and another Toulon, the home of the French navy's Mediterranean fleet. Toulon, with its sweeping harbor framed by an amphitheater of mountains and bluffs, would now be the stage for the first confrontation between the forces of French revolution and British sea power, and launch the careers of the three men who came to personify them.

The revolution had shattered the old French navy. The majority of sea officers, the aristocrats of the old *Grand Corps,* had quit or fled France. A century-old tradition of naval skill and excellence vanished. Ideological correctness took its place. The revolution abolished the "undemocratic" rank of master gunner—fatally weakening the French navy's firepower right down to Trafalgar—and offered captaincies to anyone who had been a captain in the merchant marine or even a ship's master. The old officers who stayed were always suspect: Trogoff de Kerlessy, commander of the Toulon fleet, had to watch his subordinates go constantly in and out of arrest for their supposed royalist sympathies. Not surprisingly, discipline collapsed on French ships and insubordination became common. When one admiral ordered his ship to engage Hood's squadron as they first came into the Bay of Biscay, his crew simply shot him and returned to port.

---

*This would include Tom Paine; William Godwin and his wife, Mary Wollstonecraft; William Wordsworth, who went to France and had a French wife; and other radical thinkers of the day. Many were hounded under the Sedition Acts, others under the Combination Act. Interestingly, Wordsworth, Coleridge, and others found refuge in the West Country, in Holford in Dorcetshire, where they launched the Romantic movement in poetry.

So when the anti-revolutionaries took control of Toulon and invited
Hood in, the disgusted and frustrated Trogoff decided to offer up the
fleet to his British counterpart. The news stunned and paralyzed the
French government. When rumors of the surrender reached Brest, sailors
there mutinied as well.

Pitt and the British government were jubilant. Wrote Lord Grenville,
"I am much mistaken if the business at Toulon is not decisive of the war."
Hood, however, knew his situation was untenable without more support.
Robespierre and his Committee of Public Safety were using the devastating events in Toulon to consolidate their power in Paris and formally
declare a Reign of Terror. An army had been dispatched to crush the
rebellion in the south. Hood knew that if French troops captured the
heights ringing the city, they could sweep the entire harbor with cannon.
A Spanish squadron with troop transports had arrived, ostensibly to help,
but its commander refused to recognize the British navy's authority.* So
Hood decided to send someone off to Naples to rouse the king there to
send some troops. He chose the eager young commander of the 64-gun
Agamemnon, Captain Horatio Nelson.

Nelson's promise at that time sprang as much from his background
as his personal qualities. He was from Norfolk on England's east coast,
which since the Restoration had been producing some of the navy's
outstanding officers: Christopher Myngs, Sir John Narborough, and
Cloudsley Shovell (although Hood himself came from the navy's oldest
home, the West Country and Dorset). Horatio Nelson grew up in sight
and sound of the sea. He had an uncle who was a Royal Navy captain and
a cousin on the Navy Board; he was twelve when he first went to sea on
his uncle's ship the *Raisonnable*. Although he performed well during the
American war, his family connections and influence gave him a quicker
start than most officers of his generation could hope for: lieutenant at
eighteen, first lieutenant at nineteen, post captain at twenty-one.

His precocious success fed Nelson's two least appealing characteris-
tics: his ambition and his arrogance. When he joined the Leeward
squadron in Antigua at the ripe age of twenty-five in 1784, he pronounced the admiral and senior officers there all "ninnies" (he excepted

_____

*At one point Hood had to send one of his lieutenants over with a stopwatch, to say
that unless the Spanish commander responded to Hood's orders within fifteen minutes, the British would open fire on the Spaniard's flagship—not an incident to inspire
trust on either side.

Captain Cuthbert Collingwood, who would become his closest friend and the first of Nelson's "band of brothers"). Although Nelson admired Hood—he told his brother he thought him the best sea officer in the service—the Naples assignment was a disappointment. He had wanted one of the plum combat assignments being handed out to his seniors for fortifying Toulon.

However, when he reached Naples on September 10, he changed his mind. He found the British ambassador there, Sir William Hamilton, a pleasure to work with and in no time they met with King Ferdinand and arranged for the dispatch of 4,000 Neapolitan soldiers. He also met Hamilton's wife, Emma, a captivating former artist's model who was almost forty years the ambassador's junior. "She is a young woman of amiable manners," Nelson wrote to his wife, Fanny, "who does honour to the station to which she is raised"—little realizing that one day she would drive him from his wife forever, and become a millstone that would weigh down his career and reputation.

Returning to Toulon, Nelson found British and Spanish troops dug in with the help of the local militia and the Paris government's army already at the gates of the city (Trogoff's fleet, sharply divided on the surrender, had to be disarmed and remained aloof). Hood dispatched Nelson on a raid on the French island of Corsica, for possible use as a base if Toulon fell. It was Nelson's first experience of combat, which he found he loved, and his first of independent command, as Hood sent his young subordinate off with a squadron of frigates to reinforce the blockade of Genoa.

In Toulon itself, the situation was deteriorating fast. "Shot and shell are very plentiful all over the harbor," Nelson wrote to his mentor, Captain Richard Locker, noting the uncannily accurate French artillery fire from the heights above the city. The reason for that was its commander, a gaunt and intense former lieutenant in the Royal Army who was determined to drive the British fleet out of the harbor below: Napoleon Bonaparte.

He was a decade younger than Nelson. He hailed from Corsica, the same island Nelson had just visited. As a boy he had hoped to enter the French navy; family poverty had sent him, instead to the École Militaire in Paris.* Now an admirer of Robespierre and committed ter-

---

*Indeed, his desire for a naval career was so intense that he even considered trying to enter the British navy as a cadet at the school in Portsmouth. The "what-if" possibilities of that beggar imagination.

rorist, Bonaparte was, like Nelson, razor sharp and intensely ambitious. With ruthless skill, he had ousted his commanding officer and was now acting general, directing the bombardment of Hood's positions as the French infantry took redoubt after redoubt. By the tenth Hood decided he had no choice except to evacuate Toulon, and take as many French ships with him as possible.

The city, meanwhile, was in total chaos. Bonaparte's men were shooting and bayoneting civilians as they advanced, as thousands of people swarmed on the wharf begging to be taken aboard the British ships. Hood saved almost fifteen thousand that night, although another six thousand were left behind to die by revolutionary firing squad and the guillotine. Of the surrendered war ships, Hood got away with only three. The Spanish failed to tow away or destroy the ones in their possession (on orders, as it turned out: the Spanish admiral saw no reason to help his old enemy). Nine did go up in flames, however, thanks to Lieutenant Sidney Smith, the flamboyant and voluble young naval officer Hood put in charge of the operation at the last minute.

Smith—flamboyant, ambitious, charismatic—the parallels with Nelson, even Bonaparte, are striking (later, Smith and Nelson would come to loathe each other). He had just arrived, improbably enough, from Constantinople on board his own private felucca. With Hood's orders in hand, he set his Turkish crew to work in the dark torching every French warship they could board, along with the arsenal and naval stores. French troops blazed away at them as Smith and his men reboarded their ship and sped out of the harbor on the tide. As they set their lateen sails, a great explosion rocked the quay and lit up the night. On board the *Victory*, Hood could watch the flames and destruction reflected on the water. Eight French ships of the line survived the holocaust; but the French navy had suffered a devastating blow—had lost more ships that night, in fact, than in any naval battle in its history. Sidney Smith's incendiary operation, combined with the mutiny at Brest, effectively took the French navy out of the war for the next six months.

That left the army as the French Republic's only resource. As with the navy, its aristocratic officers had left long ago; but when the revolution passed command of the army to former NCOs and penniless lieutenants like Bonaparte, they were able to reshape it into a capable fighting force. Teaching ordinary men to become efficient sailors took years, as the French navy always learned to its chagrin. Teaching them to be obedient soldiers, however, was merely a matter of months, even weeks. In a short time Bonaparte and his fellow officers were able to take the tens of thousands of unwilling new draftees the revolution gave them and turn them into the world's first mass conscript army. They also carried out key reforms which had been discussed in the military schools and on the parade ground for years, such as the use of massed artillery, but which now transformed how war on land would be waged for the next century.

By the end of 1794 French army would swell to more than one million men; it would carve out new provinces for the French republic and entire kingdoms for Napoleon and his marshals. It would dominate the battlefield everywhere it went, from Haiti to Moscow, just as the British navy dominated every sea, from the Caribbean to the Pacific. The rise of the revolutionary army constituted a military revolution on land as important as the one the British navy had achieved at sea, and it rested on its own set of ideological principles.

They were summarized by Lazare Carnot of Robespierre's Committee of Public Safety: "No more maneuvers, no more military art, just fire, steel, and patriotism." All of French society would be committed to arming, equipping, feeding, and serving in this army: even women and children were supposed to help roll bandages and old men to give the soldiers patriotic speeches. Just as the idea of the revolution "consists in exterminating everything that opposes it," so this army embodied a new military idea, that of total war. "We must exterminate!," Carnot cried. "Exterminate to the bitter end!"

Confronted by this revolutionary reality, the British Admiralty could offer no new ideas. Its outlook belonged to an earlier, less fanatical age; its best commanders were now old men. Hood was seventy years old; his brother Admiral Lord Bridport was sixty-nine; Richard Howe, commander in chief of the Channel Fleet, was sixty-eight. When war broke out, the First Lord was Pitt's brother, "the laziest man ever to hold a British Cabinet office." He was replaced by Lord Spencer, who brought youth (he was just thirty-six) but also inexperience to the board. Disgruntled and discouraged, Sandwich's old collaborator Sir Charles Middleton resigned in November 1795. Britain's army still numbered less than 50,000 men, most of whom were dispersed on diversionary expeditions to capture French possessions in the West Indies—forgetting that any La Rochelle or Brest merchant who complained about losing his Atlantic trade would only get the guillotine.

The navy did impose its usual blockade of French ports, but not the kind of close blockade that might at this point have crippled the revolution. Admiral Hawke had described how to do it: "The sooner you get to my old station off Brest, the better it will be for my country. When you are there, watch those fellows as a cat watches a mouse, and if once you can have the good fortune to get up with them, *make much of them*—and don't part with them easily." Lord Howe, who now commanded the Channel Fleet and had once served with Hawke, preferred to stay at Spithead and send frigates out to cruise off the Brittany ports. But when it came to battle, he was as ready as Hawke ever was.

"Black Dick" to his officers and men, Richard Howe was the son of an Irish peer who had married George I's mistress. Howe had spent nearly sixty years at sea. He had served with all three of the navy's modern founders—Anson, Vernon, and Hawke—and had briefly been commander in chief of the navy during the American Revolution, while his brother William was commander in chief of the army. Richard Howe's dark hooded eyes revealed nothing of his inner thoughts or personality: Fanny Nelson called him "the most silent man I ever knew." A conscientious and wise tactician, it was only in battle that he seemed to come to life.

Now, at sixty-eight, he was back in command. On May 2, 1794, he stood out to sea on reports of a crucial French grain convoy leaving the Chesapeake Bay bound for Rochefort. The recently purged and reorganized French squadron in Brest was setting out to meet them. It was commanded by Admiral Villarets-Joyeuse, one of the few officers from the old navy willing to submit to the harsh new revolutionary order. The navy's commissioner from the Committee of Public Safety, LeBon de Saint André, had crushed the Brest mutiny with characteristic brutality. Saint André had installed special political commissars on every ship to make sure everyone obeyed the orders of the republic. He also issued orders that any captain who lost his ship, *for any reason,* would go to the guillotine.

Saint André would sail on Villaret's flagship, and he had made clear the choice the admiral faced: either the convoy would get through or Villaret was a dead man. Villaret was going to sea with unskilled and inexperienced men; some of his captains had trouble keeping station, let alone executing more complicated combat maneuvers. But even more than Howe, he was prepared for a fight to the finish.

The two fleets spotted each other on May 28 and for three days Howe gave chase. Howe himself was almost constantly on deck of his flagship *Queen Charlotte,* even snatching a meal from a tray while his men took their dinner below, as he watched Villaret struggle to keep his ships together and to windward. Once, on the twenty-ninth, he nearly had them. Attacking in line ahead from leeward, with the 77-gun *Caesar* in the lead, he tried to break Villaret's line. But *Caesar*'s captain refused to make the critical turn; he sailed on past the French, with the rest of the van following as the Articles of War dictated, while officers on the *Queen Charlotte* raged and fumed.

"I desire you to hold your tongues, sirs," Howe warned them, then added, "Not to close your eyes but hold your tongues." He knew what went through a commander's mind as he steered into battle. The duties of the captain held him to the quarterdeck, the single most dangerous place on the ship. The seamen were either below handling the guns with their lieutenants and midshipmen, or scrambling aloft, which made them targets, but moving ones. The marines could crouch behind the gunwales and hammock netting as they fired, and even the officer or sailor at the helm had the ship's wheel to shield some of his body from stray bullets or flying splinters.

Only a ship's captain was completely exposed to fire from every direction. Only he stood rock-still to give his own men the image of calm authority, of courage under fire—even as iron death sped in across the gunwales. On a sailing man-of-war, it was the captain, not his sailors, who ran the first and highest risk of dying. At Quiberon Bay in 1759, the French rear admiral on the *Formidable* had been wounded in the first exchange of fire. He commanded from a chair until a cannonball took his life. Then his brother took his place until he was killed. Then the first lieutenant who took *his* place was killed—and all within an hour or so of battle. In the course of the Seven Years' War, almost thirty British captains and admirals had been killed in action.

Offering oneself up to death in this way tested any man's nerve. Sailing head on into a broadside in order to break the enemy's line, as each volley of shot and canister screamed along the deck from stem to stern while having no way to shoot back, tested it at a higher level—higher, at least, than Captain Molloy of the *Caesar* could go. So the *Caesar* sailed on and Howe lost his chance for a decisive battle. But he did manage to capture the weather gauge, so he could choose his fight the next day.

On the May 31 there was no battle, only a thick fog, which allowed Howe and his lookouts only tantalizing glimpses of the French ships. But on June 1 the fog lifted to reveal the French fleet downwind bearing east on the port tack. A sailor glanced back at the admiral and turned to one of his fellows. "I think we shall have the fight today," he was overheard to say, "Black Dick has been smiling."

Howe's plan of attack was Rodney with a twist. He would descend on the French line on the windward side and then have each ship pass the French ships by the stern, to engage them on the opposite leeward side. He knew if his captains could rake each ship as they passed, sending broadsides into sterns and bows, they would tear away enough sail and rigging to keep Villaret's fleet from escaping. Crippled and encumbered, the French would drift helplessly with the wind straight into the steady British broadsides. The result would be sheer slaughter.

His signal flags went aloft as the British fleet began its turn. "Now no more books, no more signals," Howe exclaimed as the drums rolled and the *Queen Charlotte* cleared for action. He could hear sailors on board the other ships cheering and singing "Rule Britannia." Howe caught a small boy running along the deck. "Go below," he told him, "you can be of no service here and may be killed." The boy replied, "Please sir, I am Captain Montagu's son. What would my father say if I left the deck during the battle?"

Howe let him stay. He could not know it would be Montagu the father, not the son, who would be killed on that morning of the first of June—cut down on his own quarterdeck, as his ship closed on the French line.

In fact, most of Howe's ships failed to pass through the deadly gauntlet of French fire. Like the 74-gun *Orion,* they were either too damaged to continue or found the French too tightly packed to get through—like the *Brunswick,* which collided almost head-on with the *Vengeur.* But seven did, led by Captain James Gambier's *Défense*—"Look at *Défense!*" Howe shouted, "Look how nobly she goes into action!"—and the *Queen Charlotte* herself. They managed to dismast eleven French battleships, while *Queen Charlotte* lost its own mainmast. The *Marlborough,* wedged between two French 74s and with her captain dead, fought on until she had no masts at all. An officer from one of the French ships asked the *Marlborough's* surviving lieutenant if he wanted to strike: knee-deep in the wreckage and carnage, he roared back, "I'll be damned I should ever surrender!" The sailors cheered as the *Marlborough* ran out her guns on her opponents and dismasted them both.

With the *Brunswick* literally locked anchor to anchor with *Vengeur,* the sailors on her main gun deck could not open the portals to fire. So instead they fired through them, sending their double-shotted charges straight into the French crews on the other side. Mortally stricken, the *Vengeur* managed to break loose, but it was too late. Holed through her hull, stripped of her masts, lower decks awash in blood, the *Vengeur* sank with three hundred men still on board.

Montagu's captain was dead; so was *Marlborough*'s, with *Brunswick*'s John Harvey mortally wounded. Rear Admiral Pasley on the *Bellerophon* had lost a leg. Howe, remarkably, was still alive but exhausted. The sixty-nine-year-old had spent five days continually on deck and twelve hours of unremitting violent action and risk of instant death. He had wanted a devastating victory; eleven French prizes lay helplessly to windward waiting to be taken. But before he could give the crucial order, Howe collapsed in the arms of his lieutenant, Edward Codrington, too stunned to speak. His flag captain was too worried about the survivors from Villaret's fleet, and his own dismasted ships, to follow up. In the end, the British did gather up six and returned to Portsmouth amid cheers about the "Glorious First of June." They had killed more than 1,200 French sailors and officers, and wounded and captured almost 8,000 more. But Villaret was able to tow the rest of his ships away, and the grain from America arrived safely in Rochefort.

Villaret's sacrifice on June 1 had saved the republic but doomed Robespierre's Committee of Public Safety, including navy commissioner Saint André. A victory over the Austrians at Fleurus* secured France's eastern frontier and provided an opening for a massive sweep into the Low Countries. With the victory on land and American grain in hand, the excuses for a Reign of Terror—"*La patrie est en danger*"—were waning. Robespierre and colleagues fell in the month of August (or Thermidor according to the revolutionary calendar); they would be sent to the same guillotine to which they had sent so many thousands of others.

A new, more moderate regime eventually took power, the Directory. With the Terror at an end, the incentive for counterrevolutionary revolts in France began to fade. But the price for peace and stability within France would be permanent war against the rest of Europe. Having created its Frankenstein monster, the revolutionary army, the French

---

*During the battle, the French had launched observers in a hot air balloon to keep track of the Austrian army's movements—history's first hint of military airpower.

Republic became its hostage and eventually its victim. The military force it had forged to save Liberty, Equality, and Fraternity was now the instrument for domination and conquest.

As the new year 1795 unfolded, the French army's spectacular success in the field bore diplomatic fruit. Spain dropped out of the war; Prussia dropped out. As the British army retreated back to England, Holland dropped out and was coerced into becoming France's ally. As so often happens in war, the momentum had suddenly shifted. Despite its continued command of the seas, Britain was on the defensive. It beat off an attempt to retake Corsica but had to give up the French islands it had taken in the Caribbean. Naval forces grabbed the Cape Colony from the capitulating Dutch, as well as Ceylon—momentous events in the history of Africa and Asia. But in the context of France's inexorable advance across the heart of Europe, they were hollow victories.

And worse was to come. Secure on three of its four borders, and with the last remaining royalist rebels in the Vendée in Brittany crushed, France could concentrate its magnificent war machine on Austria, Britain's one remaining ally. One army would push east through Germany toward Vienna; the other, under General Bonaparte, was sent into Italy. In his first speech to his troops, he frankly told them what they were fighting for: loot and glory. He more than delivered, crushing three Austrian armies in quick succession and in the process remaking the map of Italy. At the same time, Bourbon Spain rethought its political options and signed on as France's ally. As with the Dutch, hopes of recovering lost honor and lost imperial possessions, especially Gibraltar, made them collaborators with the new French order for Europe. With a hostile Spain at its back, the navy's position off Toulon became untenable and at the end of 1796 it withdrew. For the first time since the reign of Queen Anne, there was no British fleet in the Mediterranean. Interpreting the pullout as an abandonment of the war, Austria gave up and made peace with France.

The Directory sensed final victory. One more blow directed at Britain might do it. But how to bring its invincible army to bear against an enemy protected by the English Channel—and the fleet at Spithead? This was the problem that would perplex and baffle France's best military minds, including Bonaparte, for more than a decade. It equally baffled Hitler and his generals in 1940. Philip II and Louis XIV had each failed to find the solution, even when they enjoyed naval superiority. The various attempts to invade England in the eighteenth century provided no guidance at all. There was England with its puny army, its exposed beaches, its capital vulnerable to attack: the last barrier to complete French domination of Europe. Yet it would not give way.

So the Directory tried something else—something, in fact, not unlike Philip II's original plan for the Spanish Armada. It would dispatch the Brest squadron to escort 15,000 soldiers under the victor of the Vendée and Bonaparte's rival, General Hoche, to Ireland. After two centuries of colonial misrule, Ireland remained the soft underbelly of the United Kingdom. Irish patriot Wolf Tone promised his French masters that resentful Irishmen, Catholics and Ulster Protestants alike, would rise up to join them. So on December 16, 1796, the invasion fleet with seventeen ships of the line set sail from Brest, planning to evade Admiral Colpoys's inept western blockade by sailing south, and then to ride the easterly gales sweeping down the Channel into the open sea.

Only one British ship stood in their way. This was the 44-gun frigate *Indefatigable,* commanded by a tall, tough Cornishman named Edward Pellew. The *Indefatigable* grimly kept her station off Ushant despite the days of foul weather—the worst, Pellew later admitted, he had ever experienced at sea. Once he spotted the French ships, he knew there was no time to alert Colpoys, who had been driven far out into the Atlantic. So instead he charged in alone under the cover of night and driving rain, ducking nimbly between the bucketing French ships as they negotiated the rocks and shoals at the entrance to Brest harbor. Pellew was everywhere, firing off flares and the occasional gun in imitation of French night signals, disrupting the French fleet and creating no end of confusion. One 74, the *Séduisant,* ended up on the rocks. Many others scattered far out to sea, including the flagship carrying the French admiral and General Hoche.

By the time the rest reassembled and finally reached their landing point on Bantry Bay on December 21, it was too late. The British fleet was still not there to greet them but the weather was. Icy easterly gales pinned them at the head of the bay, unable to make landfall. For more than a week, the inexperienced French crews tried to beat into the harbor but failed. On January 2, to Tone's immense grief and disappointment, they gave up and returned to Brest.

Tone also admitted in his diary, "I am utterly astonished that we did not see a single English ship of war, neither going nor coming back." In fact, Pellew had alerted Admiral Colpoys to what was happening, but Colpoys had chosen to run back east to Spithead for orders. So Pellew and the *Indefatigable* again followed the French back to Brest virtually alone, with just one even smaller frigate, the *Amazon,* as escort. Together they picked out a third-rate from the herd, the *Droits des Hommes,* which had lost its fore and main topmasts in the storms and was "steering very wild." Although heavily outgunned, the *Indefatigable* and *Amazon* managed to engage the Frenchman on either side and then drive him onto the rocks. It was a spectacular tactical triumph, to make up for what had been a larger British strategic failure.

Yet thanks at least in part to Pellew, Ireland would never be the same. If Tone and his French allies had landed, they could easily have marched on Dublin and declared Ireland a revolutionary republic. Instead, British authorities had time to strike first. They rounded up the leaders of Tone's United Irishmen and disarmed Ulster with great ferocity; they secured Dublin and set up a spy network to undermine any future rebellion. When the French did land troops in 1798 and rebels rose up north and south, the British were ready. The rebellion was crushed and Ireland remained part of the British Crown, at the cost of nearly 12,000 Irish lives. Finally realizing how vulnerable the English position in Ireland was, Pitt and his cabinet began making plans to rule it directly from London by an Act of Union, passed in 1800. Never again would Irish Catholics and Protestants work together for independence. The Protestant Ascendancy, with all its abuses and inequities, was safe for another century.

As for Captain Pellew, his bravery and initiative reflected the bold self-confidence of the rising generation of British sailors: ready to change the course of history with a single frigate. Showing how to do it with a single ship of the line would be the destiny of Horatio Nelson.

* * *

Nelson came easily to this self-confidence, the by-product of two generations of Royal Navy dominance. As a lieutenant he had studied and absorbed Edward Hawke's aggressive approach, passed on to him by his mentor Robert Locker. Locker, who served with Hawke, taught Nelson " 'Lay a Frenchmen close, and you will beat him.' " The advice suited Nelson's own instincts. The bloodshed and violence of a yardarm-to-yardarm sea battle never appalled or sickened Nelson; on the contrary, it energized him. "I would not be anywhere else for thousands," he would exclaim in the bloodiest moments of the battle of Copenhagen. Even in the frenzy of action, he could analyze and exploit his opponent's weaknesses with the detachment of a stone-cold killer. "An enemy that commits a false step in his view," wrote his friend Cuthbert Collingwood, "is ruined."

Nelson had already displayed his love for close battle when he pitted his 64-gun *Agamemnon* against the 84-gun *Ça Ira* (named after the French revolutionary anthem) off the coast of Corsica in March 1795, crippling the larger ship and butchering more than half her crew in the process. Less than a year later he would do it again more spectacularly, making himself the most talked-about officer in the Royal Navy—and ruining any hope of a French invasion of England.

On January 19, 1796, Nelson arrived at San Fiorenzo Bay, Corsica, to meet the new commander in chief of the Mediterranean fleet, Sir John Jervis. Jervis was a leading apostle of the navy's hard and bold spirit which appealed so much to Nelson and Pellew. Dedicated to spit and polish, he was a fierce if fair disciplinarian and a stickler for protocol. He made his ships exercise at least five of their guns every day. He decreed that all officers were now to remove their hats in the presence of a superior officer— the Royal Navy's first formal salute. Although he flogged his ratings unmercifully, and did not hesitate to hang men for mutiny, Jervis also looked after their health and welfare. It was Jervis who finally introduced lemon juice as the standard antidote to scurvy on navy ships, as well as introducing soap in the lower decks. He made scrubbed and cleaned decks not just a personal fetish, as they had been for Hawke and Jervis's mentor "Old Dreadnought" Boscawen, but a navy standard.

He and Nelson took to each other at once. Jervis offered him command of one of his first rates and wanted to promote him to rear admiral. Failing that, he gave him the temporary rank of commodore and sent him on a series of vital missions that spring and summer, including capturing the ships carrying Bonaparte's siege train to Italy. But by August Spain was about to switch sides, and on September 29 the Admiralty ordered Jervis and Nelson to vacate the Mediterranean. Their withdrawal allowed Bonaparte to complete his conquests in Italy and the French to retake Corsica. Most important, the Franco-Spanish alliance raised the danger that their respective fleets might join up, outnumbering the British for the first time. One hundred and fifty-two ships of the line against one hundred and fifteen: a 6-to-4 advantage in the Atlantic alone.

As 1797 began, Jervis's urgent task was to keep that from happening. He had anchored his fleet at Lagos in Portugal, partly to encourage Britain's last remaining Iberian ally, but also to block any rendezvous of the enemy's Mediterranean and Atlantic fleets. In fact, two crucial pieces

had already connected. Pierre Villeneuve, a veteran of the Ireland expedition and admiral at only thirty-two (a sign of how the French were short
of experienced sea officers), had brought part of the Toulon squadron
safely into Brest in December. The third crucial piece, the Spanish fleet
under Don José de Cordoba, was supposed to sail out with Villeneuve but
had turned back to Cartagena. At the beginning of February Cordoba set
sail again. He had twenty-seven splendid battleships, including the largest
in the world, the 140-gun *Santissima Trinidad,* and twelve frigates, against
Jervis's fifteen ships of the line. Storms drove the Spanish far into the
Atlantic as they came out of the Gibraltar Straits. As they came back on a
westerly breeze, Cordoba found Jervis waiting for him.

Jervis put his line of battle on a south-southwest course. The 74-gun
Culloden under Captain Thomas Troubridge was in the lead, followed by
the *Blenheim,* the 98-gun *Prince George* of Rear Admiral Parker, the *Orion*
under James Saumarez, *Colossus, Irresistible,* and then Jervis's *Victory.* Twelfth
in line was Nelson's ship, the *Captain,* with Collingwood's *Excellent* bringing
up the rear.

Built at Limehouse and launched in 1787, the *Captain* was not the
most modern 74-gun ship afloat, but was still a formidable weapon of
war. Her 170-foot-long gun decks carried fourteen 32-pounders on each
side, and fourteen 18-pounders, along with two carronades. Her officers,
American-born Captain Ralph Miller and Lieutenant Edward Berry, had
both served with Nelson on the *Agamemnon.* He trusted them as implicitly
as his crew of 550 sailors and marines. As he wrote after his encounter
with the *Ça Ira,* "Nothing can stop the courage of English seamen."

Meanwhile, Jervis was bearing down with the wind on his starboard
beam to break the Spaniard's line. As he did so, Cordoba swiftly ordered
his van to steer north as his leeward squadron dropped away. He and
Jervis were now on opposite tacks; this made concentrating fire on the
passing Spanish ships almost impossible. So Jervis sent a standard signal
to his captains: "Tack in succession." This would bring the two fleets on
the same tack and moving in the same direction, as each British ship
reversed direction by passing her bows into the wind and catching the
wind on the opposite side.

It was an aggressive move, showing Jervis's desire to start the battle.
But it was not aggressive enough for Nelson. Tacking in succession took
time, as each ship made its pirouette one after the other, to remain in line.
Even as Nelson watched Troubridge turn the *Culloden*'s bows to windward,
he realized the Spanish squadron would be far to the north before they

were all done. So he did the unthinkable: he disobeyed Jervis's direct signal. Instead he ordered Miller to turn to larboard, to "wear" his ship around by bringing the stern into the wind rather than her bows. The *Captain* then deftly slipped between the *Excellent* and *Diadem* and aimed for the center of the Spanish line head-on, alone.

In ten minutes Nelson would be fighting seven Spanish ships of the line at once. Three of them had more than 100 guns, including the *Santissima Trinidad.* To the astonished Spaniards, it must have seemed suicide. His fellow officers watching from the other ships had to agree; if the Spanish did not kill him, then Jervis surely would for disobeying his order. But Nelson had carefully calculated his odds. He knew his crewmen were the best trained and motivated fighting seamen in the world, while many of the Spanish were landlubber conscripts and their officers sloppy and inexperienced. Each of his gun crews could swab, load, run out, and fire two broadsides every three minutes. The Spanish would be lucky to get off one broadside in five. Nelson also figured, as the *Captain* swung into action and the first Spanish ranging shots sang through the rigging, that once Jervis saw what Nelson was doing, he would not let him fight it out alone.

And Jervis did not. As soon as he saw Nelson's move, he realized the thinking behind it and signaled Collingwood's *Excellent* to wear around to Nelson's support, just as the *Culloden* and *Blenheim* completed their tack to join in. The signal went up from the *Victory:* "Engage the enemy more closely." By now the *Captain* was caught in a ring of fire. The Spanish three-deckers blasted away her sails and rigging, shot away her wheel and her fore topmast as the casualties mounted. Yet Nelson wanted to fight even closer. He ordered Miller to ram into the *San Nicholas,* which in the confusion of battle had run aboard the 112-gun *San Josef,* and called to the crew to prepare to board. As Miller stepped forward to lead his men, Nelson said, "No Miller, I must have that honor," and drew his sword. As a final broadside thundered out, the two ships collided with a sickening crunch, the *Captain*'s bowsprit running up over the *San Nicholas*'s stern.

Men armed with pikes and cutlasses climbed along the bulwarks and jumped for the *San Nicholas*'s rigging. A marine and a sailor nimbly scrambled up onto the *Captain*'s bowsprit. A bullet dropped the sailor into the sea but Nelson was right behind. The marine kicked open the stern galley window and leaped inside. Nelson followed with a shout of "Death or Glory!" while the other marines poured into the Spaniards' great cabin. Bullets whizzed as the desperate Spanish officers fired through the cabin door. The marines managed to pry it open, laid down a devastating volley, and then raced with Nelson onto the quarterdeck.

There he found some twenty dead Spaniards and Nelson's first lieutenant, Edward Berry, already hauling down the *San Nicholas*'s colors. From the opposite side of the deck soldiers and officers on the *San Josef* were now firing on his men, so Nelson gave the next order: take the *San Josef* as well. "Boarders away!" he shouted. Within seconds a horde of yelling, frenzied sailors and marines were leaping over the bulwark onto the *San Josef*'s main deck, scattering and hacking away at their enemy. By the time Nelson made it over, the hapless Spanish were surrendering in droves. The *San Josef*'s commanding admiral lay dying at his feet, both legs shot off, while the captain surrendered both their swords.

It was a spectacular, even theatrical, bit of derring-do. The *Victory* gave Nelson and the *Captain* three cheers as she sailed past. Yet one out of three of his crew were either dead or wounded—almost a third of all the British battle casualties. With less theatrics and bloodshed, Collingwood managed to cripple the 112-gun *San Salvador del Mundo,* forced the 74-gun *San Ysidro* to strike colors, and pounded the great *Santissima Trinidad*—"such a ship as I never saw before," Collingwood wrote later with awe—to a complete wreck. At 4:45 Jervis signaled his fleet to break off. In all, the Spanish had lost only four ships, although they were forced back to Cádiz. Yet of the four prizes the British took, two were Nelson's. He had made his fortune as well as what he really craved: his reputation.

When he arrived on the *Victory,* Jervis greeted him with a warm embrace, almost as if he were a long-lost son. When Captain Robert Calder remarked sourly that Nelson's action was a breach of orders, Jervis snapped back, "It certainly was so, and if ever you commit such a breach of your orders, I will forgive you also." Nelson basked in the praise of "every man from the highest to the lowest in the fleet," as he wrote delightedly to Fanny. Officers made jokes about "Nelson's Patent Bridge for boarding first-rates" and common seamen asked to shake his hand. For the undersized parson's son who had been sent to sea at twelve "to rough him up a bit," it was a heady experience. Yet in his own mind, it was long overdue (he was nearly forty). Nelson even saw fit to write his own highly dramatic account, entitled *A Few Remarks Relative to Myself in the Captain,* which almost made English readers believe Nelson had won the battle himself.

Nelson did win his promotion to rear admiral, while Jervis himself became an earl. The battle of Cape St. Vincent was the navy's second great victory in the war and ended French hopes of assembling a fleet large enough to protect an invasion of England, at least for now. But it hardly changed the strategic balance. Bonaparte's campaign in Italy was about to reach its triumphant climax. In October he would dictate to Austria the terms of a peace treaty at Campio Formio, securing French control over Italy, the left bank of the Rhine, and Belgium. With Austria out of the war, Britain had lost her last important ally. She had retained her naval supremacy, but France now enjoyed complete supremacy on land.

As Nelson wrote, "The French say, they are Masters on Shore, and the English at sea." By 1797 the wars of the French Revolution had resolved themselves into a life-or-death struggle between the world's preeminent land power and its preeminent sea power: what some later would call the war between the Whale and the Elephant. Which side won would be affected by many factors, some economic and military, others political and spiritual—and some a matter of chance. But two men, and two only, would decide the final outcome: the masters of the two new kinds of warfare, Napoleon and Nelson. The events of the next decade were as much a matter of a personal duel between them as a conflict between competing nations and political ideologies. Whoever won would determine the future of the globe. Either a highly centralized, bureaucra-tized military world-state would emerge, centering on Paris and dedi-cated to the glory of its ruler, or a dispersed, decentralized system of individual states, linked together by ties of trade and commerce flowing to and from London over the world's oceans.

However, just as Bonaparte's army had to be able to march to win, so Nelson's navy had to be able to sail. That suddenly became a problem in the spring of 1797, thanks to what is usually called the Great Mutiny.

The name is a misnomer. The Great Strike captures the reality better. For, beginning on April 16, sailors at the Channel Fleet's anchorage at Spithead refused to go to sea unless certain long-standing grievances were met. There was no arrest of officers or seizure of ships; precedence and rank continued to be obeyed. The fleet's frigates continued to patrol the Channel. The sailors' elected delegates swore they would call off the strike if the French fleet came out, and their officers believed them. Nonetheless, the Spithead mutiny was a national crisis. Although the French never managed to take advantage of the situation, for the first time the Admiralty was forced to deal officially with the concerns and grievances of its common seamen.

What were they? Pay (not enough), food (pilfering by dishonest ships' pursers and not enough fresh vegetables), health (still a problem on ships, which were now continuously at sea for months a time), and shore leave.* Not a word about flogging, or impressment, or the tyrannical authority of officers, although some unpopular ones were asked to leave and courteously escorted off their ships. Nothing about living under the iron law of the Articles of War, and certainly nothing about equality or the "rights of man." Although some officers grumbled about outside agitators and Jacobin insurrection, the truth was the vast majority of British seamen accepted the conditions of navy service and their duty to obey. "We are not actuated by any spirit of sedition or disaffection, whatsoever," they wrote to Whig opposition leader Charles James Fox, "it is indigence and extreme penury alone that is the cause of our complaint."

In fact, the Great Mutiny did not break out in the fleet with the sternest taskmaster and harshest discipline, Jervis's Mediterranean force (when three men did try to follow the Spithead example, Jervis hanged them at once, and got a congratulatory note from Nelson for it). In the Channel Fleet, by contrast, long months of waiting and inactivity had allowed Commander in Chief Lord Bridport and his officers to let discipline and order slip—proving, as the *Bounty* case had, that it was when officers *failed* to exercise their authority that real trouble broke out.

Besides, the grievances were hardly new. Richard Howe had received eleven petitions from seamen about low pay in early March, which he forwarded on to the Admiralty, but it failed to respond in time. In the end, it was Howe, now retired, whom the government sent to Spithead to calm the situation, bringing news of a parliamentary vote for supplementary wages and a pardon for the mutineers signed by the king. On May 10 he arrived at Portsmouth. Beginning with the *Royal George* he visited every ship in the fleet, laboriously climbing up the side to read the news and listen to the sailors' complaints against certain officers. In the end, Howe agreed to dismiss fifty-nine commissioned and warrant officers from the service, including four captains and an admiral. He then met with the strikers' delegates at the Governors' House to share a glass of wine and put the seal to the final agreement. Jubilant sailors carried "Black Dick" through the streets of Portsmouth on their shoulders: they had not won

*Shore leave was not uncommon in the prewar fleet—proving once again that navy ships were hardly floating prisons—but the demands of full-time war service made it impossible to grant it in necessary numbers. Ironically, the coppering of the fleet had also decreased the chances of getting shore leave, since ships could stay at sea longer.

everything, but they had won the attention and respect of the authorities, and were ready to go to sea again. The Spithead mutiny was over.

The outbreak at the Nore was shorter but nastier. Indeed, twenty-nine men were hanged afterward (out of four hundred arrested).* The Nore sat on the entrance to the Medway in the Thames estuary, an assembly point for navy ships coming out of the Chatham or Deptford docks and for ships blockading the Dutch coast, including those from the North Sea fleet based at Yarmouth under the command of a gigantic (six foot four in his stockings) and boisterous Scot, Admiral Adam Duncan. There was no port or docks at the Nore, just an anchorage overlooking the sandy beaches and the flowing Thames. On board the 90-gun *Sandwich* a sailor named Richard Parker managed to convince and in some cases intimidate his fellow sailors into organizing a petition similar to that of the Spithead mutineers—although those sailors had gone back to sea three days before, on May 17.

The discontent soon spread to the rest of Duncan's fleet. Interestingly, one of the first captains sent ashore by his crew was William Bligh, commander of the *Director*. When Duncan tried to sail on May 26 for his blockade of the Dutch fleet at the Texel, most of his ships hoisted a red flag and ran back to Yarmouth. For three days Duncan had to keep station with only one other ship, making signals to an imaginary fleet supposedly just beyond the horizon.

However, the nation was now impatient with mutinies and strikes, and Parker finally overplayed his hand when he threatened to blockade the Thames in order to get his demands met. Troops moved in, there were calls for volunteers to fight against the mutineers, and within two weeks the whole thing collapsed. Parker's Floating Republic, as he called the *Sandwich,* fired on ships that handed back command to their officers: "It was the most melancholy sight I ever saw," wrote an eyewitness on the *Nassau,* "Englishmen murdering Englishmen!"

On June 13, Parker surrendered. He was one of the first to be hanged, from the *Sandwich*'s yardarm, along with twenty-seven others. Yet on the *Nassau,* the lead ship in the rebellion, only twenty men were court-martialed and all except one were pardoned. All the other rebel ships, including the *Director* back under Bligh (who intervened to prevent

---

*The arrests and executions would inspire Herman Melville's novella about the British navy, *Billy Budd, Foretopman.*

twenty-one of his men from being hanged for mutiny), would fight with distinction when Duncan smashed the Dutch fleet at the battle of Camperdown on October 11. Camperdown was the navy's third great victory after the Glorious First of June and Cape St. Vincent. It effectively destroyed the Dutch navy, France's ally, as a fighting force. England was safe from any threat from the Baltic or North Sea. Only the French threat across the Channel remained. But it now faced a British navy more unified, from the foretops and lower deck to the captain's cabin and wardroom, than ever before.

That French threat was now under the command of General Bonaparte himself. Historians tend to see Napoleon's career as a series of triumphs and defeats on land. The lightning victories in Italy; seizing power in 1799 and consolidating the territorial gains of the revolution into a French empire in 1804; crushing the Austrians and Russians at Austerlitz and the Prussians at Jena; the spectacular march on Moscow and the disastrous retreat; the return from Elba to lead his army to final defeat at Waterloo. Yet through it all his real obsession was with the British navy: how to defeat it, how to circumvent it, how to break its relentless grip, and thus break Britain, "the most formidable, the most constant, and the most generous of my foes." Indeed, at the end, in exile on St. Helena, he would declare, "If it had not been for you English, I would have been Emperor of the East; but wherever there was water to float a ship, we were sure to find you in our way."

In October 1797 the Directory had named Bonaparte commander in chief of the army committed for the invasion of Britain. Not yet thirty, he was on the brink of assuming supreme power, if he could follow up his success in Italy with still more victories and triumphs. At one glance, Bonaparte realized that an attack across the Channel would only bring disaster. As he explained to the Directory in a long letter at the end of February 1798, the British navy was too dominant, and the French navy too weak, to give an invasion any chance of success. So Bonaparte had another plan to propose. "The time is not far distant," he wrote, "when we shall feel that, in order to destroy England once and for all, we must occupy Egypt."

It was a plan breathtaking in its geopolitical scope. Egypt, like the rest of the Middle East from Tunisia to Mecca and Constantinople, was part of the Ottoman Empire. No European power had even a foothold there. But the Ottoman Empire was dying a slow lingering death, as Bonaparte well knew, and Egypt's local ruling elite, the Mamelukes, paid no attention to the Sultan in Constantinople. Egypt, with its great port of Alexandria, seemed a plum ready for the taking. The Duke of Choiseul had once proposed buying it from Turkey; the Directory's foreign minister, Tallyrand, had spoken of it as a future colony for France. Egypt would give France direct access to the goods of Asia and Arabia, and a market for its own manufactured products more convenient than Haiti or the West Indies—and less vulnerable to attack from the Royal Navy.

But Bonaparte saw more. He envisioned Egypt as a springboard for joining forces with Britain's enemies in India and restoring French influence there. Then, by digging a canal across the Suez peninsula, the French could even short-circuit British trade around the Cape, forcing the "nation of shopkeepers" to its knees. To paraphrase a French foreign minister half a century earlier, Bonaparte was going to conquer England through India. The campaign would also make him the greatest conqueror since Alexander the Great.

Bonaparte estimated that with an army of 60,000 men, 10,000 horses, 50,000 camels, and 150 field guns, he could reach the River Indus in four months. However, his new ally Tallyrand persuaded him that this was far too ambitious a plan. So Bonaparte asked instead for 25,000 and the fleet at Toulon to escort them to Alexandria. On May 9, 1798, he arrived at Toulon to meet the fleet's admiral, Brueys d'Aigalliers, and supervise the loading and provisioning of his army, including a large contingent of scientists, scholars, and linguists from the French Academy (like Bougainville's voyage to Tahiti, Bonaparte's to Egypt would dramatically alter Europe's view of the non-Western world). Bonaparte set sail on May 19, by which time Jervis ordered Rear Admiral Horatio Nelson to take a squadron into the Mediterranean and see what he was up to.

Nelson was no longer the unspoiled golden boy who had breezily boarded two Spanish men-of-war off Cape St. Vincent fifteen months earlier. A failed raid on Tenerife in the Canaries had cost him his arm and nearly his life: his own son-in-law had had to tie a tourniquet to the severed stump of his right arm and row him back to his ship under enemy fire. Nelson had spent eight painful months convalescing and learning to write with his left hand; he had taken opium to sleep at night. Along with the injury from a skirmish off Corsica that had left his right eye half blind, Nelson looked older, thinner, drawn. He was still recuperating in England when the Admiralty's orders arrived to take command of an escort for merchant ships heading into the Atlantic. From there he sailed down to Tagus to rejoin the fleet.

"The arrival of Admiral Nelson has given me new life," Jervis, now Lord St. Vincent, wrote. He also had new orders for him. Spies had told the Admiralty of Bonaparte's imminent departure from Toulon, but not his final destination. Nelson was to proceed to Toulon with his flagship, the *Vanguard* of 74 guns, the *Orion* commanded by James Saumarez, and Alexander Ball's *Alexander*. Ten more ships of the line would join them later. The vital mission now was to find out whether Bonaparte and his army were headed for Italy or Brest or America, or perhaps even farther afield.

Bonaparte sailed on May 19. Nelson had in fact arrived off Toulon on the seventeenth but the French fleet's departure caught him off guard after storms had scattered and damaged his ships. What followed now was an elaborate game of cat and mouse, with Nelson constantly trying to guess where Bonaparte was going, and constantly guessing wrong. He had only three frigates to scour the entire Mediterranean for sight or sound of a French sail: without enough scouting vessels, he was sailing virtually blind in its late spring blue azure waters. It was those desperate days that inspired one of Nelson's famous quotations: "Was I to die this moment, 'Want of frigates' would be found stamped on my heart."

On June 9 Bonaparte reached Malta and expelled the famous order of Knights of St. John, who had ruled the fortress island since before Philip II, and installed a French garrison. On June 16 he set sail again; Nelson learned that on June 21 from a Genoese brig as he was passing off Cape Passaro from Naples (he did not even have time in Naples to visit his friends the Hamiltons). Nelson now had thirteen ships of the line: they included trusted friends like Troubridge on the *Culloden* and Ralph Miller, now in command of the *Theseus,* as well as Samuel Hood, the old admiral's son, on the *Zealous,* and Thomas Foley on the *Goliath.* They knew by now the French fleet was heading east. But where? Corfu? Constantinople? Perhaps Alexandria. Nelson sped off and actually passed Bonaparte's ships on the night of June 22–23, although neither fleet spotted the other. Bonaparte and Brueys were heading north toward Crete to reprovision before making for Egypt, while Nelson sailed directly south to Alexandria.

He arrived on June 28 and found no Frenchmen. "The Devil's children have the Devil's luck," Nelson wrote. "I cannot find, or to this moment learn, beyond vague conjecture, where the French fleet are gone to." Perhaps they had turned back to attack Naples after all, Nelson decided. He set sail to find out, leaving Captain Thomas Hardy with his neat little French-built brig the *Mutine,* to watch the Egyptian coast. After two days, Hardy grew impatient and sailed east to find Nelson. Two days

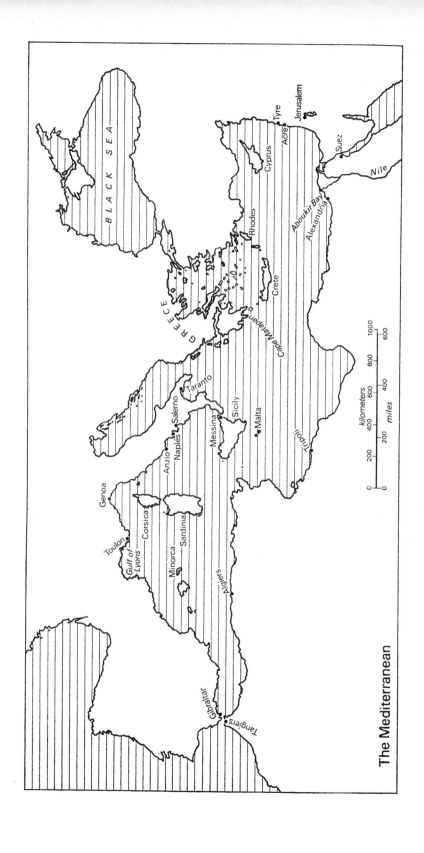

The Mediterranean

after that, the first ships of Bruey's fleet dropped anchor in Alexandria harbor.

Nelson had lost the race, partly due to his own impatience. Had he sat tight in Alexandria for a week to gather more complete information, he would have caught the French warships and transports, their crews exhausted and on short rations, as they straggled in. As it was, Bonaparte was able to land his army and artillery intact while Nelson was still fruitlessly cruising the eastern Mediterranean. It was almost another month before Nelson finally learned the truth. By then, Napoleon had routed the Mameluke rulers at the Battle of the Pyramids (July 21) and completed his conquest of Egypt.

Nelson and his squadron did not return to Alexandria until the afternoon of August 1, to find the empty transports riding high in the harbor at the mouth of the Nile and the entire French fleet anchored in a long defensive line in Aboukir Bay, with the 120-gun flagship *L'Orient* in the center: an impenetrable wall of wood and iron. The British were too late.

Or so it would have seemed to any other naval commander. To Nelson, however, the situation presented an amazing opportunity. The French fleet was immovable—but also immobilized. Nelson figured if that he brought his ships to bear at close range, his superior gunnery could pound them to pieces where they stood, or rather where they swung on their fore and aft anchor cables. It was a huge risk: the French had thirteen battleships against Nelson's fifteen, some mounting 36-pounders against his 32s. The British ships would take a horrible punishment. But Nelson loved risks—"difficulties and dangers but increase my desire of attempting them," he wrote later—especially if they brought a mad violent battle. He was sure he could beat the French: he just did not know how.

That, too, did not bother him. He had learned a valuable lesson at Cape St. Vincent: that no admiral, no matter how organized or enterprising, could control the action and tempo of a sea battle from his quarterdeck. The pace was too fast, the noise and smoke too distracting, the sudden opportunities too fleeting, and the system of signaling and communicating with his fleet too primitive, to allow him to plan and plot each move and countermove. The best an admiral could do was devise his strategy, point his ships in the right direction, and trust his captains to carry out his plan as they, not he, saw fit in the heat and smoke of battle. "I was sure each would feel for a French ship," was how Nelson put it, and that was all he wanted.

His confidence and trust in his captains sprang from the other crucial lesson he had learned, one every British admiral from Vernon and Hawke to Rodney and Howe had made part of the navy tradition. A commander's subordinates had to understand not just *what* he was planning to do, but *why*. Nelson had talked to Troubridge, Saumarez, Hood, and the others all summer about possible plans for engaging the French fleet, and how he intended to proceed. This team of trusted officers came to understand his strategic thinking almost as well as he did. Later Nelson said, quoting *King Henry V,* "I had the happiness to command a Band of Brothers"—the name by which they would be forever known.

So there was no need for a conference before the battle. Nelson could lead his ships directly into combat that very afternoon, the first of August, even though by the time they engaged the sun would be setting and twilight darkening the horizon. His men and officers were as eager for battle as he was: "The utmost joy seemed to animate every breast," Berry remembered. On the ship nearest the French, the *Goliath,* "a serious cast was to be perceived on every face, but not a shade of doubt or fear." On the *Vanguard,* Nelson overheard two sailors at their gun. "Damn them, look at them," said one. "There they are, Jack, and if we don't beat them, they will beat us." Nelson wrote afterward, "I knew what stuff I had under me, so I went into the attack."

At three o'clock, Nelson had hoisted the signal, "Prepare for battle." The British ships began to come before the wind as they entered the bay, with Foley's *Goliath* and Samuel Hood's *Zealous* jockeying for the lead. To Brueys, watching on board the *Orient,* the British ships just seemed confused. He was confident they would not dare attack in the face of an unknown lee shore and his formidable wall of ships with their starboard gun ports open, guns glaring out over the bay. But then, before the astonished admiral's eyes, the line began to take shape. First *Goliath,* then *Zealous, Audacious, Orion, Theseus, Vanguard.* Then at five came Nelson's crucial signal: "I mean to attack the enemy's van and center."

Their many discussions and debates in the *Vanguard's* great cabin made Nelson's plan clear. The leading ships would attack the French immediately to their starboard, while the rest would rush in to attack the French center. The impact would be as much psychological as tactical: concentrated fire coming too fast and in too many places for the French to react.

But as the *Goliath* spread her studding sails for every last ounce of speed in the fading light and bore down on the lead French ship, the *Guerrier,* her captain, Thomas Foley, noticed that the French were anchored far out from the shoals that lined the shore. Far enough out, in fact, that he might be able to guide the *Goliath* in and attack the *Guerrier* where she least expected, on the larboard side, where the guns ports remained closed. So the *Goliath* made her move, slipping past the *Guerrier*'s bow to put herself between the Frenchman and the shore. Then Foley dropped anchor and fired a tremendous broadside into the *Guerrier*'s unprotected side.

Nelson saw it all and hailed Sam Hood on the *Zealous*, asking if he could follow the *Goliath* into the shoals. Hood replied he would try, and raised his hat to Nelson, when a gust of wind swept it out of his hand. "Never mind, Webley," Hood said as his first lieutenant tried to catch it, "there it goes for good luck. Put the helm up and make sail." With *Zealous* leading the way, five other ships followed around on the Frenchmen's larboard flank, while *Vanguard* and the rest blasted them from starboard.

Stunned, double-teamed, and pounded from both sides at once, the French were overwhelmed. For the next two and half hours, as night fell with a blackness illuminated only by blinding stabs of gunfire, the British gunners poured out salvos that tore one ship after another apart, and filled their decks with blood and bodies. Admiral Brueys had both his legs blown off in an exchange of broadsides with the *Bellerophon.* He insisted on staying on deck, sitting in a chair with tourniquets tied around both bloody stumps, until another shot literally tore him in two. Nelson was also wounded, as a large flying splinter gashed open his forehead to the bone above his right eye. His officers quickly carried him below. Although he was out of action for the rest of the battle, he already knew he had won. The only question was whether any French ships would survive.

At nine o'clock a dark red glow began to appear at the center of the French line: the flagship *Orient* was on fire, every sailor's nightmare. "A most grand and awful spectacle," Captain Miller recalled, "such as formerly would have drawn tears down the cheeks of the victors." But now, he added, "pity was stifled as it rose by the remembrance of the numerous and horrible atrocities their unprincipled and bloodthirsty nation had and were committing."

In minutes the glow grew scarlet red, as great flames burst out from the *Orient*'s silent gun ports. At ten o'clock the *Orient* blew up—an explosion heard fifteen miles away in Alexandria. The blast threw debris over every ship in the bay. *Alexander*'s sails were set on fire by burning embers. Briefly the battle scene came to a stunned silence. Then slowly the firing recommenced and did not cease until long after midnight.

By then every ship in the French van and center had either surren-dered or was trying to do so. The last two ships in the French rear, led by Admiral Villeneuve, managed to slip their cables and flee the scene. The British left them go: Nelson's ships were too battered and his men too exhausted to follow. But they were the only ones to get away. Of thirteen French ships of the line, ten had been captured, burned, or sunk, and one had blown up. Nelson had not lost a single vessel. Despite the fierce bat-tle, he had suffered only 218 killed and 677 wounded, while French losses were six times heavier. It was the most lopsided victory in modern naval history. The Royal Navy was once again master of the Mediterranean, while Bonaparte's army was stranded and cut off. The French dreams of conquering India were gone and a new power had appeared in the Middle East: Great Britain.

The next morning, British officers and sailors, many of whom had slept at their guns, woke up to see the devastation. Battered French prizes, their masts reduced to jagged stumps, lay scattered across the bay. One ship, the *Timoléon,* which had run aground and been set on fire by her crew, smoldered in the distance. Chunks of the *Orion* floated everywhere on the water's blood-dimmed surface, along with the bodies of her sailors, "mangled, wounded and scorched, not a bit of clothes on them but their trousers." Nelson sat at his stern gallery window and looked out on what he had done from under from his bloody bandage.

He wrote: "Victory is not a name strong enough for such a scene."

CHAPTER FIFTEEN

Victory at Sea

*Now, gentlemen, let us do something today
which the world may talk of hereafter.*
—REAR ADMIRAL CUTHBERT COLLINGWOOD,
HMS *ROYAL SOVEREIGN*, OCTOBER 21, 1805

THE EMERGENCE OF Horatio Nelson as military commander marks a key event in the evolution of the modern British navy. Indeed, it may be *the* key event. As revolutionary tactician, as brilliant fleet officer, as charismatic and supportive colleague, as man and legend: no other figure has had so great an impact on the navy and its place in modern history, even today. Without Nelson the man, the British navy's rise as the supreme instrument of global power would have been incomplete. Without Nelson the myth, its transformation into a universal symbol of heroic achievement might never have begun.

Yet which was he, man or myth? This debate began soon after the Battle of the Nile, and it still goes on. Virtually every episode of Nelson's life can be presented either as the actions of a shameless self-promoter and reckless narcissist or as the deeds of a noble hero selflessly dedicated to serving king, God, and country. "He is in many points a really great man," said his friend Lord Minto, "in others a baby." Nelson himself wrote "Nelson never has, nor can change." The question is, which was the real Nelson?

The answer: he was both. One historian has called him Superman with Everyman's faults. It helps to explain the endless fascination with Nelson and his life, but it obscures the larger point. Nelson's Superman qualities flowed from the institution in which he was raised and to which he dedicated himself. While his many shortcomings were his own, his virtues, with one or two exceptions, were those of the Royal Navy. He, more than anyone, embodied what it had become after two centuries of development and conflict—not just a great and powerful fighting force, but a crucial part of Britain's national identity.

The victory in Aboukir Bay made him a national hero, starting with his colleagues. His "band of brothers" commissioned a presentation sword and portrait of Nelson to commemorate the battle. The agent who collected his prize money ordered a medal to be struck for every man who had served on August 1, in gold for captains, silver for officers, and bronze for sailors and marines—the navy's first service medal. Captain Ralph Hallowell of the *Swiftsure* found a more personal, if morbid, tribute. His carpenters had taken a massive chunk of the *Orient's* mainmast and had it fashioned into a coffin. Hallowell delivered it to Nelson with a humorous note. Nelson put it behind his chair in the great cabin. He and his officers would share many jokes about it.

The severely damaged *Vanguard* had to be towed back to Naples, where rapturous crowds greeted him while bands played "Rule Britannia" and "Hail the Conquering Hero Comes." King Ferdinand himself came on board to shake Nelson's hand, as did Ambassador Hamilton and his ravishing wife. Emma Hamilton was not prepared for the sight of Nelson with only one arm, and his bandaged head and swollen black eyes. "Oh God, is it possible?" she screamed and collapsed on deck. William Hamilton was almost as carried away with emotion. "History, either ancient or modern, does not record an Action that does more honor to the Heroes that gained the victory," he gushed. "You have now made yourself, my dear Nelson, immortal."

In England, the news of the destruction of the French fleet spread "like an electric impulse," as one newspaper put it, setting off literally hundreds of celebrations, parades, banquets, and bonfires. The king was so thrilled he read Nelson's letter aloud four times and made him a baron, with an annual pension of 2,000 pounds. Someone even created a new dance, called "the Vanguard, or the breaking of the line," and new words were added to "Rule Britannia" for the cheering crowds to sing:

> By Nelson's glorious deeds inspired,
> Fresh trophies shall thy children bring,
> And with the patriot virtues fir'd,
> Protect their Country, Laws, and King.

And indeed, the battle was a crucial breakthrough for Britain. It had not only left Bonaparte's army stranded and isolated in Egypt and crippled the French navy, it opened the way for the navy to take Malta and lay siege to Port Mahon on Minorca. The capture of both the next year would make the British navy the supreme power in the Mediterranean, with Malta controlling access to sea routes east and west.

Bonaparte, however, still had his army in Egypt. Undismayed at being cut off, he now decided to march north into Syria, to take on the Turks and break up the Ottoman Empire—part of his plan all along. He probably would have succeeded and rewritten the history of the Middle East, but for Sidney Smith. Next to Nelson, he was becoming Bonaparte's chief nemesis. As Bonaparte was fighting his way through Syria, including massacring the Turkish garrison that had surrendered to him at El Arish,* Lord St. Vincent dispatched Smith with two frigates, the *Theseus* and the captured French vessel *Tigre,* to keep an eye on the Frenchmen's progress. On March 15 Smith arrived at the harbor at Acre, just in time to prevent the city's evacuation. Smith, dressed as always in flamboyant Oriental costume complete with turban and jeweled scimitar, installed an emigré French nobleman to defend Acre with siege guns Smith had captured from Bonaparte's transports.

The result was that when Bonaparte arrived at Acre, he came under fire from his own artillery, commanded by a former classmate from the École Militaire. For sixty-three fruitless days Bonaparte besieged the city, which Smith kept provisioned from the sea. Frustrated, exhausted, and stalked by the plague, the French fell back to Cairo. Bonaparte's memory of Smith, the first man ever to beat him in battle, would remain bitter. "That man," he would say years later on St. Helena, "made me miss my destiny."

Smith refused to leave it at that. He followed the French down, and a month later landed a small Turkish army into Aboukir Bay. Bonaparte easily crushed it, but with no fleet to challenge Smith's blockade (Nelson had captured the last two French ships which had eluded him at the battle of the Nile), his days as master of Egypt were clearly numbered. To depress him further, Smith allowed a bundle of French newspapers to pass through the blockade, so that Bonaparte could read doleful accounts of his own defeat and France's deteriorating position in Italy and Germany. There were also rumors of a British expeditionary force being organized for Egypt.

Bonaparte made up his mind. He made a stirring speech to his troops,

---

*Bonaparte ordered his men to kill their prisoners with their bayonets to save on ammunition. Almost 4,500 Turkish soldiers were hacked and impaled to death, men who had thought they were surrendering in exchange for their lives.

promising never to abandon them, and was rowed out to the frigate *Muiron* moored in Alexandria harbor. Kléber, the general he left behind, was not fooled. "He's left us with his breeches full of shit," he complained. Sidney Smith had expected him to bolt. He installed his frigates out of sight, hoping to catch Bonaparte when he set out to sea. Unfortunately, they were caught reprovisioning when the *Muiron* left, and so Bonaparte made it through to Toulon.

Had Smith managed to make Bonaparte his prisoner, the history of the age might have been very different. A triumphant Britain would have forced a disorganized and unpopular Directory to make peace. There would have been no Napoleon for historians to contemplate and debate for generations, just a General Bonaparte who rose too high too fast. There would have been no Marengo, no Austerlitz, or Borodino. Certainly no Waterloo or Duke of Wellington, no War of 1812 or Andrew Jackson— and, of course, no Trafalgar.

But there still would have been Nelson. Already his identification with the British nation was so deep that when a highwayman held up the Admiralty's dispatch rider and learned he was carrying the news of the Nile victory, he let him go. "If strangers feel in this manner about you," wrote the Countess Spencer, wife of the First Lord of the Admiralty, "you can imagine how *we* of this house feel about you. . . . Every Briton feels his obligation to you, brave, gallant, immortalized Nelson." When Nelson was wounded on August 1, he had cried out to Berry, "I am killed!" Had he died at Aboukir Bay, in 1798 instead of 1805, Nelson would still have been Britain's greatest war hero. Had Bonaparte been captured that night a year later, Horatio Nelson might easily have taken his place as the dominant personality of the age.

But Smith missed the *Muiron*. Bonaparte was back in France and back in business. On October 10, 1799—or 18 Brumaire on the revolutionary calendar—he launched, and very nearly muffed, a *coup d'état* against the Directory, installing himself as First Consul of the Republic and taking supreme power. The threat of invasion against Britain revived, and the government and public naturally turned to Nelson to defend them.

Yet Nelson was busy squandering his own success. After leaving the *Vanguard*, he had moved in with the Hamiltons to recuperate in their magnificent Palazzo Sessa. The friendship with Sir William soon blossomed into his torrid affair with Emma Hamilton. Sir William was not surprised: after all, he had virtually bought Emma, as if she were one of his prize vases, from his own nephew and then, forty years her senior, made her his wife. He let the affair with Nelson happen. It was, in its own way, an act of patriotism as much as friendship or self-effacement: keeping the navy's finest admiral happy as a contribution to the British war effort.

For Nelson, however, the affair was a mistake. It shattered his marriage and poisoned his reputation. More seriously, it would affect his strategic perspective. It certainly took him out of the action after the Nile. His subordinate James Saumarez, not Nelson, would get the credit for taking Malta. His hated rival Sidney Smith would beat Bonaparte at Acre, while Captain Alexander Cochrane would be the first man ashore when British forces landed in Egypt, in the navy's first major amphibious assault since 1762.

In other respects, too, Nelson's behavior that fall and winter became erratic, almost reckless. It is possible that his wound had affected his judgment. He became locked in a lengthy lawsuit with his own commander in chief, Earl St. Vincent, over prize money. He came to identify himself with Naples and its king, who was emotionally unstable himself, and took a childish delight in the many decorations and awards Ferdinand bestowed on him, including the title Duke of Bronte. An army officer caught sight of him at Leghorn, covered with foreign stars, ribbons, and medals, "more like a prince of an opera than the conqueror of the Nile. It is really melancholy to see a brave and good man, who has deserved well of his country, cut so pitiful a figure."

Nelson also rashly encouraged Ferdinand to risk his kingdom by attacking the French army at Rome. The Neapolitans' initial success under Austrian general Mack turned into defeat and retreat; rebels in Naples declared a republic and had to be put down with brutal violence. There was a bloodbath in the streets—much of it with Nelson's active encouragement. His own fury was directed at an Admiral Caracciolo, whom Ferdinand wanted hanged as a traitor, although Caracciolo pleaded that he had been the victim of circumstances. To the disgust of his officers and sailors, Nelson ordered the wretched man to be hanged from the yardarm of his new flagship, the *Foudroyant.*

Afterward, Caracciolo's body was cut down, weighted with cannonballs, and dumped over the side. Then, in a scene worthy of a Mozart or Rossini opera, King Ferdinand and the Hamiltons came on board to dine. As they chatted and gazed out across the bay, Caracciolo's body suddenly bobbed to the surface—the cannonballs had not been attached properly— and greeted the startled guests with its staring lifeless eyes and bloated face. The king "turned pale, and, letting his spyglass fall on deck, uttered an exclamation of horror." It was not Nelson's finest moment.

The attack on Rome had also upset the balance of power across Italy and put Naples, as well as the Hamiltons, under threat. When Admiral St. Vincent ordered Nelson to take his fleet back across the Mediterranean to help with the siege of Minorca, Nelson point-blank refused, claiming he needed to protect Naples's seaward flank—and incidentally stay close to Emma Hamilton. News of Nelson's disobedience led the Admiralty to send a brusque dispatch ordering him home. On July 11, 1800, Nelson struck his flag and headed back overland for England, bringing the Hamiltons with him, including a very pregnant Emma.

In every European capital they visited—Vienna, Dresden, Hamburg— the story was the same: adoring throngs and official adulation.* In London, too, crowds mobbed him as he walked along the Strand to the Admiralty and Merchant House gave him a presentation sword worth 200 guineas. But his reception at the Admiralty itself was icy, and his presentation to the king was a disaster. Whisperings about his affair with "that Hamilton woman" and her obvious state of pregnancy followed him everywhere. It marred his own homecoming to his wife, Fanny, and it was with a sense of relief that Nelson was able to escape the gathering storm of bad publicity and scandal by hoisting his flag as Vice Admiral of the Blue and second-in-command of the Channel fleet in January 1801. French preparations for invasion across the Channel were again under way; but before that could be confronted, there was the new threat from the Baltic.

The source of the trouble was, improbably enough, the island of Malta in the Mediterranean. Czar Paul III of Russia happened to be Grand Master of the Knights of St. John who had ruled Malta before the French took the island; Bonaparte promised to give Paul back his title and income if he held out against the British. The British, who took the island in 1800, completely ignored Paul's claims. That pushed the mentally unbalanced czar out of the alliance against France and into armed neutrality—the League of Armed Neutrality, to be exact, made up of Sweden and now Russia and quite possibly Denmark. These were nations which had banded together to defy what the British, following John Selden and later, lesser authorities, called Britain's "maritime rights"—the power to

---

*In Vienna they met the composer Franz Josef Haydn, then sixty-eight, and attended a performance of his new Mass in D Minor—known ever since as the Nelson Mass.

search and seize neutral vessels in time of war. Not surprisingly, Britain's insistence on its maritime rights bred resentment even among countries who meant no harm. That insistence had provoked Holland into joining France in the American War of Independence. Now in 1800 Britain had set off a storm of hostility right where it could least afford it.

The Baltic had become a vital center for strategic materials for the Royal Navy. Iron from Sweden and Russia, mast timber from Scandinavia, flax for canvas sails, hemp for rope and cables: interrupting the flow of Baltic trade could undermine Britain's maritime supremacy. On the other hand, provocative action could provide an opening for French diplomacy and aggression. The Danish and Swedish fleets allied with Bonaparte was a scenario no one wanted to face. So Commander in Chief Admiral Hyde Parker chose a prudent course of action. He would sail to the northern tip of Denmark to blockade the sound connecting the Baltic and North Seas, and apply gentle pressure on the Danes not to sign on with the Russians and Swedes.

Nelson scoffed at such restraint. He told Parker the way to deal with any potential Danish threat was to destroy its fleet. Sail straight into Copenhagen harbor and give the Danes forty-eight hours to reject Russia's offer, he urged; if they failed to answer, blow them out of the water. Parker nervously reminded him that the Danes had some twenty men-of-war and armed hulks in the harbor, along with batteries on the shore, while he had only twelve ships of the line. And what if the Swedes or Russians also showed up? "The more numerous, the better," was Nelson's scornful reply. "I wish they were twice as many."

Although he had his misgivings, Parker was reluctant to contradict the hero of the Nile and agreed to the plan. Meanwhile, a message from the Danish court had arrived: no agreement with Britain. So on March 30 the British fleet entered Copenhagen harbor from the south (the strongest defenses were in the north), while Nelson sent his friend Captain Hardy ahead to take soundings of the crucial channel, the Holland Deep, in preparation for the attack. That night he wrote confidently to Emma, "I think I can annihilate them." On April 2 the fleet weighed anchor and moved in, while Parker watched nervously from his flagship at the entrance of the harbor to the north.

Nelson's plan, as always, was brutally simple. Each British ship, starting with the *Edgar,* would anchor opposite a Danish vessel and open fire. Once her opponent had been overwhelmed by rapid-fire broadsides, the ship was to leapfrog down the Danish line to attack the next ship. Since no Danish warship had fired a shot in anger in eighty-five years, Nelson reckoned the result would be either a slaughter or a quick surrender.

It was neither. In fact, the Danish fought hard and well, although in the end superior British gunnery was, as usual, the final margin of victory. "Here was no maneuvering," Nelson described it later, "it was downright fighting." Nelson had also overestimated the depth of the harbor's shallows. Three of his ships ran aground, including his old *Agamemnon*. Admiral Parker even raised the signal to break off combat, fearing that Nelson was in serious trouble.

But Nelson was as cocky as ever. Even with shot whipping past his head, and men and officers dying before his eyes, he told the officer standing next to him, "I would not be elsewhere for thousands!" Nelson refused to obey Parker's order: "I really do not see the signal," he said, clapping the telescope to his blind eye. By early afternoon virtually every Danish warship was crippled but the Danes still refused to give in. Their shore batteries continued to batter away at Nelson, while his ships were too damaged to evade them. So Nelson drafted a message to the Danish commanders saying that he would set the floating batteries he had taken afire, and let the Danish prisoners on board die, unless the firing stopped.

It was a ruthless gesture worthy of Bonaparte himself (although, unlike Bonaparte, Nelson was probably not really prepared to carry it out). In any case, the Danes at last agreed to a truce, which Nelson quickly negotiated into a formal capitulation. Sixteen Danish vessels were either sunk or on fire, with one, the *Holsteen,* in British hands. The Danes had suffered nearly 40 percent casualties; Nelson's came to 943 killed and wounded, although once again he had not lost a single ship. Copenhagen was Nelson's last victory before Trafalgar, and his closest scrape with real defeat. As Wellington said of Waterloo, it had been "a near-run thing." But it did shatter the League of Armed Neutrality. News of the czar's assassination and the succession of his young son Alexander I completed its demise. The Admiralty proved that nothing succeeds like success, by recalling Parker and replacing him with Nelson. Having made the Baltic safe for the British navy, Nelson returned to England to deal with the invasion threat.

Interestingly, organizing the defense of Britain did not show Nelson at his best. He understood the danger better than some of his colleagues. Earl St. Vincent had said with bold confidence, "I do not say the French cannot come. I only say they cannot come by sea." Nelson saw they could, in fact, if they rowed their transports across in a dead calm while the British fleet sat paralyzed in port. But Nelson always thought in terms of offense. Playing defense, like waiting, bored him and made him restless. He proposed an amphibious attack on the French army's assembly point at Boulogne, "until the whole flotilla be either taken, or totally *annihilated*" (fast becoming his favorite word). The French admiral in charge, La Touche-Tréville, fully expected him and stationed infantry as well as his gun crews on his ships blocking the entrance to the harbor, and then chained the vessels together. Nelson's attack was a dismal failure. His young protégé, Captain Edward Parker, lost a leg, and forty-four were dead and 126 wounded, all without damaging a single French transport.

"It is not given to us to command success," St. Vincent told him, by way of consolation. But the humiliation of defeat, his first ever, and the possibility that young Parker might die because of his mistake, was an agony to Nelson. Emma Hamilton had departed for the country; the lingering effects of his Nile wound made him more prone to seasickness than ever. At the end of September, Parker died. "My heart is almost broke," he confessed in a melancholy letter to Emma, "I know not what I am doing." He also wrote to the Admiralty, asking to be relieved of command.

Recent political events fed his pessimism. In March 1801 Pitt had resigned. Nelson, who was a dyed-in-the-wool Tory, called him "the greatest Minister this country has ever had." Yet Pitt's war against revolutionary France had largely been a failure. For eight years he had been trying to piece together a permanent coalition to stop France's domination over the Continent. Britain's command of the sea was still safe, but Pitt could find no European partner able to withstand the French assault by land. General Masséna had beaten back the Russians and Austrians in Switzerland; in 1800 Napoleon had smashed the Austrians again at Marengo, restoring French control over Italy. Austria and Russia were again pulling out of the war. Some were saying, perhaps it was time for Britain to recognize reality and do the same.

Pitt had resigned over opposition to his campaign for Catholic emancipation (his bill to end the slave trade had also gone down to defeat). But the most immediate impact was on foreign policy. The new ministry under Lord Addington opened negotiations with Napoleon. The Treaty of Amiens, when it was formally signed in October 1802, was more a truce than a peace, like that of Aix-la-Chapelle fifty-four years earlier. Britain agreed to hand back some of its key conquests: the Cape Colony, Malta, and withdraw its army from Egypt. But everyone realized that France's imperial ambitions, and Napoleon's, were as unchecked as ever.

The government kept its peacetime army up to strength, almost 130,000 men, and proceeded to refit its fleet.

The years of war on so global and intense a scale had expanded the British navy to unprecedented size and complexity. By 1800 it numbered 729 vessels of all kinds from first-rates like the *Victory* to bomb ketches, including 164 ships of the line of 64 guns or more, and 132 frigates for cruising and convoy duties. Almost all of these were still being serviced, refitted, and rebuilt at the principal royal dockyards in England: Chatham, Woolwich, Deptford, above all Plymouth and Portsmouth. The workload placed an enormous strain on the old dockyard administration and administrators. Making the dockyards more efficient and effective became a top Admiralty priority. Fortunately, new men had taken charge, bringing in new ideas and approaches that would turn the king's dockyards into models of administrative efficiency—one could even say models of the new industrial order.

The change of ministry in 1801 had also brought old Admiral Jervis, now Earl St. Vincent, as First Lord of the Admiralty, the first sailor to sit in that office since Anson. St. Vincent intended to run the Admiralty the way he ran a ship: clean, tight, and taut, obedient to his every command, with the lash or even the yardarm noose for anyone who opposed him. He quarreled with the civilian administrators and ignored the Navy Board, which he, like most sailors, considered "rotten to the core." He saw corruption and fraud everywhere, even where it was not. His official board of enquiry, launched in 1802, antagonized many in and out of the Admiralty and nearly split the ministry in two.

In the short run, St. Vincent's bull-in-a-china-shop approach caused considerable disruption and confusion. When war resumed in 1803, Sir Charles Middleton came out of retirement to smooth things over. But St. Vincent's fearless and uncompromising standards approach did end some of the old abuses, such as private fees, chips,* and kickbacks, that still stood in the way of sound dockyard management. And he stood resolutely beside his brilliant but eccentric Inspector General, Samuel Bentham, who would change not just how the dockyards were run, but the British government itself.

Bentham was the younger brother of philosopher Jeremy Bentham. He had spent considerable time in Russia doing work for Catherine the Great's advisor Count Potemkin, including naval shipbuilding. He returned to

---

*Contractors helping themselves to leftover timber (chips), sometimes as much as three-fifths of every length of rough wood.

England in 1796 to become Inspector General of the Navy Yards and brought major improvements to the navy's physical facilities and equipment. Bentham introduced steam power into the Portsmouth docks and, together with the engineer Marc Isambert Brunel, put in machine-powered tools to make the wooden blocks for the typical man-of-war's 900 or so pulleys—the first mass-production factory in the world. Bentham also installed a rolling mill for the navy's copper plates for sheathing its hulls, turning out more than 300,000 plates a year.

Bentham also challenged the old collective decision making that had governed the Navy Board since Pepys's time. Bentham saw it only as an excuse for avoiding action and for administrative logrolling. He pushed instead the idea of individual responsibility and accountability, allowing (or forcing) navy administrators to make decisions on their own, based on the good of the navy—what Jeremy Bentham would call "the greatest good for the greatest number." Indeed, Jeremy Bentham's utilitarian philosophy of "bureaucracy," a term he coined, would simply be a running commentary on his younger brother's work in the navy yards.

Samuel Bentham's efforts aroused too much opposition from vested interests; in 1807 his post was abolished. But the principle of individual accountability for administrators would force open the door to the civil service reforms of the Victorian age. In 1832, the Navy Board would disappear, its responsibilities transferred to individual members of the Admiralty—a belated triumph for the Benthamite approach.

None of this, of course, affected Nelson. He had used the coming of peace to seek some domestic peace of his own, in the country house Emma had found for them in the village of Merton in Surrey. Merton Place was just an hour's ride from the Admiralty and close to the Portsmouth Road. There his illegitimate daughter Horatia was born, and there he and Emma learned of the death of her husband in April 1803. Nelson was now completely estranged from his wife, Fanny—her letters to him imploring him to come home were returned to her unread—and whatever domestic tranquility he found at Merton Place was always overshadowed by the simmering disapproval of his conduct by elevated society, if not by the British public at large.

As Baron Nelson, however, he could take his seat in the House of Lords and he even gave a couple of speeches. Emma (who did not attend) was ecstatic, but everyone else agreed it was a disaster. "How can Ministers allow such a fool to speak in their defense?" was the reaction of

William Huskisson, former under-secretary for war, while even Nelson's friend Hardy had to agree: "I am sorry for it and I am fully convinced that sailors should not talk too much."

The truth was Nelson was out of his element. His element was war, the bloodier and fiercer the better. Only war, or preparation for war, brought out his great talents and abilities. Without it, Nelson tended to lapse into a fatuous fog, full of arrogant poses and self-important airs, of the kind which so repulsed the Duke of Wellington when they met briefly at the Admiralty. With his black cocked hat, his stars and medals, and his missing right arm, Nelson was now the most instantly recognizable public figure in Britain, the object of veneration for millions of Englishmen. Yet it meant nothing. The fame he had craved only made him uncomfortable: "How I hate to be stared at!" he confessed to Emma. For all his efforts to settle into Merton Place, supervising the work in the garden and dandling his daughter on his knee, it was battle he yearned for.

Happily for him, it was not far away. War clouds were already gathering on the horizon. Nelson was approaching the final showdown with his great rival. This was not some admiral in the French navy: there was none who dared confront him. His one worthy rival now was Napoleon Bonaparte.

* * *

The Treaty of Amiens had made Napoleon master of the continent of Europe. Only Britain and its navy still stood in the way of his next goal. Like many great egotists and tyrants, Napoleon believed in destiny and in luck (so did Nelson). But for destiny, he might have been a naval officer himself—even a British navy officer. Instead, destiny meant him to rule the world as no man had since the Roman Caesars.

Good luck, along with his genius, had seen him through every obstacle until now. He supposed they would carry him over this last remaining one as well. So when, inevitably, war with Britain resumed in May of 1803 (the pretext was Britain's refusal to evacuate Malta as promised), Napoleon focused his energies on the achievement that had eluded everyone since William the Conqueror: the invasion and defeat of Britain.

"The Channel is a ditch which one can jump whenever one is bold enough to try," he self-confidently told his generals. He threw all his powerful concentration and energy into the task. Like Philip II two centuries earlier, he summoned all the resources of his continental empire. Napoleon assembled at Boulogne the battle-hardened veterans of a dozen campaigns into a force of 160,000 men, which he dubbed the Grand Army. He poured over maps and chose the location for his beachhead landing: the northeast coast between Deal and Ramsgate, where his invasion force could anchor in the Downs in the shelter of the Goodwin Sands. He had his engineers design special boats that could get across the Channel in a dead calm—he realized, as Nelson had, that this was France's best chance for an invasion—and ordered the forests of France denuded to build them. Engineers began work on an enormous stone breakwater in Boulogne harbor so that the 1,400 or so vessels Bonaparte would need could get out on a single tide.

The First Consul was willing to listen to anyone he thought could help. That included a slightly mad American named Robert Fulton who had created a boat powered entirely by steam. It would, he told his French listeners, neutralize Britains' sailing fleet forever. On August 9, 1803, Fulton even did a trial run on the Seine, with a seventy-foot vessel with a steam engine. Thanks to bureaucratic fumbling, Napoleon did not get word of Fulton's fabulous machine until the following July. "I have just read the proposal of citizen Fulton," he wrote, "that you sent to me far too late, seeing that it could change the face of the world." It was indeed too late: Fulton was already in England, presenting his ideas to the Admiralty.

In September, Napoleon demanded a full accounting of his order of battle at Boulogne. He was told he had 114,000 men and 7,100 horses in readiness, and 1,400 boats to carry them. He also had 432 cannon, 90,000 balls and shells, 32,000 reserve muskets, 14 million cartridges, 1.3 million firing flints, 1.5 million rations of biscuits, 5,000 live sheep, and nearly a quarter of a million pints of brandy. All he needed now was to assemble a fleet large enough to cover his advance across the Channel.

That meant drawing together his three great naval squadrons at Brest, Rochefort, and Toulon. Stopping the French from doing that had been the principal aim of British naval strategy for almost a century; its method of achieving it had been a constant blockade of all three ports. Breaking that blockade would demand tremendous skill and finesse. Yet everyone recognized the key was Toulon—once again the center of action. Napoleon had his best admiral there, La Touche-Tréville, who would also command the united invasion fleet. And Britain had Nelson there, in command of the Mediterranean fleet at the end of July 1803. In fact, he had been named to the post the very same day Great Britain declared war on France.

On May 16, two days after the declaration of war, Nelson had boarded his new flagship at Portsmouth, the HMS *Victory*. Built in the aftermath of the Seven Years' War, she had been the flagship for both his mentors, Hood and Jervis. But it is to Nelson that she is permanently linked, preserved as a virtual memorial to him in Portsmouth today. At 186 feet, the *Victory* was almost twenty feet longer than the first-rates of Pepys's navy. The *Victory* had originally mounted 42-pounders, but these had been replaced in 1778 with more manageable but just as deadly 32-pounders, in addition to twenty-eight 24-pounders, thirty-eight other lighter guns, and two massive 66-pounder carronades in her bows. Altogether they gave the *Victory* a combined broadside of more than a half a ton of flying shot, which her gun crews could deliver at a rate of nearly one a minute.

The *Victory*'s crew of eight hundred would become the most famous man-of-war crew in English history. Their names are engraved in Portsmouth Harbor—although nearly one in ten was a foreigner, drawn from twelve different nationalities. Nelson's officers were typical seafaring stock: his first lieutenant, John Quilliam, was from the Isle of Man and his signal lieutenant, Thomas Pasco, from Cornwall, as was Lieutenant George Bligh, the nephew of the *Bounty*'s captain. *Victory*'s chaplain was Alexander Scott and the surgeon was William Beatty, while Nelson's trusted friend Thomas Hardy took over as captain.

When the *Victory* finally arrived off Toulon on July 29, Nelson had ten ships of the line and three frigates under his command. His goal was, as he put it in his usual style, "to keep the French fleet in check, and if they out to sea, *annihilate* him." To do this, Nelson would use a new kind of blockade, not close but loose—so loose, in fact, that it might tempt the French to break out and then fall into his trap. He also had a tool to help him: the new navy signals.

The old system, in use since James II was Lord High Admiral, had allowed an admiral to communicate to his ships by the placement and color of flags raised and lowered from his flagship's masts. Each denoted one of the articles of his Sailing and Fighting Instructions issued before the battle. Some were standard, such as a red ensign from the main topmast, pointing his captains to the Article for, "sail close-hauled." Some were devised by the admiral for his own specific purpose, the best of which, like Vernon's revolutionary signals, became standard in their turn. But they never let the admiral's captains communicate with *him,* or allowed the admiral to change his plans in the heat of battle. This was why admirals felt constrained to stick to the line ahead formation—at least everyone knew what to do next even if they could not see any signals. It was also why battles so often degenerated into a confused meleé, with no central tactical control or direction.

In 1790, however, Richard Howe introduced a new numerical system for signaling his captains, with ten flags of standard pattern and color (the basis of the International Code of Signals still used by ships today). They could now be used in combination to form more than 260 separate messages, from the admiral to his ships but also now from his ships to the admiral. There was even a signal for telling the admiral his signal had been seen and understood, resolving a confusion that had plagued every naval commander since the Spanish Armada—and which had lost Britain the battle of the Chesapeake, and the American Revolution.

In 1799 the Admiralty had adopted and expanded Howe's system to more than 340 messages. They made communication more responsive than ever, and over greater distances than ever, and gave a flag officer like Nelson unprecedented tactical control over his fleet. By November, Nelson was able to set up a chain of five frigates with the first stationed outside Toulon harbor, each using Howe's signals to send any sighting of the French fleet on to the next until it reached Nelson himself—standing on and off with his battle fleet more than one hundred and fifty miles away.

Although he did not know it, Nelson had just taken the first step in the sequence of events that would lead inevitably to battle and death off Cape Trafalgar almost two years later. A transatlantic game of hide-and-seek was about to begin, far outstripping in range and complexity the one Nelson had played with Admiral Brueys before the Battle of the Nile. This one would involve a vast ocean touching three continents; it would strain the limits of global warfare in the age of sail, just as Trafalgar would test the limits of the British navy's wooden walls.

The year 1804 would play out as a waiting game. Nelson maintained his loose blockade of Toulon without setting foot on land for almost a year; Admiral Tréville occasionally threatened to break out but never did. Admiral William Cornwallis, "Billy Blue" to the rest of the British navy because of his fondness for flying the blue pennant ordering his ships to put to sea at once, maintained a close blockade on the French squadrons at Brest and Rochefort from the Western Approaches off Ushant. Lord Keith kept an eye on the Boulogne invasion fleet from the North Sea.

The French navy, meanwhile, remained at port waiting vainly for a wind to send the British away, even as the French Grand Army continued to gather at Boulogne and other ports facing on the English Channel. It had grown to 160,000 strong, while its supreme commander, Napoleon, had had himself crowned emperor at Notre Dame. "Bonaparte, by whatever name he may choose to call himself," Nelson wrote, "general, consul or emperor—is the same man we have always known, and common disturber of the human race."

On the other side of the Channel, across from the cheering throngs of soldiers waving the tricolor and cheering, *"Vive l'Émpereur,"* Britons were grimly preparing for the worst. The threat of invasion had united Britons as never before. For the first time, Whigs and Tories came together as one. The government built an alternative capital at Weedon in Northamptonshire, complete with army barracks and a pavilion for the royal family,* and continued to fortify their southern coast and raise volunteer regiments. There were more than 410,000 recruits, including 70,000 in Ireland, where a botched insurrection led by Robert Emmet of United Irishmen had once again raised the specter of a French attack from that vulnerable flank.

In fact, Napoleon had weighed that traditional option as a diversion from his main scheme. But in August another event intervened that completely altered his perspective. The admiral at Toulon, La Touche-Tréville, suddenly died. Napoleon had lost his best admiral, and his replacement, Pierre Villeneuve, did not inspire the same confidence. At forty, de Villeneuve was young to be an admiral. He was dedicated to the revolutionary regime: he had renounced his noble origins and the aristocratic "de" in his name to remain in the navy. A trained and dedicated sea officer, alert and brave, he made a superb subordinate. Had he been English, it is easy to see him as one of Nelson's band of brothers.

But as a naval commander, Villeneuve lacked two essential qualities. The first was that he lacked a sense of independent judgment, a willingness to overturn his superiors' plan and follow his own instincts. Napoleon knew next to nothing about sea warfare, while Villeneuve was an experienced veteran. He fought Nelson at the Battle of the Nile; he knew how Nelson's mind worked better than anyone else in the French navy—indeed, he would guess Nelson's strategy at Trafalgar almost exactly. But the truth was that he was afraid of Napoleon, as was almost everyone who served him. He never dared to challenge his orders, even when he knew they were an invitation to disaster.

---

*Remains of which are still there today.

But Villeneuve was also afraid of another man: Horatio Nelson. He had witnessed the terrible destruction Nelson had unleashed at the Nile. It made an indelible impression on his mind, and on his psyche. He knew his captains and men were not as well trained as Nelson's; he knew his allies, the Spanish, were even worse. The limitations of his fleet became the excuse for his own failure of nerve over the next several months. Even when Nelson made mistakes, as he would one after another, Villeneuve could not bring himself to believe it or exploit them. At the end of the day, Villeneuve believed no matter what he did, Nelson would win. This was his second failing. In a crucial sense, he had lost the Battle of Trafalgar the very day he took command.

Napoleon, of course, suffered no such doubts or hesitations. So to finally pull together his fleet, and to enable Villeneuve to break out of Toulon, he had devised an elaborate transatlantic shell game so that each of his separate squadrons could elude the British blockade. Each depended on precise timing and luck of the weather—and since Napoleon was the master of the first, he figured he need not worry about the second. First, the squadron at Rochefort under Admiral Missiessy was to sail to the West Indies, where the squadron at Toulon under Villeneuve would dash through the Straits of Gibraltar to meet him. Then, as the hapless British scrambled after them across the Atlantic, the squadron at Brest under Ganteaume would set sail on November 23 for a diversionary attack on St. Helena, before recrossing the Atlantic to meet Missiessy and Villeneuve on the west coast of France. There the combined French fleet would leave the bewildered British behind and sail on to Boulogne. If winds were favorable, they would escort his Grand Army across the channel. If not, then they would go on through to the Texel in the North Sea, to pick up a Dutch squadron and 25,000 troops for a landing in Ireland. "One of the two operations must succeed," Napoleon said, "and we shall win the war."

It was a plan of Napoleonic scale and ambition. There was only one problem: it was never going to work. The timetable was too complicated and the sequence of rendezvous too precise to survive the uncertainties of weather (unpredictable storms made late autumn was the worst time for sailing in the Atlantic), of wind (which could limit where a fleet could sail more decisively than any enemy force), or the tenacious skill of the British blockades of all three French ports. Napoleon was used to bullying his generals over hard terrain and great distances on land in all kinds of weather. The sea, however, did not bend to human wishes or imperial command, as rulers since King Canute had found.

As a result, naval warfare and sea power had always demanded a delicate combination of organization and discipline on the one hand, and free and independent judgment on the other. Few navies or societies could manage it. The Spanish, the French under the old regime, not even the Dutch, had ever fully mastered it. The British, however, had. Their peculiar evolution as a society and nation had fostered the virtues that had fashioned them into a great maritime power—even as that maritime power fostered those same virtues in the society at large.

By 1804, the Royal Navy had spent nearly a century perfecting a naval strategy that gave it control of the seas around Europe. While Napoleon's ships sat largely idle in harbor, British crews and officers had been standing on and off for the better of a decade, constantly at the ready with continuous drills and gunnery practice. They were battle hardened and combat tested: of seventeen lieutenants and officers on the *Victory*, ten had been in a sea fight at least once. On another ship in his fleet, the *Swiftsure,* every officer had.

Even the crewmen below deck, in their cramped and dim surroundings, felt the power and confidence of the institution behind them. One of them even compared a British man-of-war to a machine, "a set of *human* machinery in which every man is a wheel, a band, or a crank, all moving with wonderful regularity and precision to the will of its machinist—the all powerful Captain." It was a vivid tribute to a tradition of excellence and skill its opponent could never hope to match. The only way Napoleon's plan could work was if someone made a major mistake.

In the event, someone did. It turned out to be Nelson. His overconfidence had left his Mediterranean squadron too far out. On January 17, 1805, Villeneuve saw his chance. On the eleventh bad weather let Missiessy get out of Rochefort and into the Atlantic; on January 7 similar storms gave Villeneuve the same opportunity and he set out heading west for Gibraltar. Nelson was watering at the Maddalena Islands on the coast of Sardinia when he learned what had happened. He proceeded to make his blunder worse by supposing Villeneuve was actually heading east and setting sail for Alexandria. Villeneuve's route for the Atlantic was now wide open; but strong westerly storms set him back and, terrified that Nelson might be catching up behind him, he returned to Toulon. Napoleon was furious. "What is to be done with admirals who hasten home at the first damage they receive?" he fumed.

But Missiessy, at least, was out with five ships of the line and three frigates. His lookouts hailed Martinique on February 20, sailing gingerly past Diamond Rock, where Lieutenant James Maurice and a hundred British seamen had set up an impregnable fortress less than a mile from the French harbor. Captain Hood of Nelson's band of brothers had seized the rock in 1803; with tremendous skill and drive his men had carried guns up sheer 600-foot cliffs—"A hundred or two of them," said an eyewitness of sailors working on land, "with ropes and pulleys, will do more than all your dray horses in London"—to fire on passing French vessels. Diamond Rock had become a symbol of British defiance and of French humiliation. The Admiralty even officially commissioned Maurice's command as HMS *Diamond Rock.* Yet even with five battleships and 3,000 men, Missiessy felt unable to take it. He captured some British merchantmen and raided Dominica and St. Kitts. But he steered clear of the other British islands and let Diamond Rock stand.

The news made Napoleon choke with fury. Once again one of his admirals had failed him, but at least he could now make a final—and critical—change in his shell game plan. He had at his disposal a new ally: Spain had declared war on Britain in December, closing Cádiz and Cartagena to the British fleet. Napoleon sternly ordered Missiessy to wait for Ganteaume, who was to sail out of Brest at once for Ferrol on Spain's northern tip, winding up in Martinique. Then Villeneuve could make his break again, but this time pick up the Spanish fleet from Cádiz. The result would be a fleet of forty French and at least twenty Spanish battleships and a dozen frigates, poised for the final approach to Ushant and the Channel. "Let us be masters of the world," Napoleon had self-confidently told La Touche-Tréville the previous spring. Now he was about to do it.

Nelson's next blunder worked in Napoleon's favor. March 29 repeated the events in January. Villeneuve again took advantage of westerly gales to leave Toulon; two frigates spotted him and reported the news to Nelson. He immediately set sail *in the opposite direction,* still imagining Villeneuve's objective was somewhere in the Mediterranean. It took him a week to realize his mistake, a crucial week. On April 18, Nelson learned Villeneuve had cleared the Straits of Gibraltar almost ten days earlier.

"If this account be true," he told the new British minister in Naples, "much mischief may be apprehended. It kills me, the very thought." To the Admiralty he wrote the same long self-exculpating letter he had done when Napoleon had escaped from Egypt to France. "I hope their Lordships," he said, "will not impute [the mistake] to any want of due attention on my part." On the contrary, Nelson claimed, thanks to his vigilance, "the enemy found it impossible to undertake any expedition into the Mediterranean." He even sent five frigates behind to cruise around Sicily. And all the while, the French were sailing farther and farther west.

If Villeneuve had been a bolder, more resourceful naval commander, he might have used this opportunity to pick up his Spanish allies at Cádiz and then sail north to challenge Cornwallis's blockade of Brest. With Villeneuve attacking from one side and Ganteaume from the other, Cornwallis would have been in a tight spot. But Villeneuve was too concerned with following his master's orders, and still worried about what Nelson was doing. He hurriedly left Cádiz on April 10 and spread sail for the West Indies.

By now, Nelson had finally turned around and was sailing west. "I am late," he confessed, "yet chance may have given them a bad passage and me a good one." In fact, Villeneuve arrived at Martinique to find no one else there. Ganteaume was still trapped in Brest by Cornwallis; Missiessy had missed Napoleon's crucial order to wait for Villeneuve and returned to Rochefort. Villeneuve took on the tasks they were supposed to share, including finally taking Diamond Rock after three days of heavy fighting and preparing to conquer the Windward Islands. Then, on June 8, he learned that Nelson had arrived with fourteen ships of the line. He had seventeen, including six Spanish; but he also figured Nelson would pick up five more ships of the line at Barbados. So, although he had only been in the West Indies for twenty-eight out of the forty days he had promised Napoleon he would stay, Villeneuve set sail back across the Atlantic. Mission failed.

Nelson, meanwhile, was searching frantically for his elusive enemy. "What a race I have run after these fellows," he wrote, "but God is just and I may be repaid for all my moments of anxiety." He knew the one way he could atone for his mistake off Toulon would be to find Villeneuve and destroy him. Yet contradictory information pointed in various directions, all of them wrong. After eight days, he concluded that the French had left again. At Antigua he wrote a dispatch to the Admiralty, saying he hoped to intercept Villeneuve on the way home, and sent the French-built brig *Curieux* under Captain Bettesworth to carry it to England.

The brig was a fast sailer, as Nelson knew, and in less than a week was 900 miles from Antigua. In the morning a lookout called Captain

Bettesworth's attention to a group of sails to their starboard. Bettesworth and his officers watched with growing wonder as the sails resolved themselves into a fleet of seventeen warships. It was Villeneuve, totally unaware of the *Curieux*'s presence and steadily making his way back to the Iberian coast.

Bettesworth was torn. Should he sail back to tell Nelson, or sail on to alert the Admiralty? Hurriedly, he decided for England. He reached Plymouth on July 7 and by first light on the ninth Nelson's dispatch was on the First Lord's desk, along with Bettesworth's news about Villeneuve. Now it was the First Lord Barham's turn to make a fateful decision. Should he act to intercept the Franco-Spanish fleet or hope that Nelson would catch up with them in time? Barham did not hesitate. He ordered Cornwallis to break off his blockade of Brest, while his squadrons patrolling off Ferrol and Rochefort were to unite under Admiral Robert Calder and take up position one hundred miles off Cape Finisterre in the hopes that Villeneuve would sail into their net.

Calder was the next person destiny put in the spotlight—the same Calder who had been Jervis's captain of the *Victory* at the Battle of St. Vincent. Early on the morning of July 22 he spotted Villeneuve's leading ships and drew up his fifteen ships of the line off Cape Ferrol for battle. Under a weak breeze and in a hot steamy haze, the engagement was intense but brief. Calder captured two Spanish vessels, and killed and wounded 640 of Villeneuve's men. But Calder lacked the kind of killer instinct that could turn advantage in battle into annihilation. In short, he lacked the Nelson touch (indeed, in 1798 he had been the one most furious with Nelson for disobeying orders). Calder had kept his fleet together and his casualties light, but Villeneuve was still able to get into Ferrol, where he picked up six more ships as reinforcements.

This news was greeted with horror in England. "There has been the greatest alarm ever known in the city of London," according to Nelson's friend Lord Minto. Calder was excoriated everywhere as a poltroon. The fear now was that Villeneuve might now try for one of the homebound merchant convoys. But what everyone wanted to know was: where was Nelson?

He in fact was making a painfully slow progress back across the Atlantic, like a man running in a nightmare. His mood was black. "Very miserable," he confessed, adding, "which is very foolish." An American schooner had told him it had spotted Villeneuve's fleet; it had no word of Calder's action on July 22 off Cape Ferrol. It was possible Villeneuve might be heading northward to batter his way into Brest, but Nelson thought Villeneuve might choose instead to slip back into the Mediterranean rather than risk a fight.

It was a shrewd guess. Despite his strong position, Pierre Villeneuve was anxious and depressed. He faced fifty-five British battleships scattered between the English Channel and the coast of Spain. Waiting in Brest was a fleet that would have given him equal numbers, with the added possibility of defeating the scattered British squadrons one by one. But doubts plagued his mind, as well as fear of the approaching Nelson. "I am about to sail," he wrote to Paris on August 13, "but I do not know what I should do." If Nelson joined the British fleet, he would be facing seventy-five battleships, not fifty-five; his confidence in his men and his Spanish allies was so low he dreaded facing twenty. "Our naval tactics are antiquated," he wailed, "we know nothing but how to place ourselves in line, and that is just what the enemy wants"—meaning Nelson. Images of British broadsides in the dark and the *Orient* exploding in a piercing blast of light at the Battle of the Nile, were already arising in his mind.

So Villeneuve made the next fateful decision. He decided to sail south, not north, toward Cádiz. Waiting there was Nelson's old friend Cuthbert Collingwood, keeping watch on the port on August 19, with six ships of the line. On August 19, he was surprised, but not dismayed, to see the succession of French and Spanish ships bearing down on the entrance to the harbor. Collingwood moved aside and let them in.

On August 22, Napoleon sent a dispatch to Villeneuve. "I hope you have arrived at Brest," it read. "Weigh, not losing an instant and, with my combined squadrons, enter the Channel. England is ours! We are ready, all is embarked. Support us for 24 hours and it will all be over." Napoleon was right; it was all over. Villeneuve was not at Brest but in Cádiz and Collingwood was deployed to keep him there. A month later, on September 21, he was joined by Robert Calder and his fifteen ships of the line. All they needed now was Nelson, and their entrapment of Villeneuve would be complete.

Yet Nelson was headed for England, not Cádiz. Now that the Villeneuve threat had dissipated, the Admiralty had granted him a brief leave to return home before the final battle. He landed at Portsmouth and reached Merton on August 20. He was mobbed everywhere he went; he had become Britain's greatest hope, her savior. Even his 8,486-mile odyssey from the Mediterranean to the West Indies and back again was being treated as an epic adventure, instead of a desperate attempt to make up for his blunder off Toulon. He spent three weeks at Merton Place with Emma and his daughter pondering his ultimate problem: how to destroy the combined French and Spanish fleet.

When young captain Richard Keats came to visit and walk in the garden, Nelson revealed to him his thinking. "No day can be long enough to arrange a couple of fleets and fight a decisive battle, according to the old system," he said. The old line ahead battle had outlived its usefulness; it gave an enemy too many ways to escape destruction. "I shall form the fleet into three divisions in three lines," he went on. "One division shall be composed of twelve or fourteen of the fastest two-decked ships, which I shall always keep to windward. . . . With the remaining part of the fleet formed in two lines, I shall go at them at once, if I can, about one-third of their line from their leading ship."

Then Nelson stopped and grinned. "What do you think of it?" Without waiting for Keat's answer, Nelson said emphatically, "I'll tell you what I think of it. I think it will surprise and confuse the enemy. They won't know what I am about. It will bring forward a pell-mell battle, and that is what I want."

A pell-mell battle was what every admiral since Blake tried to *avoid*— no way to control the action. But with the new signal system, Nelson could adjust his orders almost instantly while getting feedback direct from the heat of battle. The bond of trust and understanding he always developed with each of his captains would do the rest, "perhaps in a more advantageous manner than if he could have followed my orders." The walk in Merton Place's garden had produced a genuine revolution in naval thinking, a way to give a fleet action the maximum shock to overwhelm the enemy.

Before dawn on September 2, Captain Henry Blackwood arrived with a dispatch case under his arm. Nelson took one look at him and said, "I am sure you bring me news of the French and Spanish fleets and that I shall have to beat them yet." It was Collingwood's report that Villeneuve had returned to Cádiz. The two of them went on to London, where Lord Barham said Nelson should leave for Cádiz in the *Victory* as soon as possible. Nelson agreed. "As Mr. Pitt knows," he said, "it is annihilation that the country wants."

His last dinner at Merton Place was on Thursday, September 12. "Lady Hamilton was in tears all yesterday," observed their guest, Lord Minto, "could not eat and hardly drink and near swooning, all at table."

The next night Nelson climbed aboard a waiting post chaise and spoke his last words to Merton's stable boy: "Be a good boy till I come back again." He reached the George Inn in Portsmouth at six o'clock the next morning. An enormous crowd followed him, as always, with people kneeling and blessing him as he made his way down to the beach and the waiting boat.

The ghosts of Drake, Effingham, Blake, Russell, Anson, Hawke, and Rodney must have followed him—but also Wimbledon, Buckingham, and Byng. Portsmouth had been the embarkation point for some of the Royal Navy's most spectacular victories—but also its worst defeats. Now it was as if all its traditions, experience, and discipline were concentrated in this single rather slight individual; all its achievements in his burning desire to bring his enemy to a final decisive battle. "May the great God, whom I adore," he had written in his personal journal as he rattled along the road to Portsmouth, "enable me to fulfill the expectations of my country."

Nelson swung on board the *Victory* to the shrill whistle of bosun's pipes and stamping of Royal Marines presenting muskets. Under his remaining arm was a copy of the new navy signal book—as decisive an instrument of victory in the coming battle as any ship or cannon. On shore, an eyewitness watched a sailor coming, running up as hard as he could as the ship set out for sea. Someone asked if he had managed to see Nelson before he left. The sailor said, "No, but damn the old bugger, I should like to see him once more." The eyewitness added wryly, "This I suppose to be the ultimate expression of nautical affection."

* * *

On September 28, 1805, the British fleet off Cádiz caught their first sight of the *Victory* as she approached from the west, flying Nelson's flag from her foremast. "Lord Nelson is arrived," wrote Captain Edward Codrington of the *Orion* to his wife. "A sort of general joy has been the consequence."

Codrington had never served with Nelson. Of twenty-seven battleships and four frigates, only eight captains had ever been under Nelson's command, among them Hardy on the *Victory;* Collingwood, now ensconced in the 100-gun *Royal Sovereign;* Thomas Fremantle of the 98-gun *Neptune;* Edward Berry of the *Agamemnon;* and Blackwood, who commanded the frigate *Euryalus.* Only five officers had ever commanded a ship of the line in battle. Yet all of them, band of brothers or not, had total confidence in him.

Captivated by his reputation and charm, even his unorthodox battle plan drew only worshipful admiration and approval. "When I came to explain to them the 'Nelson touch,' it was like an electric shock," Nelson wrote exultingly to Emma Hamilton. "Some shed tears, all approved—It was new—it was singular—it was simple!" One of his officers said to him, "You are, my Lord, surrounded by friends whom you inspire with confidence."

In Cádiz harbor, by contrast, the mood could not have more bleak. Villeneuve was depressed to the point of nervous collapse. "I beg of you to believe that nothing can equal the despair that I am suffering," he wrote to the Minister of the Marine in Paris, "and the horror of the situation in which I find myself." In contrast to the discipline and confidence on British ships, in the French fleet, "the captains have no heart left to do well," said one officer, "attention is not paid to signals, which remain flying at the masthead for two or three hours. Discipline is utterly relaxed."

In contrast to Nelson's band of brothers, Villeneuve was hardly on speaking terms with most of his officers. His vice admiral, Dumanoir, was still miffed that he been passed over when Villeneuve was appointed to command. Rear admiral Magon had been so furious when Villeneuve had refused to fight the British on July 22 that he had cursed him from his quarterdeck on the 74-gun *Algésiras,* and threw his telescope and even his wig, at Villeneuve's flagship. Villeneuve's Spanish allies, Admiral Gravina and his subordinates, were outwardly respectful but silently disapproving. They sensed Villeneuve had led them into a trap from which there was no escape but death.

Villeneuve did have some fighting captains on his side, like Lucas of the *Redoutable* and Infernet of the *Intrépide* (both ships formidable 74s). He had even guessed Nelson's strategy—so exactly, in fact, that after the battle some of the Admiralty thought he must have been tipped off by a spy. But knowing Nelson's plan of attack only increased his pessimism. He sensed he was fighting not just an enormously gifted and bold opponent but an entire institution built on excellence and precision, overloading the odds from the start.

All the same, he told the Minister of Marine on September 24 he was prepared to go to sea to try again for the Channel. But then a new letter arrived from the emperor. Villeneuve was not to head north toward Brest and Boulogne but east, back into the Mediterranean. Napoleon's enemies were gathering again in central Europe; he wanted Villeneuve's fleet to land troops and supplies to cover his extreme right flank. Given the hopes and efforts of the previous two years, the order was like a rebuke, almost a punishment for the fleet and admiral who had let their emperor down. Villeneuve had learned that his replacement as commander of the fleet was already on his way from Madrid. Yet honor demanded he put the best face on the situation as Villeneuve informed his officers of their master's wishes. "I look forward eagerly," he told Paris, "to the moment when I can undertake the new mission entrusted to me."

On October 19, the combined French and Spanish fleet, thirty-three battleships strong, stood out to sea—even though a council of his admirals and captains had voted to stay in harbor rather than face Nelson. "The gaze of the Emperor is upon us," Villeneuve reminded his officers and men, most of whom had never been in a general fleet action. Indeed, many on the Spanish ships had never been to sea in their lives.

The frigate *Sirius* was the first to spot them. It immediately sent the news on to Blackwood's *Euryalus:* "To *Euryalus:* Enemy have their topsails hoisted." It took twenty-six flags to send the message, using Admiral Home Popham's revolutionary new telegraphic signal system. This had been the book tucked under Nelson's arm as he left Portsmouth. It hugely advanced Lord Howe's earlier system by using flags for letters of the alphabet. This allowed for even clearer communication across the fleet, allowing Nelson to send his individual ships where, and even when, he wanted them to go—and to get news almost instantly.

The Euryalus relayed the message on to the next frigate, the *Phoebe,* and so on until it reached the *Mars* forty-eight miles away. Lieutenant William Cumby of the *Bellerophon* then caught the *Mars*'s signal; his captain was planning to dine with Nelson on the *Victory* that very morning. Now Captain Cooke had more exciting news to pass on to his commander in chief: the French were coming.

Nelson had risen early: "What a beautiful day!" he exclaimed in a note to Collingwood. Now the day seemed even brighter with the prospect of battle. He gave the order to his fleet, "General chase, southeast." Twenty-seven ships of the line and four frigates set out to cut off Villeneuve's escape. "What think you, my dearest love?" Blackwood wrote his wife. "At this moment the enemy are coming, and as if determined to have a fair fight. . . . I have time to write to you, and to assure you that to the latest moment of my breath, I shall be as much attached to you as man can be."

On board the *Victory,* Nelson was penning a similar letter to Emma Hamilton. "My dearest beloved Emma, the dear friend of my bosom, the signal has been made that the Enemy's Combined Fleet are coming out of port. We have very little wind, so that I have no hopes of seeing them before tomorrow. May the God of Battles crown my endeavors with success; at all events, I will take care that my name shall ever be most dear to you and Horatia, both of whom I love as much as my own life."

It was not until the twenty-first, that the British finally saw all of Villeneuve's fleet before them, some twenty-one miles northeast of Cape Trafalgar. They were bearing down from windward on the opposite tack to Villeneuve's fleet, which was bunched together in three separate columns. Nelson had not slept that night: he had been busy writing out final instructions for all his captains. At 7:40 that morning, he ordered his frigate captains, including Blackwood, to come aboard to discuss final dispositions. It was during their conference that unexpected news came from one of Collingwood's ships: the French fleet was turning back!

Once he spotted Nelson's fleet, Villeneuve had ordered his ships to wear around north back toward Cádiz, to meet the British threat. Hopeless though he thought his situation was, he preferred to go down fighting rather than be caught in a race he could not win. Some of his officers were less convinced. "The fleet is doomed," Captain Cosme de Chucurra in the lead ship, the *San Juan Nepomuceno,* complained to his officers. "The French admiral does not know his business." However, his ship was now the rearmost, as the French and Spanish slowly and painfully (because of their untrained crews) came onto the same tack as Nelson.

In both fleets the crews were in a frenzy of action: stowing hammocks and stringing anti-splinter nets over the upper deck and throwing any stowed cargo overboard, breaking down bulkheads and cabins to clear the lower gun decks for battle, organizing the orlop deck, the deck above the hold, for the surgeon and his assistants, the "loblolly boys," to handle the crowds of maimed and wounded men there were certain to be that day.

Only the mood on each was different. On the French and Spanish ships, a sense of dread and doom. On the British, excitement and eagerness for combat. Villeneuve and his men were fighting for the sake of honor; Nelson's men were fighting to win. "We scrambled into battle as best we could," wrote one lieutenant, "each man to take his bird." Nelson's charismatic presence was felt everywhere in the fleet. "In fighting under him," a sailor explained, "every man thought himself sure of success." On the *Victory,* Nelson asked Blackwood, who was still on board, how many French prizes they were going to take that day. Blackwood guessed fourteen. "I shall not be satisfied with anything less than twenty," replied Nelson.

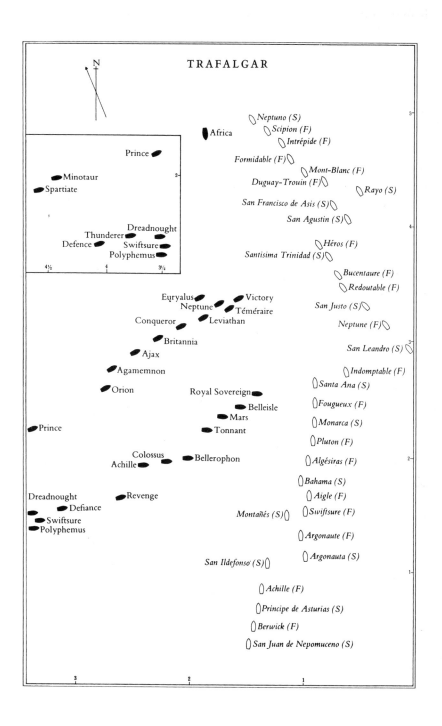

TRAFALGAR

N

Neptuno (S)
Scipion (F)
Intrépide (F)
Africa
Formidable (F)
Mont-Blanc (F)
Duguay-Trouin (F)
Rayo (S)
San Francisco de Asis (S)
San Agustin (S)
Héros (F)
Santisima Trinidad (S)
Bucentaure (F)
Redoutable (F)
San Justo (S)
Neptune (F)
San Leandro (S)
Indomptable (F)
Santa Ana (S)
Fougueux (F)
Monarca (S)
Pluton (F)
Algésiras (F)
Bahama (S)
Aigle (F)
Swiftsure (F)
Argonaute (F)
Argonauta (S)
San Ildefonso (S)
Achille (F)
Principe de Asturias (S)
Berwick (F)
San Juan de Nepomuceno (S)

Prince
Minotaur
Spartiate
Dreadnought
Thunderer
Defence
Swiftsure
Polyphemus

Euryalus
Neptune
Conqueror
Leviathan
Victory
Téméraire
Britannia
Ajax
Agamemnon
Orion
Royal Sovereign
Belleisle
Mars
Tonnant
Prince
Colossus
Achille
Bellerophon
Dreadnought
Defiance
Revenge
Swiftsure
Polyphemus
Montañés (S)

He paced the quarterdeck, as was his habit, and constantly glanced back to watch his ships. He had arranged his fleet into two large groupings, each bearing head-on into Villeneuve's port beam. The first group was led by Collingwood in his *Royal Sovereign,* with the *Belleisle* under Captain Richard Hargood, the *Mars,* the *Tonnant,* the *Bellerophon,* and nine other ships strung out aft of him. The *Victory* led the other, flanked by Fremantle's *Neptune* and Eliab Harvey's 98-gun *Téméraire,* followed by a line of ships, the 74-gun *Spartiate* being the last. It was a vulnerable position for an admiral's flagship, almost recklessly so. He and Collingwood would both be exposed to the broadside of more than two hundred French and Spanish guns until they broke Villeneuve's line, without being able to return fire. With converging fire crippling both the *Victory* and *Royal Sovereign,* an enterprising opponent might then have drawn the rest of the British fleet into the narrowing pocket, then tack to windward to double them up as they tried to pass through.

But Nelson was not facing an enterprising opponent, and he knew his opponent's standards of gunnery: slow (half as fast as his own), inaccurate, and uncertain. It was now 11:30. The tension was mounting, as the Victory was less than three miles from the nearest enemy ship—as it happened, Villeneuve's flagship, the *Bucentaure.*

"I will now amuse the fleet with a signal," Nelson suddenly announced. "Do you not think there is one yet wanting?" In the astonished silence, he suggested, "Nelson confides that every man will do his duty." Someone proposed substituting "England" for "Nelson," and Lieutenant Pasco asked to change "confides" to "expects," because "confides" would have be spelled out, flag by flag, in Popham's signal book. So the final version rose up on *Victory*'s yards and masts. Oddly enough, considering its fame, the message struck the only sour note that entire morning. "I wish Nelson would stop signaling," grumbled Collingwood, "we know well enough what to do." Seamen at their guns were seen scratching their heads and muttering, "England expects every man to do his duty?' Do his duty? I've always done my duty, haven't you, Jack?"

At 11:45 the French and Spanish ships, except the *Bucentaur,* hoisted their colors and opened fire. At 11:50 came the last signal Nelson ever sent: "Engage the enemy more closely." Nelson turned to Blackwood, as Pascoe carried away the signal books: "I can do no more," he said. "We must trust to the great disposer of all events, and to the justice of our cause."

Collingwood's *Royal Sovereign* was the first to engage the French line and came under fire from half a dozen ships at once. Collingwood ordered his men to lie down as they approached—although he, of course, remained standing on the quarterdeck, as calm and imperturbable as ever. "What would Nelson give to be here?" he asked his captain with a smile, as the shots screamed through the rigging and overhead. When one cut down a studding sail, Collingwood asked his first lieutenant to help him gather it up for future use—carefully folding it as if they were still in port.

Hargood on the *Bellelisle* ordered his men to lie down as well, even as he and his marine captain split a bunch of grapes. In ten minutes he had lost thirty men; a dozen lay dying on the deck. His lieutenant asked if they should show their broadside and fire. "No," was Hargood's answer, "we are ordered to go through the line, and go through she shall, by God!"

Finally, the *Royal Sovereign* was close enough to pour out a volley into the stern of the gigantic *Santa Ana* of 112 guns. To her starboard, she also laid out a deadly fire on the *Fougueux,* as the Frenchman desperately tried to bear away. Then Collingwood came around the leeside of the *Santa Ana,* coming so close they became locked together.

As billowing smoke enveloped the scene to starboard, Nelson and the *Victory* were bearing down on a trio of ships: the *Bucentaure, Neptune,* and *Redoutable,* all firing as furiously as they could. A blizzard of shot swept over the flagship. It carried away her fore topmast, yardarm, and mizzen topmast, stove in her launches, and smashed her wheel, making it necessary for her master and a lieutenant steer the rudder from the lower deck—just as Hawkins and Drake had steered their ships. Shot cut Nelson's secretary in two, killed and wounded a dozen marines at his side, while a stray splinter tore off the buckle on Hardy's shoe. "This is too warm work, Hardy, to last for long," Nelson said. But they both stayed on deck.

As one o'clock approached, after suffering more than fifty casualties without firing a shot, the *Victory* was now close enough to pass either the French flagship's bow or stern. "Take your choice," Nelson told Hardy, and the great ship slid into the narrowing gap between the *Bucentaure*'s stern and Captain Lucas's *Redoutable.* As the forecastle passed Villeneuve's great cabin, Hardy ordered the *Victory*'s huge port carronade to fire. A 64-pound cannonball and a keg of five hundred musket balls swept through the admiral's cabin and on down through the *Bucentaure*'s lower decks, killing and maiming her gun crews. The terrible sound of screams arose from the ships while the *Victory*'s other port guns opened fire, the French ship shuddering from the impact. Then, a moment later, the *Redoutable* rammed into the *Victory*'s starboard side, as her sailors threw their grappling hooks and surged forward with a frenzied yell.

On Nelson's leeward side, the battle seemed to be going badly. The *Royal Sovereign* and *Santa Ana* were pounding each other to pieces broadside for broadside, while the *Belleisle* had lost all her masts. The *Mars* behind had been reduced to a wreck, her captain beheaded by a stray shot, and more than seventy men, including two midshipmen and a master's mate, were dead or wounded.

But as the *Mars* drifted away out of control, Charles Tyler's 80-gun *Tonnant* broke through and headed straight for Admiral Magon's flagship, the *Algésiras*. For more than an hour the two ships fought a frenzied battle, so close together the denotations from their cannon set each other on fire. Then the plucky Magon ordered a boarding party to assemble to leap aboard the British ship. The *Tonnant*'s carronades poured out a volley of grapeshot that cut them down dead: one lone French sailor managed to jump the gap, only to be captured by one of *Tonnant*'s lieutenants. Magon himself had taken a musket ball in the arm and a splinter in the thigh, but refused to go below. Then a third shot struck him in the chest, killing him instantly, even as the *Tonnant*'s fire hose was spraying both ships, to keep the flames from enveloping them.

Captain Jean Jacques Lucas of the *Redoutable* stood only four feet ten, but he made up for his size with his blazing courage and determination. He had not trusted his undertrained gun crews to fight broadside for broadside. So when they locked yardarms with the *Victory*, he had ordered them to seize muskets and come up from below to spray bullets across the *Victory*'s main and quarterdeck. With the two ships locked in a death grapple, one of his men in the mizzenmast took aim at the small figure on the enemy ship with one arm and stars on his uniform, and fired.

At 1:35 Nelson was speaking to Hardy when he suddenly fell to his knees. "They are done for me at last," he whispered to his stunned friend. "My backbone is shot through." Hardy ordered his men to carry him below to Dr. Beatty in the orlop deck.

The *Victory* was indeed in serious trouble, even as the entire attack seemed to have stalled. But then a ship came out of the gun smoke to the rescue: Harvey's *Téméraire,* guns blazing as it came aside the *Redoutable* with a decisive crunch. Down went *Redoutable*'s fore and mainmasts and Lucas himself with a severe wound, although he refused to surrender.

Then down came the *Téméraire*'s topmasts, hopelessly entangling both ships. The two then collided with the *Fougueux*, leaving four mighty men-of-war all locked together, each frenziedly firing into the other's vitals—while the *Victory*'s port guns still wreaked havoc on the *Bucentaure*. Then the *Neptune* was pushing through; followed by *Leviathan* and *Conqueror*, each selecting her target and opening fire.

The British tide was finally rising on the leeward side, as well. The *Bellerophon*, "Billy Ruffian" to her crew, veteran of the First of June and the Nile, led the way, smashing past two Spanish warships before heaving to alongside the 74-gun *Aigle. Bellerophon*'s captain was dead, killed in the first forty-five minutes of close action. Her first lieutenant, William Cumby, was now in charge of a ship in as violent peril as any in the British fleet.

The *Bellerophon* and *Aigle* were so close that their gunners were actually fighting hand to hand through the gunports, with some of the Frenchmen throwing in deadly grenades. One killed and wounded twenty-five men; another started a fire in the gunners' storeroom and blew open the door to the magazine. Yelling men rushing through the smoke and gloom with firebuckets managed to put it out before *Bellerophon* exploded, as the *Aigle*'s fire slackened and stopped. Nearby, the *Dreadnought* was coming into action. Within fifteen minutes, she would kill Captain Churucca of the *San Juan Nepomuceno* and force her to strike her colors—fulfilling Churucca's grim prediction in a letter to a friend on the eve of the battle: "If you hear that my ship has been captured, then you know I am dead."

By 2:15 *Bucentaure, Redoutable, Fougueux,* and *Sanctissima Trinidad* were dead in the water, their masts gone and their decks strewn with corpses. The *Victory* was heavily damaged but not crippled; the sturdy old ship was ready to go into battle again. As crewmen cleared the wreckage and got the ship under way, Hardy left the quarterdeck and made his way down to the orlop, where more than two dozen wounded men lay prostrate and bleeding. With them was their admiral, Horatio Nelson.

"Well, Hardy, how goes the battle?" Nelson asked in a faint voice. The Frenchman's bullet had pierced his left shoulder and penetrated his chest into his spine. He was dying, but slowly, and he knew it; slowly enough to see the battle to its conclusion.

"Very well, my Lord," Hardy answered, crouching beside him. "We have got twelve or thirteen of the enemy's ships in our possession."

Nelson clutched his hand. "I hope none of our ships have struck, Hardy."

"No, my Lord, there is no fear of that."

Outside and above, the battle was raging to its climax. After two hours of constant hammering, the *Santa Ana* finally gave up. The *Royal Sovereign* took possession but was in no position to resume battle. The ship had lost more than 150 men and her main and mizzenmasts were gone. But Collingwood was alive and unhurt and he could see to his stern that eleven British and fourteen French and Spanish ships were still fighting it out. *Colossus, Achilles,* and *Revenge* were now in action. *Revenge* lived up to the reputation of its fierce Elizabethan namesake, taking on three ships at once, striking off the *Achille*'s mizzenmast, as *Defiance* and *Polyphemus* drew up for support.

At the other end, the rest of Nelson's column was now engaging Dumanoir's squadron—which, incredibly, had not been in action until now. Fighting together earlier on, they might have routed the stalemated British attack. Now, fighting one on one, they were outgunned and overwhelmed.

The *Intrépide* under Captain Infernet was one of the last to engage, as she fought past the 64-gun *Africa* and took on Codrington's *Orion*. By four o'clock the two ships were locked in a deadly duel, as one after another of the other British ships abandoned their French and Spanish prizes to join in. By five o'clock the *Intrépide* was under fire from seven ships. Infernet strode around the deck with his sword, threatening to kill anyone who spoke of surrender. As the shots flew and men screamed and died, the officer in command of the soldiers on board, a decorated veteran of Marengo, lost his nerve and tried to hide behind Infernet. "Colonel," he exclaimed in mock surprise, "do you think I am made of metal?" and roared with laughter.

However, Infernet had by now lost his wheel as well as his tiller and all his masts. At 5:35 he struck his colors. Minutes later, the stricken *Achille* blew up, "expanding into an enormous globe," said one awestruck eyewitness, "representing, for a few seconds, a prodigious tree in flames, speckled with many dark spots"—pieces of timber and the bodies of her crew suspended in the air. Then nothing but a gathering silence.

The last shots of the Battle of Trafalgar were fired at around six o'clock, after nearly seven hours of continuous fighting. Two hours earlier Horatio Nelson had died in the arms of his heartbroken captain, Thomas Hardy. It was a scene worthy of operatic tragedy; in fact, it would be reproduced in paintings, engravings, woodcuts, porcelain plates, needlework quilts all across Britain and the English-speaking world. Its elements would be embedded in the collective English memory. Nelson bandaged and stripped to the waist, propped against the main beam of the cockpit, Doctors Beatty and Scott on one side, Hardy on the other, and grieving seamen gathered around in the gloom (one man on the *Royal Sovereign* remembered the reaction of his fellow sailors, hardened veterans, when they heard Nelson was dead: "They have done nothing but blast their eyes, and cry, ever since he was killed.")

Before he died, Nelson asked about the final tally of enemy ships. Hardy told him fourteen or fifteen (in fact, it would be eighteen, out of the enemy's thirty-three ships of the line—just two shy of Nelson's goal). "Don't throw me overboard," Nelson begged.

"Oh, no, certainly not," said Hardy, shocked.

"Then you know what to do. And take care of my dear Lady Hamilton, Hardy."

Then Nelson said, "Kiss me, Hardy," as a gesture of farewell. Hardy kissed his forehead and stood for a minute or two in silence as Nelson drew a few last breaths. Hardy was back on deck when Nelson spoke his last words to the chaplain, Dr. Scott: "Doctor, I have not been a *great* sinner." After saying that he wished to leave Emma and Horatia as a legacy for his country, Nelson whispered, "Thank God I have done my duty," and was dead.

He had just lived long enough to learn that he had won the decisive battle he yearned for: the greatest fleet battle of the age of fighting sail. In a body of water not more than a mile and a half square, sixty great men-of-war had slugged it out for control of the oceans. The British navy had suffered more than 449 killed and 1,214 wounded, while inflicting almost ten times that number on the enemy. Losses on the *Victory* alone came to 57 dead and 102 wounded; almost one in four of the captains in the British fleet was either dead or wounded. Yet to those still alive, it had been worth it, despite their admiral's death. In their minds, they had smashed the enemy's fleet as a fighting force and buried any chance of Napoleon's invasion of England. "It makes us feel," as Collingwood said later, "as if the welfare of all England depended on us alone."

What they did not know was that earlier that August Napoleon had already given up his invasion plans. Trouble had been brewing in central Europe with Prussia, Austria, and Russia; he had given orders to strike the camp at Boulogne even as Villeneuve was making his way into Cádiz harbor. As the first shots were fired at Trafalgar, his Grand Army was on the march into Germany. England was already safer than it had been since the outbreak of war in 1793; while Napoleon's position on the continent would be even stronger after his victory over the Austrian and Russian armies under the "glorious sun of Austerlitz" in December.

So in a sense, it had all been for nothing.

CHAPTER SIXTEEN

Succession

To any other nation, the loss of Nelson would have been irreparable;
but in the British fleet off Cádiz, every captain was a Nelson.
—ADMIRAL PIERRE VILLENEUVE

NELSON WAS DEAD. The tiny sloop with the strange name, HMS *Pickle,* bore the news back to England, along with the dispatches describing the overwhelming victory off Cape Trafalgar.* The commander, Lieutenant Lepenotiere, reached the Admiralty at one o'clock on the morning of November 6, and burst in on Lord Barham's secretary who was just finishing up work for the night. "Sir, we have gained a great victory," he said in a choked voice, "but we have lost Lord Nelson."

The news stunned the nation and plunged it into a deep mourning it had not known for any public figure, not even Queen Elizabeth I. "The great and gallant NELSON is no more," read the *Times* headline in bold letters. Another paper exclaimed. "Not a man would not have surrendered every part of the victory (except the honor of Britain) to save the life of Lord Nelson." The defeat of the French fleet was completely overshadowed by the collective sense of grief and loss. "The death of Nelson was felt in England as something more than a national calamity," wrote the poet Robert Southey. "It seemed as if we had never, 'til then, known how deeply we loved and reverenced him." Lady Bessborough confessed to her diary, "I hardly imagined it possible to feel so much grief for a man I did not know."

The grief was more intense, of course, in the navy. Jane Austen's

---

*Blackwood of the *Euryalus* had hoped to have this honor, but it was not to be. However, he would take the captured admiral Villeneuve to England. Villeneuve was paroled back to France a broken man. He wrote to his wife, "The fact is, I have reached a point where life is a disgrace and death a duty." His body was found in his hotel room in Rennes, the victim either of suicide or (some would argue) of the vengeful Napoleon's secret police. Either way, he was Trafalgar's final fatal casualty.

brother Frank was captain of the *Canopus*. He had sailed with Nelson to the West Indies in pursuit of the French fleet, but had missed Trafalgar to reprovision at Gibraltar. He wrote to his fiancée: "I never heard of his equal, nor do I expect to see such a man." For those who called themselves Nelson's band of brothers, it was even more painful. It was said to be the first time anyone had seen Cuthbert Collingwood shed tears; Codrington told his wife that Ralph Hallowell could barely support himself. Someone asked William Hoste, on duty off Algiers, how he was taking the sad news. "I am as well as a man can be who had lost the best friend he ever had."

Meanwhile, the men of the *Victory* prepared to return Nelson's body to England. Surgeon Beatty cut off the hair to give to Lady Hamilton and preserved the body as best he could with brandy, camphor, and myrrh in a water cask. The bosun's mate was too grief-stricken to pipe hands to quarters. "Hang me, I can't do it!" he exclaimed. "To lose him now!" There was a suggestion that the flagship might be too damaged to make the trip back, but her sailors almost mutinied. "We told the Captain as we had brought him out," seaman James Bayley remembered, "we would bring him home."

So with the cask containing his body lashed to the mainmast, and a Royal Marine keeping guard day and night just as if their admiral were still alive, the *Victory* arrived at Portsmouth on December 5, 1805. "If ever there were a hero who merited the honor of a public funeral," declared one newspaper, "it is the pious, the noble and the gallant NELSON." By the time the *Victory* reached the Downs, Beatty and his assistants had put Nelson's body in its full dress uniform and in the casket carved from the mainmast of the French warship *Orient*—the same casket that Ralph Hallowell had given Nelson after the Battle of the Nile as a sick joke.

Except now it was no joke. On Christmas Eve it was sealed with lead and placed in a larger second coffin, then made its way up the Thames to Greenwich Hospital. It lay in state there for three days, drawing more than 30,000 mourners. On January 8, a black-draped funeral barge carried the body up river to the Admiralty, with a two-mile train of barges following in its wake. With the body were two silent mourners: Admiral Peter Parker, who had given Nelson his first ship and had thought of him almost as a son, and Admiral Hood, now almost eighty, who had given him his first independent command.

They landed at Whitehall Stairs in a driving hailstorm. But the next day was clear and calm, as the funeral procession got under way. It was more than a mile and a half long, so long that its head reached St. Paul's Cathedral before the last carriage had pulled out of the Admiralty gates.

The Royal Dragoons rode in front, followed by four regiments of infantry, more than 10,000 soldiers marching in their red uniforms and black shakos to the Dead March from Handel's *Saul* played on fifes and muffled drums. Then came forty-eight crewmen from the *Victory*, bearing the white St. George's ensign that had flown from the mainmast during the battle, and occasionally showing the thronging crowds its gaping shot holes as they passed. Then thirty-one admirals and one hundred sea captains, followed by a contingent of peers and nobles, and then the funeral car itself. Modeled on the hull of the *Victory*, its figurehead was emblazoned FAME, and on its sides were gilt escutcheons bearing the names of ships Nelson had beaten in battle: *San Josef, Orient, Santissima Trinidad,* and Villeneuve's flagship at Trafalgar, *Bucentaure*. Columns in the shape of palm fronds, symbolizing the Nile victory, supported the swaying canopy overhead, while the ensign at the funeral car's stern flew at half-mast.

Nelson had once jokingly said as he went into battle, that it would bring him either "a peerage or Westminster Abbey." Now, England did him one better. The funeral service in St. Paul's lasted four hours. His coffin was then laid in a sarcophagus originally made for Henry VIII's Cardinal Wolsey. At the end, the sailors of the *Victory* were supposed to fold up the battle ensign and place it on the coffin as it was lowered into the crypt. But they did not. Instead, they impulsively tore it up into strips, so each man would have a personal memorial of his beloved admiral. The thousands who watched were stunned; some were outraged. But Edward Codrington's wife, watching in the gallery, and the assembled naval officers approved. As she told her husband afterward, "*That* was Nelson."

Since John Foxe, English Protestantism did not permit the worship of patron saints, or the cult of holy relics, or the saying of masses for the dead. But in 1806 it was ready to embrace a secular martyr. That was Horatio Nelson. The role suited a man who had been a church-going Tory (his great prayer on the eve of Trafalgar would be reprinted all across Britain); a man who had sincerely believed that he was the instrument of God's will, and who had self-consciously lived his life in order to become a hero. "A glorious death is to be envied," he had once said, and he had risked his life accordingly. On the other side, his unorthodox lifestyle (Emma Hamilton was excluded from attending the funeral), his vanity, his arrogance and recklessness, might have eventually destroyed his reputation had he lived.

In death, however, his sins were forgotten, his virtues magnified, his status elevated to that of virtual sainthood—one could even say, an English Christ. His demise at the very moment of triumph turned the quarterdeck of the *Victory* into the nation's Calvary. The last scenes on the orlop deck with Hardy and Beatty became as fixed in the English imagination as the Stations of the Cross for a Roman Catholic; "Kiss me, Hardy" and "Thank God I have done my duty" as familiar as the Seven Last Words. Even at the time, some pointed to the parallel between the twelve in the band of brothers and the twelve Apostles. It was not difficult for sympathetic biographers to turn Emma Hamilton into a slightly louche Mary Magdalen.

The dead Nelson, "the Immortal Memory," would become a crucial part of the fabric of national culture. Today, there are still more than fifty streets, squares, terraces, passages, and alleyways named for Nelson in London alone, and the great column in Trafalgar Square looms overhead, the familiar one-armed figure in the cocked hat gazing impassively down at the Admiralty across the road. Not Wellington, not Gordon or Kitchener, not even Winston Churchill, would become so all-embracing a symbol of how Englishmen wanted to see themselves and the virtues they sought to uphold—nor would they be so symbolic of Britain's dependence on the Royal Navy for its power and greatness.

The navy itself became a kind of Nelson shrine. It repainted all its ships into the colors he had personally chosen for the *Victory*: black with yellow squares around the portholes. October 21 became an official day of naval celebration and mourning, with chaplains opening services with the words: "We are also met together to give thanks for the life of Viscount Horatio Nelson." When the uniform for Royal Navy seamen was first introduced in 1857, it was widely, if incorrectly, believed that its black hat band was a badge of mourning and that the three tabs on the sleeve symbolized his three great victories at the Nile, Copenhagen, and Trafalgar.

His every action and command would be studied and hailed as inspired genius, his every word treated as Holy Writ. The needless risks and reckless gambles he often ran became acts of superior vision and intuition. In short, Nelson in death could do no wrong; those who criticized or did differently at the time, could do no right. His posthumous hold on the institution he had loved and served would be one of the most arresting features of the modern British navy. It would inspire, uplift, and unify; it would give the navy a common identity, one that touched the very heart of the nation. But as time went on, it would also shackle, blind, and blinker. As Joseph Conrad observed, "He is a terrible ancestor." From this point on, Nelson became the navy's ancestor, for better or worse—a legacy without parallel or mercy.

And although no one wanted to admit it, the truth was that Trafalgar, for all its drama, had not altered the larger picture. It was Napoleon's change of plans in August, not the battle, that had lifted the threat of invasion. He remained the master of Europe; indeed, the victories at Ulm and Austerlitz made him even more so. At sea, sixteen French and Spanish ships had escaped back to Cádiz and were ready to fight again, while Napoleon's dockyards soon replaced the ones he had lost. With thirteen ships of the line, the Brest squadron was still a formidable force. The possibility it might yet unite with the squadrons in Toulon and Cádiz remained a serious worry. The post-Trafalgar British fleet would face challenges as daunting and complex as it ever had, over distances and in regions of the world that stretched even its resources to the ultimate limit.

Fortunately, the British navy soon discovered, somewhat to its own surprise, it could do without Nelson. After the Age of Nelson, there followed what could almost be called the Age of Nelson*s*, as a series of bold and brilliant naval commanders stepped forward and won the war he had left unfinished.

They began with Nelson's own band of brothers. Troubridge was dead, drowned when his flagship *Blenheim* went down in a storm off Madagascar—"I shall never see Troubridge's like again," said Admiral St. Vincent. "I loved that invaluable man"—and Ball died of fever in Malta in 1809. But James Saumarez, who in 1801 had won the *first* battle near Cape Trafalgar at Algeciras by destroying three Spanish three-deckers and capturing a French 74, although outnumbered two to one, took over the *Victory* as commander in chief of the Baltic squadron. By dint of blockade and patrols, Saumarez would frustrate Napoleon's ambitions in northern Europe. Collingwood, now commander in chief of the Mediterranean squadron, did the same in southern Europe, skillfully maintaining the crucial blockades of Cádiz and Toulon until the constant strain undermined his health (he died in 1810).

Samuel Hood lost an arm in action in 1806 but served with distinction at the second battle of Copenhagen and as Saumarez's second-in-command in the Baltic. He was a beloved by his men as Nelson had been by his: "You would have really thought that every man in the ship was his brother," remarked one eyewitness. In 1809 he became a baronet and was briefly reunited with Hallowell, Fremantle, and Blackwood in the Mediterranean fleet. William Hoste scored a brilliant victory over a French squadron at Lissa, in which he unfurled the famous signal, "Remember Nelson." As for Hardy, he went on to command various squadrons in the Atlantic, including the Halifax station during the War of 1812, and eventually rose to become First Lord of the Admiralty. Taken together, the band of brothers formed a living legacy for the British navy. Direct descendants of five—Hood, Fremantle, Blackwood, Thompson, and Troubridge—would be naval officers on the eve of World War I.

Others were just as good, even better. Richard Strachan caught up with the remainder of Admiral Dumanoir's squadron from Trafalgar two weeks after the battle and bagged all four ships. Admiral Home Popham, who invented the alphabetic signal code that had revolutionized battle at Trafalgar and after, would together with David Baird retake the Cape Colony, making it the key base for operations in the South Atlantic. They then sailed on to take Buenos Aires. Admiral John Duckworth encountered a squadron from the Brest fleet off Santo Domingo in early 1806 and destroyed it in true Nelson fashion, sinking or running aground five ships of the line.

There was still the irrepressible Sidney Smith, who led an amphibious expedition to Calabria in 1807 that proved that British soldiers could beat a superior force of Napoleon's men in battle—a lesson not lost on army officers like Arthur Wellesley, the future Duke of Wellington. Smith then took charge of the South American station, although quarrels with the English minister there led to his recall in the summer of 1809. In 1810 he became a rear admiral; in July 1812 he became second-in-command in the Mediterranean under Lord Exmouth, the former Edward Pellew. Earlier Pellew had taken a squadron into the Pacific and conquered Java from the Dutch, opening the way for the founding of Singapore.

Then there was Thomas Cochrane, Lord Dundonald, after Pellew the most brilliant frigate commander of the age and the master of small ship tactics and the *ruse de guerre*. He was the nephew of Admiral Alexander Cochrane, who led the naval forces in General Abercrombie's landing in Egypt after the Nile and brilliantly assisted Duckworth in his victory at Santo Domingo. Uncle and nephew were not to everyone's taste. Lord St. Vincent said, "They are mad, romantic, money-getting, and not truth-telling."

But Thomas Cochrane would make himself a legend in his little 14-gun sloop the *Speedy*, snapping up merchant prizes all across the western Mediterranean and then outfighting and capturing the Spanish frigate *El Gamo*, although she had outnumbered his crew by six to one, and threw a broadside of 190 pounds to his twenty-eight (Cochrane used to joke he could carry his broadside around in his pocket). With the *El Gamo*, he had his men seize and strike her colors as they boarded, fooling the Spanish into laying down their weapons because they thought their captain had surrendered the ship. Another time, he eluded capture by flying the Danish flag and telling his pursuer he had the plague on board. As he said, "No device can be too minute, even if apparently absurd, provided it have the effect of diverting the enemy's attention whilst you are concentrating your own."

The number of prizes he took on his three-year cruise with the frigate *Imperieuse* made it the single most valuable commission in Royal Navy history. His midshipmen included future admiral Houston Stewart and future naval writer Frederick Marryat, as well as Henry Cobbett, nephew of parliamentary reformer William Cobbett, and William Napier, the nephew of another future admiral and later to be Britain's first ambassador to China. "Well do I recollect the powerful frame of Napier with his claymore," Marryat later wrote, "bounding in advance of his men and cheering them on to victory." As for Cochrane, he was "a sailor every inch of him."

Marryat's bestselling novels turned the fearless, flamboyant Cochrane into the archetype fictional naval hero, the model for both Horatio Hornblower and Patrick O'Brian's Jack Aubrey (the novels also inspired Joseph Conrad). But Cochrane was more than just a self-promoting swashbuckler. As Marryat said, "I never knew any one so careful of the lives of his ship's company as Lord Cochrane, or any one who calculated so closely the risks attending any expedition. Many of the most brilliant achievements were performed without the loss of a single life." A sharp contrast with Nelson, although Cochrane's action in the battle of the Aix Roads in April 1809 was classic Nelson in its boldness and daring, single-handedly destroying three French ships of the line and knocking the Rochefort squadron out of the rest of the war.

So was the quarrel Cochrane had afterward with his commanding admiral, Lord Gambier, whom Cochrane accused of cowardice for not annihilating the rest of the French fleet. Yet it was Gambier whose *Defence* first broke the French line at the Glorious First of June, and who, together with Samuel Hood, led the daring amphibious attack on Copenhagen in 1807, which denied Napoleon use of the Danish fleet for the second time in the war.

By then, Napoleon had realized that even with Nelson gone, no conventional naval strategy was going to break this British navy's grip. Theoretically, at least, the fleets of France and its allies should have

outnumbered the British fleet by 160 battleships to 110. Practically, however, they were too scattered, and too hemmed in by the British blockade,
to ever combine into an effective force. So Napoleon announced he
would instead "conquer the sea by the land." If Britain's trade was the life
blood of the nation, including its government and navy, then Napoleon
would choke that trade until Britain no longer had the will or resources to
fight. He would beat the British navy before it left port.

Of course, his predecessors in the Committee of Public Safety and in
the Directory, even Napoleon himself, had tried to do this with the standard *guerre de course,* but the results had been disappointing. Altogether,
French privateers and cruising frigates and ships of the line would take
more than 11,000 British merchantmen from 1793 to 1815. Yet that was
only 2.5 percent of Britain's total shipping, while the British merchant
fleet actually grew over the same period, and the port of London alone
saw more than 14,000 ships come and go every year. At the same time,
the British navy's blockade had incapacitated the merchant fleet of nearly
every country facing the Mediterranean, Atlantic, or Baltic. By 1806, the
only way a desperate Europe could get its overseas exports, even food, was
in British bottoms. The French war on British trade had, ironically,
turned the British merchant marine into the grocers of Europe, even as
the Admiralty's convoy system eventually defeated the *guerre de course.*

Parliament's Convoy Act of 1798, renewed and expanded in 1803,
made every British merchantman engaged in foreign trade except those
from the East India Company, which organized its own armed convoys,
the Hudson's Bay Company, or those fast and sleek enough to outrun any
privateer, sail under the protection of an armed convoy. Every spring hundreds of British ships would gather at the Nore or the Portsmouth road
under the watchful eye of their navy escorts, to make for points west or
east. Keeping track of the convoys' routes, and which ships should be sailing where, represented an administrative nightmare. Fortunately, the
Admiralty had a partner in Lloyd's of London, whose *Lloyd's Register,* begun
in the 1760s, kept track of virtually every ship with a cargo worth insur-
ing. Together the men of Lloyd's and the Admiralty planned everything:
the convoys' composition and routes, their ports of call, eventually even
their balancing of Britain's exports and imports. It was a bureaucratic triumph for the Admiralty and gave the government for the first time a
sense of British trade as a manageable whole. It also made Lloyd's the
umpire of the world's maritime commerce, right down to today.

For the truth was that the wars of the French Revolution grew

Britain's economy as never before. Trade boomed in 1798–1802 as the navy's control over the Mediterranean and the captured French colonies in the West Indies opened key new markets for the goods of the Industrial Revolution. In the Far East, another addictive substance was playing the same role sugar had in expanding the Atlantic economy, namely tea. In the seventeenth century it had been a great luxury. Samuel Pepys thought drinking a cup momentous enough to record in his diary. But with the East India Company carefully organizing the traffic with China from its base in India, the exports of tea grew steadily, along with a flow of other goods from the East.

By 1784 tea was part of the diet of all classes of English society. By the time of Trafalgar, Englishmen were consuming more than two pounds per person a year. With the Royal Navy denying France and Holland their trade links to the Far East and India, including capturing Ceylon, Java, and the Cape Colony, the big player in any future east-west trade in Asia was clearly going to be Great Britain. A truly international trading network was taking shape, from the Caribbean to Ceylon and Canton, and all converging in London. All this, while Britain was supposedly engaged in a life-or-death struggle with its archenemy, Napoleon Bonaparte.

So on November 21, 1806, on the heels of his decisive defeat of Prussia at the battle of Jena, Napoleon struck back. The Declaration of Berlin established the outline of what would come to be his Continental System. From that day forward, all European trade with the British Isles would cease. All ports and harbors subject to the French empire and its allies were now shut to British merchants; his next edict ordered all British goods and ships in Europe confiscated. From the Baltic to the Mediterranean and Black Sea, Europe was to become a self-sufficient fortress, impervious to British maritime power while producing all the goods and services it needed—or rather, all the ones Napoleon's armies needed. It was in effect a close blockade from the inside out. Deprived of customers, Napoleon figured, Britain must starve or sue for peace.

The British response was swift and devastating. An executive order from the Privy Council in 1807 proclaimed "All the countries where French influence prevails to exclude the British flag shall have no trade but to and from this country and its allies." Any merchant ship on the high seas headed for Europe and not flying the Union Jack would now be seized or sunk. If Europe wanted anything that had to come from overseas, from luxuries like Chinese porcelain to essential foodstuffs like American grain, it would have to get it from a British merchant or not at all. Cooperate with Napoleon, Britain said in effect, and you will be reduced to poverty. Cooperate with us, on the other hand, and we will find a way to keep you supplied with what you need.

This was a dramatic raising of the stakes. In 1807 the principle of total war had found a new weapon, the total blockade aimed as much, or even more, against civilians as against armies and navies. Napoleon's Continental System, and the British response, had pushed John Hawkin's "method of Jason" to its next level, further even than the *guerre de course*. The object was no longer just to seize a king's revenue or cut off his trade, but to disrupt the normal workings of an entire society, so that public opinion would have to force its government's hand or face ruin. Far from trying to halt revolution and social chaos, the total blockade now deliberately encouraged it as a way to cripple the enemy and its allies. The destinies of other nations would now be pawns in the deadly geopolitical duel between the Elephant and the Whale.

All this was made possible by the fact that the economic systems of Britain and Europe were so much larger and globally connected than in the past. The interdependency that brought affluence and economic growth in the eighteenth century could suddenly be made to implode, triggering worldwide depression. The struggle between France and Britain after 1807 would transform the lives of tens of millions of people around the planet who had no stake in the fate of either nation. This was world war on a truly titanic, and potentially catastrophic, scale: the harbinger of the global conflicts of the twentieth century.

Economic war as total war also dramatically raised the workload for the Royal Navy. It now held the key for victory or defeat, both by shutting down seaborne trade for the entire continent of Europe *and* poking holes in Napoleon's Continental System so that British merchants, and eventually British armies, could get in. Since it was already blockading most of Napoleon's ports and controlled the sea lanes, the first task proved relatively easy—although the navy had to balloon to an unprecedented size of more than nine hundred ships, with two hundred frigates and cruisers.

It was the second task, cracking open Napoleon's Europe, that proved more challenging. Efforts at the southern end, in the eastern Mediterranean, proved disappointing. In 1807 John Duckworth sailed his squadron up the Dardanelles to Constantinople, to keep the Turks out of French clutches or even to sink the Turkish fleet before it could be handed over to Napoleon. Duckworth failed, although he did open the way to seizing the strategically important Ionian Islands in 1809, which allowed Britain to control access to the Adriatic and Aegean. A similar effort at denying Napoleon the Danish fleet for a second time, with Gambier's raid on Copenhagen, did succeed, forcing Napoleon to send troops to invade Denmark and threaten Sweden. It was in order to seal up northern Europe against the British that Napoleon signed his fateful alliance with Czar Alexander I of Russia at Tilsit, making the Baltic the ultimate test of his Continental System.

There were good geopolitical reasons for making the Baltic the fulcrum of his anti-British strategy. Its importance to the British navy, of course; its importance as a British export market as well. But the Baltic Sea was also Russia's "window on the West" and its point of maritime access to the global economic system. As Napoleon's hegemony over Europe expanded eastward, it was increasingly converging on Alexander's plans for expanding Russia's influence westward. By turning the Baltic into a French lake, Napoleon believed he could not only cripple his British nemesis but contain a future Russian one at the same time.

"Sire, I hate the English as much as you do," were Alexander's first words to Napoleon when they met at Tilsit on June 25, 1807. "In that case," Napoleon replied, "peace is established." Yet his Continental System, which looked so grand and impregnable on paper, was already springing leaks, thanks to the British navy. His efforts to get Prussia to close its ports to British goods in 1806 had revealed the extent of the problem. When Prussia agreed, the Royal Navy immediately retaliated by seizing seven hundred Prussian merchant ships in port or at sea and blocking their access to the North Sea. Facing economic collapse, the Prussian king then turned his wrath on Napoleon, rescinding their agreement and ordering the French out. That in turn led to war, Napoleon's trouncing of the Prussian army at Jena and Auerstadt, and the creation of the Continental System in the first place, after his triumphant Grand Army marched into Berlin.

But the dilemma remained. Napoleon could boast that every port, every river estuary and inlet on the continent of Europe now lay within reach of his sword. But they were also within reach of the British navy and its enterprising protégé, the British merchant. Despite Napoleon's best efforts, Englishmen were able to use navy outposts like Malta in the Mediterranean and the German island of Heligoland in the North Sea to run a profitable smuggling trade with the increasingly desperate population of Europe. By 1808, in fact, there were so many British merchants living on Heligoland that they opened a branch of the Chamber of Commerce.

The truth was that the Continental System was backfiring. Far from crippling Britain's economy, 1809 proved to be a boom year, especially for trade in northern Europe—ironically, the very place where Napoleon hoped to do the most damage. After dropping off in 1808, as the shutdown of Baltic ports began to take effect, business picked up again, rising by 1810 to the same level as before Napoleon's ban had gone into effect.

Far from unleashing the economic potential of continental Europe, Napoleon's anti-British embargo was propelling Europe into ruin. The harbors of the great cities facing the North Sea, which had dominated European trade since the Middle Ages, became ghost towns. Fleets of great merchant ships rotted idle in the docks, their owners too terrified of being seized by British warships to go to sea. Amsterdam, Rotterdam, Antwerp, Hamburg, and Bremen were devastated by the economic impasse. So were La Rochelle, Lorient, Bordeaux, Venice, Marseilles, and Genoa—anywhere Napoleon's garrisons and secret police held sway and where the British blockade froze out any outside contact.

Further inland, Europe's incipient industrial revolution faltered and ground to a halt. The British navy's blockade would set the economies of European rivals, including France, back by more than a generation, thus ensuring that Britain would emerge as the leading industrial power in the world when the war ended.

The most glaring gap in Napoleon's system, however, was on the Iberian peninsula. Portugal was an old British ally and, although neutral in this current fight, it maintained cordial trade relations with her former protector. Spain walked a fine line between an opportunistic alliance with Napoleon and avoiding overt hostility toward Britain, so that its traffic from the Americas could continue to flow. In 1807 Napoleon decided to take drastic action. As he told Tallyrand, "The English say they will not respect neutrals at sea; I will not recognize them on land." He sent an army into Portugal to take Lisbon and grab the Portuguese fleet. He was foiled again, however, by his old nemesis, Sir Sidney Smith, who with a squadron of nine battleships scooped up the Portuguese royal family, as well as the entire Portuguese navy, and carried them off to safety in Brazil. A new chapter in Latin American history was about to be written, thanks to Smith's daring action, and it forced Napoleon to make another fateful decision.

Since the death of Philip II, Spain had known nothing but decline, defeat, depression, and humiliation. Once the world's greatest superpower, Spain was now a standing joke on the international stage. Spain had watched England displace it in the New World, strip away key dependencies like Minorca, usurp its colonial trade, and even establish a naval base on Spanish soil at Gibraltar while its own lifeline of silver from America finally dried up and expired (the last official *flota* sailed in 1778). In the eighteenth century Spain had tried to recover her prestige through an alliance with France; that had only brought more defeat and humiliation, most recently at Trafalgar.

Now Napoleon demanded that Spain again bow down to French wishes, and sign on to his Continental System. Spain's merchant classes in Cádiz and Barcelona and Madrid knew this meant their ruin; they seethed as they watched Napoleon bully their wretched King Carlos IV into arresting his own son for treason for opposing the French ultimatum. Yet Carlos himself balked at the final step and so, losing patience, Napoleon ordered three army corps into Spain in February 1808. The people of Madrid responded by forcing King Carlos to abdicate in favor of his son; Napoleon replied by occupying the city and forcing both Bourbons to abdicate in favor of his own brother Joseph.

On May 3, 1808—a day Francisco Goya would commemorate in one of his most famous and powerful paintings—French soldiers fired into the Madrid crowds who had attacked them with any weapons they could find, and executed others *en masse.* As the news spread, the entire country, city and village rose up against the hated French invader. A new kind of war, of soldiers against armed civilians—as the Spanish called them, *guerrilleros*—had begun, with terrible atrocities and murderous reprisals on both sides. Napoleon had opened the Spanish Ulcer, which would consume one-quarter of his army and resources for the next five years—and provide a golden opportunity for the British army and navy to at last carry the war to their enemy.

In August a navy squadron landed an expeditionary force of 9,000 men north of Lisbon. They were under the command of the officer who would give the British army the same reputation for invincibility as the British navy, and rise to a place in public respect almost equal to, but not quite, that of Nelson: Arthur Wellesley, the future Duke of Wellington. In just one month he would drive the French out of Portugal, using a new type of musket, the rifle, and a new type of cannon, directly modeled on the navy's carronade, firing a devastating new anti-personnel artillery charge developed by an army lieutenant named Henry Shrapnel.

As the blue columns of French infantry went down to volleys of rifle fire and hailstorms of exploding shrapnel, General Sir John Moore took over to join up with the insurgent Spanish army and drive to Madrid. Instead, Moore ran afoul of Napoleon, who descended into Spain with his Grand Army and drove the British back to Corunna in Spain's extreme northwest tip. A bloody siege followed that cost Moore his life and might have cost him his army if the navy had not been able to provide vital support and evacuate his bulk of his troops—foreshadowing the role it would play at Dunkirk more than one hundred and thirty years later.

Like Dunkirk for Hitler, Corunna was for Napoleon only an illusory victory. Moore's death meant the return of Wellington, who took over in February 1809 and, with an army of 20,000 well-trained and disciplined soldiers, began to roll back the French tide. Meanwhile, Collingwood had worked out an arrangement with his Spanish counterparts in Cádiz, allowing him to enter the harbor he had been blockading continuously since Trafalgar and dock his fleet. Within months there was a British garrison in Cádiz. It would become the navy's base for operations all along the Iberian coast, supplying and moving Wellington's forces almost at will.

Napoleon's empire was at last coming apart at the seams. The vicious war he waged against Spain's population revealed to the world the true face of his regime. The arrogant mask of glory and imperial pageantry had been stripped away to reveal, as Thomas Cochrane, who saw the suffering firsthand, bitterly said, "The wanton devastation committed by a military power, pretending to high notions of civilization." Spain was not the only example. Napoleon had ruled his entire empire for years as its virtual colonial master, stripping subject nations in central Europe of the resources and men he needed, even as the deprivations of the Continental System and British blockade pushed populations to the brink of despair.

Now, with the Spanish example and Britain's steadfast support before them, people began to dream of liberation. Johann Fichte's *Addresses to the German Nation,* announcing that a people united by culture and language had the right to determine their own destiny, found a ready audience among the students and urban classes of Germany. Similar ideas circulated in Switzerland and Italy. The British blockade was stirring to the surface a new political force in Europe, that of nationalism, which was only waiting for an opportunity to rise up against its hated French oppressor.

The Austrians were the first to try, mobilizing for war in February 1809 with the help of secret British subsidies. Napoleon was able to beat them, but just barely, at Aspern and Wagram that summer, and force the Austrian emperor to give him his daughter Marie Louise in marriage (he quickly and brusquely divorced Josephine to make it happen). He also repulsed a British attack at Walcheren in the Scheldt estuary, although the last British troops did not leave the island until December. But by then the British blockade had unleashed the forces of resentment and nationalism in another part of the world, this time against the British themselves: in the United States of America.

* * *

This was itself a strange twist of events. Since independence America had become a virtual economic dependency of Britain. America was the single largest customer of British industry, taking nearly one-quarter of all Britain's manufacturing exports. The two countries were so close, in fact, that when the French revolutionaries put their embargo on British goods they automatically extended it in 1795 to the Americans. With its merchants open to French attack and no Royal Navy to protect them, America was forced to create its own standing navy. The Congress had authorized six modern frigates to be built, including three with 44 guns and based on the most advanced designs: the *Constitution*, the *President*, and the *United States*. They were twenty feet longer than their British cousins and two to three feet wider in the beam. They also had one continuous upper deck, instead of the usual forecastle and quarterdeck joined by two gangways, which allowed them to mount twenty or so carronades, in addition to thirty 24-pounders in the gun deck below. Fast, heavily armed, and sturdily built (hence the *Constitution*'s nickname "Old Ironsides"), they immediately outclassed any other frigate afloat.

Although the coming of peace with France halted Secretary of the Navy Benjamin Stoddert's more ambitious building program, the frigates made Stoddert, not John Paul Jones, the real founder of the United States Navy. Together with their 38-gun sisters, *Constellation*, *Congress*, and *Chesapeake*, and the 32-gun *Essex*, they gave the Americans the confidence to push their resentments against Britain to the brink of war by the beginning of 1812.

The Royal Navy's impressment at sea of sailors who considered themselves American citizens, but whom the navy considered British subjects and deserters, so often cited as a cause of the War of 1812, was only a part of the story. The real problem was the draconian Order in Council, which empowered the navy to stop and seize American merchantmen as well as those of any other neutral power. Secretary of State James Madison and President Thomas Jefferson foresaw the American merchant marine reduced to ruin, just like those of Holland, Hamburg, Prussia, and every other community squeezed by the British blockade. They countered with their own embargo of British goods, particularly timber, tar, and other naval stores, just as Napoleon was shutting down the British navy's other strategic source in the Baltic.

It was an act of extreme provocation. Yet the Americans felt they had no choice. They had come to resent their dependence on Britain. They believed their future dominion over the North American continent, what Jefferson called their "empire of liberty" and others would later call their "manifest destiny," meant breaking the shackles that still bound them to Britain's economic and military will. By the time Madison took office as president in 1809, he was ready to do a deal with Napoleon for opening the continental blockade to American ships. Napoleon made the appropriate convincing noises; Madison pushed a reluctant Congress to declare war in June 1812, unaware that the British government had already decided to suspend the Order in Council. And so the two English-speaking maritime powers, their economies closely interlinked, found themselves in a war which neither side particularly wanted, but the outcome of which was, unfortunately for the United States, never in doubt.

The Americans did well in the small things, especially their navy. Their super frigates and enterprising privateers like Samuel Nicoll and David Maffet swept the North Atlantic of British shipping, and beat every British warship they met. Commodore John Rodgers in the *President* bested the 36-gun *Belvidera* in a sharp battle on June 23 one hundred miles southwest of Nantucket Shoals, while the *Constitution* outduelled the *Guerrière* and then the *Java* five months later. Stephen Decatur's *United States* scored another spectacular success over the 38-gun *Macedonian* in October.

The humiliation the Royal Navy suffered from these defeats was offset somewhat by HMS *Shannon*'s hard-fought triumph over the *Chesapeake*, after calling her out of Boston harbor in a personal challenge to her captain. It was a bloody fight, with the American captain killed and the British captain, John Broke, seriously wounded, and more than a quarter of *Shannon*'s crew dead or injured. But as the *Shannon* sailed with the captured *Chesapeake* into Halifax harbor, "every housetop and every wharf was crowded with groups of excited people, and as the ships passed, they were greeted with vociferous cheers." Everyone in Britain felt the pride of the *Shannon*'s success, and Broke recovered from his wounds to become a national hero. Humiliation for the Royal Navy, after all, was humiliation for the nation, and teaching the upstart Americans a lesson became a national priority second only to beating "Boney."

So inexorably the wheels of British naval supremacy began to turn. Even with all its commitments in Europe, the Royal Navy was still able to impose a blockade of the entire American seaboard from New England to New Orleans, shutting down even light coastal trade. America's cities reeled from a nation-wide depression, while the country's poorly trained army flubbed its attempt to invade Canada. American sailors, particularly Oliver Perry, managed to score some success on the Great Lakes in 1813. But by then it no longer mattered. The American war had become a permanent sideshow. Back across the Atlantic, Napoleon's empire was entering its death throes, as his invasion of Russia proved his final undoing.

The reason for the invasion was, again, the British navy's success in turning the Continental System into a continental failure. Czar Alexander I had signed on at Tilsit in 1807 because he assumed an alliance with Napoleon would allow him to draw togther his own empire in Eastern Europe. Instead, it virtually wrecked his economy. Industries that had been built around Russia's export trade to England, such as pig iron, collapsed. The ruble fell to one-third of its pre-blockade level while the urban classes in St. Petersburg and Moscow had to make do without their beloved colonial imports, particularly coffee and sugar. Napoleon had also refused to gratify Alexander's ambitions in Turkey, Poland, and the Baltic. And so in December 1810 the Czar opened Russia's ports to neutral shipping. Unless Napoleon could stop him, the Continental System would fall apart.

In December 1810, Napoleon was at the pinnacle of power. His Grand Army had crushed every opponent. The crowned heads and aristocrats of Europe who had once dismissed him as usurper and "the monster" groveled at his feet—the Habsburg emperor had even given him his daughter in marriage. He had rearranged the map of Europe; his brothers and former marshals sat on the thrones of Spain, Holland, Naples, and Sweden. Only the dispatches about Wellington's steady advance along the Iberian peninsula, and the sight of British frigates along every coastline and harbor entrance, reminded him that he was still not master of the world.

Yet the economy of France itself was now a shambles, thanks to the British blockade, as was that of nearly every other European country. The Continental System had failed to break the Royal Navy as he had hoped; he needed some other extreme gesture to convince Britain the struggle was hopeless and to beg for peace. To crush Russia would demonstrate France's resolve to fight to the finish, he told his marshals and advisors. It would also open the door to India. "Essentially all that is needed," he declared, "is a swift stroke of the sword for the entire British mercantile apparatus in the East to collapse."

So even as Napoleon began to assemble his massive army, 675,000 strong, on the banks of the Niemen for its thrust into Russia, his real attention was, as always, focused on Britain. The invasion came on June 23, 1812—less than a week after the United States had declared war on England. It was Napoleon's supreme miscalculation. But it also demonstrated how little he understood the implications of sea power, and how British naval supremacy limited his options, even on a campaign across the landlocked Russian heartland. James Saumarez's continuing blockade of the Baltic meant that while British goods could get through to Alexander's forces, Napoleon's army had no hope of supplying itself from a nearby seaport or coastal base. Everything depended on long overland supply routes, which easily broke down; for essential food and shelter, his men had to rely on outright plunder. Discipline in the Grand Army gave way. By the time it reached Moscow, it was an armed rabble.

Retreating that winter along the burned-over route on which they had advanced completed its destruction. Napoleon abandoned his doomed army on December 5, 1812, just as he had abandoned it in Egypt. By the time he got back to Paris, the news of his calamitous defeat was spreading across Europe. One nation after another rose up against him— Prussia, Austria, Germany, Italy—all with London's encouragement and subsidies. The day of liberation was at hand.

Meanwhile, the British navy was gathering up the remains of Napoleon's continental empire like a shroud. It had already gathered up the French possessions in the Caribbean, and seized the naval bases at Mauritius and Réunion, driving the last French privateers out of the Indian Ocean. The Baltic blockade crippled Napoleon's efforts in Russia, while virtually everything Wellington needed for his advance across Spain, from men and horses to food and ammunition, was brought to him by the Royal Navy. For five years it kept him equipped and supplied, while mopping up points of resistance along the coast. Afterward Wellington wrote, "If anyone wishes to know the history of this war, I will tell them that it is our maritime supremacy [that] gives me the power of maintaining my army while the enemy is unable to do so." By July of 1812 he was in Madrid. Less than a year later, his victory at Victoria drove the last French army back across the Pyrenees. With the help of Lord Exmouth and the Mediterranean squadron, Wellington began to plan the invasion of France from the south.

By 1814 Britain was not only fighting and winning a major war in Spain and another one in America (Admiral Sir George Cockburn led a brilliant amphibious assault on the mid-Atlantic coast, capturing Baltimore and providing logistical support while a British army burned the American capital at Washington). It was not only paying for more than 130,000 sailors and officers serving on more than 700 ships, including 150 ships of the line, and half a million men in arms. It was also providing more than 10 million pounds a year to Austria, Prussia, and Russia, to keep their armies in the field and keep their rulers from making any last-minute deals with Bonaparte. The cost of war had mounted to nearly ten times the amount spent in 1793. Yet Britain was able to pay for it, and grow the national debt to over 800 million pounds, without setting off a political or economic crisis.

On the contrary, Britain's economy was booming. The wheels of the Industrial Revolution were humming ever faster and Britain's landscape was crisscrossed with new roads, bridges, canals, and iron rail tracks to carry its goods to markets and ports. War had given Britain the biggest economy, as well as the biggest navy, in the world, dwarfing the rest of Europe put together.

From that point of view, the events of 1814 and the next year were anticlimactic. Wellington's army entered Bordeaux on February 27, while coalition forces boxed in Napoleon's last remaining army around Paris. On April 6 Napoleon abdicated. The allies dispatched him into exile on the tiny island of Elba in the Mediterranean while diplomats gathered in Vienna to draw up a final peace. At the end of February 1815, Napoleon managed to give the allied naval patrol around Elba the slip and land back in France. On March 20 he was in Paris. On June 12 he left to prevent the junction of the Prussian and British armies under Wellington. On June 15 came his crushing defeat at Waterloo. On June 22 he abdicated in favor of his son and fled for his palace at Malmaison, which he left on the twenty-ninth. For a few days he disappeared completely.

HMS *Bellerophon* of 74 guns had been keeping station in the Aix Roads on the French west coast for almost a month, as part of the blockade of the naval base at Rochefort. It had been a dull uneventful wait—that is, until the morning of July 15, 1815, when the crew watched the ship's barge row up with a short, plump man in a gray greatcoat and black cocked hat sitting in her stern. It was Napoleon. As he clamored aboard, he announced to the *Bellerophon*'s captain, Frederick Maitland, "I have come to throw myself on the protection of your Prince and laws."

It was a fitting finish. The *Bellerophon* had fought at the Glorious First of June, the Nile, and Trafalgar, and paid for it dearly each time. The first battle had cost her all her masts and her captain a leg; the second brought her new captain a severe head wound, while 47 of her officers and men died, and another 143 fell wounded. At Trafalgar another new captain, John Cooke, had lost his life along with 27 others and 123 wounded. Across her decks had poured a river of blood and gore, all in order to defeat the man who now walked those decks as her prisoner—the man who had been the greatest conqueror in European history.

Yet now he was merely an object of curiosity as he roamed the *Bellerophon*. Napoleon said nothing about his own desire to join the Royal Navy as a boy. He merely remarked on the clean decks and orderly discipline as the hands went aloft and they got under way. "What I admire most in your ship," he told Maitland, while sails were set to take him to Plymouth and into captivity, "is the extreme silence and orderly conduct of your men; on board a French ship everyone calls and gives orders, and they gabble like so many geese." He smiled. "Well, gentlemen," he said, "you have the honor of belonging to the bravest and most fortunate nation in the world."

At that moment Maitland and his crew belonged to the most powerful nation in the world as well. Now everyone wanted to see what Britain meant to do with that privilege and position.

*   *   *

The answer would be unveiled many miles away from Plymouth, at the Congress of Vienna in 1814–15. It was a glittering gathering of crowned heads, princes, princelings, diplomats, and statesmen from every corner of Europe to arrange a treaty with France and reestablish the map of Europe that Napoleon and the French Revolution had so violently scrambled. They included Czar Alexander I and the most prestigious statesmen of the age, Tallyrand and Prince Metternich. There were even representatives from the pope and the Sultan of Turkey.

But the two most important figures were both Englishmen born in Ireland. The first was the Duke of Wellington, whose decisive defeat of Napoleon at Waterloo made him the most respected soldier in Europe. The other was Britain's foreign secretary, Lord Castlereagh. Political scientists like to present Prince Metternich as the great architect of European order after 1815. In fact, Metternich's system for a "Europe restored" and a Holy Alliance to hold it together lasted barely thirty years. Castlereagh's version prevented a general war in Europe for a century and has served as the basis of international politics ever since.

It rested on a basic fact: it was Britain's navy that had beaten Napoleon and made Britain the most powerful nation on the planet—and a basic principle. It was a principle Castlereagh had absorbed from his dead friend William Pitt, who first enunciated it in a memorandum drawn up back in 1805, when the prime minister began to consider the face of the future once Napoleon was finally gone, as Pitt knew he one day would be. It was "security not revenge." Europe's war had been with Napoleon, not France. What Europe needed now was peace, based on a new stable international order that would "bring the world back to peaceful habits." A restored France, not a defeated or humiliated one, should be as much a part of that order as Austria, Prussia, Russia, or Britain.

France would have to return to her pre-revolution borders, and to rule by the Bourbons. But Napoleon would be allowed to return to exile—this time exile at a safe distance on St. Helena in the South Atlantic, with a pair of Royal Navy brigs to keep permanent watch over him—and France would pay no indemnities nor give up any territory as punishment for disrupting the life of Europe for a quarter-century. Castlereagh even insisted on giving back all the colonies the British navy had take from France (the one exception being Mauritius, to keep watch over the western approaches to the Indian Ocean). All this was part of achieving a lasting peace in Europe, which also meant peace and security for Britain.

Castlereagh's second goal was to use the Congress of Vienna to create a true and permanent balance of power within Europe itself. "The establishment of a just equilibrium in Europe [is] the first object of my attention," he explained. No single power should ever again be allowed to enjoy unchallenged sway over the Continent. The rise of Russia in the east and any future French ambitions in the west was to be counterbalanced by strong, independent "Great Powers" in the center, which in 1815 meant Austria and Prussia. Later, it would be adapted to include Germany and Italy. Meanwhile, Britain's own security would be safeguarded by a neutral Holland (and after 1830, a neutral Belgium), which no aggressor could ever again use for staging an invasion across the Channel.

As for Britain, the greatest Great Power of all, she was to remain fundamentally *outside* Europe. "The power of Great Britain to do good,"

Castlereagh wrote in 1813, "depends not merely on her resources but her impartiality and the reconciling character of her influence." For Castlereagh believed Britain did have the power to do good. Under the circumstances, Britain could decide to use its unprecedented supremacy to aggrandize its power and dictate terms to its neighbors. Or, alternatively, Britain could use it to umpire the balance of power of Europe and maintain the general peace, while protecting the worldwide bonds of trade and commerce, on which the prosperity of Europe now depended— not to mention Britain itself.

Just as Britain had fought the last twenty years to defend what it saw as a fundamental moral order, so Castlereagh and his successor, George Canning, wanted to make sure that the future world order embraced the same moral principles. Without perhaps knowing it, they were about to make Britain's seaborne empire unlike any empire that preceded it.

The defeat of Napoleon had been a dramatic repudiation of one of the oldest assumptions about government in human history: that maintaining a large standing army, led by a charismatic ruler and serviced by a centralized bureaucracy, was a natural and effective way to organize the political community. Such an organization, it was believed, allowed a community both to defend itself and dominate its neighbors by either physically occupying them or forcing them to pay tribute—the only kind of relations with neighbors worth having. In the final analysis, all power was about domination, and all domination about control of land and territory. This had been the ancient formula for tyranny from Mesopotamia and Persia to Egypt and Rome. It had underpinned the assumptions about empire under Philip II of Spain and Louis XIV of France—not to mention the rule of English kings from the Plantagenets to the Stuarts.

The French Revolution and Napoleon had modernized this formula for land-based empire, and perfected it. They stripped it of its traditional religious trappings and harnessed it to objectively progressive forces— mass mobilization based on ideas about nationalism and citizenship, advanced systems of science and technology, invocations of the General Will, even of the Rights of Man—to pursue an even more impressive and sophisticated grand design. This was the complete domination of the world system—the great interlocking network of trade, commerce, and communication that western Europe had created since the Renaissance and the age of exploration. The stakes were now larger than just Europe, or even Europe's overseas colonies. They were coming to include the entire global community.

This was the great dream of power that Britain had checkmated at Trafalgar, and definitively defeated at Waterloo (although it would revive again in German hands a century or so later). Instead, what emerged after 1815, thanks to the British navy, was a very different view of how the political community could be constituted, and how the world system should be organized.

Instead of a charismatic ruler and his centralized bureaucracy, Britain could offer the world the idea of limited government, with a strong parliamentary sanction and a deep suspicion of authoritarian leadership except in times of crisis. This was a direct legacy of the British navy, since the island kingdom's reliance on maritime strength had made building large standing armies seem unnecessary, even dangerous, rather than a natural part of governance.

Instead of dividing society into those who serve the state—soldiers, courtiers, and bureaucrats—and those who obey it, Britain had made the defining social element the ownership of property. These included mobile and dynamic forms of property associated with commerce and trade, as well as static forms of land ownership. In fact, the more mobile the form of property, the more dynamic and flexible the social structure becomes. This was a point Adam Smith had made in his *Wealth of Nations,* the bible of the new British world order. But at its foundation was the Royal Navy's historical role as the defender of the most valuable and mobile part of the nation's wealth, its overseas trade.

Indeed, trade and commerce had increasingly become Britain's principal relationship with its neighbors and outside world. That, too, could be articulated as a principle for a new global order. Underlying the British championship of Free Trade, of course, was the fact that Britain was bound to be the major beneficiary of any expansion of free markets, since it was the world's leading trading nation. Castlereagh also refused to budge on so-called maritime rights to stop other people's trade in case of war.

But free trade also reflected a belief that relations with other sovereign states can be based on cooperation for reciprocal benefit, rather than aggression, plunder, and conquest. Trade could be something more than just war by other means, as it had been for centuries. Britain's sea power, which had been built around that older harsher principle, could now be used to promote that cooperation for the benefit of all. Again, this is not where England had started. But beginning at the Congress of Vienna, it was where it wanted to lead the world in the future.

Many even at the time were skeptical; others found Castlereagh's altruistic vision laughable. Napoleon, in exile at St. Helena, scoffed: "The peace he has made is the sort of peace he would have made if he had been beaten. What great advantage, what just compensations, has he acquired for his country?" The truth was that Britain had all the advantages it needed or could handle. Having nothing more to win and much to lose, Britain could afford to shed its old pugnacious aggressiveness. It could settle into a conservative, detached position, with a vested interest in world peace, trade, and prosperity. "She was strong enough to discourage aggression in others," as Sir Harold Nicholson once put it, "and vulnerable enough not to practice aggression herself."

At any rate, Castlereagh was determined to stump the critics and take the first positive steps toward this new moral world order. He would begin where the British navy could have the most direct impact, with the very business in which the modern Royal Navy had its ancestral roots: the slave trade.

CHAPTER SEVENTEEN

New World Order

A nobler achievement now awaits us.
—SIR THOMAS FOWELL BUXTON, 1839

L IEUTENANT ROBERT HAGAN had been at sea since he was
thirteen. He was a veteran of the Napoleonic Wars—wars that
started before he was born. As a midshipman he had been on the
ship that brought the Duke of Wellington to Portugal, and as midshipman
and master's mate he fought all through the Peninsular Campaign, only
making his lieutenant's grade after the coming of peace, in October 1816.

Now it was June 1819, and Hagan was in Sierra Leone taking command of the brig *Thistle* as part of a new kind of war, a war against the
slave trade. Indeed, at any given moment for the next forty years, some
twenty or so Royal Navy vessels would be on patrol along the Atlantic
coast of Africa, trying to stop the trade in human cargo with which the
navy's founder, John Hawkins, had launched his career, and on which the
Atlantic economies had been built. Ending that trade would be the first
real test of the Royal Navy in the new world order, the first test of its
transition from the world's dominant military force to world policeman.

All this was the result of the intense lobbying effort foreign minister
Castlereagh had unleashed at the Congress of Vienna. Britain had abolished its own slave trade in 1807. The antislavery campaign of the late eighteenth century had been the most recent fruit of the English Protestant
evangelical tradition, with William Wilberforce, Zachary Macaulay, and
other reformers drawing on support from Tories like William Pitt and
Whigs like Henry Brougham. Its success in the face of strong arguments for
keeping what was a highly profitable business, made it the godmother of all
future social reform movements, from the repeal of the Corn Laws to child
labor laws and slum clearances. It also put Britain in the spotlight as the first
nation to embrace a humanitarian cause against its own economic self-
interest.

Castlereagh had been a late convert to it. But once he was convinced that the slave trade truly was evil, he committed himself heart and soul to wiping it out. He believed Britain could and should use its unprecedented command over the seas to stop it everywhere. At Vienna he persuaded and cajoled four major slave trading powers, France, Holland, Spain, and Portugal, to accept abolition in principle. France at first only agreed to abolish its trade in ten years' time. But then during his Hundred Days' return to power, Napoleon tried to prove his bona fides to the world by banning the trade in all French dominions. After Waterloo, Louis XVIII had little alternative but to uphold the ban "the little corporal" had forced upon him.

Holland agreed to end its trade as the price for getting the East Indies back. Spain and Portugal agreed to be bought out gradually at 400,000 and 300,000 pounds each. Castlereagh also got the Vienna summiteers to sign a general statement condemning the trade, and at least to consider imposing a trade embargo on nations who failed to abolish it—the first invocation of economic sanctions in diplomatic history. He also set up a Conference of Ambassadors to monitor the agreements that had been signed—another diplomatic first—and a series of international admiralty courts to enforce the ban.

But it was Castlereagh's commitment of the Royal Navy to shutting down what Thomas Cochrane's friend Lord Brougham called, "the worst of all crimes ever perpetrated by man," that made history—and gave the diplomatic agreements whatever teeth they had. They became the driving priority of the fledgling Colonial Office and, more reluctantly, the Admiralty. In 1811, even at the height of the wars against Napoleon, there were British warships based at Sierra Leone to enforce the British ban. Freetown, Sierra Leone's capital, was the first settlement in Africa explicitly set up as a home for freed slaves. By 1815 it had grown to 10,000 people.

After Waterloo, the navy's West African station faced a much more daunting task. The war on slavers demanded many of the same skills as the close blockade, but with a very different range of ships. The navy had learned the lessons of its failure to stop American smugglers. Frigates, sloops, two-masted brigs, brigantines, and schooners were small enough to work the palm tree–lined inlets and sluggish river estuaries where slave ships hid and picked up their illicit cargo, and fast enough to run them down in open sea. Ships of the line were useless for this kind of work; only once did a mighty 74 put in a cameo appearance. Instead, the burden of being world policemen would increasingly fall on the Royal Navy's smaller vessels, and the dedicated, independent-minded captains, commanders, and even lieutenants who officered them.

Robert Hagan was one of the earliest and one of the best. From 1819 to 1823, with his 12-gun *Thistle,* he single-handedly ran down and seized more than forty slaving vessels and freed some four thousand human beings—although they were only a fraction of those who were still being carried off across the Atlantic. When he left his command, the grateful merchants of Freetown, black and white, presented him with a 100-guinea ceremonial sword, much like the one Nelson had received after the Nile.

Others, like Captain Leeke of the sloop *Myrmidon,* regularly led their men with cutlass in hand to board an armed slaving vessel at sea or charge a slaver's fort on land. They willingly risked their lives for a cause which, whatever their feelings when they started, became a passion, even an obsession, as they experienced the slave trade firsthand. Boarding one ship, young Thomas Pasley (later an admiral) wrote:

> In my life I have never witnessed anything so shocking. About 450 people were packed into that small vessel as you would pack bales of goods; and diseases of all sorts became rife with them. One hundred had died before she was taken, and they were and are still dying daily. . . . Some children were in the last stages of emaciation and sores. It was dreadful, and so distressing I could have cried.

Even as the West African station expanded to fourteen ships in 1836, and thirty-two by 1847, navy officers found the work deeply frustrating. Death from disease along this mosquito-ridden coast was far more a certainty than death from gunfire. The patrol was also hampered by overly technical rules. Until 1822 it could not seize a slave ship unless there were actually captives on board. This meant often slavers threw their prisoners into the sea before a navy vessel could board them. The navy also faced indifferent judges (every case had to be heard before a judge from the seized ship's nation, who could and often did nullify the vote of the presiding British magistrate) and local African chiefs who worked hand in hand with the slavers. The law even made a navy commander personally liable if a search-and-seizure case went against him. To cap it all, the United States, which still tolerated slavery, flatly refused to allow any of its ships to be searched under any circumstance—a bitter legacy of the

War of 1812. That soon meant that every slaver, no matter what his nationality, was flying the Stars and Stripes.

Studying the raw numbers, it is easy to see the campaign against the slave trade as a failure. Between 1810 and 1849 the Admiralty estimated it freed more than 116,000 slaves. But almost a million more evaded their net. Over the same years the volume of slave traffic actually *increased*. Thanks in part to the ban, a single illegal voyage with 800 captives could net more than 60,000 pounds in gold. As long as slaving could generate profits on this scale, and as along as slave markets like Havana and Zanzibar on Africa's east coast remained open for business, it was impossible to do more than hamper the flow.

But successive British governments, Whig and Tory, simply refused to give up. By the 1840s the navy's African squadron, now thirty-five vessels strong, was starting to have a real impact. In 1833 Britain had abolished slavery in all its possessions, including the West Indies (it had been illegal in Britain since 1772). Britain had also forced other nations to accept an "equipment clause" as part of the slave trade ban, finally allowing ships to be seized and condemned simply for carrying the equipment of the trade, such as shackles in the hold or ventilation gratings between decks, or even just extra water and food casks.

Foreign minister Lord Palmerston then told the British navy it was free to stop and search any ship flying the Stars and Stripes, as long as it had good reason to believe its captain and crew were not actually American nationals. This in turn forced the American government to set up its own anti–slave trade patrol, to stop and inspect its merchants crossing the Atlantic before the British did. It was not until 1862, when President Abraham Lincoln agreed to allow search and seizure by Royal Navy vessels, that this major leak in the slave traffic ban was finally shut down. But Palmerston's forthright action had forced the Americans to confront their own consciences and shifted the diplomatic focus to the slave trade's source of demand, the plantation economies of the Western Hemisphere.

In 1849 Palmerston sent in a flotilla of navy ships to bully Brazil into enforcing the ban it had already signed on paper. When the government in Rio de Janeiro protested, Palmerston replied he was simply helping Brazil to enforce its own laws. Fortunately, he had British public opinion on his side, as well as that of Brazil's middle class, who were fed up with the slave owners' paralyzing grip on their government. In 1850 only eleven slavers slipped through Admiral Reynold's net—and all eleven were later seized, burned, or sunk. Brazil's importation of slaves fell from 24,000 to 3,000 in 1851; by 1853 it had effectively come to an end.

Slavery would persist in Brazil for another thirty years. The last open slave market in the Americas, at Havana, was finally closed down in 1869, thanks again to British pressure. By then, the British navy was shutting down the slave trade along Africa's eastern coast as well.

Indeed, it was the navy's campaign to plug the remaining holes that would lead Britain to annex Lagos in 1861 and to begin opening the so-called Dark Continent to European colonization. At the same time, a new trading economy was springing up along Africa's western shores, with merchants from London and Liverpool carrying in inexpensive manufactured goods and taking away palm oil instead of human beings, to grease the whirling wheels of the Industrial Revolution. The end of West Africa's slave trade, the last surviving servant of the old world system, marked the close of one era. The arrival of direct British rule marked the opening of another. For all its setbacks and occasional hypocrisies, the campaign against the slave trade had succeeded, giving the Royal Navy an altruistic humanitarian gloss it never quite lost. It also marked the triumph of what would come to be known as "gunboat diplomacy," the assertion of Britain's will through the mere appearance of its all-powerful navy.

Its masterful pioneer was Lord Palmerston. His success in bullying Brazil was followed by the Don Pacifico case in 1850. Pacifico, a Portuguese-Jewish merchant born in Gibraltar, had had his life threatened and his house destroyed in an anti-Semitic riot in Athens. Since his birth in Gibraltar made him a British subject, the British government demanded that the Greeks pay restitution. When the Greeks were slow to act, Palmerston dispatched part of the Mediterranean fleet to seize Greek shipping in Athens's port of Piraeus and display its guns across the harbor.

The international outcry was tremendous. France withdrew its ambassador from London; even the House of Lords raised a vote of censure against Palmerston. But Palmerston replied that just as in the days of the Roman Empire, a Roman citizen was free from any unlawful arrest or attack, "so also a British subject, in whatever land he may be, shall feel confident that the watchful eye and strong arm of England will protect him against injustice and wrong." The remark made Palmerston the most popular politician in Britain.

It was more than just British arrogance. A Tory serving in Britain's last Whig administration, Palmerston hated tyranny and oppression in all its forms. It had made him a dedicated enemy of the slave trade—indeed, as prime minister he would threaten to resign rather than give up the struggle against it—and a keen foe of czarist Russia. It also led him to risk his public career for the sake of a Portuguese Jew he had never met but who just happened to be British, and to stand up for a principle that established the political baseline of the new world order, the *Pax Britannica*. There was no longer any place on the planet that was "beyond the line," as far as the British government was concerned. The rule of law was to be upheld everywhere and anywhere British interests were touched. Indeed, anywhere it wished to exert its moral will.

The means to do it, "the watchful eye and strong arm of England," as Palmerston phrased it, was the Royal Navy. Even with its new global responsibilities, the end of the war against Napoleon had shrunk it to a hint of its former bulky self. At the time of Waterloo, it still had ninety-nine ships of the line in commission, and more than 140,000 seamen on the pay lists. Just two years later, in 1817, there were only thirteen active battleships and 19,000 men. Ships that had been the pride of the fleet, like the Collingwood's old flagship *Royal Sovereign,* became mastless hulks, never to sail to sea again. The *Defiance,* brave veteran of Trafalgar, lost her guns and became a hospital ship; the *Bellerophon* a floating prison. Hundreds of others less renowned were laid up or broken up, their cannon rusting in rows by the thousands in the dockyards at Plymouth, Deptford, and Chatham.

For discharged sailors, at least, there was service on Britain's expanding fleet of merchant ships to take up the slack. The coming of peace was far harder on the officers. Literally thousands found themselves without commands or even the prospect of one. As early as 1813, nearly 50 percent of all commissioned officers in the Royal Navy were unemployed. By 1817, that figure was 90 percent, as the bottleneck of promotion slowed to a bare trickle.

Nor was there much prospect of the trend being reversed. The defeat of Napoleon had not only destroyed Britain's greatest naval rival, but the navies of her only other competitors, Spain and Holland. Castlereagh and his successors still adhered to a "two-power" standard in assessing naval strength. But until 1835, and even after, that could be comfortably met by keeping a dozen or so ships of the line anchored in home waters. All the rest of the navy's duties around the globe required only nine battleships, thirty-three frigates, and sixty sloops and brigs, spread out over eight squadrons in North America, South America, the West Indies and East Indies, Gibraltar, Malta, the Cape Colony, and West Africa.

This contraction left the navy dangerously top-heavy. The end of the war against France stranded 242 flag officers atop the Navy List, where there had been sixty-four when it started. Captains found themselves waiting on average ten years between assignments, and of 3,000 lieutenants only eight or nine hundred were being employed at any given time. To secure the precious few available posts, family and political connections counted more than ever. Some lucky men found alternative employment in the one sea service that actually expanded after the war, the Coast Guard, created in 1822 to control the coastal smuggling that burgeoned with the coming of peace. That was what Robert Hagan ended up having to do after he returned from West Africa; for all his exemplary record and courage, he would not make post captain until 1843. Certainly for anyone from an obscure family or the wrong social class, choosing a life in the Royal Navy now might seem a big mistake.

All this posed a potential death blow to the navy's morale, and its tradition of excellence. Its entire character had been shaped by the notion that it would always need *more* officers and more ships to command, because there would always be more wars to fight. For every well-connected nonentity who landed a commission, another was bound to make it on sheer talent. The old system of interest and private patronage had worked because the Admiralty was willing to bend the rules in order to win a war, as when it chose Rodney to take over the West Indies fleet in 1779, or replaced poor Peter Parker with Horatio Nelson. And everyone, rich or poor, born sailor or born idiot, would inevitably face the ultimate test of courage and skill, a battle at sea.

Now the reverse was true. The last of Nelson's band of brothers, Thomas Hardy, died in 1839. That still left an entire generation of men who had been commanders or lieutenants at the time of Trafalgar, men who would serve out their lives in a peacetime navy for the next three decades. Having found their way to the top, they stayed there, usually unemployed, sometimes unemployable. Their sheer numbers prevented others from pressing forward. By 1843, the youngest admiral in the fleet was sixty-five; the average age of the first three hundred captains on the Navy List was sixty.

The navy did not have much alternative. These old sea veterans preserved a nautical knowledge which, if war did come, the navy would desperately need. They were the last generation of officers who knew how to keep a fleet of ships close-hauled in line ahead or how to get them to tack in succession. That was why Edward Codrington, now Admiral Sir Edward Codrington, and Sir William Parker were ordered in 1831 to form a special squadron of eight ships of the line and four frigates to practice these "battle evolutions." Codrington was less than impressed by what he saw and complained of a "falling off of discipline since he had last served afloat . . . which quite astonished him." But ten years later the Admiralty was considering bringing him back out of retirement, in his mid-seventies, to teach the fleet again this vanishing art.

A navy at war had honed skills and instincts no textbook could teach. This was why Thomas Cochrane was put in charge of the West Indies station when he was seventy-six, and why he confidently put his name forward, at age seventy-nine, for command of the Baltic squadron at the outbreak of the Crimean War. The Admiralty thought about giving it to him, too, before turning him down—not because it thought him too old, but because it thought he would be too wild and reckless!

Giants like Codrington and Cochrane still gave the navy of Queen Victoria the fading spirit of the age of Nelson. But no armed service, no institution, could survive at this rate. So to avert a crisis, the Admiralty was forced to take a series of measures which, almost without anyone realizing it, would finally turn the Royal Navy officer into a full-time career professional, a man who met uniform standards of recruitment, service, and efficiency. He was about to shed his last vestiges of private enterprise and amateur spontaneity, his last links to a service Raleigh or Pepys or even Anson might have recognized. His life would now belong to the state; it and no one else would dictate how he got in the navy and how he left it.

It began with the decision in 1847 to get rid of a bloc of two hundred senior but unemployable captains at the top of the Navy List by promoting them to rear admiral and relegating them to half-pay. The old pretense of "Admirals of the Yellow," still in service but without a squadron, gave way to a recognition that "Flag Officer on Half-Pay" meant the end of the line, with half-pay as a kind of retirement pension. Then came the next step: establishing in 1851 a numerical ceiling of active captains at 450. Compulsory retirement, either as Flag Officer on Half-Pay or "Superannuated" or simply "Retired," became a reality by 1852. That same year, the same status of reserve half-pay was extended to lieutenants. The old title of "master and commander" (as distinct from permanent or "post captain") was modified into the formal rank of commander, allowing the navy to promote its best senior lieutenants and distribute them throughout the fleet.

The result flushed out and consolidated the Navy List. In 1842, the number of unemployed post captains was at 85 percent; by 1865 it had dropped to 55 percent, or little more than half. Instead of nearly two-thirds of all navy lieutenants sitting idle, by 1865 they were down to one-fifth. Then, having found a way to control how many officers reached the top of the ladder, the Admiralty set about establishing new rules about how they came in at the bottom. The navy could no longer afford to have its captains bring a half-dozen sons of friends on board every voyage to start their careers in the Royal Navy or enter their own children on the ship's roll to collect their pay, as James Cook had done. Those easy informal days had to end.

The Admiralty began by establishing formal exams (not very rigorous at first) for anyone seeking the rating of midshipman. In 1843 these examinees became known as cadets, and in 1848 the number admitted each year was set at one hundred. There was, however, still no official naval academy to train them. The Royal Naval College at Portsmouth, which had taught the rudiments of naval seamanship to aspiring teenagers since the 1770s (both of Jane Austen's brothers were graduates), closed in 1837. But in 1830 an alternative appeared, which had a profound effect on the future of the Victorian navy and on its evolution as an institution.

HMS *Excellent* was originally tied up in Portsmouth harbor to teach young officers and a select body of able seamen the art of naval gunnery. The choice of ship was fitting: it was the old command of Cuthbert Collingwood, who had demonstrated to the Trafalgar generation how rapid, accurate gunfire was the key to victory at sea. Under Captain Thomas Hastings, HMS *Excellent* became a laboratory for the study of the latest gunnery techniques. Its officers and crew learned mathematics, ballistics, and mechanics, even philosophy. Every year it turned out a crop of master gunners and skilled and eager gunnery officers, who understood their business with scientific precision and who became, by the 1840s, a source of technological innovation throughout the navy. The *Excellent* approach puzzled and alarmed some older admirals.* But formalized professional training had come to stay in the Royal Navy, and with it a new kind of officer. He was the technician, whose expertise and specialized training the navy would need in an increasingly complex world.

---

*There is the famous story of two admirals puzzling over some examination papers from the *Excellent*. "Pray, sir, what is the meaning of the word *impact*?" asked one. "And what in the name of good fortune is meant by initial velocity?" "I'll be hanged if I know," replied the other, "But I'll tell you what I think we had better do—we'll just go at once to Lord de Grey [who was First Lord] and get the *Excellent* paid off."

One area was gunnery, which became particularly vital with the introduction of the explosive shell in the 1830s. No warship used these before that simply because they were considered too dangerous. One mishap in the powder magazine would mean instant self-annihilation, and blowing an enemy ship to pieces at fifty or one hundred yards might blow up one's own ship as well.

But then the French began to experiment with explosive shells in 1824. At the same time, after a half-century in which navy guns had gotten shorter, they got longer again, allowing more accurate fire at a greater and safer range. In 1838 HMS *Excellent*'s Thomas Hastings used explosive shells to demolish the old *Prince Regent* at a range of 1,200 yards. The navy took the hint: explosive shells became standard ordnance that same year. New shells, new guns: the long 32-pounder (standard on ships of the line after 1825), the 68-pounder, followed by the 10-inch gun and the 12-inch gun able to fire a 100-pound shell, were all part of the explosive mix that might upset the balance of naval power, and put the officer who understood them at a premium.

Steam was next. The Admiralty had set up a special commission, with Joseph Banks at its head, to hear Robert Fulton's proposal for a steam-propelled vessel after he arrived from France in 1804. Like Napoleon's Ministry of the Marine, it had turned him down. The navy's resistance to steam power became legendary. When the Admiralty declared that "the introduction of steam power is calculated to strike a fatal blow at the naval supremacy of the Empire," the remark seemed to prove that it was blind to the need for technological change.

Yet at the time its objections were quite sensible. The first steam-powered vessels were paddle steamers. No broadside of guns could be fitted on the ship's side where the paddle wheel was mounted, while a single volley from an enemy ship might disable the paddles and leave her helplessly adrift. The navy had no objections to using steamers as coastal packets and tugs; it even appointed its first Chief Engineer and Inspector of Machinery in 1835. But it also saw no reason to alter the overall profile of its fighting fleet of sail. So in 1840, as Isambart Kingdom Brunel's 10,000-ton *Great Western* was beginning regular transatlantic service and Lloyd's Register listed 720 large seagoing steamships in the British merchant fleet, the Royal Navy had not a single one.

Yet in just five years it would launch the world's first steam battleship, the *Ajax*, and four years after that, in 1849, a screw propeller battleship, the *Agamemnon*. The danger that another country such as France* or the United States might deploy a steam fleet first to challenge Britain's naval supremacy had prodded the Admiralty into action—a pattern that would become all too familiar in the future.

The question was what to do about the engineers who tended these alarming new machines. The first ones brought on board were usually civilians who knew nothing about the navy. That made the Admiralty reluctant to give them any grade except warrant officer (although with much higher pay than the ship's bosun or carpenter). It was only in 1847 that they were deemed worthy to be officers and gentlemen and allowed to enjoy the rank and promotion scale of their counterparts who spent their day above deck and with salt spray, not coal dust, on their cheek.

Since many came out of the urban middle class, more aristocratic and tradition-minded officers still liked to dismiss them as vulgar mechanics. They routinely referred to the lieutenant or the commander in charge of the engine room as "the plumber" or even the "cuckoo in the nest." But there was fear mingled with their contempt. These men looked aloft at their warships' magnificent display of sails, masts, and rigging, the product of centuries of nautical art and all tended with expert and loving care, and wondered how long before it would all have to come down, to be replaced with funnels, ventilators, and choking black clouds of smoke.

They resisted the end of a way of life as best they could. But the Crimean War showed that the steam-powered warship was here to stay, as was the engineering officer. Yet it was not until 1880 that a Royal Naval Engineering College was set up, and no engineering officer, no matter how senior his rank or extensive his experience, was ever allowed to command a navy ship. He still cannot, even today.

Yet an expertise in engineering, like expertise in gunnery, was one way an enterprising and ambitious young officer could stand out from the rest of the pack in the nineteenth-century navy. Another was an interest in science: the navy came to put a premium value on its officers with scientific pursuits, from hydrography and astronomy to botany and geology. More than anyone else, the man behind this new appreciation was John Barrow, permanent First Secretary of the Admiralty for more than forty years. His personal mission was to use the Royal Navy's unchallenged sea power not

---

*France finished its screw propeller battleship, the *Napoleon,* just three months before the *Agamemnon* was launched.

just to patrol the boundaries of a new global order and defend a growing British Empire but also to push forward the frontiers of human knowledge. Under Barrow's influence, the navy's officers and ships became instruments "for the acquisition of knowledge, not for England alone," as he put it, "but for the general benefit of mankind."

• • •

Tall and thin with dark imposing eyes, Barrow was the living link between the age of Cook and the age of Charles Darwin. He was a friend and protégé of Sir Joseph Banks when he entered the Admiralty on the eve of Trafalgar; indeed, he was the last Admiralty official to meet with Nelson before he boarded the *Victory*. Barrow would go on to found the Royal Geographic Society in 1830 and remain in office until almost the eve of the Crimean War, when he was eighty-one. Politically astute but without personal ambition, he would serve thirteen different ministries and a succession of First Lords, Whig and Tory, with the same dedication and skill. He became the prototype modern British civil servant: selfless and hardworking, a master of bureaucratic detail (he gathered together the moldy bundles of documents and scattered papers of the Admiralty's archive and shaped them into the British government's first true Record Office, with his son at its head), yet also a man of cultivated tastes and a wide-ranging knowledge of the world.

It was Barrow who first suggested Napoleon be exiled to St. Helena; Barrow had visited the island himself on his way to China as part of Lord McCartney's famous embassy to Peking in 1792. He wrote books about his travels both in China and South Africa, which made him an easy choice for Fellow of the Royal Society and the acquaintance of worthies such as its president Joseph Banks, royal astronomer Neville Maskeleyne, architect John Rennie, chemist Humphrey Davy, and Hydrographer of the Navy and Cook's old rival, Alexander Dalrymple.* Indeed, it was Barrow who finally saw to it that Dalrymple left the Hydrography Office in 1808, to be replaced by a trio of men—Sir Thomas Hurd, Captain Edward Parry, and Admiral Sir Francis Beaufort—who made Admiralty nautical charts the best and most accurate in the world.

---

*Barrow also wrote the first detailed account of the voyage of the *Bounty*, introducing Victorian readers for the first time to that other Banks protégé, Captain William Bligh, and the notorious mutiny, setting off the storm of controversy and debate that has continued ever since.

But his most dramatic and ambitious project was born in 1817, when Barrow received a report from British whaling captains that the seas around Greenland that year were remarkably free of ice. Barrow argued that this was the perfect opportunity to search once more for a Northwest Passage from the Atlantic to the Pacific, by sailing up through Baffin Bay to the west, while another expedition would try to penetrate the polar seas north of Spitzbergen to the east. The last remaining mystery about the nature of the earth and its oceans might finally be solved.

Barrow's plan links him not just to James Cook but to Martin Frobisher and John Dee—even Richard Chancellor. It put the British navy at the center of the modern age of Arctic exploration. To do the job, he turned to a pair of hardy Scotsmen, naval officers who would not be daunted by subzero temperatures, ice-covered decks and rigging, or miles of impassable ice floes fifty-feet thick. Alexander Buchan (the first man to cross Newfoundland) took charge of an ex-whaler renamed HMS *Dorothea* and the fifth-rate *Trent* for the Spitzbergen expedition. However, it was halted by fierce polar gales and accomplished nothing.

Captain John Ross's expedition with the *Isabella* and *Alexander* managed to get to the far western end of Baffin Bay before Ross turned back, convinced it ended in a cul-de-sac. Barrow was disappointed, but two of the officers with Ross, his nephew Midshipman James Ross and Lieutenant Edward Parry, would carry out a series of daring and dangerous Arctic voyages over the next two decades. Parry alone made five trips between 1818 and 1827, penetrating to longitude 110 degrees West. He was the first captain ever to winter in the polar ice. James Ross would take the explorations southward, discovering the Ross Sea and charting most of the coastline of Antarctica.

However, the most famous, and most ill-fated, of "Barrow's boys" was John Franklin. He had been a nineteen-year-old midshipman on the *Bellerophon* at the battle of Trafalgar and served as lieutenant on Buchan's failed voyage from Spitzbergen. Franklin made his first trip to the Arctic in 1819, to try to find the Northwest Passage by traveling over land. His party of fifteen French-Canadian *voyageurs,* four Royal Navy officers, including a doctor, and one able seaman, John Hepburn, covered more than 5,500 miles under appalling conditions of ice, blizzards, and virtual starvation. None of the fifteen trappers, sons of the frigid north, returned alive; yet all the sailors survived except one, Midshipman Robert Hood, who was shot by one of the *voyageurs* who had turned cannibal (he had already killed and devoured two other men). The other navy men sur-

vived by scraping off the bits of lichen they could find clinging to the
Arctic tundra. "We used it as an article of food," remembered Doctor
John Richardson, "but . . . it proved nauseous to all, and noxious to several
of the party, producing severe bowel complaints."

Undaunted, both Franklin and Richardson volunteered for the next
expedition in 1825. This time they were better prepared. Franklin had
learned from the natives how to make pemmican, which became their
equivalent of ship's biscuit, the food of last resort, and how to use snow-
shoes. The second Franklin expedition also discovered how sledges pulled
by teams of hardy Indian dogs speeded up overland travel and the carrying
of supplies. At one stroke, Franklin established the basic equipment of
polar exploration for the next century, down to Shackleton, Amundsen,
and Scott.

Yet his second expedition was no more successful than the first. The
Northwest Passage still eluded every attempt to find a way through the
ice, either from the Atlantic or the Pacific side, where Captain F. W.
Beechey was working up from the Bering Strait. At one point Beechey
and Parry were only 160 miles apart, yet both were turned back by the
winter ice (Parry also lost his ship, the *Fury,* although he saved her crew).
Franklin tried one last time in 1844, although he was now nearly sixty.
Edward Parry told the Admiralty they had to let him go or "the man will
die of disappointment."

He sailed in May 1845, with two ships, the *Erebus* and *Terror,* and 134
men and supplies for three years. He was to sail through the Barrow
Strait (discovered by Parry and named after the Admiralty secretary) and
then head either south or north, via either the Wellington Channel or
what would be called the Franklin Channel. The Wellington Channel to
the south failed; a year later Franklin was still stuck in winter ice in the
northern passage. He died, exhausted and disappointed, on board the
Erebus on June 11, 1847. His men abandoned their ships and struck out for
the mainland. They were never seen alive again. It was not until almost a
decade later, the year of the Indian Mutiny, that their remains were found
and the fate of Franklin finally known.

John Barrow himself died in 1848. During his unparalleled duration
in office, he had reshaped the Admiralty into a modern bureaucratic
institution and turned the Royal Navy into a wellspring of scientific talent and exploration. One of his most important appointments was his
friend Francis Beaufort to the Hydrography Office. Beaufort was the
finest scientist-navy officer since Home Popham. He had devised a sys-

tem for classifying the strength of storms at sea, the gale force system, which is still in use today. Beaufort was also a keen and experienced chart maker. He would turn loose a far-flung team of brilliant young officers who would literally remake the map of the oceans, and give safe passage to sailors and navigators of every nation in the world.

Until 1795 the British navy still relied on whatever maps and charts its captains could find or buy, or make themselves. Pitt's Order in Council that year set up the navy's first hydrography office, in charge of standardizing and distributing accurate charts. In 1817 its head, Thomas Hurd, created a separate Surveying Service, with its own ships. But it was the West African squadron's need for accurate charts to track the slave traders in unknown waters that made nautical surveys a major priority of the peacetime Royal Navy.

Beaufort had done his own extensive surveying in the eastern Mediterranean; in his almost quarter-century as navy hydrographer, he made sure the work continued across the rest of that ancient sea. But Beaufort also insisted that whatever new and accurate information his men developed must also be available to the public. He had already done this with tide tables and a series of published amendments to published charts known as Notices to Mariners. His predecessor, Edward Parry, had done the same with lists of lighthouses.

Now Admiralty charts, which a century before would have been top secret and classified, were to be available to everyone. They would eliminate the last mysteries of navigation for the mariners of every nation on earth—including, of course, mariners in the French, Russian, and United States navies. That was the risk Beaufort and the Admiralty were willing to run. Theirs was a magnanimity born of self-confidence and the conviction that safety of the seas was necessary for freedom of the seas. It would ultimately be the British navy's most tangible legacy. Until the advent of satellite imaging, anyone venturing by sea across the Mediterranean or Baltic was probably using charts first drawn up by one of "Beaufort's boys" in the 1830s, with the captain's name and that of his ship still in the margin.

Beaufort's best surveyors worked farther afield. Like John Franklin, William Fitzwilliam Owen was a warrior as well as an explorer and had served with Edward Pellew during the Napoleonic Wars. But as a prisoner on Mauritius he had met Captain Matthew Flinders, who had charted the last unknown stretches of the coastline of Australia (in fact, it was Flinders who gave that continent its name). Flinders had learned his craft from William Bligh, making Owen a protégé of Cook by just two degrees of separation. In 1821 Owen set out in the sloop *Leven* and the brig *Barracouta* to survey the entire east coast of Africa, from the Cape to the Horn of Africa. It took three and a half years to sound and chart nearly five thousand miles of coastline, during which time Owen fought off disease, hostile natives, and marauding slavers.

Owen hated slavery with a passion and struck two major blows against the trade in eastern Africa, where Arabs had been carrying off their human cargo from ports like Zanzibar and Mombasa for centuries before Europeans got into the business. His first was a treaty with a local chieftain in Mozambique, placing the territory under British protection as a way to stop the slave trading (in 1872, an international treaty passed Mozambique to the Portuguese).

Owen did the same at Mombasa, working out a treaty that allowed the Mazrui nation to abandon its allegiance to the Sultan of Oman in exchange for abolishing slavery. The Sultan was understandably upset, but not to the point of breaking off relations with Britain. The war against the slave trade had turned him into a British client, the first in the Middle East. He had agreed to close the slave markets at Muscat in exchange for help in building up his navy, including a two-decker built to his specifications in Bombay. Barrow even arranged for him to be elected to the Royal Geographic Society. With the sultan's help, the Royal Navy could now operate freely in the western reaches of the Indian Ocean, and close the vise around the remaining routes for Arab slave dealers.

Owen returned home in August 1825. He and his team, including future surveying stars like Alexander Vidal, William Mudge, and Owen's nephew Richard, had put together some three hundred separate charts. He had lost more than half his crew to tropical diseases such as malaria and yellow fever, together with thirty-one of his forty-four officers. As a later hydrographer put it, Owen's African charts had truly been drawn in blood. But the work did not stop. Alexander Vidal returned to chart the Madagascar coast in 1826. Beaufort sent another team out to start work along the Arabian peninsula into the Persian Gulf. By 1850 the entire coastline of the Indian Ocean had been surveyed and mapped.

Philip Parker King began his career as a navy surveyor working on the Australian coast. In 1826 he was shifted to the coast of South America, where the newly independent nations freed from Spanish rule were opening up to British merchants who would need accurate charts. King took two ships with him, HMS *Adventure* and the 10-gun brig *Beagle*. The *Beagle* was an unimpressive little ship, built in Woolwich in 1820 as the kind of vessel the Royal Navy needed for anti–slave trade patrols. But she never sailed as a brig. Instead, she was converted to a bark, with square-rigged fore and mainmasts and a small mizzen with a fore and aft driver sail.

Ninety feet long from stern to stem, and twenty-four feet across the beam, the *Beagle* was too clumsy and slow to be an effective anti-slaver. Instead, she was converted to surveying work. Together with the *Adventure,* the *Beagle* reached the southern tip of South America in December 1827, to begin charting the Magellan Straits.

These were the violent storm-tossed waters that had defied the likes of Francis Drake and William Bligh, and nearly cost them their lives. Now they cost the *Beagle*'s captain, Pringle Stokes, his. The frustrations of bad weather and constant stress drove him to despondency and suicide. When the two ships returned for repairs to Rio de Janeiro, home of the South American station, King appointed his lieutenant, Robert Fitzroy, as the *Beagle*'s new commander.

Fitzroy was every inch an aristocrat, descended from the dukes of Grafton (one of his grandfathers had been prime minister) and nephew to Lord Castlereagh on his mother's side. But he was also an accomplished sailor—"one of the best practical seamen in the service," said a friend—and a product of Portsmouth's Royal Naval College. The college's curriculum had brought out his scientific side, with a passion for geology as well as meteorology and hydrography. The duties of the *Beagle* suited him perfectly: he virtually took over the survey from King and by August 1831 they were done. After returning to Plymouth, Fitzroy and the *Beagle* were recommissioned for a second voyage to complete their South American survey and follow though on one of John Barrow's pet projects. This was to circumnavigate the world and fix precisely a complete chain of meridian distances by chronometer: yet another step to make the globe more measurable, more compact.

Barrow and Beaufort agreed that Fitzroy was the man for the job. Fitzroy said he wanted a naturalist to identify and study the flora and fauna they would meet on their way. Beaufort asked a Cambridge friend if he could recommend anyone; he said he could. So on September 1, Beaufort wrote to Fitzroy: "I believe my friend Mr Peacock has succeeded in getting a 'savant' for you . . . a Mr Darwin."

Since Banks had sailed with Cook, it had become standard practice for naturalists or other civilian scientists to accompany navy ships to the remote and exotic places they had to visit. Many signed on as ship's surgeon, like botanist and future director of Kew Gardens Joseph Dalton

Hooker, who sailed with James Ross on his voyages in the South Seas. Future evolutionist Thomas Huxley signed on as assistant surgeon of the HMS *Rattlesnake* for a four-year surveying voyage around New Guinea (he complained shipboard life was fit for neither man nor beast; he gave up the navy to return to Oxford, and abandoned medicine for biology). Benjamin Bydnoe, the *Beagle*'s surgeon, was a skilled amateur botanist, while Fitzroy was a careful geologist. In fact, geology was the principal bond between himself and his new passenger, Charles Darwin, a Cambridge- and Edinburgh-trained naturalist who still thought he might prefer a career in the ministry. Fitzroy lent the twenty-two-year-old Darwin his own copy of Charles Lyell's *Principles of Geology*, the latest work on the subject, as the two made sail from Plymouth under bright skies and a full breeze on December 27, 1831.

"I loathe, I abhor the sea and all ships which sail in it," Charles Darwin wrote to his sister Susan. "I hate every wave of the ocean," he told a cousin. Even clear calm seas left him helplessly ill in his hammock or on the sofa in Fitzroy's cabin. "Not even the thrill of geology," he confessed, "makes up for the misery and vexation of spirit that comes with seasickness." By the time they reached South America, Fitzroy realized his new friend was never going to get proper sea legs. So as they started their coastal surveys, he thoughtfully arranged for Darwin to spend as much time on land as possible, often three or even six weeks at a time. Indeed, Darwin would spend almost four-fifths of the *Beagle*'s voyage ashore, gathering specimens, walking, watching, and thinking.

The product of that time ashore would be a new understanding of nature, which today is still called Darwin's theory of evolution. It was inspired by Lyell's geology, and sharpened by constant conversation and debate with Captain Fitzroy. Lyell had seen the present state of the earth as the product of a long, gradual transformation, with the land rising slowly from the seabed and volcanoes and earthquakes marking great formative events in the planet's geologic history. Darwin's insight was to transfer the Lyellian theory of gradual change to the earth's biological species, based on his observations of the plants and animals that the *Beagle*'s landfalls brought him in all their range and diversity. Yet without Fitzroy's copy of Lyell and his own bouts with seasickness, his vision of evolution might never have happened.

At first, Fitzroy was half convinced. He, too, was impressed by Lyell's theories (he had spoken to Lyell before they left England and agreed to do some geological observations for him), enough to begin to doubt the validity of the biblical account of the Great Flood as the most important event in the natural history of the planet. But when they returned to England in 1836 via Australia and the Cape of Good Hope, Fitzroy, a deeply believing Christian, was having second thoughts. He and his assistant, Philip Gidley King, published the first two parts of the scientific account of their voyage with the *Beagle*. Darwin finished the third, on natural history, which was an immediate bestseller—to Fitzroy's growing distress. He published his objections to Darwin's views at the end of his own book, trying valiantly to reconcile his geological discoveries with the literal account of Earth's creation in Genesis. Even as the *Beagle* was being outfitted for a third voyage, Fitzroy watched Darwin's reputation grow, as well as the controversy. The two were friends no longer, as Fitzroy's dismay at what he felt to be a direct challenge to the revealed Word of God grew into an obsession, even a mania.

His uncle, Lord Castlereagh, had been touched by a similar mental disease—the painful price, it was believed, for carrying the great responsibility of restoring peace to England and the world. In the end, Castlereagh's doctor had had to remove all firearms and razors from his possession, but missed a small pen knife he kept in a drawer in his washstand. On August 12, 1822, his doctor had found the foreign minister in his dressing room, his throat cut from ear to ear.

Forty-three years later, on April 30, 1865, Fitzroy, now a vice admiral, did the same—the price, Fitzroy believed, for having helped Darwin to undermine the Protestant faith in which he had believed so fervently, and on which the navy had been built. Anti-Darwinism had claimed a martyr, and the *Beagle* had lost her second captain to suicide.

For Fitzroy and the navy, it was a tragedy. For the rest of the world, it was the birth of a revolutionary theory of nature, one which would make the *Beagle* the most famous navy ship of the nineteenth century. Yet Darwin's presence was, we should remember, only secondary to the *Beagle*'s main purpose: charting the world's oceans. Its third and last voyage under Captain John Wickham ended in 1843, after nearly six years of charting the reefs and shoals of western and northern Australia and exploring the waters of the south Pacific.

The *Beagle* was now a quarter-century old: not bad for a ship experts had once pronounced worthless. She returned to Sheerness for her bottom to be recoppered one last time and joined the Coast Guard as a watch vessel. In 1870, she finally went to the breakers' yard, along with a sister surveying ship, the *Chanticleer,* another unsung hero of the struggle to make navigating the oceans safe in the new world order, and to give true meaning to the phrase "freedom of the seas."*

• • •

Freedom of the seas. For Whigs and liberal Tories like Castlereagh's successor George Canning, it was more than just a broad invitation for British merchants to make a profit wherever they could sail a ship or land a cargo. Their notion of free trade and markets was inseparable from political freedom and the idea of civilized peoples round the world choosing their own destinies. So this, too, became a role for the British navy, promoting the self-determination of nations within the framework of a stable international order and British security—which were, after all, pretty much the same thing.

They started in the same place the *Beagle* did, in South America. Napoleon's invasion of Spain in 1808 had set in motion a chain of events across the Atlantic, as one Spanish colony after another used the opportunity to break free from Spanish rule. One of the first was Chile. In 1817, just as the British navy was settling into its new duties of surveying the seas and policing the slave trade, Chile's leaders asked the irrepressible Thomas Cochrane to create a navy to defend them against the Spanish, while a Royal Marine major, William Miller, organized the army. Cochrane and Miller's victory over Spanish forces at Valdivia a year later secured Chile's independence; Cochrane went to do the same for Peru, standing triumphantly beside José San Martín as the city of Lima proclaimed its freedom on July 28, 1821. The dissolution of Spain's empire in the New World, begun by Hawkins, Drake, and the Royal Navy two and half centuries earlier, was complete.

What remained was to make it permanent. In 1820, after a half-decade of Bourbon misrule, Spain was trying out its own democratic revolution. Metternich's Holy Alliance, together with France, intervened to crush it in the bud. Canning could not stop them. Naval supremacy, as

---

*Two years later in 1872 another small ship, HMS *Challenger,* left Portsmouth on an even more ambitious mission. *Challenger* would spend three and a half years circling the globe, recording almost 69,000 nautical miles. Her study of the oceans' temperatures and depths (including discovering the Marianas Trench) would form the basis of modern oceanography right up to the present.

always, did not bring omnipotence on the European stage. But Canning was determined to prevent restored Bourbon Spain from reclaiming its American colonies. Even as a French army was marching on Cádiz in August 1823, Canning wrote to the United States ambassador, suggesting that Britain and America declare that any attempt to reestablish Spain's empire in the Western Hemisphere would meet with a hostile response from both countries. President James Monroe consulted with former presidents Jefferson and Madison, who urged him to accept Canning's offer. But Secretary of State James Quincy Adams said the declaration should be by America alone.

And thus the Monroe Doctrine was born, a British idea inspired by Canning's belief that a permanent world order would require a close cooperation between the two Anglo-Saxon Atlantic powers. As Canning put it, "I called the New World into existence, to redress the balance of the Old." Yet Washington's rejection of European interference in American affairs was only posturing without the backing of British sea power. The Royal Navy's frigates and battleships in Halifax, Jamaica and the Leeward Islands, and Rio de Janeiro gave the Monroe Doctrine whatever force it had. America's first venture onto the geopolitical stage had taken place under the protection of British naval guns.

Spain never recovered its South American colonies. Only Cuba and Puerto Rico, and the Philippines in the Pacific, remained loyal to the Spanish flag. In 1825 Canning persuaded Portugal to let Brazil go, with the help of the British naval squadron in the Tagus overlooking Lisbon.

Greek independence was another cause dear to the hearts of British romantics and liberals. Lord Cochrane would go to Greece to fight for it; so would the poet Byron, and leave his bones there. But it was Britain's overwhelming naval presence in the Mediterranean that stopped the Turks from crushing the Greek rebels and also prevented a meltdown of the Turkish Empire from "destabilizing the region"—a concept, if not a phrase, crucial to the new diplomacy based on balance of power.

This time Britain was determined not to act alone. It put together an international coalition, including rivals France and Russia, to oversee the Greek war of independence. When Edward Codrington, Nelson's old frigate commander, confronted the Turkish fleet in Navarino Bay in October 1827, he was joined by Russian and French battleships. But when battle was joined, it was Codrington's ships of the line, especially the *Asia, Albion,* and *Genoa,* who did most of the fighting. They sank or destroyed more than sixty Turkish vessels, while seventy-five British sailors died and another 197 were wounded—all for a cause far removed from any definable British interest. Codrington narrowly missed death three times. His ship's master and the captain of marines were both killed standing beside him; his son, a midshipman, was badly wounded. But Greek independence was now assured.

Navarino was the last battle of Nelson's navy; certainly the last before the advent of ironclads and exploding shells changed the nature of sea warfare forever. Yet in just thirteen years the British navy would be back to *defend* the Turks, this time to stop an Egyptian invasion of Syria and bombard the fortifications at Acre—the same place where Sidney Smith had halted French ambitions in the region. Propping up Turkey had become vital to prevent another empire from reaching into the Mediterranean, namely Russia. Fear of Russian expansion made the navy's presence in the eastern Mediterranean as important as its traditional dominance of the western end. In the first full decade of Victoria's reign Malta would overshadow Gibraltar in Royal Navy activity and planning, and Russia would overshadow France. The stage was set for the Crimean War, as well as the building of the Suez Canal.

The navy's role in securing Greek independence also signaled the final defeat of Mediterranean piracy. Ending piracy went hand in hand with ending the slave trade; captains and crews engaged in one were almost inevitably drawn to the other. The Algerian corsairs had for generations sold their prisoners to the same Arab slave markets that brought black captives out of Africa. Many of their prisoners were seamen, particularly English seamen. No wonder the Royal Navy hated the Mediterranean slavers even more than the African traffickers. "My blood boils that I cannot chastise these pirates," said Nelson. "Never let us talk about the cruelty of the African slave trade while we permit such a horrid war." When Thomas Cochrane showed up (uninvited) at the Congress of Vienna in 1814, he spoke about closing the Algerian pirates nests to anyone who would listen, and even wrote a book about it.

Yet curiously, Africa, not Algeria, took top priority; curiously, since the majority of the victims of the North African corsairs were white, not black. But inevitably no new world order could tolerate the world's second-oldest nautical profession, no matter where piracy happened or who was involved. The navy struck the first blow right after the coming of peace, in 1815. Lord Exmouth, the former Edward Pellew, sank the entire Algerian navy and forced the local dey of Algiers to sign an agreement banning the corsairs.* The war to save Greek independence freed the eastern Mediterranean from the same menace. The British navy's complete dominance over the Caribbean after 1806 wiped out the last pirate dens in those islands.

Nowhere was piracy more persistent and dangerous than in the Indian Ocean, especially in the Malay Straits and around the great jungle-covered islands of the Dutch East Indies: Sumatra, Borneo, Celebes, Java, and Timor. They were the last remaining jewels of Holland's once-proud seaborne empire. To the fury of many Britons, including the directors of the East India Company, Castlereagh had insisted in giving them back to the Dutch for the sake of stability in Europe. What British merchants in Asia wanted, however, was not stability but growth and expansion, even as the Dutch were moving swiftly to cut them off in the Malay Straits. "I much fear the Dutch have left us hardly an inch of ground to stand upon."

That sentence was penned in 1818 by an employee of the East India Company named Thomas Stamford Raffles. He had literally been born to a life at sea, on board his father's ship, the *Anne,* off Port Morant in Jamaica in 1781. Raffles became a clerk for the East India Company at age fourteen, and in 1806 was sent to Penang, the East India Company's outpost on the Malay Peninsula, just as Holland's alliance with Napoleon offered the opportunity for Britain to expand its influence in the eastern seas.

Raffles advised Pellew and the British fleet on the capture of Java and was made lieutenant governor of the island when it fell in September 1811. He abolished the Dutch system of forced labor, reformed many old abuses, and even established trial by jury—all reforms that the Dutch kept when they returned to power and Raffles was left without a job. However, in 1819, with the help of India's new governor general, he set up a trading colony at Singapore, an ancient but obscure site at the tip of the Malay Peninsula, to be a beacon of free trade and an anchor of British influence in Asia. "Our object is not territory, but trade," Raffles proudly wrote, adding, "Our free port in these seas must eventually destroy the

---

*The Americans under President Jefferson made an effort to rescue American captives there in 1805, with their famous storming of "the shores of Tripoli." The British effort was more comprehensive, yet only marginally more effective. The dey repudiated his agreement almost as soon as the British fleet left. Ironically, it was only with the coming of French colonization in the 1830s, which Britain tried to stop, that the Algerian corsairs were finally scoured out and relegated to the pages of history.

spell of Dutch monopoly, and what *Malta* is in the West, that may Singapore become in the East. . . . Our commerce will extend to every part [of Asia], and British principles will be known and felt throughout."

Indeed, Singapore quickly outstripped Malta in geopolitical importance. It would become the crossroads of virtually all trade between India and China, Japan, Indonesia, and Australia, and a key station for the British navy. By 1862 it had a population of 90,000 of all races and colors. With the opening of the Suez Canal, it became crucial to Middle East trade as well.

A visit to Singapore inspired another former East India employee, James Brooke, to bring British commerce and influence to the embattled northern shores of the island of Borneo at Sarawak. He arrived from England at Kuching, Sarawak's capital, in August 1839, in a private schooner he had bought with his inheritance from his father. A Spanish official once said that John Hawkins was a man to whom it was impossible to say no; the same was true of James Brooke. By sheer force of personality and obvious selflessness of motive, he gained the confidence of the people and their local governor. He was able to abolish slavery, carry out land reform, and launch a campaign to root out the pirates who infested every inlet and river along the Borneo coast and who had made native life a living hell.

"They are indifferent to blood, fonder of plunder, but fondest of slaves," Brooke wrote. The Borneo pirates were also headhunters who preyed on local populations, Brooke knew destroying them would also end centuries of intertribal violence and civil war. In this, Brooke was entirely on his own. He had no standing with the British government or the Colonial Office. But he found a willing ally in Henry Keppel, descendant of one of the Royal Navy's most illustrious dynasties, and commander of the 18-gun corvette HMS *Dido* of the East Indies squadron. In 1843 they joined forces to take on the worst pirate nests. Keppel's sailors and marines stormed one Dyak fort after another, as Brooke personally led his own peculiar army of adventures, idealists, and devoted natives in their support. By 1849 they had largely eliminated the pirate menace. Despite criticism from some in Parliament of his strong-arm tactics, Brooke had a stout defender in Lord Palmerston and in Queen Victoria herself, who gave him a knighthood.

Brooke, the "White Rajah of Sarawak," showed what could happen when the drive of a Hawkins or Drake combined with the humanitarian passion of a Wilberforce. Twenty years later Keppel returned to Kuching.

"In 1842," he remembered, "piracy, slavery, and head-hunting were the order of the day. The sail of a peaceful trader was nowhere to be seen. . . . Now how different!" Merchants and fishermen plied their trade in peace; families were able to build farms and enjoy a settled life for the first time in memory. Kuching had grown from barely 800 inhabitants when the *Dido* first dropped anchor there to more than 20,000.

Many people, of course, doubted that the British were doing all this out of sheer selflessness. Many, if not most, still do. Who, after all, was going to benefit from global free trade more than the world's biggest trading nation? Who had rejected the notion of freedom of the seas for more than two centuries, while enforcing its Navigation Acts by war and violence? Who had insisted on upholding its "maritime rights," to stop and seize neutral ships in time of war? Yet successive British governments were determined to show that they could uphold the principles of free trade and freedom of the seas even in the face of Britain's own national and corporate interests.

*   *   *

The Whig government of Lord Grey, which also passed the great Parliamentary Reform Bill, began in 1833 by abolishing the East India Company's trade monopoly with China. The lone survivor of the great merchant adventurer companies of the Elizabethan age, and once the bastion of England's seaborne empire in Asia, the company had been steadily losing profits and influence. In the eighteenth century it stayed in business by trading opium for tea in China. In the short term, the end of its monopoly brought an explosion in the volume of opium exports from India, as Portuguese, American, and other British merchants jumped into the business. It also meant increasing instability within China. The first Opium War was just around the corner. But the founding of Hong Kong in its aftermath would bring a huge expansion in China's trade with the rest of the world in a whole range of commodities. With Singapore and Hong Kong, and British naval squadrons based in both, the age of free trade had finally arrived in Asia. The tentacles of the modern global system were stretching to every corner of the eastern seas.

In 1809 Britain renounced its right to demand that foreign vessels "dip their colors" as they entered the English Channel. It was a largely symbolic, yet significant, decision: a surrender of Britain's ancient claims to sovereignty over the narrow seas, which it had upheld at gunpoint since the reign of Henry VIII and which had been the cause of at least two wars. In 1849 Parliament repealed another vestige of its aggressively mercantilist past, the Navigation Acts.

Then in 1856 British diplomats pledged to renounce Britain's so-called maritime rights to stop and seize goods in neutral vessels in time of war. Many were shocked and horrified, and not just in England. Karl Marx was so incredulous he assumed the Liberal government must be in the pay of imperial Russian agents. Yet the Liberals refused to be deterred. It was, said one in the House of Lords, the abandonment of a policy "hostile to commerce, and as unfavorable as possible to a mitigation of the evils of war"; it was a crucial "step in the progress of civilization," said another. For in exchange, Britain and the other signatories had agreed to end all forms of state-sponsored privateering or seizure of merchant vessels for profit. The seas were henceforth to be open and free from threats by national governments as well as private individuals, by navies as well as roving corsairs.

The Declaration of Paris ended one of the gaudiest and longest-running chapters in nautical history, not to mention in the evolution of the British navy. The *guerre de course* and letters of marque were now things of the past. No longer could a sea captain look forward to war as a way to make his fortune, as Nelson, Cochrane, and Edward Pellew did, or sail his ship up the Thames to Greenwich with sails of silk damask from a captured galleon, as Thomas Cavendish had. Instead, admiralty courts would now spend their time punishing pirates and slave traders—punishing them for the very things that Raleigh and Hawkins had done to make England a maritime power.

Meanwhile, their successors in the Royal Navy would devote themselves to protecting merchants of every nation, escorting their vessels through war-torn regions and rescuing their crews in storm-tossed waters. They would bring help and supplies to distant places hit by famine or earthquake (including six Royal Navy vessels dispatched to carry food to Ireland during the Potato Blight of 1847). They would carefully survey and chart the shorelines of every remote island and inlet. They would pull together the disparate parts of the British Empire into a single community. They were the policeman of the new world order. But what about their oldest obligation, to defend Britain itself?

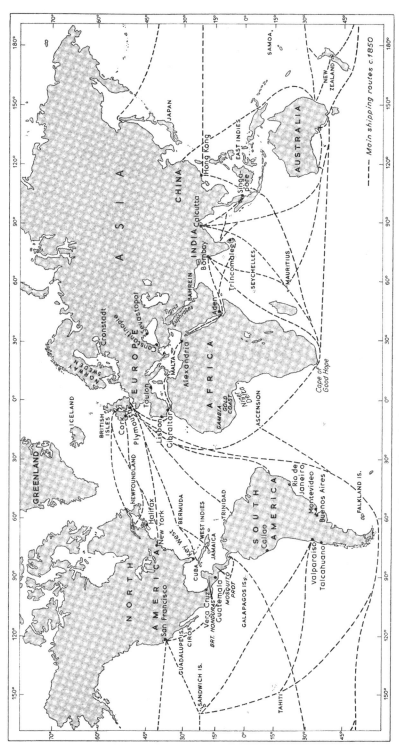

The World, with Shipping Routes and Naval Bases

CHAPTER EIGHTEEN

The Sun Never Sets

How glorious is the title of "Englishman"—and yet we are not loved.
—Captain Cooper Astley Key, R.N., 1848

O**N A COLD** wintry day in November 1849, Herman Melville stood on London Bridge and gazed down into the Thames, the commercial superhighway of the world. Below him, on the north bank, stood the church of St. Magnus, designed by Christopher Wren and the burial place of Miles Coverdale, first translator of the English Bible and godfather of John Foxe's English Reformation. Farther down on the fog-shrouded shore, was Limehouse, where on a similar cold winter day Humphrey Gilbert showed his friend George Gascoigne his project for finding a Northwest Passage. Even farther down was Black-wall Stairs, where Captain John Smith boarded three ships bound for the James River colony in America. Over Melville's other shoulder, upstream, lay Whitehall Stairs, where Nelson's body had been brought back to the Admiralty.

Downstream, just visible when the thick yellow and blue fog lifted, was Greenwich Naval Hospital, Britain's monument to its naval seaman and Wren and Hawksmoore's architectural masterpiece. Farther still lay Woolwich and Deptford, where Henry VIII first commanded docks be built, and Tilbury, where Captain Kidd's bones had rotted to frighten potential pirates. Then Chatham, where John Hawkins had watched shipwrights build the first race-built galleons and Tromp had burned and humiliated the English fleet. Then beyond Chatham, this river of history widened out into the Warp, the Nore, and the open sea.

Melville was visiting his London publisher, Richard Bentley, who was about to come out with Melville's memoirs of serving on an American frigate, *White Jacket*. In a year or two Bentley would also be the first to publish Melville's fiction masterpiece, *Moby Dick*. It is the story of brave men at sea, of great hopes and catastrophic defeat. Yet in 1849 neither Melville nor anyone else could have gazed on the scene below, the great forest of masts and teeming wharves stretching from the Upper Pool past the Tower of London to St. Katherine's Docks and the West and East India docks beyond, and imagined any catastrophe capable of disrupting the great geopolitical and financial certainties it represented.

The ebb and flow of the Thames had become the life rhythm of the world's economy. Already by 1790 more than forty ships a day loaded and unloaded cargoes bound for every corner of the globe. For the next century, teams of dockworkers would disgorge the riches from ships of every nation. Chinese porcelain, Thai silks, Persian carpets, African ivory, Norwegian timber, bundles of feathers and furs, crates of ambergris and seashells, bales of Alabama cotton and Australian wool jammed the warehouses and over-flowed onto the wharves. Stevedores swarmed past man-made mountains of grain, sugar, tea, and hides, and stepped over fragrant puddles oozing from oak casks of wine, sherry, port, and Madeira. The resources of the world flowed up the Thames and spilled out across the country in a river of wealth and material goods, meeting the outflow from Britain's other major seaports: Liverpool, Manchester, Glasgow, and Bristol.

Yet these did not come at the command of some king or emperor, as in the past, or even of a ruling class. They came in exchange for the goods that British merchant ships carried to every corner of the world, goods that were the fruits of its Industrial Revolution. By 1850, Britain was pro-ducing two-thirds of the world's coal, half its iron, five-sevenths of its steel, two-fifths of its metal hardware, and half its commercial cotton cloth. Merchants around the world, British and non-British, very often white but also yellow, brown, and black in skin, passed those wares on to their customers, and grew rich and respectable in their turn. In the 1850s world trade boomed at an 80 percent growth rate, with Britain leading the way. By 1875 British capitalists had more than one billion pounds invested abroad. One out of every five English workers was engaged in trade or transport, including the merchant marine. By 1890, Britain had more registered shipping tonnage then the rest of the world combined.

Britain's industrial affluence spread across every social class, includ-ing (contrary to Marxist myth) its working class. As everyone knows, it had come at the cost of severe economic dislocation, especially in rural areas and in the preindustrial trades, and considerable social unrest.* But

---

*It had not begun to touch Ireland. That island was still suffering from the greatest famine in British history, which killed upwards of two million people, thanks in part to the obstinacy of the British government and Irish landowners (including men like

Britain's parliamentary system was able to absorb, defuse, and sort out the conflicts in the ordinary workings of politics. The government's own statistical Blue Books, first created to keep track of the navy's campaign against the slave trade, became tools for measuring every aspect of British society and mobilizing public opinion behind reforms, from abolishing child labor to regulating the mining industry and clearing urban slums.

So while continental Europe lay wracked by the revolutions of 1848, Britain was able to watch with serene detachment. This would later be known as Britain's sense of "splendid isolation"—although this was a sensation no previous century of Englishmen could afford to feel. It was made possible above all by naval supremacy. Britain would lose the title of the world's biggest industrial power before the century was over. Yet its self-confidence remained undimmed. The reason was that its navy still sat in unchallenged, even unchallengeable, mastery over the seas.

From that point of view, Britain was not "isolated" at all. The Royal Navy had wrapped itself around the globe, intertwined with the trade routes it protected as they grew and flexed. By 1851, as Queen Victoria and Prince Albert were opening the Great Exhibition, the navy had bases at Gibraltar, Malta, Bombay, Trincomalee, Mauritius, Aden (added in 1839 to patrol the entrance to the Red Sea), Singapore, Hong Kong (the spoils of the first Opium War), Sydney, the Sandwich Islands, Valparaiso, Buenos Aires, Rio de Janeiro, Jamaica, Antigua, Bermuda, Halifax, and a dozen ports and islands in between. These were outposts of empire but also watchtowers guarding the main shipping routes of the world. As the world's economy grew, so did the navy's presence overseas. In 1817 it had sixty-three ships serving in foreign stations; by the time Melville was in London, that number had more than doubled to 129.

Some in England were troubled by this growth in global reach, and in the responsibilities and liabilities it entailed. Radicals in Parliament complained of the costs and arrogance of power, just as they do today. But one of their own number, philosopher John Stuart Mill, answered them in 1853 by comparing Britain's maritime empire to the preeminent role Athens played in classical Greece. "Under the protection of the powerful Athenian navy," he wrote, the other Greek city-states "enjoyed a security never before known." When Athens lost its supremacy, Greece fell into

---

Palmerston and the Castlereaghs). But for those able to escape the horror of Ireland for the industrial cities of England and Scotland, the Industrial Revolution would enable them to make new lives for themselves and their families.

chaos and then under the heel of tyranny, first from Alexander the Great and then Rome.

The future of civilization, Mill warned, always depended on keeping power in the right hands. What democratic Athens had been then, Great Britain was at the dawn of the Victorian age, the instrument for the "permanent improvement of mankind." Britain had a duty to make sure its sea power remained more dedicated to "the service of others, than of itself"—and that the Royal Navy continued to rule the waves.

The foreign stations over and over again demonstrated this power at the service of others. The year before Melville arrived in London, the Admiralty had sent one of its ships to the Italian coast to watch out for British interests in Rome, where riots had broken out. "You cannot imagine the effect of a British man-of-war," her captain enthused afterward. "People wrote to the Minister at Florence and Naples, and a large number said that my presence at Rome kept the City tranquil, though my ship was fifty miles off!"

This was the agreeable face of British naval supremacy in the mid–nineteenth century. But its real source was the battle fleet concentrated at home in England and in the Mediterranean. Often sitting idle but bristling with guns, this "fleet in being" was the epitome of the military doctrine of deterrence: keeping the peace with a fighting fleet larger than any three rival fleets combined.

It was easy to forget this. Periodically British newspapers and parliamentary debates were filled with "invasion alarms" and worries about dire threats from this or that country. Palmerston and other politicians liked to publicly excoriate opponents for having weakened the navy to a state of abject prostration. Indeed once, when a diplomatic tiff with France in 1844 threatened to spill over into war, the Mediterranean fleet found itself with precisely one ship of the line. But the truth was that the British navy ruled the waves by its determination to bring overwhelming force to bear on any opponent, anywhere, and at any time. The foreign stations were puny compared to the navies of neighboring powers, like the United States in the case of Halifax, or even Argentina in the case of the South American squadron. But anyone challenging them knew that inevitably he would have to face that implacable battle fleet. Like Villeneuve at Trafalgar, foreign admirals sensed defeat even before a British ship appeared on the horizon.

In the nineteenth century the Admiralty learned the fine art of staying on top while working within budget. Even with Liberal governments eager to cut "waste" from the naval estimates, Britons were able to enjoy their maritime supremacy at an annual cost of less than a pound a head. The Admiralty's own self-confidence grew from the knowledge that even if some other Great Power made a bid for naval rivalry, Britain's industrial might could outbuild and overmaster them. Its members lived by the motto of Nelson's friend Thomas Hardy, when he was First Sea Lord: "Happen what will, England's duty is to take and keep the lead."

Three nations, and only three, made them nervous. The first was France. Since 1815, it had committed itself to rebuilding its fleet and its navy's shattered morale; some French officers even dreamed of a rematch to expunge the memory of Trafalgar. French naval engineers looked for any possible competitive edge. They were the first to experiment with explosive shells and the use of armor plate; British engineers had to scramble to catch up. But France never regained the political stability needed for a long-term naval comeback. From 1815 to 1871, France would go through three revolutions and one civil war, plus a half-dozen constitutions. By default its naval strategy reverted back to various scenarios for a *guerre de course*. Its battle fleet had no hope of facing the British in the Channel or anywhere else.

The same was true of the United States. Its super frigates from the War of 1812 had formed the core of a small but effective modern fleet, including a battleship, the *Pennsylvania,* which set a new standard for the ship of the line. For a while American clipper ships seemed poised to challenge Britain's mercantile shipping edge, even as Commodore Perry's naval squadron opened Japan and the routes to China to American business. But then in 1861 the United States too became bogged down in a civil war; a self-imposed naval blockade ruined merchant trade. The war produced a generation of steam-powered ironclads, like the USS *Monitor,* that were essentially coastal vessels; the British version came a year earlier and outclassed them in every respect. Indeed, the coming of steam, which Americans and Europeans had hoped might erode that British naval edge, ended up only making it more secure.

Russia posed a different problem. Unlike France, it had no great naval tradition or desire to avenge past wrongs by Britain. Unlike the United States, Russia was essentially landlocked, with access to the world's sea lanes limited by the season of the year or by narrow and diplomatically sensitive corridors like the Dardanelles. Instead, the Russian czars had built their navy to support their continental empire as it expanded to the borders of southern and eastern Europe, and into the geopolitical vacuum created by the decline of Turkey in the Middle East. Like France earlier, Russian ambitions seemed to pose a threat to the stability of Europe, "the just equilibrium" on which Britain's long-term security depended.

No British government was going to stand for this. Politicians vacillated on how to halt Russian expansion, either by becoming their friends, as Lord Aberdeen's Tories tried to do, or by declaring a virtual crusade against them, as Liberals and Radicals did. So when a series of incidents in Palestine over holy sites grew into a full-blow diplomatic crisis in 1853, Britain made common cause with France and Turkey to halt the Russian menace.

Popular history presents the Crimean War as the British army's most disastrous campaign, with the blundering charge of the Light Brigade and the suffering soldiers at Balaclava saved only by Florence Nightingale. In fact, it was a naval war from start to finish, with naval strategy dictating the time and place of action throughout. The Royal Navy would come under nearly as much criticism as the army did afterward; the British public expected it to deliver decisive victories on the scale of Trafalgar and was furious when it did not. Admiral Charles Napier, commanding the Baltic fleet, and James Dundas, his counterpart in the Black Sea, were attacked as being too old to serve effectively. Both were in their sixties, hardly too old for previous generations that had seen Richard Howe go to sea at nearly seventy and Samuel Hood still running the Greenwich Naval Hospital at ninety-one. It was true they lacked the dash and daring of a Nelson. The admiral commanding the Asian squadron, David Price, committed suicide rather than face the terrible responsibility of leading his ships into battle.

But the war they faced was different, too. The Admiralty used a two-pronged strategy, with Napier moving into the Baltic to catch the Russian fleet at Revel and then blockade the Denmark straits, while the combined British and French fleets sailed from Constantinople for the Russian naval base at Sebastopol on the Black Sea. The Russians feared the British fleet so much they surrendered both bodies of water without a shot. The problem was what to do then. Conventional thinking opted for a blockade strategy: after a year or two, maybe three, victory was "certain in the end." But Russia was more immune from the effects of naval blockade than any other European power. Since its fleet refused to fight, the British yielded to the French strategy of besieging Sebastopol by land.

From that decision all the subsequent disasters followed. The Royal Navy was reduced to being the British army's valet, just as it had been in America in 1776.

Yet the Crimean War accomplished more than its critics allowed. It ended in stalemate, but it did block the gathering Russian threat on the eastern horizon for another one hundred years. It made the unification of Germany possible, and the creation of the Austrian-Hungarian Dual Monarchy, without Russian interference. It closed the Mediterranean to the Russian fleet for good.* Crimea also led to the signing of the Declaration of Paris in 1856 renouncing privateering, a major victory for the freedom of the seas. The Royal Navy's success further showed that steam power had come to stay (Britain's best battleships were now all steam and screw propeller driven) and that its naval bombardments could overwhelm the most modern naval bases in the world such as Odessa and Sebastopol. The St. George's Day naval review at Spithead in 1856 displayed a fleet still without equal. Yet in just two years, the Admiralty was laying out plans for the next great generation of warship.

This was HMS *Warrior*. Everything about her was a shock to the system. Launched in 1860, the ship was as revolutionary in design as the *Sovereign of the Seas* had been when she came down the slips at Chatham in 1637, or as Jack Fisher's *Dreadnought* would be in 1906. When French emperor Napoleon III saw her anchored at Portsmouth, surrounded by the wooden warships of the previous age, he said she looked like "a black snake sitting among the rabbits." The *Warrior* still does, at her Portsmouth mooring, not far from the *Victory*—the kind of wooden man-of-war the *Warrior* made obsolete forever.

The *Warrior* was the world's first iron-hulled battleship. Characteristically, she had been ordered in response to French efforts to build a seagoing iron warship, the *Gloire*. Admiral Baldwin Walker even admitted, "It is not in the interest of Britain—possessing as she does so large a navy—to adopt any important change in ships of war . . . until such a course is forced upon her." In the case of iron, Walker added, "this time has arrived." But the *Gloire* had been clad with iron plates around a wooden hull, whereas builder Isaac Watts made the *Warrior* entirely of iron, with longitudinal and transverse framing to make her as strong as possible.

---

*The strong British navy presence in the Mediterranean also prevented France from interfering when Garibaldi's army of liberation crossed over to Italy from Sicily, opening the path to Italy's independence.

In fact, the *Warrior* outclassed the *Gloire* in every respect, along with every other warship in the world. She displaced nearly 9,200 tons, compared to 5,630 for the *Gloire,* and less than 2,000 tons for poor old *Victory.* She was also twice *Victory's* length, but with long clipper ship lines, and forty 68-pounders and four 110-pounder breech loading guns (*Gloire* had only 6¼-inch muzzle loaders). *Warrior's* 5,200 horsepower engines gave 14½ knots in open sea, making her the fastest warship afloat. She still had masts and sails, with the rigging for an 80-gun ship of the line, and retractable funnels in case her captain wanted a full spread of canvas. But those masts were now of iron, and with 4½-inch-thick plating extending from five feet below the waterline to the upper deck, the *Warrior* seemed an impregnable iron fortress. She was impervious to the newest exploding shells yet sleek, fast, and maneuverable. The *Warrior* had begun a new era for warship technology, just as her crew represented a new era for the British sailor.

The men who served on the *Warrior* were, for the first time, professional navy seamen. The Admiralty had been forced to this by the Crimean War, when it had to man its ships without using impressment which, in the age of Dickens and liberal humanitarian reform, would have made it a political pariah. So in 1853 it allowed new entrants to sign on for ten-year service, in exchange for a pay raise (until then still stuck at the 1797 level) and a pension at the end of twenty years. The volunteers came slowly at first. It was hard for sailors to shake off the habit of thinking of the queen's service as merely temporary and of looking forward to being paid off at the end of a commission to sign on with a merchantman instead. But within a decade the Royal Navy had set up a way to create its own full-time professional ratings, while regularly turning volunteers who had never been to sea before into genuine seamen.*

All of this, of course, meant standardized training, not just in the tra-

---

*This brought two immediate changes in seaboard life. First, everyone on Her Majesty's ships was now a Briton. The days of multinational, multiracial crews collected from every seaport around the world (in 1808 Byam Martin noted that the seamen on his 74-gun *Implacable* came from twenty-three non-British nationalities, including five from Portugal and two from Bengal) were over. It also made crews exclusively male. Women were a regular feature of life on old navy ships. Most were the wife or girlfriend of a crewman or warrant officer; but one or two disguised themselves as men and served as ordinary ratings. All were expected to pitch in, even in battle. When two women in the 1840s applied for the navy's General Service Medal on the grounds they had served at Aboukir Bay and at Trafalgar, the Admiralty had to turn them down, saying the precedent would prompt "innumerable applications" from other women veterans.

ditions of seacraft but also for handling the new guns or stoking and tending the new steam engines. HMS *Excellent* provided one avenue for training gunners; it soon branched out into drilling recruits in fighting with cutlass and rifle. In 1854 HMS *Illustrious,* also moored at Portsmouth, taught them how to hand, reef, and steer. Soon, almost every navy home port had an old timber "liner" on which the new recruits could get their introduction to sea service and to the conditions of the Royal Navy. Those, too, had to improve to attract and keep volunteers; beginning in the 1850s life below decks, for new entrants and old hands alike, changed more dramatically than it had in three centuries of life at sea.

A pay raise was part of that. So was a better diet. The era of meatless or "banyan" (a Hindu word from the navy's days in India) days came to an end, and the introduction of tinned foods made everything the men ate better and safer, with vegetables available even after months at sea. Changes came the other way as well. The beer ration was abolished in 1831, and the rum ration halved in 1825. The navy introduced tea and cocoa instead, which many sailors actually preferred. In 1850 the navy was able to cut the rum ration again without too much grumbling. As a result, drunkenness on board ship became almost unknown (drunkenness ashore, of course, remained a sailor's right and duty).

Flogging, too, disappeared from Her Majesty's new professional navy. In 1831 Charles Darwin had been shocked and sickened when after they had been less than twenty-four hours at sea, Captain Fitzroy ordered four men on the *Beagle* flogged. The Victorian age had no more stomach for this kind of brutality, any more than it had for the press gang. In fact, the Admiralty was deeply reluctant to abolish flogging altogether, insisting the threat of it remained essential for discipline while urging "a safe forbearance" in its application. But bit by bit, the legal restrictions on its use tightened; certainly the end of impressment, which had filled generations of Royal Navy ships with unwilling and unruly men, made flogging and other forms of corporal punishment less and less necessary. "Starting" men with a bosun mate's rope end had been abolished in 1809. Putting them in irons became much harder to do after 1853, and soon disappeared altogether.

Indeed, the Admiralty for the first time wanted to keep its new sailors not just well ordered, but happy and content. In 1859 a series of disturbances broke out across the fleet over men's leave. Sailors refused to obey orders, threw linchpins and gun sights overboard; on one ship, HMS *Marlborough,* they refused to change their clothes and rolled shot down hatchways. The Admiralty's reaction was extraordinary. It sentenced the main offenders to hard labor: in the old days, it would have been death. When the captain of the *Princess Royal* punished his men with flogging, the board censured him and pardoned and released the culprits. The Naval Discipline Act of 1860 then liberalized leave so that sailors could have a week or two away from their ships when they were in home port. It also replaced the old Articles of War and imposed a naval judge advocate to oversee all future courts-martial.* For the first time, the navy also allowed sailors to find their own counsel for the defense.

All this reflected the consensus in the Admiralty, and in the public at large, that the new navy seaman was healthier, better educated, more sober and self-directed than his predecessor in the age of Nelson. In 1847, one old sailor could write, "The system of manning ships has improved with the march of intellect, and men who join the Navy, in nine cases out of ten, gladly remain." In 1870 the number of cases of flogging dropped to just fifty-seven for the entire fleet; the next year the Admiralty suspended all flogging in peacetime. It was never formally abolished; but by 1879, when it was suspended for wartime as well, the only place one could find the venerable nine-tailed cat was in naval fiction.

In 1870 a Royal Navy able seaman received a pay double that of his 1830 counterpart, almost fifty shillings a month. He had learned how to march in step, how to salute his officers, and how to wear shoes (although some ships were still doing small-arms drill barefoot in the 1870s). He also had a uniform, which the Admiralty created for him in 1857 and which has remained the basic pattern until today. However, his ready-made one did not arrive until 1907. Instead, he was expected to make his own, since seamen were traditionally master sewers, and the cost of the blue serge and white duck was still deducted from his wages.

In so many respects, he seemed a very different creature from his predecessors. Yet in others, he was not. The seamen on the *Warrior* and the other warships of the 1860s were the last breed to go aloft just as sailors had done on the *Victory* and the *Royal James* and the *Golden Hind* before them. In another twenty years these men would be looked on as heroic giants from a vanished world. The officers who grew up as midshipmen and lieutenants among them, would remember them with respect and awe.

---

*Although the Naval Discipline Act went through revisions until 1866, it still kept the same framework as the old 1749 version; even when it was replaced in 1957, the new act kept the same structure and much of the old language.

They "had great arms and shoulders," remembered one. "They could climb but they could not march. They had steady hands aloft, and very unsteady heads ashore. They were artisans in rope and leather." Admiral Charles Beresford could recall them swinging from the rigging like trapeze artists. "I once saw the captain of the maintop hurl himself bodily down from the cap on a hand who was slow in obeying an order," he later wrote. He also remembered their sense of initiative and independence: "If a seaman of the old days noticed anything wrong up aloft, up he would run to put it right without waiting for orders."

Above all, their skill and daring sprang from a pride in their craft. It was not just their officers who would regret the coming of steam. When ships of the line spread their sails for home out of the Grand Harbor in Malta, it was tradition for the upper yard man of each mast to balance himself on the topmost part, the royal truck. "Many a time have I seen these men," wrote an eyewitness, "balanced more than 200 feet in the air, strip off their shirts and wave them" to the multitude gathered on the docks below. One of those foretopmen, as an old man, later wrote to Admiral Beresford:

> I am doubtful if there are many men in the Navy today who would stand bolt upright upon the royal truck of a line-of-battleship. I was one of those who did so. It was perhaps a foolish practice. But in those days fear never came our way.

Their officers, too, came from the same heroic mold, the last generation for whom "the age of fighting sail" was more than just legend. They were also the first for whom professional selection and training was a matter of course. In 1858 the HMS *Illustrious* made way for the *Britannia,* a training ship specifically for naval cadets. Together with HMS *Excellent, Britannia* turned out class after class of young midshipmen ready for a modern, technologically advanced navy, yet rooted in the traditions that reached back to Nelson and Blake. Its early graduates included future luminaries as Beresford, Percy Scott, and fourteen-year-old John Jellicoe, who boarded the wooden frigate *Newcastle* as a midshipman in 1874. After five years as midshipmen, they faced an examination board allowing them to take the new rank of sublieutenant. Those who failed left the navy: never again would men be allowed to remain midshipmen into their early forties. Those who passed went on to the Royal Naval College at Greenwich, which opened its doors in 1873 on the grounds of the old Naval Hospital.

Graduates liked to complain, then and later, about the quality of education at Greenwich and the standards of the midshipman exam. Jellicoe said the captains who examined him seemed more intent on reading their mail than on quizzing him on seamanship. Yet it all represented the navy's effort to come to grips with the changes that seemed to beset it from all sides, in the new era of technological competition and scientific specialization. The School of Naval Architecture and Marine Engineering also moved down to Greenwich; HMS *Excellent* developed courses on mines, torpedoes, and electrics for its technically inclined cadets. Officers were expected to choose a speciality, whether in engineering (still the least prestigious), gunnery, or navigation, with the navigation officer replacing the ship's master after 1867. At the other end, every captain not reaching flag rank at age fifty-five went permanently on the beach. Dead wood would no longer be tolerated at the top, any more than well-connected loungers at the bottom.

These, then, were the officers and men who took over the *Warrior,* and all the other ships that marked the transition from steam to sail, and from wood to iron.

Britain's iron industry had begun by making guns for the Royal Navy. The greatest iron founders of the eighteenth century, the Crowley family, had made their fortune supplying the needs of the navy and its dockyards. Now fully industrialized, Britain's foundries could turn out iron and steel for Britain's warship in quantities no other country could match. As with steam, the introduction of a new technology to challenge British naval supremacy ended up working in Britain's favor. The *Warrior* was joined by a series of new iron vessels ordered in the 1860s; by 1865 the Royal Navy had thirty ironclad ships of the line versus France's eighteen.

And yet they were all obsolete almost as soon as they were built. The reason had to do with guns. While the *Warrior* and her sister ships represented the peak of warship design, naval gunnery had already leapfrogged ahead. The *Warrior*'s armor plate had been tested against 200-pound shells. But a year after she went into service, guns were being tested that could fire 300-pound shells capable of punching through eight-inch-thick armor—nearly twice as thick as the *Warrior*. The British navy was facing a problem on a scale never confronted before. Industrial technology was introducing change faster than the admirals, policy makers, or even the engineers and designers could deal with. The modern age of the "arms race" had arrived, with each new innovation forcing everyone else to scramble to regain the lead with innovations of their own. New ships came down the slips every year, each equipped with a bewildering array of new features and changes, as technology more and more dictated the terms of naval strategy.

Confronted by the problem of bigger and more accurate guns, British shipbuilders literally went back to the drawing board. The result was the *Bellerophron*, with six-inch-thick armor (still not enough for the heaviest guns), but also with a new gun arrangement. The designer, Edward Reed, abandoned the old broadside concept for a single central battery, thickly armored with ten nine-inch rifled guns. The new *Bellerophron* was shorter and stubbier than the *Warrior*—more a battle tub than a battleship. But a ship with a big central battery no longer needed a long keel for long rows of guns. Firepower was becoming a matter of a small number of very powerful pieces, which steam power could deliver in range of their target without regard to the weather gauge.

The problem now was how to increase that central battery's range and rate of fire. The answer was the turret, first developed by a Royal Navy captain named Cowper Coles for a small coastal vessel used to bombard enemy forts during the Crimean War. Swedish engineer Ericsson used a similar design for the first American ironclad, the *Monitor*. The *Monitor*, however, was not properly seagoing (when it ventured out in a storm, it capsized and sank). It was British engineers who found a way to mount a gun turret over the center line of an oceangoing warship; first on the *Royal Sovereign*, an existing three-decker, then on a brand-new ship of revolutionary design, HMS *Captain*.

The *Captain* was born of controversy, as indeed almost all these ships were. The days of treating new military technologies as top secret had not yet arrived; the planning of each brought acrimonious debate in the newspapers and Parliament. The *Captain* had triggered a power struggle between First Lord of the Admiralty Hugh Childers and Chief Naval Architect Reed, the Navy Controller, and the rest of the Board of Admiralty. They opposed adopting Coles's unusual design with its long, low freeboard which made the *Captain*, Coles argued, less of a target at long range. Childers, a civilian who believed he was pushing the Royal Navy into the modern age in spite of itself, overruled them.

Less than six months after her first voyage the *Captain* foundered and sank in the Bay of Biscay in September 1870, taking with it 472 officers and crew, including Coles and Childers' own son. The British public was stunned and demanded that political heads roll. Prime minister Gladstone forced the Controller, Spencer Robinson, to resign, while Reed had quit the year before—even though the feature they had most warned about, the low freeboard in a ship made top-heavy by turret and masts, had caused the accident. Childers resigned in May 1871, a broken man mentally and physically. The Admiralty had lost the one man strong enough to hold its tiller to a single course, even though it had been the wrong one. It would not see another for the next quarter-century. Yet the technological innovations went ahead.

If a turreted ship was too top-heavy with masts, then they had to build one without them. Removing them also allowed the gun turret to turn for a much wider range of fire. The *Devastation,* launched in Portsmouth in 1871, was the first warship ever designed without masts or rigging. She had two turrets, one forward and one amidships, each packing two 12-inch guns, the largest guns ever put afloat. Each gun weighed 35 tons and was capable of firing a 700-pound shell. They were so large they had to be muzzle loaded: no breech-loading gun that size could stand the impact of the blast on the breeching (by 1891 they could). The *Devastation*'s turret armor was more than a foot thick, with plating almost as thick running the length of the waterline and five feet below. Her 800-horsepower steam engine ran two independent screw propellers, giving the ship slightly less speed (albeit more than 13 knots) but much increased turning power and maneuverability.

Devastation was every inch a formidable weapon of war. Even her prow was designed for ramming other vessels. Yet even this was no longer enough. In 1873 work began on the *Inflexible,* a 11,880-ton monstrosity with four 16-inch guns and six 20-pounders. She carried the thickest armor ever put on a British ship, almost two feet thick around the central citadel with its two huge turrets, and three feet of teak backing. *Inflexible* was also the first warship to have electric lights. Although she still had masts and stuck to the central citadel battery concept, the *Inflexible* pointed the way to the future of the battleship more than any previous vessel. "Imagine a floating castle," wrote her designer, "which the progress of invention in artillery has finally driven us to resort to."

Floating castles like the *Alexandra,* a central-battery battleship with two 11-inch guns and ten 10-inchers mounted on two decks and the fastest capital ship in the navy, and the *Dreadnought,* launched in 1879 as the most formidable battleship in the world and, at $14^1/_2$ knots, one of the fastest. The *Alexandra* was also the first capital ship to carry tubes for self-propelled torpedoes, developed by a Scotsman named Whitehead in the 1870s—ironically, the weapon that would threaten the future of the battleship more than any other. In 1880 technological innovation was still keeping the British navy on top. But the twists and turns in the race for the supreme battle fleet were getting tighter. One mistake or missed opportunity, some were beginning to sense, would leave the course open for others—and put the British Empire at risk.

. . .

At one end, the impact of technology on sea power spawned iron behemoths like the *Devastation* and *Dreadnought*. At the other, it produced the gunboat. Never more than 200 feet long and usually with a crew of only thirty or forty, the steam-powered gunboat became the ubiquitous symbol of the Victorian navy's global responsibilities. More than two hundred were built between 1855 and 1856; many more would appear before the end of the century. Usually commanded by a single lieutenant, often in his twenties, the gunboat not only gave its name to a new form of international diplomacy, "gunboat diplomacy," it also gave the Royal Navy its last dying sense of swashbuckling adventure.

This was only appropriate, because the steam-powered gunboat made its first appearance in that most piratical of all Victorian wars, the Opium War of 1841–42. Built at Birkenhead and weighing 660 tons with two pivot-mounted 32-pounders and two 60-horsepower Forrest engines, the *Nemesis* was a private venture by the East India Company. But its captain, William Hall, was a former Royal Navy officer, who took the *Nemesis* up the Pearl and Wampoa rivers to bombard Chinese forts and open up China to British trade—which in 1840 largely meant opium from India. Hall enthused to the East India's directors about the *Nemesis* and her devastating effect on the Chinese: "They are more afraid of her than all the line-of-battleships put together," he chortled. "She's worth her weight in gold."

The *Nemesis,* joined later by a flotilla of navy ships, played an essential part in forcing Chinese concessions to Western traders—the first in a long, dismal history—and creating the port of Hong Kong. The navy soon had its own versions. A fleet of them went up the Irrawaddy River during the Anglo-Burmese War of 1852–53;* they were crucial for attacking Russian coastal positions during the Crimean War. Twenty-five were

---

*The fleet's commander was Jane Austen's brother Charles, now a Rear Admiral and a stalwart seventy-three year old. Alas, not stalwart enough—he died on the voyage upriver.

deployed in the second Opium War in 1856–60, to attack Canton and the Taku forts near Peking.

What made the gunboat so indispensable was its ability to enter shallow waters and river estuaries. A two-mast sailing rig gave it speed and maneuverability in open sea. The steam engine allowed it to chug upriver, past impenetrable jungle and villages of hostile natives to bring firepower to bear on anyone defying the Union Jack. The gunboat made the Royal Navy for the first time a power on land as well as at sea.

Without the gunboat, the navy could never have fulfilled its role as global policeman, intervening at the request of British officials and merchants virtually anywhere in the world:

> In one year, for example, 1858, such requests came (among other places) from New Zealand, Jamaica, Panama, the Kooria Mooria Islands (to protect the guano trade), Honduras, Siam, Brazil, Sarawak, Alexandria, Vancouver (because of the excitement of a gold rush), Vera Cruz, Morocco, and the fishing grounds off Newfoundland; and every one of these far-flung demands was granted.

Gunboats that year helped Dr. Livingstone to secure the Zambezi River against slave traders, the British Museum to protect archaeologists on a dig in Cyrene, and the Archbishop of Canterbury to get some missionaries out of trouble in Borneo.

A gunboat's young lieutenant and crew were the instant heroes of Britons, and many non-Britons, everywhere—and interfering villains to others. The gunboat *Lynx* sailed 400 miles up the Niger to deal with a fight among local palm oil merchants; the *Lee* and the *Dove* went 500 miles up the Yangtze to put down rebels against the Manchu Dynasty. They became symbols of British justice in far-off tropical or polar places—and sometimes injustice.

Lieutenant Herbert Brand was put in charge of suppressing a riot against colonial rule in Jamaica in 1865. He treated it like an armed mutiny on shipboard. One hundred and seventy-seven Jamaican blacks were condemned to hang, and hundreds more were flogged. Troops from the West African regiment, most of them black themselves, were allowed to run amok. Liberal public opinion in Britain demanded that Brand and the governor, Edward Eyre, face trial; white Jamaicans rallied around the men they believed had saved them from revolution and massacre. For the first time since 1776, a line was publicly drawn between the interests of Britain and its white colonists. It was a fault line that would grow and deepen over the next century, as the size and number of British colonies continued to expand.

The advent of the gunboat allowed Great Britain to penetrate and dominate larger tracts of the world than ever before, while letting other countries such as France follow its example. After 1865 the British Empire grew on average more than 100,000 square miles a year. Over the next couple decades, thanks to the gunboat, the familiar schoolroom map of the world "colored red" by British possession took shape.

Canada, Australia, New Zealand, India, and the Cape of South Africa were the first large patches of scarlet. To these were added between 1870 and 1900: Cyprus, Somaliland, Kenya, Uganda, Rhodesia, Nyasaland, Transvaal, Ghana, Nigeria, Papua, Sarawak, Burma, Egypt, and the Sudan— more than 4.5 million square miles of territory, inhabited by more than 66 million people. "England," wrote J. B. Seeley in 1882, well before the job was finished, "has left Europe altogether behind it and has become a world state." It was bound together by allegiance to the Union Jack, by steam power, which had cut the typical transatlantic crossing from four to six weeks to ten days, and the trip from London to Cape Town from forty-two days to two and half weeks, and after the completion of the first transatlantic cable in 1866, the telegraph. That device would allow the Colonial Office in London to read messages direct from India, and get a reply to the viceroy in New Delhi the next day.

To this world-state empire, the Royal Navy was more indispensable than ever. Indeed, it was as if *two* British empires had appeared. The first consisted of great port cities and naval bases, like Singapore, Hong Kong, Sydney, Cape Town, and London, centers of commerce and international exchange where the White Ensign of the British navy and the Red Ensign of the British merchant marine presided over flags and ships of a dozen other nations. The second consisted of vast hinterlands, even trackless desert, which demanded army garrisons and the Colonial Office to command and control.

Unlike the first, this second empire was indeed like others in history. It was the product of a self-consciously imperial will and calculation, with soldiers and bureaucrats conducting endless "brushfire wars" against hostile populations, from the Burmese and Afghans to Boers and Zulus, and with missionaries and traders picking up the pieces. It required far fewer soldiers to maintain than any of its predecessors—in 1898 less than 100,000 men to govern one-quarter of the world's population, plus the 148,000 in the native Indian army—and it tried to be more humane than its European or American counterparts. But it was an empire nonetheless. Like all the rest, its only claim to legitimacy was its own self-interest and its military power—in Hilaire Belloc's immortal phrase, that "we have the Maxim gun and they do not."

Yet that empire too would not have existed without the Royal Navy. Without the 100,000 sailors and officers, the 154 commissioned ships, and thirty-eight naval bases and coaling stations, the entire Victorian enterprise of empire building would have quickly flown apart. The navy already guaranteed the safety of a global economic system, a new world order based on British values, along with the gold standard. After 1870, more and more of the navy's resources had to protect the boundaries of this larger land-bound empire as well.

Two brothers, both naval officers, understood this. Philip Colomb had served against the African slave trade and with Henry Keppel rooting out the last pirates in the Chinese seas in the 1860s. John Colomb had been a Royal Marine before entering the new field of naval intelligence. Beginning in 1878, they published a series of books and articles, warning colleagues and contemporaries that the old ways of thinking about the navy's responsibilities had to change. The navy's principal job now had to be to "keep open the great sea-routes to and from the heart of the Empire—the islands of Great Britain."

In the event of any future war, they argued, a global strategy involving the defense of British commerce and suppression of enemy commerce by naval blockade would be the key to victory. Unless Britons realized that "command of the seas" was the secret of their survival as an empire and a nation, the new maritime technologies would become enemies, not allies. "Keep command of the sea as you value the national life," wrote Philip Colomb. "With it you can do everything. Without it you will be speedily blotted from the list of great countries."

The Colomb brothers gave sea power a new visibility in the minds of many—including an American navy captain named Alfred T. Mahan. They had had little effect on the Admiralty as yet. But they and their strategic successors made it clear that Britain and its empire now relied on the Royal Navy more than ever.

Not that the government and the British public were ungrateful. The Victorian army may have produced individual heroes like Kitchener and Gordon of Khartoum, but the navy produced them *en masse*, as an ascribed class of heroes. The navy seaman went from being the drunken violent thug from an alien world of Nelson's day to becoming Jolly Jack Tar, a sturdy reliable fellow of unflinching courage. His ruddy smiling face, ringed with sideburns, punctuated by a smoldering pipe, and crowned by a black tarpaulin hat, appeared on porcelain figurines, songbooks, advertisements for soap, coffee, tea, and cigarettes, and on children's board games. His basic uniform, with bell-bottom trousers and striped blue kerchief over a white or blue tunic, and black hat or sennet straw boater emblazoned with his ship's name, became the model for children's clothing around the world—both boys and girls, including the sons of the German Kaiser and the children of the Russian czar.

The Victorian craze for everything naval began with Victoria herself. Her uncle William IV, "the Sailor King," had gone to sea as a midshipman and rose to be Lord High Admiral (the last individual ever to hold that ancient title) before ascending the throne. She and Prince Albert sent their son Alfred to sea; as Duke of Edinburgh he became an efficient if eccentric officer, famous for having a pet elephant on board his frigate the *Galatea* that helped with raising and lowering the sails. From Alfred on, every generation of the royal family would make sure someone carried on the navy tradition, King George V and Louis Mountbatten being the most famous and Prince Philip the most recent.

Victoria and Prince Albert adored their royal yachts, some of which had engines of the most sophisticated design, and after Albert's death she went on to build a total of seven. For the navy, a royal yacht like the 2,470-ton *Osborne* was as much a commissioned ship as any man-of-war. Indeed more so during the long years of peace, when they were plum commands for the ambitious and well-connected officer, and glamorous symbols of the spit-and-polish peacetime British navy.

The Royal Navy officer himself was an object of almost universal fascination and admiration, the modern equivalent of the knight in shining armor. With the beatified Nelson as his model, he was supposed to be brave in battle, stoic in defeat, and compassionate in victory. Appearing on the horizon in his frigate or gunboat, he became the protector of the oppressed and avenger of the wronged. Certainly that was how officers were taught to think of themselves. "Our job was to safeguard law and order throughout the world," remembered one, "safeguard civilization, put out fires on shore and act as guide, philosopher, and friends to the merchant ships of all nations."

The British naval officer was steeped in tradition yet on the cutting edge of modern science and technology. He was renowned for being cheerful in the face of danger and resourceful in the pursuit of victory. Yet at the same time, he was a soldier with a conscience, a sailor with a sober sense of duty. The Western military tradition had acquired a new human face, one unlike any other fighting man in history.

No one contributed more to this cult of the navy officer than Frederick Marryat, whose series of nautical novels began appearing in 1829, with *The Naval Officer: Or Scenes and Adventures in the Life of Frank Mildmay.* They were far more than just escapist juvenilia. Marryat had served with Lord Cochrane. He had commanded the frigate that carried home the news of Napoleon's death on St. Helena. His descriptions of navy life sprang from close experience, and made the British public aware of their navy's dark side as well as its virtues. Marryat's novels went a long way to prevent the navy from ever thinking of impressing men again; they certainly forced it to give up flogging.

But it was Marryat's fictional naval heroes, most of them modeled on Cochrane, who struck the most resonant chord with the British public. They would spawn a long line of imitators, from Lord Jim (reading Marryat inspired Joseph Conrad to go to sea) to Horatio Hornblower and Patrick O'Brian's Jack Aubrey. They had their genuine Victorian counterparts, men like Henry Keppel and William Owen and Captain George Maclean, the Scottish naval officer who single-handedly wiped out the slave trade on the Gold Coast in the 1830s and whose word was law to black and white alike. But Marryat's books reached backward for their themes of heroism, to the age of Nelson. They made the old navy's ideal of grace under pressure and courage under fire part of the British national character.

A "stiff upper lip" was unknown to the Tudors and Stuarts: tears and tantrums were part of ordinary, even especially aristocratic, life. The same was true for the eighteenth century and the Romantics. But the imperturbable stoicism of Anson and Hawke and other navy captains on the quarterdeck found ready support among Victorian values, and became the British masculine ideal both in fact and fiction. Indeed, for the next hundred years nearly every hero in popular English fiction, whether a soldier or civilian, on land or at sea, would have to exhibit the same steely-eyed calm, the same imperturbable phlegm, the same "aquiline good looks you associate with the bridge of a destroyer." It is not for nothing that the most famous British superhero, Ian Fleming's master spy James Bond, is also a Royal Navy commander.

The admiration for the navy spilled over into comedy as well. HMS *Pinafore* had its first performance in 1878, and was the making of Gilbert and Sullivan as a musical team. Its success, both in Britain and abroad, was certainly due to the enormous popularity of its subject. *Pinafore* poked gentle fun at lawyers turned First Lords of the Admiralty like James Graham and W. H. Smith (the original model for Sir Joseph Porter), who had never gone to sea but still became rulers of the queen's navy, and the navy's class-bound attitudes, as protagonist Rex Rackstraw, a lowly tar yet "the smartest man in all the fleet," turns out to be Captain Corcoran's long-lost brother. But the overall tone of *Pinafore* was enormously respectful, and its chorus of sailors and petty officers are the play's true heroes.

> *For a British tar is a soaring soul*
> *And free as a mountain bird;*
> *His energetic fist should be ready to resist*
> *A dictatorial word!*

The British navy had become a self-conscious symbol of the nation itself. Half a century after Herman Melville gazed at ships in the Thames passing downstream from London Bridge, Rudyard Kipling watched a brace of British cruisers making their way upstream, passing those same merchantmen one after another in "the leisurely, rolling slow-march of the overlords of all the seas." Kipling realized the power they represented was "mine to me by right of birth. Mine were the speed and power of the hulls, not here only but the world over; the hearts and brains and lives of the trained men; such strength and such as we and the world dare hardly guess at."

Any other people or nation, Kipling guessed, would have unleashed that terrible force long ago, for their own gain and glory, and brought a terrible holocaust on humanity. But not England, not Great Britain. "Thus I stood," he concluded, with just the requisite touch of irony, "astounded at my own moderation, and counted up my possessions with most sinful pride."

• • •

One navy, two British empires. The seaborne one connected the main trading routes of the global economy; the other, land-based one, spread out over great plateaus, mountains, savannah, desert, and jungle and covered almost a fifth of the earth's land surface. These empires overlapped in many places, but by 1880 they had come to converge in the eastern Mediterranean and the Suez Canal. The canal was originally French-built and financed: Napoleon's dream of a Mediterranean route to India brought into reality. But like the Panama Canal a couple of decades later, what was supposed to be a display of Gallic enterprise became instead an imperial prize for Anglo-Saxons.

Fearful of the effect on their Cape trade, the British had at first opposed the canal. But once it opened in 1869, the ships that took the most advantage of the shorter route to Asia (it trimmed almost 3,000 miles and two months off the journey from England to Singapore) of course turned out to be British. In 1870, English traffic was less than 300,000 tons; in 1875, it was 2 million tons. Ten years later, it was approaching 3.5 million. Britain bought out the Egyptian ruler's half of the canal company in 1875; it now had a stake in the canal's smooth operation even greater than its French rival. The Royal Navy, as usual, became its ultimate guarantor and its Mediterranean fleet more crucial to British interests than ever.

This growing European presence fed deep resentments in Egypt, spawning the first great nationalist movement in what would come to be called the Third World. Egypt's military leader, Colonel Arabi Pasha, threatened to seize power and drive the foreigners out. The cry of "Egypt for the Egyptians" found sympathetic ears in England, including liberal Prime Minister Gladstone. But Gladstone was forced to follow the lead of his French counterpart, who wanted the revolt crushed. Gladstone turned first to the Turks to restore order in Egypt. But the French said no, we must do it together, which meant (in effect) that the Royal Navy must do it alone.

In May 1882 a joint French and British squadron under Admiral Sir Frederick Seymour was dispatched to Alexandria. On June 11 riots broke out in the city, Arabi Pasha seized power, and some fifty Europeans were massacred. The French lost heart and withdrew. On September 13 a British force under General Garnett Wolsely, including the Royal Marine Light Infantry and a naval brigade, defeated Arabi Pasha at the battle of Tel-el-Kebir. Britain was sole master of Egypt and the Suez Canal. With Suez at one end of the Red Sea route and Aden at the other, Great Britain had become the arbiter of power from the Middle East to East Africa.

Yet none of it would have been possible without Seymour's bombardment on July 11 of Alexandria's massive fortifications guarding the entire sweep of the bay from Fort Marabout in the west to Pharos, the site of Alexandria's ancient lighthouse, in the east. He had seven battleships to do the job, all ironclads. His own flagship, the *Invincible,* had been built in 1869 and now seemed small at 6,000 tons, compared to monsters like the *Alexandra* and *Sultan* at 9,000 tons each. The most advanced was the 11,880-ton *Inflexible,* commanded by the navy's most technically adept senior officer, Captain John Fisher. Not one of the ships, however, had ever fired a shot in anger. Seymour also had five large gunboats, which he ordered to keep watch on the western corner of the harbor, while his battleships moved in to open fire.

July 11 began bright and clear, with a slight breeze out of the northwest. At seven o'clock the *Alexandra* fired the first shot, as the *Invincible* raised the signal for general combat. For the next ten hours the British ships carefully directed their fire from one fort to the next, some of them more than a mile away, with officers in the mast tops passing on information on hits to the gunners below. The northwest breeze kept the smoke blowing inshore, making seeing the targets difficult. Fisher's *Inflexible* found her 16-inch guns could not be fired much faster than five minutes per round. "For a long time after they had been fired the whole ship would be enveloped in a yellow fog, while the projectile could be seen soaring away in the distance like a huge bird." The reverberations were so great that they shattered *Inflexible*'s lifeboats, throwing up clouds of flying splinters, and damaged her superstructure.

Yet hour by hour the shells began to tell, even though many were defective and failed to explode. At 8:30 the *Monarch* blew up the magazine of one fort, while *Inflexible* and *Téméraire* were able to move east to pound the emplacements around Pharos and Ada. Captain Charles Beresford of the gunboat *Condor,* noticed the harassing fire from Fort Marsa in the west had not slackened. So at ten o'clock he charged in and anchored so close to shore that Marsa's guns could not bring their sights low enough to fire at him. Beresford had his men warp the *Condor* back and forth, like a duck in a shooting gallery—except that it was Beresford, not the Egyptians, who was doing the shooting. Seymour ordered the other gunboats to join him.

By 4:30 the last Egyptian fortress had been silenced. An hour later the *Invincible* ran up the signal to cease firing. As Beresford rejoined the rest of the fleet, he got three cheers from the flagship and the signal: "Well done, *Condor.*" The next day Arabi Pasha's forces evacuated the city and abandoned most of the fortifications. The way into Alexandria was open, at a cost of only fifty-three British casualties. It was hardly Trafalgar. Everyone agreed that if the forts had had European gunners, or mines or torpedoes, the battle might have told a different story.

But Victoria's navy had fought her last great battle, the last won by ships of iron and ships with sails. Seymour's battleships became a kind of roll of honor, latecomers to the feast of Royal Navy invincibility, but participants nonetheless. *Inflexible, Invincible, Monarch,* once *Captain's* sister ship but then modified to avoid the same fate; *Alexandra,* the empress of the central battery ironclads, *Superb,* and *Sultan.*

And finally *Téméraire.* The ship carried one of the most renowned names in the British fleet. She had been built at Chatham in 1875 with just two masts, armored and iron-hulled but with the largest fore and aft sails ever set on a British warship. In the light of 1882, she was modern and up to date, with torpedoes, searchlights, and 11-inch guns. Everyone, including the observers on a United States corvette, agreed that *Téméraire's* fire had been among the most accurate. The Americans commented she was "a very efficient ship."

On October 3, 1890, at Suda Bay in Crete she was the last Royal Navy ship to stand into harbor under sail alone. Her captain obtained permission from his admiral to sail rather than steam in, and for five hours she leisurely beat to windward until she was home, with her crew handling sails, sheets, bowlines, and braces as efficiently as they might have in Hawkins's or Nelson's day. The rest of the fleet, including the commanding admiral himself, stopped everything to watch.

• • •

It was fitting that *Téméraire* should be the last. The first *Téméraire,* a French 74, been taken as a prize off Lagos by Boscawen and served faithfully through the American war until she was sold in 1784. Then, following navy custom, a new ship of 98 guns was built bearing her French name, to battle the French again. The "fighting *Téméraire*" experienced mutiny (with eighteen of her crew hanged at the yardarm in 1802) and blockade before her captain, Eliab Harvey, took her into action at Trafalgar and fought both the *Fougueux* and *Redoutable* to a standstill, saving the *Victory* but not Nelson himself.

Despite her name, the *Téméraire* had been a truly British ship. Of 718 hands at Trafalgar, 339 were Englishmen and a third of those men from Devon; 220 others were Irishmen, 53 Scots, 38 Welsh—and 28 Americans. After the war, they were paid off and *Téméraire* faced the fate of the vast majority of fighting sail. For a while, she became a receiving and victualing ship at Sheerness. In 1838, forty years after she had been built, the *Téméraire* was finally sold to a breakers' firm in Rotherhithe. The painter

John Turner was out on the Thames with some friends when he saw her being towed into her last berth by a steam tugboat, as the sun slowly set in the west. The great men-of-war of the Royal Navy, with their massive oak hulls and spreading masts, had been Turner's earliest visual inspiration as a boy. Now he decided to leave a permanent record of what those wooden walls had meant to him, and to the nation.

The result was one of Turner's most popular and influential paintings. Everyone realized it marked the passing of a heroic age, and Britain's departure to a future destination unknown. William Thackeray admired how Turner's tugboat, "little, spiteful, diabolic," pulled the *Téméraire* from the gold-bathed sunset toward the gathering darkness, as "slow, sad, and majestic, follows the brave old ship, with death, as it were, written on her . . ." John Ruskin wrote: "Never more shall sunset lay golden robe on her, nor starlight tremble on the waves that part at her gilding."

On his second visit to London in 1857, Herman Melville also saw Turner's painting. It inspired him to write his own tribute to the wooden ships on which he himself had sailed, and to the era vanishing before his eyes:

> *O ship, how brave and fair,*
> *That fought so oft and well,*
> *On open decks you manned the gun*
> *Armorial.*
> *What cheering did you share,*
> *Impulsive in the van,*
> *When down upon leagued France and Spain*
> *We English ran. . . .*
>
> *But Fame has nailed your battle flags*
> *Your ghost it sails before:*
> *O, navies old and oaken,*
> *O Téméraire no more!*

CHAPTER NINETEEN

Edge of Battle

*Don't you worry about either the British Empire or the British Navy!
(THEY ARE SYNONYMOUS TERMS!) Our Navy at this
moment could take on all the Navies of the World! Let 'em all come!*
—ADMIRAL JOHN FISHER, 1911

CAPTAIN ALFRED THAYER MAHAN was a tall beanpole of a man, with a great bald dome rising above calm hooded eyes and a small chin with neat pointed beard—an egghead literally and figuratively. He was a naval officer who detested going to sea as much as he loved thinking about the sea and sea power. Although an American, his passion was the history of the British navy, and the lessons it taught about the relationship between sea power and national dominance.

He offered the first fruits of his study as a set of lectures at the American Naval War College in 1887, and then published them under the title *The Influence of Sea Power Upon History.* Other books, including a biography of Nelson, followed, but the theme of each was always the same: naval supremacy as the key to power in the modern world. Like Darwin's view of nature, Mahan's view of history was of a perpetual struggle for dominance and survival. "The history of seapower," he explained, "is . . . a narrative of contests between nations, of mutual rivalries, of violence frequently culminating in war." Every nation and empire able to exert its will over the seas had thrived and prospered, from ancient Rome to modern Britain. Those that did not, like Hannibal's Carthage and Napoleon's France, or who lost that power, like Spain and Portugal, had withered and died. In 1890 the British still ruled the waves. The issue Mahan left for his readers to ponder was: What if they faltered? Who would be the next nation to use sea power to dominate the world?

For, like any great historian, Mahan offered not just an explanation of the past but also a lesson for the future. "The principal elements which affect, favorably or unfavorably, the growth of sea power in nations . . .

belong to the unchanging order of things," he proclaimed, "They belong, as it were, to the Order of Nature . . . as though laid upon a rock." What Britain had done in building a navy to control the world's sea lanes, others could do—indeed, *must* do if they were to keep up with the race for wealth and empire in the future.

It was not as if every statesmen read Mahan one day and rushed out to build warships, the next. But they certainly gave that impression. One of Mahan's most devoted disciples was Theodore Roosevelt. He had written his own earlier book on British sea power, his *Naval War of 1812,* and would become the most influential advocate of a "blue water" American navy as an expression of its national destiny. In 1895 Roosevelt's friend, Senator Henry Cabot Lodge, set up a map of the Pacific in the Senate chamber with each British naval base marked by a red cross. "It is sea power which is essential to every splendid people," Lodge told his colleagues, "We are a great people; we control this continent; we are dominant in this hemisphere: we have too great an inheritance to be trifled with . . . It is ours to guard and extend"—which meant, in Mahan's terms, building a modern battle fleet.

That had begun the year Mahan's book was published, in 1890. The American Congress authorized the building of three new battleships with a fourth, the *Iowa,* to be built two years later. Each was to be the equal to the most advanced British vessels of the day, as were the armored cruisers that followed. Then in 1898 the battleship *Maine* was in Havana harbor protecting American citizens there, British navy–style, when it mysteriously blew up and sank. The incident would propel America into war with Spain, its first major appearance on the geopolitical stage. Admiral George Dewey, whom Mahan personally recommended to then secretary of the navy Theodore Roosevelt, sailed his six modern battleships and cruisers into Manila Bay and destroyed the entire Spanish fleet before breakfast. The Mahan Doctrine had scored its first success, and America was now a world naval power.

The Japanese made *Influence of Sea Power* a textbook in their naval and military colleges. Its themes seemed to speak directly to them. Like Britain, they were an island nation. Like America, they were recently industrialized and anxious to enter the race for empire and hegemony. The navy became the focus of Japan's geopolitical hopes, and in 1873 Britain set up a naval mission in Tokyo under Lieutenant Commander Archibald Douglas to help. In 1882 nineteen of Japan's twenty-eight warships were bought in Britain. The Japanese navy copied the Royal Navy's uniforms, signals, band tunes, and even used special red bricks imported from England to build their naval academy. The Japanese navy's lightning defeat of its Chinese counterpart in 1894–95 gave Japan control over Korea. "Master and pupil have just reason to be proud of each," wrote the London *Times* approvingly. The victory also convinced Britain to sign a naval alliance with the new rising power in Asia.

On May 14, 1905, Admiral Heirachiro Togo, who had been trained on HMS *Britannia,* took his Vickers-built flagship *Mikasa,* four other battleships and ten cruisers, and wiped out the Russian fleet at the battle of Tsuchima.* The effects reverberated around the world. It set off riots and revolution in Russia. The emergence of the world's first non-white modern power stirred the hopes of men like Mohandas Gandhi and W. E. B. DuBois. But Tsuchima also demonstrated how quickly and catastrophically the new naval technologies could shift the balance of power against those who could not keep up. Just five years earlier the Russian fleet had been considered state of the art; now it was scrap metal at the bottom of the ocean. Mahan seemed even more the prophet with honor in his own time.

Nowhere with more honor, in fact, than in Germany. Its new ruler, Kaiser Wilhelm, had virtually been raised by the Royal Navy. His happiest memories included visiting his grandmother, Queen Victoria, and touring her navy's ships with their gleaming brasswork and teak decks, surrounded by smiling admirals in blue frock coats and plumed hats. "Wilhelm's one idea," his mother wrote, "is to have a Navy which shall be larger and stronger than the British Navy."

Alfred Thayer Mahan became his guru. "I am just now not reading but devouring Captain Mahan's book and am trying to learn it by heart," the kaiser wired a friend in 1894. "It is on board all my ships and constantly quoted by all my captains and officers." Wilhelm wanted Germany to have her rightful place in the leadership of nations, her "place in the sun." Reading Mahan had showed him how to do it. In 1898 came the first German Navy Act; two years later a second doubled the number of ships to be built, to nineteen battleships and twenty-three cruisers in the next twenty years. In another decade, Germany would go from a naval

---

*Even Togo's last signal before the battle consciously echoed Nelson's before Trafalgar: "The fate of the Empire depends on this battle. Let every man do his utmost."

ranking lower than Austria to having the second largest battle fleet in the world. For the first time since Trafalgar, Britain had an aggressive and truly dangerous naval rival to worry about.

Not that Britons were complacent about the situation. In 1884, just two years after the bombardment of Alexandria, W. T. Stead's *Pall Mall Gazette* ran a series of stories entitled "The Truth About the Navy" by "One Who Knows the Facts." The author was Stead himself, the most reputed journalist in England. The series offered lots of cold hard data to show that the British navy, far from being the unchallengeable ruler of the waves, was desperately short of everything, from first-class battleships to torpedo boats. Its vital coaling stations around the world were unprotected; its guns were antiquated and poorly used; it lacked enough cruisers to protect British trade. In a war, Stead averred, the navy's top admirals secretly believed they would be trounced.

Much of this was journalistic hype, supplied by disgruntled officers outside the Admiralty. The navy did have its problems. It was too class-bound and tradition-minded for its own long-term good. Many of its ships in outlying stations were slow and superannuated. Gunnery practice, when it happened, was still geared around the ranges of Nelson's navy, while modern guns were hitting targets at distances of a mile or more. Standards suffered as a result. Gunnery expert Captain Percy Scott claimed that of the three thousand navy shells fired at the bombardment of Alexandria, exactly ten were direct hits. More gravely, taking on the duties of the old Navy Board had reduced the Victorian Admiralty to examining bureaucratic trees, instead of considering the larger strategic forest. There was still no Chief of Naval Staff and no one to think about long-term planning.

But there was little to justify the hysterical tone of Stead's articles, or the kind of national sensation they set off—far greater, as Stead admitted, than that of any articles he had written in his life. "A cry of patriotic anxiety" went up across the country, the *Daily Telegraph* reported, "to which no Ministry can close its ears." The result was the Naval Defense Act of 1889, which formally reestablished the old two-power standard for British naval superiority and dedicated some 21.5 million pounds to building ten new battleships and thirty-eight other vessels. Britain's naval future had become the hot political issue for the 1890s. It would split the Liberal party as severely as Irish Home Rule did, and give the British public a taste of the stark fear of defeat its Georgian predecessors had known. That fear would become familiar again in the darkest days of the Blitz.*

Then came Mahan. He left an ambivalent legacy at best. On the one hand, his history of modern sea power was a tribute to Britain's rise from island obscurity to world greatness. As someone said, the discovery of "sea power" was for Britons like the discovery of oxygen: after breathing it for centuries, it was exciting to learn what it actually was. The term itself entered intellectual fashion. The Latin essay prize at Cambridge University for 1895 was on "British Sea Power" (in Latin, of course). When Mahan came to England in 1893, it was a triumphal progress. Prime Minister Lord Rosebery gave him a private dinner, where he and Mahan talked until midnight. Mahan dined not once but twice with the queen, and was the first foreigner ever to be hosted by the Royal Yacht Squadron, with a hundred admirals and captains swarming to shake his hand. He met future prime ministers Asquith and Balfour, and he was the first person ever to receive honorary degrees at Cambridge and Oxford in the same week.

Yet for Britain's future, Mahan's words offered cold comfort. It was as if this American had let the secret of her greatness out of the bag; now he was inspiring at least three other nations to try the same thing, including his own. Could Britain remain on top? "The oceans," as former Liberal minister Charles Dilke put it in an influential book, "are in fact a British possession." Britain's vast merchant fleet, traveling to every part of the globe, was not just the material foundation of its status as a world power, as Mahan argued; it kept the island nation clothed and fed. Not only world peace or the empire, but Britain's very survival, depended on its navy ruling the waves. That was what the Colomb brothers and the Admiralty's Carnavon Commission† had pointed out; now Mahan made the same point in a more chilling way.

In 1895 the Navy League sprang up, to encourage public awareness of the need for maintaining British naval supremacy—and to counter a sim-

---

*The sense that the navy was running out of control was reinforced on June 22, 1893, when the battleship *Camperdown* collided with Admiral Sir George Tyron's flagship *Victoria* because of Tyron's faulty signal, which no one had the courage to countermand—although the collision cost Tryon his life and those of 358 officers and men. One who barely survived was *Victoria*'s second-in-command, John Jellicoe.
†Set up by Admiral Sir Alexander Milne in 1878, the commission urged that the navy plan and allocate resources for a systematic defense of British trade. The Admiralty largely ignored it.

ilar Navy League in Germany. The annual navy budget or "estimates" poured into building one uniform "class" of battleships and cruisers after another, in the frenetic search for the right technical combination in the proper numbers to hang on. There was a *Renown* class (using nickel steel for the first time instead of iron, for greater protection); a *Royal Sovereign* class; a *Majestic* class (using, ironically, German Krupp steel for its turrets and mounting two 12-inch guns); a *Duncan* class; and a *King Edward VII* class, capable of 18½ knots. Ships ever stronger, ever faster, more heavily armed: yet each made a little weaker by the appearance of the next, even as other industrial powers were doing the same.

So the great naval review of June 1897 for the queen's Diamond Jubilee, took place in an atmosphere of unease and uncertainty. On the one hand, it was a pageant of naval supremacy of unparalleled splendor. The queen, her son the future Edward VII, and his son the future George V, toured the warships of twenty-two invited nations, including Germany, and a magnificent British fleet of 21 battleships and 53 cruisers, which had been assembled at Spithead without diminishing a single foreign station. On the other, Britain sensed it was surrounded by competitors and imitators, even enemies. The Germans had demonstrated a determination to meddle in the affairs of South Africa. The collision of British and French forces at Fashoda in the Sudan in 1898 might have led to war, except for Britain's naval edge. That led to the kaiser's quip: "The poor French. They have not read their Mahan!" But that same edge also kept Germany from intervening when the Boer War broke out the next year.

But how was Britain going to stay ahead? That was the agonizing question to which Mahan only offered half-answers. In 1902, the man who thought he had the answer was about to take the stage, as the Admiralty's Second Sea Lord. He was already sixty-one; respected and feared, he was known as a man with a gift for finding talented subordinates and for making enemies. In fact, he was the man who had supplied the data for Stead's sensational articles in 1884, which had thrown the navy into such an uproar. He was John Arbuthnot Fisher.

• • •

Everything about Jack Fisher cut against the grain. There was his appearance: short, stout, with narrow slit eyes, a mocking smile, with yellow skin from bouts with malaria and dysentery in colonial service. Since he was born in Ceylon, there were rumors in that racially conscious era that he had Oriental blood. The German naval attaché in London would refer to him as "that unscrupulous half-Asiatic." In fact, Fisher was the son of an impoverished former captain in the 78th Highlanders who sent him to live with relatives in England, and into the navy at age thirteen to earn his own bread.

Then there was his career. In an age when the service still considered sailing and navigation an officer's most essential skills, Fisher had specialized in gunnery—becoming gunnery officer on the *Warrior,* a gunnery instructor on HMS *Excellent,* and then head of Naval Ordnance in 1886— and in the development of the torpedo. Most officers could not be bothered to deal with the Whitehead torpedo when it made its first appearance in 1869. Fisher remembered one old admiral telling him, "There were no torpedoes when I came to sea and I don't see why the devil there should be any of the beastly things now." But Fisher saw how these sixteen-foot-long explosive tubes, equipped with an independent screw propeller and a reliable warhead, could revolutionize sea warfare. Even the largest battleship would be vulnerable to a single torpedo-armed craft. "History," Fisher would say later, "is a record of exploded ideas." The new naval technologies were not just making the old ships obsolete, but also the old rules and assumptions behind them.

Finally, there was his personality. When he became commander in chief of the Mediterranean fleet in 1899, at age fifty-eight, he terrified virtually everyone who dealt with him. On board ship, "He prowled around with the steady, rhythmical tread of a panther. The quarterdeck shook and all hands shook with it. The word was quickly passed from mouth to mouth when he came on deck. 'Look out, here comes Jack.' " He wanted his officers and men think of themselves as a fighting fleet once again, to make them the prototype of the modern technological navy he wanted. Everything was about "tactics, strategy, gunnery, torpedo warfare," remembered one subordinate, "it was a veritable renaissance and affected every officer in the fleet." When one of them failed an exercise, Fisher told him that he was sorry for the man's wife and children but "if it had been in a time of war, I would have had you shot."

As Second Sea Lord in 1902, commander in chief at Portsmouth the next year, and then First Sea Lord the year after that, his energy and drive swept aside all opposition. He was never at his desk later than five in the morning, and rarely left earlier than nine in the evening. On slow days, he would wander the halls of the Admiralty with a sign around his neck, reading I HAVE NOTHING TO DO or GIVE ME SOMETHING TO SIGN. He

dashed off letters in a broad impulsive hand, signing them "Yours til charcoal sprouts" or "Burn this!" The Admiralty was going to be "the house
that Jack built," he told everyone; "so we must have no tinkering! No pan-
dering to sentiment! No regard for susceptibilities! . . . We must be ruthless, relentless, and remorseless!"

Fisher was there to shake things up. That was why, despite their misgivings, the politicians had put him there in order to keep the British navy
on top. Fisher brought remorseless energy to the vision of others; at
times, too much energy. He was a man convinced of his own rightness and
refused to suffer fools or opposition gladly—in his mind, the same thing.
In the years leading up to 1914, he would force the navy to undergo a
series of revolutionary changes and reforms. Most of them were necessary, although not all of them were good.

Fisher tried to broaden the navy's social and intellectual base. He
brought engineering and executive officers together as one class of cadets
at the Royal Naval College at Dartmouth, as HMS *Britannia* became an
off-shore establishment, the equivalent of the American Naval Academy
at Annapolis. Cadets were still only twelve or thirteen when they entered,
for a grueling physical and mental course of study: "An austere method of
ensuring the survival of a certain kind of fittest," as one graduate ruefully
noted. But Fisher now made sure cadets postponed choosing among gunnery or navigation or engineering until their posting as lieutenants; it was
an attempt, not entirely successful, to close the social and intellectual gap
between the engine room and the bridge. Fisher did the same when he
allowed senior warrant officers to apply for lieutenancies; with the disap-
pearance of ship's masters, that plebeian route to a commission had
closed. In the eighteenth century, that despised century for the new technological navy, a common sailor could find a way to move from the lower
deck to the quarterdeck. Now it was almost impossible, even under
Fisher. The sea service was decidedly still a "class act"—with all the good
and bad that implies.

Even before Fisher arrived, there had been a new emphasis on gunnery. It was Admiral Tromp in the seventeenth century who said, "No one
can command at sea farther than his guns can reach." It was Percy Scott,
director of gunnery at HMS *Excellent,* who taught the new navy how to
shoot, how to use telescopic sights, and how to hit the target. Scott
showed his students that they could use the fall of shot and the splash it
made behind, beside, or in front of the target to judge distance and range.
Before Scott, captains practiced their guns, when they practiced at all, on

stationary targets at ranges under 1,500 yards—less than a mile. But in naval warfare the enemy ship is constantly on the move, and while steam had trebled the speed of battleships and quadrupled that of cruisers, the range of guns had increased by tenfold.

As commander in chief in the Mediterranean, Fisher set his gunners practice at the unheard-of ranges of 5,600 to 7,000 yards and on moving targets. In March 1905 he made Scott Inspector of Target Practice, an office Fisher created for him, and put Scott to work creating shooting competitions between ships and fleets. Gunnery officers underwent a big jump in prestige and importance in the British navy. Like Fisher, Scott was incapable of tact. He made many enemies, and generated more complaints. But Fisher was adamant. "I don't care if he drinks, gambles, and womanizes," he said. "He hits the target."

So did Scott's gunners. In a short time Scott had raised the percentage of practice hits from 30 to 80 percent, at ranges from 2,000 to 7,000 yards—almost four miles. At that range, no gunner could see what he was shooting. Therefore, Scott introduced long-range optical devices mounted in the foremast to measure distance and judge impact. The civilian engineer Arthur Pollen, whose brother was a naval officer, worked on a machine to calculate the direction and speed of enemy ships, since at those formidable distances, the shell had to fall where an enemy ship was going, rather than where it was when the gun was fired. By 1908, thanks to Fisher and Scott, British capital ships were hitting moving targets at 8,000–9,000 yards, while steaming at 14 knots. And Scott was looking at ways to centralize the ship's fire control, so that every shot from the big guns fell where they could do the most damage.

Fisher's other big breakthrough was in submarines. There had been experiments in submersible naval craft since the American Revolution. In the 1880s John Philip Holland, a fiery Irish nationalist, had created a working submarine with a single torpedo tube to sink British warships. Ironically, it was the British Admiralty that made the most of Holland's design, buying in 1900 the rights for its oil-fuel engine and electric battery for operating underwater (other countries soon followed: Japan, Sweden, and the Dutch in 1906 and Russia in 1907). The Holland boat was inferior in every respect to the underwater craft the French were trying out, but it had the advantage—important in any arms race—of being ready for trials at once.

Admirals like Sir Arthur Wilson of the Mediterranean fleet, considered the submarine "underhanded, unfair, and damned un-English." But

Fisher grasped its significance at once. Even with old Whitehead torpe-does of limited range, the first submarine trials in March 1904 proved devastating against surface ships (including Admiral Wilson's very English *Majestic*-class battleships). With new gyroscopically guided torpe-does able to hit a target at a range of a mile or more, the submarine could turn naval warfare upside down. "My beloved submarines," Fisher wrote, would "magnify the naval power of England seven times more than pre-sent." The submarine, in fact, gave Fisher his first great strategic vision, of flotillas of submarines and torpedo boats shutting down enemy ports and coasts, and making the major waterways of the world impassable to enemy warships. "Suffice it to say," Fisher predicted in April 1905, "in three or four years of this date . . . the English Channel and the western basin of the Mediterranean will not be habitable by a fleet or squadron."

Fisher's vision of submarine warfare, like Scott's of a battleship with all guns turning and firing at the press of a single button, demanded more technology than British engineers could provide. Fisher saw the Royal Navy "saturating" the narrow seas with one hundred submarines and a hundred fast torpedo craft. In 1904 Britain had fewer than twenty. But at least Fisher was thinking ahead of the game, not reacting to it like every-one else. And in June 1905 Captain Henry Jackson, one of the pioneers in the development of shipboard wireless technology, began negotiating with Vickers for the construction of a new oceangoing submarine, the 600-ton D Class, capable of doing 18 knots. When its modified 800-ton variant, the E class, went into service in 1908, it would give Britain the lead in submarine service over the rest of the world.

"On the British Navy rests the British Empire," said Fisher when he was commander in chief of the Mediterranean. In his mind there were "five strategic keys" to the empire and the world economic system: Gibraltar, Alexandria and Suez, Singapore, the Cape of Good Hope, and the Straits of Dover. England possessed them all. His job as First Sea Lord was to make sure it kept them. To do that, he decided there had to be a radical consolidation of the navy and reorientation of its strategic focus.

He began by scrapping more than 150 of the navy's old gunboats and sloops scattered around the world; ships, he said in a famous phrase, "too weak to fight and too slow to run away." In the event of war, "an enemy cruiser would lap them up like an armadillo let loose on an ant-hill." For Fisher was thinking in terms of war, not just showing the flag. Just as he decided other inessential navy services and personnel "must be extirpated like cancer—cut clean out," so the old distribution of ships and stations demanded a reshuffle. Australia, China, and the East Indies stations became the Eastern Fleet, based at Singapore; the same happened with the North and South American stations. The Mediterranean fleet shrank from fourteen battleships in 1902 to eight in 1904, and six in 1907. The most modern ships, Fisher's new *Dreadnought* and the battle cruisers, were concentrated in the Nore squadron of what he designated the Home Fleet, which included the old Channel Fleet and a large reserve of par-tially manned capital ships and cruisers. All the navy's biggest and best, including its torpedo boats, submarines, and anti-submarine destroyers, were now stationed along the North Sea. And all their gray steel hulls and turreted guns pointed in one direction, toward Germany.

Fisher said later that he first divined Germany's intentions to rule the world when he met its military delegates at the international disarma-ment conference at The Hague in 1899. The Foreign Office had made up its mind in 1902; an official visit to the German shipyards at Kiel and Wilhelmshaven convinced the Admiralty that the kaiser's naval preparations were aimed at England, and England alone. No amount of diplomatic niceties or warm family feelings (the German kaiser was Edward VII's nephew) could disguise the fact that Wilhelm II's imperial ambitions centered on knocking the Royal Navy from its global perch. Fisher, not surprisingly, pushed for a preemptive strike, and argued that his ships could "Copenhagen" the German fleet as it lay at anchor at Kiel. "The Germans are our natural enemies everywhere," he exclaimed, "we ought to unite with France and Russia."

Indeed, it was time for a major reassessment of Britain's strategic position. Of the rising naval powers, America was the least probable enemy. After Tsuchima, the Russian threat, which had haunted Palmer-ston and Disraeli, had shrunk to nothing. France had dropped out of the naval arms race. Their checkmate at Fashoda had pushed French politi-cians into a *crise de conscience* and left them with a choice. They could continue their rivalry with Britain for overseas empire, or confront the growing German menace on their eastern flank. France's leaders opted to confront Germany. In 1904 France signed an Entente Cordiale with Britain, ending an enmity stretching back to the Hundred Years' War. Britain had a new continental ally—actually two, since friendship with France brought in Russia as well—as the shape of any future conflict in Europe became clear.

The Entente Cordiale was signed in May. In September Fisher became First Sea Lord. The following year he began to draw up plans for possible war against Germany.

What would that conflict look like? Fisher had no doubt it would be a classic naval war, with Germany deploying its forces to sever Britain's trade and the Royal Navy moving into the Baltic and North seas to close down Germany's access to the sea. Fisher relied on his future flotillas of submarines and torpedo boat destroyers, and the older cruisers could do that job. So the role of Britain's main battle fleet was to act as a highly visible deterrent. "Germany keeps her whole fleet always concentrated within a few hours of England," Fisher told the Prince of Wales in 1906. "We must therefore keep a Fleet twice as powerful concentrated within a few hours of Germany."

But the composition of that battle fleet would have to change. His submarine expert, Reginald Bacon, had taught him that any large capital ship within twenty miles of a submarine was effectively doomed. So, "What is the use of battleships as we have hitherto known them?" Fisher asked. "NONE! Their one and only function—that of ultimate security of defense—is gone—lost!"

So Fisher proposed to scrap the lot and start over, with a new kind of warship: the fast battle cruiser. "The first desideratum in every type of fighting ship is *speed*," Fisher explained. "It is the *weather gauge* of the old days." Equipped with the large-caliber guns of the battleship, but light and fast as a cruiser, the battle cruiser hybrid could outpace any opponent at sea, while blowing them out of the water with powerful guns, using Percy Scott's new central-control firing system. It would be a decisive change in naval warfare—and a cheap one, too, since the battle cruiser's light armament would cost less than two-thirds of the old battleship design. A win for the navy, a win for taxpayers and politicians, and Britain rules the waves again. "Supreme—unbeaten!"

Fisher recognized that his idea was far ahead of its time. "At the present moment," he wrote, "naval experience is not sufficiently ripe to abolish totally the building of battleships," especially since other powers were still building them, not least Germany. So Fisher's compromise was the *Dreadnought,* launched at Portsmouth in 1906. His real design, the battle cruisers of the *Invincible* class, did not appear until two years later. *Dreadnought* took a year and a day to build, a record time and in conditions of top secrecy. Even after she was launched, Frederick Jane, who first began publishing data on the world's navies in *Jane's Fighting Ships* in 1898, was not allowed to reveal all her specifications. All Britain needed anyone to know was that *Dreadnought* made all other warships in the world obsolete.

Steam turbine engines made the *Dreadnought* the fastest capital ship afloat, capable of doing 21 knots—certainly faster than any threatening submarine. She carried ten 12-inch guns, whereas her biggest and closest competitors carried only four. This too was important, because as Percy Scott had shown, the bigger the caliber of gun the more accurate it was at greater ranges, as well as more devastating at the point of impact. The *Dreadnought's* guns were set up on five turrets, allowing her to blast enemies from end-on, as well as broadside. This meant that a fleet of ten *Dreadnought*s could match the forward-firing power of thirty pre-*Dreadnought* battleships—and Fisher had plans for many more *Dreadnought*s, as well as the slightly smaller battle cruisers. "We shall have ten *Dread-noughts at sea* before a single [foreign] *Dreadnought* is launched, and we have thirty percent more cruisers than Germany and France put together!"

Depressing news for Germany, certainly. Yet the response of Fisher's German counterpart, Admiral Tirpitz, was far different from what the British had hoped. Without intending to do so, Fisher had started the first great arms race in modern history. Without knowing it, he had put Europe on the path to war.

Tirpitz had often visited Portsmouth as a naval cadet and admired and envied the Royal Navy. Like his kaiser, Tirpitz believed Germany's future dominant role in the world depended on a navy powerful enough to challenge it. "The military situation against England demands battle-ships in as great a number as possible," he had declared back in 1897 when he took office ("Why was Nelson then always calling for frigates?" Kaiser Wilhelm, who knew his naval history, wanted to know. "Because he *had* a battle fleet," was Tirpitz's reply). The appearance of the *Dreadnought* made the fifteen battleships he had already built little more than British tar-get practice. But Tirpitz refused to be intimidated. He believed that Germany's industrial and technological might would allow it ultimately to outbuild Britain ship for ship. Germany had been close to developing a *Dreadnought* type of battleship, as was America. So, using the threat of his own resignation, Tirpitz forced the German Reichstag to expand his naval estimates to include three *Dreadnought*-type battleships and a battle cruiser. Ominously, Tirpitz also put aside money to create a German sub-marine branch.

In July 1906 the first German dreadnought, the *Nassau,* was laid down at Kiel. The next year work on three more dreadnoughts, *Westfalen, Posen,*

and *Rheinland,* was started under stealthy security. So, too, the first
German battle cruiser, the *Von der Tann,* with eight 11-inch guns, making
her the match to Fisher's *Invincible.* At this rate, Tirpitz would have nine
dreadnoughts by 1909; Britain would have twelve. Even if Germany continued at the same rate, it would have thirteen in 1912, to Britain's sixteen. If it built even faster (and Germany had seven shipyards capable of
building a dreadnought every two years), it could pull just about even—or
with the battle cruisers thrown in, slightly ahead.

When word of what was happening leaked out in the spring of 1909,
the result was a massive public outcry. All the new fears about British vulnerability, all the worries about someone else's ambitions for world domination, came to the surface. Ugly attacks were directed at the Asquith
government and at Fisher in particular for being too complacent and
unaware of what the Germans were up to. Instead of building four new
dreadnoughts for next year, as the government had planned, the public
demanded doubling that number. "We want eight and we won't wait,"
was the rallying cry, while the *Daily Telegraph* cried defiantly, "We are not
yet prepared to turn the face of every portrait of Nelson to the wall."

On the other side, Liberals like Lloyd George worried that the naval
race with Germany was eating up money that ought to be used for social
programs—not the last time this argument would be heard. But Foreign
Secretary Lord Grey gave what would become the standard reply: "If we,
alone among the great powers, gave up the competition and sank into a
position of inferiority . . . we should cease to count for anything amongst
the nations of Europe, and we should be fortunate if our liberty was left."
After beating a vote of censure in the House of Commons, Asquith
agreed to build four dreadnoughts in 1910 and authorize money for four
more, if the Germans continued to build. As Home Secretary Winston
Churchill, an opponent of the additional ships, put it, "The Admiralty
had demanded six ships; the economists offered four; and we finally com-
promised on eight."

The pro-navy party had won. But the implications for the future were
grim. Tirpitz would have no choice but to consider Britain's new dreadnought program as a threat aimed directly at Germany. He was bound to
respond in kind, raising the stakes yet again. More seriously, the commitment of funds to outbuild the Germans meant Britain was abandoning
any notion of a two-power standard for naval superiority. No amount of
money could enable Britain to compete with Germany *and* the United
States or Russia or even Italy. A new policy, of dominance over the world's

second-leading naval power by a 60 percent margin, went into effect. For the first time since the seventeenth century, England would have to find allies to preserve its strategic edge at sea.

Japan was one; the naval alliance was renewed in 1911, securing Britain's Pacific flank. France was another; the government signed a controversial naval alliance, letting France take over some of Britain's strategic responsibilities in the Mediterranean. The Admiralty also began approaching the Dominions, like Canada and Australia, to contribute to their own defense. The plan included having them pay for two battle cruisers, the *Australia* and *New Zealand,* which the navy actually wanted for itself.

It was a grim season all the way around at the Admiralty. All the resentment Fisher had built up by his brusque refusal to tolerate any opposition to his plans finally and publicly descended on his head. The anti-Fisher forces were headed by Sir Charles Beresford, commander in chief of the Channel Fleet, who called Fisher "our dangerous lunatic" and told the First Lord the scheme for creating the Home Fleet was "a fraud upon the public and a danger to the Empire." Ugly enough, but when Beresford managed to organize a public inquiry into Fisher's conduct in office, Fisher found the final report insufficiently exculpatory and blamed Asquith for the lack of support. The "Eight Won't Wait" campaign was the final straw. On January 25, 1910, Fisher left the navy, after fifty-five years of continuous service. Percy Scott quit later that year. The navy had lost its two most outstanding leaders, just as the race against Germany was coming into the final turn.

Fortunately, a third figure was ready to step forward to offer the kind of leadership the British navy and nation so desperately needed. This came as a surprise to almost everyone who knew him. At thirty-six, Winston Churchill had a long reputation as a self-seeking publicity hound and as an unscrupulous political adventurer. The idea of "Winston" having convictions or principles at all, said the king's private secretary, "is enough to make anyone laugh." When Asquith switched him from the Home Office to the Admiralty in 1911, it was assumed he would be the prime minister's hatchet man in cutting the navy budget and dispatching anyone who stood in his way.

Instead, the experience transformed Churchill's life. Later, he recalled his first visit to the Home Fleet as it lay in anchor at Portland: "The whole harbor . . . alive with the goings and comings of launches and small launches of every kind" around the great gray ships, "and as night fell ten thousand lights from sea and shore sprang into being and every masthead twinkled as the ships and squadrons conversed with one another." Who, Churchill asked himself, could fail to work for such a service? He remembered how it had stood between Napoleon and the dominion of the world. Now it stood in the way of another nation's bid for world power, a Teutonic nation "and all that a Teutonic system meant."

For the Germans and Mahan's other disciples, a navy represented power and dominion. For the British, it was existence itself. "All our long history built up century after century," Churchill wrote, "all our great affairs in every part of the globe, all the means of livelihood and safety of our industrious, active population depended upon" those navy ships. How best to serve them? For advice Churchill turned to Jack Fisher, now Baron Fisher of Kilverstone. The two became inseparable friends and colleagues, as the older man guided the younger through the steps of consolidating the earlier reforms and branching out into new ones. They were the most important dual Admiralty act since Sandwich and Anson. Together they forged a navy ready to fight a modern world war.

The most important part was launching the new class of dreadnought battleships, the *Queen Elizabeth* class, in 1912. Armed with 15-inch guns, the largest mounted on any modern warship (the latest American and Japanese dreadnought-types carried 14-inchers), they were the first true fast battleships. They were the fruits of the "Eight Won't Wait" campaign, which Churchill had opposed at the time. Now he recognized ruefully he had been wrong. The *Queen Elizabeth* and her powerful sisters would give the British navy the edge it would need in a decisive battle with a German dreadnought fleet—as Jutland would demonstrate four years later.

The *Queen Elizabeth* also had oil-fired engines. This increased her range, her speed, and ease of refueling: no more daylong stops at remote coaling stations as the entire crew wrestled the sacks of anthracite coal below decks and a black sooty powder covered the entire ship. But it also made building petroleum reserves a naval priority. The British navy bought a controlling share in the Anglo-Persian Petroleum Company, as Churchill dispatched teams to search for new sources in the region. It was the birth of the oil industry in the Persian Gulf: an unintended legacy of the British navy's need for fuel and a new focal point for global economic forces.

Meanwhile, two new bases were taking shape for concentrating the fleet in the North Sea, Rosyth in Scotland and Scapa Flow in the Orkney Islands. Fisher had concluded that the new German submarines would make the old-style close blockade impossible. Shutting down Germany's access to the sea was going to require operations farther from the enemy coasts than ever before, including operations of the main battle fleet. Rosyth, and particularly Scapa Flow, would become the long-range bases where the Home Fleet could wait to go into action in case the German High Seas Fleet dared to venture out. By 1914 this combined home force had swollen to 22 dreadnoughts and 14 modern battle cruisers, plus another 22 older battleships and 160 cruisers and destroyers in reserve. No wonder Churchill would officially dub it "the Grand Fleet" on the eve of war—the greatest and most powerful naval force ever assembled.

Yet long-range operations imposed another burden: finding where the enemy was going and why, before it became too late. The advantages of wireless telegraphy, now on almost every warship, and high-powered optics were offset by the fact that the British would never actually see their opponents until they were almost at the point of action. This meant a new reliance on naval intelligence. Churchill would write the new charter for the Naval Intelligence Division, and appoint the man who would turn it into the prototype of every other modern intelligence service, Reginald "Blinker" Hall. The submarine service, which Churchill, under the influence of both Fisher and Reginald Bacon, continued to expand and upgrade, assumed a new role as unseen advance scouts. So did the "destroyer," a new class of fast warship that Fisher had transformed from a torpedo boat into an anti-submarine escort vessel. Increasingly, they would take the old frigate's place as the eyes and ears of the battle fleet. Churchill's first naval estimates included money for twenty new destroyers, and plans for many more.

The need for long-distance eyes also got the navy into the field of aviation. The Germans were experimenting with lighter-than-air craft, in the shape of their massive Zeppelin airships. Churchill saw the utility of dirigible scouts, but he believed the real future of naval aviation lay with the airplane, which was more maneuverable, less vulnerable, and also cheaper. The first flight off a ship's deck took place in June 1912; in March 1913, the world's first seaplane carrier was unveiled, as the converted cruiser HMS *Hermes*. Churchill wrote to Fisher, "In a few months the Navy List will contain regular flights of aeroplanes attached to the battle squadrons." From communications and intelligence to the submarine and airplane, the British navy now had the future of modern warfare in its hands.

Churchill also tried to bring forward the right men for the future. When he first met David Beatty, he remarked, "You seem very young to be an Admiral." Beatty, who was four years older than Churchill, cheekily replied, "And you seem very young to be First Lord." Churchill made him his naval secretary. John Jellicoe was a Fisher disciple, who had worked with him on everything from gunnery to submarine tactics. Churchill made him second-in-command of the Home Fleet, as Fisher assured him, "He is the future Nelson SURE!" Churchill also saw the need for men who could organize the navy's resources as well as use them. He set up the Admiralty's first Naval War Staff in 1912, and even took steps to open a naval staff college. But Churchill understood as little about staff work as the Admiralty did. His Chief of Naval Staff reported to him but not to the Sea Lords; on matters of policy they remained as much out of the loop as before. No one had yet found a way to get the navy as an *organization* to come to grips with the complexities of modern war. If Churchill or Fisher weren't thinking about it, no one else was.

At the same time, the dreadnoughts continued to thunder down the slips. In 1912 came the *Queen Elizabeth, Warspite, Barham, Valiant,* and *Malaya,* all oil-fired and all packing eight 15-inch guns. Another five, the *Royal Sovereign* class, were slated for 1913. The most recent German battleships had only 12-inch guns. Meanwhile, HMS *Thunderer* had been outfitted with Scott's Director Fire system, with a single key firing all primary guns at the press of a button. In its first test maneuvers, *Thunderer* scored six times more hits than the dreadnought with the best gunnery record in the navy. Soon Director Fire would be installed on every dreadnought, old or new. Once again, the British had jumped ahead.

Across the North Sea, Tirpitz watched and wondered. It was not that he gave up the arms race in 1913. He still believed that, given time, German industry and technology could defeat the British navy. The first 15-inch gun German battleships, beginning with the *Baden,* were slated to be built that year. But Tirpitz saw no point to trying to outdo the British ship for ship—certainly not until the critical Kiel canal had been widened to permit his dreadnoughts to pass direct from Kiel to Wilhelmshaven. So he told the Reichstag Budget Committee in February that he was ready to accept British naval superiority according to the 60 percent standard.

It was a stunning concession. Outwardly, the British government refused to be impressed. As foreign minister Grey said, "The reason for his saying it is not the love of our beautiful eyes." Churchill's new estimates still included the largest jump in the navy estimates yet, to more than 50 million pounds. Lloyd George almost resigned when he saw them. But Churchill also proposed a one-year moratorium of all dreadnought construction. "If for the space of a year . . . no new ships were built by any nation," Britain would cancel its four projected battleships, he said. "The finances of every country would obtain relief," he stated, and added:

> As thinking men, we have the foreboding that, in the long run, exceptional expenditure on armaments, carried to an excessive degree, must lead to catastrophe, and may even sink the ship of European prosperity and civilization.

With the world sensing it teetered on the brink of a great war, Churchill's proposed "naval holiday" offered a chance for hope. Not for the Germans, however. Their rise to power demanded war. General von Bernhardi had authored a book, *Germany and the Next War,* which stated flatly that war was a necessity for the triumph of German power and *Kultur.* "Only fighting yields happiness on earth," Friedrich Nietzsche had written. Sociologist Ernst Troeltsch saw war as the place where "the fullness of contending national . . . spirits unfold their highest spiritual powers."

Charles Darwin's view of nature, as the emergence of the most fit through the struggle for survival, was the outgrowth of his voyage with HMS *Beagle;* now it had become the official German view of man. War determined the destiny of nations and races, General von Bernhardi stated, and the defeat of Britain would determine Germany's destiny in the next era. Yet now the crucial instrument for victory, the Imperial Navy, was dropping out of the struggle. When General von Heeringen asked Admiral Tirpitz what Germany's chances were in a war with England, and Tirpitz answered "Not great," Heeringen was horrified, as was the rest of the German military establishment. The view of von Moltke, chief of the general staff, was, "War, the sooner the better!" And so in 1912 the army unveiled to the kaiser its own secret strategy to win the war, the Schlieffen plan.

The German army had almost militarized German society to a degree no society had known since Napoleon, with every German male conscripted to serve two full years in barracks and training, then five years as active reserve, and then in the *Landwehr* second reserve until he was thirty-nine. The Schlieffen plan was a triumph of Prussian ruthlessness and discipline and German industrial organization, mobilizing an obedient army of five million men by rail to points west for a sweep into neutral Belgium to capture Paris, and points east for a sweep into Russia. In a matter of weeks the generals believed, Germany's two most dangerous land rivals, France and Russia, would be crushed. Britain would have no time to send its puny army to help them. Instead, it would be forced to sue for peace or face an onslaught from a German navy no longer restrained by budgetary concerns.

Here at last was an infallible plan to make Germany master of Europe and force Britain to admit it as equal partner in ruling the world—to succeed finally where even the great Napoleon had failed. Tirpitz had his doubts; his navy would not be ready for at least another year, he warned. But the kaiser gave his assent and preparations got under way. In 1913 another 170,000 men were added to the peacetime German army, bringing its total to 870,000 men—an army poised to conquer Europe. All it needed was an excuse to go into action.

Meanwhile, the relations between the German and British navies were never more cordial. There seemed to be a break in the dark clouds of enmity and rivalry, with Britain's dominance conceded at last. When the Kiel canal was finally completed in June 1914, the Admiralty announced it was sending its Second Battle Squadron under Admiral Sir George Warrender, to share in the German celebrations. Warrender arrived on June 23, with four of Britain's latest dreadnought battleships: *King George V, Ajax, Audacious,* and *Centurion.* British sailors cheered the kaiser as he cruised past on his yacht, the *Hohenzollern,* and he raised his hand in respectful salute. British officers allowed their German counterparts to tour every inch of their ships virtually without restriction. One German officer, Captain von Hase, would years later say, "I shall never forget the fatherly, affectionate hospitality" of Warrender and the other English officers.

Then on June 28 came the news that Archduke Franz Ferdinand had been assassinated. The kaiser decided to cancel the day's yacht race. He left for Berlin the next morning; Warrender and Tirpitz shook hands and said good-bye. As the English squadron pulled out of Kiel harbor, the German warships ran up the signal, "Pleasant journey." Warrender sent his by wireless:

FRIENDS TODAY.
FRIENDS IN FUTURE.
FRIENDS FOREVER.

The next time these sailors met they would be lobbing 1,000-pound shells at each other for control of the North Sea.

CHAPTER TWENTY

Armageddon—Again

Something seems to be wrong with our bloody ships today.
—ADMIRAL DAVID BEATTY AT JUTLAND, MAY 31, 1916

THE GREAT WAR. The phrase conjures up images of trench warfare, of shell-pocked fields in Flanders strewn with barbed wire and rotting bodies; of mud, lice, and poison gas; the chatter of machine-gun fire and the roar of high-explosive artillery. Verdun, the Somme, Paschendaele; the Argonne and Belleau Wood. A gruesome struggle, which eventually cost the lives of upward of ten million men between 1914 and 1918.

Yet it is by no means the whole story. Behind the horror and stalemate of the First World War's land battles, another great war was being fought on the seas. To the officers and men of the British navy, it had a familiar feel. This was their second world war in just a hundred years. It was fought with new weapons, new technologies, and against a new opponent. Yet the strategies were virtually the same as those of the war against Napoleon: blockade, *guerre de course,* cruisers patrolling the high seas from the China coast to the Dardanelles, and two great battle fleets lying in wait for each other, preparing for the great decisive battle that would settle the contest once and for all.

Yet this time, to its own surprise, the Royal Navy nearly lost the match. It began the war with all the tools for victory—including unprecedented access to its enemy's most secret plans. Yet its opponent proved more resourceful than the Admiralty expected. Tirpitz and the Germans grasped the ruthless spirit of modern technological warfare, if not all its implications. In contrast, it was as if the Royal Navy had never left its wooden walls. It still lingered in the shadow of the "Immortal Memory," still hoping that Nelson, or someone like him, would magically appear at Portsmouth and lead the fleet to victory and glory.

But he did not come. Instead, the British navy would find its habit of "muddling through," its reliance on the habits of class and tradition, were no longer enough. The Admiralty realized to its horror that while it could not win the war single-handedly, it could certainly lose it. In the end, Britain would have to turn for help from two allies, which had managed to clone the virtues of the Royal Navy with fewer of its vices: Japan and the United States. World War I would set the balance of global naval power for the next generation. The British navy would survive and regroup after its nearly disastrous test of fire—even grow to unprecedented size. But it would not rule the waves again.

• • •

The problems began even before England declared war on Germany on August 3, 1914, and they started at the top. The British navy found itself with an unprecedented supremacy in all the world's oceans and regions. Protecting that supremacy had become vital for the sake of the empire; as Churchill had said, "Our naval power involves British existence." So its formal plan for war, first drawn up in 1906 and approved by then First Sea Lord Fisher, was an essentially defensive strategy. The issue was keeping what one already had, as one of its architects and the godfather of modern British naval history, Sir Julian Corbett, put it, rather than taking it from someone else. In 1914, there was no one else. Instead, the navy would defend the main arteries of Britain's trade and lock a long-distance blockade on Germany, in order to "strangle the whole national life of the enemy," from its businesses and banks to its ability to supply its army and navy. The Grand Fleet would only fight if its German counterpart tried to break the blockade. Otherwise, the navy would play prevent-defense until the German economy collapsed.

This, of course, left all initiative to the Germans. Unfortunately for Britain, they were poised to use it. Tirpitz had few illusions about his naval inferiority, but as he told the kaiser, the British navy was spread so thin that it could not "concentrate all its striking force against us." He had a core battle fleet of thirteen dreadnoughts against the Grand Fleet's twenty-one, and five modern battle cruisers against Britain's nine. But Tirpitz also knew they were better armored than their British counterparts, and crewed by men who were at the peak of training (as were the British).

More strikingly, unlike every other admiral in the world since Beachy Head, Tirpitz was unafraid of fighting and losing a showdown against the main British fleet. Even in defeat, Tirpitz figured, his dreadnoughts would so cripple the British that they would have to give ground elsewhere. He could afford to put his High Seas Fleet at risk, knowing that he had his cruisers, his surface raiders, and submarine *Unterseeboot* (U-boat) branch, which would grow from twenty boats in 1914 to more than a hundred at the end of 1916, ready to play havoc with the British sea lanes.

Neither the Admiralty's brand-new Naval War Staff nor its Operations Division understood the implications of Tirpitz's "risk theory." They followed the ancient tradition of letting admirals on the scene decide what to do, even if that meant ignoring what their colleagues in the British army called "the big picture." Instead, the only men with their eyes on larger strategy were the two at the top, Churchill and Fisher, who been reinstated as First Sea Lord. Unfortunately, the partnership that had worked so well behind the scenes broke down when it became official. Churchill and Fisher quarreled incessantly, and with increasing bitterness, as the war ran badly from the start.

At the declaration of war, a fast German battle cruiser, the *Goeben,* and its light cruiser escort *Breslau* led a merry chase around the Mediterranean, while the Admiralty frantically signaled the admirals on station there to stop them. However, neither Commander in Chief Archibald "Arky Barky" Milne nor second-in-command Ernest Troubridge, descendant of one of Nelson's immortal band of brothers, was really up for the job of stealthy cat-and-mouse, as *Goeben*'s captain brought her triumphantly into asylum in the neutral Dardanelles. The *Goeben*'s escape was a humiliation for the Royal Navy, but its geopolitical consequences were even worse. The Turks were already riled about the Asquith government's decision to confiscate two dreadnoughts Vickers was building for the Sultan, the *Agincourt* and *Erin.* The arrival of the powerful *Goeben,* with its 11-inch guns, tipped the Turks into joining the Central Powers. The Dardanelles and entrance to the Black Sea, and the eastern coast of the Mediterranean as far south as Gaza, became enemy territory.

Things were no better in the Pacific. A squadron of German armored and light cruisers under Admiral Graf von Spee broke out of Chinese waters and, after detailing the cruiser *Emden* as a commerce raider, quickly destroyed a force of four British cruisers off the coast of Chile on November 1, 1914, without losing a single sailor. Von Spee's ships were of pre-dreadnought design; the four British cruisers were older than that. But Britain's first exchange of hostile shots in the modern era, at an effective ship-killing range of 12,000 yards or nearly five miles, had ended in disaster. Britain had also lost control of the trade routes in a crucial region of the world. Tirpitz's hunch that the Royal Navy had stretched itself too thin was coming true.

But nowhere was the Admiralty's failure to anticipate or control events more apparent than in the submarine menace. Everything Fisher and Reginald Bacon had said about these new stealth weapons, which could now dive to depths of 200 feet, make 15 knots on the surface with their diesel engine, and enjoy a range of 5,000 miles, proved true. Except that it was the Germans, not the British, who proved the masters of the U-boat. Every British warship, even the biggest, was suddenly vulnerable to surprise attack.

On the morning of September 22, 1914, Captain Otto Weddigen of the submarine *U-12* peered out of his periscope and saw three British cruisers drawn up in a row. They were part of the Royal Navy's blockade off the Dutch coast. Firing five torpedoes from his submerged position, he sank all three in quick succession: *Aboukir*, *Cressy*, and *Hogue*—the last, ironically, named after one of the navy's most glorious victories. They were older cruisers, only 10,000 tons each. But more than 1,400 British officers and men died that morning, not one of whom even saw his killers. Indeed, *Cressy* and *Hogue* were both sunk when they stopped to rescue survivors.

The Admiralty flew into a panic. Julian Corbett said he could never remember an incident in the history of naval warfare in which "had so great a result been obtained by means so relatively small." There was a frantic scramble to string anti-submarine nets and other defenses at the new bases at Rosyth and Scapa Flow. Captains in other British ports had to wonder. Were they safe even in home waters? On October 27 the brand-new battleship *Audacious* struck a mine—another stealth weapon against surface ships—and sank.

With the loss of *Audacious* and mechanical troubles with other dreadnoughts, the Grand Fleet's advantage over the High Seas Fleet had shrunk from 60 to just over 20 percent. Admiral Beatty at Rosyth told his wife that the Admiralty was in panic mode. "We are nervous as cats," he wrote, "afraid of losing lives, losing ships, and running risks." Commander in Chief Jellicoe said later that if the High Seas Fleet had taken full advantage of the situation its submarines and mines had created, "we should now be a German colony."

However, the German U-boats were actually shifting their target. With the British fleet effectively buttoned up at Rosyth and Scapa Flow, they needed easier meat. They found it in the great open sea lanes surrounding the British Isles. On February 4, 1915, Germany declared that any vessel found in designated waters close to Great Britain, neutral or not, would be subject to attack without warning.

This first declaration of "unrestricted" submarine warfare caught the Admiralty, once again, completely unprepared. The time-tested antidote to any *guerre de course* was the convoy. This, however, was the one legacy of the Nelson era the Royal Navy had abandoned. After the international ban on privateering in 1856, the Admiralty dropped convoys from any future war plans. It assumed its fast cruisers could run down any surface raiders foolish enough to try to prey on British shipping. No one thought about the possibility of *under*-surface raiders.

The numbers of British ships sunk by U-boats rose slowly at first. The Germans had only twenty boats available for commerce raiding, with just two or three operating in the Western Approaches, Irish Sea, and English Channel at any given time. Yet in March and April they managed to sink thirty-nine vessels, all without warning. Back in 1903 Jack Fisher had imagined the terror a submarine attack could inspire: "Sudden—awful—invisible—unavoidable! Nothing conceivably more demoralizing!" In the late spring every merchant ship captain in the western Atlantic sailed with his heart in his mouth, zigzagging for his life as he made for home port.

On May 7, 1915, one of them was Captain William Turner of the passenger ship *Lusitania*, pride of the Cunard line and inbound from New York City. Turner had made the route five times already, relying on the *Lusitania*'s famous speed to elude the U-boats. This time he was not so lucky. The *Lusitania* was already in sight of the Irish coast when *U-20* struck her with a single torpedo. Within twenty minutes she went to the bottom, taking 1,198 civilian passengers and crew with her, including 128 Americans.

International horror and outrage swept over German embassies and into the dispatch boxes of the German Foreign Office. The killing of innocents, especially women and children, as a matter of deliberate policy was something new to Western warfare. The outcry was not deflected by German charges that the *Lusitania*, ostensibly sailing from a neutral port, had secretly been carrying arms (which turned out to be true) or the fact that the British Admiralty had done nothing to protect the *Lusitania*, although its own intelligence service knew U-boats were hunting in the area. President Woodrow Wilson of the United States delivered a sharp rebuke to the German ambassador in Washington, which grew sharper when another liner, the *Arabic,* was sunk in August, killing more innocent

Americans. Terrified that the United States might be pushed into renouncing their neutrality, Germany's chancellor agreed to lift the unrestricted U-boat campaign.

The end came just as the campaign was becoming effective, and just in time for Britain. The navy slowly started to develop anti-submarine tactics and scored some success against individual boats, including the destruction of Weddigen's *U-12* by the *Dreadnought:* it was her one contribution to the war she had done so much to start. But it was American outrage, not British warships, that had halted the U-boat menace—at least for now.

In fact, 1915 found the Admiralty confused and adrift. This, in spite of the fact that its Naval Intelligence Office had cracked the German naval cipher at the very start of the war and stayed on top of it right to the end.* Each time the Germans smelled a rat and changed the code, the navy's master code breaker Sir Alfred Ewing, managed to break it again. Housed in Room 40 in the Old Admiralty Building, Ewing's and "Blinker" Hall's hardworking wranglers provided priceless information on German naval plans, intentions, and movements.

The problem was what to do with it. No official system for distribution existed. Much of it went directly up to the Admiralty Board itself but never made it down again, to be put into the hands of those who could act on it. The navy's head of operations despised the men and women in Room 40 and mistrusted their reports. "Thank God," he was overheard to say when the Germans changed their codes again, "I shan't have any more of that damned stuff." He even forbade his own staff to meet with them.

Churchill and Fisher were too busy quarreling to pay much attention. Fisher's reinstatement as First Lord at the end of October 1914, such a perfect idea at the time, had probably been a mistake. Far more than Mahan, Fisher had foreseen the future of modern naval warfare. He understood that the era of the big battleship was over and that all sea warfare would be determined by three factors: *firepower, speed,* and *stealth.* The fast battle cruiser had secured the first two for the British navy; the submarine, the third.

---

*This would not have been possible without the accidental capture of three German cipher books: one from a merchant ship in Australia, the second from a light cruiser, the *Magdeburg,* wrecked on the Russian coast, and the third from a torpedo boat salvaged from the English Channel.

Had he been ten years younger, Fisher might have found the energy to make them work efficiently together in a war situation and figure out ways to incorporate the new advantages of naval intelligence and air power. But at seventy-three, Fisher contented himself with firing off directives and criticizing the plans of his former protégé turned foe, Winston Churchill. Sadly, he was generally on the mark. For Churchill, who had been so brilliant and resourceful in the ramp-up to war, was a disaster when it came.

Unlike so many at the Admiralty, his problem was not too little imagination, but too much. As 1915 began, he saw Britain's naval situation deteriorating fast. So he revived a classic Pitt-Anson strategy to reverse the trend: using the navy's ubiquity to launch an unexpected amphibious strike, disrupting the enemy's plans and straining his resources to the breaking point. The place he chose was Turkey, Germany's new ally in the eastern Mediterranean. Once a British army was landed, Turkey's capitulation "is then only a matter of time," Churchill reasoned. "We cannot be content with anything less than a surrender of everything Turkish in Europe," he added, as he envisioned the British navy sweeping into the Black Sea to join the Russian fleet.

The plan, which involved threading the Dardanelles Straits with a fleet of battleships and then landing a large combined force on the beaches on the peninsula at Gallipoli, might conceivably have worked had the British army backed it early on. But the generals did not. Instead, the force of dreadnoughts under the command of Admiral Sir Ian Hamilton took on the Dardanelles forts and minefields alone at the end of February 1915—just as the German unrestricted U-boat campaign was getting started. Turkish mines sank two British battleships, the *Irresistible* and *Ocean,* and a French one, the *Bouvet.* They almost sank the battle cruiser *Inflexible* as well. By the time the first troop ships arrived at the end of April, the Turks and their German military advisors were well fortified and ready for them.

Almost a quarter of a million British, Australian, and New Zealand troops would die in vain over the next year, without once breaking out of their beachhead trenches. More ships, including battleships *Triumph* and *Majestic,* would be lost in the Gallipoli fiasco to U-boat torpedoes. There were also two political casualties. First Jack Fisher, who had turned bitterly critical of the expedition and resigned when Churchill overrode his objections. Then it was Churchill's turn. His departure was widely celebrated: "The navy breathes freer now it is rid of the succubus Churchill," David

Beatty said. He was ignoring the good work Churchill had done in the three years before the war. Critics also ignored that he was being blamed for a scheme that everyone on the War Cabinet and in the Admiralty, including Fisher, had enthusiastically embraced as a way to break the bloody stalemate on the Western Front—and to get the Royal Navy back in the game.

As 1915 wound down, Grand Admiral Tirpitz should have been content with his navy's performance, especially its U-boat branch, and the serial failures of the British. There had been a few German setbacks. The hopes that Germany might remain a power in the Pacific ended when Von Spee's squadron was intercepted on the way home off the remote Falkland Islands in December 1914 by the modern battle cruisers, *Inflexible* and *Invincible* (they had been sent at Fisher's orders, over the protests of both Beatty and Jellicoe). It was almost as lopsided a slaughter as the fight at Coronel had been. Four German warships and 2,200 men killed, including von Spee himself, or taken prisoner, against ten British killed and injured. The same hope for the Indian Ocean ended with the destruction of cruisers-turned-raiders *Emden, Karlsruhe,* and *Königsberg.* In addition, the abandonment of the unrestricted submarine campaign was a bitter blow.

But what was most frustrating to Tiripitz is that the great decisive battle, the *Entscheidungsgeschlacht,* which he anticipated between his High Seas Fleet and the British Grand Fleet, had not taken place. Everything he had read in Mahan suggested that would be the turning point of the war, with the smaller but more effective fleet beating or at least fatally weakening the larger one. Even if Germany lost the battle, Tirpitz believed, the British navy's strategic position would be shattered—and its image of invincibility destroyed.

Hence a strange irony. The British Admiralty and the commander of the Grand Fleet, who expected to win the great sea battle, did everything to avoid it, including moving the fleet up to Scapa Flow. Tirpitz, who expected to lose the battle, yearned for it with all his heart. Yet his kaiser and his general staff would have none of it. The kaiser regarded the High Seas Fleet as his own personal property; he was not going to risk its magnificent ships against a superior British force, Mahan or no Mahan. Likewise, Germany's generals wanted it preserved as a "fleet in being" to keep the British from landing troops on the North Sea or Baltic coasts. So Tirpitz silently fumed and raged, as one cautious High Seas Fleet commander in chief and then another obeyed the kaiser's wishes. That is, until January 1916, when the fleet got a commander who was eager to find a way to bring about the kind of showdown Tirpitz wanted, but without endangering the entire German fleet.

Reinhardt Scheer was a tough, confident, and quick-thinking sea officer, someone who would have made a fine brother-in-arms to a Hawke or Nelson. He faced a difficult strategic situation. The Grand Fleet was tucked away far out of his reach, at Scapa Flow. The German fleet would have to spend a full day steaming into the North Sea to get at them, exposing their ships to submarine and torpedo attack all the way up and all the way back—or with battle cruisers from Harwich or the Nore cutting off the line of retreat. So Scheer devised a different plan. He now had only thirteen battleships against Jellicoe's twenty-eight. But his were better armored and faster, dreadnought for dreadnought, with more reliable range-finders for more accurate fire. If he could lure out a portion of the British fleet, and then pounce on it before it could get away, he could even the odds for a bigger sea fight later on. Enough, at least, to convince the Kaiser finally to unleash his fleet for the final *Entscheidungsgeschlacht*—a battle even more decisive for world history than Trafalgar.

Without planning to, the Germans had almost succeeded in doing this off the Dogger Bank the previous January. Three German battle cruisers under Admiral Franz Hipper, plus the older cruiser *Blücher,* had set out to make a sweep of waters they thought infested with British spy ships (the Germans never quite realized that the reason the British always seemed to anticipate their moves was not due to spies but Room 40) and then lay mines in the Firth of Forth, entrance to the naval base at Rosyth. Ewing's code breakers picked up the news of their departure and gave it to David Beatty, who set out in the cold North Sea waters to meet them.

He had with him six of the best battle cruisers: *Lion, Tiger, Queen Mary, Princess Royal, New Zealand,* and *Indomitable.* Compared to the warships nations had been building just ten years earlier, they were weapons of unbelievable power and speed. Their prototype, the *Invincible,* had appeared in 1909 with eight 58-ton, 45 caliber, 12-inch Mark X guns, capable of hitting a target eight and a half miles away with 5,100 pounds of shell every sixty seconds— more than twice the weight of broadside of the entire battle fleet at Trafalgar combined. The longest warship in the world, *Invincible* had a top of speed of 25 knots. Fisher called her "my greyhound of the sea." Together with her sister ship *Inflexible,* she had wiped out von Spee's entire squadron without having to get nearer than 10,000 yards.

Yet the *Invincible,* like all battle cruisers, had sacrificed armor for speed. The steel plate around her waist was only six inches thick; her German counterpart, the *Von der Tann,* had 10-inch side and 9-inch turret armor. Later British versions, like Beatty's *Lion* and *Princess Royal,* had more, but they were still woefully thin-skinned compared to Hipper's cruisers. How thin-skinned the British were about to find out, as the first real battle between modern dreadnoughts got under way.

Beatty caught up with Hipper around eight o'clock in the morning and opened fire at the unprecedented range of 20,000 yards—almost twelve miles. His ships were faster than the Germans, capable of speeds up to 30 knots, and the Germans took a ferocious pounding as they closed the range, especially the older and slower *Blücher* and the *Seydlitz,* whose aft and midship turrets both blew up in a "great glowing mass of fire," killing 160 men. But then about ten o'clock the German gunners began to score. One of the first ships hit was the *Lion,* Beatty's flagship. "The whole ship seemed to lift and shake violently," remembered his staff commander, William Chalmers, as two 850-pound projectiles from the *Seydlitz*'s sister ship *Derfflinger* hit home. A midshipman in the *Lion*'s fire control foretop thought they had been torpedoed. "The ship seemed to stop, and the mast, to which the foretop was secured, rocked and waved like a tree in a storm."

More shells rained in as the damage reports poured in to Beatty on the bridge. "Armour belt pierced on the waterline in several places, switchboard room flooded, port engine reducing speed and shortly to stop, 'A' turret magazine on fire, ship making water heavily along port side, all lights gone out . . ." The *Lion* had lost her electric power, as she dropped out of line while Beatty signaled the rest of his cruisers to press ahead. The *Indomitable* stopped to finish off *Blücher,* and *Tiger, Princess Royal,* and *New Zealand* now had the other fleeing German cruisers, including the wounded *Seydlitz,* in their sights.

But then a lookout on the *Lion* spotted a periscope on the starboard bow. Beatty had worried that Hipper might be drawing him into a trap, a cul-de-sac of submarines and hidden mines: dangers made more intimidating by being unseen. He ran up the signal to his battle cruisers, "Turn together eight points to port," as they broke off action to obey. They reassembled around the *Blücher* and finished her off in a spectacular end to the battle, as she rolled over and took nearly 800 men with her. But the rest of Hipper's squadron had escaped and the lessons of Dogger Bank went unlearned. The need for more armor plating; the need for better protection against flash fires in magazines and turrets (with the *Seydlitz* as a vivid warning, the Germans did learn this lesson); the need for ways to prevent the threat of submarine or torpedo attack from disrupting a fleet action.

And above all, the need for naval officers willing to press home the attack regardless of the risk to themselves and their ships, even in the face of a direct order. Fisher in particular was furious at the response to Beatty's panicky signal. "In war the first principle is to disobey orders," he thundered. "Any fool can obey orders." That was after all how the whole Nelson legend had begun, more than a hundred year earlier off Cape St. Vincent. For all their training, all their confidence and esprit de corps, a century of peace and playing world policeman seemed to have sapped away some of the Royal Navy officer's love of combat.

Then, of course, the scale had changed. "A modern sea battle," wrote one young officer about Dogger Bank, "is extremely difficult to describe, partly because it is like nothing else in human experience and partly because that amazing adaptability and power of adjustment which enables mankind rapidly to alter its standard of what is possible or endurable causes men to pretend, even to themselves, that things are nothing which are, in fact, something very terrible." A yardarm to yardarm battle on an old wooden man-of-war could be violent and terrible. But there was something even more horrifying, as Midshipman Filson Young would remember, about a fight among steel dreadnoughts. "Nowhere else do men, banded together in such numbers and wielding such powers, contend with one another at so extreme peril to themselves."

> Each man commits himself with a thousand others to a vulnerable shell, and launches it into a arena sheeted and bolted with flame and concussion. . . . A single stroke of a single weapon might wipe out a thousand lives . . . He may die by a blow, by asphyxiation, by flaying, by boiling, by mutilation, by drowning, or may be instantaneously consumed in a glory of mauve flame, accompanied by the thunder of a detonation which he never hears.

Quite apart from the gunfire, the steel warship had introduced a host of new ways for men to die. One man on the *Seydlitz* watched the effect of the tremendous air pressure from an internal explosion as it swept "roaring through every opening" and every corridor on the ship. "As one poor wretch was passing through a trap-door a shell burst near him. He was exactly halfway through. The trap-door closed with a terrific snap."

Horrible death at an instant. Young believed it was the supreme glory of the British navy that "thousands and thousands of men are always ready to do this as a matter of course; do it easily, desire to do it." So they had done at Dogger Bank, and so they were about to do on a far larger and bloodier scale, in the waters off Jutland on the Danish coast in late May of 1916.

• • •

The fight at Dogger Bank in January 1915 had been indecisive. Admiral Scheer was determined not to let that happen again. He would use Hipper to lure out Beatty's battle cruisers again. But this time, Scheer would follow at a distance, unseen, with the rest of the battle fleet. By the time Beatty realized his mistake, it would be too late. Broadsides and an advance screen of mines and U-boats would annihilate him. If Admiral John Jellicoe tried to get his fleet out to save him, Scheer's scout Zeppelins would radio him in time to escape. Like a game of three-dimensional chess, Scheer's combined underwater-surface-air operation would start on May 15, with the deployment of fifteen U-boats off the Scottish coast, and get into high gear on May 31, when Hipper and Scheer put to sea.

What Scheer could not know was that the Admiralty had already picked up news of his plans from Room 40 and passed it on to Beatty and Jellicoe, and that high winds would prevent his Zeppelins from taking to the air. Yet, characteristically, the message delivered to the British admirals was incomplete: it noted only the departure of Hipper's battle cruisers, not the rest. So both men left harbor in the predawn hours of May 31 assuming that they were going to face a single German squadron, not the thirteen other dreadnoughts in Scheer's High Seas Fleet. As late as two o'clock, when both fleets were less than 120 miles apart, neither had a clue of the existence of the other. In fact, the British fleet had just received a signal from the director of operations "confirming" that Scheer was still anchored at Wilhelmshaven. "What am I to think," Beatty said later in a rage, "when I get that telegram and in three hours' time meet the whole German Fleet well out at sea?"

For, at 2:20 P.M., that was exactly what he and his six battle cruisers found. The *Lion* was hit twice in the first five minutes. "All around us huge columns of water, higher than the funnels, were being thrown up as the enemy shells plunged into the sea," remembered Chalmers, "Occasionally, above the noise of battle, we heard the ominous hum of a shell fragment and caught a glimpse of polished steel as it flashed past the bridge." Beatty signaled frantically to his other cruisers to concentrate their fire on the lead German ship, Hipper's flagship *Lützow*. Foolishly, Beatty used his signal flags instead of his wireless, as if he were commanding at Copenhagen or Quiberon Bay. In the heat of the chase, *Tiger* and *Queen Mary* missed the signal and fired on their opposite numbers, as Hipper began to turn to draw them south. That left *Derfflinger* free for a quick barrage at *Lion* that smashed through the roof of Q turret and ignited the cordite in the gun cages. Almost everyone inside was horribly mutilated or killed, and the fire would have touched off the magazine if the officer in charge, Marine Major F. J. W. Harvey, both legs severed at the knees, had not ordered the magazine flooded with his dying breath. Neither Beatty nor his officers knew how close they came to annihilation until afterward. Harvey was awarded a posthumous VC.

Indefatigable was not so lucky. She was engaged with the *Von der Tann*, whose thicker armor and better optical range-finding equipment gave a decisive advantage. At 4:02 three 11-inch shells hit *Indefatigable*'s upper deck, where the steel plate was only an inch thick. The German shells all exploded in her hull, even as another shell hit A turret, setting off a tremendous explosion.

In an instant, all that remained of *Indefatigable* was a "colossal pall of thick smoke." Then, twenty minutes later, it was the *Queen Mary*'s turn, as the *Derfflinger* and *Seydlitz* turned their guns on her and she went up in a tremendous explosion. *Tiger* and *New Zealand* watched horrified as they passed the *Queen Mary*'s stern rising up for the final plunge, the propeller still turning. Only seven men could be rescued from a crew of 1,266. It was at this moment that Beatty turned to Chalmers with his famous remark, "There seems to be something wrong with our bloody ships today."

Even so, the course of battle was starting to turn. Admiral Evan-Thomas's Fifth Battle Squadron of fast battleships was coming up and into range. They cheered as they passed the wreck of the *Indefatigable*, thinking the ship was German: "We never dreamt that it was one of our own battle cruisers," an officer confessed afterward. Then *Barham*, *Warspite*, *Malaya*, and the others opened up with their 15-inch guns and it was the Germans' turn to take a pounding. Although their thicker armor saved them from the fate of *Queen Mary* or *Indefatigable,* the *Seydlitz* took hits that left her sinking by the stern and *Von der Tann* had all her guns knocked out. Her German captain bravely still kept her in line, however, to draw fire away from the others. Beatty's destroyers also raced in, closing to a range of only 600 yards to pepper the German cruisers with their 4-inch guns (one officer on the *Derfflinger* found an unexploded 4-inch shell in his bunk). German destroyers charged in to meet them, as a vicious "dog-fight" developed in the waters between Hipper's line and Beatty's, even as the *Lion* led the way north to join Evan-Thomas's battleships.

Meanwhile, a line of British light cruisers was moving south to screen Beatty's retreat. Suddenly the flag lieutenant on HMS *Southampton* turned to the squadron commander, Admiral Goodenough: "Look, sir, this is the day of a light cruiser's lifetime! The whole of the High Seas Fleet is before you!"

Goodenough raised his binoculars. Sixteen German battleships were emerging out of the hazy late afternoon mist, with destroyers spread out on each bow, and another six battleships in line to the rear—Scheer's entire battle fleet. The *Southampton* was only 13,000 yards from them— less than seven miles—when Scheer, as startled as Goodenough, opened fire. Goodenough managed to keep his ship safe by steering toward the splashes left by falling shells and signaled Beatty by wireless that the Germans were coming.

It was not until almost 5:00 P.M. that Scheer's lead battleships, *König* and *Kaiser,* began to engage the British cruisers and battleships silhouet-ted against the western horizon. For the next hour shells rained down on Beatty and Evan-Thomas's ships as they turned farther north to escape— and to where Jellicoe and the main fleet must be. The *Barham* took hits that put her wireless out of action and mortally wounded her navigation officer. A 12-inch German shell struck *Malaya*'s forward turret and nearly blew her up, while two more punctured her below the water line. Another shot smashed into the *Lion*'s plotting room and tore the nav-igation chart out of Lieutenant Chalmers's hands, as one ripped half blew out the window, "fluttering over the sea like a frightened seagull." Admiral Horace Hood, fourth-generation scion of the great naval dynasty, had brought his squadron of older battle cruisers, including *Invincible* and *Indomitable,* into action against the Germans. But that was not what everyone was waiting for. "Where was our Grand Fleet?" a mid-shipman on the beleaguered *Barham* was asking himself. "Would they never come?" Then, "Suddenly out of the mist, almost melted into view Admiral Jellicoe's great battleships. Ship after ship, twenty-seven in all, firing their broadsides."

For most of the afternoon Jellicoe had been almost unaware of the great battle that had been raging to his south. As late as six o'clock he was still plaintively signaling Beatty by wireless telegraph: "Where is enemy battle fleet?" and receiving no answer. Then, as he paced the bridge of his flagship *Iron Duke,* her captain drew his attention to a ship appearing out of the mist. It was the *Lion,* with smoke pouring out of the forecastle's port side. Then they could make out the other battle cruisers, their guns blazing with faint flashes as "grey, ghost-like columns of water thrown up by heavy enemy shells pitched amongst these great ships." The *Iron Duke's* searchlight flashed out: "Where is the enemy's battle fleet?" As Beatty was telling him, Jellicoe turned to the Fleet Signal Officer: "Hoist equal-speed pendant SE" and then to his flag captain: "Dreyer, commence the deployment."

Two short siren blasts rang out over the water as the main battle fleet, steaming in four groups, turned to port to form themselves in a single line of battle—the last line head battle formation in the history of the British navy. Not wooden walls this time, but walls of steel, with streamlined gray hulls instead of gilded stern galleries and figureheads, and funnels belching black smoke instead of sails close-hauled. But it was a formation Blake or Rooke or Rodney would have recognized, and approved. *King George V* and *Ajax* were first, followed by *Orion, Royal Oak, Iron Duke, Superb, Thunderer, Benbow, Bellerophon, Téméraire, Collingwood, Colossus, Marlborough, St Vincent*— twenty-seven in all, names redolent with the navy's past (the first *Royal Oak* had been burned by the Dutch at Chatham in 1667), names of admirals and generals, Greek heroes and Roman virtues. And all slowly bringing their guns to bear as they steamed into harm's way—just as their predecessors had for so many centuries in exactly the same sea.

They were arriving just in time. The older cruiser *Defense* had gone up in a sheet of smoke and flame, while *Warrior* was badly disabled and steaming to the rear. At 6:25 *Invincible,* Fisher's "greyhound of the sea," suffered a tremendous explosion that literally tore her in two. Then Scheer saw through his bridge screen on the *Friedrich der Grosse* a great ring of fire stretching across the horizon from north to east. It was Jellicoe's battleships, still not visible except for the gun flashes, which lit up the sky as they crossed his line of advance.

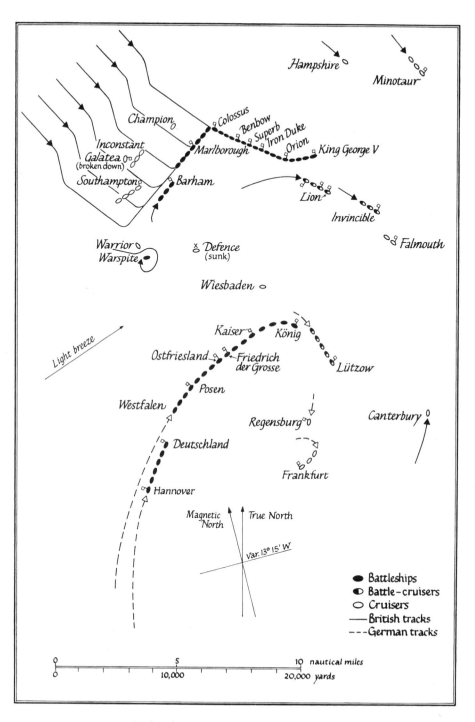

Jutland, May 31, 1916: situation at 6 P.M.

Scheer's position was dangerous but hardly hopeless. The combined fire of twenty-seven battleships, and Beatty's surviving battle cruisers and Evan-Thomas's dreadnoughts, could be devastating. But if the experience of Jutland proved anything, it was the difficulty of hitting anything at these tremendous ranges, even with central fire controls and machines for calculating distances and speeds. The *Barham* would fire 337 15-inch shells that day and score no more than a couple dozen direct hits, none of them fatal. *Lion* and *Tiger* would fire more than 300 each, *Seydlitz* and *Moltke* even more than that. A modern battleship doing 25 knots made an elusive target at open sea, especially in the heat of battle, when range-takers were guessing distances by their own falling shot, and often guessing wrong.

By charging in to close the distance with Jellicoe, Scheer might have looked to his heavier armor to protect his ships from British shells (many of which were defective and failed to explode), while overpowering theirs with his own faster and more accurate fire. Certainly this was the moment of decisive battle he and Tipitz had been yearning for.

But as Scheer gazed out at the flashing fire along the horizon, he saw something else. He saw before him the entire history of the British navy, a fighting force with an unequaled reputation for invincibility in battle and bravery under fire. "The English fleet," he wrote later, "had the advantage of looking back on a hundred years of proud tradition which must have given every man a sense of superiority based on the great deeds of the past." His own navy's fighting tradition was less than two years old. At that fateful moment, Scheer was confronting not John Jellicoe but the ghosts of Nelson, Howe, Rodney, Drake, and the rest; and he backed down.

At 6:38 P.M., Scheer gave the order for the entire German fleet to turn simultaneously to port, as his destroyer surged ahead to fire their torpedoes and lay down a smoke screen. In another ten minutes, the German fleet disappeared in the mist, as Jellicoe's line veered east sharply to avoid the torpedo attack. At ten minutes to seven Jellicoe resumed his course. He still could not see Scheer's forces, but he assumed he could cut off their retreat by sailing south and west. Just before seven the two fleets saw each other and Jellicoe re-formed his line. Scheer gave his second order for a *Gefechtskehrwendung* (a simultaneous turn) and this time disappeared for good, as Jellicoe swerved to avoid another destroyer torpedo attack. As darkness fell, elements of both fleets remained in intermittent contact. There was a fierce night battle as British destroyers managed to put a torpedo in the old German battleship *Pommern* and sink her. The cruiser *Black Prince* had gone down hours earlier, victim to an encounter with the battleship *Thüringen*. But the last great battle of surface fleets was over. By morning Scheer's fleet was back in Wilhelmshaven largely unscathed, while Jellicoe and the Admiralty exchanged accusations about what had gone wrong.

In material terms, the battle of Jutland was a German victory. Scheer could point out that he had lost a single battle cruiser, the *Lützow* (although the *Seydlitz* was so badly damaged she had to beach herself as she came home), the pre-dreadnought *Pommern,* four light cruisers, and five destroyers: 2,500 men lost in all. The British, by contrast, had lost three modern battle cruisers, four armored cruisers, eight destroyers, and more than 6,000 officers and crew—the bulk of them on the *Invincible, Indefatigable,* and *Queen Mary.* Their ships had proved vulnerable, especially the battle cruisers, their shooting inaccurate, their shells defective, their method of signaling ludicrously antiquated, and their admirals cautious and bemused, especially Jellicoe. (in November he would be moved upstairs to First Sea Lord). The kaiser could, with justifiable pride, hand out Iron Crosses to the High Seas Fleet, the Pour le Mérite to its admiral, and officially christen Jutland "the North Sea Battle of 1 June," a self-conscious echo of Howe's "Glorious First of June."

But in moral terms, the British navy had won. Despite its mistakes and shortcomings, its image of invincibility had stayed the hand of its ablest opponent in more than a century. The High Seas Fleet ventured forth once more on August 16; but when word reached Scheer that the Grand Fleet had put to sea, he set off at once for home. That day Jellicoe, too, had been reluctant to press forward for fear of possible U-boat attacks (a torpedo narrowly missed the *Iron Duke* as she picked him up off the Firth of Forth). Just a year earlier, Alfred Mahan had died in America, still believing that big battleships were the key to sea power. Jutland had proved the opposite. As one German officer put it right after the battle, "It is senseless to build 30,000-ton ships which cannot defend themselves against a torpedo shot." Yet however obsolete, as long as the Grand Fleet was strong and intact, "a fleet in being," Germany's High Seas Fleet was useless. As Scheer told the kaiser in his official report, nothing it could do now would force England to make peace.

Two weeks later on June 16, General Douglas Haig launched his great offensive along the River Somme. Almost 16,000 British soldiers died the first day—the bloodiest single day in the history of the British army.

The British, French, and German armies would be drawn into a pro-longed stalemate at the Somme, costing hundreds of thousands of casualties and tons of ammunition and materiel, with no result. On Easter Sunday, a bloody revolt had broken out in Dublin sounding the death knell of British rule in Ireland after six centuries. But German hopes of exploiting the rebellion faded as the conspirators were caught and executed. Earlier in April, a German offensive at Verdun had also bogged down in stalemate.

At the same time, the noose of the British navy's blockade was beginning slowly but inexorably to tighten. German civilians felt the pinch first, as supplies in the cities of the most basic goods ran out. In 1916 German troops remained fed and armed. But Germany had to break the stalemate. Having failed on land, then at sea at Jutland, only one decisive weapon remained: the U-boat.

The German government had so far refrained from renewing its unrestricted submarine campaign, out of fear of American wrath. Even so, they now had nearly one hundred U-boats in action and in September sank almost a quarter-million tons of British and neutral shipping, their highest total ever. In December, losses jumped to 355,000 tons. German experts calculated that they would need to sink 600,000 tons if they were going to make a significant dent in the Allied war effort. The German admirals and generals put the pressure on Chancellor Bethmann Hollweg to take the gloves off. The Chief of the Naval Staff said, "In spite of the danger of a breach with America, unrestricted submarine war, started soon, is the . . . only way to end the war with victory." And so with great misgiving, the government announced on February 1, 1917, the beginning of the next round in the U-boat wars. Any ship at sea from any nation would, in effect, be sunk on sight.

The first two months of the campaign devastated British shipping, while the Admiralty was at a loss as to how to stop the slaughter. It had deployed more than 3,000 ships, including armed yachts, fishing smacks, and merchantmen all across the oceans to find the U-boats, and strung anti-submarine nets throughout the English Channel. Yet in the last six months of 1916, the Germans lost only fifteen U-boats, and most of those to accidents. They simply dived away from their pursuers at sea or ducked under the mined nets along the harbors and coasts. In the meantime, the killing mounted. In the first month of unrestricted warfare, the Germans sank 250 ships; in March, 330, very close to the magic number of 600,000 tons. In April they broke through. More than 430 British, Allied, and neutral ships went down to torpedoes and gunfire, carrying 881,000 tons of vital supplies to the bottom. The Admiralty was near despair. First Sea Lord Jellicoe said, "It is impossible for us to go on with the war, if losses like this continue."

Yet British naval intelligence was already holding the winning hand. On January 17, 1917, Reginald Hall entered Room 40 and found Lieutenant Commander Nigel de Grey in a state of high excitement.

"D'you want to bring America into the war?" de Grey asked.

"Yes, my boy," Hall remembered answering. "Why?"

"I've got something here which," de Grey stammered, "well, it's a rather astonishing message which might to do the trick if we could use it."

Hall had a look. It was a telegram from German foreign minister Zimmermann to his ambassador in Washington which Room 40 cryptographers had intercepted and deciphered. It warned him that the restrictions of submarine warfare were about to be lifted, and that this might push the United States into the war. If it did, Zimmermann averred, then Germany was going to propose a counter-alliance with Mexico for an invasion of the United States, allowing the Mexicans to recover Texas, New Mexico, and Arizona with German help. "Blinker" Hall had in his hand the document that could turn around American public opinion, and with it the course of the war.

On February 23 a copy of the Zimmermann telegram reached the desk of the American ambassador in London, Walter Hines Pages. When President Woodrow Wilson was shown the contents of the original, his only exclamation was: "Good Lord! Good Lord!" It is possible the German unrestricted submarine campaign might have pushed the United States into war—possible, but doubtful. The Zimmermann telegram erased any lingering hesitations Wilson might have had. On April 6, 1917, he asked Congress to declare war on Germany.

Of all the industrialized nations, America was the least prepared for a modern war. Its vaunted "blue water" fleet with its magnificent battleships and cruisers numbered less than 200 vessels, and these were totally unsuited for the kind of naval war the Allies were facing. The navy's attaché to London, Admiral William Sims, discovered this on his trip across the Atlantic, when his ship struck a German mine inside Liverpool harbor. Sims was one of the original architects of America's battle fleet. But when he asked Prime Minister Lloyd George what England needed most from the United States and Lloyd George said, "Ships, ships, ships," what he meant were smaller and faster craft that could help deal with the U-boat threat.

Particularly destroyers. The Royal Navy had pioneered the use of destroyers as anti-submarine vessels, equipping them with hydrophones to track the U-boat underwater, and pressure-detonated depth charges. What they needed now was more of them. On May 4, 1917, the first six United States destroyers turned up at Queenstown in Ireland. By July, there were thirty-four stationed there. Meanwhile, the Americans were doing the British one better. The young assistant secretary of the navy, Franklin D. Roosevelt, had approved the design for what would be one of the classic warships of World War I, the subchaser.

"The prettiest little ships I ever saw," said one grateful passenger, who watched them working off the coast of Ireland. One hundred and ten feet long and built of wood, they displaced only 85 tons—not much more than half of Drake's *Golden Hind.* Carrying a crew of two officers and twenty-four men, they were armed with two 3-inch guns and a Y-shaped depth charge gun mounted on the stern. More than 400 subchasers would be deployed during the war, from Ireland and the Mediterranean to Archangel in Russia. Meanwhile, American shipyards were turning out new destroyers, the famous "four-stackers," in record numbers.

Sims and his London assistant, Captain Harold Stark, found that the Royal Navy had the right experience and technology for the anti-submarine war. But all the right tools and tactics could not make any difference, unless they served the proper strategy. Jellicoe and the Admiralty's opposition to the use of convoys was a major stumbling block. They argued that assembling forty or fifty merchant ships together only created a more inviting target for the U-boats, that merchants had better odds of avoiding detection by sailing across alone. But in fact the opposite was the case. The larger number of individual sailings actually *increased* the chance of U-boats finding a target. What the convoy did was replace multiple targets with only one; one which, in the broad stretches of the Atlantic and Pacific, could virtually hide itself unless the U-boat captain knew where to look.

The convoy also solved another problem: how to find the U-boats. "The thing to do," as Sims wrote, "was to make the submarines come to the anti-submarine craft and fight in order to get merchantmen." Sailors in Nelson's day had known this when they were fighting privateers and surface raiders; now the convoy would allow the destroyers, corvettes (a smaller version of the destroyer), subchasers, and by 1918, flying boats, to take on their submerged prey. With Sims and the Americans throwing their weight behind the pro-convoy forces at the Admiralty, Jellicoe finally relented. On May 10, 1917, the first convoy sailed from Gibraltar. Not a single ship was lost. The strategic breakthrough everyone had been waiting for had finally come.

The Admiralty's Convoy Room became "the central nervous system of a complicated but perfectly working organism which reached to the remotest corners of the world." It created eight oceanic "gateways" for routing convoys to the British Isles, France, and the Mediterranean, assembly points for all the world's merchant shipping. The four biggest were Sierra Leone for ships coming to Europe from the Cape of Good Hope, where they met ships coming from South American ports; Gibraltar for shipping from Suez and the Mediterranean headed for Britain or France; Halifax and Cape Breton for Canadian shipping; New York City for merchantmen coming out of Boston, Philadelphia, and Portland; and Hampton Roads for ships out of the Panama Canal, the Gulf of Mexico, Baltimore, and Norfolk. There they met their British and American escorts and set out on regularly fixed schedules, leaving New York every sixteen days and Hampton Roads every eight.

By the autumn, the losses to U-boats started to drop. After the peak in April 1917, the tonnage sunk had fallen to 557,000 in July. Many were frustrated that U-boats were still sinking ships and killing passengers and crews in record numbers; talk about the "failure" of the anti-submarine war was rampant. But in November the losses fell to 289,000 tons. Even more important, the British and American navies were killing U-boats faster than they could be built. In June 1918 losses were still at 255,000 tons. But in April 1917 the Germans had been sinking a ship every two days. In June 1918, it was one every two weeks. And during the last nine months of the war, of 1,133 merchant ships sunk only 10 percent were in convoys: Convoys were also deploying the first units of the American Expeditionary Force to reinforce the Allied armies in the trenches.

Germany had run out of options. The British blockade, now reinforced by the Americans, had forced the German army under General Ludendorff to take almost total control of the German economy in order to keep itself supplied and in the field. Ludendorff had realized as early as February that the U-boat was not going to win the war. So in March 1918 he launched his Saint Michel offensive, a last desperate attempt to win the war before the Americans arrived in sufficient numbers. It broke the trench stalemate, but the German soldier, who had not seen a square meal in months, lacked the morale and stamina to sustain the drive that took him to within fifty miles of Paris.

On August 8, 1918, the British launched their counteroffensive at Amiens. With British regiments on the left, Canadians on the right, Australians in the center, and Americans in reserve, and 450 tanks in front, they decisively broke the German line. By September, the Germans were reeling back toward their Rhine frontier, as all hope of reversing the Allied advance disappeared.

Meanwhile, the German High Seas Fleet was still sitting idle at Kiel and Wilhelmshaven. Sailors began to hear rumors that they were going to be sent out against the Grand Fleet, which had been reinforced by American battleships, on a final "death ride." Embittered by official neglect after Jutland, poor food, and miserable living conditions (most German junior officers had to bunk four or six in a cabin), and two years of enforced idleness, the High Seas Fleet rose up and mutinied.

The German naval mutiny on October 29, unlike its British counterpart one hundred and twenty years earlier, really did alter the course of the war. The rebellion soon spread to Germany's cities; Marxist rebels, inspired by the example of the Russian Revolution, joined with disaffected sailors and soldiers to seize the capital at Berlin. Facing ruin on the battlefield and revolution at home, the German High Command forced the kaiser to abdicate and asked for an armistice.

For the High Seas Fleet, there was one final humiliation. On November 21, 1918, ten days after the armistice was signed, it sailed *en masse* to surrender to the Grand Fleet at Scapa Flow, in accordance with the armistice terms. Ninety thousand British officers and sailors gathered on deck to see eleven dreadnought battleships, once the pride of the German nation, and five battle cruisers enter the harbor—some in such poor condition they could barely get to sea. *Friedrich der Grosse, Kaiser, Markgraf, Nassau, Ostfriesland*—names soon to be entered in the annals of history's vanquished navies, their guns silenced and their challenge to British sea power ended forever.

For David Beatty, now commander in chief of the Grand Fleet, it was a bittersweet moment, as he raised his cap and received the cheers of his men. In 1914, Beatty had bet his fellow officer Ernle Chatfield a five-pound note there would be no war. "He yearned for it," Chatfield remembered. "We had not fought for a century; it was time we repeated the deeds of our forefathers." The British navy had won—some were even saying it had won the war. But not in the way Beatty or anyone else had anticipated; certainly not with the kind of grand victory at sea Beatty had hoped would put his name in the annals alongside that of Nelson. It was the small vessels, not the big ones, that ended up holding the scales of victory and defeat in World War I: the destroyer, the submarine, the sub-chaser, the light cruiser on blockade duty—even the seaplane and air-plane, as the fledgling Royal Naval Air Service helped to mop up the U-boat threat in the last months of the war.

Something else unexpected had come out of this war. The fight against the submarine had woven a close bond of trust and cooperation between the Royal and U.S. Navies. Until then, the two had seen each other as at least theoretical rivals for command of the sea—even, given the bitter legacy of John Paul Jones and the War of 1812, enemies with an old score to settle. All that now changed. Indeed, the "special relation-ship" between the United States and Britain in the twentieth century really begins in the confidence the experience of war built up between men like William Sims and his counterparts in the British Admiralty, between American destroyer and cruiser captains and the officers of the navy the Americans admiringly called "the senior service." As the com-mander of the American fleet, Admiral Hugh Rodman, wrote, "Our friendship ripened into a fellowship and comradeship, which in turn became a brotherhood." When the Americans left the North Sea for home, Beatty warmly thanked them, urging them not to "forget your comrades in the mist" and to "come back soon"—never dreaming just how soon that would be.

For the unpleasant truth was, the British navy would have lost the war without the Americans—or indeed the Japanese, who dispatched their own destroyers to escort British merchantmen and even helped in the anti-submarine campaign in the Mediterranean. The navy had won the war and saved the empire. But unless they got more help, they were about to lose the peace.

CHAPTER TWENTY-ONE

Into the Twilight

God of our fathers, known of old—
Lord of our far-flung battle-line—
Beneath whose awful hand we hold
Dominion over palm and pine—
Lord God of hosts, be with us yet,
Lest we forget, lest we forget!
—RUDYARD KIPLING, "RECESSIONAL"

I T WAS A bright clear morning on June 21, 1919, at Scapa Flow. A party of schoolchildren from the Stromness Higher Grade School were out on a tour of Scotland's biggest naval base on a local steamer. The main body of the Grand Fleet had set out to sea for torpedo practice but the harbor was by no means empty. Arranged before the boys and girls in neat rows was the German High Seas Fleet, interned at Scapa Flow since the previous November. The fleet's great black shapes loomed up on the bow as the steamer entered the Brings Deep channel at noon, framed by the blue-gray mountains of Stromness behind them.

Another ship, a British armed trawler, was in Brings Deep at the same time, carrying a marine artist named Gribble to do a series of sketches of the German ships, as a record of their captivity and that of their officers and crew, done over the last seven months. As the trawler drew up to the first, the *Friedrich der Grosse*, Gribble noticed something odd. The big battleship was surrounded by little lifeboats, into which the German sailors overhead were busy throwing their duffel bags as if they were headed for the shore. Gribble turned to the trawler's commander, Sub-Lieutenant Leeth, and asked, "Do you allow them to go for joy rides?"

Leeth watched for a moment and then said, puzzled, "No, but by Jove it looks as if they were." Then they glanced over at a cruiser, the *Frankfurt,* where the same thing was happening. Some German sailors were even leaping into the water. Leeth stared at Gribble. "I've got it!" he exclaimed. "They're scuttling their ships!"

All across the harbor the same scene was being played out, with the Germans abandoning their ships as quickly as they could. Traditions in the Royal Navy die hard. Leeth at once ordered his men to "get the cut-lasses and rifles ready" if the Germans tried to board the trawler. He bawled out across the water to the men in the small boats: "Return to your ships at once!" When one of the German boats drew too close, Leeth's men fired a volley of shots, hitting four sailors and dropping them into the water. Leeth yelled out again for the Germans to go back to their ships. "We can't go back," cried out one of their officers, "they are sinking."

Indeed they were. The crews of every capital ship in the German fleet had opened her sea-cocks on orders of their commanding officer, Admiral von Reuter, letting the gray-green waters of the North Sea rush in. The *Friedrich der Grosse*, Reinhardt Scheer's proud flagship at the battle of Jutland, was the first to scuttle at 12:10 P.M. Leeth and his men were help-less to do anything as she turned over and sank. Then, the boys and girls of Stromness Higher Grade School watched with fascination as "suddenly and without warning and almost simultaneously, those huge vessels began to list over to port or to starboard." One of the schoolchildren remem-bered years later: "Some heeled over and plunged headlong ... others were rapidly settling down in the ocean, with little more showing than their masts and funnels."

Then "a dreadfully roaring hiss" rose up, as billows of steam poured up through the ships' vents. The sea around the boat was "turning into one vast stain of oil, which spread outward as if the life blood of some sea monster mortally wounded." Minutes later the sea became covered for miles around with boats and hammocks, life belts and sea chests, spars and reams of paper, along with hundreds of German sailors still strug-gling for their lives. At once "the air was rent by the lusty cheering of long lines of sailors drawn up on the deck of one of the largest German ships ... bidding farewell to a sister ship whose decks were now under water."

By the time the Grand Fleet returned from torpedo practice, they found a strange and horrifying sight. The last German battle cruiser, the *Hindenburg*, went down at five o'clock. By then fifty-two of seventy-seven German ships were at the bottom of Scapa Flow. The British admiral in charge, Sydney Fremantle (great-grandson of the "band of brothers" Fremantle), was as furious as he was uncomprehending. He gave Reuter a violent tongue-lashing when the German admiral was brought aboard his flagship *Revenge:* "a breach of naval honor" was only one of the charges

Fremantle leveled at his head. Yet Reuter and his officers were unperturbed. "They stood with expressionless faces," Fremantle said afterward, "clicked their heels and descended the accommodation ladder without a word," as British marines escorted them into captivity.

Why had they done it? Partly to cleanse away the humiliation of surrender; in its way, it was a backhanded tribute to Britain's naval supremacy, still intact despite every attempt to break it. At war's end, the Royal Navy still had half of the total effective warships anywhere in the world.

But it was also a gesture of collective German rage and defiance. News of the general peace treaty signed at Versailles had reached Scapa Flow at the end of May. "For a couple of days it lay like lead on the minds of the men," Admiral Reuter would remember. They had hoped their voluntary surrender might mitigate the terms of settlement with the Allies. Instead, they had read like a prison sentence. Germany was to be stripped of territory east and west; it would be allowed no army larger than 100,000 men and no navy (above all, no submarines). Outraged and betrayed, Reuter and his men lashed out in the only way they could.

The German fleet was gone, but the bitterness remained. In that sense, the Grand Scuttle was less the final act of the Great War than the first act of a greater, even more destructive conflict. In just twenty years, the world would again be at war. And once again, the Royal Navy would have to protect the world from its own follies and ambitions.

• • •

Versailles had failed precisely where the Congress of Vienna had succeeded. In 1919, it was the United States, not Britain, that set the agenda for a new moral world order, but Woodrow Wilson was no Castlereagh. Britain's goal in 1815 was a "just equilibrium" in Europe and collective security. Wilson's was "to make the world safe for democracy" — a much more ambitious, and nebulous, aim. Despite the years of bloodshed France had caused, Castlereagh had reserved his moral outrage for fighting the slave trade. Wilson, by contrast, felt a deep bitterness toward Germany, especially after a U-boat sank the Irish Mail Steamer *Leinster,* killing 450 men, women, and children in October 1918—just eleven days after the German government had asked Wilson to mediate a peace. The incident scarred everyone's opinion of the Germans. "Brutes they are," said the usually philosophical Arthur Balfour, "and brutes they remain."

Yet Wilson also harbored a bitterness toward Europe's other rulers and politicians, for having allowed so destructive a war to happen. He cared little about how they finally punished Germany. He believed it was his League of Nations, not the peace treaty, that would make this the War to End All Wars. Wilson carried the self-righteous legacy of John Calvin and John Foxe into the complexities of twentieth century diplomacy—not an entirely happy combination. Others saw the creation of the League as a matter for negotiation. Wilson saw it as a solemn covenant, a commitment of heart and soul. When the American Congress refused to accept his terms, he decided, not unlike the German sailors at Scapa Flow, to scuttle the entire treaty.

Hence the new world order was born in 1919 with its most powerful godparent, the United States, missing at the font. It was a bad beginning for the future, made worse by the horrors of revolution, civil war, and famine in Russia and a worldwide economic depression. In the absence of the Americans, it was the British navy that had to guard peace and stability around the world. But this time, for the first time, it was not up to the task.

It was not the navy's fault. In 1918 it was still the largest and most effective fleet in the world. More than 37,000 officers and 400,000 men were actively serving, and the navy's first postwar budget for 1918–19 was 344 million pounds—almost seven times the amount Winston Churchill had presented to a shocked House of Commons in 1912. But in 1919–20 the estimates tumbled to 154 million; in 1920–21 to 76 million. As literally hundreds of ships went out of commission, by 1932 the total number of active personnel in the navy was less than 100,000.

The government justified these cuts by invoking a Ten Years' Rule, passed by the cabinet in 1919 and ordering the armed services to set their budget requests on the assumption that Britain would not fight a major war in the next decade.* The measure reflected a sense of war weariness, not to say pacifism, which would sweep over British politics until the late 1930s. It was the midwife of appeasement, and it led sucessive governments to disregard the Admiralty's warnings that unless the budget cuts stopped, Britain would become the second naval power in the world after America.

The politicians in fact had already made that inevitable by signing the Washington Naval Treaty in 1922—the treaty which, even more than

---

*The rule would be extended again in 1928, and finally abandoned in November 1933—eight months after Hitler came to power in Germany.

Versailles, set the stage for World War II. The government was terrified that the Americans would use their postwar economic surge to build a navy bigger than Britain's, so they were delighted to get them to agree to stop at one just as large, with the navy of imperial Japan only slightly behind. The treaty set a 5:5:3 parity ratio between American, British, and Japanese capital ships, respectively, and a 5:1.75 ratio with France and Italy. David Beatty, First Sea Lord, was outraged, particularly when he learned that he would actually have to scrap ships in order to bring the American and British fleets into balance. Eventually, the Washington treaty would cut the British navy's seventy cruisers to fifty. Instead of 443 destroyers at war's end, it would have barely 120 by 1931—and fifty-five of those would be obsolete in five years.

Beatty saw the treaty as abject surrender, but the politicians forced him and the Admiralty to swallow this deeply bitter pill. The goal was to prevent an expensive arms race with America, though in fact it crippled the navy's ability to do its job. Unlike the Americans, Britain had a vast empire to protect and defend, an empire swollen even larger with captured German colonies, from Southwest Africa, the Cameroons, and Tanganyika to New Guinea and a string of atolls in the Pacific. Nor could it rely on the Japanese to help. One of the conditions of the Washington treaty was an end to the naval alliance with Japan. When it came up for renewal in 1921, it was allowed to lapse—again over the strenuous objections of the Admiralty.

Like most arms limitation treaties, the Washington treaty made the world not a safer but a more dangerous place. Yet British politicians of all parties seemed to believe that the navy had become irrelevant in the new postwar world. Even Winston Churchill applauded rounds of "swinging" budget cuts, which sapped the navy's resources in the 1920s, including cuts in seaman's wages.* He had pushed through the Ten Years' Rule and scoffed at the Admiralty's worries that the Washington treaty would "starve" the empire. "We cannot have a lot of silly little cruisers," he told a cabinet secretary, "which would be of no use anyway."

Churchill's casual attitude toward the naval base at Singapore was typical, and ultimately tragic. In 1922, David Beatty had wanted its for-

---

*These cuts would trigger the so-called Invergordon mutiny on ships in the Atlantic fleet in September 1931, in which sailors refused to go to sea unless the cut was rescinded.

tifications and large dockyards finished in three years; Singapore, he believed, would be even more crucial to the empire now that the alliance with Japan had lapsed. Prime Minster Stanley Baldwin, however, considered it expensive and unnecessary, and said no. In 1924 the Labor prime minister, Ramsay MacDonald, canceled work altogether. In November, Baldwin's new Tory government reopened the case for Singapore, but wanted nothing done until 1926. Churchill, meanwhile, had assured Baldwin there was "not the slightest chance" of a war with Japan in their lifetimes. He wanted the whole thing put off for another six years.

In 1928 the naval chiefs of staff, worried about other budget priorities, recommended more delays. In 1929 a Labor government stopped work on Singapore's fortifications again, pending the outcome of yet another naval treaty; the Tories did the same for all of 1929 and 1930. The result was that it was not until 1933 that the concrete foundations for Singapore's defensive shore batteries were laid, even though British naval strategy assumed the only way an enemy could take the city would be from the sea. The batteries were budgeted to be finished by 1935, ten years after Beatty's original deadline. Even then, Singapore would have no adequate drydocks for Britain's biggest ships—and the British navy no other modern base east of the Malay Straits.

In April 1931 First Sea Lord Sir Frederick Field drew up a list of the navy's current state, and a doleful list it was. In terms of quality and quantity of ships and resources, the Royal Navy was at its lowest point in more than a century. It was down to fifty cruisers and 120 destroyers, and only three new battleships. By treaty, the navy could build no warship larger than 38,000 tons. The fleet's Air Arm, once the largest in the world, had shrunk to only 159 aircraft, while Japan's had grown to more than four hundred. There was not a single adequately defended port in the entire Commonwealth, and for the first time since the reign of Queen Anne, the Admiralty no longer sat at cabinet meetings. In less than five months, the mutiny by sailors at Invergordon would trigger a loss of confidence in the government, a run on the pound, take Britain off the gold standard, and force the Bank of England to temporarily shut its doors—proof that the navy could still shape political events in Britain. Yet at almost the same time, Japan felt free to invade Manchuria.

Britain and the rest of the world were about to find out what happened when the Royal Navy no longer ruled the waves. The decline of the navy in the 1920s meant the effective end of the *Pax Britannica.* Into the

vacuum would rush a series of totalitarian powers, each eager for conquest and empire.

The Japanese were the first. For half a century, Japan had been
Britain's eager naval protégé. Britain built Japan's best warships, trained
its officers, and gave vital intelligence to help Japan win the Russo-
Japanese War. Admiral Togo had told his officers: "The English navy is
very great. . . . Study it. See all you can. Learn all you can. . . . All other
navies are negligible beside it." But Royal Navy officers noticed that
though their Japanese counterparts were eager to learn whatever they
could about naval technology, strategy, and tactics, they had no interest in
the Western civic values that went with them. Japan remained a nation
driven by the samurai code of Bushido, the warrior values of its violent
feudal past. Armed with the tools of modern warfare, including a powerful navy, the Bushido spirit would propel Japan on an imperialist course
of unparalleled ferocity and brutality.

For it was power, and power alone, that attracted Japan. It had joined
the Allies in World War I in order to seize the German naval base in
China at Tsingtao, and Germany's islands in the Pacific—the Marshalls,
Marianas, and Carolines. Only naval ties with Britain kept Japan on a
course of international propriety and rule of law, and constrained its
thirst for empire. In 1921, however, under pressure from Canadians and
Americans who feared this new emerging power in the Pacific, Britain
declined to renew their two-decade alliance. The government hoped
that Japan's naval ambitions would be satisfied by the ratios in the
Washington naval treaty, and collective security in the Pacific by a Nine-
Power Treaty guaranteeing the integrity of China—a treaty that specifically excluded Japan.

It was an act of breathtaking stupidity. The Nine-Power Treaty left
Japan feeling isolated and vulnerable. By 1930, Japan had become a military dictatorship, ruled by a clique of imperialist-minded generals and
admirals. Since its entire economy depended on imported resources,
from iron ore and oil to wheat and rice, they believed Japan would have to
expand its sea power or die.

As the British navy withered from neglect, Japan's grew to ten modern battleships, 36 heavy and light cruisers, 113 destroyers and 63 submarines. In addition, it built no fewer than ten aircraft carriers, compared
to six for the United States and four for the United Kingdom. Indeed,
both Japan and America were far more committed than the Royal Navy
to developing this vital new instrument of sea power, which U.S. Admiral

William S. Sims predicted back in 1924 would be the capital ship of the future.

This was all the more puzzling because Britain had been the great pioneer and innovator in naval aviation. The Royal Navy made its first flight from the deck of a ship in 1912, and launched the world's first carrier for fixed-wing aircraft, the HMS *Furious*. Even before the war, the Royal Naval Air Service had conducted experiments with airborne torpedoes against surface ships. On Christmas Day 1914 it launched the first attack by seaborne planes on the Zeppelin sheds at Cuxhaven; in 1915 its seaplanes sank three Turkish steamers in Istanbul harbor. Admiral Beatty even wanted to use carrier-based planes to knock out the High Seas Fleet in 1917, with 121 aircraft launched from eight carriers—the first inkling of the revolutionary tactics of Pearl Harbor. The war ended before the RNAS could muster an effective force that large. Nonetheless, by April 1918 it numbered more than 3,000 aircraft and 55,000 personnel.

Yet in 1933 this had shrunk to less than 160 planes. Part of the reason was the same belief that had affected the budget of all the armed branches in the interwar years, that international treaties and bodies like the League of Nations made military preparation an unnecessary expense. It was also due to a disastrous bureaucratic decision in 1921 to give the Royal Air Force control over the navy's planes and pilots, renamed the Fleet Air Arm. Thereafter, whatever money was available for new planes and facilities went to the RAF; the Fleet Air Arm was left with whatever loose change it could wrench from the grip of the Air Ministry. For sixteen crucial years, British naval aviation came to a virtual halt.

Meanwhile, Japan was surging ahead with its seaborne aviation—thanks, ironically, to the Royal Navy. In 1921 it had sent an unofficial mission of navy aviators to its erstwhile ally, led by a brilliant flier, William Francis Forbes, who also bore the ancestral Scottish title of Master of Semphill. Lord Semphill reorganized Japan's naval air service along advanced British lines, and for three years trained its pilots in the latest techniques, including aerial torpedo attacks. During his stay Semphill held the rank of captain in the Japanese navy, and for his efforts won the Order of the Rising Sun.

Semphill was impressed with his Japanese pupils. "Nerves seem conspicuous by their absence," he reported afterward. "Pilots are ever ready to undertake the most difficult maneuvers." The average level of skill was "perhaps higher than we are accustomed to find in the West," he averred, and "their courage and determination to carry out orders under any conditions are most noticeable." At first, the Japanese air naval service used British planes. Then the Japanese company of Mitsubishi came up with a design crafted by an English engineer. The Mitsubishi Type-10 fighter, ancestor of the famous Zero, first flew off the deck of the Japanese carrier *Hosho* in 1923, while one of Semphill's aides, Lieutenant Commander Brackley, followed in a Vickers Viking.

The Japanese naval air service rapidly grew in size and confidence. A Royal Air Force officer noticed their skill in torpedo bombing in trials in Yokohama harbor in 1931. But the Air Ministry and Admiralty refused to believe there was a threat. Meanwhile, before their eyes and those of the world, Japan was evolving into an aggressive hostile power. In 1931 it unleashed its unprovoked invasion of Manchuria. In 1933, Japan withdrew from the League of Nations; in 1934 it announced it would no longer abide by the Washington treaty. Britain finally awoke to the danger to its empire in the East and restarted work on the naval base at Singapore. Yet this new vigor, after years of sloth, only made Japan more paranoid. Its military planners now added Britain to their hit list, and made Singapore itself a key focus of their Pacific strategy.

Italy's Benito Mussolini noted how the world failed to act to stop Japanese aggression in China. He also noted how stretched the British navy's resources were, with its Mediterranean bases at Alexandria and Malta looking more and more impotent and isolated. Greedy for his own empire, Mussolini began to grow the Italian fleet and probed the crumbling *Pax Britannica* for signs of weakness. He found them in Britain's reaction to his invasion in Ethiopia in 1935. Britain loudly endorsed the League of Nation's sanctions against Italy; it was uniquely positioned to enforce them, since everything Mussolini needed for his war on Ethiopia had to pass through the Suez Canal. Yet no one tried to close the canal or impose a naval blockade. Those who had cut the navy estimates now clamored the loudest for action, only to learn that in their haste to save money they had created a navy terrified of risking its dwindling resources. The First Sea Lord told the cabinet he had only *seven* capital ships available for action. Any fight with the Italians for control of the canal, he said, would only make the navy weaker. He was particularly worried about Italian air strikes.

The navy did reinforce its fleet at Alexandria; ironically, Mussolini told his admirals not to risk a fight if it ventured out. But it did not. Emperor Haile Selassie fled to London on May 4, 1936; Italian troops marched into his capital, Addis Ababa, the next day. The failure to stop

Mussolini meant the death of the League of Nations. Italy was now the leading power in the Horn of Africa, and Britain's most important rival in the Mediterranean. Its navy continued to expand, ending up in 1940 with seven heavy and 12 light cruisers, 61 destroyers, 105 submarines, and six battleships, two of which—the *Littorio* and *Vittorio Veneto*—had 15-inch guns and were among the most modern in the world. Alfred Mahan had belatedly found a new disciple as the balance of power in the Mediterranean seemed about to shift for the first time since Nelson's victory at the Nile.

None of this was lost on Adolf Hitler, either. He had become German chancellor in January 1933, as German resentment against the Treaty of Versailles and the Western democracies reached its height. Rebuilding Germany's military might was his first priority, and his way of getting the Fatherland out of economic depression. His plans included a new army, a new air force or *Luftwaffe,* as well as a strong navy. Hitler had sensed when he wrote *Mein Kampf* that the Washington naval treaty marked a watershed, that Britain had surrendered command of the seas. He also believed that it had no stomach for another war for the sake of Europe. The refusal of Cambridge students to repudiate the resolution of their debate union in 1933, that "under no circumstances will this house fight for King and Country," confirmed this. His naval strategy aimed to make sure they never did.

The flashy centerpiece were the three compact 11,700-ton "pocket battleships," the first of which, the *Deutschland,* was finished in 1934. But the real core of Hitler's navy was to be its resurrected U-boat force. Almost his first act as chancellor was to order twenty-four of them, to be built and designed by German engineers in Finland. Yet the Versailles treaty dictated that Germany was to have *no* submarines. So Hitler announced Germany would no longer abide by the Versailles restrictions, and with diabolical skill made Britain his accomplice in rearming the German navy.

The Anglo-German Naval treaty was signed in June 1935 by Stanley Baldwin's new government. Hitler, had formally proposed limiting his new *Kriegsmarine*'s capital ships to just 35 percent of Britain's, and its U-boat force to 45 percent. The British were all too eager to sign on. The treaty seemed an easy way to limit Hitler's maritime expansion; "For Germany," Hitler had announced to the Reichstag, "this is final." Britain ignored the fact that having just violated one formal treaty, Versailles, there was nothing to stop Hitler from violating another. The treaty also permitted a massive expansion of Germany's navy. Far from limiting

Hitler's ambitions, the Anglo-German Naval Treaty made Germany once again a major naval power.

Two back-benchers, and two only, grasped this: former prime minister Lloyd George, who made an impassioned speech against the treaty, and Winston Churchill. Churchill had spoken out before about the danger of ignoring what Hitler was doing in Germany, and the threat he posed to European peace. But now the successive governments' weakness and "appeasement" (the new key word in British politics by the mid-1930s) of German demands threatened a subject close to Churchill's heart, Britain's naval strength. It also awakened him to the gathering threat at the other end of the empire. "What a windfall this has been for Japan!" Churchill exclaimed, since a large portion of the British fleet would now have to remain in the North Sea to keep watch on the growing German menace— growing, he pointed out, in accordance with the very terms of the treaty. Churchill noted that Baldwin had been quoted as saying, "We shall have to give up certain of our toys—one is 'Britannia rules the waves.' " Churchill warned, "If the idea 'Rule Britannia' is a toy, it is certainly one for which many good men from time to time have been ready to die."

The question was, of course, whether they were ready to do the same now. Hitler was banking that they were not, a hunch confirmed by Britain's supine response in Ethiopia. In 1935, Hitler unveiled to the world his new German army, the Wehrmacht, more than thirty-six divisions strong, and his Luftwaffe, with more than 1,888 planes to sweep the skies. He also appointed Karl Dönitz, a hardened veteran of the unrestricted submarine campaign of the First World War, to head the new U-boat service. The plan was to use the threat of the U-boats to blackmail Britain into staying out of the way of his ambitions in Europe. His pocket battleship program was fully under way, with two super battleships, *Bismarck* and *Tirpitz,* on the horizon. In 1936 he turned to the triumphant Mussolini as his ally; the "Rome-Berlin axis" became the linchpin of Europe's new power politics. Hitler was about to unleash his Third Reich in a drive for domination of Europe. No one, certainly not Britain, seemed prepared or even willing to stop him.

From his reoccupation of the Rhineland in 1936 to his *Anschluss* with Austria and dismemberment of Czechoslovakia in 1938, Hitler's ambitions met with only more accommodation and appeasement—all born of a sense of military impotence, especially naval impotence. Britain's one lever of influence on the continent of Europe had been fear of its overwhelming naval strength. Once that disappeared power passed to those aggressive and ruthless enough to use it—not only Germany and Italy but Soviet Russia as well.

The British navy meanwhile was reduced to being a mere spectator to events: evacuating British subjects when the Japanese bombed Shanghai in 1937, and shepherding British ships in and out of ports like Cádiz and Corunna as the Berlin-Rome Axis's ally General Franco overran Spain. Almost too late, the Admiralty awoke to the dangers Britain and the empire now faced and began a desperate race to prepare for war. The Ten Years' Rule had at last been scrapped, and construction of new ships got under way. The first new aircraft carrier, the *Ark Royal,* appeared in 1937; the second, HMS *Illustrious,* in 1939. A new class of battleship, the 35,000-ton *King George V* class, was launched with 16-inch guns to match those of the latest American and Japanese ships, and in 1937 a new class of destroyers. The RAF created a Coastal Command to coordinate its fighters and bombers with the navy's need for air support around the British Isles—although the planes the RAF provided were few in number and obsolete in design. And on the very evening war was declared against Germany, the navy took on its old friend as First Lord of the Admiralty. The ecstatic signal went out across the fleet: "Winston's back."

Yet even after the failure of Munich reversed the course of appeasement, it was still Hitler who held the initiative and controlled the time and place of future conflict. By striking at Poland in September 1939, Hitler ensured that Britain and France remained on the defensive. His generals and admirals still wanted to delay another two years until their buildup was complete; ironically, that would also have given Britain more time to finish its own prewar preparations. Instead, Britain would have to rely on France to hold down the Germans on land, while the Royal Navy deployed to protect its sea routes. "Thank God for the French army," was the constant refrain from Churchill and others.

So when the Germans unleashed their ground campaign in the West in May of 1940, it was a rude awakening. The tank had been a British invention: naval engineer Reginald Bacon, one of Fisher's brilliant protégés, built the first "land-ship" in September 1914, to which Winston Churchill gave its famous code name. The British had pioneered its offensive use in World War I; the first theorists of mass tank warfare had been two British army officers, J. F. C. Fuller and Captain Basil Liddell-Hart. But as with the submarine, the Germans took a British technology and showed how its ruthless application could change the face of war.

The German blitzkrieg led to France's collapse in less than five weeks. Britain was now alone and vulnerable against the totalitarian threat—even more vulnerable than in 1588, because now it had so much more to lose. Italy declared war in the closing days of June, exposing Malta, Suez, and the Mediterranean to its powerful fleet. The Germans occupied France's western coast, giving Dönitz's U-boats direct access to the Channel and Atlantic. The previous year the battleship *Royal Oak* had been sunk by a U-boat in Scapa Flow itself; the aircraft carrier *Courageous* was also lost to a torpedo and the *Ark Royal* narrowly escaped the same fate (it would succumb in November 1941 to the *U-81*). The fall of France dramatically increased the chances of more such attacks, in addition to increasing the danger to merchant shipping. Already in June, the losses came to almost 600,000 tons. The numbers fell back again in July but on August 17, 1940, Hitler lifted the last restrictions on his submarine war against Britain. Germany's U-boat captains were about to embark on what they would call "the happy time," and there was no one this time, including the Americans, who were going to stop them.

Britain's status as the world's greatest maritime nation, the legacy of four hundred years of voyaging, piracy, slave trading, naval warfare, empire-building, and overseas trade—a legacy the British navy had defended since the days of Hawkins and Drake—was about to be turned against it. Sea power, which had once seemed to make Britain invincible, now left it vulnerable to its enemies. Winston Churchill, the new prime minister, also recognized the larger stakes involved. "Upon this battle depends the survival of Christian civilization," he told Britons on June 18, as the French were asking Hitler for peace. "Hitler knows he will have to break us on this island or lose the war.... If we fail, then the whole world, including the United States, including all we have known and cared for, will sink into the abyss of a new Dark Age.... Let us brace ourselves to our duties, and so bear ourselves that ... men will say: 'This was their finest hour.'"

Impressive words. It was up to the Royal Navy to see that they did not ring hollow. The evacuation of Dunkirk left Britain without an effective army; the Royal Air Force was outnumbered and outclassed by its Luftwaffe rival. Only the navy could both defend the British Isles from invasion *and* keep them linked to the rest of the empire and their lifeline of the sea.

It was by far the most daunting task the Royal Navy ever faced—one ultimately it could not face without American help. But in the meantime, its success, and the survival of the free world, turned on the leadership of a handful of men, truly a "band of brothers" as much as Nelson's. They were a generation of flag officers as supremely gifted, yet as strikingly different, as any in the navy's history. Unusually, they came from army as well as navy backgrounds; one's father had been a professor at Edinburgh University. Another was a Jew. But all of them were trained in the skills and assumptions of Fisher's post-dreadnought navy. They were the kind of officers Fisher had wanted: smart, aggressive, and unfazed by new technology. Bruce Fraser began as a gunnery specialist; James Somerville in wireless communications. The others made their way commanding the small ships, not the big ones: Andrew Cunningham, John Tovey, Bertram Ramsay, and Philip Vian on destroyers, Max Horton on a submarine. It would give the admirals of World War II some of the same independent, ruthless, almost piratical, instincts of an earlier British navy (Max Horton liked to record U-boats sunk by his Western Approaches Command with a skull and crossbones).

Unlike Nelson's band, there was no single charismatic leader to pull them together. It might have been Churchill, who is usually seen as Britain's wartime savior—and rightly so. But the sad truth was that Churchill distrusted the Admiralty and promoted quarrels and controversy throughout its high command. It was to the credit of First Sea Lord Sir Dudley Pound that he managed to nip some of Winston's wilder ideas in the bud, although a few, like Narvik and Greece, slipped through. Pound would later be criticized for not offering the kind of tough strong leadership at the top his fleet officers showed at sea. But in the end, it was Pound and the navy who got the British nation, and Winston Churchill, through the war's darkest years.

Max Horton was the first to show what this new generation could do. As vice admiral in charge of British submarines, in March 1940, he was the only commander to figure out that the Germans would first attack Norway, and on his own initiative sent out ten subs into Norwegian waters to intercept them. Horton's force would sink or cripple sixteen German warships and transports, and might have foiled Hitler's plan altogether if the Admiralty had not pulled six of his submarines away for duty in the North Sea.

Captain Philip Warburton-Lee led a daring destroyer charge up the Ofotsfjord to Narvik on April 10, catching unaware a force twice his size as they were guarding the offloading of German troops, and sank two German destroyers and severely damaged four more. It was the sort of thing Nelson or Thomas Cochrane might have done, and should have launched Warburton-Lee's career as the navy's foremost fighting admiral. But the attack had taken his life, and ultimately German airpower would tip the balance in Norwegian waters, with the British task force, including the battleship *Warspite,* fleeing without fighter cover from the Nazi bombers. However, it was Churchill's strategy, not the navy's tactics, that made Narvik a disaster and Norway the northern arm of Hitler's European empire.

Admiral Bertram Ramsay took on the almost impossible job of evacuating the British army from Dunkirk in early June 1940. Popular myth says it was yachts and fishing trawlers that brought the beleaguered troops safely home; in fact, almost half were carried out on Ramsay's warships, and most of the rest on Royal Navy—manned vessels. The Admiralty had hoped to get out 45,000 men; Ramsay managed almost 340,000, in addition to 4,000 troops from Boulogne and 1,000 from Calais. Never before had a navy carried away an entire army from a hostile shore—and again without proper air cover. It came at grievous cost: six destroyers sunk and another fourteen damaged by bombs. Dunkirk thinned a naval force already lean from interwar neglect, even thinner. But it had turned humiliating defeat into a moral victory. The British army lived on to fight another day, and Bert Ramsay earned himself a place in naval history.*

Less than a month later Admiral James Somerville faced a more distasteful task: convincing the French Mediterranean fleet in Algeria to surrender to the British before Hitler could get his hands on it, or to destroy it if the French refused. The French fleet included two large battleships and two modern battle cruisers, *Dunkerque* and *Strasbourg.* Together with the Italian fleet, they would have given Germany unchallengeable control of the Mediterranean. Churchill wanted Britain to have those ships, and no one else. So Somerville's Force H, with *Ark Royal,* battleships *Valiant* and *Resolution,* and Britain's most advanced battle cruiser, HMS *Hood,* arrived at Mers-el-Kebir harbor on July 3, 1940, to negotiate a French surrender. The French admiral felt honor-bound to refuse.

The fight was over in less than an hour. One French battleship was sunk, another damaged and run aground, along with the *Dunkerque. Strasbourg* got away but took several torpedoes from *Ark Royal's* Swordfish bombers. More than a thousand French sailors were dead. It was the last time the British navy fought its French rival, the fleet it had once contested

---

*Four years later, Ramsay would go back the way he came, as commander of all naval forces in the D-Day invasion.

for mastery of the world. But this time it was the fleet of a vanquished ally, not a jealous foe, and a fleet trapped in its own safe harbor. Somerville said afterward, "We all feel thoroughly dirty and ashamed." Churchill called the decision to attack "heartbreaking." Certainly Somerville's ruthless attack made France's new Vichy government more vehemently pro-Hitler and anti-British. But it also proved to the world that Britain meant to fight on, rather than surrender. Mussolini's son-in-law Count Ciano was awestruck and wrote in his diary that it showed "the fighting spirit of His Majesty's fleet is still quite alive, and still has the aggressive ruthlessness of the captains and pirates of the seventeenth century."

It also saved Winston Churchill. "Up till this moment the Conservative Party had treated me with some reserve," he remembered later. After the fall of France, many talked of replacing him with Lord Halifax. But when Churchill entered the house on July 4, he received a tremendous standing ovation. Former supporters of Chamberlain and Halifax rallied around their new leader, throwing aside their remaining doubts. Britain now had a wartime prime minister in the tradition of the elder Pitt. "Winston's dominance over the House," said Harold Nicolson, was total. Having unified the government at home and impressed observers abroad, Mers-el-Kebir marked the first real turning point in Britain's war for survival.

The sinking of the French fleet had also impressed another foreigner: President Franklin Roosevelt. The day after Churchill had become the Admiralty's First Lord Roosevelt had sent a congratulatory note, appealing to their common navy background (Roosevelt had been assistant secretary of the navy during World War I). They had confidentially remained in touch ever since, using the mutual code name "Former Naval Person." On June 15, as France fell, Churchill wrote to FDR: "The successful defence of this island will be the only hope of averting the collapse of civilization as we define it."

On July 1, two days before Mers-el-kebir, his ambassador in London, Joseph Kennedy, had told Chamberlain, "Everyone in the U.S.A. thinks [England] will be beaten in a month." Now President Roosevelt and his advisors had to rethink their timetable. Roosevelt sent a trio of American military advisors to London on July 14 to assess Britain's ability to continue the war and whether American aid might make a difference: above all, Roosevelt did not want to see the British fleet or its bases in the Atlantic under Nazi control. By the end of the month Churchill knew that America stepping in to save the day was a real possibility.

Meanwhile, the navy's still strong presence in the narrow seas frustrated any hopes for a German crossing of the Channel, even with Luftwaffe support. This forced Hitler to turn in August to Göring's plan to break Britain's will and ability to fight from the air alone—a plan which, despite thousands of British casualties and devastated cities, including Portsmouth and Plymouth, had no chance of success as long as the Royal Navy stood firm.

Then in the Mediterranean, Commander in Chief Andrew Cunningham dealt decisively with the Italian threat. Later, people would treat the Italian war effort in World War II, especially the Italian army, as a joke. But in 1940, the Italian navy was large—in battleships and cruisers, larger than Germany's—active, and technically accomplished. Britain could do nothing to protect Malta and the vital lifeline of the Suez Canal until it had been neutralized.

Cunningham had the boldness and imagination to do the job. Just before midnight on November 11, 1940, torpedo bombers from HMS *Illustrious* struck the Italian fleet unawares in Taranto harbor, sinking one battleship and severely damaging two more at the cost of only two Swordfish planes. In another carrier strike on March 28, 1941, this time off Cape Matapan, Cunningham knocked out a fourth Italian battleship and crippled the heavy cruiser *Pola,* while his capital ships finished off the *Pola* and sank two more cruisers sent to its rescue. Taranto and Matapan effectively put the Italian navy out of the war and proved to any lingering doubters the effectiveness of carrier-based aircraft against the biggest surface ships. They also sent naval planners in Japan scurrying to their desks until late in the night.

Unfortunately, Taranto also allowed Winston Churchill to ignore objections to one of his most disastrous ideas: a British landing in Greece. The sudden crippling of the Italian navy had imperiled Mussolini's empire everywhere. His armies in Libya collapsed under attack from the British Eighth Army; his invasion of Yugoslavia stalled, then stalemated. Hitler was forced to intervene to save his increasingly feeble ally, as the Wehrmacht unleashed once more its devastating blitzkrieg tactics. In February 1941 General Erwin Rommel would drive his Afrika Korps to the border of Egypt. German air attacks began on Malta and sank the carrier *Illustrious,* while another German army descended into Yugoslavia and then pushed on into Greece.

"Things went well for us," Cunningham would say later, "as long as we pursued one object. When we started pursuing two or more at one time catastrophe resulted." Churchill hoped Greece would do what his other brainschild, Gallipoli, had failed to do in the first war: unexpectedly open an enemy's soft flank with a single bold amphibious stroke. The first British troops arrived there on March 4, 1941. Yet in less than a month they had to be taken away again in Cunningham's ships, as it turned out the Aegean was not Germany's soft flank, but Britain's.

Greece collapsed; German paratroopers dropped into Crete. Cunningham beat off the Nazi attempt to take Crete by sea, but once again had to evacuate British troops while enduring a blizzard of air attacks from German bases in Greece and North Africa. At one point some of his captains suggested breaking off, as the Stukas took out yet another of his destroyers. "It takes the Navy three years to build a ship," Cunningham replied, "it would take three hundred years to build a new reputation. The evacuation will continue." So it did, at the cost of three cruisers and eight destroyers lost, and two battleships, a carrier, and five cruisers put out of action. A British army had been saved again. But Cunningham's fleet had been crippled and the new dominant power in the eastern Mediterranean was Nazi Germany.

It was a crucial moment. The future of the world economic system was suddenly in play—more in play than at any time since Rodney had won the Battle of the Saintes in 1782. Yet Germany had done it without deploying a fleet of any kind, and in the teeth of Britain's naval superiority—what Mahan and his disciples had confidently predicted could never happen. Air power, and the speed and precision of the new technologies of land warfare, had shifted the military balance, and with it the geopolitical balance. Cairo, the Suez Canal, Palestine and Syria, the oil fields of Iraq and the Persian Gulf, and the route to India all lay within Hitler's grasp. Significantly, it was his *naval* advisors, especially Grand Admiral Raeder, who now urged him to seize the Suez Canal and hurl his panzers into the Middle East. It would strike Britain "a deadlier blow than the taking of London," Raeder said. If Hitler had taken their advice, the result would very probably have been permanent German control of half the world's trade and all the world's oil resources. Ultimately, Germany and Japan could have divided up the resources of Asia—from Afghanistan and Bombay to Singapore and Australia—between them.

But Hitler did not take their advice. His geopolitical vision belonged to an even earlier era, that of land-based empire and dominion. Like Napoleon a century and a quarter before, he had his eye fixed on Russia. By destroying it, he would be free to create his vast, racially pure Aryan empire in eastern Europe. And like Napoleon, Hitler believed the Soviet Union's defeat would convince Britain that further resistance was useless. "England's hope is Russia and America," he told his generals on July 31, 1940. Taking out Russia would also take out America, since then it would then have to deal with a Japan reigning supreme in the Pacific. "England's last hope," Hitler said, would be extinguished. "The quicker we smash Russia the better," he concluded and ordered them to prepare to move their armies east.

So Hitler missed his opportunity to have Germany replace Great Britain as the biggest geopolitical player in the world. Indeed, even as the Battle of Britain was starting in August, Hitler was losing interest. Besides, while the German army secretly deployed along the Russian border in May and June of 1941, he still had another weapon to prevent Britain from interfering with his plans: the U-boat.

• • •

For nearly three hundred years the ports of Brittany at Brest, Lorient, Rochefort, Nantes, and St. Nizaire had been home to the French Atlantic fleet, and sortie points for its struggle against the British navy for control of the oceans. With France's defeat in 1940, they became home to another challenger to British naval mastery. This time however, it was submarines, not frigates and ships of the line, in a ruthless battle for the Atlantic such as only the Third Reich could conceive and execute.

The U-boats' commander, Karl Dönitz, had learned the brutal lessons of unrestricted submarine warfare in the First World War. His guru, Walter Forstmann of the *U-39*, had told him: "One must energetically put aside all sympathy, all pity, and every other feeling of the kind." From his headquarters at Kerneval near Lorient, the old French naval base, Dönitz applied the hard logic of a war of attrition to the classic *guerre de course*. With fifty U-boats on patrol at any given time, each sinking three ships a month, he could destroy half the British merchant fleet in a year. The merchant marine was already a quarter smaller than it had been in the first war; the rate of 150 ships lost per month was twenty times what it could replace with new building. At that rate, Dönitz knew, Britain would be doomed.

From July to October 1940, "the happy time" for German U-boat captains, sinkings rose steadily to one hundred ships a month, more than half of them in the North Atlantic. Nor did convoys help, for Dönitz was using the new tactics of the *Rudel* or "wolf pack," with ten or fifteen

U-boats attacking a single convoy at a time. His problem was not having enough of the new medium-size boats, the Type VII and Type IX, to keep up the rate of attack. However, as 1941 dawned, Dönitz had more than a hundred U-boats in service, easily enough to kill British ships at twice the rate they could be built.

The man who had to stop him was Admiral Sir Percy Noble, head of Western Approaches Command, the front line in the anti-U-boat war. Noble was a soft-spoken, understated man, in sharp contrast to his flamboyant successor, Max Horton. But in his own quiet way Noble oversaw the changes in the campaign that would gradually halt, and then reverse, Dönitz's successes.

Liverpool, once the hub of Britain's slave trade, now became the navy's window onto the Atlantic. Noble kept track of the battle from his headquarters at Derby House, while in the nearby Liver Building Rear Admiral Ritchie and his staff organized and routed the convoys. Noble also brought RAF's Coastal Command under his control, to better coordinate air and sea operations. He often went up with Coastal Command's Beauforts and Sutherlands on patrol, and saw for himself how the use of airpower could have a decisive impact on the war against the submarine. Radar, too, for tracking submarines on the surface: Noble had it installed on his destroyers and escorts, which he organized into Escort and Support Groups, so that the navy could concentrate its forces against the wolf pack attacks.

Thanks to the Americans and Canadians, Noble was also getting the ships he needed. In September of 1940 Roosevelt and Churchill had struck a deal, giving Britain fifty old American "four-stacker" destroyers in exchange for leasing British navy bases in Bermuda, the West Indies, and Newfoundland. The Canadians meanwhile were building dozens of new anti-submarine corvettes for the convoys. By May Noble had enough ships to provide escorts for the convoys all the way across the Atlantic.

Yet even this might not have been enough—in April 1941 shipping losses were such that meat and eggs had virtually vanished from the tables of British families—if not for a major breakthrough far to the south of Liverpool, at Bletchley Park near London. There a young Cambridge-trained mathematician named Alan Turing was working to break the German naval code, a cipher generated by a machine called Enigma. Turing had already cracked the German army and Luftwaffe Enigma codes by employing a counter-machine, which he had built with the help of some Polish mathematicians in exile, "a bronze colored column surmounted by a larger circular bronze-colored face, like some Eastern Goddess" and which made "a noise like that of a thousand knitting needles." In March, Turning and his machine, the ancestor of all computers, enabled the code breakers at Bletchley Park to decipher all of Dönitz's submarine communications for the month of February. By May they were reading his signal traffic with a delay of only three to seven days.

The "invisible war" was invisible no longer. Since the wolf pack tactics depended on close radio communication between headquarters and submarines to coordinate attacks, cracking Enigma now allowed the Admiralty to monitor the U-boats' every move—even reroute convoys if they were too close to a wolf pack patrol area. The losses, which had risen to 109 ships in June 1941, dropped off dramatically to only 43 in July, 41 in August, down to 35 in November. U-boat losses, on the other hand, began to climb. Dönitz had lost three of his best aces in March: by August "North Atlantic U-boat operations sank to their lowest level of effectiveness," as an authority later wrote. Noble had more than 400 British, Canadian, and American vessels on patrol against the U-boat menace.

In May 1941 the war in the Atlantic had taken another major turn for the better, thanks to Admiral Sir John Tovey, commander in chief of the Home Fleet and James Somerville's Force H. Together they had tracked down and destroyed Hitler's most potent battleship, the *Bismarck,* which had broken out into the Atlantic to take on the convoys. She had managed to blow up the *Hood* and seriously damage *Prince of Wales* before a Swordfish from the *Ark Royal* struck her with a torpedo, disabling her steering. On May 27, Tovey and his flagship, the mighty *King George V* along with the *Rodney,* caught up with the *Bismarck* as she wandered in a long slow circle to port. Their combined 14- and 16-inch guns pounded her to a wreck; only 110 out of 2,200 German crewmen survived. That same month HMS *Devonshire* caught and destroyed the Nazis' most successful surface raider, the *Atlantis,* off the Cape of Good Hope.

Then on September 11 came the biggest break of all. After German planes attacked and sank an American merchant ship in the Gulf of Suez, President Roosevelt made a speech to the nation. America had been preparing for this moment for more than a year. Every policy maker from Roosevelt down was worried about what would happen if Britain lost the war—and the British navy became Hitler's hostage. In June 1940 Chief of Naval Operations Admiral Stark had put in a request to Congress for the largest naval appropriation in American history, some four billion dollars to expand the fleet to almost 700 ships. Roosevelt's deal with

Churchill for the fifty "four-stackers" opened a new era of Anglo-American cooperation at sea and of American preemptive response to events outside its borders. In February 1941, the American naval attaché in Berlin noted that Germany's war was "now not only against England but also against the United States which is the only strong force left against [its] New Order."

On September 11, Roosevelt addressed that point directly in terms of sea power: "To be ultimately successful in world-mastery, Hitler knows he must get control of the seas," he said. That inevitably meant conflict with America over "the bridge of ships we are building across the Atlantic." Roosevelt added: "We have sought no shooting war with Hitler. We do not seek it now." But any German or Italian submarine entering waters "the protection of which is necessary for American defense," would be fired upon. It amounted to a virtual declaration of war against the Axis.

The *Bismarck* sunk; the U-boat threat contained; Hitler's panzer divisions bogged down in the mud in Russia; Rommel stalemated in North Africa; America about to enter the war—in November 1941 it seemed the British navy had the war well in hand and had succeeded in stemming the Nazi tide. With American help, it could even begin reversing it. What it was *not* prepared to do was to fight a whole other war at the same time on the other side of the world, in the Pacific. Yet, in a few weeks, that was precisely what it faced.

• • •

This was ultimately America's fault, not Britain's. Japan's brutal war in China had alienated the American public opinion for a decade; Japan's naval buildup had American strategists worried longer than that. When the fall of France in 1940 gave Japan the use of airfields in French Indochina, Roosevelt imposed economic sanctions against the island nation. In June 1941 Japan overran the rest of Indochina, giving them access to all of Southeast Asia. Roosevelt retaliated by imposing an embargo on all strategic goods to Japan, including oil, 80 percent of which Japan imported from the United States. Until this point, only the Japanese army had wanted to expand Japan's war outside China. Now, thanks to the American ban, the navy faced total immobility. "The Navy is consuming four hundred tons of oil an hour," said its chief of staff in a secret minute. Seizing the oil fields in the Dutch East Indies would certainly mean war with America, and probably with Britain. But "there is no choice left but to fight and break the iron chains strangling Japan," he said.

Britain had tried to do everything to avoid provoking Japan into hostilities. It could not afford another major war at sea. Now, as war loomed the Admiralty begged the United States to shift some of its fleet to Singapore. The American admirals, however, refused. They had doubts that Singapore, "the Gibraltar of the East," could really hold out against a determined Japanese assault, especially with Japanese bombers poised for action in Indochina. But in the end they did agree to send more ships into the Atlantic, to allow Britain to form an Eastern Fleet to protect Singapore.

The proud flagship of the new fleet was to be the *Prince of Wales,* sister ship of the *King George V,* the first new battleships Britain had built since 1925. She was so new she still had dockyard workers and engineers on board finishing work when she went into action against the *Bismarck* in May. *Prince of Wales* carried ten 14-inch guns, capable of hitting a target at 35,000 yards or more than twenty miles. She carried the latest antiaircraft weaponry, and had been built with special bulkheads and watertight compartments to make her safe against torpedo attack. Indeed, *Prince of Wales* was considered largely unsinkable—always a dangerous boast. Her complement of 1,502 seamen and 110 officers was headed by Captain John Leach, a burly West Country navy man, and diminutive Admiral Thomas "Tom Thumb" Phillips, whom Churchill had called "his little cock sparrow" (although he and Churchill had quarreled about the operation in Greece and Philips was now out of favor).

Prince of Wales's companion in fate, *Repulse,* was a quarter-century older. She had been built at Clydebank in 1916 and had missed Jutland by only a couple of months. But she had undergone two major refittings since then, at a cost of two million pounds, and was still among Britain's best fighting ships. *Repulse* was a typical Fisher-era battle cruiser, with six 15-inch guns and engines still capable to bringing her up to 29 knots. She also had nine 4-inch guns which, together with three mounts of 2-pound "pom pom" guns, were supposed to provide antiaircraft cover. A special protective bulge around her main hull was *Repulse*'s defense against torpedo attack. Her captain, William Tennant, was a hero of the Dunkirk evacuation, and known affectionately as "Dunkirk Joe" to his crew, who were largely West Country men themselves.

Taken together, *Prince of Wales* and *Repulse* summed up almost a quarter-century of British naval technology and three centuries of tradition and pride. The ships were more than just leaders of a task force. They were symbols of the men and nation that had dominated the sea lanes of the

Pacific since the days of Anson and Cook, symbols of a navy whose word was still law across the oceans of the world.

They were supposed to be joined by another powerful representative of the modern navy, the brand-new aircraft carrier *Indomitable*. In fact, Pound and the other sea lords had envisaged a much larger and more diverse Task Force G, with another two battleships (*Nelson* and *Rodney*) and four more cruisers. But Churchill had overruled them. He thought "the smallest number of the best ships" would be enough to "exert a paralyzing effect upon Japanese Naval action" when they appeared in the Indian Ocean. Then, however, *Indomitable* struck a reef at Kingston Harbor, Jamaica, on November 3 and had to be taken to the American facilities at Norfolk for repairs. So *Prince of Wales* and *Repulse* sailed on alone, with only four destroyers as escorts.

They reached Singapore on December 2, 1941, to find extensive for-tifications and an imposing garrison of more than 100,000 men but no personnel, spare parts, or machine tools to service big warships, and a totally inadequate air force. Far from securing Singapore, *Prince of Wales* and *Repulse* were now themselves vulnerable. Indeed, the very next day the Admiralty quietly urged Phillips to leave: they had word that the Japanese were building up their aircraft and submarines in the area. On the fourth Phillips flew to Manila to confer with the Americans, and *Repulse* set off on a cruise for Australia. It was during the meeting with General Douglas MacArthur that they learned that Japanese troop transports had been seen sailing south for Malaya. War was coming, and coming fast.

Phillips left hurriedly for Singapore—so hurriedly that one of his plane's aircrew got left behind. He signaled Tennant to bring the *Repulse* back; she was just returning into Singapore harbor when Philips got news that the Japanese were landing on the Malay Peninsula to the north, at Kota Bharu. Later came further news that the Japanese had crippled the American fleet with a surprise air attack on Pearl Harbor on the 7th—borrowing the same plan the British had employed at Taranto two years before. That next day, December 8, Japanese planes bombed Singapore itself.

With the Americans out of the picture and more Japanese air attacks certain, Phillips's position had become untenable. He had a choice. He could stay and die fighting, or he could run *Prince of Wales* and *Repulse* out to sea to try to intercept the Japanese troop transports and disrupt their inva-sion. Such a move would take place in submarine-infested waters, and without any air cover. "Nonetheless," he told a meeting of his staff,

Captains Leach and Tennant, and his destroyer captains, "I feel that we have got to do something." One lieutenant from the destroyer HMS *Tenedos* remembered there was "a long silence after this." Everyone was thinking the same thing, he thought: this was the impossible situation into which Churchill's rash confidence in British naval supremacy had put them.

Force G left Singapore on the eighth, but reports they had been spotted by a Japanese submarine convinced Phillips to break off his move north. Instead, he decided to make south for Kuantan, where Singapore had heard more Japanese troops were landing. There Phillips found a deserted beach with no sign of Japanese transports, but also no sign of Japanese planes. He sent one destroyer closer to shore to investigate and another, the *Tenedos,* back to Singapore to refuel. The ships were just getting back under way when just after 10:00 *Tenedos* radioed she was under air attack and that a massive wave of planes and bombers was headed right for Phillips and Force G.

These were Japanese navy planes, 34 bombers and 51 torpedo planes, all land-equipped from bases in Saigon—although Phillips had thought they could not possibly reach him from 500 miles away. It was a fatal miscalculation. As the planes appeared in the bright December sky, Phillips ordered *Repulse* and *Prince of Wales* both to turn away 30 degrees to starboard, although this meant that antiaircraft guns on the starboard side would be unable to fire. Bombs hit the *Repulse* first, while Phillips tried to correct his mistake by ordering both ships to port as the first wave of torpedo bombers swept in—too high and too fast for *Prince of Wales*'s 5-inch guns or *Repulse*'s 4-inchers to hit.

One torpedo struck *Prince of Wales,* flooding the aft compartments and knocking out electrical power—including power to the guns. Leach found he could no longer steer the ship, as she took on a huge list to port. The next wave of bombers put three torpedoes into *Repulse*'s hull; then at 12:20 P.M. *Prince of Wales* took no fewer than four, leaving her with only one engine. Then *Repulse* took another three torpedoes on the port side, and one from starboard. The anguished men on the *Prince of Wales* could see her sinking, but their own agony had just begun. Two squadrons of bombers passed high overhead and unloaded their deadly cargo. A 500-pound bomb smashed through the *Prince of Wales*'s five-inch-thick deck armor and exploded in X Boiler Room, putting out the battleship's last remaining engine. The doomed ship was now awash from stem to stern. A little after one o'clock *Repulse* rolled over and sank. Fifty minutes later

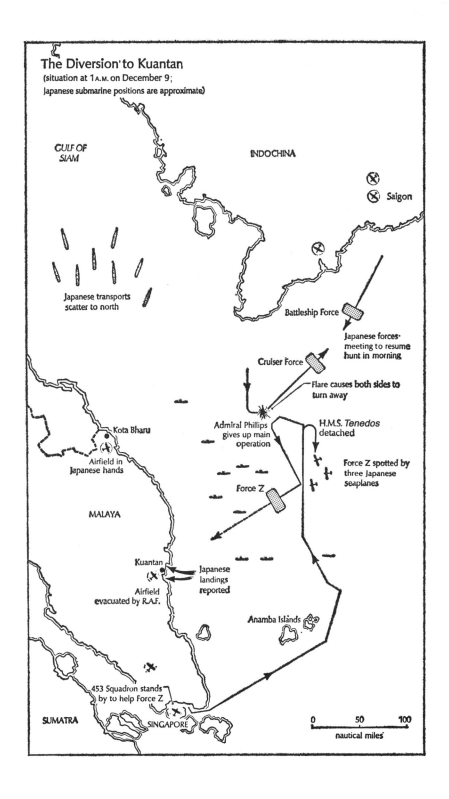

The Diversion to Kuantan

(situation at 1 A.M. on December 9;
Japanese submarine positions are approximate)

GULF OF
SIAM

INDOCHINA

⊗
⊗ Saigon

⊗

Battleship Force

Japanese transports
scatter to north

Japanese forces·
meeting to resume
hunt in morning

Cruiser Force

Flare causes both sides to
turn away

H.M.S. *Tenedos*
detached

Admiral Phillips
gives up main
operation

Kota Bharu

Airfield in
Japanese hands

Force Z spotted by
three Japanese
seaplanes

Force Z

MALAYA

Kuantan
(X)

Japanese
landings
reported

Airfield
evacuated by R.A.F.

Anamba Islands

453 Squadron stands
by to help Force Z

SUMATRA
SINGAPORE

0   50   100
nautical miles

Prince of Wales did the same. Almost one thousand men went down with them, including Philips and Captain Leach.

For the Japanese naval airmen, it was a moment of supreme triumph—but also respectful silence for the defeat of the navy they had all been raised to emulate and envy. Almost uniquely among Japanese air operations, there was no machine-gunning of survivors or bombing of the destroyers picking them up as their boats bobbed in the oil-slickened waters. Even more extraordinary, the next day Lieutenant H. Iki of the Third Torpedo Squadron dropped a wreath over the scene. It was a gesture of gallantry almost unknown to the Japanese, but then it was the Royal Navy's Forbes-Semphill who had taught them the techniques of naval airpower, both here and at Pearl Harbor. As Pearl Harbor's planner, Minoru Genda, told a British officer after the war, "It was the grandsons of the Master of Semphill who sank the *Prince of Wales* and *Repulse*."

In fact, the sinking of the two British warships was a far greater Japanese victory than Pearl Harbor. The Allies' position in the eastern Pacific would quickly recover; the one in the western Pacific would not. It doomed the garrison at Singapore. On February 15, 1942, they surrendered to the Japanese army: the greatest surrender in British military history. On the nineteenth Japanese bombers struck Port Darwin in northwest Australia, severing the sea link between Australia and Java. On March 8 the Dutch East Indies, the anchor of the Atlantic world's presence in Asia since the sixteenth century, capitulated. The last remaining American garrison in the Philippines at Corregidor gave up on May 6, and the week before that Japanese troops took Mandalay in Upper Burma.

The Japanese advance would finally be checked on May 8, when American planes from the carriers *Yorktown* and *Lexington* stopped an invasion force headed for Port Moresby in New Guinea at the battle of the Coral Sea. The Battle of Midway was less than a month away. Yet the face of modern Asia would never be the same. White colonial rule was finished. Even after final victory, neither the French nor the Dutch nor the British would be able to restore authority over their old possessions again. The Japanese invasion of Burma forced Britain to commit its remaining resources to a long slow campaign of jungle fighting for the next two years, and to promise independence to India in exchange for Indian help. Indeed, without the sinking of the *Prince of Wales* and *Repulse* there might not have been an India or a Pakistan—or a Vietnam War.

In any case, the era of the great battleships was definitely over, and with it the kind of sea power on which the Royal Navy had built its strength and reputation, and built and preserved an empire. A new kind of decisive power had arisen: airpower, operating both from land and sea. By 1942 Germany and Japan had shown just how decisive it could be; but neither would remain masters of the situation for long. The sinking of *Prince of Wales* and *Repulse* did indeed pass mantle of world power—but not to Japan. Japan was already at the limit of its resources, and Hitler had thrown away his last chance to dominate the world when he chose to invade Russia instead of the Middle East.

Instead, it would be the United States that would turn airpower into the key to victory, both in Europe and Asia. It did this by using airpower as an *extension,* rather than a substitute, for sea power. The British navy had started on that course three decades earlier with the aircraft carrier, but then faltered and almost dropped out. Japan and Germany had the will but lacked the material resources to keep up technologically with the Americans in either arena. After an early lead, both would fall further and further behind. Only the United States had the wealth and productive capacity to wage a land, sea, and air war against *two* major industrial powers at once, while keeping all the others armed and supplied at the same time.

It was an incredible, almost miraculous feat, although the British had done something similar a century and a half earlier in their war against Napoleon. After 1942 the resources of the global economic system would flow to America's military-industrial complex; victory over totalitarianism would be the result. The United States Navy, just like its Royal Navy ancestor, would grow to become the largest and most dominant in the world. It would take over the job of protecting the postwar *Pax Americana,* which replaced the *Pax Britannica,* and carry it on into the cold war era and beyond. The British navy, by contrast, would shrink to a shadow of its former self, no longer wanted or needed, its power to shape the world at an end.

Yet it still had a few tricks to teach the world's newest superpower and the offspring of its naval loins. The first was in military intelligence, particularly cryptography and code breaking. British naval intelligence became the grandfather of all modern intelligence services. In particular, the men and women of Room 40, and at Bletchley Park in World War II, showed the priceless value of code breaking. Since modern armed services depended more and more on radio communication, intercepting and interpreting those messages offered opponents a huge advantage on the battlefield or at sea. American army cryptographers had very nearly forewarned Washington of the attack at Pearl Harbor; navy code breakers enabled Admirals Nimitz and Halsey to outwit the Japanese at Midway, destroying four of their carriers and killing the best of their planes and pilots. British decrypts of the German Enigma, code-named ULTRA, ensured Hitler's defeat in Russia and provided the key to victory over the U-boats. By the end of the war the code-breaking wing of United States naval intelligence in Washington had more than 5,000 employees. The British navy had shown that covert brains count as much, or even more, than overt brawn in deciding who won wars and who lost them, right down to today.

The second set of lessons offered by the Royal Navy was in the war against the submarine. Hitler had declared war against America four days after Pearl Harbor as part of his plan to finish off Britain's maritime links to the outside world. German U-boats were now free to kill American merchant ships and their escorts with impunity, operating only a few miles from the eastern seaboard, from New York to Cape Hatteras— ironically, the old home waters of Blackbeard and Captain Kidd. From mid-January to the end of April, Germany's Operation Drumbeat (*Paukenschlag*) sank eighty-seven ships, totaling 515,000 tons of cargo—cargo that Britain urgently needed to stay alive. Chief of Naval Operations Ernest King said, "The situation approaches the desperate." The United States Navy was completely unprepared for this kind of stealth warfare in its own home waters. It had to learn again from the British navy, almost from scratch, the techniques and tactics of anti-submarine warfare.

The British introduced the Americans to the use of radar and ASDIC, the ancestor of sonar, in tracking U-boats both above and below the surface. They demonstrated how High-Frequency Direction Finding equipment allowed them to pick up the U-boats radio signals and get their bearing, and how the Leigh light could be used for spotting them at night. They revealed their Enigma decrypts, which, after a one-year hiatus, began reading German signals again in January 1943. And they taught the Americans how the airplane decisively altered the balance against the submarine, delivering firepower and surprise against surfaced boats without giving them time to dive. The Admiralty had been forced to conclude that German's success with the U-boat, both in 1917 and 1942, proved that *"ships alone were unable to maintain command at sea."* To regain it, the British introduced small escort carriers for convoy duty, which by May 1943 had closed the "air gap" in the mid-Atlantic.

With Max Horton now firmly in charge of Western Approaches

Command, the tide of war decisively turned. In April 1943 the Germans lost thirty-four U-boats, most of them to air attacks. In May Dönitz decided he could no longer risk his captains and crews in the North Atlantic convoy routes, and withdrew. It was, he said, a temporary redeployment. In fact, as one of his aides put it, "He was in despair. He saw how things were going." The U-boat war was far from over. From June 1943 until the end of the war U-boats would sink another 337 merchant ships. Yet that was only fifty more than they had killed in the single month of March 1942. At the same time, British and Americans would destroy more than 530 German submarines—including two commanded by Dönitz's own sons. Germany's bid for underwater mastery of the Atlantic had failed.

In the Pacific, meanwhile, American submarines were bringing Japan's economy to a halt. They would sink more than 1,300 Japanese ships, including eight aircraft carriers and eleven cruisers, and almost two and three quarter million tons of shipping in 1944 alone. Half of Japan's merchant fleet was gone by the end of 1944, and three-quarters of its precious oil tankers. Jack Fisher's vision of the submarine scouring the seas clean of enemy warships and merchant vessels had at last become a reality—but in American hands, not British or even German. By war's end, just 2 percent of U.S. Navy personnel in the submarine service had accounted for 55 percent of Japan's naval losses. Japan, which had tried to use British-style sea power to build its empire, had ended up being trapped by it; it suffered the fate that Britain itself had barely escaped.

The third area where the Royal Navy blazed the trail for its American counterpart was with the aircraft carrier. The Americans had not planned to make the aircraft carrier the decisive instrument of the war in the Pacific. The crippling of their powerful battleships at Pearl Harbor had left them no choice. But the American carriers were built with planked wooden flight decks, which made them vulnerable to fire and structural collapse. One by one the great American carriers would succumb, or nearly succumb, to enemy attacks: *Lexington, Hornet, Yorktown, Enterprise* (twice), and *Franklin*.

British carriers, by contrast, had heavy armor plating on their decks and plane hangers—learning the hard lesson from their capital ships. This meant British carriers had fewer than half the planes of their American or Japanese counterparts. But in 1943 the navy at long last wrested control of its air arm from the RAF and were able to outfit their

carriers with the best and latest aircraft, including American-built bombers and fighters. Their defensive advantage over their American cousins
would make itself felt when the British joined forces for the invasion of
Okinawa in March 1945—the last great appearance of a British war fleet
in the Pacific.

Andrew Cunningham, now First Sea Lord, had appointed Sir Bruce
Fraser commander in chief of the Pacific fleet. Fraser hoisted his flag on
the *King George V* at Ceylon in November 1944, relieving James
Somerville, who had been sent to Washington to take Percy Noble's place
dealing with the Americans—a duty now as vital to the British Empire as
commanding any task force.* When Fraser's fleet joined Admiral Chester
Nimitz's Americans for the invasion of Okinawa, it included two battleships and four aircraft carriers: *Victorious, Indefatigable, Illustrious,* and
Indomitable. Indomitable was supposed to have been with *Prince of Wales* and
Repulse in 1941, and might have saved them if she had. When those two
ships had left for Singapore, Britain's navy was still the largest in the
world. Now, just four years later, Nimitz's single fleet of ten aircraft carriers, six light carriers, seven battleships, and eighteen cruisers, was more
powerful than the entire Royal Navy put together.

The fact was that years of unremitting war had bled the British navy
white. The fate of its "Tribal" class of destroyers, built in the late 1930s,
tells the ugly story:

> *Maori,* sunk in an air raid on Malta, 1942; *Cossack,* torpedoed off Gibraltar,
> 1941; *Mashona,* sunk by bombs in the North Atlantic, 1941; *Mohawk,* sunk
> in destroyer torpedo action off Tunisia, 1941; *Sikh,* sunk by gunfire off
> Tobruk, 1942; *Zulu,* sunk by aircraft in the eastern Mediterranean, 1942;
> *Matabele,* sunk by a U-boat in the Barents Sea, 1942; *Punjabi,* sunk by colli-
> sion in the North Atlantic, 1942; *Bedouin,* sunk by aerial torpedoes in the
> central Mediterranean, 1942; *Somali,* sunk by torpedo off Iceland, 1942;
> *Afridi,* sunk by aircraft off Norway, 1940: *Gurkha,* sunk by aircraft off
> Norway, 1940. *Matabele . . .* was torpedoed in a northern Russian convoy
> in mid-January; she sank immediately; two of her 4,000 men were
> picked out of the Arctic water.

---

*The same was true in the choice of Allied Supreme Commander in Southeast Asia,
Admiral Louis Mountbatten. Mountbatten, a member of the royal family, had a cred-
itable record as a destroyer captain early in the war (his exploits inspired Noël
Coward's movie *In Which We Serve*) and as chief of Combined Operations, including
Britain's secret commandos. But the main reason behind his appointment in August
1943, at age forty-two, was that he was popular with the Americans.

Of sixteen ships in the *Tribal* class, only four would survive the war. In all, more than 1,525 British warships would be lost, and 50,000 navy seamen and officers.

Britain had permanently lost its lead in the race of naval technology, as well. It had not built a single new cruiser since 1941; no new aircraft carriers since 1940. The once-great naval dockyards in Plymouth, Portsmouth, and Chatham had been devastated by Nazi air raids. By 1944, more than a third of the Royal Navy's ships were American-built. As for the rest, they were now slower, their machinery more antiquated and poorly protected, their methods of supply and refueling more cumbersome than their American counterparts. And yet, as historian Corelli Barnett notes, "The seamanship and fighting spirit of the officers and men of the Royal Navy itself had never been greater." They would prove it again in this closing campaign of the war, the Royal Navy's last stand as a major player on the world stage.

Japan had pinned its last hope of stopping the Allies with its kamikazes, most of them raw recruits flying obsolete machines—the old skill and precision of the British-trained Naval Air Service was now only a memory. In the first five days of the Okinawa operation, kamikaze attacks grew in size and intensity. At first the destroyer pickets took the brunt of it, but then the Japanese began to reach the heart of the invasion fleet, the carriers. With their wooden flight decks, the American carriers suffered worst. Admiral Mitscher had to shift his flag twice when both *Bunker Hill* and *Enterprise* were put out of action. But the British carriers held up and even continued to send planes aloft in the midst of the hell-storm. One kamikaze crashed on the flight deck of the *Formidable,* killing and wounding fifty-five sailors and starting a fire among the parked aircraft. Yet six hours later planes were once again taking off from *Formidable.*

Indomitable was hit as well, but the Japanese plane simply bounced off her deck and blew up over the side. Then it was *Formidable*'s turn again; and again if she remained fully operational. Finally, on May 9, 1945, HMS *Victorious* took three deadly kamikaze hits, including one that opened a twenty-five-foot hole on the flight deck. But *Victorious* was able to put planes in the air in less than an hour and was fully back in action two days later. The performance of the British carriers, and the persistence and courage of their crews, was one of the miracles of the Okinawa campaign. Without their three-inch-thick deck armor, all three might have been lost. It was a lesson the Americans would remember when they built their first carriers after the war.

The Americans, however, were careful to keep Fraser's fleet far from the main action. As Admiral Halsey put it privately, they did not want Britain claiming "she had delivered even a part of the final blow that demolished the Japanese fleet." America, not Britain, was going to dictate the shape of the postwar Pacific—and "one thing we are sure we are *not* fighting for," said *Life* magazine, "is to hold the British Empire together." After Okinawa, *King George V* helped with the bombardment of Japan's home islands; she was the last Royal Navy capital ship to fire a shot in anger. Other-wise, the British Pacific fleet had become very much a minor supporting player.

On September 2, 1945, Admiral Bruce Fraser stood beside General Douglas MacArthur and Admiral Nimitz to witness the signing of the Japanese surrender in Tokyo Bay. It was a sobering moment in world history, and in the history of the British navy—the two were, after all, so much intertwined. One hundred and seventy years before, another Scot, Archibald Douglas, brought the first British naval mission to that same spot. Then, the Royal Navy had been the envy and admiration of the world, the symbol of invincible military power and global hegemony.

In 1945, the pride and expertise were still there.

In Southeast Asia, Admiral Louis Mountbatten had overseen combined Allied operations, including the liberation of Burma, Indonesia, Indochina, and Singapore. In Europe, although the bulk of the 284 warships, 7,500 landing ships and amphibious craft, 175,000 soldiers, and 9,500 airplanes for the D-Day invasion were American, and most of the rest American supplied or built, it was a British admiral, Bert Ramsay, who planned and carried it out—drawing on two and a half centuries of experience in amphibious landings for the biggest military operation ever.

But the mantle of power had definitively passed. The signing of the Japanese surrender was on an American battleship, the *Missouri,* not a British one. Indeed, while America's might and influence would only grow after 1945, the British navy's ability to shape events would steadily ebb away, until it could barely make its voice heard across the waters.

Conclusion:

Long Voyage Home

It is not the beginning but the continuing of the same unto the end.
—FRANCIS DRAKE

I T WAS MARCH 31, 1982. The meeting in Prime Minister Margaret Thatcher's office that evening was gloomy. She and her defense minister John Nott, junior Foreign Office minister Richard Luce, and the foreign minister's spokesman in the House of Commons, Sir Humphrey Atkins, had all received the dire news. After months of growing tension with Argentina over the status of the Falkland Islands, Britain's last remaining South American outpost, that country's military junta had taken unilateral action. A large task force of Argentine ships was headed for the islands: a military invasion was imminent.

Yet Britain was helpless to stop them. It no longer had an effective naval force to stop any aggressor. There was no military garrison in the Falklands except a handful of Royal Marines. The closest RAF planes were in Gibraltar, more than 7,000 miles away, and even when they arrived there was no airfield in the islands big enough to handle them. Drawing together a task force from Britain's depleted army and navy, might take weeks, and by then it would be too late.

In 1744, Admiral George Anson had predicted these bleak little islands in the South Atlantic would be "of great consequence to this nation." But when he first saw them from the quarterdeck of the *Centurion,* Britain had been an emerging world power, self-confident and eager, in Anson's words, to be "master of the seas." He could never have guessed that 240 years later an Argentine attack on the Falklands would demonstrate just how impotent and inconsequential the navy had become—nearly as weak as when Francis Drake first plied those same waters under Queen Elizabeth I.

The great naval power of the Atlantic was now America, which was just embarking on its quest to build a 600-ship navy, the most powerful and sophisticated in modern times. But President Reagan's advisors were largely unsympathetic with Britain's desire to keep the Falklands British. If the Americans won't intervene, was the meeting's growing consensus, then the government had no choice but to try for some face-saving deal.

Just then the door opened. In strode First Sea Lord Admiral Sir Henry Leach. He had just returned to his office at the Ministry of Defense from a visit to the Admiralty's Surface Weapons Establishment at Portsmouth— one of the navy's last remaining active bases in England—when he heard the news. He had grabbed his papers and headed to the defense minister's office, only to find he had left for the House of Commons. So Leach set out after him, taking the hundred yards or so to the Houses of Parliament with a long confident pace.

The Royal Navy was in Leach's blood. He was, as was fitting, from the West Country. His father John Leach had been captain of the *Prince of Wales* when Japanese bombers caught her off Kuantan on December 10, 1941. Henry Leach was an eighteen-year-old midshipman when he saw his father for the last time at Singapore at the base swimming pool. "I remember my father saying, 'I am going to do a couple of lengths now; you never know when it mightn't come in handy. . . .' Afterwards we had a final Gin Sling . . . and he introduced me to Captain Bill Tennant of the *Repulse* . . . I never saw him again." John Leach ended up facedown in the Pacific, with a broken neck and a half-inflated life vest. His son's war took him to the frigid waters of the North Atlantic and the savage duel between the *Duke of York* and the battle cruiser *Scharnhorst* in December 1943, with Admiral Bruce Fraser on the bridge, when the *Duke's* fifty-three salvos finally cracked the tough German's side and steam poured out from a ruptured line, as torpedoes from the destroyer *Jamaica* finally put the *Scharnhorst* to the bottom.

A lifetime in the Royal Navy. A lifetime of watching it fade into irrelevance and neglect. No one had even thought of inviting him to Thatcher's meeting, but Leach was determined to be there. A policeman stopped him at the door and ordered him to sit and wait. A junior Tory whip noticed the head of the navy sitting patiently in a chair in front of the prime minister's door and invited him into his own office for a whisky and soda while he made a phone call. Finally, Ian Gow showed Leach into the throne room, where Leach told the prime minister and anyone who would listen that the Royal Navy could get a task force off to the Falklands not in one week or two, but in seventy-two hours.

The arguments back and forth went on until after midnight. Finally Margaret Thatcher sat back and asked, "First Sea Lord—what precisely is it you want?"

"Prime Minister, I would like your authority to form a task force which would, if you so required, be ready to sail for the South Atlantic at a moment's notice."

"You have it," she said.

Admiral Henry Leach turned and left the room. On Friday, Rear Admiral John "Sandy" Woodward received word that he would command the Falklands task force. Woodward, as it happened, was also from the West Country from Cornwall, and engaged in NATO exercises in the Atlantic when the order arrived directing him to "prepare covertly to go south." Earlier, a phone call went to the man who would command the land forces in the operation, Royal Marine Brigadier Julian Thompson— also from Cornwall. Four centuries after they started Britain on this path, the men of the West Country were coming to its rescue. And after almost four decades of neglect and humiliation, the Royal Navy was back.

. . .

The truth was after 1945 Britain was exhausted. For five long years Britain had, in the words of historian A. J. P. Taylor, "sacrificed her postwar future for the sake of the world." Britain had spent more than a quarter of its national wealth waging war against the Axis powers; its empire was in a shambles, never to be reassembled or repaired; its people had made a sacrifice they never wished to make again. With their mighty army, navy, and air force, the Americans would have to do the heavy lifting from now on. They were the inevitable successors to Britain as guarantor of the new world order, a *Pax Americana* to follow the *Pax Britannica,* as a new threat to that order emerged with Soviet Communism.

Yet Britain's role could still have been decisive. At war's end, it had a navy of unprecedented size and firepower. From aircraft carriers and battleships to submarines, destroyers, and minesweepers, it was the biggest Britain had ever enjoyed: more than 900 vessels, including fifty-two aircraft carriers, and nearly 900,000 men and women in uniform. Many of those ships were antiquated and would have to be replaced; Britain's battered economy could never have sustained a navy of such mammoth size. But the Royal Navy still controlled access to Fisher's five strategic keys: Gibraltar, Suez, Singapore and the Malay Straits, the Dover Straits, and the Cape of Good Hope, as well as Aden on the Persian Gulf, gateway to the world's oil supply. If Britain had wanted, it could have shrugged off the burden of its great territorial empire, including Africa and India, and still maintained guardianship of vital links of the world economic system, as it had for the past 150 years.

Instead, the dawn of the cold war pushed British politicians into an understandable but disastrous decision. Europe, not the sea, became the focus of strategic priorities, signalized by the signing of the NATO treaty in 1949. Britain's NATO commitment originally involved seven divisions, or more than 150,000 men. Although that number eventually had to be scaled back, Britain's forces on the ground remained enormous. In addition to maintaining a large army in Germany, British troops were garrisoned in Italy and Austria. Around the globe, they found themselves enforcing the post-war peace in multiple hot spots, from Greece and Palestine to India and Malaysia, while the British navy scrambled to keep them supplied and secure. The army ended up devouring nearly half the defense budget, while the navy was swiftly dropping into third place, behind the Royal Air Force.

This was a radical change in British strategic thinking. Since the days of the elder Pitt, the navy had always been the dominant face of British power. "Blue water" strategists had treated the army as a small mobile force the navy could put into action anywhere around the globe—in the vivid image of Foreign Secretary Grey, "a projectile to be fired by the navy." Maintaining a large standing army in peacetime had seemed absurd—keeping one in Europe, unthinkable. Yet in order to meet its commitments in Germany and around the world and then to NATO, Britain in 1947 had to reimpose the draft. Fighting Communist terrorists in Malaysia alone required two full divisions of troops; almost 4,000 British soldiers would be killed or wounded in the Korean War. By 1953, maintaining Britain's global posture was going to require an additional doubling of the defense budget—a price no one could pay.

These were truly the years of imperial overstretch, and with the army and air force as top priorities, the effect on the British navy was devastating. Over the next two decades, literally hundreds of every type of ship would be scrapped, never to be replaced. Battleships (none by 1959), battle cruisers, aircraft carriers (down from twelve in 1950 to three in 1970), cruisers (gone completely by 1980), destroyers, corvettes, submarines, and landing craft—a long and dismal list. The Home Fleet almost vanished; the West Indies station shrank to one cruiser and a pair of frigates; the Pacific Fleet could show only two cruisers, two destroyer flotillas, and a handful of submarines in 1949. Only the Mediterranean fleet kept some shadow of its former self, because it still had to secure the Suez Canal and block a Russian breakout from the Black Sea. Once the British gave up the canal in 1956, however, even that excuse was gone.

One by one the substance and symbols of British naval supremacy, the embodiments of three centuries of tradition and pride, vanished. The mighty battleship *Queen Elizabeth* had served thirty-three years and carried the flags of sixteen admirals, including David Beatty the day he received the surrender of the German High Seas Fleet in 1918—the greatest bloodless naval victory in history. As her ensign came down the last time in March 1948, a Royal Marine band played "Auld Lang Syne" and "God Save the King" as the commander in chief and other senior officers stood at attention.

HMS *Renown* had been *Repulse*'s sister ship; *Rodney* was one of two battleships that had sunk the *Bismarck*. Both were gone by 1948. *Bismarck*'s other opponent, the *King George V*, lingered on for a while in reserve. She was finally sold for the breaker's yard in 1958. HMS *Vanguard* had been finished too late to see action in World War II but she managed to survive the budget cuts until 1959 as Britain's last remaining battleship. Then it was decided the *Vanguard* too had to go. As she was being tugged out of Portsmouth harbor, she ran aground and would not move for more than an hour—as if in silent protest against her sad fate.

But none were sadder, perhaps, than that of HMS *Implacable*. Like the rest, the ship had held the king's commission during the war: but her heart was not of steel but oak. The *Implacable* was the last survivor of Trafalgar still afloat. She had been a French-built 74, launched from the Rochefort dockyards as the *Dugay Trouin* in 1800. She escaped annihilation at Trafalgar but was captured by Richard Strachan on November 3, 1805, after her French captain was killed and her masts shot away. She was refit and relaunched as HMS *Implacable,* and saw action in the Baltic before being retired with the coming of peace in 1815. Somehow she managed to avoid the fate of *Téméraire* and *Bellerophon* and her other warrior sisters. Instead, in 1855, *Implacable* was refitted as a training vessel for boy seamen at Devonport. For fifty years she taught young men the art of handling sails and going aloft on it, on the very sound where Hawkins, Drake, and Raleigh had begun the modern age of fighting sail.

By 1908 that era had closed for good. The navy put the *Implacable* on

its disposal list. However, a millionaire bought the ship and refurbished
her at his own expense, so that she was able to serve as a training ship
again in 1932, this time at Portsmouth. When war came, she was still in
service as a coal hulk—the oldest wooden warship afloat. Then in 1947,
the Admiralty decided it could no longer afford to keep her. There was a
public outcry, but in an era of economic austerity, no money could be
found to save her. The government offered her to France. The French
refused, although *Implacable* was the last surviving example of the French
shipwright's art, once considered the finest in the world.

And so on December 2, 1949, she was towed out into Portsmouth
harbor, as the *Victory* watched the only other survivor of Trafalgar pass by
for the last time. *Implacable* was flying both the Union Jack and the French
tricolor—and carrying four hundred tons of pig iron and a set of scuttling
charges in her hull. After the two national anthems were played, the
charges were detonated. But *Implacable* fooled her would-be executioners.
As Nelson or Blake could have told them, the wooden ship of old did
not sink like her modern steel descendants. Instead of turning over and
plunging when her bottom blew out, *Implacable* stubbornly remained
afloat, and stayed afloat, for several days until workers finally had to go in
and break up her mighty timbers so she would not be a navigation haz-
ard. *Implacable* had died unwanted but not unmourned: the most venerable victim of imperial overstretch.

For the effort to keep Britain's empire and status as a great power
while shrinking the navy was doomed to failure. In 1947 the Labor government announced Britain could no longer keep troops in Greece and
Turkey (the United States had to step in, and the Truman Doctrine was
born). A year later Britain passed the Palestine problem over to the
United Nations. Independence for India was next; Suez was only just
around the corner. In fact, the failure in 1956 to maintain British control
over the Suez Canal, even with French and Israeli help, marked the crucial watershed in Britain's imperial decline.

Militarily, Suez's Operation Musketeer had been a success. The navy,
army, and air force performed the kind of deft joint operation British
politicians always dreamed about. Diplomatically, however, it was a farce.
American political and economic pressure forced Britain and France to
back down; the mere threat of American disapproval caused Prime
Minister Eden to resign just twenty-four hours after the invasion was
launched. Britain had tried the time-honored technique of gunboat
diplomacy to restore its authority in world affairs. Instead, it had only

exposed its own impotence. The United States, not Britain, became the dominant power in the Middle East; and without the canal, the excuse for keeping a Royal Navy presence in the Mediterranean seemed to have vanished. Indeed, some were saying, the excuse for keeping a Royal Navy presence anywhere.

The Suez debacle led directly to the Defense White Paper of 1957, a radical rollback of Britain's independent military posture. It abolished conscription over three years, cutting in half an army Britain could no longer afford, but also affecting the navy's ability to man its ships for the first time since the eighteenth century. Meanwhile, Britain's military future was more bound to NATO than ever. The White Paper claimed this commitment could now be met by building up Britain's arsenal of nuclear weapons both in Europe and in the air, with bombers and ballistic missiles. Defence minister Duncan Sandys insisted this was a matter of modernizing Britain's armed deterrent; in fact, he and the government chose the nuclear option because it was cheap. As for the navy, the entire Reserve Fleet of 550 ships was to be scrapped, 1,750 officers would be forced to leave in the next five years, and the navy itself reduced to 75,000 officers and ratings.

The uproar in naval circles was tremendous. First Sea Lord Mountbatten had the prestige and political clout to get the cuts scaled back. However, he also conceded that the need "to provide a separate kind of Navy specialized in the tasks of total war" no longer existed, thus setting the stage for another round of cuts. Mountbatten also pointed the way to the next fateful decision for the future of the British navy: the shift from the aircraft carrier to the submarine, particularly the nuclear submarine.

Mountbatten assumed they represented the future of sea power; he also assumed they would provide a strategic and technological bond with the Americans. The Americans and Russians were both building them, and later would arm them with ballistic missiles. So Britain, too, had to get into the act. The first British-built nuclear submarine was commissioned in 1963, bearing one of the most venerable names in the Royal Navy: *Dreadnought*. Jack Fisher's *Dreadnought*, however, had represented a strategic revolution, a technological leap ahead to guarantee British naval supremacy. Mountbatten's *Dreadnought* only committed Britain to a highly sophisticated technological race that it could not win, as its relative economic and industrial position continued to decline.

Dreadnought alone took four years to build and commission; its reactor

and most of her machinery ended up being American-made, which virtually put a halt to Britain's own nuclear research (as the Americans
intended all along). Henceforth, the Royal Navy would end up squandering its share of a dwindling defense budget on successive generations of
American-built submarine technology, from Polaris missiles to the
Trident submarine.

Meanwhile, the cuts in the fleet continued. None were more short-
sighted than the scrapping of its aircraft carriers. Carriers were the
preeminent weapon in the new age of sea power, with their "three-
dimensional" projection of land, sea, and air forces—and with it the projection of geopolitical influence. Able to strike enemies on land or at sea
without the need for a fixed base, prepared to escort troops and supplies
or land them directly by helicopter, and a majestic presence on the horizon or in harbor, the aircraft carrier was everything the battleship had
been in the previous century, and more. Britain had been a pioneer in carrier aviation; it had developed further innovations after World War II,
including introducing the first carrier-borne jet fighters and the steam
catapult for getting planes aloft. Above all, the carrier demanded technologies Britain's scaled-back shipbuilding industry could still have met.
Britain had twelve carriers in 1950; no other force could have allowed
Britain to maintain its unique maritime place and the Royal Navy to continue to shape the world.

But instead they were scrapped, and only rarely replaced. In 1950
there had been twelve; in 1970 there were just three. America, meanwhile,
had thirty-one of them, including 80,000-ton behemoths like the
Constellation and the nuclear-powered *Enterprise,* to guarantee its naval
supremacy in every region. By now, however, naval decline was becoming
official British doctrine. In 1966 a Labor government announced the most
sweeping abdication of global responsibilities since King James I. Defense
minister Dennis Healey swore Britain would never again embark on any
major operations without its American or NATO allies, and undertake no
military assistance to any country unless it was given the necessary facilities beforehand. The sole purpose for maintaining an independent navy
was now "for day-to-day tasks of peacekeeping throughout the world,"
since in so many international hot spots, Healey said, "the visible presence
of British forces by itself is a deterrent to local conflict"—forgetting that
Britain's role as world policeman had always depended on the strength of
its battle fleet.

Both the navy minister and First Sea Lord resigned in protest at the sweeping cuts and the closing of bases, but the eclipse of the British navy was now virtually complete. For the first time in three hundred years it was no longer a weapon of offensive war.

Then, having shed the empire and scrapped the navy, Harold Wilson's government prepared to hand over Fisher's remaining strategic keys. Aden, watchtower over the Horn of Africa, was abandoned in 1967. The Singapore naval base was handed over in 1971; the navy's last remaining base in the Persian Gulf at Bahrain was shut that same year. The navy's 230-year presence "east of Suez," so crucial to Britain's geopolitical and economic status, was at an end. Meanwhile, control of the navy's base at Simonstown at the Cape of Good Hope had been transferred to South Africa in 1955, and when a new Labor government imposed an arms embargo on the apartheid regime, all military cooperation between Britain and South Africa ceased. For the first time since 1798, no British warship patrolled the waters of Sub-Saharan Africa.

And for the first time since the seventeenth century, there was no permanent British naval presence in the Mediterranean. In 1975 decisions were made to phase out bases and forces there, including Malta. Of a naval presence that had once dictated the destiny of southern Europe and the Middle East, only Gibraltar remained. However, its dockyards were ready for the budgetary chopping block, and the future of the colony itself very much in doubt. The world could afford the change, since the United States had taken over the job of global policeman. But the British navy's once-ubiquitous overseas presence had shrunk to Hong Kong and a couple of harbors in the West Indies and Caribbean, and a handful of remote islands like Diego Garcia and the Falklands.

Meanwhile, at home the navy was losing not only ships and men, but its own unique identity. In 1948 it cut its last link to its entrepreneur origins, when it discontinued paying prize money for captured enemy ships to its captains and crews. In 1950 it got rid of officers' ceremonial uniforms, which a Nelson or a Codrington would have recognized and worn, on the grounds that they were too expensive.

Then in 1962 Mountbatten endosed the idea of abolishing the separate service departments and merging all the military services into a single Ministry of Defense, along American lines. Nothing in the plan worked to the advantage of the Admiralty. Far from it: the proposal was one way for the War Office and Air Ministry to rein in their senior naval partners, who were still furious over their steadily shrinking fleet. Everyone admitted the Admiralty was the most efficient of the three service headquarters, with a deep sense of its own traditions and history. As Britain's oldest continuous department of state, it was still "an absolutely first-class organization," said one outside observer, and "in a class by itself."

But the pressure to conform to the demands of modern bureaucracy was too much. On March 31, 1964, the Admiralty Board met for the last time, surrendered its letters patent, and hauled down its flag, after three hundred and thirty-six years of continuous existence. From now on, it was just one more set of dreary offices in the Ministry of Defense, looking forward with dread every year for the next Defense Survey and the next round of cuts.

A year later the administration and financial control of the Greenwich Observatory was transferred to the Science Research Council, severing the link between the British navy, astronomy, and navigation dating back to John Dee and Humphrey Gilbert. In 1970, so was the last remaining link to its sail seafaring past, the rum ration.*

Britain's merchant marine had slid into permanent decline as well. Its share of the world's export of manufactures slid from nearly 30 percent in 1948 to less than 13 percent in 1966. In 1971 it still had 1,356 general cargo ships; in 1981 it was down to 720. Their place had been taken by fleets of Japanese, American, and Panama-registered tanker and container ships, while the great dockyards of London, which had once dazzled Herman Melville, closed one by one. As in Tudor days, England's economic destiny was increasingly in the hands of others, which British politicians actively encouraged by courting links with the European Community.

Even the fishing fleet was entering an eclipse. When tiny Iceland declared a twelve-mile territorial fishing limit—the first major breach in the principle of freedom of the seas in a century—trawlers from ports like Grimsby and Hull faced ruin. They called on the Royal Navy to protect

---

*The daily rum ration was not as venerable as some liked to claim. Although instituted by Admiral Vernon, and mentioned in Anson's revised regulations in 1756, it did not become general and official until 1844. In 1825 rum rations had been cut from half a pint to a quarter, and in 1831 the issue of alcohol other than rum had ceased; in 1850 it was to be served only once a day at noon (officers and sailors younger than eighteen were also excluded). Thus things stood until July 31, 1970, when to the bitter disappointment of many, it was issued for the last time. The Royal Canadian navy held out a little longer: their last issue was on March 31, 1972.

them. The Icelandic navy consisted of exactly seven ships with one gun each, most manned by policemen and civilian volunteers. Yet the navy ended up being humiliated in not one but three "cod wars," as each time the British government yielded to international pressure and backed down.

And so Britain, having effectively crippled its navy, found herself adrift in the waters where the whole adventure had begun. Back in the cod banks off Iceland, where men from Bristol had made their living long before Hawkins and Drake, and long before John Dee had dreamed of a Petit Navy Royale to dominate the waters; before Henry VIII had decided to build a royal dockyard at Deptford, or his father Henry Tudor decided to purchase space for warehouses at Greenwich or issue letters patent to John Cabot to set out for his New Found Land. Or even before one Bristol merchant, John Lloyd, first had the idea of sailing west to a new horizon.

> *Lo, all our pomp of yesterday*
> *Is one with Nineveh and Tyre!*
> *Judge of the nations, spare us yet,*
> *Lest we forget, lest we forget!*

That was in 1973. Now, in 1982, Admiral Sandy Woodward and an even smaller navy found themselves with a far more daunting task, one many were saying could not be done. Some in the cabinet thought Leach should have put an older, more experienced admiral in charge. Yet Woodward was a fitting choice to restore the navy's reputation of honor, not just because he came from the West Country but because he was one of the last to give his life to the navy and its traditions. He been been just thirteen, a year older than Nelson, when he first donned a navy uniform, as a cadet at the Royal Naval College in 1946. Then it was still called HMS *Britannia,* although the old two-decker was long gone, replaced by a red and white brick building that formally opened its doors in 1905—the year construction began on Jack Fisher's *Dreadnought.* Woodward had been taught to think of Nelson and Hood and Rodney, of Codrington and Beatty and Jellicoe, not as remote historical figures but as professional models. "These are the kinds of men who have *always* commanded the Fleets of the Royal Navy," Woodward would remember his instructors saying, "and the kind of men you should try to emulate"—never dreaming he would end up joining that list.

Certainly he never imagined he would end up commanding a fleet of surface ships. After brief stints on cruisers *Devonshire* and *Sheffield,* he had entered the submarine service, the one branch of the navy that suffered least from the cuts and retirements in the 1950s and 1960s. Yet command of the task force for the Falklands was the job First Sea Lord Admiral Leach and Commander in Chief Admiral John Fieldhouse had given him, partly because he was already in charge of the surface flotilla that would lead the battle group. He did not even have charts of the Falklands aboard his flagship, the 8,000-ton guided missile destroyer *Glamorgan.*

Indeed, the force itself was puny compared to the splendid fleets that had once roamed the Mediterranean: just five destroyers and four frigates. Even the two aircraft carriers slated to join them, *Hermes* and *Invincible* (carriers which, had the Argentines waited another three months to attack, would have been sold or scrapped) were small and underequipped compared to the fleet carriers the Americans now used to command the waves. Together they would only be able to carry thirty-four Sea Harrier aircraft, all that stood between the task force and the 220 jet fighters of the Argentine air force, since there would be no land-based planes to help.

Indeed, the RAF deemed the whole enterprise hopeless without proper air cover, just as the British army considered it hopeless to land troops without proper air protection. The U.S. Navy, studying the situation and the odds, deemed retaking the Falklands "a military impossibility." But Leach, Fieldhouse, and Woodward were determined to keep the government's promise to the Falkland inhabitants. There were fewer than 1,800 of them, living a dreary existence on these bleak, stormswept islands. They were true "orphans of post-imperialism," as one writer put it. But they wanted to remain Britons, and fiercely resisted any attempt to hand their homes over to the Argentinians (who called the islands the Malvinas). Principles of self-determination and the rule of law were involved; so was the issue of just what it meant to be British in the postmodern world.

It was a motley scratch group that assembled in the Atlantic off Ascension Island* in mid-April, more like one Drake or Raleigh might

---

*At the last minute, sensing the British resolve, the Americans allowed Woodward's task force to use Ascension Island as a forward base. While the American State Department remained hostile to the whole enterprise, the Pentagon stoutly backed their old comrades-in-arms. Defense Secretary Casper Weinberger also ordered his staff to give the Royal Navy "every possible assistance in terms of hardware and intelligence." The Special Relationship, stretching back to Admirals Sims and Jellicoe, remained intact.

have commanded than the kind of battle fleet Jellicoe or Fraser or Cunningham would recognize—and following the same route into the South Atlantic. The two aircraft carriers and a single amphibious assault ship, HMS *Fearless* (which the defense minister had also slated for the scrap heap), were the core of the task force. Sixteen destroyers and frigates were there to protect them and the troop transports, all of which were converted merchant and cruise ships, including the Cunard liner *Canberra,* since the Royal Navy no longer had any of its own transport ships. There were even four deep-sea fishing trawlers, converted into minesweepers—offering another layer of necessary protection for *Hermes* and *Invincible.*

For the carriers were, as Woodward realized, his one hope for success. Without them, no air cover; and without air cover, no operation. Already the Argentine navy with its aircraft carrier *Veinticino de Mayo* (ironically, the former British-built HMS *Venerable*) and its cruiser *General Belgrano* were positioned to try to cut the task force off. However, on May 2, the submarine HMS *Conqueror* on Woodward's orders put three torpedoes into the *Belgrano,* which sank, taking 336 officers and crew with her. The *Veinticino* and the other ships promptly turned around and headed for port. With one blow Woodward had taken the Argentine fleet out of the picture— and restored in the British public a sense of confidence in its navy that it had not known since World War II.

The Argentine air force was another matter. It was small by superpower standards, but it would enjoy air superiority over the Falklands, and it came equipped with the latest sophisticated weapons systems. Many of Woodward's ships had the same gadgetry. But no one had waged this kind of high-tech warfare at sea before, with planes attacking not with bombs but guided missiles—especially the super-lethal French-designed Exocet—and ships defending themselves with similar missiles, while radar controls locked on and tracked targets almost automatically as computer screens lit up and flashed. Woodward, his captains, and his crews did not know what to expect; they only knew they had better prepare for the worst.

And on May 4, only two days after the *Belgrano* sank, the worst came when two Argentine Super Étendard fighters slipped in undetected and launched their Exocet missiles just east of the fleet. HMS *Glasgow's* radar picked up the Étendards as they turned away and fired off chaff to confuse the missiles' guidance radar and alert the rest of the fleet. But then she lost contact as the Argentine fighters ran in the other direction, leav-

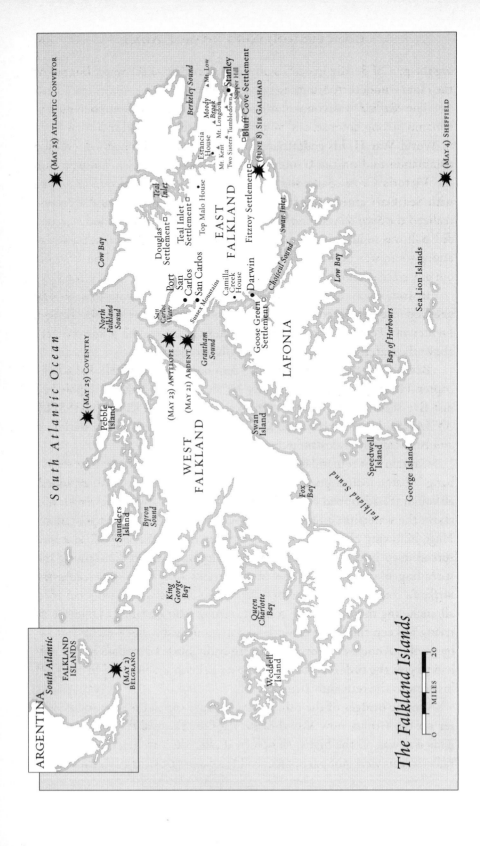

The Falkland Islands

ARGENTINA
South Atlantic
FALKLAND ISLANDS
(MAY 2) BELGRANO

South Atlantic Ocean

(MAY 25) ATLANTIC CONVEYOR

(MAY 4) SHEFFIELD

(MAY 25) COVENTRY

Pebble Island

(MAY 23) ANTELOPE
(MAY 21) ARDENT

Saunders Island

Byron Sound

King George Bay

Queen Charlotte Bay

Fox Bay

Weddell Island

WEST FALKLAND

Falkland Sound

Swan Island

North Falkland Sound

San Carlos Water

Port San Carlos
San Carlos

Sussex Mountains

Grantham Sound

Cow Bay

Berkeley Sound

Teal Inlet

Douglas Settlement

Teal Inlet Settlement

Top Malo House

EAST FALKLAND

Camilla Creek House

Darwin

Goose Green Settlement

Choiseul Sound

Swan Inlet

Fitzroy Settlement

Estancia House

Mt Kent

Two Sisters

Mt Longdon

Moody Brook

Mt Low

Stanley

Sapper Hill

Tumbledown

(JUNE 8) SIR GALAHAD

Bluff Cove Settlement

LAFONIA

Low Bay

Bay of Harbours

Speedwell Island

George Island

Sea Lion Islands

MILES
0   20

ing the pair of deadly Exocets skimming along above the water but below the radar—undetected, unseen, unexpected.

The *Sheffield* was commanded by Sam Salt, a five-foot-four human dynamo, strong, intense, and voluble. His father had died in a submarine in World War II, his godfather was "Red" Ryder, who had led a daring commando raid on the U-boat base at St. Nazaire, which had won him the Victoria Cross. Salt's ship was a Type 42-class destroyer, equipped with Sea Dart antimissile missiles; but they were useless until someone realized the *Sheffield* was under attack. For a crucial thirty minutes no one did. Salt was in his cabin, unaware of *Glasgow's* frantic warnings; the operations room was hooked up to its satellite communication link, blotting out any trace of the Exocet's own radar path on *Sheffield's* radar screen.

In fact, since there was no sign of planes or enemy activity no one believed they *could* be under attack until the officer on the bridge, Lieutenant Peter Walpole, noticed a smudge of smoke about six feet above the water a mile away, headed right for them.

Beside him was Brian Layshon, commander of *Sheffield's* Lynx helicopter. He saw it, too, and thought: "My God, it's a missile!" Walpole had just five seconds to grab the ship's microphone and shout: "MISSILE ATTACK! HIT THE DECK!" before the Exocet struck starboard amidships at 680 miles an hour.

Captain Salt remembered it hitting with "a short, sharp, unimpressive bang." Later, some guessed the warhead might not have exploded, although it had ripped a gash in the hull four by fifteen feet across, just above the waterline, and set an intense fire in the forward engine room. Huge billowing clouds of smoke poured up out of the *Sheffield's* side and spread deep into her hull. Almost as many men would die fighting the spreading blaze—made worse by the miles of plastic wire cable for *Sheffield's* computerized systems—than from the missile blast. Twenty in all, including the men in the computer room who had died at their posts trying to keep the ship's defense system going until they were overcome by smoke. Another twenty-three were badly hurt. By midafternoon Salt had to give the order to abandon ship, as helicopters hovered to carry off his crew to the remaining frigates.

On the bridges of the other British ships, and in the operations center on the *Hermes,* now Woodward's flagship, the reality was sinking in. This was war on the high-technological seas; the tiny green blips on the radar screen were not part of some video game but signs of death sudden and sure. As one weapons officer remembered, "We began to see that war is ghastly, that people do get killed," even in a war fought on computer displays and with satellite links.

Indeed, the sophisticated computerized systems on the *Sheffield* had not saved her or her men. On the contrary, they had left them overconfident and vulnerable, and literally fanned the flames that eventually took the ship to the bottom. The sinking of the *Sheffield* changed the tenor of the Falklands War, and made the odds clear to everyone—including the British public. If the British navy was going to win this war, it was going to have to rely on the human factor, the courage and endurance of its officers and men.

Woodward now had to make another crucial decision. He would have to pull the carriers back out of Exocet range. Everything would now depend on the amphibious landing, and the 3,000 men the task force would have to escort into harm's way. Three thousand men against an estimated 10,000 Argentine troops, who were now well entrenched on the islands and who enjoyed full air cover from their bases 400 miles away.

At the head of the amphibious forces was Julian Thompson and his Royal Marines of the 3 Commando Brigade. They were among the toughest and best-trained troops in the world. As a fighting force, the Royal Marines had a long if erratic history. Before the eighteenth century, the navy's seaborne regiments had been dissolved as soon as they returned from war. The men who served on Restoration ships with the Admiral's Regiment or who stormed the fortifications at Gibraltar in 1704 had been paid off afterward, just like the sailors with whom they served. They had left no institutional trace on the history of the British navy.

It was George Anson who made them a permanent part of the navy and Admiralty—ironically so, since he hoped to use them to solve his manning problems and as menial help on shipboard. Instead, they became the navy's main "projectile" for engaging the enemy on shore. The marines began their first amphibious operations in the 1750s, and soon they were going everywhere the navy went. They even established the first fort on the Falklands at Port Egremont in 1767. Yet in the minds of most sea captains, the marines were basically landsmen who helped with raising the anchor and handling the guns in a sea fight; otherwise, they were an afterthought. Their officers never received the social prestige of their naval counterparts, let alone equal pay.

However, the Napoleonic Wars and the rise of the Victorian Empire transformed the status of the Royal Marines. As the British navy found itself more involved in land campaigns, and sailors themselves were organized into naval brigades for duties onshore, trained and disciplined marines became for the first time an essential part of naval strategy. In 1810 they were 30,000 of the navy's 145,000 men at sea. After the Crimean War, they were more than a third.

At the same time, they were evolving into the prototype military force of the future. Instead of soldiers who were either mass conscripts or a militarized warrior caste, the Royal Marines were a small force of highly trained and motivated professionals, ready and able to be delivered quickly into battle by ship, steam gunboat, diesel transport, or, in the twentieth century, by helicopter. They were the secret of success behind the Royal Navy's most successful amphibious operations and the ancestor of all special operations forces—the British navy's final military legacy to the modern world. While the Falklands force included many of Britain's elite military formations, from two battalions of paratroopers to the Special Air Service (SAS) and Special Boat Service (SBS), the Royal Marines with their green berets were the true prototype for them all.*

These were the landing force Woodward's task force now brought forward on D-Day, May 21, 1982, The air attacks had intensified since the attack on the *Sheffield.* On May 12, the destroyer *Glasgow* took a near fatal hit as she was bombarding the Port Stanley airfield on the east side of East Falkland. She was commanded by Paul Hoddinot, still another West Country man, whose family could trace their seafaring tradition all the way back to the days of Raleigh. As the attack came in, Hoddinot and his advanced warfare officer, Lieutenant Commander Nick Hawkyard, had seen the tiny green blobs on their radar screen—showing approaching Argentine air force Seahawks carrying a deadly cargo of missiles and bombs. Hawkyard gave the order to fire his Sea Darts, but the microswitch on the launcher had become encrusted with sea salt and refused to work. He gave the order to his chief to override the computer. But then the computer failed to respond.

Hawkyard hit the "Launch" button anyway, muttering "Please work, please work." When it did not, "it was," Hawkyard remembered, "the

---

*And not just in Britain. The Americans' version of Special Forces would adopt the green beret as their symbol of elite status; the army's Rangers would do the same and color it black.

biggest silence I ever heard in my life." Undaunted, Captain Hoddinot ordered the ship's 4.5-inch gun to open fire, as the nearby *Brilliant* managed to lock onto the Argentine bombers with *her* defense system and open fire. The first bomber blew up, as did the second; the third swerved to avoid the Sea Wolf missile but lost control and dived straight into the sea. "Christ," said one young seaman watching from the gun direction platform, "it's like a fucking war film up here!" But this was not a film, it was real—and deadly. The fourth Seahawk managed to release its bombs but they missed, one bouncing out of the water and flying thirty feet over the *Glasgow*'s upper deck.

Then the second wave of bombers appeared in the sky. The main gun had by now jammed; the entire computer system on the *Glasgow* had crashed. Houddinot ordered his men on deck to man machine guns, rifles, anything to keep firing as the Argentines closed in. Their gunfire actually did cripple one Seahawk but could not stop it from releasing its bomb. "In the Ops Room they feel their ship shudder and hear the WHHOOMMFF of the bomb as it crashes through the hull and travels clean out the other side." The lights went out, then flickered back on.

Miraculously, the bomb did not detonate; but it had cut two gaping holes through the *Glasgow*'s hull, as the icy seawater rushed in. For an hour or two, it seemed the ship might not survive. Then Hoddinot and his crew pulled her back from the brink of death, while her computer team managed to get all their systems back on-line in less than thirty minutes—including the truant Sea Darts. The *Glasgow* limped back toward the *Hermes,* with the *Brilliant* (whose Sea Wolf system had also failed at the critical moment) acting as escort. Woodward gave Hoddinot sea room to make his repairs. "Don't worry," Hoddinot said stoutly, "we'll be patched up in a couple of days, and back out there."

Nine days later, on the west side of East Falkland, Thompson's marine commandos were scrambling ashore along San Carlos Water in the pre-dawn darkness. Within hours they were digging in with the Third Paratroopers on a ten-mile front on some of the most desolate terrain in the world. In fact, *digging in* was the wrong term; most of the ground around them was too rocky to permit anything but the shallowest fox holes. Fortunately, two of Thompson's battalions were experienced hands with Arctic warfare training; his 45 Commando had run exercises in Norway every winter since 1973. It got the marines ready for the kind of bleak conditions in which they would have to fight, as the Falklands winter was creeping up day by day.

Meanwhile, *Hermes* and *Invincible* had moved in to less than one hundred miles from shore, while Woodward's destroyers and frigates stood in close by to give support to the landing craft. When the Argentine counterattack came, it would be directed at them. As an officer on the *Broadsword* put it, "all hell was let loose." Wave after wave (by one estimate, almost sixty sorties) of American-built Seahawks, French-built Mirages and Étendards, and Israeli-built Daggers swarmed in, all concentrating on their attacks on the ships in what would come to be known as "Bomb Alley," while the navy's Sea Harriers struggled desperately to drive them away and the marines and paratroopers opened up from shore.

By nightfall the Argentines had lost between thirteen and sixteen aircraft. The navy had paid a grievous price. The frigate *Ardent* was sinking; destroyer *Antrim* and *Argonaut* were out of action, with unexploded bombs lodged deep in their hulls; *Brilliant* and *Broadsword* were both damaged. The air attacks would continue. On May 25 they would sink HMS *Coventry*; nineteen men would be killed before she went under. But the navy had held on through the biggest naval battle since the end of World War II. Woodward and his men had decisively turned the tide of battle. Now it was up to the men on the ground to finish the job.

This they did in conditions worse than almost any under which the British army had ever fought. The Argentine forces were larger than anyone had guessed. But they were totally unprepared for the toughness and tenacity with which the marines, paratroopers, and other elite units closed on the Falklands' two principal towns, Goose Green and Darwin. Spearheading the assault was the Second Paratroopers' commander, who also happened to be from Devon: Lieutenant-Colonel Herbert Jones or "H." The son of American and Welsh parents; smart, outspoken, and impulsively brave, Jones had grown up in a house overlooking Start Bay on the River Dart opposite the Royal Naval College. He might have joined the navy but chose the army instead (his brother was in the task force as a naval officer). "H" would die in the desperate fighting around Goose Green, shot down as he led his men into action and earned the task force's first posthumous Victoria Cross.

Goose Green fell on May 29; the fighting for Port Stanley dragged on until June 14, when the demoralized Argentinian garrison finally surrendered. They had suffered more than a thousand dead; another 13,000 were now prisoners—five times the size of the British force that had defeated them.

The Britons had lost 255 dead—eighty-seven of them navy officers and men—and 777 wounded. Their deaths, including the beloved Jones, were made less painful by the reality of victory. "I never thought we would lose," Julian Thompson remembered later, because "I knew the political will was there." For now, the most common sentiment was "We're alive!" Marines and paratroopers milled around the streets of Darwin and Port Stanley, as the inhabitants greeted them with discreet rapture. Bottles of whisky and red wine appeared; some soldiers were even brewing up tea. For their defeated enemies, most British soldiers and sailors felt nothing stronger than pity. Being less well trained, the Argentine conscript soldiers had suffered worse from the weather and frostbite; many units had run out of food. Their government had suffered an international humiliation; Argentina's military dictatorship was doomed, sounding the death knell for the other military dictators in the hemisphere. For Argentina and South America, an era was ending. For Britain and its navy, another was just beginning.

On the bridge of the *Hermes,* Admiral Woodward could already feel the change in the wind—literally. He had contacted Leach and Fieldhouse with the news of the surrender and to tell them the job was done, the job the Americans and others had said was impossible. Now the wind was picking up as the *Hermes* rose with the swell. Woodward could hear the sleet start to patter against his cabin window. He looked out.

The Falklands winter had arrived, less than seven hours after the Argentine surrender. The war had ended just in time. The wind barreling up from the Antarctic was dropping the temperature to sixteen degrees below freezing. At times the gusts rose to one hundred miles an hour, whipping snow and sleet against everything that stood upright on the island: houses, the soldiers' tents, the guns and armored vehicles now silent, and the small pile of stones that marked the grave of Herbert Jones. Eventually after the war, it would have a proper limestone marker with an epitaph Jones had chosen from the prayer usually ascribed to another Devonshire man, Francis Drake: "It is not the beginning but the continuing of the same unto the end."

Meanwhile, snow and sleet blanketed the fleet as it rocked back and forth in the gale. Waves crashed against the bows hour after hour, lashing every fixture and straining every fitting, especially on those still repairing the hits from "Bomb Alley." Sailors on deck in their parkas and oilskins ran to tie up lifelines from bow to stern, while sailors below tied down vital equipment and secured doorways and bulkheads. A moonless night settled over the ships, as the satisfaction of victory gave way to a far older imperative, survival in the face of the elemental forces of the sea.

Storm-tossed ships. Desolate islands eight thousand miles from England. Tiny flyspecks on the face of the global system, which the British navy had done so much to build but no longer had the power to secure and protect.

That responsibility was now in other hands. Yet at this moment, even after the mantle of global power had passed, its original possessor had proved it could still act, and not without honor.

NOTES

1. INCIDENT AT SAN JUAN DE ULLOA

2 *fish were able to swim:* Cotton manuscript Otho E VIII (British Library), transcribed and reprinted in J. Williamson, *Sir John Hawkins: The Time and the Man* (Oxford: Clarendon Press, 1927), 530.

2 *largest form of commerce:* P. McGuire, *Experiment in World Order* (New York: William Morrow, 1948), 50.

2 *"The voyage I pretend":* Letter of September 16, 1567, quoted in R. Unwin, *The Defeat of John Hawkins* (New York: Macmillan, 1960), 138.

3 *one hundred ducats per head:* Williamson, *Hawkins,* 84.

3 *shirts and shoes:* Ibid., 95.

4 *60 percent:* Williamson, *Hawkins,* 107.

5 *split the prisoners:* Cotton ms., 510–11.

5 *"governor was so strait":* John Hawkins, *A True Declaration of the Troublesome Voyage . . .* London, 1569, reprinted in Edward Arber, *An English Garner* (Birmingham, Eng.: 1882), vol. 5, 218.

7 *three lanterns:* Hawkins's rules of sailing are described in John Spark's account of the second voyage, reprinted in Richard Hakluyt, *Principal Navigations, Traffiques, and Discoveries* (New York: Macmillan, 1904), vol. 10, 10.

7 *northerly storms:* Unwin, *Defeat of John Hawkins,* 165.

8 *"everyone would recite":* Williamson, *Hawkins,* 148.

8 *"a bowshot across":* Hawkins, *True Declaration,* 219.

9 *only the battered royal standard:* Cotton ms., 532.

9 *two fourteen-foot bronze culverins:* Admiralty Court Deposition, reprinted in Arber, *English Garner,* vol. 5, 238; Michael Lewis, *Armada Guns* (London: Allen, Unwin, 1961).

10 *700 tons:* Williamson, *Hawkins,* 186.

10 *"Queen of England's ships":* *The Rare Travels of Job Hartop, an Englishman,* London, 1591, reprinted in Arber, *English Garner,* vol. 5, 315–6.

11 *"None of you knows John Hawkins":* Unwin, *Defeat of John Hawkins,* 148.

12 *"between two dangers":* Hawkins, *True Declaration,* 220.

12 *"I represent":* Job Hartop, 316.

13 *"on pain of death":* Ibid.

13 *a little surprise:* Unwin, *Defeat of John Hawkins,* 184.

13 *as one eyewitness:* "A Discourse Written by one Miles Phillips, Englishman," reprinted in Arber, *English Garner,* vol. 5, 268.

14 *at a moment's notice:* Unwin, *Defeat of John Hawkins,* 187.

15 *twenty yards away:* Hawkins, *True Declaration,* 233.

15 *"You are quite right,":* Unwin, *Defeat of John Hawkins,* 193.

16 *"God and St George!":* Job Hartop, 317.

17 *five minutes:* Lewis, *Armada Guns.*

18 *something to drink:* Job Hartop, 318.

18 *"If you had done so":* Ibid.

19 *Job Hartop watched:* Ibid., 319; Hawkins, *True Declaration,* 235–36.

19 *Young Horsewell:* Unwin, *Defeat of John Hawkins,* 210.

21 *A Spanish eyewitness:* Williamson, *Hawkins,* 202.

21 *Hawkins was able to send:* Unwin, *Defeat of John Hawkins,* 228–29.

21 *The men Hawkins had left behind:* J. Williamson, *Hawkins of Plymouth* (London: A. and C. Black, 1949) 151–52.

21 *Hawkins's nephew:* Ibid., 155.

22 *Robert Barrett and Job Hartop:* Unwin, *Defeat of John Hawkins,* 254–56.

23 *a little more than twenty-three years:* Helen Miller, *Captains from Devon: The Great Elizabethan Seafarers* (Chapel Hill, N.C.: Algonquin Books, 1985), 29.

2. BEGINNINGS

24 *nautical expert:* P. E. Pérez-Malliana, *Spain's Men of the Sea,* trans. C. R. Phillips (Baltimore: Johns Hopkins University Press, 1998), 24.

24 *clear to the universe:* Norman MacLean; *Young Men and Fire* (Chicago: University of Chicago Press, 1992), 28.

25 *four hundred:* J. Youings, *Raleigh's Country: The South West of England in the Reign of Queen Elizabeth I* (Raleigh, N.C.: N.C. Dept. of Cultural Resources, 1986), 9.

27 *the most extensive deep-water anchorage:* D. Parker, *The West Country* (London: Batsford, 1973).

27 *mythical founder:* W. G. Hoskins, *Devon* (London: Collins, 1954), 200.

27 *death trap:* Ibid., 206.

27 *large enough to quarter:* M. Oppenheim, *The Maritime History of Devon* (Exeter: University of Exeter Press, 1968), 37.

27 *Lord John Russell:* Youings, *Raleigh's Country,* 29.

28 *equal partners:* N. A. M. Rodger, *The Safeguard of the Sea: A Naval History of Britain* (New York: W. W. Norton, 1998), 141–42.

28 *Ancient philosophers:* Specifically Anacharsis the Scythian (sixth century B.C.), in Sarah Arenson, *The Encircled Sea: The Mediterranean Maritime Civilization* (London: Constable, 1990), 106.

28 *A recruit:* N. A. M. Rodger, *The Wooden World: Anatomy of the Georgian Navy* (London: Fontana, 1986), 37.

28 *"Fouler ways":* Youings, *Raleigh's Country,* 33.

28 *who was drawn:* Hoskins, *Devon,* 202.

28 *During the Hundred Years' War:* Rodger, *Safeguard,* 100, 111.

29 *"the most infamous":* Christopher Lloyd, *The British Seaman 1200–1800: A Social Survey* (London: Collins, 1968), 27.

29 *supplied the navy with more officers:* Michael Lewis, *The Navy in Transition 1814–1864: A Social History* (London: Hoddart and Stoughton, 1965), 37–38.

30 *a "Guz ship":* Martin Middlebrook and Patrick Mahoney, *Battleship: The Sinking of the Prince of Wales and Repulse* (New York: Scribner, 1979 [1977]), 31.

30 *resplendent in a scarlet:* Michael Foss, *Undreamed Shores: England's Wasted Empire in America* (London: Harrap, 1974), 16.

30 *the conditions sailors met:* J. H. Parry, *The Age of Reconnaissance* (1963; London: Sphere Books, 1973), 109–10, 115, 120.

31 *On July 15:* Foss, *Shores,* 20.

31 *Ylha de Brasil:* Peter Russell, *Prince Henry "The Navigator"* (New Haven: Yale University Press, 2000), 100–101.

31 *the following July:* Quinn, *Discovery,* 74–75.

32 *Robert Thorne:* Ibid., 11.

32 *In 1956:* Ibid., 5–6.

32 *Columbus himself:* Ibid., 105.

33 *"whatsoever lands":* Foss, *Shores,* 23.

34 *Eskimos:* Ibid., 25.

35 *not a thing but an event:* David Loades, *The Tudor Navy: An Administrative, Political & Military History* (Aldershot: Scholar Press, 1992), 11.

35 *Admiral . . . first appears:* Rodger, *Safeguard,* 131.

36 *a boy of seven:* this was Henry's illegitimate son, Henry Fitzroy, Duke of Richmond; Loades, *Tudor Navy,* 75.

36 *formidable fighting machine:* John Guilmartin Jr., *Galleons and Galleys* (London: Cassell, 2002).

37 *half a century:* Rodger, *Safeguard,* 156.

37 *until the 1420s:* Ibid., 162.

37 *Henry VII did not ignore:* Richard Harding, *The Evolution of the Sailing Navy* (London: St. Martin's Press, 1995), 9–10.

38 *his model was . . . Scotland:* Rodger, *Safeguard,* 167–8.

39 *first English ship:* Ibid., 207.

39 *long pointed stakes:* Alexander McKee, *King Henry VIII's Mary Rose* (London: Souvenir, 1973), 30.

40 *new shipyards:* Arthur Nelson, *The Tudor Navy: The Ships, Men, and Organization 1485–1603* (Annapolis, Md.: Naval Institute Press, 2001), 50.

40 *"wherein shall ride":* Rodger, *Safeguard,* 224.

41 *No such corporate body:* Ibid., 226–27; Loades, *Tudor Navy,* 82.

41 *"hoping that":* McKee, *Mary Rose,* 66.

42 *make Channel travel safer:* Harding, *Evolution,* 13.

42 *his idea:* Rodger, *Safeguard,* 227.

42 *met Sebastian Cabot:* J. A. Williamson, *The Age of Drake* (London: A. and C. Black, 1960), 14.

43 *Protestant gentlemen in Devon:* David Loades, *Two Tudor Conspiracies* (Cambridge: Cambridge University Press, 1965), 17–19, 37, 43–44.

43 *force foreign ships:* Rodger, *Safeguard,* 188.

3. UNKNOWN LIMITS

45 *Black Bull:* A. L. Rowse, *The Expansion of Elizabethan England* (New York: Harper and Row, 1971), 46.

46 *a Champernowne:* D. B. Quinn, *Raleigh and the British Empire* (London: Houghton and Stoddard, 1947), 1; Raleigh Trevelyan, *Sir Walter Raleigh* (London: Allen Lane, 2002), 4.

46 *sons of the Duke of Surrey:* Warren Wooden, *John Foxe* (Boston: Twayne, 1983), 1–5.

46 *most widely read book:* William Haller, *Foxe's Book of Martyrs and the Elect Nation* (London: J. Cape, 1963).

46 *"It cannot be":* G. Williamson, ed., *Foxe's Book of Martyrs* (London: Secker and Warburg, 1965), 456.

46 *Walter Raleigh's mother:* Edward Edwards, *The Life of Sir Walter Raleigh* (London: Macmillan, 1868), vol. 1, 19.

47 *"If all these miseries":* John Hawkins, *A True Declaration of the Troublesome Voyage . . .* London, 1509, reprinted in Edward Arber, *An English Garner* (Birmingham, England, 1882), 5.

48 *changed England's relationships:* Carol Z. Wiener, "The Beleaguered Isle: A Study of Elizabethan and Early Jacobean Anti-Catholicism," *Past and Present* (May 1971): 27–62.

48 *evil empire:* The classic work is William Maltby, *The Black Legend in England: The Development of Anti-Spanish Sentiment 1558–1660* (Durham, N.C.: Duke University Press, 1971).

49 *In June 1570:* J. Williamson, *Hawkins of Plymouth,* (London: A. and C. Black, 1949), 173–75.

49 *"Their practices":* Alan Haynes, *Invisible Power: The Elizabethan Secret Services 1570–1603*

(London: Sutton, 1992), 9. Harry Kelsey, in *Sir John Hawkins: Queen Elizabeth's Slave Trader* (New Haven: Yale University Press, 2003), argues unconvincingly that Hawkins's contacts with Spain were genuine.

50 *sent some help:* Williamson, *Hawkins of Plymouth,* 169–70.

50 *"by God's grace":* Sir Herbert Richmond, *Statemen and Sea Power* (Oxford: Clarendon Press, 1946), 4.

50 *"Who are you?":* Lionel Casson, *The Ancient Mariners* (London: Gollancz, 1961), 198, 199–201.

51 *Medieval kings:* N. A. M. Rodger, *Safeguard of the Sea: A Naval History of Britain* (New York: W.W. Norton, 1998), 127–28.

51 *Even old William Hawkins:* Williamson, *Hawkins of Plymouth,* 34–35.

52 *most recent biographers:* Harry Kelsey, *Sir Francis Drake: The Queen's Pirate* (New Haven: Yale University Press, 1998).

52 *"If there be cause":* John Cummins, *Francis Drake: The Lives of a Hero* (New York: St. Martin's Press, 1995), 39.

52 *"I am not going to stop":* C. Lloyd, *The Nation and the Navy* (London: Cresset, 1954), 22.

53 *the Spanish saw themselves:* Elliott, *The Old World and the New,* (Cambridge: Cambridge University Press, 1970), 94.

54 *The convoy system developed:* Richmond, *Sea Power,* 7–8.

55 *A letter from Mexico:* Geoffrey Parker, *The Grand Strategy of Philip II* (New Haven: Yale University Press, 1998), 50.

55 *"If death came":* J. H. Elliott, *Spain and Its World 1500–1700* (New Haven: Yale University Press, 1989), 14.

55 *a Cornish name:* A. L. Rowse, *The Expansion of Elizabethan England* (New York: Harper & Row, 1971), 40.

57 *the first white man:* Cummins, *Francis Drake,* 64.

59 *"I will be one":* Ibid., 62.

60 *"news of the captain's return":* Rodger, *Safeguard,* 243.

60 *young Richard Hakluyt:* David Armitage, *The Ideological Origins of the British Empire* (Cambridge: Cambridge University Press, 2000), 70–71.

61 *Richard Eden:* James McDermott, *Martin Frobisher, Elizabethan Privateer* (New Haven: Yale University Press, 2001), 20.

62 *not an entirely new idea:* J. H. Parry, *The Discovery of the Sea* (London: Weidenfield and Nicholson, 1974), vi–vii.

63 *interruptions of trade:* K. R. Andrews, *Drake's Voyages,* (London: Weidenfield and Nicholson, 1967), 8–9.

63 *East India Company:* T. O. Lloyd, *The British Empire 1558–1983* (Oxford: Oxford University Press, 1984), 13.

64 *he and a group:* A. L. Rowse, *Sir Richard Grenville of the Revenge: An Elizabethan Hero* (London: Jonathan Cape, 1937), 155.

64 *Quid non?:* Douglas Bell, *Elizabethan Seamen* (Philadelphia: Lippincott, 1951), 265.

65 *Robert Thorne of Bristol:* McDermott, *Martin Frobisher,* 96.

65 *Mercator:* Ibid., 102.

65 *"By the Northwest":* Sir Humphrey Gilbert, *A Discourse of a Discoverie for a New Passage to Cataia* (London: 1576), 42, 38.

65 *The Englishman's Strait:* E. G. R. Taylor, *Tudor Geography 1485–1583* (New York: Octagon Book, 1930; 1968), 33–34.

65 *cold winter's day:* Gilbert, Preface, *Discourse,* [iv].

65 *"Such a monstrous mind":* Benjamin Woolley, *The Queen's Conjuror: The Science and Magic of Dr. John Dee, Advisor to Queen Elizabeth I* (New York: Henry Holt, 2001), 99.

66 *"reputation . . . of almost unremitting blackguardry"*: McDermott, *Martin Frobisher,* 118.

66 *cargo for trade:* Ibid., 128–29.

67 *wife of one of his partners:* Woolley, *Queen's Conjuror,* 109.

67 *"hot metal":* McDermott, *Martin Frobisher,* 157.

67 *four separate locks:* Ibid., 189, 156.

4. "INCOMPARABLE EMPYRE"

69 *Oxenham returned:* Derek Wilson, *The World Encompassed: Francis Drake and His Great Voyage* (New York: Harper and Row, 1977), 35.

70 *asked him about:* Ibid., 36.

71 *"make the name":* Nicholas Canny, "The Ideology of English Colonization: From Ireland to America," in *Theories of Empire 1450–1800* ed. D. Armitage (Aldershot, England: Ashgate, 1998), 186.

71 *single largest movement:* D. B. Quinn, *The Elizabethans and the Irish* (Cambridge: Cambridge University Press, 1966), 12.

71 *"man, woman, and child":* Ibid., 127, 109.

72 *Those he spared:* Canny, "Ideology," 182.

72 *said God had made:* Canny, *The Elizabethan Conquest of Ireland: A Pattern Established 1565–1576* (New York: Barnes and Noble, 1976).

72 *The Earl of Essex:* John Sugden, *Sir Francis Drake* (London: Barnes and Jenkins, 1990), 81–82.

73 *One recent biographer:* Harry Kelsey, *Sir Francis Drake: The Queen's Pirate* (New Haven: Yale University Press, 1988), 74.

73 *Another points out:* John Cummins, *Francis Drake: The Lives of a Hero* (New York: St. Martin's Press, 1995).

73 *Richard Grenville in 1574:* A. L. Rowse, *Richard Grenville of the Revenge: An Elizabethan Hero* (London: Jonathan Cape, 1937), 94.

74 *"To plant the Christian religion":* Peter Mancall, *Envisioning America: English Plans for the Colonization of North America 1580–1640* (Bedford Brooks, England: St. Martin's Press, 1995), 39.

74 *"How Her Majesty":* M. Foss, *Undreamed Shores: England's Wasted Empire in America* (London: Harrap, 1974), 113–14.

74 *Some were pirating:* Ibid., 115–17.

75 *said poisoned:* Kelsey, *Sir Francis Drake,* 75.

75 *"He feared God":* Wilson, *World Encompassed,* 40–41.

76 *"I would gladly be revenged":* Ibid., 23.

76 *The queen told Drake:* Kelsey, *Sir Frances Drake,* 76.

77 *"the south sea":* J. Hampden, ed., *Francis Drake, Privateer: Contemporary Narratives and Documents* (London: Methuen, 1972) 111–17.

78 *meant to carry heavy armament:* Guilmartin, *Galleons and Galleys,* 158–59.

78 *sixty-eight feet in length:* Hampden, *Francis Drake,* 119–20.

78 *"not the wisest man":* Kelsey, *Sir Francis Drake,* 83.

78 *its international flavor:* Cummins, *Francis Drake,* 73.

78 *usual supplies: Sir Francis Drake . . . An Exhibition to Commemorate Francis Drake's Voyage Around the World* (London: British Museum, 1977), 40.

78 *"If we bring home gold":* Kelsey, *Sir Francis Drake,* 96.

79 *medieval geographers:* J. H. Parry, *The Age of Reconnaissance* (London: London Sphere Books, 1973).

79 *finding out where you are:* McDermott, *Martin Frobisher, Elizabethan Privateer* (New Haven: Yale University Press, 2001) 133.

80 *astrolabe: Drake . . . British Museum*, 45.

80 *cross staff:* Ibid., 44–45.

80 *the greatest obstacle:* David Waters, "Elizabethan Navigation," in *Sir Francis Drake and the Famous Voyage 1577–1580,* ed. N. Throwe (Berkeley: University of California Press, 1984), 27.

81 A Regiment for the Sea: Ibid., 18.

81 *pricked out his course:* Waters, "Navigation," 17.

81 *a copy sits today in the British Museum:* Waters, *The Art of Navigation in England in Elizabethan and Early Stuart Times* (London: Hollis and Carter, 1958), 121.

81 *probably Ortelius's:* Wilson, *World Encompassed,* 39.

82 *spent long hours together:* Ibid., 63.

82 *Drake later told the queen:* H. Wallis, "The Cartography of Drake's Voyage," in Thrower, *Sir Francis Drake,* 131.

83 *"Let us not be thus used":* Kelsey, *Sir Francis Drake,* 100.

83 *a witch and a poisoner:* Ibid., 105.

83 *"No, that hath he not":* Cummins, *Francis Drake.*

84 *"This is not law":* Kelsey, *Sir Francis Drake,* 107.

84 *silently prayed:* Ibid., 108.

85 *unity of command:* Christopher Lloyd, *Nation and the Navy* (London: Cresset, 1961), 3–4.

85 *a twisting, winding channel:* Douglas Bell, *Elizabethan Seamen,* (Philadelphia: Lippincott, 1951), 153.

87 *naval supremacy:* Kelsey, *Sir Francis Drake,* 146.

87 *John Doughty:* Bell, *Elizabethan Seamen,* 163.

87 *"no one in the world":* Waters, *Art of Navigation,* 535.

87 *"would give me a greater joy":* Bell, *Elizabethan Seamen,* 161.

87 *named Sant Juan de Anton:* Kelsey, *Sir Francis Drake,* 151.

88 *"What English demands":* Ibid., 157.

88 *these things happen in war:* Bell, *Elizabethan Seamen,* 160.

89 *a Drake biographer:* Kelsey, *Sir Frances Drake,* 161.

89 *mulled over the problem:* Ibid., 162.

89 *A leading expert:* Wallis, "Cartography," 130.

89 *doubts he got farther:* Kelsey, *Sir Frances Drake,* 185–86.

90 *"so tractable and loving a people,"* Wilson, *World Encompassed;* J. Hampden, *Francis Drake,* 182.

90 *"bred great fear":* Benjamin Woolley, *The Queen's Conjuror: The Service and Magic of Dr. John Dee, Advisor to Queen Elizabeth I* (New York: Henry Holt, 2001), 115.

91 *claimed to have discovered:* Waters, *Art of Navigation,* 274.

91 *voodoo doll:* Richard Deacon, *John Dee* (London: F. Muller, 1968).

91 *a national hero:* Christopher Dean, *Arthur of England: English Attitudes to King Arthur and the Knights of the Round Table in the Middle Ages and the Renaissance* (Toronto: University of Toronto Press, 1987), 26–27, 163.

91 *Humphrey Lloyd:* Armitage, *The Ideological Origins of British Empire* (Cambridge: Cambridge University Press, 2000), 46–47.

92 *When he finished:* Ibid., 106.

92 *"What a privilege":* Wilson, *World Encompassed,* 20.

92 *"No King, no Kingdom":* Lesley Cormack, *Charting an Empire: Geography at the English University 1580–1620* (Chicago: University of Chicago Press, 1997), 1–2.

92 *"three score tall ships":* John Dee, *The Petty Navy Royal,* reprinted in Edward Arber, *An English Garner,* (Birmingham, England: 1882), vol. 2, 61.

93 *"Master Key":* Ibid., 66.

93 *Elizabeth was still excited:* Woolley, *Queen's Conjuror,* 121–22.

93 *10 degrees:* Wallis, "Cartography," 131.

94 *"The fairest cape":* Bell, *Elizabethan Seamen,* 167.

94 *47 pounds:* Lloyd, *Nation and the Navy,* 23.

95 *sworn to secrecy:* Wallis, "Cartography," 124, 133.

95 *"At present":* T. K. Rabb, *Enterprise and Empire* (Cambridge, Mass.: Harvard University Press, 1967), 20–21.

96 *new trading companies:* Ibid., 23–24.

5. THE WORLD IS NOT ENOUGH

97 *"very delicately":* Henry Kamen, *Philip of Spain* (New Haven: Yale University Press, 1997), 171.

97 *"I don't know how":* Ibid., 176.

97 *ten newly built fighting galleons:* Geoffrey Parker, *The Grand Strategy of Philip II* (New Haven: Yale University Press, 1998), 167.

98 *first naval battle:* Lloyd, *The Navy and the Nation* (London: Cresset, 1961), 25.

98 *"You should follow up":* Parker, *Grand Strategy,* 168.

98 *Spanish expeditionary force:* J. H. Adamson and H. F. Holland, *Shepherd of the Ocean: Sir Walter Ralegh and His Times* (Boston: Gambit, 1969), 63–66.

99 *for 150 years:* G. R. Elton, *England Under the Tudors,* 364, 361.

99 *"Our enemies are many":* quoted in Haller, *Foxe's Book of Martyrs and the Elect Nation* (London: Jonathan Cape, 1963), 221.

100 *"book for sea causes":* David Loades, *The Tudor Navy: An Administrative Political & Military History* (Aldershot, 1992), 179.

100 *no longer a major anchorage:* Ibid., 185.

100 *a U-shaped bend:* J. A. Williamson, *Hawkins of Plymouth,* (London: A. and C. Black, 1949), 255.

100 *under Edward VI:* J. A. Williamson, *Sir John Hawkins: The Time and the Man* (Oxford: Clarendon Press, 1927), 232, 530.

101 *professional rat catcher:* Loades, *Tudor Navy,* 187.

101 *beakhead prow:* Ibid., 189.

101 *"head of a cod":* Martin and Parker, *Spanish Armada,* 2nd ed., 34.

101 *"majesty and terror":* Garrett Mattingly, *The Armada* (Boston: Houghton Mifflin, 1959), 195.

101 *use of plans:* Rodger, *Safeguard,* 219, 335–36.

102 *Cannon had been going to sea:* Kennedy, *British Sea Mastery,* 15–16.

102 *look for an alternative:* Rodger, *Safeguard,* 213–17; Lewis, *Armada Guns.*

102 *the Greys [n.]:* Roger Whiting, *The Enterprise of England: The Spanish Armada* (New York: St. Martin's Press, 1988), 140.

103 *at 350 to 400 yards:* Lewis, *Armada Guns,* 39.

103 *only six:* Loades, *Tudor Navy,* 197.

103 *"Thomas Pitt":* Rodger, *Safeguard,* 216–27.

103 *official investigation:* Williamson, *Sir John Hawkins,* 347–48.

103 *"I protest it before God":* Martin and Parker, *Spanish Armada,* 36.

104 *as early as 1570:* Williamson, *Sir John Hawkins,* 384–85, 396.

104 *"The greatest traffic":* Simon Adams, "The Outbreak of the Elizabethan Naval War Against the Spanish Empire," in *England, Spain, and the Gran Armada 1585–1604* (Edinburgh: J. Donald, 1991), ed. Simon Adams and Rodriguez-Salgado, 53.

105 *twenty-two fighting vessels:* Loades, *Tudor Navy,* 234–36.

105 *a counter-embargo:* Adams, "Outbreak," 46.

106 *enlisted local Indian tribesmen:* Kelsey, *Sir Francis Drake,* 267.

106 *a lone French prisoner:* John Cummins, *Francis Drake: The Lives of a Hero* (New York: St. Martin's Press, 1995), 157–58.

107 *fifteen shillings to the pound:* Loades, *Tudor Navy,* 236.

107 *"I keenly regret":* Parker, *Grand Strategy,* 181–82.

107 *Two illuminated clocks:* Ibid., 28–30.

108 *"this is the ink":* Mattingly, *Armada,* 387.

108 *silver fleet, could not sail: Ibid.,* 84.

108 *"England's chief defense":* Martin and Parker, *Spanish Armada.*

108 *"I will emerge victorious":* Parker, *Grand Strategy,* 182–84.

109 *already ordinary citizens:* Martin and Parker, *Spanish Armada,* 114.

109 *ingenious counterplan:* Parker, *Grand Strategy,* 186–87.

109 *ships, supplies, and men:* F. Fernández-Armesto, *The Spanish Armada. The Experience of War* (Oxford: Oxford University Press, 1988), 10.

110 *original plan:* Ibid., 11–12.

111 *news that Mary Queen of Scots:* Parker, *Grand Strategy,* 190.

111 *nine new ships:* Loades, *Tudor Navy,* 193.

111 *Taking a page:* Parker, *Grand Strategy,* 193.

111 *Lord Burghley had built up:* Elton, *England Under the Tudors,* 363.

111 *a force of 23,000 infantry:* Whiting, 72, 75.

112 *"God send us":* Ibid., 70.

112 *"I thank God":* Mattingly, *Armada,* 90.

112 *decided to make for Cádiz:* Kelsey, *Sir Francis Drake,* 289.

112 *furling all English banners:* Mattingly, *Armada,* 95; Kelsey, *Sir Francis Drake,* 290.

113 *Cape Sagres:* Peter Kemp, *The Campaign of the Spanish Armada* (New York: Facts on File, 1988), 60.

113 *The old story [n.]:* Rodger, *Safeguard,* 253.

113 *But Drake's raid:* Parker, *Grand Strategy,* 195.

114 *He did not hesitate:* Ibid., 184.

114 *twenty times:* I. A. A. Thompson, "The Spanish Armada: Naval Warfare Between the Mediterranean and the Atlantic," in Adam and Rodrigo-Salgado, *England, Spain,* 70–71.

114 *armed merchantmen:* Fernández-Armesto, *Spanish Armada,* 17–18.

114 *eight months' supplies:* Thompson, "Spanish Armada," 81.

115 *He scrounged up cannon:* Martin and Parker, *Spanish Armada,* 129.

115 *only six ships:* Loades, *Tudor Navy,* 244.

115 *already preparing arguments:* Rodger, *Safeguard,* 257.

115 *He had seen the hand of God:* Parker, *Grand Strategy,* 102.

116 *"Things hang in the balance":* Ibid., 203.

116 *At least one:* Mattingly, *Armada,* 217.

6. ARMADA: THE VICTORY THAT NEVER WAS

112 *was patroling:* Garrett Mattingly, *The Armada* (Boston: Houghton Mifflin, 1959), 265.

117 *"a hearty Gentleman":* Robert Kenny, *Elizabeth's Admiral: The Political Career of Charles Howard, Earl of Nottingham 1536–1624* (Baltimoore: Johns Hopkins University Press, 1970), 36.

117 *"for all conditions":* Colin Martin and Geoffrey Parker, *The Spanish Armada,* 2nd ed. (New York: W.W. Norton, 1988), 36.

117 *"I have been aboard":* Kenny, *Elizabeth's Admiral,* 133.

118 *"here is the gallantest":* A. L. Rowse, *Sir Richard Grenville of the Revenge: An Elizabethan Hero* (London: Jonathan Cape, 1937), 260.

118 *amazing feat:* Ibid., 112.

118 *not pleased:* Mattingly, *Armada,* 262.

119 *"The advantage of time and place":* Ibid., 259.

120 *the tide was running:* Ibid., 265–66.

120 *"making enquiry":* Martin and Parker, *Spanish Armada,* 38.

121 *five miles in three days:* David Howarth, *The Voyage of the Armada: The Spanish Story* (1981; New York: Lyons Press, 1991), 60.

121 *Four captured fishermen:* A. L. Rowse, *The Expansion of Elizabethan England* (New York: Harper and Row, 1971) 274.

121 *They assumed:* Peter Kemp, *The Campaign of the Spanish Armada* (New York: Facts on File, 1988), 92–94.

122 *Bow chasers fired first:* N. A. M. Rodger, *Safeguard of the Sea: A Naval History of Britain* (NY: W.W. Norton, 1998), 265.

122 *shot an hour:* Ibid., 270.

122 *"their ships so fast":* Mattingly, *Armada,* 282.

122 *did not dare:* F. Fernández-Armesto, *The Spanish Armada: The Experience of War* (Oxford: Oxford University Press, 1988), 141.

122 *"durst not adventure":* Kemp, *Campaign,* 107.

123 *although rumors had it:* Ibid., 109.

123 *Night had fallen:* Ibid., 110.

123 *Later he would claim:* Mattingly, *Armada,* 293–95.

123 *"Like a coward":* John Cummins, *Francis Drake: The Lives of a Hero* (New York: St. Martin's Press, 1995), 191.

124 *But Frobisher's heavy guns:* Kemp, *Campaign,* 116.

125 *"line ahead":* Rodger, *Safeguard,* 267; Kemp, *Campaign,* 116.

125 *the Owers:* Mattingly, *Armada,* 309.

125 *resplendent in white velvet:* Ibid., 349.

126 *The answer he got back:* J. R. Whiting, *Enterprise of England: The Spanish Armada* (New York: St. Martin's Press, 1988), 128.

126 *Parma had given up:* Mattingly, *Armada,* 319–22.

126 *One version:* Whiting, *Enterprise of England,* 133.

126 *On each was a single man:* Mattingly, *Armada,* 317.

127 *"within musket shot of the enemy":* Padfield, *Maritime Supremacy and the Opening of the Western Mind* (New York: Overlook Press, 2002), 43.

127 *More than 260 ships:* Whiting, *Enterprise of England,* 137.

127 *a wake red with blood:* Mattingly, *Armada,* 333.

127 *"Not a man among us":* Whiting, *Enterprise of England,* 142.

127 *107 separate shots:* Padfield, *Maritime Supremacy,* 52.

128 *"Their force":* Mattingly, *Armada,* 336.

128 *"So our half-doing":* Ibid., 351.

128 Elizabeth Jonas: Whiting, *Enterprise of England,* 151.

129 *110 of the 117 ships:* Jose Lus Casado de Soto, "Atlantic Shipping in Sixteenth-Century Spain and the 1588 Armada," in S. Adams and Rodriguez-Salgado, eds. *England, Spain, and the Gran Armada, 1585–1604* (London, 1991), 120.

129 *only one captain:* Fernández-Armesto, *Spanish Armada,* 18.

129 *The map of Ireland:* Whiting, *Enterprise of England,* 170.

129 *"Many were drowning":* Ibid., 184.

130 *cemetery at Fort Hill:* Ibid., 186.

130 *Some crews were so exhausted:* Padfield, *Maritime Supremacy,* 55.

130 *"The troubles and miseries":* Whiting, *Enterprise of England,* 205.

130 *"I sent my ships":* Mattingly, *Armada,* 388.

130 *less than 20 percent:* De Soto, "Atlantic Shipping," 122.

130 *supposed to have remarked:* Fernández-Armesto, *Spanish Armada,* 269.

131 *Medina Sidonia swore:* In a letter to Juan de Idiáquez, quoted in Peter Pierson, *Commander of the Armada: The Seventh Duke of Medina Sidonia* (New Haven: Yale University Press, 1989), 171.

131 *Rumors swirled:* Parker, *The Grand Strategy of Philip II* (New Haven: Yale University Press, 1998), 229.

131 *As for Philip:* Mattingly, *Armada,* 389.

131 *"It lost us the respect":* Parker, *Grand Strategy,* 230.

131 *Flevit Deus:* Wallace McCaffrey, *Elizabeth I* (London: Edward Arnold, 1993), 241.

131 *Dee's friend:* F. Yates, *Astraea,* 85–86.

132 *"stop the mouths":* G. B. Parks, *Richard Hakluyt and the English Voyages* (New York: American Geographical Society, 1928), 124–26.

132 *legends of King Arthur:* Parks, *Hakluyt,* 126.

132 *Anyone reading:* Brian Penrose, *Travel and Discovery in the Renaissance 1420–1620* (Cambridge, Mass.: Harvard University Press, 1952), 318.

132 *"in searching the most opposite corners":* Rowse, *Expansion of Elizabethan England,* 161.

133 *prose epic:* Parks, *Hakluyt,* 187.

133 *"There is no doubt":* Quoted in P. Johnson, *A History of the American People* (New York: HarperCollins, 1997), 21.

133 *particularly celebrated:* Ibid., 186; Lesley Cormack, *Charting an Empire: Geography at the English Universities, 1580–1620* (Chicago: University of Chicago Press, 1997), 7.

7. PIRATES

137 *set sail from Plymouth:* H. Kelsey, *Sir Francis Drake: The Queen's Pirate* (New Haven: Yale University Press, 1998), 349.

138 *"el gran cosario":* Winston Graham, *The Spanish Armadas* (New York: Doubleday, 1972), 194.

138 *Martin Frobisher's turn:* N. A. M. Rodger, *Safeguard of the Seas: A Naval History of Britain* (New York: W.W. Norton, 1998), 275, 278.

138 *Rumors that Spaniards:* J. R. Whiting, *The Enterprise of England: The Spanish Armada* (New York: St. Martin's, 1988), 210–11.

138 *"the method of Jason":* R. B. Wernham, *After the Armada: Elizabethan England and the Struggle for Western Europe* (Oxford: Clarendon Press, 1984), 236.

138 *share of the budget:* Elton, *England Under the Tudors,* (London: Methuen, 1959), 362–63.

139 *every Spanish treasure convoy:* Whiting, *Enterprise of England,* 211.

139 *"God hath many things":* Foss, *Undreamed Shores,* 180.

139 *"like a soldier":* Cummins, *Francis Drake,* 256–57.

140 *"The Spanish shall have no peace":* Richard S. Dunn, *Sugar and Slaves* (New York: W.W. Norton, 1973), 11.

140 *From 1589 to 1591:* K. R. Andrews, ed. *English Privateering Voyages to the West Indies 1588–1595* (London: Hakluyt Society, 1959), 16–17.

140 *One Dutch expert:* Wernham, *After the Armada,* 249.

141 *Robert Dudley:* Rodger, *Safeguard,* 301.

141 *Sir Kenelm Digby:* R. D. Thomas, *Digby: The Gunpowder Plotter's Legacy* (London: Janus, 2001), 89–93.

141 *Cumberland's greatest moment:* Charles Corn, *The Scents of Eden: A History of the Spice Trade* (New York: Kodansha, 1998), 115.

141 *transferring more than 400,000 pounds:* Wernham, *After the Armada,* 250.

142 *poet John Donne:* Graham, *Spanish Armadas,* 215.

142 *Earl of Cumberland:* Kenny, *Elizabeth's Admiral,* 174.

142 *on June 1:* Rodger, *Safeguard,* 284–85.

142 *twelve million ducats:* Graham, *Spanish Armadas,* 214–15.

142 *subordinates watched helplessly:* J. F. Adamson and H. F. Folland, *The Shepherd of the Ocean, An Account of Sir Walter Raleigh and His Times* (Boston: Gambit, 1969), 278.

142 *Her commitments to war:* Richmond, *Statesmen and Seapower,* 18–19.

143 *More than 4 million pounds:* Elton, *England Under the Tudors,* 362.

143 *undying enmity of the Dutch:* D. H. Willson, *King James VI and I* (Oxford: Oxford University Press, 1967), 274–75.

143 *up to his neck:* K. R. Andrews, "Elizabethan Privateering," in *Raleigh in Exeter 1585: Privateering and Colonisation in the Reign of Elizabeth I,* ed. J. Youings, (Exeter, England: Exeter University Press, 1985), 10.

143 *For three years:* Rodger, *Safeguard,* 338.

144 *Sir Robert Mansell:* Ibid., 364–66.

144 *"everyone practiceth":* David Loades, *England's Maritime Empire: Seapower, Commerce & Policy 1490–1690* (New York: Longman, 2000), 151.

144 *out of forty-three navy ships:* C. Lloyd, *The Nation and the Navy* (London: Cresset, 1954), 53.

144 *England's ability:* Rodger, *Safeguard,* 348–49, 350.

145 *Between 1609 and 1616:* Lloyd, *Nation and the Navy,* 36.

145 *Mansell had not been to sea:* D. B. Quinn and A. N. Ryan, *England's Sea Empire* (London: Allen & Unwin, 1983), 226.

145 *real beneficiaries:* Padfield, *Maritime Supremacy,* 57.

146 *Even Philip II:* Ibid., 58.

146 *three-quarters:* Kennedy, *The Rise and Fall British Sea Mastery* (London: Allen Lane, 1976), 50.

146 *"He who possesses":* Elliott, *Old World and the New,* 97.

146 *75 percent:* Padfield, *Maritime Supremacy,* 60.

147 *the 1600s:* Kennedy, *Sea Mastery,* 30.

147 *Five separate admiralties:* Padfield, *Maritime Supremacy,* 74–75.

148 *three times the taxes:* Ibid., 66.

148 *"Jesus Christ is good":* Angus Calder, *Revolutionary Empire* (New York: E. P. Dutton, 1981), 117.

148 *They sold rope:* Violet Barbour, *Capitalism in Amsterdam in the 17th Century* (Ann Arbor: University of Michigan Press, 1963), 31–34, 131.

149 *routinely excluded:* Ibid., 118.

149 *A full-scale battle:* Willson, *King James VI & I,* 360.

149 *"greatest scholar in the country":* A. L. Rowse, *Four Caroline Portraits* (London: Duckworth, 1993), 125.

149 *license for Dutch piracy:* Donald Petrie, *The Prize Game* (New York: Berkley, 1998), 41.

149 *"the King of Great Britain":* Armitage, *Ideology,* 113–17, 118.

150 *When Francis Drake:* Kelsey, *Sir Francis Drake,* 277.

151 *He had envisaged:* Calder, *Empire,* 82–83.

151 *"Walter Raw Lie":* Ibid., 84.

152 *"nothing [is] more glorious":* Armitage, *Ideology,* 76.

152 *within striking distance:* Loades, *Maritime Empire,* 119.

152 *His father:* Andrews, "Elizabethan Privateering," 8.

152 *"journeys of pickery":* Ibid., 9.

153 *Chesapeake Bay:* Ibid., 11–12.

153 *leaked to Parliament:* T. Rabb, *Jacobean Gentleman: Sir Edwin Sandys 1561–1629* (Princeton, N.J.: Princeton University Press, 1998), 319.

154 *"for all their multitude"*: Ibid., 323.

154 *Within a year*: Loades, *Maritime Empire*, 141.

154 *extraordinary character*: Waters, *Art of Navigation*, 467–88.

154 *"The eyes of all Europe"*: Calder, *Empire*, 138.

155 *West Country puritans*: Bridenbaugh, *Vexed and Troubled Englishmen, 1590–1642* (Oxford: Oxford University Press, 1968), 436.

155 *Bermuda was the first*: Calder, *Empire*, 137–39.

155 *probably less than*: *Sir Francis Drake: An Exhibition*, 24.

155 *1.5 percent*: Bridenbaugh, *Englishmen*, 395–96.

155 *Boston alone*: Loades, *Maritime Empire*, 144.

155 *Sir Ferdinando Gorges*: Quinn and Ryan, *Sea Empire*, 175.

155 *Christopher Newport*: Rodger, *Safeguard*, 295.

8. ROCK THE NATIONS

157 *On November 19, 1630*: A. P. Newton, *The Colonizing Activities of the English Puritans* (New Haven: Yale University Press, 1914), 58, 34.

157 *thirty English overseas trading companies*: David Loades, *England: Maritime Empire: Seapower, Commerce, and Policy 1490–1690* (New York: Longman, 2000), 117.

157 *John Winthrop*: Newton, *Colonizing*, 65.

158 *"the extraordinary importance"*: Quoted in Karen Kuperman, *Providence Island 1630–1641: The Other Puritan Colony* (Cambridge: Cambridge University Press, 1993), 198.

158 *Fully two-thirds*: J. H. Hexter, *The Reign of King Pym* (Cambridge, Mass.: Harvard University Press, 1941), 78.

158 *contemplated emigrating*: Christopher Hill, *God's Englishman: Oliver Cromwell and the English Revolution* (1970; New York: Harper, 1972), 33.

158 *"War with Spain"*: Quoted in Robert Ruigh, *The Parliament of 1624* (Cambridge, Mass.: Harvard University Press, 1971), 205.

158 *a future director*: Newton, *Colonizing*, 58.

159 *"to cut him up"*: Quoted in D. B. Quinn and A. N. Ryan, *England's Sea Empire* (London: Allen & Unwin, 1983), 227.

159 *"Spain is rich"*: N. A. M. Rodger, *The Safeguard of the Seas: A Naval History of Britain* (New York: N. W. Norton, 1998), 356.

159 *goaded James into arresting*: D. H. Willson, *James VI and I* (Oxford: Oxford University Press), 374–75.

159 *"Spain must be the enemy"*: Quoted in Ruigh, *Parliament of 1624*, 181.

159 *the annual tonnage*: Ralph Davis, *The Rise of the English Shipping Industry in the Seventeenth and Eighteenth Centuries* (London: Macmillan, 1962).

159 *the Tre Kroner*: Rodger, *Safeguard*, 386–87.

160 *spent its tax*: J. H. Elliott, *Imperial Spain* (Harmondsworth: Penguin Books, 1970), 326.

161 *promoted him to earl*: G. P. V. Akrigg, *Jacobean Pageant* (1962; New York: Atheneum, 1974), 205–6.

161 *at his instigation*: Quinn and Ryan, *England's Sea Empire*, 223–24.; Rodger, *Safeguard*, 368.

162 *only 140,000 pounds*: Rodger, *Safeguard*, 370.

162 *40,000 strong*: Lloyd, *Nation and the Navy*, 63.

162 *the trumpeter*: Rodger, *Safeguard*, 406.

162 *"this intolerable scum"*: Ibid., 407.

163 *stretched the manpower*: Andrews, *Ships, Money, and Politics: Seafaring and Naval Enterprise in the Reign of Charles I* (Cambridge: Cambridge University Press, 1991), 8.

163 *relied on it far more*: Rodger, *Safeguard*, 398–99.

163 *"We are used like dogs":* Ibid., 402.

163 *Buckingham ordered it raised:* Lloyd, *Nation and the Navy,* 48; Rodger, *Safeguard,* 403.

163 *attacked his carriage:* Roger Lockyer, *Buckingham: The Life and Political Career of George Villiers, First Duke of Buckingham 1592–1628* (London: Longmans, 1981), 342–43.

163 *on Wednesdays and Fridays:* Lloyd, *Nation and the Navy,* 63.

164 *one-half of all shipwrecks:* Ibid., 45.

164 *Viscount Sitstill:* Rodger, *Safeguard,* 358.

164 *decided to split:* Nicholas Tracy, *Nelson's Battles,: The Art of Victory in the Age of Sail* (Annapolis: Naval Institute Press, 1996), 50.

165 *leaking so badly:* Rodger, *Safeguard,* 359.

165 *half a million pounds:* K. R. Andrews, *Ships, Money & Politics: Seafaring and Canal Enterprise in the Reign of Charles I* (Cambridge: Cambridge University Press, 1991), 8.

165 *Buckingham's protégé:* Harold Hulme, *The Life of Sir John Eliot* (London: Allen & Unwin, 1957), 98.

165 *"Our honor is ruined":* Lockyer, *Buckingham,* 309.

165 *"the ships are unprovided":* Quoted in Lockyer, *Buckingham,* 363.

165 *Desperate to ingratiate himself:* Harding, *Evolution of the Sailing Navy,* 43–44.

166 *"I vow to God":* Quoted in Lloyd, *Nation and the Navy.*

166 *"more than lives":* Hulme, *John Eliot,* 190.

166 *not entirely new:* Quinn and Ryan, *Sea Empire,* 235–36.

167 *even published John Selden's:* Rodger, *Safeguard,* 382.

167 *almost 80,000 pounds:* Quinn and Ryan, *Sea Empire,* 237.

167 *seventy large ships:* Lockyer, *Buckingham,* 364.

167 *a system of regular patrols:* Rodger, *Safeguard,* 382.

167 *the only way:* Newton, *Colonizing,* 37.

167 *Ship money created:* Rodger, *Safeguard,* 409–10; Wheeler, *The Making of a World Power* (London: Sutton, 1999), 36.

168 *Rainsborough and three other "tarpaulin":* Rodger, *Safeguard,* 385.

168 *"For safety's sake":* Quoted in Armitage, *British Empire,* 116.

168 *In October:* Padfield, *Maritime Supremacy,* 61, 62.

169 *as day by day:* Ibid., 63.

169 *one-third of the 1638 levy:* Quinn and Ryan, *Sea Empire,* 237.

169 *Yet the afternoon:* J. R. Powell, *The Navy in the English Civil War* (London: Archon, 1962), 5.

170 *Within twenty-four hours:* Wedgwood, *The King's Peace,* 1637–1641 (London: Collins, 1978), 329.

170 *with a single exception:* Rodger, *Safeguard,* 414.

170 *cut off royalist bases:* Richard Harding, *The Evolution of the Sailing Navy* (London: St. Martin's, Press, 1995), 63–64; Rodger, *Safeguard,* 415.

171 *Power passed:* Andrews, *Ships, Money & Politics,* 13.

171 *something drastic:* Wheeler, *World Power,* 160; Rodger, *Safeguard,* 417.

171 *far-flung operations:* Wheeler, *World Power,* 43–44.

172 *the largest full-time navy:* Harding, *Evolution,* 70.

172 *smaller faster vessels:* Rif Winfield, *The 50-Gun Ship* (London: Chatham, 1997), 7–8. The very first example was built in 1612, but it was the capture of the swift Dutch privateer *Swan* in 1635 that prompted the king to order two more of a similar design. Wheeler, *World Power,* 40–41.

172 *Vane worked best:* Lloyd, *Nation and the Navy,* 55; Wheeler, *World Power,* 39.

172 *"not placed in employment":* Quoted in Christopher Hill, *A Century of Revolution 1603–1714* (New York: W. W. Norton, 1980), 119.

172 *raised the pay:* Peter Padfield, *Tides of Empire* (London: RKP, 1979), vol. 1, 214.

172 *a sense of deomocratic solidarity:* Bernard Capp, *Cromwell's Navy: The Fleet and the English Revolution* (Oxford: Clarendon, 1989), 213.

173 *"The meanest of them":* Quoted in Capp, *Cromwell's Navy*, 214–16.

173 *"not let slip":* Quoted in Hill, *God's Englishman*, 163.

173 *"160 sail of brave ships":* Ibid., 86.

174 *a political union:* Padfield, *Maritime Supremacy*, 92.

174 *"too much trade":* Quoted in Kennedy, *Naval Mastery*, 48.

174 *first English translation:* Armitage, *British Empire*, 118; John Selden, *Of the Dominion of the Sea,* trans. Marchamont Nedham (London: 1652). Britannia appears with the banners of Scotland, Ireland, and Wales at her feet and a winged victory in her hand.

174 *had removed Warwick:* Lloyd, *Nation and the Navy*, 39–40.

175 *a trio of generals:* Capp, *Cromwell's Navy*, 46.

176 *appeal of the broadside:* Michael Baumer, *General at Sea: Robert Blake and the Seventeenth-Century Revolution in Naval Warfare* (London: John Murray, 1989), 116–19.

176 *no foreign vessel:* Ibid., 119.

176 *made their cannon shorter:* Rodger, *Safeguard* 389; Baumer, *General at Sea,* 116.

176 *Blake was furious:* Capp, *Cromwell's Navy*, 79; Baumer, *General at Sea,* 158.

177 *become the Articles of War:* Capp, *Cromwell's Navy*, 219.

177 *"much dyed":* Ibid., 80–81.

178 *"Why should I":* Admiral de Witt, quoted in Padfield, *Empire*, vol. 1, 229.

178 *"all ships":* Baumer, *General at Sea,* 182; Brian Tunstall, *Naval Warfare in the Age of Sail,* ed. Nicholas Tracy (Edison: Wellfleet Press, 2001), 18–19.

178 *a line of bearing:* Baumer, *General at Sea,* 182–83, 184.

178 *The effect was spectacular:* D. Howarth, *Men of War* (Alexandria, Va,: Time Life Books, 1978), 62–63.

178 *a cousin of the Grenvilles:* *Dictionary of National Biography,* vol. XII, 594.

178 *ships crashed through:* Tunstall, *Navy Warfare,* 21.

179 *"all their masts gone":* Quoted in Padfield, *Empire*, vol. I, 230.

179 *1,500 Dutch merchants:* Loades, *Maritime Empire,* 177.

179 *presence in the Mediterranean:* Hill, *God's Englishman*, 162.

180 *"Most men cry up war":* Loades, *Maritime Empire,* 177.

180 *"rock the nations":* Quoted in Hill, *God's Englishman*, 155.

180 *proof of how much:* Loades, *Maritime Empire;* Calder, *Revolutionary Empire,* 241–42, says four thousand.

180 *Stayner sank three ships:* Howarth, *Men of War,* 87.

180 *a feat of seamanship:* Capp, *Cromwell's Navy*, 3.

181 *cost of endless war:* Baumer, *General at Sea,* 211.

9. MR. PEPYS'S NAVY

182 *"All the world":* *The Diary of Samuel Pepys,* ed. Robert Latham and William Matthews, vol. I.

183 *"The weather being good":* Ibid.

183 *"in a melancholy fit":* Pepys, *Diary,* April 10, 1660.

184 *"the first time":* Pepys, *Diary,* May 22, 1660.

184 *Montagu ordered Pepys:* Pepys, *Diary,* May 27, 1660.

184 *"We must have a little patience":* Pepys, *Diary,* June 2, 1660.

185 *someone whose name:* N. Rodger, *The Admiralty* (Lavenham: Terence Dalton, 1979), 30–31.

185 *crucial decisions:* Frank Fox, *Great Ships: The Battlefleet of Charles II* (Greenwich, England:

Conway Maritime Press, 1980), 155–56. See also D. Davies, *Gentlemen and Tarpaulins: The Officers & Men of the Restoration Navy* (Oxford: Oxford University Press, 1991), 40–41.

185 *"right hand of the Navy"*: Quoted in Stephen Coote, *Samuel Pepys: A Life* (London: Hodder and Stoughton, 2000), 154.

185 *more than one hundred and twenty*: Wheeler, *Making of a World Power*, 54. Sixty-six were in active service and sixty "in Ordinary," meaning in storage for wartime use.

185 *growth of English shipping*: Ralph Davis, *The Rise of the English; Shipping Industry in the Seventeenth and Eighteenth Centuries* (London: Macmillan, 1962); R. Harding, *Seapower and Naval Warfare 1650–1830* (Annapolis: Naval Institute Press, 1999), 14.

185 *Royal Navy's budget*: Wheeler, *World Power*, 64.

185 *trade numbers rebounded*: S. Horenstein, *The Restoration Navy and English Foreign Trade 1674–1688* (Aldershot: Scholar Press, 1991), 48.

186 *largest single employer in England*: Davies, *Gentlemen and Tarpaulins*, 15.

186 *entire forest industry*: R. G. Albion, *Forest and Sea Power: The Timber Problem of the Royal Navy 1652–1862* (Cambridge, Mass.: Harvard University Press, 1926).

186 *burnt coal, or coke*: L. A. Wilcox, *Mr. Pepys's Navy* (South Brunswick, England: A. S. Barnes, 1968), 90.

186 *told his sister*: Quoted in Robert Bliss, *Revolution and Empire: English Politics and the American Colonies in the Seventeenth Century* (Manchester England: Manchester University Press, 1990), 171.

186 *version of the Navigation Acts*: Christopher Hill, *Century of Revolution, 1603–1714* (New York: W. W. Norton, 1980).

186 *expensive naval arms race*: J. Glete, *Navies and Nations: Warships, Navies, and State Building in Europe and America 1500–1860* (Stockholm: Almquist and Wilcell, 1993), vol. 1, 178–79.

187 *by size and armament*: The rating system had begun in the 1640s as a way to determine officers' pay. Those who captained or served on larger ships were deemed worthy of higher pay. Fox, *Great Ships*, 20.

187 *the Naseby*: D. Howarth, *Men of War* (Alexandria, Va.: Time-Life Books, 1978), 33.

187 *"head, waist, quarter"*: Quoted in N.A.M. Rodger, *Safeguard*, 38.

187 *rather than serving*: Fox, *Great Ships*, 29.

187 *Getting rid of the bonaventure*: Rodger, *Safeguard*, 388.

188 *as many on a ship*: Lavery, *Arming and Fitting*, 144–47

188 *more than 60,000 pounds*: Rodger, *Safeguard*, 388.

188 *overhauled Navy Board*: Rodger, *Admiralty*, 19–20; Coote, *Samuel Pepys*, 61.

188 *Chatham Chest*: Coote, *Samuel Pepys*, 92.

188 *two books*: Pepys, *Diary*, March 13, 1660 and November 29, 1661.

188 *slide rules*: Pepys, *Diary*, July 18, 1663.

189 *lessons on how to draw them*: Claire Tomalin, *Samuel Pepys: The Unequaled Self* (New York: Knopf, 2003), 139.

189 *twelve hours a day*: Philip MacDougall, *Royal Dockyards*, (Newton Abbott: David & Charles, 1982), 13.

189 *toasted themselves*: Wilcox, *Pepys's Navy*, 55.

189 *Epping Forest*: Pepys, *Diary*, August 18, 1662.

189 *broke the contract*: Coote, *Samuel Pepys*, 144.

189 *did not hesitate to take*: Coote, Ibid., 144.

190 *"My delight"*: Ibid.

190 *more than 450,000 pounds a year*: Wheeler, *World Power*, 54

190 *less than two-thirds*: Pepys learned this in his conversations with Sir Philip Warwick: *Diary*, 1664.

190 *"The want of money"*; Pepys, *Diary*, September 30, 1661.

190 *"The trade of the world"*: Captain George Cocke, in Pepys, *Diary*, February 2, 1664.

190 *"We all seem"*: Pepys, *Diary*, April 30, 1664.

190 *on June 3*: Or June 11 according to the new style calendar. Harding, *Seapower*, 86.

191 *more than five miles*: Howarth, *Men of War*, 126.

191 *written instructions*: B. Tunstall, *Naval Warfare in the Age of Sail*, ed. Nicholas Tracy (Edison, N.J.: Wellfleet Press, 2001), 32, 39.

192 *"Without a miracle"*: Quoted in Peter Padfield, *Maritime Supremacy and the Opening of the Western Mind* (New York: Overlook Press, 2002), 160.

192 *meet the Dutch on the same tack*: Howarth, *Men of War*, 128.

192 *"they had attentively listened"*: J. Dryden, *An Essay of Dramatic Poesy*, (London, 1668), 3.

193 *heard in the Hague*: Howarth, *Men of War*, 128.

193 *"a great victory"*: Pepys, *Diary*, June 1665.

193 *recriminations began*: Davies, *Gentlemen and Tarpaulins*, 138–39.

193 *"a distinction"*: J. R. Tanner, ed. *Samuel Pepys's Naval Minutes*. Quoted in Coote, *Samuel Pepys*, 269–70.

193 *disastrous attempt*: Davies, *Gentlemen and Tarpaulins*, 140.

194 *Officers close*: Ibid., 145.

194 *seriously undermanned*: Ibid., 136.

194 *"The lamentable moans"*: Quoted in Lloyd, *Nation and the Navy*, 54.

194 *funeral of Captain Myngs*: Pepys, *Diary*, June 13, 1666.

194 *"It seemed"*: J. Dryden, *Annus Mirabilis*, published in 1666.

195 *"help for God"*: Pepys, *Diary*, June 11, 1666.

195 *guns on Upnor Castle*: Howarth, *Men of War*, 157.

195 *"We were paid"*: Pepys, *Diary*, vol. 8, June 14, 1666.

195 *"the most dismal spectacle"*: Howarth, *Men of War*. 157–58.

195 *"This is what comes"*: Pepys, *Diary*.

195 *"intolerable neglect"*: Davies, *Gentlemen and Tarpaulins*, 151.

196 *He sensed the hostility*: Pepys, *Diary*, March 5, 1668.

196 *more than one hundred and fifty*: Richard Ollard, *Man of War. Sir Robert Holmes and the Restoration Navy* (London: Hodder & Stoughton, 1969), 148–51.

197 *great-grandfather*: R.J. Knecht, *Richelieu* (London: Longmans, 1991), 157.

198 *"pierced the heart"*: Quoted in Ibid., 155.

198 *sixty sailing warships*: John Lynn, *The Wars of Louis XIV 1667–1714* (London: Longmans, 1999), 84.

198 *ten by 1712*: J. Rule, "Louis XIV, Roi-Bureaucrat," in *Louis XIV and the Craft of Kingship*, ed. J. Rule (Columbus: Ohio State University Press, 1969), 34.

198 *a registry*: Lynn, *Wars*, 89.

198 *more than eighty ships*: Glete, *Navies and Nations*, vol. 1, 189–90.

198 *the Brest yards*: Lynn, *Wars*, 88.

199 *trade itself as a form of warfare*: Paul Sonnino, *Louis XIV and the Origins of the Dutch War* (Cambridge: Cambridge University Press, 1988), 59.

199 *"only of their own interests"*: Quoted in Padfield, *Maritime Supremacy*, 98.

199 *"natural hatred"*: Quoted in Sonnino, *Louis XIV*, 58.

199 *certain ports in Zeeland*: Padfield, *Maritime Supremacy*, 100.

200 *drowning in debt*: Ibid.

200 *Anthony Deane*: Fox, *Great Ships*, 140–41.

201 *"General, Soldier"*: Quoted in Padfield, *Maritime Supremacy*, 109.

201 *Order of the Garter*: Richard Ollard, *Cromwell's Earl: A Life of Edward Mountagu 1st Earl of Sandwich* (New York: HarperCollins, 1994), 262.

201 *saved the Dutch Republic:* Padfield, *Maritime Supremacy,* 115.

201 *"a very pretty boy":* Pepys, *Diary,* May 14, 1660.

201 *"damned cowards":* Frank Kitson, *Prince Rupert: Admiral and General-at-Sea* (London: Constable, 1998), 288.

202 *"this is* your *war":* K. H. D. Haley, *The First Earl of Shaftesbury* (Oxford: Oxford University Press, 1968), 33.

202 *"The interest of the king":* Padfield, *Maritime Supremacy,* 117.

202 *"I see":* Coote, *Samuel Pepys,* 229, 280.

202 *offices to Derby House:* Arthur Bryant, *Samuel Pepys: The Years of Peril* (New York: Macmillan, 1935), 120.

202 *"The French and Dutch":* Coote, *Samuel Pepys,* 278.

203 *most successful class of ships:* Fox, *Great Ships,* 156–58.

203 *Jonas Moore:* Clive Aslet, *The Story of Greenwich* (Cambridge, Mass.: Harvard University Press, 1999), 124–28.

203[n.] *avid horticulturalist:* Albion, *Forests and Sea Power: The Timber Problem of the Royal Navy 1652–1862* (Cambridge, Mass. Harvard University Press, 1926), 131–32.

203 *The original idea:* Aslet, *Greenwich,* 141; Coote, *Samuel Pepys,* 165–66.

204 *The volunteer per order system:* Summarized in Davies, *Gentlemen and Tarpaulins,* 29–30.

205 *"sobriety":* Coote, *Samuel Pepys,* 271. Pepys introduced a similar examination for pilots and masters in Rodger, *Admiralty,* 24.

205 *Navy List:* Lloyd, *Nation and the Navy,* 59–60.

205 *watched his success:* Bryant, *Pepys,* 110; Haley, *Shaftesbury,* 362–3.

205 *An organized opposition:* J. R. Jones, *The First Whigs. The Politics of the Exclusion Crisis 1678–1683* (Westport, Ct.: Greenwood, 1985); Mark Knights, *Politics and Opinion in Crisis, 1678–81* (Cambridge: Cambridge University Press, 1994).

206 *take over the fleet:* Coote, *Samuel Pepys,* 286.

206 *"Mr. Speaker":* Tomalin, *Samuel Pepys,* 312.

206 *His friends:* Coote, *Samuel Pepys,* 291–92.

207 *built a Royal Navy:* The figures are from Glete, *Navies and Nations,* 195.

207 *all-powerful Secretary:* Rodger, *Admiralty,* 27.

207 *analysis of tides:* Margaret Deacon, *Scientists and the Sea 1650–1900* (New York: Academic Press, 1971).

10. REVOLUTION

208 *"It is from England":* Quoted in Nescia Robb, *William of Orange: A Personal Portrait,* vol. 2 (New York: St. Martin's Press, 1966), 254.

208 *to prevent a union:* Peter Padfield, *Maritime Supremacy and the Opening of the Western Mind,* (New York: Overlook Press, 2002), 120–21.

209 *at his accession:* Wheeler, *Making of a World Power,* (London: Sutton, 1999), 59.

209 *worked to make:* Pepys, *Memoires to the State of the Royal Navy . . . 1688* (London, 1690); Rodger, *Admiralty,* 31–32, 33.

209 *"this hell":* Quoted in Davies, *Gentlemen and Tarpaulins,* 177.

209 *a practice Pepys tried to ban:* Ibid., 180–82; Coote, *Pepys,* 319–22.

210 *rising generation:* Davies, *Gentlemen and Tarpaulins,* 178.

210 *strong burst of public support:* J. R. Jones, *The Revolution of 1688 in England* (New York: W. W. Norton, 1972), 59–61.

210 *Catholic courtiers:* W. A. Speck, *James II* (London: Longmans, 2002), 61.

210 *fatal error:* Jones, *Revolution,* 61.

210 *three years earlier:* This was Louis's 1685 revocation of the Edict of Nantes, which had protected the rights of French Protestants for eighty-seven years. Stories of French

soldiers terrorizing helpless Huguenots to force them to convert to Catholicism circulated widely in England and had a sharp impact on public opinion. See Guy Dodge, *The Political Theory of the Huguenots of the Dispersion* (Lexington, Mass: Heath, 1971).

210 *Sir Roger Strickland:* Davies, *Gentlemen and Tarpaulins,* 200–201.

211 *strongest supporters:* Jones, *Revolution,* 102.

211 *Herbert was offended: Bishop Burnet's History of His Own Time* (London, 1910) vol. 3, 95–97.

211 *"A man who lives":* Macaulay, *History of England,* vol. 2, 194.

212 *Pepys's bitter objections:* Davies, *Gentlemen and Tarpaulins,* 202.

212 *near mutiny:* Jock Haswell, *James II: Soldier and Sailor* (London: Harnish Hamilton 1972), 268.

212 *grown by 50 percent:* Davis, *Shipping Industry,* 15–18.

212 *until a month before he sailed:* Padfield, *Maritime Supremacy,* 123.

212 *had declined:* Glete, *Navies and Nations,* vol. 1, 195.

212 *"It is now or never":* Literally, *"Autnunc aut numquam,"* quoted in Robb, *William of Orange: A Personal Portrait* (New York: St. Martin's Press, 1960), vol. 2, 257–58.

212 *"The nation cannot be beaten":* Quoted in Padfield, *Maritime Supremacy,* 120.

213 *the champion of international Protestantism:* Pincus, *Protestantism and Patriotism: Ideologies and the Making of English Foreign Policy, 1650–1688* (Cambridge: Cambridge University Press, 1993).

213 *told Russell:* Robb, *William of Orange,* 257–58.

213 *95 percent:* Jones, *Revolution,* 240–41.

213 *The French ambassador:* Ibid., 176–77.

214 *"great and sudden invasion:* Padfield, *Maritime Supremacy,* 124.

214 *Sir John Berry:* Davies, *Gentlemen and Tarpaulins,* 203, 207.

214 *"The kingdom has always depended":* Quoted in David Ogg, *England in the Reigns of James II and William III* (Oxford: Oxford University Press, 1963), 214.

214 *three-foot-high letters:* Macaulay, *History of England,* vol. 2, 427.

214 *William had intended:* Padfield, *Maritime Supremacy,* 124.

214 *huge crowds:* Macaulay, *History of England,* vol. 2, 432.

215 *Monmouth uprising:* Jones, *Revolution,* 59–60.

215 *actually in sight:* Davies, *Gentlemen and Tarpaulins,* 216.

215 *"Well, Doctor":* Macaulay, vol. 2, 438.

215 *Swedes:* Macaulay, *History of England,* vol. 2, 439.

215 *paralyzed by indecision:* Jones, *Revolution,* 296.

215 *Great Seal of State:* Ibid., 305.

216 *local fishermen:* Ogg, *England,* 219.

216 *the Mutiny Act:* This was a largely symbolic measure for establishing Parliament's control over the army. See J. P. Kenyon, *Stuart England* (Harmondsworth, England: Penguin Books, 1978), 278.

216 *"France is at the bottom":* Quoted in Julian Hoppitt, *A Land of Liberty? England 1689–1727* (Oxford: Clarendon Press, 2000), 92.

216 *40,000-man:* Ibid., 102.

216 *secret agreement:* Davies, *Gentlemen and Tarpaulins,* 214–15.

217 *naval war by default:* Ibid., 227; J. R. Jones, "Limitations of British Sea Power in the French Wars, 1689–1815," in *The British Navy and the Use of Sea Power in the Eighteenth Century,* ed. J. Black and P. Woodfine (Leicester England: Leicester University Press, 1988), 35–36.

217 *La Hoste:* Tunstall, *Naval Warfare,* 59–60.

218 *Louis took the opportunity:* Davies, *Gentlemen and Tarpaulins,* 225; Padfield, *Maritime Supremacy,* 128.

218 *most trusted officers:* Shovell was covering the Ireland invasion; Henry Killigrew was escorting merchantmen from the Mediterranean: Padfield, *Maritime Supremacy,* 129.

218 *fifty-eight ships of the line:* Ogg, *England,* 353.

219 *His plan:* Tunstall, *Naval Warfare,* 53–54.

219 *70-gun Anne:* Anon., *A Plain Relation of the Late Action at Sea . . . From June 22 to July 5 last . . . ,* (London, 1690), 5–6.

219 *fifteen vessels:* Philip Aubrey, *The Defeat of James Stuart's Armada 1692* (Leicester, England: Leicester University Press, 1979), 50.

219 *Panic set in:* Macaulay, *History of England,* vol. 3, 453–55.

220 *"fleet in being":* Padfield, *Maritime Supremacy,* 138.

220 *"They dare not":* Quoted in Daniel Baugh, "The Eighteenth-Century Navy as a National Institution, 1690–1815," in *Oxford Illustrated History of the Royal Navy,* 120.

220 *nearly two million pounds a year:* Ibid., 121.

220 *Events at sea:* Ogg, *England,* 388–90; Lloyd, *Nation and Navy,* 83.

221 *the most important:* Wheeler, *Making of a World Power,* 59–63.

221 *to 176 ships:* Baugh, "National Institution," 123.

221 *over the long haul:* Wheeler, *Making of a World Power,* 145.

222 *"I am for":* Quoted in Hoppitt, *Land of Liberty?,* 101.

222 *"The Navy is of so great importance":* George Savile, Marquis of Halifax, *A Rough Draft of a New Model at Sea,* in *Halifax: Complete Works,* ed. J. P. Kenyon (Harmondsworth, England: Penguin Books, 1969), 159.

222 *complicated maneuvers:* Padfield, *Maritime Supremacy,* 141.

222 *immediate invasion:* Aubrey, *Defeat,* 78–80.

223 *45,000 men:* Lynn, *Wars of Louis XIV,* 89.

223 *"and I wish it":* Padfield, *Maritime Supremacy,* 143.

223 *shook hands with each:* Ibid.; Aubrey, *Defeat,* 91.

224 *more than 7,000 guns:* Nigel Calder, *The English Channel* (Harmondsworth, England: Penguin Books, 1986), 102.

224 *"God preserve your person":* Macaulay, *History of England,* vol. 4, 316–17.

224 *George Churchill:* Aubrey, *Defeat,* 98.

225 *"began to run":* Ibid., 97.

225 *"Fight the ship":* Macaulay, *History of England,* vol. 4, 317.

225 *"none but my brave English":* Calder, *English Channel,* 105.

226 *Famine would break out:* John B. Wolf, *Louis XIV* (New York: W. W. Norton, 1968), 476.

226 *"If you take":* Quoted in Lloyd, *Nation and Navy,* 54.

226 *twenty years ahead:* Lavery, *The Arming and Fitting of English Ships of War 1600–1815* (Annapolis, Md.: Naval Institute Press, 1987), 7; on the ship's wheel, see 18–19.

226 *siege expert Vauban:* Geoffrey Symcox, *The Crisis of French Sea Power 1688–1697* (The Hague: M. Nijhoff, 1974), 177–87.

227 *"is so placed":* Quoted in Kennedy, *British Naval Mastery,* 79.

227 *cut by half:* Padfield, *Maritime Supremacy,* 153.

227 *four thousand:* This was the Admiralty's estimate. Davis, *Shipping Industry,* 316.

227 *In the Caribbean:* Jones, "Limitations," 39.

227 *Cruiser Act:* Ibid., 40; Kennedy, *British Naval Mastery,* 80.

228 *two and a half million:* Padfield, *Maritime Supremacy,* 155.

228 *raids on Brest and Saint-Malo:* John B. Hattendorf, "The Struggle with France, 1689–

1815," in *Oxford Illustrated History of the Royal Navy,* ed. J. R. Hill (New York: Oxford University Press, 1995), 86–87.

228   *trapped at Toulon:* Padfield, *Maritime Supremacy,* 156.

228   *"If the world":* The second Earl of Shaftesbury, quoted in J. Hattendorf, *England in the War of the Spanish Succession* (New York: Garland Publishers, 1987), 7.

229   *"the Pyrenees":* Wolf, *Louis XIV,* 507.

229   *Canada and Nova Scotia:* Harding, *Seapower,* 118–19.

229   *first serious operation:* Hattendorf, *Spanish Succession,* 69–70.

230   *not an entirely novel idea:* J. Corbett, *England in the Mediterranean 1603–1713* (London: Longmans, 1917), vol. 2, 517–18; J. H. Owen, *War at Sea Under Queen Anne* (Cambridge: Cambridge University Press, 1938), 91.

230   *On August 1, 1704:* Henry Kamen, *The War of Succession in Spain 1700–1715* (Bloomington, Ind.: Indiana University Press, 1969), 14.

231   *joined battle off Malaga:* Tunstall, *Naval Warfare,* 66.

11. GOING GLOBAL

233   *boucaniers:* David Cordingly, *Under the Black Flag* (New York: Random House, 1995), xviii.

233   *Henry Morgan their leader:* Peter Earle, *The Sack of Panama* (New York: Viking, 1982), 47–48.

234   *twelve ships and five hundred men:* Cordingly, *Black Flag,* 45–46.

234   *Spain was now England's ally:* Earle, *Sack of Panama,* 53; Calder, *Revolutionary Empire,* 315.

234   *even more ambitious attack:* Cordingly, *Black Flag,* 46–47.

235   *"the famous and ancient city":* Ibid., 52.

235   *his connection:* Dudley Pope, *The Buccaneer King: The Biography of Sir Henry Morgan* (New York: Dodd and Mead, 1978), 264–66.

235   *if not all:* On Bartholomew Sharp's exploits, see James Burney, *History of the Buccaneers of America* (1816; New York: Dover, 2002), 121–43.

235   *stamp out buccaneering:* Anna Neill, *British Discovery Literature and the Rise of Global Community* (New York: Palgrave, 2002), 37–38.

235   *twenty-two-gun salute:* Pope, *Buccaneer King,* 347.

235   *lost its appeal:* And not just Britain: see Janice Thomson, *Mercenaries, Pirates, and Sovereigns* (Princeton, N.J.: Princeton University Press, 1994).

236   *The story of sugar:* The single best book remains Sidney Mintz, *Sweetness and Power: The Place of Sugar in Modern History* (New York: Penguin, 1985).

236   *found a home:* J. H. Parry, *Trade and Dominion, The European Overseas Empire* in the Eighteenth Century (London: Weidenfield and Nicolson, 1971), 32–34.

236   *landholders gave way:* Richard S. Dunn, *Sugar and Slaves: The Rise of the Planter Class in the English West Indies 1624–1715* (New York: W. W. Norton, 1973), 64–67.

236   *the death toll for crews:* The relevant data can be found in Philip Curtin, *The Atlantic Slave Trade* (Madison: University of Wisconsin Press, 1969).

237   *first large-scale:* T. O. Lloyd, *The British Empire* (Oxford: Oxford University Press), 72.

237   *four pounds of sugar:* Mintz, *Sweetness and Power,* 67.

237   *twenty-five by 1750:* Kenneth Morgan, *Bristol and the Atlantic Trade in the Eighteenth Century* (Cambridge: Cambridge University Press, 1993), 185.

237   *a glass industry:* Ibid.

237   *number two by the 1790s:* Ibid., 188–89.

238   *monopoly in 1697:* Lloyd, *British Empire,* 56.

238   *a hundred slave ships:* Morgan, *Bristol,* 132.

238   *the biggest demand:* Dunn, *Sugar and Slaves,* 165.

238 *70,000 a year:* Lloyd, *British Empire,* 71.

238 *The South Sea Company:* D. W. Jones, *War and Economy in the Age of William III and Marlborough* (Oxford, England: Blackwell, 1988), 67; Parry, *Trade and Dominion,* 102.

239 *"No African Trade":* Quoted in Richard Sheridan, "Caribbean Plantation Society 1689–1714," *Oxford History of the British Empire: The Eighteenth Century,* 409.

239 *twice the size:* Harding, *Seapower,* 184.

239 *half of what they had been:* Davis, *Shipping Industry,* 316.

239 *building more frigates:* Daniel Baugh, "The Eighteenth-Century Navy as a National Institution, 1690–1815," in *Royal Navy,* ed. J. R. Hill (Oxford: Oxford University Press, 1995), 124.

239 *almost three to one:* Harding, *Seapower,* 176.

240 *the first Englishman:* Cordingly, *Black Flag,* 84.

240 *almost 150,000 pounds:* Rogers saw only 1,600 pounds—proof of how unpredictable prize money could be for a privateer, versus the standard share for a navy captain. Harding, *Seapower,* 176; Douglas Botting, *The Pirates* (Alexandria, Va.: Time-Life Books, 1978), 139.

240 *French attacks grew so bad:* Kennedy, *Naval Mastery,* 85.

240 *ten parliamentary boroughs:* Rodger, *Admiralty,* 61.

240 *"no ways of making":* Quoted in Jack P. Greene, "Empire and Identity from the Glorious Revolution to the American Revolution," in *British Empire: Eighteenth Century,* 216.

240 *largest industrial organization:* The classic study is Daniel Bough, *Naval Administration in the Age of Walpole* (Princeton, N.J.: Princeton University Press, 1965).

241 *unprecedented continuity:* Rodger, *Admiralty,* 65–66.

241 *Rodney wanted a post:* Rodger, *Wooden World,* 333.

241 *the one profession:* Ibid., 253–54.

241 *John Pasco:* Ibid., 267, 272.

242 *"When a Gentleman hath":* "A Rough Draught of a New Model at Sea," in *The Works of George Savile, Marquis of Halifax,* ed. Mark Brown (Oxford: Clarendon, 1989), 305.

242 *Any loyalty they felt:* Rodger, *Wooden World,* 119.

243 *George Shelvocke:* Kenneth Poolman, *The Speedwell Voyage* (New York: Berkley Books, 2000), 92.

243 *success in battle:* Rodger, *Wooden World,* 294.

244 *Chatham alone had four:* Baugh, "National Institution," 269.

244 *fourteen-week process:* Ibid., 128.

244 *mast pond:* Philip MacDougall, *Royal Dockyards* (Newton Abbot, England: David and Charles, 1982), 11.

244 *grew the fastest:* Ibid., 76–77; Baugh, "National Institution," 273–75.

244 *"a very handsome street":* Macdougall, *Royal Dockyards,* 101.

244 *Great Northern War:* Harding, *Seapower,* 188–89.

245 *harbor at Chebuco:* Julian Gwyn, "The Royal Navy in North America, 1712–1776," in *The Royal Navy and the Use of Naval Power,* ed. Black and Woodfine (Leicester: University Press, 1988).

245 *on permanent station:* Ibid., 133.

245 *led the first squadron:* Parry, *Trade and Dominion,* 99.

245 *"honest rough seaman":* *Dictionary of National Biography,* vol. 2, 210.

246 *had shattered Benbow's leg:* Ruth Bourne, *Queen Anne's Navy in the West Indies* (New Haven: Yale University Press, 1939), 154–57.

246 *his story was the opposite:* The most recent account is Richard Zacks, *The Pirate Hunter: The True Story of Captain Kidd* (New York: Hyperion, 2002).

247 *"take particular care":* Cordingly, *Black Flag,* 185–86.

247 *solved any awkwardness:* Ibid., 187.

247 *willed his black slave:* Zacks, *Pirate Hunter,* 387–88.

247 *His investors included:* Cordingly, *Black Flag,* 181–82.

247 *"I am the innocentest":* Zacks, *Pirate Hunter,* 379.

247 *a new Piracy Act:* Thomson, *Mercenaries,* 50–51.

248 *100 pounds:* Cordingly, *Black Flag,* 195.

248 *More than six hundred:* Botting, *The Pirates,* 143.

248 *"hardly one ship":* Quoted in Ibid., 138.

248 *to clean out the remaining:* Cordingly, *Black Flag,* 152–53.

248 *four navy ships:* The 32-gun *Milford* had been built as the *Scarborough* in Woolwich in 1694, was captured by the French in 1694 off the coast of Ireland, and recaptured in 1696. A 1705 rebuilding made the ship bigger and gave it a new name. Colledge, *Ships of the Royal Navy* (London: Greenhill Books, 2003), 290.

248 *Teach came from Bristol:* Botting, *The Pirates,* 144.

248 *"covered his whole face":* Charles Johnson, *A General History of the Robberies and Murders of the Most Notorious Pirates,* ed. Arthur Hayward (New York: Dodd and Mead, 1926), 57. This account used to be thought the work of Daniel Defoe under a pseudonym, but modern scholars have dispelled this notion.

248 *his private pirate lair:* Botting, *The Pirates,* 148.

248 *still smaller sloop:* The best account is in Johnson, *General History,* and Cordingly, *Black Flag,* 196–98.

249 *a Scottish Highlander:* This according to the *Boston News Letter,* quoted in Ibid., 198.

250 *from fifty in 1718:* Ibid., 203.

250 *normal business practice:* W. A. Cole, "Trends in Eighteenth Century Smuggling," in Walter Minchinton, *The Growth of English Overseas Trade in the Seventeenth and Eighteenth Centuries* (London: Methuen, 1969), 121–43. Cole estimates that only one-fifth of the tea consumed in Georgian England paid any customs duty.

250 *Respectable merchants:* William McClellan, *Smuggling in the American Colonies at the Outbreak of the American Revolution* (New York: Moffat Ward, 1912), 33.

250 *The center:* Lance Grahn, *The Political Economy of Smuggling* (Boulder, Colo.: Westview Press, 1997), 3.

250 *not a single registered:* Ibid., 44.

250 *stopped one of the latter:* Herbert Richmond, *The Navy in the War of 1739–48* (Cambridge: Cambridge University Press, 1920), 3–4.

251 *"as essential to our Safety":* Quoted in Philip Woodfine, *Britannia's Glories: The Walpole Ministry and the 1739 War with Spain* (London: Woodbridge, 1988), 235. I thank Professor N. A. M. Rodger for this reference.

251 *the dual nature:* Richard Harding, "Edward Vernon," in *Precursors of Nelson,* 152–53; Richmond, *Navy in the War* 39–40.

252 *"Destroy their settlements":* Quoted in Douglas Ford, *Admiral Vernon and the Navy* (London: Fisher Unwin, 1907), 124.

252 *"Let who will":* quoted in Richmond, *Navy in the War,* 44.

252 *to see his old mentor:* Harding, *Precursors of Nelson,* 165.

252 *"will be good news"* Quoted in B. Ranft, ed., *The Vernon Papers.* (London: Naval Records of Society, 1958), 5.

252 *the last English captain:* This was the *Santa Cruz,* taken off in a night battle off Cartagena, on May 29, 1707. Harding, *Precursors of Nelson,* 111–13.

252 *"to commit all hostilities":* Richmond, *Navy in the War,* 40.

252 *foresaw a great revolt:* Glyn Williams, *The Prize of All the Oceans* (New York: Penguin, 2001), 10–11; Daniel Bough, "Admiral Sir Charles Wager," in *Precursors,* 121–22.

253 *"Lay aside all thoughts"*: Richmond, *Navy in the War,* 44.

253 *even Spanish authorities:* Ibid., 49.

253 *"the formidable Dragon":* Quoted in Harding, *Precursors of Nelson,* 167.

253 *a half-pint of rum:* The order is quoted in Richmond, *Navy in the War,* 56, *n.* 1.

254 *"the scourge of Spain":* Dictionary of National Biography, vol. 20, 267.

254 *sugar-cake ships:* G. Jordan and N. Rogers, "Admirals as Heroes: Patriotism and Liberty in Hanoverian England," *Journal of British Studies* 28/3 (1989): 205, n. 16.

255 *vetoed an attack:* Williams, *Prize,* 8.

255 *Wager had his doubts:* Harding, *Precursors of Nelson,* 122.

255 *had learned his business:* N. A. M. Rodger, "George, Lord Anson," in *Precursors of Nelson,* 177.

255 *only eight guns:* Colledge, *Ships of the Royal Navy,* 354.

255 *buy property:* Williams, *Prize,* 9.

255 *"The misfortune and vice":* Quoted in Hattendorf, *Spanish Succession,* 142.

255 *largely pensioners:* Williams, *Prize,* 20–21, 22.

256 *Flies from the rotting stores:* Ibid., 30, 33, 36.

256 *a large Spanish squadron:* This was under Admiral Don José Pizzarro; see *Documents Relating to Anson's Voyage Around the World,* ed. G. Williams (London: Naval Records Society, 1967), 48, 53.

256 *starboard chain plates:* Ibid., 77; Howarth, *Sovereign of the Seas,* 217.

256 *onto the Gilstone Rocks:* Rodger, *Precursors of Nelson,* 72.

256 *more than six weeks:* Kenneth Carpenter, *History of Scurvy and Vitamin C* (Cambridge: Cambridge University Press, 1986).

257 *On May 3:* Log, *Centurion,* National Maritime Museum.

257 *"To so wretched a condition":* Williams, *Prize,* 55.

257 *suffered worst:* The full story is in ibid., 76–93.

258 *carried his field artillery:* Ibid., 105.

258 *a nautical legend:* Ibid., 122–23.

258 *They waited three weeks:* Howarth, *Sovereign of the Seas,* 221.

259 *English merchant captain:* Williams, *Prize,* 160–61.

259 *morning of June 20:* Log, *Centurion,* June 20, 1743.

259 *"My lads":* Williams, *Prize,* 174.

259 *at 700 tons:* Ibid., 172.

259 *enough men: Centurion* was supposed to have a 400-man crew; Anson had only 227. *Anson's Voyage,* 188.

259 *"black as a Mulatto":* Williams, *Prize,* 167, 175.

259 *only four of them:* Ibid., 202.

259 *a dismal flop:* Richmond, *Navy in the War,* 134–37; see also Richard Harding, *Amphibious Warfare in the Eighteenth Century: the British Expedition to the West Indies 1740–1742* (London, 1991).

260 *put its admiral:* This was Admiral Thomas Mathews. See chapter 12.

260 *Thirty-three great wagons:* Williams, *Prize,* 206, 217, 218.

261 *named Tobias Meyer:* A good account is in Parry, *Trade and Dominion,* 226–27.

261 *made the Greenwich meridian:* Dara Sobel, *Longitude* (New York: Walker, 1995) 166–67.

261 *the first time:* Williams, *Prize,* 156, 183–85, 209–10.

12. DIVIDE AND CONQUER

263 *more than double:* Padfield, *Maritime Supremacy,* 188.

264 *still the largest:* Richard Harding, *Seapower and Naval Warfare 1650–1830* (Annapolis, Md.: Naval Institute Press, 1999), 14, table 2.1.

264 *"mere poltroons":* Quoted in Woodfine, "Naval Power and the Conflict with Spain," in *Use of Naval Power,* ed. Black and Woodfine, 83.

264 *the Spanish reverted:* Ibid., 70–71.

264 *Horace Walpole remarked:* Letter of April 18, 1742, in *Correspondence,* vol. 17, 390.

265 *"For God's sake":* Quoted in Black and Woodfine, *Naval Power,* 82.

265 *largest navy in the world:* Baugh, *Naval Administration,* 496. In 1740 its total tonnage was 195,000, versus 91,000 for the Dutch navy and 91,000 for the French; Baugh, "National Institution," *Royal Navy,* 123.

265 *growing even faster:* Padfield, *Maritime Supremacy,* 189.

265 *By 1740:* Harding, *Seapower,* 291; appendix, table A.2.

265 *mood plummeted:* Jeremy Black, "Naval Power and British Foreign Policy," in *Use of Naval Power,* ed. Black and Woodfine, 94–95.

266 *"If Norris can get":* Quoted in Woodfine, "Conflict with Spain," *Naval Power,* 86.

266 *Elisabeth was carrying:* David Daiches, *Charles Edward Stuart: The Life & Times of Bonnie Prince Charles* (London: Thomas and Hudson, 1973).

266 *"the greatest example":* Tunstall, *Naval Warfare,* 83.

266 *rushed in alone:* Ibid., 88.

267 *still recovering: Precursors of Nelson,* 181; S. W. C. Pack, *Captain George Anson* (London: Cassell, 1960), 128–29. Pack points out he was at once appointed Rear Admiral of the Blue, backdated to June 1744.

267 *Pepys's memory:* Rodger, *Admiralty,* 65.

267 *"tyranny of custom":* Quoted in J. R. Jones, "Limitations of British Sea Power in the French Wars, 1689–1815," in *Use of Naval Power,* ed. Black and Woodfine, 33.

267 *he told Anson:* Rodger, *Admiralty,* 60.

267 *Navy Board to heel:* Rodger, *Precursors of Nelson,* 189–90.

267 *a uniform tonnage:* Pack, *Captain George Anson,* 141–42.

268 *a basic problem at the top:* Rodger, *Precursors of Nelson,* 186.

268 *persisted until 1806:* Lloyd, *Nation and the Navy,* 59.

268 *finding more sailors:* Rodger, *Wooden World,* 113, and 145–82, passim; R. D. Merriman, ed. *Queen Anne's Navy: Documents Concerning the Administration of the Navy of Queen Anne 1702–1714* (London: Naval Record Society, 1956), 170–71.

268 *took over the Royal Marines:* Pack, *Captain George Anson,* 184.

269 *The new articles:* Brian Lavery, ed., *Shipboard Life and Organization 1731–1815* (London: Naval Records Society, 1998).

269 *"The surest means":* Rodger, *Precursors of Nelson,* 173.

269 *The prevailing winds:* Ibid., 182.

270 *pulled together:* Pack, *Captain George Anson,* 156–57, 158.

270 *"having called them all":* Ibid.

270 *he had drawn up:* Harding, "Admiral Vernon," in *Precursors of Nelson,* 166; *The Vernon Papers,* 286, 291.

271 *Hawke's career:* Ruddock McKay, "Edward, Lord Hawke," in *Precursors of Nelson,* 201–4.

271 *But King George:* Ibid., 204.

272 *"so young an officer":* Ibid., 205.

272 *new French 74s:* Tunstall, *Naval Warfare* 98–99.

272 *from a Dutch trading vessel:* Rodger, *Precursors of Nelson,* 207.

272 *"I immediately made":* Ibid.; Pack, *Captain George Anson,* 167–68.

272 *"at pistol shot":* Rodger, *Precursors of Nelson,* 208.

273 *"she called for quarter":* Pack, *Captain George Anson,* 169.

273 *"no ships behaved":* Padfield, *Maritime Supremacy,* 196.

273 *"Commanders, officers"*: Pack, *Captain George Anson,* 171.

273 *took more than forty:* Burns, *West Indies,* 481.

274 *entered the Indian Ocean:* Harding, *Seapower,* 198, 200.

274 *more a truce:* Parry, *Trade and Dominion,* 113.

274 *Dutch were finished:* Jones, "Limitations," 46; Lloyd, *Nation and Navy,* 46.

274 *French were rebuilding:* Padfield, *Maritime Supremacy,* 197.

274 *governor of Madras:* O'Gorman, 181.

275 *"wicked madman"*: This was philosopher David Hume: quoted in J. G. A. Pocock, "Hume and the American Revolution: Thoughts of a Dying North Briton," *Virtue, Commerce, and Liberty* (Cambridge: Cambridge University Press, 1985), 137.

275 *"a self-conceit"*: Jeremy Black, *The Elder Pitt,* (Cambridge: Cambridge University Press, 1992), 113.

275 *"Is this any longer"*: O. A. Sherrard, *Lord Chatham: A War Minister in the Making* (London: Bodley Head, 1952), 69.

275 *"All the maxims"*: In Jonathan Swift, *Political Tracts 1711–1713,* ed. Herbert Davis (Oxford, England: Blackwell, 1951), 22.

276 *"the vastness"*: Greene, "Empire and Identity," in *Oxford History of the British Empire: The Eighteenth Century,* ed, P. J. Marshalle (Oxford: Oxford University Press, 1999), 216.

276 *John Oldmixon:* Ibid.

276 *a deeply militarized:* Guy Chaussinand-Nogaret, *The French Nobility in the Eighteenth Century* (Cambridge: Cambridge University Press, 1985), 46–50.

277 *"Kingdoms are not conquered"*: Quoted in A. N. Wilson, *French Foreign Policy During the Administration of Cardinal Fleury* (Cambridge, Mass.: Harvard University Press, 1936), 333; Parry, *Trade and Dominion,* 118.

277 *By 1756:* Harding, *Seapower,* 204–5.

277 *What set it off:* Parry, *Trade and Dominion,* 115, 116.

278 *dispirited council of war:* Lloyd, *Nation and the Navy,* 99.

278 *"Had I stayed out"*: Quoted in Padfield, *Maritime Supremacy,* 200.

279 *"Distress, infinite distress"*: Black, *The Elder Pitt,* 120.

279 *no strong ally:* Kennedy, *Naval Mastery,* 101.

279 *equal to the entire:* Parry, *Trade and Dominion,* 120.

279 *"Our Colonies"*: Quoted in Padfield, *Maritime Supremacy,* 200.

280 *"Except for one"*: Ibid., 204.

280 *was not blameless:* Rodger, *Precursors of Nelson,* 193–94.

281 *Walpole wrote:* Quoted in Lloyd, *Nation and the Navy,* 100.

281 *Hawke would alter:* Padfield, *Maritime Supremacy,* 201.

281 *new fighting ship:* Brian Lavery, *The Ship of the Line* (Annapolis, Md.: Naval Institute Press, 1983), vol. 1, 96–97.

281 *"the greatest breakthrough"*: Ibid., 97.

282 *Thanks to George Pocock's:* Parry, *Trade and Dominion,* 165.

282 *joint army-navy siege:* Padfield, *Maritime Supremacy,* 202.

282 *thought impossible:* Richard Hough, *Captain James Cook,* 24–25; Parry, *Trade and Dominion,* 122.

283 *only to meet:* Tunstall, *Naval Warfare,* 113–14.

283 *"Our bells are threadbare"*: Letter to George Montagu, October 21, 1759 in W. S. Lewis ed. *Horace Walpole's Correspondence* (New Haven: Yale University Press, 1941), vol. 1, 250–51.

283 *actually increased:* Kennedy, *Naval Mastery,* 105.

283 *"No trade left"*: Quoted in Walter L. Dorn, *Competition for Empire 1740–1763* (New York: Harper, 1940).

284 *no staying power:* "Sources of funds ebbed and flowed according to public confidence." See James Pritchard, *Louis XV's Navy 1748–1762: A Study in Organization and Administration* (Montreal: McGill, 1987), 206–7, 208.

284 *"The moment we lose":* Some Remarks on the Late Conduct of the Fleet in the Mediterranean (London: 1756), 4.

284 *last reckless gamble:* Summarized in Padfield, *Maritime Supremacy*, 202–3.

286 *Hawke's system of close blockade:* Geoffrey Marcus, *Quiberon Bay* (London: Hollis and Carter, 1960), 40.

286 *brought overland:* Padfield, *Maritime Supremacy*, 204.

286 *"perfect and unparalleled":* Mackay, *Precursors of Nelson*, 214.

287 *"fought for glory":* "Je combattrai avec toute la gloire possible." Quoted in Padfield, *Maritime Supremacy*, Padfield, 206.

287 *"At first the wind":* R. R. Lawrence, ed., *Mammoth Book of Naval Battles* (London: Robinson, 2003), 141.

287 *"Monsieur Conflans":* Ibid., 142.

288 *ran up his white flag:* McKay, *Hawke*, 245.

288 *"At half-past":* R. R. Lawrence, ed., *Mammoth Book of Naval Battles*, 142.

288 *"like a cullender":* Marcus, *Quiberon Bay*, 152.

288 *Hawke spotted:* Mackay, *Precursors of Nelson*, 219.

289 *A similar disaster:* Padfield, *Maritime Supremacy*, 210–11.

289 *"At about four o'clock":* Lawrence, ed., *Naval Battles*, 142.

289 *"The confusion was awful":* Padfield, *Maritime Supremacy*, 209.

289 *"I made the signal":* Lawrence, ed., *Naval Battles*, 142.

290 *desperately throwing:* Padfield, *Maritime Supremacy*, 211.

290 *lost his flagship:* Marcus, *Quiberon Bay*, 160.

290 *"When I consider":* Lawrence, ed., *Naval Battles*, 147.

291 *In the navy:* Lloyd, *Nation and the Navy*, 107.

291 *"There is an extraordinary":* Quoted in Rohan Butler, *Choiseul Volume I: Father and Son 1719–1754* (Oxford, England: Clarendon, 1980), 246.

291 *"it gave me great pleasure":* Mackay, *Precursors of Nelson*, 195.

292 *a unique honor:* Rodger, *Admiralty*, 59.

292 *"To his wisdom":* Pack, *Captain George Anson*, 253.

13. CLOSE ENCOUNTERS

293 *age of eight:* Richard Hough, *Captain James Cook* (London: Hodder and Stoughton, 1994), 3.

293 *The old story:* It first appears in G. Young's *Captain Cook*, published in the 1830s.

294 *million tons a year:* Hough, *James Cook*, 7.

294 *skilled coasters:* Parry, *Trade and Dominion*, 247.

294 *work on a naval vessel:* Rodger, *Wooden World*, 116, 154. The usual ratio of men to tonnage on a line of battleship was three to one; merchantmen in European were often ten to twenty to one.

294 *largely competitive:* Ibid., 137.

294 *fifteen guineas:* Williams, *Prize of All the Oceans*, 208.

295 *girls of Gosport:* Rodger, *Wooden World*, 136.

295 *needed 85,000:* Ibid., 149.

295 *Entire categories:* Ibid., 177.

296 *the Tasker:* Ibid., 176.

296 *"I do not believe":* Hough, *James Cook*, 13.

296 *"can make himself"*: Brian Lavery, *Nelson's Navy: The Ships, Men, and Organization 1793–1815* (Annapolis, Md.: Naval Institute Press, 1989), 129.

297 *fourteen inches*: Ibid., 207.

297 *part of life*: "A line of battleship might have on board fifty or more boys aged from six to eighteen." Rodger, *Wooden World*, 68.

297 *system of divisions*: Ibid., 216–17.

297 *"the confidence and affection"* Quoted in ibid., 120.

297 *gave him lessons*: Hough, *James Cook*, 15, 22.

298 *only from a Spanish snow*: Ship's log, HMS *Eagle*, May 29, 1756.

298 *forty-five minutes*: Ibid., May 30, 1757.

298 *army officer*: This was Lieutenant Samuel Holland. Hough, *James Cook*, 22.

298 *last unknown ocean*: Parry, *Trade and Dominion*, 237–38.

299 *also lay claim*: "You are also with the Consent of the Natives to take possession of Convenient Situations in the Country in the Name of the King of Great Britain; or if you find the Country uninhabited take Possession for His Majesty." Additional Instructions for Lt. James Cook, July 30, 1768, in A. Grenfell Price, ed. *The Explorations of Captain James Cook in the Pacific as Told by Selections of His Own Journals 1768–1779* (New York: Dover, 1971), 19.

299 *found Pitcairn Island*: Oliver Allen, *The Pacific Navigators* (Alexandria, Va.: Time-Life Books, 1980), 79–80.

299 *inspired by Anson's voyage*: Ibid., 82.

300 *"goddess's celestial form"*: Ibid., 87.

300 *"born essentially good"* Philibert Commerson, quoted in ibid.

300 *vital contribution to the science of navigation*: Peter Aughton, *Endeavour: The Story of Captain Cook's First Great Epic Voyage* (London: Orion Books, 1999), 3.

300 *enthusiastic believer*: Parry, *Trade and Dominion*, 242.

300 *"would rather cut off his right hand"*: Hough, *James Cook*, 45.

300 *"First Lieutenant Cook"*: Hawke to Cook, May 25, 1768, quoted in ibid., 47.

300 *paper on solar eclipses*: Aughton, *Endeavor*, 5.

300 *106 feet long*: Allen, *Pacific Navigators*, 109–10.

301 *twenty-two men die of it*: Hough, *James Cook*, 19.

301 *latest instruments*: Derek Howse, "The Principal Scientific Instruments Taken on Captain Cook's Voyages of Exploration, 1768–80," *Mariners' Mirror* 65:2 (1979): 119–35.

301 *helm indicator*: Lavery, *Arming and Fitting*, 27.

301 *modern hydrographers*: Parry, *Trade and Dominion*, 249.

302 *where to put them*: Alan Villiers, *Captain James Cook* (New York: Scribner, 1967), 90–91.

302 *leave their sea chests*: Allen, *Pacific Navigators*, 110.

302 *lion's share of the credit*: Hough, *James Cook*, 213–14.

302 *a turning point*: Gannath Obeyesekere, *The Apotheosis of Captain Cook* (Princeton, N.J.: Princeton University Press, 1992), 5.

302 *"He was never afraid"*: Price, ed., *Explorations*, 289.

302 *flies flew so thick*: Hough, *James Cook*, 124.

303 *tried to have sex*: Ibid., 121–22.

303 *"every kind of Civility"*: Price, ed., *Explorations*, 19.

303 *navy seamen*: Obeyesekere, *Apotheosis*, 30.

303 *"What a pity"*: Quoted in Hough, *James Cook*, 114.

303[n] *enterprising thief*: Ibid., 128.

303 *"We introduce among them"*: Quoted in Howarth, *Sovereign of the Seas*, 250.

303 *under secret orders:* Parry, *Trade and Dominion*, 248–49.

304 *many of his officers:* Hough, *James Cook*, 157.

304 *no European:* Padfield, *Maritime Supremacy*, 233.

304 *only four cases:* Allen, *Pacific Navigators*, 131–2.

304 *an exact model:* Dava Sobel, *Longitude* (New York: Walker, 1995), 145, 150.

305 *the lowest latitude:* Hough, *James Cook*, 287.

305 *"Thus fell":* Price, ed. *Explorations*, 268.

305 *"His paternal courage":* Ibid., 287.

306 *wealthiest per capita:* Niall Ferguson, *Empire*, (New York: Basic Books, 2002), 89.

306 *Every year:* Mark Kurlansky, *Cod: A Biography of the Fish That Changed the World* (Harmonsworth, England: Penguin, 1997), 82–86, 94–95.

306 *rum trade:* Angus Calder, *Revolutionary Empire*, 646; Oliver Dickerson, *The Navigation Acts and the American Revolution* (Philadelphia: University of Pennsylvania Press, 1951), 294, 296.

306 *tea trade:* Peter Thomas, *Tea Party to Independence: The Third Phase of the American Revolution 1773–1776* (Oxford: Clarendon Press, 1991), 14.

306 *two hundred dollars:* N. Stout, *The Royal Navy in America 1760–1775* (Annapolis, Md.: Naval Institute Press, 1973), 17.

307 *Grenville decided:* Ibid., 27.

307 *elaborate new regulations:* Edmund and Helen S. Morgan, *The Stamp Act Crisis: Prologue to Revolution* (1953; New York: Collier Books, 1962), 39–40; Stout, *Royal Navy*, 27.

307 *"well-known mobbish Disposition":* Stout, *Royal Navy*, 28, 41.

307 *"has caused a greater alarm":* Morgan, *Stamp Act*, 43.

307 *Philadelphia merchant:* Quoted in Stout, *Royal Navy*, 88–89.

308 *navy schooner:* Morgan, *Stamp Act*, 63–64.

308 *"set people a thinking":* Ibid., 52–53.

308 *Grenville may have:* Ibid., 76–78.

309 *a smugglers' lobby:* Calder, *Revolutionary Empire*, 646; Morgan, *Stamp Act*, 167–69.

309 *morale in the North American squadron:* Stout, *Royal Navy*, 126.

309 *wealthiest man in America:* William Fowler, *The Baron of Beacon Hill: A Biography of John Hancock* (Boston: Houghton Mifflin, 1980), 48–49; Calder, *Revolutionary Empire*, 648.

309 *his brig Lydia:* Oliver Dickerson, *The Navigation Acts and the American Revolution* (Philadelphia: University of Pennsylvania Press, 1951), 232–33, 234–35.

309 *It arrived on October 1:* Stout, *Royal Navy*, 122–23; Fowler, *Baron of Beacon Hill*, 95–96.

310 *"There seems to be":* *The Works of John Adams* (Boston: Little, Brown, 1865), vol. 3, 460, 464.

310 *the navy sloop:* W. E. May, "The *Gaspée* Affair," MM 63:2 (1977): 129–35.

310 *smuggler friends were fearful:* Thomas, *Tea Party*, 14.

311 *one-third of a ton:* Piers Macksey, *The War for America 1775–1783* (Cambridge, Mass.: Harvard University Press, 1965), 66.

311 *12.5 percent:* Brewer, *Sinews of Power*, 41.

311 *In 1777 alone:* David Syrett, "The Failure of the British Effort in America, 1777," in *Use of Naval Power*, ed. Black and Woodfine, 185.

311 *Even the uniform:* S. E. Morison, *John Paul Jones: A Sailor's Biography* (Boston: Little, Brown, 1959), 71–72.

312 *revanchist zeal:* Padfield, *Maritime Supremacy*, 230.

312 *"a restless and greedy nation":* Quoted in ibid., 239.

312 *Since 1763:* Nicholas Tracy, *Navies, Deterrence, and American Independence: Britain and Seapower in the 1760s and 1770s* (Vancouver: University of British Columbia, 1988), 12.

312 *the French Toulon squadron:* Padfield, *Maritime Supremacy*, 255.

312 *another thirty-one:* Glete, *Navies and Nations,* vol. 2, 640–41.

313 *"with trembling":* Padfield, *Maritime Supremacy,* 246–47, 249.

313 *"It will be asked why":* Daniel Bough, "Why Did Britain Lose Command of the Sea During the War for America?" in *Use of Naval Power,* ed. Black and Woodfine, 149, 159–60.

313 *"Capacity is so little":* Quoted in Rodger, *Wooden World,* 31.

314 *a linguist and art connoisseur:* Rodger, *The Admiralty,* 73–74.

314[n.] *invented the meal:* N. A. M. Rodger, *The Insatiable Earl: A Life of John Montagu, Fourth Earl of Sandwich 1718–1792* (London: HarperCollins, 1993), 79.

314 *Carron Iron Works:* Padfield, *Maritime Supremacy,* 250.

314 *The hulls of wooden:* Lavery, *Arming and Fitting,* 56–61.

315 *the sloop* Hawke: Rodger, *Insatiable Earl,* 295–96.

315 *1,500 pounds sterling:* Lavery, *Arming and Fitting,* 62–63. In this decision, as with the carronade, it was Sir Charles Middleton of the Navy Board who deserves the credit for proposing and then persuading Sandwich to adopt the policy in question. But it was Sandwich who made the final decision and faced the consequences if either had failed.

315 *a third less:* Rodger, *Insatiable Earl,* 296.

315 *"Yesterday the British fleet":* G. R. Barnes and J. H. Owen, ed. *The Private Papers of John, Earl of Sandwich, First Lord of the Admiralty 1771–1782* (London: Navy Records Society, 1932–8), vol 4, 189.

316 *age twenty-three:* This was at Spithead, on March 31, 1745: Kenneth Breen, "George Bridges, Lord Rodney, 1718?–1792," in P. Le Fevre and R. Harding, ed. *Precursors of Nelson* (London: Chatham Publishing, 2000), 228.

316 *stole from captured prizes:* Rodger, *Wooden World,* 325.

316 *seventeen years:* David Spinney, *Rodney* (Annapolis: Naval Institute Press, 1969), 302.

316 *reliable flag captain:* This was Walter Young, ibid., 297.

316 *specifically warned him:* Insatiable Earl, 287.

316 *new battle signal:* Spinney, Rodney 306–7.

317 *"When the British fleet":* Quoted in Padfield, *Maritime Supremacy,* 252.

317 *thirty-six ships of the line:* Spinney, Rodney 392.

317 *new flintlock firing system:* designed by Sir Charles Douglas, Rodney's captain of the fleet; Padfield, *Maritime Supremacy,* 274.

317 *sudden subtle wind shift:* D. MacIntyre, *Admiral Rodney* (London: P. Davis, 1962), 231–32.

318 *"one peal of thunder":* Quoted in Padfield, *Maritime Supremacy,* 276.

318 *The* Marlborough: MacIntyre, *Admiral Rodney,* 234.

318 *"That nation":* Quoted in Padfield, *Rodney,* 277.

319 *captured French frigate:* Richard Hough, *Captain Bligh and Mister Christian* (1972; London: Chatham Publishing, 2000), 58.

320 *Even James Cook did it:* Hough, *Captain James Cook,* 57.

320 *"a fatal turn":* Explorations, 267.

320 *"a most infamous lie":* Hough, *Captain Bligh,* 51.

320 *"I can only assure you":* Caroline Alexander, *The Bounty* (New York: Viking Press, 2003), 43.

320 *cheaper food staple:* Ibid., 327. For a different view of the global aspects of this arrangement, see Greg Dening, *Mr Bligh's Bad Language* (Cambridge: Cambridge University Press, 1992), 12–13.

321 *remarkably good:* Wooden World, 82–86.

321 *careful research:* Ibid., 80–81.

322 *probably 80 percent:* Ibid., 78.

325 *Lieutenant Ralph Dundas:* Ibid., 209; 225.

323 *"all in good order":* Hough, *Captain Bligh,* 78.

324 *Fryer's instigation:* Dening, *Mr Bligh's Bad Language,* 22.

324 *"It adds much":* Quoted in S. McKinney, *Bligh: A True Account of Mutiny Aboard His Majesty's Ship Bounty* (Camden: International Marine Publishing Co., 1989), 28.

325 *seven years old:* Hough, 112.

325 *"such neglectful":* Hough, 122.

325 *"You are all a parcel":* Ibid., 140; 142–43.

326 *"What is the meaning":* Hough, 21–22.

327 *"I am in hell":* Alexander, *The Bounty,* 141.

327 *thirty men:* Hough, *Captain Bligh,* 158–60.

327 *"I felt an inward happiness":* Ibid., 163.

327 *"What an emotion":* S. McKinney, *Bligh,* 123.

327 *first English colony:* Ibid., 132.

328 *two of Pandora's midshipmen:* Ibid., 152.

329 *only three:* These were Tom Ellison, who had been only sixteen when he joined the mutineers; John Millward, and Tom Burkett. Hough, *Captain Bligh,* 282.

329 *case that eerily parallels:* Alexander, *The Bounty,* 384–85.

14. THE ELEPHANT AND THE WHALE

330 *Two men:* Malcolm Cook, *Toulon in War and Revolution* (Manchester, England: Manchester University Press, 1991), 140–41.

331 *he was predicting:* G. J. Marcus, *The Age of Nelson* (London: George Allen Unwin, 1971), 16.

331 *"dreadful outrage":* February 1, 1793, in W. Pitt, *Orations on the French War* (London: Dent, n.d.), 1.

331 *after French revolutionary troops:* Ibid., 13–14.

332 *Pitt himself was born:* on May 28, 1759, the year Wolfe and Saunders took Quebec.

332 *"threatened to overwhelm":* Pitt, *Orations,* 53.

332 *"not a contest":* Ibid., 37.

332 *"Although we might one day":* Joseph Callo, ed., *Nelson Speaks* (London: Chatham, 2001), 64.

333 *Pitt would bring forward:* Fletcher Pratt, *Empire and the Sea* (New York: Henry Holt, 1946), 285.

333 *The revolution had shattered:* Cormack, *Revolution and Political Conflict in the French Navy 1789–1794* (Cambridge: Cambridge University Press, 1995).

333 *offered captaincies:* Pratt, *Empire,* 12.

333 *watched his subordinates:* Cormack, *Revolution,* 185–86.

333 *When one admiral:* This was Admiral Duval of the Brest fleet; Pratt, *Empire,* 43–44.

334 *"I am much mistaken":* Quoted in Nathan Miller, *Broadsides: The Age of Fighting Sail 1775–1815* (New York: John Wiley, 2000), 112.

334 *using the devastating events:* R. R. Palmer, *Twelve Who Ruled* (Princeton, N.J.: Princeton University Press, 1977), 43.

334 *refused to recognize:* Pratt, *Empire,* 18.

334 *grew up in sight:* This was Burnham Thorpe, where his father Edmund Nelson was minister. Tom Pocock, *Horatio Nelson* (London: Bodley Head, 1987), 1–2.

334 *"ninnies":* "The Admiral [Sir Richard Hughes] and all about him are great ninnies," quoted in ibid., 65.

335 *the best sea officer:* Nelson to Fanny Nelson, September 1794, in G. P. B. Naish, ed., *Nelson's Letters to His Wife* (London: Navy Records Society, 1958); Pratt, *Empire,* 90.

335 *a disappointment:* "I may have lost an appointment by being sent off." *Nelson's Letters,* September 7, 1793, 89.

335 *"She is a young woman":* Ibid.

335 *"Shot and shell are very plentiful":* Edgar Vincent, *Nelson: Love and Fame* (New Haven: Yale University Press, 2003), 113.

335 *hoped to enter:* Frank McLynn, *Napoleon: A Biography* (New York: Arcade, 1997), 21, 72–73, 81–82.

336 *saved almost fifteen thousand:* Cormack, *Revolution,* 213–15.

336 *He [Smith] had just arrived:* Pratt, *Empire,* 22–23.

337 *carried out key reforms:* Michael Howard, *War in European History* (Oxford: Oxford University Press, 1977), 76–78.

337 *more than one million men:* Ibid., 80.

337 *"We must exterminate!":* Ibid., 81.

337 *"the laziest man":* Rodger, *Admiralty,* 82.

337 *Britain's army:* David Chandler, ed. *The Oxford Illustrated History of the British Army* (Oxford: Oxford University Press, 1994), 133.

337 *most of whom were dispersed:* Miller, *Broadsides,* 119–20. It was in the West Indies that Vice Admiral Sir John Jervis emerged into prominence, capturing Martinique in February 1794 and then St. Lucia and Guadeloupe in April.

338 *Admiral Hawke:* Quoted in Marcus, *Quiberon Bay,* 178.

338 *"the most silent man I ever knew":* Precursors of Nelson, 280.

338 *He also issued orders:* Pratt, *Empire,* 46.

338 *spotted each other on May 28:* Miller, *Broadsides,* 125.

339 *"I desire you to hold your tongues":* Ibid., 127.

339 *single most dangerous place:* Rodger, *Wooden World,* 245–46.

339 *the French rear admiral:* Marcus, *Quiberon Bay,* 152.

339 *almost thirty:* Rodger, *Wooden World,* 256. Seventeen were killed by enemy fire; fifteen drowned. More than one-third of post captains ended up either dead or in disgrace.

340 *"Black Dick has been smiling":* Marcus, *Age of Nelson,* 28.

340 *tear away enough sail:* Davies, 67; Nicholas Tracy, *Nelson's Battles: The Art of Victory in the Age of Sail* (Annapolis, Md.: Naval Institute Press, 1996), 90–91.

340 *"Go below":* Pratt, *Empire,* 63.

340 *"Look at* Défense!": Quoted in Miller, *Broadsides,* 130.

340 *"I'll be damned":* Ibid., 132.

341 *sank with three hundred:* The legend that they died shouting, "Vive la République!" seems to be largely that, a legend—started, ironically, by an account in a British newspaper.

341 *Rear Admiral Pasley:* See the account in John Cordingly, *Billy Ruffian: The "Bellerophon" and the Downfall of Napoleon* (New York: Bloomsbury, 2003), 81, where Pasley curtly tells two sailors who commiserated with their admiral's loss, "Thank you, but never mind my leg: take care of my leg."

341 *collapsed in the arms:* For Codrington's own account of what happened, see Christopher Lloyd, *Barrow of the Admiralty* (London: Collins, 1970), 176.

341 *saved the republic:* Palmer, *Twelve Who Ruled,* 345–46.

342 *what they were fighting for:* McLynn, *Napoleon,* 110.

342 *For the first time:* J. Hattendorf, "Struggle with France, 1689–1815" in *Oxford Illustrated History of Royal Navy,* 109.

343 *promised his French masters:* Davies, *Fighting Ships,* 79.

343 *Tone also admitted:* Lloyd, *St. Vincent,* 21; Richard Woodman, *The Sea Warriors* (London: Robinson, 2001), 87–91.

343 *"I am utterly astonished":* Lloyd, *St. Vincent,* 23.

344 *could easily have marched:* O'Gorman, *The Long Eighteenth Century,* 320.

344 *passed on to him: Precursors of Nelson,* 221.

344 *"An enemy that commits":* Tracy, *Nelson's Battles,* 10.

345 *first formal salute:* Touching one's hat (or forelock, if bareheaded) was normal custom of social deference. However, Jewis was dissatisfied with its lax performance on shipboard. Hence, the order to remove hats.

345 *introduced lemon juice: Precursors of Nelson,* 332–33.

345 *wanted to promote him:* Pocock, *Nelson,* 126–27.

345 *outnumbering the British:* Kennedy, *Naval Mastery,* 126; Davies, 78.

346 *south-southwest course:* Vincent, *Nelson,* 184–85.

346 *Built at Limehouse:* Lavery, *Ship of the Line.*

346 *as each British ship:* Tracy, *Nelson's Battles,* 54.

347 *he ordered Miller:* Vincent, *Nelson,* 187.

347 *seven Spanish ships:* Pocock, *Nelson* 130.

347 *a shout of "Death or Glory!":* Others claim he said, "Westminster Abbey or Glorious Victory"—a near enough prophecy of his ultimate fate, if true. Ibid.

348 *The Victory gave Nelson:* Padfield, *Maritime Supremacy,* 125–27.

348 *"such a ship as I never saw before":* Lloyd, *St. Vincent,* 78.

348 *remarked sourly:* Pocock, *Nelson,* 132.

348 *own highly dramatic account:* Vincent, *Nelson,* 192.

349 *"The French say": Nelson's Letters,* June 1796.

349 *The Great Strike:* The best account is still James Dugan, *The Great Mutiny* (London: Andre Deutsch, 1966).

349 *The fleet's frigates:* Davies, *Fighting Ships,* 53.

349[n.] *not uncommon:* See Rodger, *Wooden World,* 137–44.

349 *"We are not actuated":* Quoted in Lloyd, *St. Vincent,* 98.

349 *a congratulatory note:* Pocock, 137. Nelson did add this justification: "The particular situation of the service requires extraordinary measures."

350 *received eleven petitions: Precursors of Nelson,* 297–98.

351 *twenty-nine men:* Lloyd, *St. Vincent,* 111–14, 116.

351 *"most melancholy sight":* Quoted in ibid., 115.

352 *fight with distinction:* Davies, *Fighting Ships,* 95.

352 *"If it had not been":* Howarth, *Nelson: The Immortal Memory,* 295.

352 *"The time is not far distant':* McLynn, *Napoleon,* 167.

353 *digging a canal:* Ibid., 168.

353 *Jervis ordered:* Lavery, *Nelson and the Nile: The Naval War Against Bonaparte 1798* (London: Caxton, 1998), 63.

353 *taken opium:* Pocock, *Nelson* 147.

353 *half blind:* Vincent, *Nelson,* 129. Contrary to legend, Nelson never wore an eye patch: the eye, although sightless, remained intact.

354 *"The arrival":* Lavery, *Nelson and the Nile,* 62.

354 *on the seventeenth:* Ibid., 65.

354 *only three frigates:* These were the *Emerald,* commanded by Thomas Waller, the *Terpsichore,* commanded by William Gage, and a captured French ship, the *Bonne Citoyenne.*

354 *from a Genoese brig:* Pocock, *Nelson,* 156.

354 *"The Devil's children":* Quoted in ibid., 158.

354 *Hardy grew impatient:* McLynn, *Napoleon,* 176.

356 *"difficulties and dangers":* Excerpted from his *Sketches of My Life,* for John MacArthur's biography in 1799.

356 *"I was sure":* Howarth, *Immortal Memory,* 281.

357 *"The utmost joy":* Lavery, *Nelson and the Nile,* 168–69.

357 *jockeying:* Ibid., 170; Pocock, *Nelson,* 162.

357 *Foley noticed:* According to one of his midshipmen, Foley also had a French chart of Aboukir, which helped to eliminate the guesswork. Lavery, *Nelson and the Nile,* 171–72.

358 *hailed Samuel Hood:* Pocock, *Nelson,* 163.

358 *"A most grand":* Ibid., 165.

358 *Alexander's sails:* Lavery, *Nelson and the Nile,* 199.

359 *ten had been captured:* Pocock, *Nelson,* 167.

15. VICTORY AT SEA

360 *"He is in many points a really great man":* Quoted in David and Stephen Howarth, *Lord Nelson: The Immortal Memory* (New York: Viking, 1989), 368.

360 *One historian:* Tom Pocock, in *Nelson and His World* (New York: Viking, 1968), 126.

361 *presentation sword and portrait:* Ibid., 168.

361 *agent who collected his prize:* Ibid., 184–85.

361 *played "Rule Britannia":* Lavery, *Nelson and the Nile,* 269.

361 *"History either ancient or modern":* Pocock, *Nelson.*

361 *"like an electric impulse":* Howarth, *Lord Nelson,* 200–201.

361 *new words:* The dance called vanguard; Pocock, *Nelson,* 182–83.

362 *"That man":* Quoted in Pocock, *Terror Before Trafalgar* (London: John Murray, 2002), 223.

363 *"He's left us":* McLynn, *Napoleon* 198.

363 *He installed his frigates:* Tom Pocock, *Thirst for Glory: The Life of Admiral Sir Sidney Smith* (London: Aurum Press, 1996), 121.

363 *dispatch rider:* Howarth, *Lord Nelson,* 201.

363 *one of his prize vases:* The nephew was Charles Greville. Pocock, *Nelson,* 175.

364 *first man ashore:* Pocock, *Thirst for Glory,* 137–38. Captain (later Admiral) Cochrane was the uncle of an even more famous Cochrane, Thomas, Lord Dundonald. See chapter 16.

364 *his wound had affected his judgment:* Tracy *Nelson's Battles,* 123.

364 *lengthy lawsuit:* Edgar Vincent, *F. Nelson: Love & Fame* (New Haven: Yale University Press, 2003), 381, 405–6, 438. St. Vincent won the case.

364 *"more like a prince":* This was Sir John Moore, later defender of Corunna. Ibid., 369.

364 *Nelson's active encouragement:* Pocock, *Nelson,* 180.

365 *"turned pale":* Ibid., 205.

365 *a brusque dispatch:* Ibid., 212.

365 *the island of Malta:* Howarth, *Lord Nelson,* 244–45; Vincent, *Nelson,* 391.

366 *provoked Holland:* Padfield, *Maritime Supremacy,* 256.

366 *"The more numerous, the better":* Vincent, *Nelson,* 416.

366 *he wrote confidently to Emma:* Quoted in Howarth, *Lord Nelson,* 247.

367 *in eighty-five years:* Davies, *Fighting Ships,* 120.

367 *"Here was no maneuvering":* Quoted in Tracy, *Nelson's Battles,* 147.

367 *raised the signal:* There is, admittedly, still great controversy over why Parker did what he did, but none about Nelson's response. See Davies, *Fighting Ship,* 127–28; also Tracy, *Nelson's Battles,* 147–48.

367 *drafted a message:* Pocock, *Nelson,* 237.

367 *Nelson at his best:* Howarth, *Lord Nelson,* 262–63.

368 *"until the whole flotilla":* Pocock, *Nelson,* 248–50; see also T. Pocock, *The Terror Before Trafalgar,* 15–19.

368 *"It is not given":* Quoted in Howarth, *Horatio Nelson,* 264.

368 *"My heart is almost broke":* Pocock, *Nelson,* 255, 257.

368 *Pitt had resigned:* O'Gorman, *Long Eighteenth Century,* 236.

369 *numbered 729 vessels:* R. A. Morriss, *The Royal Dockyard during the Revolutionary and Napoleonic Wars* (Leicester: Leicester University Press, 1983), 12.

369 *"rotten to the core":* Rodger, *Admiralty.*

369 *did end some:* For a more measured judgment of St. Vincent's efforts, see Morriss, *Dockyard,* 194–96, 198.

370 *Bentham introduced steam:* Ibid., and Morriss's article in Bulletin of the Institute of Historical Research, "Samuel Bentham and the Management of the Royal Dockyards" (1981) 226–40.

370 *300,000 plates:* Morriss, "Management," 234.

370 *collective decision making:* Ibid., 239.

370 *"How can Ministers":* Pocock, *Nelson,* 267.

371 *repulsed the Duke of Wellington:* Howarth, *Lord Nelson,* 369–70.

371 *"How I hate":* Pocock, *Nelson,* 247.

371 *Napoleon believed in destiny:* McLynn, *Napoleon,* 289–91.

371 *"The Channel is a ditch":* Pocock, *Terror,* 90.

372 *northeast coast:* Ibid., 91.

372 *"I have just read":* Georges Blond, *La Grande Armée,* trans. Marshall May (London: Cassall, 1995), 30–31.

372 *a full accounting:* Ibid., 13.

373 *for both his mentor:* Tracy, *Nelson's Battles,* 40–43.

373 *crew of eight hundred:* R. H. Mackenzie, *The Trafalgar Roll* (Annapolis, Md.: Naval Institute Press, 1989).

373 *The old system:* Tracy, *Nelson's Battles,* 49–51.

375 *"by whatever name":* Quoted in M. Nash's introduction to J. Callo, ed., *Nelson Speaks* (London: Chatham, 2001), xv.

375 *renounced his noble origins:* Howarth, *Trafalgar,* 83–85.

375 *guess Nelson's strategy:* John Keegan, *The Price of Admiralty* (New York: Penguin, 1988), 61.

376 *transatlantic shell game:* The best summary of Napoleon's original plan is in ibid., 19–20; for its 1805 modification, see Howarth, *Trafalgar,* 49.

376 *"One of the two operations":* Alan Schom, *Trafalgar: Countdown to Battle 1803–1805* (New York: Atheneum, 1990), 175.

377 *seventeen lieutenants:* Keegan, *Price of Admiralty,* 36.

377 *"a set of human machinery":* This was Samuel Leech, in *A Voice from the Main Deck,* published in 1844, and quoted in Ibid., 39.

377 *On the eleventh:* Schom, *Countdown,* 184.

377 *at the Maddalena Islands:* Pocock, *Terror,* 167.

377 *"What is to be done":* Keegan, *Price of Admiralty,* 21.

378 *"A hundred or two":* Rodger, *Wooden World,* 250.

378 *choke with fury:* "I choked with indignation when I read he had not taken the Diamond Rock." Quoted in Pocock, *Terror,* 168.

378 *a fleet of forty French:* Davies, *Fighting Ships,* 149–50.

378 *"Let us be masters":* Pocock, *Terror,* 145.

378 *Nelson's next blunder:* Keegan, *Price of Admiralty,* 21.

378 *"If this account be true":* Vincent, *Nelson,* 541.

379 *"I am late"*: Quoted in Pocock, *Nelson*, 303.

379 *on June 8*: Alfred T. Mahan, *The Life of Nelson* (Boston: Little, Brown, 1897), vol 2, 301.

379 *"What a race"*: Ibid., 300.

379 *French-built brig* Curieux: Ibid., 312.

380 *First Lord Barham's turn*: Keegan, *Price of Admiralty*, 25.

380 *hot steamy haze*: Schom, *Countdown*, 230–35.

380 *"the greatest alarm"*: Quoted in Mahan, *Life of Nelson*, vol. 2, 307.

380 *"Very miserable"*: Ibid., 310.

381 *"I am about to sail"*: Keegan, *Price of Admiralty*, 27.

381 *he was surprised*: Howarth, *Trafalgar*, 53, 60.

381 *"I hope you have arrived"*: Blond, *Grande Armée*, 39–40.

381 *his 8,486-mile odyssey*: As calculated by Julian S. Corbett, *The Campaign of Trafalgar* (London: 1919), vol. 1, 170–71, 204–5.

382 *captain Richard Keats*: Dudley Pope, *Decision at Trafalgar*, 113–14.

382 *Before dawn*: Pocock, *Nelson*, 313.

382 *"Lady Hamilton was in tears"*: Ibid., 314.

383 *people kneeling*: Dudley Pope, *Decision at Trafalgar* (1959; New York: Henry Holt, 1999), 126.

383 *"May the great God"*: Oliver Warner, ed., *Nelson's Last Diary* (Kent, Ohio: Kent University Press, 1971), 23.

383 *watched a sailor*: Pocock, *Terror*, 189.

383 *"Lord Nelson is arrived"*: Howarth, *Trafalgar*, 69.

383 *only eight captains*: Tunstall, *Naval Warfare*, 248.

384 *"When I came to explain"*: Pocock, *Nelson*, 318.

384 *point of nervous collapse*: "I cannot pull out of this deep depression into which I have fallen," he confessed to a friend in August. Quoted in Schom, *Countdown*, 241.

384 *"the captains have no heart"*: Dispatch of General Lauriston, quoted in Keegan, *Price of Admiralty*, 32.

384 *threw his telescope*: Howarth, *Trafalgar*, 89.

384 *he must have been tipped off*: He had, in fact, a manuscript signal book captured from the schooner *Redbridge* in 1804. Tracy, *Nelson's Battles*, 181.

385 *"I look forward eagerly"*: Howarth, *Trafalgar*, 93.

385 *never been to sea in their lives*: Keegan, *Price of Admiralty*, 37.

385 *twenty-six flags*: Howarth, *Trafalgar*, 103.

385 *his captain was planning to dine*: Cordingly, *Billy Ruffian*, 183.

385 *"What a beautiful day!"*: Howarth, *Trafalgar*, 104.

385 *"What think you"*: Ibid., 109.

385 *"My dearest beloved Emma"*: N. H. Nicholas, *The Dispatches and Letters of Vice-Admiral Lord Viscount Nelson* (1846; London: Chatham, 1998), vol. 7, letter of October 19, 1805, 132.

386 *At 7:40*: Schom, *Countdown*, 317.

386 *ordered his ships to wear around*: Ibid., 314–15.

386 *"The fleet is doomed"*: Howarth, *Trafalgar*, 135.

386 *"We scrambled into battle"*: Ibid., 130.

386 *"I shall not be satisfied"*: Pope, *Decision at Trafalgar*, 223.

388 *"I will now amuse"*: Howarth, *Trafalgar*, 150–51.

388 *"I can do no more"*: Ibid., 151.

389 *"What would Nelson give"*: Schom, *Countdown*, 338; Howarth, *Trafalgar*, 163.

389 *split a bunch of grapes*: Howarth, *Trafalgar*, 151–53, 166.

389 *Shot cut Nelson's secretary*: Pocock, *Terror*, 204; Schom, *Countdown*, 324.

389 *more than fifty casualties:* Ibid., 325.

390 *The Mars behind:* Keegan, *Price of Admiralty,* 82.

390 *Tonnant's fire hose:* Ibid., 82–83.

390 *had not trusted:* Ibid., 76–77.

390 *men in the mizzenmast:* Schom, *Countdown,* 327, says 1:25; other authorities agree 1:35.

390 *Harvey's Temeraire:* Howarth, *Trafalgar,* 175–77.

391 *killed in the first forty-five minutes:* Cordingly, *Billy Ruffian,* 193–95.

391 *throwing in deadly grenades:* Keegan, *Price of Admiralty,* 84.

391 *"Well, Hardy, how goes":* Howarth, *Trafalgar,* 187.

392 *The ship had lost more than 150 men:* Schom, *Countdown,* 331.

392 *The Intrépide:* Howarth, *Trafalgar,* 201–3.

392 *At 5:35 he struck:* Keegan, *Price of Admiralty,* 88.

392 *"expanding into an enormous globe":* Tracy, *Nelson's Battles,* 199.

393 *it would be eighteen:* Including the *Indomitable,* which ran ashore two days later. Ibid.

393 *"Doctor, I have not been":* Pope, *Decision at Trafalgar,* 320–21.

393 *not more than a mile:* Howarth, *Trafalgar,* 160–61.

393 *almost one in four:* Keegan, *Price of Admiralty,* 96–97.

393 *"It makes us feel":* Howarth, *Horatio Nelson,* 371.

16. SUCCESSION

395[n.] *some would argue [n.]:* Howarth, *Trafalgar,* 239.

395 *"Sir, we have gained":* Pope, *Decision at Trafalgar,* 30.

395 *"The great and gallant":* Howarth, *Lord Nelson,* 356.

395 *"The death of Nelson":* Quoted in ibid., 369.

396 *"I never heard":* Quoted in Audrey Hawkridge, *Jane and Her Gentlemen* (London: Peter Owen, 2000), 81.

396 *the first time anyone:* Ludovic Kennedy, *Nelson's Captains* (New York: W. W. Norton, 1951), 352; Pocock, *Horatio Nelson,* 335.

396 *"I can't do it!":* Howarth, *Immortal Memory,* 356, 357, Pocock, *Horatio Nelson,* 333.

396 *sealed with lead:* Pocock, *Horatio Nelson,* 339.

397 *funeral car itself:* Kennedy, *Nelson's Captains,* 353–54.

397 *"a peerage":* Vincent, *Nelson,* 188.

397 *Cardinal Wolsey:* Pocock, *Horatio Nelson,* 340.

397 *"That was Nelson":* Howarth, *Lord Nelson,* 360.

398 *twelve in the band of brothers:* Pocock, *Horatio Nelson,* 335, 336.

398 *more than fifty streets:* L. Foreman and E. B. Phillips, *Napoleon's Lost Fleet: Bonaparte, Nelson, and the Battle of the Nile* (New York: Roundtable, 1999), 181.

398 *"We are also":* Howarth, *Immortal Memory,* 359.

398 *it was widely:* Howarth, *Sovereign of the Seas: The Story of Britain and the Sea* (New York: Atheneum, 1974), 329.

398 *"He is a terrible":* Howarth, *Lord Nelson,* 370.

399 *thirteen ships:* Miller, *Broadsides,* 307.

399 *"I shall never see":* Kennedy, *Nelson's Captains,* 359.

399 *"You would have really":* Ibid., 364.

399 *"Remember Nelson":* Pocock, *Horatio Nelson,* 342.

400 *descendants of five:* Keegan, *Price of Admiralty,* 127.

400 *Strachan caught up:* Davies, *Fighting Ships* 168, 170, 171–72.

400 *a lesson not lost:* G. J. Marcus, *Age of Nelson* (London: George Allen & Unwin, 1971), 298.

400 *Uncle and nephew were not:* Christopher Lloyd, *Lord Cochrane* (London: Longmans, 1947), 28.

400 *Cochrane used to joke:* Ibid., 12.

401 *single most valuable:* Paul Johnson, *The Birth of the Modern: World Society 1815–1830* (New York: HarperCollins, 1991), 20.

401 *"Well do I recollect":* Lloyd, *Lord Cochrane,* 39, 37.

401 *Yet it was Gambier:* Miller, *Broadsides,* 130, 314–15.

402 *outnumbered the British:* Keegan, *Price of Admiralty,* 105.

402 *"conquer the sea":* Marcus, *Age of Nelson,* 309.

402 *11,000 British merchantment:* Kennedy, *British Naval Mastery,* 131.

402 *the grocers of Europe:* Francois Crouzet, "The Impact of the French Wars on the British Economy," in *Britain and the French Revolution,* ed. H. T. Dickinson (Basingstoke: England; Macmillan, 1989), 192–93.

402 *Convoy Act of 1798:* Patrick Crowhurst, *The Defense of British Trade 1689–1815* (London: Davon, 1977), 71.

402 *whose Lloyd's Register:* J. R. Jones, "Limitations," 42.

403 *Trade boomed:* Crouzet, "Impact," 193.

403 *two pounds per person:* Ralph Davis, *The Industrial Revolution and British Overseas Trade* (Leicester: Leicester University Press, 1979), 46–47. From 14,200 pounds in 1784–86 annual imports jumped to 25,600 pounds in 1804–1806.

403 *Napoleon struck back:* Paul Schroeder, *The Transformation of European Politics 1763–1848* (Oxford: Clarendon Press, 1994), 307–9.

403 *"All the countries":* Marcus, *Age of Nelson,* 310.

404 *nine hundred ships:* Morriss, *Royal Dockyards,* 12.

404 *John Duckworth:* Davies, *Fighting Ships* 172–73.

405 *"I hate the English":* McLynn, *Napoleon,* 377.

405 *When Prussia agreed:* Marcus, *Age of Nelson,* 308. The seven hundred figure comes from McLynn, *Napoleon,* 354.

405 *so many British merchants:* Marcus, *Age of Nelson,* 326.

406 *became ghost towns:* Ibid. 442. The details are in A. D. Harvey, *Collision of Empires: Britain in Three World Wars 1793–1945* (London: Hambledon, 1992), 58–61.

406 *Further inland:* This is the argument in Kennedy, *Naval Mastery,* 161. Crouzet, "Impact," insists on some modification.

406 *"The English say":* Quoted in McLynn, *Napoleon,* 389.

406 *nine battleships:* Ibid., 390.

407 *the last official flota:* Stanley and Barbara Stein, *The Colonial Heritage of Latin America* (New York: Oxford University Press, 1970), 100.

407 *ordered three army corps:* McLynn, *Napoleon,* 390.

407 *force of 9,000 men:* Padfield, *Maritime Power and the Struggle for Freedom* (London: John Murray, 2003), 271.

407 *directly modeled:* They were in fact manufactured in the same foundry, the Carron Iron Works in Scotland. On Shrapnel, see Gordon Corrigan, *Wellington: A Military Life* (London: Hambledon, 2001), 366, n.1.

408 *cost him his army:* Davies, *Fighting Ships,* 180–81.

408 *worked out an arrangement:* Ibid., 177.

408 *"The wanton devastation":* Quoted in Lloyd, *Lord Cochrane,* 45.

408 *dream of liberation:* See Harold Nicholson, *The Congress of Vienna: A Study in Allied Unity: 1812–1822* (New York: Viking, 1946), 22–23.

409 *single largest customer:* Padfield, *Maritime Power,* 291, 294.

409 *six modern frigates*: Ibid., 294.

409 *38-gun sisters*: Robert Gadiner, ed., *The Naval War of 1812* (London: Chatham, 1998), 34.

409 *foresaw the American*: Padfield, *Maritime Power*, 291. Exports dropped from 9.3 million pounds in 1810 to less than two million in 1811.

410 *ready to do a deal*: Ibid., 298–99.

410 *after calling her out*: Ibid. Gardiner, ed. *War of 1812*, 57.

410 *"every housetop"*: Ibid., 61.

411 *impose a blockade*: Padfield, *Maritime Power*, 313.

411 *fell to one-third*: Marcus, *Age of Nelson*, 443.

412 *"Essentially all that is needed"*: Quoted in McLynn, *Napoleon*, 498.

412 *675,000 strong*: According to ibid., 502.

412 *Everything depended*: Padfield, *Maritime Power*, 301–3.

412 *the last French privateers*: Kennedy, *Naval Mastery*, 132,

412 *"If anyone wishes"*: Quoted in Davies, *Fighting Ships*, 181.

413 *130,000 sailors*: Crouzet, "Impact," 195.

413 *more than 10 million pounds*: Kennedy, *Naval Mastery*, 174.

413 *entered Bordeaux*: Corrigan, *Wellington*, 273.

413 *he disappeared completely*: Nicholson, *Congress of Vienna*, 230–31.

414 *a severe head wound*: This was Captain Henry Darby. Cordingly, *Billy Ruffian*, 147.

414 *"What I admire most"*: Ibid., 253.

414 *Political scientists*: The best example is Henry Kissinger, *A World Restored* (New York: Grosset and Dunlop; 1964), but the best corrections are Paul Schroeder, *Transformation of European Politics*, and Harold Nicholson's classic *Congress of Vienna*.

415 *back in 1805*: Summarized in Edward Gulick, *Europe's Classic Balance of Power* (1955; New York: W. W. Norton, 1967), 143–45.

415 *"bring the world back"*: Quoting Castlereagh, in Schroeder, *Transformation*, 52.

415 *pair of Royal Navy brigs*: McLynn, *Napoleon*, 639.

415 *"The establishment"*: Gulick, *Balance of Power*, 204.

415 *No single power*: Nicholson, *Congress of Vienna*, 124.

415 *"The power of Great Britain"*: Quoted in ibid., 258.

416 *modernized this formula*: Schroeder, *Transformation*, 441.

418 *"The peace he has made"*: Quoted in Nicholson, *Congress of Vienna*, 234.

418 *"She was strong enough"*: Ibid., 123.

17. NEW WORLD ORDER

419 *Lieutenant Robert Hagan*: William O'Bryne, *A Naval Biographical Dictionary* (London: John Murray, 1849), 440. Hereafter cited as *NBD*.

419 *made it the godmother*: Niall Ferguson, *Empire* (New York: Basic Books, 2003).

419 *late convert*: Harold Nicholson, *Congress of Vienna*, 210, 213, 214; Paul Johnson, *The Birth of the Modern: World Society 1815–1830* (New York: HarperCollins, 1991), 328. Spain got the same amount as Portugal for suppressing the trade north of the equator, but signed a further treaty in 1817 pledging to abolish to the south by 1820 as well. Neither country seriously intended to carry out the treaty.

420 *"the worst of all crimes"*: Quoted in Christopher Lloyd, *The Navy and the Slave Trade* (London: Longmans, 1949), 89.

420 *Freetown, Sierra Leone's capital*: Johnson, *Birth of the Modern*, 330.

420 *only once*: W. E. F. Ward, *The Royal Navy and the Slavers* (New York: Pantheon, 1969), 25.

421 *seized more than forty*: O'Byrne, *NBD*, 440.

421   *Captain Leeke of the sloop* Myrmidon: Ward, *Slavers,* 65–68.

421   *Thomas Pasley:* Quoted in Peter Padfield, *Rule Britannia: The Victorian and Edwardian Navy* (1981; London: Pimlico, 2002), 114, n. 17.

421   *technical rules:* Ibid. 110–12; Ward, *Slavers,* 138.

422   *Between 1810 and 1849:* Lloyd, *The Navy,* 117.

422   *single illegal voyage:* According to Johnson, *Birth of the Modern,* 327.

422   *"equipment clause":* Ward, *Slavers,* 119–25.

422   *told the British navy:* Padfield, *Rule Britannia,* 113; Ward, *Slavers,* 140, 149. Palmerston made his announcement in May 1841; agreement on an American squadron was reached in 1842.

422   *to bully Brazil:* Ward, *Slavers* 164, 165–66.

423   *Havana:* Ibid., 216; 216–19.

423   *"a British subject":* Hansard, *Parliamentary Debates,* vol. 112 (3rd series), 380–444.

423   *hated tyranny:* A. J. P. Taylor, *Essays in English History* (New York: Penguin, 1982), 106.

424   *ninety-nine ships of the line:* According to Johnson, *Birth of the Modern,* 336, 337.

424   *nearly 50 percent:* Michael Lewis, *The Navy in Transition 1814–1864: A Social History* (London: Hodder and Stoughton, 1965), 69.

424   *nine battleships:* Johnson, *Birth of the Modern,* 338.

424   *242 flag officers:* C. J. Bartlett, *Great Britain and Sea Power 1815–1853* (Oxford: Clarendon Press, 1963), 44; Lewis, *Navy in Transition,* 81.

425   *Some lucky men:* Ibid., 89–90.

425   *patronage had worked:* Ibid., 52–53.

425   *died in 1837:* Kennedy, *Nelson's Captains,* 369–70.

425   *ordered in 1831:* Bartlett, *Sea Power,* 43–44, 46.

426   *Cochrane was put in charge:* Lewis, *Navy in Transition,* 116.

426   *rid of a bloc:* Ibid.

426   *at 85 percent:* Ibid., 118.

427   *commander Thomas Hastings:* Bartlett, *Sea Power,* 41.

428   *too dangerous:* Keegan, *Price of Admiralty,* 109.

428   *demolish the old:* Bartlett, *Sea Power,* 216.

428   *a special commission:* Pocock, *Terror Before Trafalgar.*

428   *"is calculated":* Bartlett, *Sea Power,* 202.

428   *first Chief Engineer:* Ibid., 209.

428   *So in 1840:* Howarth, *Sovereignty,* 318.

428   *screw propeller:* Bartlett, *Sea Power,* 223; J. P. Baxter, *The Introduction of the Ironclad Warship* (1933; New York: Archon Boots, 1968), 11–16, 120.

429   *much higher pay:* B. Greenhill and A. Giffard, *Steam, Politics, and Patronage: The Transformation of the Royal Navy 1815–54* (London: Conway, 1994), 88.

429   *"cuckoo in the nest":* Lewis, *Navy in Transition,* 176.

429   *not until 1880:* Padfield, *Rule Brittannia,* 177.

430   *"not for England alone":* C. Lloyd, *Mr. Barrow of the Admiralty* (London: Collins, 1970), 129.

430   *last Admiralty official:* Ibid., 84.

430   *moldy bundles:* Ibid., 107–9.

430   *first suggested:* Ibid., 90.

431   *received a report:* Ibid., 124, 130–31, 141, 142–46.

433   *experienced chart maker:* Roger Morris, "Endeavour, Discovery, and Idealism, in J. R. Hill, ed., *Oxford Illustrated History of the Royal Navy* (Oxford: Oxford University Press, 1995), 235.

433   *in the 1830s:* Howarth, *Sovereign,* 325.

433 *it was Flinders:* Morris, "Endeavour," 233.

434 *three and a half years:* Ibid., 236–37. See E. H. Burrows, *Captain Owen of the African Survey* (Rotterdam: A. A. Baalkema, 1979).

434 *elected to the Royal Geographical Society:* Johnson, *Birth of the Modern,* 335.

434 *the entire coastline:* Ibid., 334.

434 *unimpressive little ship:* Keith Thomson, *HMS Beagle: The Ship That Changed the Course of History* (London: Phoenix, 1995), 26–27.

435 *"one of the best":* Ibid., 94.

435 *"I believe my friend":* Charles Darwin, *Voyage of the Beagle,* ed. J. Browne and M. Neve (New York: Penguin, 1989), 5; Thomson, *HMS Beagle,* 143.

436 *complained shipboard life:* Lloyd, *Mr. Barrow,* 164.

436 *geology was the principal:* Darwin, *Voyage,* 12.

436 *"I loathe, I abhor":* Ibid., 17.

436 *Lyell's geological theories:* Ibid., 19–20.

437 *published the first two parts:* Thomson, *HMS Beagle,* 205.

437 *Castlereagh's doctor:* Nicholson, *Congress of Vienna,* 270–71.

437 *recoppered one last time:* Thomson, *HMS Beagle,* 264–65.

438 *irrepressible Thomas Cochrane:* Lloyd *Lord Cochrane,* 143–50, 155.

439 *wrote to the United States ambassador:* Johnson, *Birth of the Modern,* 646.

439 *Canning persuaded Portugal:* Bartlett, *Sea Power,* 76.

439 *in Navarino Bay:* Johnson, *Birth of the Modern,* 697–98.

440 *went hand in hand:* Lewis, *Navy in Transition,* 13.

440 *"My blood boils":* Quoted in Johnson, *Birth of the Modern,* 287.

440 *even wrote a book:* Pocock, *Thirst for Glory,* 219–20.

441 *"I much fear":* Quoted in Johnson, *Birth of the Modern,* 347.

441 *Raffles advised Pellew:* NBD, vol. 16, 604–5.

441 *"Our object is not territory":* Quoted in Johnson, *Birth of the Modern,* 348.

442 *By 1862:* John Bowle, *The Imperial Achievement. The Rise and Transformation of the British Empire* (Boston: Little, Brown, 1975), 280–81.

442 *in a private schooner:* Dictionary of National Biography, vol. 2, 1,336–37.

442 *"They are indifferent to blood":* Quoted in Padfield, *Rule Britannia,* 100, 101.

442 *gave him a knighthood:* DNB, vol. 2, 1,337.

443 *"the order of the day":* Quoted in Lloyd, *Nation and Navy,* 228–29.

443 *explosion in the volume:* Johnson, *Birth of the Modern,* 775.

443 *renounced its right:* Kennedy, *Naval Mastery,* 163.

445 *Marx was so incredulous:* Bernard Simmel, *Liberalism and Naval Strategy* (Boston: Allen and Unwin, 1986), 64–65.

445 *"step in the progress":* Quoted in ibid., 58.

445 *now things of the past:* Francis Stark, *The End of Privateering and the Declaration of Paris* (New York: Macmillan, 1897). The Royal Navy, however, continued to pay its officers and crew prize money for enemy ships captured in action through World War II. That privilege was only finally abolished in 1948. But even today, an enemy vessel captured in wartime can legally be dubbed a prize and be auctioned off—although the proceeds go not to the nation but to the officers and crew of the captor. See Donald Petrie, *The Prize Game* (New York: Berkley Books, 1999), 142.

18. THE SUN NEVER SETS

446 *cold wintry day:* Jay Leyda, *The Melville Log: A Documentary Life of Herman Melville* (New York: Harcourt Brace, 1951), 326. This description follows H. M. Tomlinson, *London River* (London: Cassell, 1951), 2, 10.

446 *In a year or two:* The Whale was published first in London in October 1851; it only appeared under the title *Moby Dick* in the United States in November 1851.

447 *two-thirds of world's coal:* Kennedy, *Naval Mastery,* 151, 152.

447 *One out of five:* Peter Mathias, *The First Industrial Nation: An Economic History of Britain 1700–1914,* 2nd ed. (London: Methuen, 1983), 224.

448 *Blue Books:* Johnson, *Birth of the Modern,* 342.

448 *sixty-three ships:* Kennedy, *Naval Mastery,* 171.

448 *John Stuart Mill:* B. Semmel, *Liberalism and Naval Strategy: Ideology, Interest, and Seapower During the Pax Britannica* (Boston: Allen and Unwin, 1986), 61–62.

449 *"You cannot imagine":* Quoted in Padfield, *Rule Britannia,* 107.

449 *precisely one ship of the line:* Andrew Lambert, "The Shield of Empire, 1815–1895," in Hill, ed., *Oxford Illustrated History of the Royal Navy* (Oxford: Oxford University Press, 1993), 171.

449 *compared to the navies:* Robert K. Massie, *Dreadnought* (New York: Random House, 1991), 462.

450 *less than a pound a head:* Kennedy, *Naval Mastery,* 150.

450 *"Happen what will":* Quoted in Rodger, *Admiralty,* 100.

450 *some French officers even hoped:* C. Hamilton, *Anglo-French Naval Rivalry 1840–1870* (Oxford: Clarendon, 1993), 1, 13.

450 *ruined merchant trade:* Mathias, *First Industrial Nation,* 286.

450 *the coming of steam:* Lambert, "Shield of Empire," 163.

451 *it was a naval war:* Ibid., 172–73.

451 *committed suicide:* This was Admiral David Price. Lambert, "Shield of Empire," 179.

452[n.] *also prevented France:* R. Fiennes, *Sea Power and Freedom* (New York: Putnam, 1918), 234.

452 *"It is not in the interest":* Quoted in *Royal Navy,* 211, 212.

453 *14½ knots in open sea:* Ballard, *The Black Fleet,* 53, says 14.3 knots.

453 *without using impressment:* Bartlett, 305–6, 309.

453 *came slowly at first:* For the problems, see ibid., 309–10.

454 *era of meatless:* John Winton, "Life and Education in a Technically Evolving Navy, 1815–1925," in Hill, ed., *Royal Navy,* 259; Howarth, *Sovereign of the Seas,* 297.

454 *ordered four men on the Beagle:* The men had been drunk and broke their leave. Peter Nichols, *Evolution's Captain* (New York: HarperCollins, 2003), 143–44.

454 *"Starting" men:* Eugene Rasor, *Reform in the Royal Navy* (Hamden, Ct.: Archon Books, 1976), 56–57.

454 *a series of disturbances:* Ibid., 64–66.

455 *naval judge advocate:* Ibid., 40, 116.

455 *"The system of manning ships":* Quoted in Colin White, *Victoria's Navy: The End of the Sailing Navy* (Annapolis, Md.: Naval Institute Press, 1981), 74. Another who joined in 1872 wrote twenty years later: "I now have to answer the question whether we should send our boys to the Navy. I say *Yes,* emphatically *Yes*" (p. 79).

455 *number of cases of floggings dropped:* Padfield, *Rule Britannia,* 183.

455 *a pay double:* White, *Sailing Navy* 70.

455 *expected to make his own:* Padfield, *Rule Britannia,* 182.

455 *"great arms and shoulders":* Ibid., 20.

456 *"I once saw":* The Memoirs of Admiral Charles Beresford (Boston: Little, Brown, 1914), vol. 1, 21–22, 25. He adds: "I have seen a man fall off the maintop sail yard and be caught in the bight of the main sheet in the main rigging, and run aloft again. And this was at sea" (p. 26).

456 *fourteen-year-old John Jellicoe:* A. Temple Patterson, *Jellicoe: A Biography* (London: Macmillan, 1969), 17.

457 *the captains who examined him:* Royal Navy, 269. The author of a scathing article published anonymously in *MacMillan's Magazine* in 1878 branded the whole program at Greenwich "a farce."

457 *developed courses:* The torpedo course began in 1872 on the frigate HMS *Vernon;* in 1876 it became an independent command. Winton, "Life and Education," 270.

457 *the Crowley family:* M. Daunton, *Progress and Poverty: An Economic and Social History of Britain 1700–1850* (Oxford: Oxford University Press, 1995), 214.

457 *working in Britain's favor:* Andrew Lambert, *Battleships in Transition: The Creation of the Steam Battlefleet, 1815–1860* (Annapolis, Md.: Naval Institute Press, 1984).

457 *thirty ironclad ships:* Padfield, *Rule Britannia,* 154.

457 *300-pound shells:* Ibid., 155–56.

457 *eight-inch-thick armor:* G. A. Ballard, *The Black Battle Fleet* (Annapolis, Md.: Naval Institute Press, 1980), 63; Winton, "Life and Education," 212–23.

458 *a battle tub:* This is Ballard's term, *Black Battle Fleet,* 63.

458 *Cowper Coles:* Ibid., 88–89, 101.

458 *a power struggle:* Rodger, *Admiralty,* 110–11.

459 *35 tons:* Ballard, *Black Battle Fleet,* 224.

459 *no front-loading gun:* Padfield, *Rule Britannia,* 156.

459 *thickest armor ever:* David Brown, "Wood, Soil, and Cannonballs to Steel, Steam, and Shells, 1815–1895," in Hill, ed., *Royal Navy,* 217.

459 *"Imagine a floating castle":* Padfield, *Rule Britannia,* 164.

459 *the fastest capital ship:* Ballard, *Black Battle Fleet,* 233.

460 *Never more than:* Howarth, *Sovereign,* 322–23.

460 *the Nemesis:* Daniel Headrick, *The Tools of Empire: Technologies and European Imperialism in the Nineteenth Century* (Oxford: Oxford University Press, 1981), 47, 49–50.

460 *A fleet of them:* Ibid., 54.

461 *"In one year":* Howarth, *Sovereign,* 323.

461 *Herbert Brand:* Bernard Semmel, *Jamaican Blood and Victorian Conscience: The Governor Eyre Controversy* (Boston: Houghton Mifflin, 1963).

462 *between 1870 and 1900:* Kennedy, *Naval Mastery,* 181.

462 *"England . . . has left Europe":* J. R. Seeley, *The Expansion of England,* ed. John Gross (Chicago: University of Chicago Press, 1971), 231.

462 *read messages direct from India:* Robert Kubicek, "British Expansion, Empire, and Technological Change," in Andrew Porter, ed., *Oxford History of the British Empire,* (Oxford: Oxford University Press, 1999), vol. 3, 254, 200–201.

463 *they published a series:* Semmel, *Liberalism and Naval Strategy,* 88, 91.

464 *a pet elephant:* Massie, *Dreadnought,* 376.

464 *the most sophisticated design:* White, *Sailing Navy,* 99.

464 *"Our job was":* Vice Admiral Humphrey H. Smith, quoted in Arthur Marder, *The Anatomy of British Sea Power* (New York: Knopf, 1940), 15–16.

465 *Frederick Marryat:* The best biography remains Oliver Warner, *Captain Marryat: A Rediscovery* (London: Constable, 1953), 195.

465 *Captain George Maclean:* W.E.F. Ward, *The Royal Navy and the Slavery* (New York: Pantheon, 1969), 166.

465 *"the bridge of a destroyer":* The quotation is from Ian Fleming, *Doctor No* (New York: Macmillan, 1961), 13.

466 *the original model:* Rodger, *Admiralty,* 112.

466 *"the leisurely, rolling":* Rudyard Kipling, *A Fleet in Being* (London: Macmillan, 1899), 34.

467 *almost 3,000 miles:* Robert Kubicek, "British Expansion," 254, 252.

467 *first great nationalist movement:* P. Knaplund, *The British Empire, 1815–1939* (1941; New York: Fertig, 1969), 417–18.

468 *July 11 began:* W. L. Clowes, *The Royal Navy: A History,* vol. 7 (London: Sampson Low, 1903), 328–29.

468 *"For a long time":* Padfield, *Rule Britannia,* 173.

468 *So at ten o'clock he charged in:* Clowes, *Royal Navy,* 330.

469 *built at Chatham:* Ballard, *Black Battle Fleet,* 204, 211.

469 *for five hours:* Ibid., 212.

469 *experienced mutiny:* R. H. Mackenzie, *The Trafalgar Roll* (Annapolis, Md.: Naval Institute Press, 1989), 48.

469 *a truly British ship:* Pope, *Decision at Trafalgar,* 205.

470 *John Ruskin:* Quoted in *Trafalgar Roll,* 50.

470 *second visit to London:* Herschel Parker, *Herman Melville: A Biography,* vol. 2, 1851–1891 (Baltimore: Johns Hopkins University Press, 2002), 341, 561.

19. EDGE OF BATTLE

471 *detested going to sea:* Barbara Tuchman, *The Proud Tower* (New York: Putnam, 1978), 133.

471 *"the history of sea power":* A. T. Mahan, *The Influence of Sea Power upon History 1660–1783* (Boston: Little, Brown, 1918), 1.

471 *"The principal elements":* Ibid., 88.

472 *"It is sea power":* Quoted in Tuchman, *Proud Tower,* 135.

472 *the battleship* Maine: Actually an older vessel, built in 1890 and weighing less than 7,000 tons. H. and M. Sprout, *The Rise of American Naval Power 1776–1918* (Princeton, N.J.: Princeton University Press, 1967), 189.

472 *before breakfast:* Captain V. Gridley's account of the battle is reprinted in R. R. Lawrence, ed., *The Mammoth Book . . . of Naval Battles* (London: Robinson, 2003), 314.

472 *set up a naval mission:* A. Marder, *Old Friends, New Enemies: The Royal Navy and the Imperial Japanese Navy,* vol. 1 (Oxford: Clarendon, 1981), 3.

473 *trained on HMS* Britannia: Lawrence, *Naval Battles,* 319.

473 *"Wilhelm's one idea":* Quoted in John Keegan, *Price of Admiralty* (New York: Perguin, 1988), 112–13.

473 *"I am just now":* Tuchman, *Proud Tower,* 133.

473 *first German Navy Act:* Gerard Fiennes, *Sea Power and Freedom,* (New York: Putnam, 1918), 259.

474 *series of stories:* Arthur Marder, *The Anatomy of British Sea Pour: A History of British Naval Policy in the Pre-Dreadnought Era* (1940; London: F. Cass, 1964), 121.

474 *ranges of Nelson's navy:* 350 yards represented "point-blank" range for the Napoleonic man-of-war, i.e., the range at which it could reach its target without elevating its muzzle and the easiest to fire at the ship's roll. Nicholas Tracy, *Nelson's Battles,* 43.

474 *exactly ten:* Robert Massie, *Dreadnought,* 399.

474 *"A cry of patriotic anxiety":* Marder, *Anatomy,* 121.

475 *like the discovery of oxygen:* Tuchman, *Proud Tower,* 132, Marder, *Anatomy,* 47.

475 *Latin essay:* Marder, *Anatomy,* 53.

475 *"The oceans":* Quoted in Semmel, *Liberalism and Naval Strategy* 91.

475 *the Navy League sprang up:* Marder, *Anatomy,* 49–50.

476 *using nickel steel:* David Brown, "Wood, Sail, and Cannonballs to Steel, Steam, and Shells, 1815–1895," in Hill, ed, *Royal Navy,* 222–23.

476 *without diminishing:* Padfield, *Rule Britannia,* 196.

476 *"The poor French":* Massie, *Dreadnought,* 256.

476 *who had supplied the data:* Padfield, *Rule Britannia,* 193.

477 *"that unscrupulous half-Asiatic":* Massie, *Dreadnought,* 403, 414.

477 *"He prowled around":* Padfield, *Rule Britannia,* 219.

477 *Everything was about:* Massie, *Dreadnought,* 439, 450.

478 *"the house that Jack built":* Marder, *Anatomy,* 488.

478 *Fisher tried to broaden:* Padfield, *Rule Britannia,* 220, 230.

478 *new emphasis on gunnery:* Marder, *Anatomy,* 386, 422.

479 *steam had trebled:* Keegan, *Price of Admiralty,* 123.

479 *unheard-of ranges:* Marder, *Anatomy,* 521.

479 *"I don't care":* Quoted in Massie, *Dreadnought,* 466.

479 *30 to 80 percent:* Keegan, *Price of Admiralty,* 118.

479 *civilian engineer:* Royal Navy, 284.

479 *while steaming at 14 knots:* Padfield, *Rule Britannia,* 227.

479 *John Philip Holland:* Keegan, *Price of Admiralty,* 253.

479 *the French were trying out:* Nicholas Lambert, *Sir John Fisher's Naval Revolution* (Columbia, S.C.: University of South Carolina Press, 1999), 50.

479 *"underhanded, unfair":* Dreadnought, 452.

480 *"My beloved submarines":* Quoted in Lambert, *Naval Revolution,* 83, 123.

480 *one of the pioneers:* Ibid., 41.

480 *"On the British Navy":* Massie, *Dreadnought,* 450.

480 *"lap them up":* Quoted in Kennedy, *Naval Mastery,* 216, 217.

481 *Mediterranean fleet shrank:* James Goldrick, "The Battleship Fleet: The Test of War, 1895–1919," *Royal Navy,* 287.

481 *divined Germany's intentions:* Marder, *Anatomy* 460, 498.

481 *left them with a choice:* See A. J. P. Taylor, "The Entente to Cordiale," in *From Napoleon to Lenin* (New York: Harper & Row, 1966),

482 *"Germany keeps her whole fleet":* Massie, *Dreadnought,* 500.

482 *"What is the use":* Marder, *Anatomy,* 528.

482 *"The first desideratum":* Padfield, *Rule Britannia,* 224, 222.

482 *"At the present moment":* Marder, *Anatomy* 528.

483 *doing 21 knots:* Massie, *Dreadnought,* 493, 472–73.

483 *"We shall have ten":* Padfield, *Rule Britannia,* 227.

483 *envied the Royal Navy:* Massie, *Dreadnought,* 166, 167.

483 *first German* Dreadnought: Ibid., 611, 616, 617.

485 *60 percent margin:* Goldrick, "Battleship Fleet," 289, 292.

485 *"our dangerous lunatic":* Massie, *Dreadnought,* 520.

485 *"make anyone laugh":* Ibid., 614.

485 *"The whole harbor":* Winston Churchill, *The World Crisis* (London: Library of Imperial History), 119–20.

486 *the* Queen Elizabeth *class:* Royal Navy, 291; Massie, *Dreadnought,* 785.

487 *combined home force:* Padfield, *Rule Britannia,* 222.

487 *write the new charter:* See Patrick Beesley, *Room 40: British Naval Intelligence 1914–18* (New York: Harcourt Brace, 1982).

487 *first naval estimates:* Goldrick, "Battleship Fleet," 292.

488 *"You seem very young":* Massie, *Dreadnought,* 770, 772.

488 *Naval War Staff:* Rodger, *Admiralty,* 127–28.

488 HMS Thunderer: Massie, *Dreadnought,* 786–87.

488 *He still believed:* Ibid., 829, 832.

489 *General von Bernhardi:* Padfield, *The Great Naval Race,* 287, 288.

490 *never more cordial:* Massie, *Dreadnought,* 851–52.

491 FRIENDS TODAY: Padfield, *Naval Race,* 316.

20. ARMAGEDDON—AGAIN

493 *"Our naval power":* Quoted in Peter Padfield, *The Great Naval Race: The Anglo-German Naval Rivalry, 1900–1914* (New York: D. McKay, 1974), 281.

493 *drawn up in 1906:* Simmel, *Liberalism and Naval Strategy,* 141.

493 *"concentrate all":* Quoted in Gerard Fiennes, *Sea Power and Freedom* (New York: Putnam, 1918), 260.

493 *a core battle fleet:* Richard Hough, *The Great War at Sea 1914–1918* (Oxford: Oxford University Press, 1983), 55. Four of the British battle cruisers were with the Grand Fleet, the other five in other stations.

493 *Tirpitz figured:* Keegan, *Price of Admiralty, 113–14.*

494 *humiliation for the Royal Navy:* Barbara Tuchman, *The Guns of August* (1962; New York: Ballantine, 1990), 160–61.

494 *pre-dreadnought design:* His flagship *Scharnhorst* of 11,616 tons and sister ship *Gneisenau* were launched in October 1907 and June 1906, respectively.

495 *range of 5,000 miles:* Keegan, *Price of Admiralty,* 255.

495 *stopped to rescue survivors:* Hough, *Great War,* 62.

495 *"so great a result":* Corbett, *History of the Great War, Naval Operations* (London: 1920–31), vol. 1, 177.

495 *shrunk from 60:* Hough, *Great War,* 63.

495 *"nervous as cats":* William Chalmers, *Life and Letters of David, Earl Beatty,* (London: 1951), 161.

495 *"we should now be":* Hough, *Great War,* 172.

496 *the Admiralty dropped convoys:* James Goldrick, *Royal Navy,* 295. Churchill was one of those who believed cruisers could deal with any anti-merchantmen menace. Paul Kennedy, *The Rise and Fall of British Naval Mastery* (London: Allen Lane, 1976), 253.

496 *only twenty boats:* John Terraine, *The U-Boat Wars, 1916–1945* (New York: Putnam, 1989), 9.

496 *"Sudden—awful":* Quoted in Hough, *Great War,* 173.

496 *five times already:* Ibid., 174–75.

496 *although its own intelligence:* Beesley, *Room 40,* 91–92, 103–4.

497 *destruction of Weddigen's U-12:* This was on March 18, 1915.

497 *right to the end:* The entire story is in Beesley, *Room 40.*

497 *"Thank God":* Rodger, *Admiralty,* 131. Room 40 was also the first department in the Admiralty to employ women.

498 *a classic Pitt-Anson strategy:* Kennedy, *Naval Mastery,* 256–57.

498 *"only a matter of time":* Hough, *Great War,* 153.

498 *the generals did not:* Goldrick, "Battleship Fleet," 303.

498 *"The navy breathes freer":* quoted in Hough, *Great War,* 167.

499 *at Fisher's orders:* Goldrick, "Battlefield Fleet," 301.

499 *Everything he had read:* See V. E. Tarrant, *Jutland: The German Perspective* (London: Cassell, 1995), which shows the Germans assumed the British fleet would precipitate the decisive battle by attacking first: "This could be accepted as certain from all the lesson of English naval history," according to Admiral Scheer, 21.

499 *his own personal property:* Hough, *Great War,* 121–22.

500 *spend a full day:* Keegan, *Price of Admiralty,* 125.

500 *infested with British spy ships:* Hough, *Great War,* 202–3.

500 *the* Invincible: V. E. Tarrant, *Battlecruiser Invincible: The History of the First Battlecruiser, 1909–16* (Annapolis, Md.: Naval Institute Press, 1986), 16.

501 *10-inch side:* Ibid., 20.

501 *unprecedented range:* Keegan, *Price of Admiralty,* 132; Hough, *Great War,* 133–34.

501 *"great glowing mass of fire":* Filson Young, *With the Battle Cruisers* (Annapolis, Md.: Naval Institute Press, 1986), 191, 194.

501 *"Armour belt pierced":* Hough, *Great War,* 135.

502 *"In war the first principle":* Keegan, *Price of Admiralty,* 134.

502 *"A modern sea battle":* Young, *Battle Cruisers,* 218.

502 *One man on the Seydlitz:* Keegan, *Price of Admiralty,* 134.

503 *"thousands and thousands":* Young, *Battle Cruisers,* 219.

503 *scout Zeppelins:* Hough, *Great War,* 203.

503 *"What am I to think":* Beesley, *Room 40,* 153–55, 156.

503 *"All around us":* Hough, *Great War,* 220, 221.

504 *an inch thick:* Ibid., 222.

504 *"colossal pall of thick smoke":* Chalmers, *Life and Letters,* 233.

504 *"We never dreamt":* Keegan, *Price of Admiralty,* 158.

505 *one officer on* Derfflinger: Ibid.

505 *by steering toward:* Hough, *Great War,* 227–28.

505 *A 12-inch German shell:* Ibid., 231–32.

505 *"fluttering over the sea":* Lawrence, ed., *Naval Battles,* 365.

505 *"Where was our Grand Fleet?":* Ibid., 373.

506 *As late as six o'clock:* Hough, *Great War,* 234.

506 *"grey ghost-like columns":* Ibid., 240–41.

506 *a great ring of fire:* Scheer, *Germany's High Seas Fleet in the World War* (London: Cassell, 1920), 151–52.

508 *The Barham would fire:* John Campbell, *Jutland: An Analysis of the Fighting* (1986; New York: Lyons Press, 1998), 347, 348.

508 *were defective:* Hough, *Great War,* 276–77.

508 *"The English fleet":* quoted in Keegan, *Price of Admiralty,* 128.

508 *At 6:38 P.M.:* Lawrence, ed., *Naval Battles,* 374.

509 *"the North Sea Battle":* Keegan, *Price of Admiralty,* 176.

509 *narrowly missed the* Iron Duke: Kennedy, *Naval Mastery,* 247.

509 *"It is senseless":* Ibid.

510 *inexorably to tighten:* on the pros and cons of the British blockade, see Kennedy, *Naval Mastery,* 253–55.

510 *in September sank:* John Terraine, *U-Boat Wars,* 766.

510 *"In spite of the danger":* Memorandum of December 22, 1916, quoted in ibid., 15.

510 *more than 3,000 ships:* Hough, *Great War,* 303.

510 *sank 250 ships:* Keegan, *Price of Admiralty,* 256.

511 *"It is impossible":* Hough, *Great War,* 314.

511 *entered Room 40:* Beesley, *Room 40,* 204–5.

511 *his only exclamation:* Ibid., 221.

511 *less than 200 vessels:* A. B. Feuer, *The United States Navy in World War One* (Westport, Ct: Praeger, 1999), 2.

511 *his ship struck a German mine:* Robert W. Love, *History of the United States Navy* (Harrisburg, Pa.: Stackpole, 1992), 484.

512 *"Ships, ships, ships":* Feuer, *United States Navy,* 3.

512 *pioneered the use:* Terraine, *U-Boat Wars,* 27–30. The Allied Submarine Detection Investigation Committee in June 1917 turned to a more advanced technology using sounds beamed in a fan-shaped pattern into the water in front of the ship to detect enemy submarines with a returning echo. This was ASDIC, an acronym the com-

mittee that recommended its use. Used extensively in World War II, ASDIC is the ancestor of sonar.

512 *the first six:* Feuer, *United States Navy,* 17–8.

512 *Admiralty's opposition:* W. S. Sims, *The Victory at Sea* (New York: 1920); Hough, *Great War,* 306–8.

512 *"The thing to do":* Sims, *Victory at Sea,* 110.

513 *On May 10, 1917:* Love, *United States Navy,* 485.

513 *"the central nervous system":* Sims, *Victory at Sea,* 130, 131–33.

513 *After the peak:* Terraine, *U-Boat Wars,* 766.

513 *sinking a ship every two days:* Ibid., 131.

513 *as early as February:* Keegan, *Price of Admiralty,* 259.

514 *British regiments on the left:* James Stokesbury, *Navy and Empire* (New York: Morrow, 1983), 328–29.

514 *Embittered by official neglect:* Hough, *Great War,* 319.

514 *Ninety thousand British officers and sailors:* Ibid., 320–21.

515 *"Our friendship":* Quoted in ibid., 313.

515 *the Japanese:* Kennedy, *Naval Mastery,* 262.

21. INTO THE TWILIGHT

516 *A party of schoolchildren:* Dale van der Tat, *The Grand Scuttle* (London: Hodder and Stoughton, 1982), 171.

516 *marine artist named Gribble:* The (London) *Times,* 23–25 June 1919, in Gregor Dallas, *1918: War and Peace* (New York: Overlook, 2001), 485.

517 *first to scuttle:* Marder, *Dreadnought to Scapa Flow,* (London: Oxford University Press, 1961–70), vol. 5, 280.

517 *One of the schoolchildren:* Vat, *Grand Scuttle,* 171.

517 *"a breach of naval honor":* Marder, *Dreadnought* 283–84.

518 *half of the total effective:* In 1918, Britain more than 781 ships and submarines in commission, including sixty-one battleships and four aircraft carriers. The United States, France, Germany, Japan, and Italy together had 117 cruisers; Britain 120. Geoffrey Till, "Retrenchment, Rethinking, Revival 1919–1939," in Hill, ed., *Oxford Illustrated History of the Royal Navy,* (Oxford: Oxford University Press, 1993), 319. After Scapa Flow, the margin increased even more.

518 *"For a couple of days":* Tat, *Grand Scuttles* 160–61.

518 *Versailles had failed:* This is the underlying theme of Harold Nicholson, *Peacemaking 1919* (New York: Grosset and Dunlap, 1965).

518 *after a U-boat sank:* Ibid., 24.

519 *When the American Congress:* Paul Johnson, *Modern Times* (New York, 1983), 32–34.

519 *More than 37,000:* Till "Retrenchment," 319; Barnett, *Engage the Enemy More Closely: The Royal Navy in the Second World War* (New York: W. W. Norton, 1991), 19–20.

519 *Ten Years' Rule:* It was approved by the cabinet on August 15, 1919; Till, "Rethinking," *Royal Navy,* 319.

519 *Admiralty's warnings:* Barnett, *Engage the Enemy,* 20.

520 *seventy cruisers:* Ibid., 24.

520 *over the strenuous objections:* Barnett, Ibid., 21–23.

520 *"We cannot have":* Quoted in Johnson, *Modern Times,* 174.

520 *naval base at Singapore:* Summarized in Barnett, *Engage the Enemy,* 23. The two excellent books on the subject are W. David McIntyre, *The Rise and Fall of the Singapore Naval Base* (London: Macmillan, 1979) and James Neidpath, *The Singapore Naval Base and the Defense of Britain's Eastern Empire* (Oxford: Clarendon Press, 1981).

521 *drew up a list:* Barnett, *Engage the Enemy,* 27–28.

521 *for the first time:* Rodger, *Admiralty,* 150.

522 *Admiral Togo had told:* A. Marder, *Old Friends, New Enemies: The Royal Navy and the Imperial Japanese Navy* (Oxford: Clarendon Press, 1981), vol. 1, 7.

522 *Only naval ties:* Johnson, *Modern Times,* 188.

522 *under pressure:* Ibid., 174.

522 *Japan's grew:* These were the totals by 1941. Kennedy, *Naval Mastery,* 294.

523 *Sims predicted:* Donald McIntyre, *Aircraft Carrier: The Majestic Weapon* (London: Ballantine, 1968), 25.

523 *made its first flight:* Barnett, *Engage the Enemy,* 10–11.

523 *disastrous bureaucratic decision:* McIntyre, *Aircraft Carrier,* 24–25.

523 *a brilliant flier:* Marder, *Old Friends,* vol. 1 343–44.

524 *an English engineer:* Mitsubishi's top test pilot was also an Englishman. McIntyre, *Aircraft Carrier,* 26–27.

524 *noticed their skill:* Marder, *Old Friends,* 344.

524 *Britain's reaction to his invasion:* Barnett, *Engage the Enemy,* 31–33; Johnson, *Modern Times,* 320–21.

524 *had told his admirals:* James Stokesbury, *Navy and Empire* (New York: Morrow, 1983), 353.

525 *in 1940:* Kennedy, *Naval Mastery,* 294.

525 *wrote* Mein Kampf: See *Mein Kampf* (New York: Reynal and Hitchcock, 1940), 929.

525 *Almost his first act:* John Keegan, *Price of Admiralty* (New York: Penguin, 1988), 261, but see Terraine, *U-Boat Wars,* 169.

525 *"For Germany":* William Manchester, *The Last Lion* (Boston: Little, Brown, 1988), 144–45.

526 *Two back-benchers:* Ibid., 146.

526 *more than 1,888 planes: The Rise and Fall of the German Air Force* (London: Public Record Office and Air Ministry, 1948), 11.

527 *shepherding British ships: Royal Navy,* 331, 334.

527 *obsolete in design:* Barnett, *Engage the Enemy,* 49.

527 *a British invention:* This was in September 1914. Terraine. *U-Boat Wars,* 108–9.

528 *battleship* Royal Oak: Till, "Retrenchment," 350, 351, 359.

528 *Already in June:* Terraine, *U-Boat Wars,* 767.

528 *"Upon this battle":* Manchester, *Last Lion,* 685–86.

529 *one's father:* This was Andrew Cunningham. Max Horton was the first Jewish admiral in the history of the Royal Navy.

529 *Bruce Fraser began:* Martin Stephen, *The Fighting Admirals: British Admirals of the Second World War* (Annapolis: Md.: Naval Institute Press, 1991), 180.

529 *Max Horton liked:* Ibid., 197.

529 *later be criticized:* S. W. Roskill, *Churchill and the Admirals* (New York: Collins, 1977).

529 *As vice admiral in charge:* Stephen, *Fighting Admirals,* 44–45.

529 *daring destroyer charge:* Barnett, *Engage the Enemy,* 116.

530 *Ramsay took on:* Stephen, *Fighting Admirals,* 58–60.

530 *more distasteful task:* Barnett, *Engage the Enemy,* 175–81.

531 *"We all feel":* Stephen, *Fighting Admirals,* 70.

531 *"the fighting spirit":* Quoted in John Lukacs, *The Duel* (New York: Ticknor and Fields, 1990), 162.

531 *"Up till this moment":* Ibid., 163.

531 *The day after: Churchill and Roosevelt:* Warren Kimball, ed., *The Complete Correspondence* (Princeton, N.J., Princeton University Press, 1984), vol. 1, 24, 56, 51.

531 *Roosevelt sent a trio:* Lukacs, *Duel,* 185.

532 *frustrated any hopes:* Eric Grove, "A Service Vindicated, 1939–1946," in Hill, ed., *Royal Navy,* 354.

532 *Just before midnight:* McIntyre, *Aircraft Carriers,* 50–51.

532 *Cape Matapan:* Grove, "Vindicated," 359–60.

533 *The first British troops:* Stephen, *Fighting Admirals,* 98.

533 *"It takes the Navy":* Ibid., 98, 100.

533 *"a deadlier blow":* Quoted in Joachim Fest, *Hitler,* trans. Richard and Clare Winston (New York: Harcourt Brace Jovanovich, 1974), 645. See also Allan Bullock, *Hitler: A Study in Tyranny,* 638–39.

534 *"England's hope":* Lukacs, *Duel* 198–99.

534 *guru, Walter Forstmann:* Keegan, *Price of Admiralty,* 262.

534 *more than half:* Terraine, *U-Boat Wars,* 767.

535 *at twice the rate:* Keegan, *Price of Admiralty,* 266.

535 *the navy's window:* Terraine, *U-Boat Wars,* 304–7.

535 *He often went up:* Ibid., 306.

535 *all the way across the Atlantic:* Grove, "Vindicated," 356.

535 *meat and eggs:* Keegan, *Price of Admiralty* 267.

535 *named Alan Turing:* Terraine, *U-Boat Wars,* 323–25.

536 *109 ships in June 1941:* Ibid., 767.

536 *"sank to their lowest level":* Quoted in ibid., 311.

536 *James Somerville's Force H:* Stephen, *Fighting Admirals,* 112.

536 *largest naval appropriation:* Stephen Howarth, *To Shining Sea: A History of the United States Navy* (New York: Random House, 1991), 375, 380–81.

537 *America's fault:* Ronald Spector, *Eagle Against the Sun: The American War with Japan* (New York: The Free Press, 1985), 68–69.

537 *"The Navy is consuming":* Quoted in Johnson, *Modern Times,* 391.

538 *They had doubts:* Spector, *Eagle Against the Sun,* 67.

538 *first new battleships:* Martin Middlebrook and Patrick Mahoney, *Battleship: The Sinking of the Prince of Wales and the Repulse* (New York: Scribner, 1979), 33–35.

538 *"little cock sparrow":* Stephen, *Fighting Admirals,* 121.

538 *built at Clydebank:* Middlebrook, *Battleship,* 29.

539 *much larger:* Barnett, *Engage the Enemy,* 393, 394.

539 *"exert a paralyzing effect":* Ibid., 394.

539 *more than 100,000:* Basil Collier, *The War in the Far East, 1941–45* (New York: William Morrow, 1969), 190.

539 *the very next day:* Middlebrook, *Battleship,* 69.

539 *borrowing the same plan:* McIntyre, *Aircraft Carriers,* 72–73.

539 *"I feel we have got to":* Middlebrook, *Battleship,* 89.

540 *just after 10:00:* Barnett, *Engage the Enemy,* 414–15. According to Middlebrook, *Battleship* (p. 134), the Japanese pilot logs show they spotted the destroyer at 9:43.

540 *too high and too fast:* Middlebrook, *Battleship,* 142, 148–49.

540 *in X Boiler Room:* Ibid., 187.

542 *Almost uniquely:* Ibid., 209–10, 227.

542 *"It was the grandsons":* Ibid., 237.

542 *greatest surrender:* Collier, *War in the Far East,* 199.

543 *already at the limit:* As noted in Johnson, *Modern Times,* 395–96.

543 *grandfather of all:* Philip Knightley, *The Second Oldest Profession* (New York: W. W. Norton, 1986) and Patrick Beesley, *Very Special Intelligence* (London: 1977).

544 *more than 5,000 employees:* Spector, *Eagle Against the Sun,* 454.

544 *sank eighty-seven ships:* Howarth, *Shining Sea,* 394.

544 *completely unprepared*: Terraine, *U-Boat Wars*, 410–11.

544 *High-Frequency*: The Americans were developing a similar system, thanks to an exiled French scientist, Professor Deloraine. However, the British had tested theirs in March 1940, and had it deployed on anti-submarine vessels in early 1942. Terraine, *U-Boat Wars*, 438–39.

544 *"ships alone"*: Ibid., 442.

545 *"He was in despair"*: Captain Hans-Rudolf Rosing, quoted in Lawrence, ed., *Naval Battles*, 512.

545 *Dönitz's own sons*: Peter Dönitz was killed with *U-954* on May 19, 1943, Klaus Dönitz on May 14, 1944.

545 *economy to a halt*: Spector, *Eagle Against the Sun*, 486–87.

545 *fewer than half*: HMS *Ilustrious*, for example, carried a maximum of 36 aircraft (Barnett, *Engage the Enemy*, 244); an American *Essex* class carriers first launched in 1943, had room for more than one hundred.

546 *more powerful*: Ibid., 879.

546 Maori, *sunk in an air raid*: Stokesbury, *Navy and Empire*, 376.

547 *not built a single new cruiser*: Barnett, *Engage the Enemy*, 879.

547 *"The seamanship and fighting spirit"*: Ibid., 880–81.

547 *shift his flag twice*: McIntyre, *Aircraft Carriers*, 151.

548 *put it privately*: Barnett, *Engage the Enemy*, 894.

548 *it was a British admiral*: Howarth, *To Shining Sea*, 447–48; Stephen, *Fighting Admirals*, 204–6.

CONCLUSION: LONG VOYAGE HOME

549 *The meeting*: Martin Middlebrook, *Operation Corporate: The Falklands War, 1982* (New York: W. W. Norton, 1985), 66.

550 *"I remember my father saying"*: Middlebrook, *Battleship*, 88.

550 *fifty-three salvos*: Stephen, *Fighting Admirals*, 189.

550 *Finally Margaret Thatcher*: Admiral Sandy Woodward, *One Hundred Days* (Annapolis, Md.: Naval Institute Press, 1992), 72.

551 *"prepare covertly to go south"*: Max Hastings and Simon Jenkins, *The Battle for the Falklands* (New York: W. W. Norton, 1983), 71.

551 *in the words of*: Quoted in Kennedy, *Naval Mastery*, 316.

551 *quarter of its national wealth*: John Pimlott, ed., *British Military Operations* (New York: Bison, 1984), 12.

551 *Britain had ever enjoyed*: Eric Grove, "A Service Vindicated, 1939–1946," in Hill, ed., *Oxford Illustrated History of the Royal Navy* (Oxford: Oxford University Press, 1993), 377.

552 *some eighteen divisions*: Pimlott, *British Military Operations*, 108.

552 *"a projectile"*: Quoted in Kennedy, *Naval Mastery*, 255.

552 *Almost 4,000*: Pimlott, *British Military Operations*, 46.

552 *The Home Fleet almost vanished*: Cecil Hampshire, *The Royal Navy Since 1945* (London: William Kimber, 1975), 26–27.

553 *As her ensign came down*: Ibid., 29, 163.

554 *on February 12, 1949*: J. J. Colledge, *Ships of the Royal Navy* (London: Greenhill, 2003), 166.

554 *resign just twenty-four hours*: Paul Johnson, *Modern Times* (New York: Harper, 1983), 493.

555 *a radical rollback*: Desmond Wettern, *The Decline of British Sea Power* (London: Jane's, 1982), 137–39.

555 *"a separate kind of Navy"*: Ibid., 138.

555 *assumed Mountbatten*: Eric Grove, *Vanguard to Trident: British Naval Policy Since World War II* (London: The Bodley Head, 1987), 230, 386.

555 *took four years to build*: Hampshire, *Royal Navy*, 147.

556 *as the Americans intended:* Grove, *Vanguard,* 233.

556 *most sweeping abdication:* Wettern, *Decline,* 266.

557 *control of the navy's base:* Kenneth Speed, *Sea Change* (Bath: Ashgrove Press, 1982), 62–63.

558 *Everyone admitted:* Rodger, *Admiralty.*

558 *the Greenwich Observatory:* Hampshire, *Royal Navy,* 37.

558 *world's export:* Kennedy, *Naval Mastery,* 339.

558 *In 1971:* Speed, *Sea Change,* 68.

558 *tiny Iceland:* Mark Kurlansky, *Cod: A Biography of the Fish That Changed the World* (Harmondsworth, England: Penguin, 1997), 160–69.

558 *red and white building:* Admiral Sandy Woodward, *One Hundred Days* (Annapolis, Md.: Naval Institute Press, 1992), 23.

560 *not even have charts:* Ibid., 73.

560 *carry twenty Sea Harrier:* Middlebrook, *Operation Corporate,* 72–73.

560 *deemed the whole enterprise:* Woodward, *One Hundred Days,* xvii.

560 *"orphans of post-imperialism":* Hastings, *Falklands,* 12.

561 *four deep-sea:* Middlebrook, *Operation Corporate,* Appendix 1, 398.

561 *HMS Glasgow's radar:* Woodward, *One Hundred Days,* 10–11; Middlebrook, *Operation Corporate,* 158.

563 *"Red" Ryder:* See John Parker, *Commandos: The Inside Story of Britain's Most Elite Fighting Force* (London: Headline, 2000), 69, 75.

563 *the operations room:* Woodward, *One Hundred Days,* 13, 14; Hastings, *Falklands,* 153.

563 *made worse:* Hastings, *Falklands* 155, 156.

564 *established the first:* Julian Thompson, *No Picnic* (London: Lee Cooper, 1985), 2.

564 *never received:* Rodger, *Wooden World,* 67, 215.

565 *In 1810:* The figures are from *The Memoirs of Admiral Charles Beresford* (Boston: Little, Brown, 1914), 40.

565 *highly trained and motivated professionals:* Michael Howard, *War in European History* (Oxford: Oxford University Press, 1976), 127, 133.

565 *another West Country man:* Woodward, *One Hundred Days,* 6–7, 212–13.

565 *"In the Ops Room":* Ibid., 214–215, 216.

566 *experienced hands:* Thompson, *No Picnic,* 8–9.

567 *less than one hundred miles:* Middlebrook, *Operation Corporate,* 217; Hastings, 204.

567 *by one estimate:* Middlebrook, *Operation Corporate,* 226, 227.

567 *He had grown up:* John Wilsey, *H. Jones VC: The Life and Death of an Unusual Hero* (London: Arrow Book, 2002).

567 *another 13,000:* Woodward, *One Hundred Days,* 334.

568 *could already feel the change:* Ibid., 333.

INDEX

Page numbers in *italics* refer to illustrations.